CULTURAL COMMUNISM IN BENGAL 1936–1952

Cultural Communism
IN BENGAL
1936–1952

Anuradha Roy

PRIMUS
BOOKS

PRIMUS BOOKS
An imprint of Ratna Sagar P. Ltd.
Virat Bhavan
Mukherjee Nagar Commercial Complex
Delhi 110 009

Offices at
CHENNAI LUCKNOW
AGRA AHMEDABAD BANGALORE COIMBATORE
DEHRADUN GUWAHATI HYDERABAD JAIPUR KANPUR
KOCHI KOLKATA MADURAI MUMBAI PATNA
RANCHI VARANASI

First published 2014

ISBN: 978-93-80607-88-7

Published by Primus Books

Laser typeset by Guru Typograph Technology
Crossings Republic, Ghaziabad 201 009

Printed at Manipal Technologies Ltd., Manipal

To the memory of

CHINMOHAN SEHANABIS

and to

ASOK SEN

the two Bengali Communists I admire most

Contents

Acknowledgements

I WOULD LIKE to thank the University Grants Commission for granting me a research fellowship for four years (1982–6), without which this work would not have been possible. I am also grateful to Professor Binay Bhushan Chaudhuri of the Department of History, Calcutta University, for his patient and careful guidance during the course of my research. My eternal gratitude to my parents, Srikumar Roy and Sukla Roy, for the support they gave me despite their considerable reservations about the subject.

I would also like to acknowledge the staff of the libraries and archives where I worked and all the others who helped me by providing research material, information and encouragement. Quite a few of them were my interviewees too, and have been mentioned in the main text. I am particularly grateful to Gautam Chattopadhyay, Chinmohan Sehanabis and Sudhi Pradhan who gave me so freely of their time and inside knowledge.

Last but not the least, to the Maulana Abul Kalam Azad Institute of Asian Studies, Kolkata, and the then Director, Hari Vasudevan, for an honorary fellowship in 2011, which enabled me to take leave from my university and revise the work, I am truly thankful.

ANURADHA ROY

Introduction

A Personal Reflection

THIS BOOK DRAWS upon my Ph.D. dissertation written more than a quarter of a century ago, in the early 1980s. I had just returned to my home city Calcutta having finished my post-graduation in History from University of Delhi. There, Professor Randhir Singh and Professor Sumit Sarkar had given me the impression that Communism was the destiny of mankind. I knew that Bengal had a rich tradition of Communism and was happy that recently it had entered upon a new phase. True, it was a phase of parliamentary democracy and true Professor Parthasarathi Gupta had taught us in his European History class that the path of parliamentary democracy was fraught with many a trap for Communists. Yet, I optimistically thought that the Bengalis would surely escape those traps and irresistibly move towards Revolution. Weren't the Bengalis revolutionary to the core? Though their revolutionary urge was yet to achieve social or political fruition, it had long been gloriously manifest in their literary and artistic activities, the legacy of which seemed very vital in my personal life too. So I decided to research the

*Here I must apologize for beginning a research-based book on a personal note. I know that this is not done and I could have written a separate 'Preface' for related personal reminiscences. But this research was carried out not so much with a view to making a career in academia but from an inner urge emanating somewhere from the depth of life itself. And I publish it after so many years, because I can still feel that urge very strongly in my mind, maybe quite foolishly. This is an urge for a unity between 'I' and 'we', with its corollary of that between 'is' and 'ought'. Even if this unity is ultimately unattainable, I believe that this is a primordial urge of human beings and that the living existence of the individual can be meaningful only through a harmonious communion with universal humanity (which, of course, is manifested in specific times and places). Is this what has been called the 'Truth' by great thinkers from Aristotle to Rabindranath? Is this what appeared to Christopher Caudwell (who laid down his life in the Civil War of Spain and whose book *Illusion and Reality: A Study of the Sources of Poetry*, 1937, became a big influence in the Communist cultural movement that I will be studying) as the 'matrix of poetry', where the individual poet withdraws into the deepest layers of the self and hence into the formative and most fruitful phase of Communist culture in Bengal—from the middle of the 1930s to the early 1950s—the period that saw nothing less than a 'cultural uprising'—an invigorating and widespread Communist cultural movement. Let the Bengalis be conscious and proud of this cultural heritage, which would inspire them to progress towards a just and equitable society. A UGC fellowship at the Department of History, Calcutta University, facilitated this project. While the research was a very rewarding experience, at the same time it made me conscious of the limitations of Bengal Communism. The dissertation that was ultimately written was a sympathetic but critical one. The award of the degree took more than two years largely due to a near-anarchical situation at Calcutta University headed by a Vice Chancellor who was considered a renegade by the left-front government and thus opposed in every possible way. Ultimately, however, I did get my degree despite some caustic remarks made by my foreign examiner, a reputed historian gracing one of the universities in the US, to the effect that it was a pity to have so much of admirable scholarship wasted on people belonging to the same abominable category as Stalin or Pol Pot.

No, it was not the foreign examiner's comments that disheartened me and kept me from publishing the dissertation for all these years. It was something else—a reason nearer home and more potent. I will try to explain in this 'Introduction'.

A Conjunction of Cultural and Political Activism

The precise subject matter of my research and hence of this book is the Communist-inspired cultural activism in Bengal during the period 1936–52 that greatly stimulated the creative talents of the Bengalis and at the same

---

wellsprings of the 'genotype', and also into illusion in order to find a desired reality? Anyway, this urge of my own insignificant mind found a resonance in the subject matter of my research and sought to gratify itself by trying to understand it. For me, this research was an exercise of 'linking life with life' through an understanding of some people of the past, who had tried to forge similar links in their own way, an exercise of feeling those people and their minds at least partly in the present through oral history, and all this with a hope that all our lives and many others would flow to meet some day at a confluence of some immensely better future. The recession of this hope in the course of my research was also an integral part of the research experience. Indeed I think that without a clarification and justification in terms of this personal urge, the related hope and also its betrayal, the book would have very little value. If the reader thinks that I am unduly emphasizing my own involvement in the research work, I would at least answer that a historian is after all a product of his/her time and place and this needs to be understood in the reading of any work of history.

time induced a kind of social and political commitment in writers and artists. In fact, the cultural scene of Bengal had been showing a distinct change of attitude since the end of the First World War. With the maturing of the freedom movement, the awakening of peasants and workers within and outside of the Gandhian movement, the growth of fascism abroad, the global depression and so on, writers and artists could no longer live in their ivory tower. The middle-class to which they belonged was itself engulfed by a deepening crisis. The diminishing income from land, unemployment, migration to the city with all its complications and uncertainties, dissolution of joint families, etc., constituted this crisis. The growing communal bitterness at both the elite and popular levels was also quite disturbing. Abroad, it was all turmoil too. The European economy had been facing several structural pressures and political uncertainties had been growing since the War. The naked territorial aggression by the fascist forces of Germany, Italy and Japan shocked common people everywhere. The crises all around forced into the ideological and cultural self-representations of the middle-class an acute sense of disjunction and self-criticism. Breaches in the middle-class consciousness made room for an interest and concern for the labouring 'other' in their mind. It often seemed that the future of the world was bound up with that of the latter. On the whole, an awareness of the social, economic, national and international problems, a courage to face them and to examine them in some depth, was gradually developing in the cultural and intellectual arena. Socialism that had been slowly forcing its way into Bengal since the Bolshevik Revolution played a more or less important role in the growth of this consciousness. A warm admiration for the Soviet experiment and a left-oriented world view was shared by a large section of Bengali intellectuals of that time and not only by those who called themselves Communists. They showed an urge to integrate the struggle for political freedom with the socio-economic aspirations of the poor as well as with the worldwide struggle against imperialism and its most rabid manifestation fascism.

Of course, these developments took place over many years. But if out of such a tense period it is possible to choose one particular year as marking an abrupt intensification of the crisis as also the beginning of a collective resistance to the ominous threat to civilization, that year arguably was 1936. In March 1936, Hitler pushed German soldiers into the demilitarized Rhineland. In May, Mussolini attacked Abyssinia. In July, General Franco rebelled against the lawful government of the Spanish Republic. The Communists, who had formulated the 'United Front' theory in the face of the fascist threat a year back, now promoted a literary equivalent of the Front in the form of the International Brigade, consisting largely of eminent writers and intellectuals fighting in defence of Spain, some of them even dying in that cause. Just before the Spanish outburst had appeared the first number of

New Writing in Britain, self-declaredly 'independent of any political party', but predominantly run by leftist liberals, if not actually fellow-travellers or members of the Communist Party of Great Britain. The Left Book Club was also formed about this time. This too was a 'United Front' standing 'for World Peace and against Fascism'. Such activities in Britain need to be mentioned specially, because international Communism made its way to India largely through the British Communists.

At home, at the venue of the historic Lucknow Congress session in April 1936 marking the 'Indian Summer' of socialism, the All India Progressive Writers Association (AIPWA) was inaugurated under the initiative of some left-minded youths inspired by the international anti-fascist resistance movement that reputed intellectuals like Rolland, Barbusse and Gorky had been organizing for quite some time. The AIPWA was a cultural front of the Communist Party of India that had emerged as the principal Communist Party in India about the middle of the 1930s. But by no means was this writers' body restricted to Communist writers only. It was a broad-based movement, consisting of left-radicals, left-liberals, but also many not-so-left and non-left intellectuals and writers standing against fascism and to that extent believing in the interconnectedness between arts and politics and aligning themselves with the Communists. Thus, the new culture was given an organized shape and gradually crystallized into a cultural movement with strong national and international links. It was a movement in the sense that it was based on the perception of a set of common goals by a collectivity, at least a sense of collective commitment. It is this cultural movement—its origin, nature and eventual decline—that constitutes the subject of this book.

Hundreds of writers and intellectuals joined the movement responding to the troubled times and the intensified political climate at home and abroad, agonizing over the grim socio-political reality, and realizing the wide possibilities of creative practices afforded by the PWA project. They united on this platform in the cause of anti-fascist resistance in particular and human progress in general. Indeed, they called themselves 'progressive'. The vision of progress was rather inchoate and vague and by no means uniform for all. Only for some was it equated with the agenda of the Communist Party. But a number of them joined the movement with hegemonic aspirations to effect some fundamental and yet not very well-defined changes in both cultural and social terms. And they all paid attention to current problems and almost all of them tried to enter the hard lives of the poor and ordinary people. New themes led to bold experiments spanning a range of art forms at the hands of a set of idealistic people, middle-class in origin but sensitive to the problems of the poor and downtrodden. They did not want their movement to remain the mere intellectual and aesthetic exercise of a handful of middle-class people, but set themselves the objective of reaching down to the masses through their cultural activities and inspiring the fight for a better society.

As the decade of the 1940s began amid the Second World War and piled ruin on Bengal and the world, the cultural movement went from strength to strength. This demanding period—the War, the Japanese air raids on Assam and Chittagong, the Quit India Movement (even though the Communists opposed it), the traumatic Bengal Famine, the final collapse of fascism, the final and most militant phase of the Indian freedom movement, communal riots, independence accompanied by partition—greatly stimulated creative activities. The Communists admittedly played an important role throughout this momentous period by fighting fascism, famine, and communalism, and by leading the post-War popular upsurge, and thus had ample opportunity to draw people to their fold. The Bengal Famine (1943) in particular led to a broadening of the scope of the movement, as the Communists drew very close to the common villagers in the grip of the famine in the process of providing relief to them and trying to understand their problems. The Communist efforts in this direction impressed a number of writers and artists. In 1943, the Indian People's Theatre Association (IPTA) was established, complementing the AIPWA and extending the reach of the movement. It not only provided a platform for dramatic and musical artistes, but also pushed the boundaries of the Communist cultural movement to include people lower down the social scale. Given the material conditions of literacy in the country, performing arts bringing alive social realities proved to be more useful for mass contact than printed materials. The IPTA even tried to identify creative talent from among the peasants and workers. In Bengal, the IPTA was part of the Anti-Fascist Writers' and Artists' Association (AFWAA) which included practitioners of pictorial art and sculpture too. The PWA, IPTA, AFWAA and other cultural and political organizations of the Communists provided the organizational underpinning of the cultural movement under discussion.

Apart from the fact that it was the Marxists who took the initiative to provide the movement with the very many organizations through which it flourished and also won the admiration of many writers and artists by trying to the address current problems, there were other factors operating in their favour. The heroic war-efforts of the Soviet Union, then the only Communist State in the world, were found particularly inspiring. Moreover, whatever was understood as Marxism in those days gave the Marxists an apparently deep insight into the problems of exploitation at different levels—fascism, imperialism, capitalism and feudalism—by connecting one with the other. Also, to fight the crisis they needed a profound faith in man's positive possibilities and a teleological assumption of humanity's inevitable progress. And although these are largely attitudes of minds and by no means exclusive features of the Communist ideology, Communism could more effectively provide these than any other contemporary thought. In fact, humanism became manifest in Bengal during those days in the form of Marxism. Tarasankar Banerjee, a prominent fiction-writer, was certainly a non-Communist and, in his later years, even anti-Communist. And yet he asserted in his presidential speech at the 1942 conference of the AIPWA—'I have been drawn towards Russia before 1930; but it was a kind of romantic and therefore a rather impermanent fascination. Since 1930, I have had a new understanding, have rendered homage to the Soviet Union as the depository of humanity's greatest good.'

Thus Bengal in the 1930s and the 1940s saw a veritable Renaissance (to use the word very loosely, of course) in the cultural fields. It involved talents like Manik Banerjee, Tarasankar Banerjee, Nani Bhowmik and Gopal Haldar in prose; Bishnu Dey, Samar Sen, Subhas Mukherjee and Sukanta Bhattacharya in poetry; Manoranjan Bhattacharya, Sambhu Mitra and Bijan Bhattacharya in theatre; Jyotirindra Moitra, Salil Chowdhury, Debabrata Biswas and Hemanta Mukherjee in music, Chittaprosad Bhattacharya, Somenath Hore and Paritosh Sen in pictorial art, to name only a few. The roster of names associated with the movement—closely or remotely, at one point of time or another, individually, or organizationally—is simply a galaxy. However, the real strength of the movement perhaps lay more in quantity than quality—in the large number of people it attracted. This of course means that much that was produced was trash. But in some cases, literary, performing, auditory and visual art forms did attain a striking aesthetic height.

I would like to reiterate that of all the writers and artists who assembled under the banner of the movement, some were predisposed towards Communism, and some grew up to be close to or part of the Communist movement. But not all of them had a strong partisan identity, though most were more or less sympathetic to the Communist cause or at least to the way the Soviet Russia was fighting Hitler. But ultimately, perhaps, it was the open humanist terrain of the movement rather than a political agenda that attracted most writers and artists, and the strength of the movement too perhaps lay precisely here. Or we can say that it was a rather vague ethical-socialism and not a congealed socialist ideology that provided strength to the movement. However, as we would see later, this distinction eventually culminated in a schism between the personal ideological perspective of the writer or artist and the collective direction of the Party.

Responding to the Hard Times more than a Political Ideology

The movement has usually been related to the Communist political movement of the time. To a certain extent it did owe its existence to Marxian ideas and the political and cultural organizations of the Communists. But as a whole it was perhaps shaped and influenced more by the historical situation of the time than by any particular political ideology. This must be stressed for a better understanding of the movement.

This time factor was given due importance in the novel *Ekada* written by Gopal Haldar in the Presidency Jail in September 1933.[1] Here, the narrator-hero observed in the course of a discussion on the contemporary Bengali literature: 'Those who have been able to devote their lives to any definite current of national endeavour, are relieved. Half of those who have not been able to do so are being burnt within themselves—their lives are inflammable like a house of lac. They are being burnt to ashes like Hamlet—"*The time is out of joint. O cursed time! That ever I was born to set it right!* The tragedy of their lives is *to be or not to be*." The other half have saved themselves from this tragedy at the cost of their souls—by writing poems and stories. This is escapism. They are proving that they are *spiritually destitute, emotionally defunct, morally banal*.... Thought is our second best substitute. It is an age of action.'[2] The author was not really recommending thoughtless action, nor was his a blanket condemnation of creative writing. Actually, he was seeking in his anguish a new kind of literature that would complement action by analysing the crisis of man's social, political, national and international existence. In fact, Gopal Haldar himself became one of the trendsetters by writing *Ekada*. Here we see an assemblage of various middle-class characters: some settled in life like the 'sand-buried cities of Khotan', engaged either in the luxury of vapoury intellectualism or in the worship of 'that bitch-goddess, success'; some sensitive to the common people's struggle of the time—one of them profoundly stirred by the Civil Disobedience Movement, another engaged in underground activities of militant nationalism and also some labour leaders and Communists of different shades. The narrator of the novel is a tormented soul, sympathetic to all forms of struggle, but unable to choose a particular form for himself. The novel borrowed the 'Stream-of-Consciousness' form of Marcel Proust and James Joyce to describe what was going on within and outside the narrator's mind. It was a new experiment with regard to both theme and style. It was an intellectual analysis of hard reality, responding to hard times. The mechanism of this response was provided by artistic activities, which were soon to be given an organized shape in the PWA movement.

Ekada was the first volume of a trilogy. In the last volume titled *Ar Ek Din*, Gopal Haldar made the protagonist put aside all hesitation and profess Communism—a reflection of the author's own conversion from militant nationalism to Communism during the period 1937–8.[3] Haldar became well-known not only as a Communist writer and intellectual, but also as an activist in the party's peasant front. But all the writers would not think and act in his way. Many of them developed their art largely independent of politics, at least Communist politics. On the whole, the creative space provided by the PWA seemed more important than the political space in facilitating their response to the difficult times. Through their creativity, some of them could even run ahead of politics in some respects. Thus, in the novels *Dhatri Devata*, *Gana Devata* and *Panchagram*,[4] Tarasankar Banerjee, though not a Communist but rather a Gandhian, could clearly mark off the enemies of the poor people in the country's agrarian sector, which the CPI with all its jargon could not do so well. So it was the time, the troubled and shifting time, that deeply stirred the people of Bengal, including its writers and artists.

And when we talk of the time, we must keep in mind not only the social, economic and political crises, but also the intellectual influences it brought in. Since the First World War, Bengal had been overwhelmed by the intrusion of powerful forces of modernity and also opened up to the strange new world of Western culture, particularly some influential currents of contemporary Western thought that were revolutionizing man's understanding of his material, mental and physical realities. The three major currents were Freudian psychoanalysis, Einstein's theory of relativity and Marxism-Leninism. The westerly wind also blew in new literary thoughts and modes. One example is T.S. Eliot's preoccupation with decline and death, which found a parallel in the disillusionment and uncomfortable self-consciousness of the *bhadralok* intelligentsia and led to impatience with their romantic-sentimental-harmonic literary tradition. As has been shown by a scholar in a recent book on Bengali culture, on the whole they felt that the existing social order, the accepted value system and the established world view were moving towards a crisis point. A kind of anti-establishment, anti-exploitation, anti-prudery and anti-status-quo sensibilities and perceptions thus germinated during the 1920s and 1930s.[5] Its political expression was Marxism-Leninism, which was perhaps the most popular among the new trends. But actually the entire gamut of intellection and creation bore the mark of the scintillating discourses of the modern, the international and the scientific. The writers and artists naturally aspired for a modernist breakthrough in their own works, though the indigenous tradition of creative practices had a role to play too.

So, on the whole, the time was perhaps more important than any political ideology in forging this cultural movement. This was good in a way, for it strengthened the movement both quantitatively and qualitatively. It drew a great many number of writers and artists to the movement even beyond the ranks of the left and made it very broad-based. It also helped the movement to largely avoid the straitjacket of any pre-formulated ideological line in its creative practices. In any case, it was natural for a cultural movement to develop a dynamism of its own and to acquire a certain autonomy. Experiments in various art forms, could not, because of their very nature, be wholly decided by the specific policies of the Communists. Controlled by the Communists only very loosely, the movement could thus play a positive role in the context of those times.

Cultural Communism

As a student of history one could simply contend that the movement well-served the need of the times, particularly for the middle-class. The suffering of humanity during those hard times could have made this class utterly insensitive. Instead, the cultural movement helped sensitize them to the current problems and indeed made them address some of those problems, albeit in a small way. Describing the movement in this way would have satisfied my own middle-class self too, which in the case of the Bengalis has long been associated with a progressive, leftist and even Communist self-image, alongside a very culture-loving one. The cultural movement under discussion—a response to a particular historical context—definitely stands out in the cultural history of the Bengali middle-class. But because I took up this research primarily from an ideological perspective—an ideology that works not on a short-term basis, but has a long-term aspiration, an ideology that cannot rest valorizing the historical past but must look forward to a better future—it did not take me long to realize the limitations of the movement from this perspective. Viewed from such a perspective, the movement would indeed look inconsequential.

Doubts started clouding my mind soon. Did the organizers and activists really want to change the society at a fundamental level? Of course, those were turbulent times and the days of capitalism seemed numbered due to its own inherent contradictions. At one level, those people, at least many of them, had the vision of an equitable world in a not very distant future. But did they think of striving for it seriously except through cultural engagement? How seriously did they want to redirect the course of the freedom struggle towards a socialist vision? We must remember that Communism at that time was being dominated by the Stalinist orthodoxy, an aberration of Marxism. Its epistemology emphasized a historicism in a very unilinear sense, couched in 'scientific' terms. This meant that revolutionary transformation seemed not a question of the people's conscious control over history, but a 'natural and inevitable phenomenon'. So there was nothing much for the Communists to do about it, except wait for the mature moment to come. Till then, they could suitably engage with other people's politics, i.e. national, communal and fascist politics, and fight to realize some limited economic demands of workers, peasants and petty bourgeoisie, and above all, focus on cultural activities. For the Bengalis, Communism at its best has always been cultural Communism, largely dissociated from real life and its struggle.[6]

Even in the cultural field, how serious were they about forging links with the masses? They radicalized artistic pursuits in many ways. But how far did their culture represent the voices of people lower down the social scale? How far did it succeed in reaching out to those people? Wasn't the movement's success in this regard very limited? One thing is certain though. The Communists destroyed this vital cultural movement that was largely their own creation with the ostensible aim of bringing it closer to the masses and their struggle. How did this happen? The answer I found was certainly curious.

The Communists hardly ever questioned their own class position in society and their own prospective role in bringing about a social revolution. They had always remained an 'invisible intelligentsia' without ever theorizing themselves in their discourse of class and Revolution. Therein perhaps lay their greatest subterfuge and one of the biggest problems of Marxian theory and practice from the very beginning.[7] However, the Bengali Communists during the period of our study did apply the Marxist class theory congealed into 'economic determinism' (an important aspect of the 'science' of Stalinist Marxism) most enthusiastically in the cultural field. They liberally distributed labels like 'feudal' and bourgeois' to writers and artists who had joined their cultural front and also to those of the past (of course, always sparing themselves!) and condemned them as anti-people and anti-revolutionary. Alongside, they evolved a very repressive and bigoted cultural policy in the name of Socialist Realism, which was the aesthetic aspect of Stalinism. Based on a deterministic theory of direct superstructural reflection of society, Socialist Realism' asserted that the art and literature of bourgeois society *reflected* its economic decadence and that present-day art and literature *must reflect* socialist reality. So this was a highly contradictory aesthetic theory—a representational reflection theory on the one hand, and a Utopian conception on the other. The Utopian assertion involved rejection of all new artistic experiments leading to complex and advanced aesthetic styles as undemocratic 'formalism' and also any depiction of despair and despondency in arts as 'reactionary'.[8] In their application of Socialist Realism, the Marxist aesthetic theorists seemed more keen on removing all differences within the united cultural front to make it a veritable Party organization than attacking real reactionary forces. They were intolerant enough to often use grossly insulting language in denouncing even reputed and friendly writers and artists.

This happened particularly after the defeat of fascism. Now the United Front policy seemed unnecessary, or rather the Communists now thought in terms of a more profound political liberation. The popular movements taking place all around against economic and social inequalities also convinced them of the imminence of Revolution. On the one hand, this led to extreme valour and sacrifices by a number of Communists charged by the vision of a Revolution. On the other hand, this set in a process of alienation of the writers and artists. With the broadening of its aim, the broad social base of the cultural movement shrank considerably and now became indistinguishable from the Communist political movement.

However, a total war for political liberation in a broad sense called for a choice of proper strategies and tactics, which the Marxists miserably failed to formulate. They seem to have thought that it was only art and literature that was standing in the way of their cherished Revolution, which would automatically come only if the right kind of art and literature was produced. Though they emphasized science, culture attracted most of their attention. Though theoretically they considered culture as merely a part of a superstructure that did not have any autonomy, in practice they made every effort to monitor and control it. Culture, however, can never lead to a big social revolution directly. At best it can help establish a counter-hegemony in society by way of preparing people for that revolution. We will see that a couple of important cultural activists of the period of this study (namely Hiren Mukherjee and Bijan Bhattacharya) did compare their task to preparing the soil before sowing the seed (and reaping the harvest). Needless to say, this is no mean task. And the more broad-based a cultural movement is, the more effective it can be in its hegemonizing drive. The Communists during the 1930s and 1940s did try to forge a broad-based cultural movement. But by destroying the movement very early, they left their hegemonic aspirations unfulfilled.

Also, culturalism could offset political wrongs. The wrong politics of the Communists will be gradually unfolded in this study. The Communists themselves have admitted many mistakes of their politics later in self-critical moods. The mistakes include the passivity of the 'People's War' period and the ineffectual revolutionary excitement of the Post-War period that partly created the conditions for the acceptance of the status quo during the early 1950s. This acceptance was marked by the participation of the Communist Party in the general elections of 1952. That is why I have taken 1952 as the terminal year of my work. Without the earlier political fervour the Communist cultural movement could not survive as a *movement* after this.

The Communists not only failed to achieve their aim of counter-hegemony, but also got hegemonized themselves by the cultural mainstream. After Independence, having come out of a short sectarian phase of adventurous ultra-leftism, a number of Communist and broadly leftist artists and writers made a space for themselves in the new dispensation. Quite a few of them were gradually co-opted in the Bombay film industry, others became close to the new Indian state structure by joining government-sponsored cultural institutions and academies. Ultimately, all that the Communist cultural activists could achieve was making some mark in the cultural world, not much in the political or social arena. With more privileges and power came more complacency. In Bengal in particular, Communist politics lost its oppositional nature since 1977, and the project of cultural counter-hegemony became a routine ritual before getting gradually dismantled.

There was an anti-culturalist strand in Italian Communism during the 1920s. Communists like Amadeo Bordiga believed that cultural activities were a diversion in the struggle for a socialist society.[9] If this is an extreme view, then the Bengali Communists' belief that only correct art and literature can bring about Revolution represents an opposite extreme. Culture is of course useful in preparing people for big social changes. Communist politics without a cultural dimension can indeed be very barren. Indeed, in my opinion, the capitalist order that Communism pledges to confront and change has reached perfection and completion more in cultural terms than economical. So a cultural intervention in society is imperative for Communism. But that is culture in a very broad sense and not just literary, performative and pictorial practices. This narrow kind of culture without a real political mission can be quite useless (and even harmful) as far as Communism is concerned.

A Personal Note Once Again

Some personal reflections may once again be in order. As I have already said, my research experience during the 1980s was very rewarding. Getting a feel of the excitement of that cultural movement of bygone days was very exciting. A number of cultural activists of those days were still alive and I would meet all sorts of people belonging to all the factions of the once-undivided CPI, even a number of people who had left politics for good, many of whom had never been very political. Indeed, I met many apolitical people in the process of my research. Some of my interviewees were cultural stars like Salil Chowdhury, Sambhu Mitra and Paritosh Sen. I sought to understand the aesthetic intricacies of their respective art-forms by talking to them. Most of them admitted that their association with the Communist cultural movement during those days had ignited their creativity. I remember, for example, Purnendu Pattrea, who was a neighbour of mine and whom I admired for his multifarious contributions to poetry, painting, cinema, etc., saying once—'If I had not come close to the Communist cultural movement in the early 1950s, I would have been just a petty clerk today in some obscure office.' Of course, I had to admit that such deep and wide influence in the field of culture was a measure of the success of the movement. But I also found a number of my interviewees (and those who had reminisced in writing about those days) highly self-critical. Some of them seemed quite bitter about the movement. Gradually, the limitations of the movement sketched above became evident to me.

And as I wrote or talked about these limitations, I faced humiliation and marginalization myself. For example, at a seminar I talked about the play *Nabanna*, the prized production of the IPTA (1944) and tried to make the point that though it was about Famine-stricken peasants, the latter did not get much of a chance to watch the play. This was a mere statement of fact and by no means an opinionated view. The session was being chaired by a historian who had been a leader of the Students' Federation during the 1940s and thus had the opportunity to see the cultural movement from close quarters. He had always been very affectionate towards me and had helped me considerably in my research. Now, however, he vehemently protested and claimed that he himself had seen *Nabanna* being enacted at street corners by using the backdrop of a mere jute curtain. This rendered me speechless. Of course, the jute curtain of *Nabanna* had become famous in the history of Bengali theatre. It was innovative and at the same time involved very little expenses which suited the pocket of the hard-up IPTA. But there was no question of arranging street-corner shows of *Nabanna*, for it was a big 5-act play involving a huge cast and elaborate props. I realized that the cultural movement of the 1940s was being turned into a myth. An objective history of it was neither desired nor welcome. Bengal in the 1980s saw the consolidation of the power of the Communists through a process of gradual politicization of the society, which was correlative of a process of de-ideologization (that seemed absolutely irreversible after the fall of the Soviet Union and the satellite regimes). The cultural movement of the earlier period was a source of nostalgia for the Communists of the 1980s, a tale of great sacrifices and creativities, to justify their present position of power.

During the period of my study, i.e. the long 1940s, a number of Bengalis had a holistic vision of a more equitable and better world, which was responsible for a strong emotional and ideological commitment in them, however ineffectual this may have proved. During the period in which I was doing this study, this emotion and sense of commitment was fast-eroding. Still, I found a continuity between the two times. First, the lack of serious theoretical and practical thoughts about the ideology in its theoretical and applied aspects. Second, the tendency to suppress any critical voices. Third, making culture a channel of escape rather than an aid to real struggle.

I felt very bitter and did not want to publish my research in Communist Bengal. What use could my fellow Bengalis have for it? Taking lessons from past wrongs in order to correct them? But if the wrongs can lay the foundation of a huge and seemingly permanent structure of power, then of course wrongs are right, and my criticism would naturally be considered as subversion. I did publish a few small articles and books drawing upon the dissertation. But the main body of the thesis remained stowed away in a corner of my study.

Over the last couple of years, however, a wind of change has been blowing. Disillusionment with Bengal Communism and readiness to accept critical evaluation is discernible. The 34-year-old Communist regime has given way to a non-Communist one. So I have revised my research in the light of the altered state of Bengal and the rest of the world, further thoughts, and of course, new materials that have been published. I have not found the task too difficult. For the new materials are generally reminiscences, some complacent and a few anguished. Not one proper full-fledged academic work has emerged on the subject. The long Communist regime in Bengal did not encourage an objective history of Communist culture.

Of course, I may be wrong in thinking that Bengal has at last become ready for such a history. Sometimes it seems to me that as far as Communism is concerned, it will always be difficult for the Bengalis to be free from prejudices—either for or against it. I remain optimistic. At the same time I brace myself for many brickbats.

Presenting the Book at Last

I am publishing this book, because I think that politics motivated by some kind of ethical socialism and charged by the vision of an alternative is still needed, maybe even more so, and that the pursuit of such politics can indeed be helped by cultural practices, particularly of a kind that bridges the gap between the middle-class and the poor in emotional, ideational and physical terms. In this connection, the Communist cultural movement of the long 1940s can be looked upon as a source of both inspiration and caution.

Apart from the first chapter that sketches the historical-cum-organizational background to the movement, the book has three chapters on three different art forms—music, theatre, and pictorial art. I have left out literature where the movement had many achievements. This is indeed an indefensible omission, and anomalous too, because the study begins from 1936, the most apparent significance of which in the Indian context was the organizational beginning of the progressive writers' movement. I will say only this much in self-defence that the omission was partly a question of convenience. I thought it would be discreet not to undertake a critical analysis of the vast literary output of the time, in view of the large mass of materials I had to sift and analyse in my study of the other art-forms. More importantly, however, the Communist cultural movement as a consciously planned and organized cultural movement was more directly involved in the aural and visual arts than in literary ones. It was a country where the masses were generally illiterate. As reaching out to the masses was the central concern of the movement, literature had hardly any direct role to play. Rather, performing and pictorial arts had always constituted an important part of public entertainment and education in India. Moreover, these arts (performing more than pictorial) can create an interactive relationship with the viewers and audience, which generates an immediate response and hence are more effective for a cultural movement that seeks to give people political directions. Theatre, music and art could more directly communicate to the people the message of the movement.

There is another reason for my choice. I know of at least one scholar who has worked extensively on the literary aspect of the Communist cultural movement of Bengal that I am trying to understand. I have read and appreciated a number of Rajarshi Dasgupta's articles that try to understand the Communist literary culture of pre-colonial and early post-colonial Bengal as an important aspect of Bengali middle-class culture and underscore its limitations as well achievements.[10] As far as the performing arts are concerned, I have come across a few articles by Malini Bhattacharya[11] and at least one by Aishwarj Kumar.[12] But a lot remains to be done. Amit Gupta's book *Crises and Creativities: Middle-class Bhadralok in Bengal c. 1932–52*[13] is a very ambitious book dealing with the entire spectrum of the creative activities in Bengal within the time-frame. Here, the Communist cultural movement is treated as a segment of middle-class culture and is placed in relation to other segments. This makes the book interesting indeed, though the treatment of this particular segment seems inadequate.

However, the Communist cultural movement was not confined to Bengal alone and had an all-India character. So works related to other regions need to be mentioned too. Most of such works are focused on the Urdu language and literature and on the Muslims of north India. One may mention Ralph Russell, Priyambada Gopal and Talat Ahmed in this connection.[14] In India, all cultures are region- and history-specific. The Communist cultural movement in the late colonial and early post-colonial period brought forth the regional/linguistic cultural diversity of India. But at the same time it aimed at being a national cultural movement. Sometimes we find some scholars working on the Urdu linguistic zone of the movement trying to establish that this was the primary linguistic area of the movement from where it broadened out to incorporate other languages.[15] This historical view of the movement is not really acceptable. A Bengali or a Telegu-speaking or a Hindi-speaking historian may well have a very different view of the movement.[16]

Then there are scholars who think that the movement represented a sharp break from the previous cultural traditions,[17] which was not the case at least in Bengal, nor most probably anywhere else. This view emanates from the scholar's lack of knowledge and understanding about indigenous cultural traditions.

Some scholars indicate that the movement was a mere transmission belt of Communist ideas emanating from Moscow. Some, on the other hand take great pains to establish that the movement was not at all subservient to the party machine. Of course, it is true that the movement was largely autonomous and was enriched by non-Communist writers and artists. But the role of the Communist Party in forging and destroying the movement was vital too and has to be understood.

A related problem is the undue stress on the nationalist character of the movement. Of course, it can be treated as part of the national movement. But it evidently had many problems with nationalism. The cultural activists working within the movement stressed the part of their ideology that spilled over nationalism—their international and socialist perspective was more important than their nationalism, and at least during the 'People's War' period they failed to combine anti-fascism and nationalism satisfactorily. Similarly, in some works the popular character of the movement is also unduly exaggerated. On balance, the history of the movement has remained a shade too adulatory, showing a tendency to uncritical valorization.[18]

A notable exception is G.P. Deshpande[19] who was an activist himself in the 'progressive' cultural tradition. In one of his articles 'Of Progress and the Progressive Cultural Movement' he points out some of the limitations of the movement just mentioned. He stresses the need to recognize the movement both as a national movement and a diverse one and regrets that plurality was a mere slogan rather than a useful concept for the movement which failed to internalize and analyse this plurality and generate a proper historiography of the movement on its basis. In this connection he criticizes the essentially North-Indian character of the progressive cultural movement, for its failure to take up a position in the Aryan-Dravidian language divide.[20] He also shows how the exercise of reducing the political in art to mere 'reacting and responding' (rather than to 'think the political culturally') merely produced simplistic manifestos and posters at the hands of the lesser artists within the movement. He further regrets that the movement could not really become a people's movement and that in fact it made a travesty of the notion of people's theatre. He points out that it did not take long for the activists to co-opt in the new dispensation after India's Independence and that the movement gradually became mere nostalgia instead of a real urge to change the society. And finally, he says, 'The PCM (progressive cultural movement) still awaits its proper cultural and political history.'

Here I try to write one to the best of my ability, with reference to Bengal only. Perhaps the work would appear more cultural than political. I must, however, admit that I do not have the expertise for dealing with all the three art-forms discussed in this book. Mine is necessarily a 'Jack of all trades' approach. But as I have already made clear, the starting point of my work was a political aspiration. This book is not music history, theatre history and art history. Its priority is the Communist movement. Here music, theatre and pictorial art are treated as objects of politics, and not so much as subjective creations. In any case, the kind of cultural expressions

I have chosen to deal with were not objects belonging to the domain of pure aesthetic contemplation. The music and theatre discussed in this book are the music and theatre of politics. These two art forms were regarded as a frontal site of political engagement by the Communists. But the results were interestingly different in the two fields. The music sponsored by the Communist Party came closest to becoming a mass movement during the 1940s. But People's Songs constituted, after all, just a minor category of Bengali songs among many others (*adhunik* or modern, *ragpradhan* or classical-based, *Rabindrasangeet* or Tagore's songs, and so on). So there was no overall change in the field of music during those days. People's Theatre could not really become a people's movement. However, it was able to bring about big overall changes in terms of artistic experimentation in theatre. Pictorial art was rather neglected by the Party and hence could hardly become a mass movement, but the art scenes too underwent big changes during the period of this study; and perhaps did so more successfully due to the comparatively little intervention by the party. All the three art forms were, however, more or less affected by the politics of the Communists and suffered because of this. The three chapters 'The music of politics and politics of music', 'The theatre of politics and politics of theatre' and 'The political *within* pictorial art and the pictorial art in politics' will hopefully reveal this influence.

I owe the reader some more words of apology at this point. All the chapters of the book are rather narrativistic, and the analytical parts flow from and are subsumed under the narrative. This is often considered an outdated style of writing history. Perhaps I myself would not have adopted this style today, had I written the thesis all over again. However, I feel that such a narrativistic style has an advantage. It tends to ground history firmly in empirical data and thus makes it more reliable than vapory theoretical analysis, which more often than not tries to compensate for the writer's lack of grasp over flesh-and-blood reality. I say this even while keeping in mind and largely agreeing with Haydn White's exposition of history as a sort of storytelling, which involves the historian in a hierarchical arrangement of selected events and assignment of a specific motific characterization to the set.[21]

But having said this, I must admit that the narrative in my book is sometimes overburdened with data. Long lists of activists and their acts have perhaps curbed the readability of the book at places, particularly in the first chapter dealing largely with the membership and working of different cultural organizations, but also to some extent in the chapters on music, theatre and pictorial art. My youthful enthusiasm as a researcher in the early 1980s perhaps generated a kind of data fetishism. But this was also because, apart from understanding the movement and revealing its historical significance, a major purpose of my research was simply to document the movement.

I felt that the people who had been responsible for creating it were fast getting lost in the oblivion of history, and that a handful of people were trying to project themselves as its leading personalities. Also, without retrieving the names, it would have been difficult to establish the broad-based character of the movement, i.e. its claim to be a movement in the first place. Above all, when a researcher makes forays into an entirely new subject area of history, shouldn't documentation become an essential academic responsibility? I think these reasons remain valid even today. Hence, I retain most of those lists of names in the present book, which may look somewhat like a 'roll of honour'. But I actually want to honour the small and obscure actors of history alongside big and famous ones, particularly because this is the history of a movement which apparently tried to win the world for the ordinary people. The reader is of course at liberty to skip those lists of names.[22] However, I append small bio-notes at the end of the first chapter to make the names in it more meaningful in as many cases as possible.

It must be remembered that when this thesis was written, cultural history was defined very narrowly and the culturalist turn in academics was yet to come. I had to do the research and write the dissertation in my own way, which may look a bit conventional now. However, looking back, I feel that being able to retain my intellectual autonomy was not really a bad thing. Later, I have benefited from a number of works of cultural studies, which of course strongly relates culture to politics and in this sense look relevant for a project like mine. But I consider its tendency to find 'cultures of resistance' everywhere a bit too far-fetched. It is rather timidity and conformity that draw my attention. Maybe it is my innate pessimism that makes me see the cup half-empty whereas others see it half-full. But actually the question that above all bothers me is whether we believe that it is a fundamentally immoral social order and whether we want to change it fundamentally. Or should we just call for some minor reforms and happily acquiesce in the existing order of things on the whole? And I address this question in terms of Bankimchandra Chattopadhyay's concept of politics rather than that of the scholars of 'cultural studies'. Bankim, the 'literary monarch' of nineteenth-century Bengal talked about two kinds of politics—the politics of the bull and that of the dog. He placed the politics of his fellow Bengalis in relation to colonial rule in the dog category.[23] It seems to me that we Bengalis are still continuing with this tradition. Can we ever metamorphose into a bull?[24]

Notes and References

1. Published in 1939, though written six years earlier.
2. The emphases are original. English-educated as he was, the narrator was in the habit of breaking into English quotations or words while speaking in Bengali.

3. Haldar could not get down to write the last two volumes until 1948–9 when he was arrested as a member of the illegal Communist Party of India and thus enjoyed forced leisure inside the Alipore Presidency Jail where he had once written *Ekada*.
4. *Dhatridevata*, *Ganadevata* and *Panchagram* were published in 1939, 1942 and 1943 respectively.
5. Amit Gupta in his *Crises and Creativities: Middle-class Bhadralok in Bengal c.1932–52* (Orient BlackSwan, Hyderabad, 2009) has emphatically made this point.
6. I have discussed and analysed the theoretical flaw of Bengal Marxism and how it affected the movement related to it from the very beginning in my forthcoming book *Bengal Marxism: Early Discourses and Debates* to be published by Stree-Samya, Kolkata.
7. 'The ultimate false consciousness of Marxism is that the historical role attributed by it to the proletariat was assigned by an invisible intelligentsia that never made an appearance in its own theory, and whose existence and nature are therefore never systematically known even to itself', says Alvin W. Gouldner in *The Two Marxisms: Contradictions and Anomalies in the Development of Theory*, originally published 1980, OUP, 1982.
8. I have discussed Marxian aesthetics as practiced in Bengal at that time in my forthcoming book *Bengal Marxism*, op. cit.
9. Amadeo Bordiga was a leading figure in Italian Communism. He opposed electoralism and was criticized by Lenin for left extremism. Later, he accused Stalin as the 'gravedigger of Revolution' and considered the Soviet Union as a capitalist society.
10. Rajarshi Dasgupta, 'Inventing Modernity in a Colony: The Marxist Discourse on the Bengal Renaissance', *Contemporary India*, vol. 3, no. 1, 2004; 'Rhyming Revolution: Marxism and Culture in Colonial Bengal', *Studies in History*, vol. 21, no. 1, February 2005; 'Manik Bandyopadhyay', *Journal of History*, University of Burdwan, vol. VI, no. I, 2005. 'Marxbader Bhut Banam Marxbadir Gotra', *Ababhas*, April–September 2006. Dasgupta tries to show how Marxism has adapted to specific concerns of Bengali middle-class and taken on a distinctive middle-class character.

    While talking about Bengali literature's response to the turbulent 1940s, one may also mention Srimanjari's article 'War, Famine and Popular Perceptions in Bengali Literature, 1939–45', in *Issues in Modern Indian History for Sumit Sarkar*, Biswamoy Pati, ed., Mumbai: Popular Prakashan, 2000. But this is not really an attempt to specifically understand the Communist-sponsored cultural movement.
11. For example, Malini Bhattacharya, 'Changing Roles: Women in the People's Theatre Movement in Bengal (1942–51)', in Lata Singh, ed., *Theatre in Colonial India: Playhouse of Power*, New Delhi: OUP, 2009.
12. Aishwarj Kumar, 'Visions of Cultural Transformation: The IPTA in Bengal, 1940–44', in *Turbulent Times: India 1940–44*, ed., Biswamoy Pati, Mumbai: Popular Prakashan, 1998.
13. Amit Gupta, op. cit.

14. (a) Ralph Russell, *Pursuit of Urdu Literature: A Select History*, London: Zed, 1992 and 'Leadership in the All-India Progressive Writers' Movement', in *Leadership in South Asia*, B.N. Pandey, ed., New Delhi: Vikas Publishing House, 1977.
    (b) Priyambada Gopal, *Literary Radicalism in India: Gender, Nation and the Transition to Independence*, London: Routledge, 2005.
    (c) Talat Ahmed, *Literature and Politics in the Age of Nationalism: The Progressive Episode in South Asia, 1932–56*, London, New York and New Delhi: Routledge, 2009.
15. As for example, Talat Ahmed does, see her book, p. 13.
16. I must mention, however, Sumangala Damodaran's commendable efforts to research and document the old IPTA songs in at least five languages (including Bengali and her own Malayalam). I had the opportunity to attend one of her lecture-demonstrations and also read an online article by her.
17. Again, Talat Ahmed can be cited as an example. She does say that the movement has crystallized since the days of *Angare* (Burning Coal), a collection of Urdu short stories by some young and radical writers in 1932. But apart from *Angare*, the movement seems to lack a history from the way she has presented it.
18. Carlo Coppola, '*Urdu Poetry, 1935–1970: The Progressive Episode*', unpublished Ph.D. thesis, referred to by Talat Ahmed, suggests that the movement was largely controlled by Communists adhering to policies emanating from Moscow. Ahmed rightly says that this downplays the motivation of the writers, particularly those who were beyond the ranks of the Left. It is also true that a cultural movement should have some dynamism of its own. However, if Coppola's is an extreme view, so is that of Ahmed, who stresses the nationalism of the movement and glorifies it rather simplistically. She stresses the activists' close identification with Nehru and the Congress Socialists. In her opinion, they tried to shape the nationalist project through the infusion of populist ideas and the creation of a popular base among the masses (particularly after the IPTA was formed). In fact, this tendency to project the movement above all as a nationalist one seems quite common among scholars today. Aishwarj Kumar too can be cited as an example.
19. G.P. Deshpande, *Talking the Political and other essays*, Kolkata: Thema, 2009, particularly the essay titled 'Of Progress and the Progressive Cultural Movement'.
20. Deshpande calls for the Punjabi, Marathi, Telegu, Malayalam, Hindi and all other language areas of the movement to be given due attention, which would lead to a historiography recognizing the diversity of the movement and at the same time not denying its unity. He shows how interesting such a history would be by giving special attention to two language areas:

    In Maharashtra a big achievement of the movement was crossing the caste barrier—mobilizing lower caste talents like Annabhau Sathe, Shahir Gavankar and Omar Shaikh in the movement alongside middle-class literati. This was a very meaningful intervention in the caste situation. It is Deshpande's regret that the Left or the PCM (Progressive Cultural Movement) failed to realize its own achievement in this respect. Thus, Sathe was later appropriated by caste radicals, de-idealized and depoliticized and claimed by the contemporary Dalit caste politics rather than the working class movement. He was made into a great Mahang (a Dalit caste) leader. The Mahangs would rather deny any connection between Sathe and the progressive movement sponsored by the Communists.

The second example of regional specificity given by Deshpande is the PCM in north India that stressed the shared heritage of Hindi and Urdu, which were being projected as binary opposites at that time. The PCM also tried to bring both the languages as close as possible to the people's own mode of expression and was a major protagonist of Hindustani as the lingua franca for north India. This was a major contribution to the process of democratization of languages in India that had been going on for a long time. But again, as Deshpande points out, the PCM was unaware of its own historical contribution in this respect. He cannot but conclude that PCM did not have a critical understanding of history.

21. Hayden White, *Metahistory: The Historical Imagination in Nineteenth Century Europe*, Baltimore and London: The Johns Hopkins University Press, 1973, pp. 7–8.
22. But sometimes the reader may find to his delight a name or two not so famous and yet familiar to him personally—maybe someone from his own extended family or someone he has heard about from his father or grandaunt. I say this because I have actually come across such reactions from quite a few friends and acquaintances who have read parts of this thesis or with whom I have discussed it.
23. Bankimchandra Chattopadhyay, 'Politics' in *Kamalakanta*, available in *Bankim Rachanabali*, 2nd vol., Sahitya Samsad, 1st edn. 1361, Bengali Year 1954.
24. I must mention two crucial omissions of my work at least in this footnote. These too may be considered as hazards of publishing an old research work.

Any explanation of cultural practices necessitates the inclusion of the category of gender which is also constructed by culture in a broad sense. In political terms also the progressive cultural movement was supposed to question both class-based and gender-based inequality. However, when I did this study, I was not quite gender-conscious. Later, I wrote a long article in Bengali on the involvement of women in the progressive cultural movement, which is included in my Bengali book *Sekaler Marxiya Sahitya Andolan*, Kolkata, 2000. But this dimension is largely missing in the present book. I can say only this much here that women did make a space for themselves in this cultural movement particularly in the arena of performative practices. To some extent the movement did have a liberating effect on women activists (here I mean mostly middle-class women, as only they were present in the cultural movement), leading to a high level of creativity and a profound sense of political commitment, which also made them challenge the limits of their roles within their families and society. There were severe limitations, however, in this respect. Women did remain very marginal in this movement. Even a more sympathetic study, Malini Bhattacharya's 'Changing Roles: Women in the

People's Theatre Movement in Bengal (1942–51)', in *Theatre in Colonial India: Playhouse of Power*, Lata Singh, ed., New Delhi: OUP, 2009, that dwells on the women's gains from this movement rather than their marginalization, admits that there was 'perhaps a certain implicit acquiescence with stereotyped gender roles'. Bhattacharya points out that the IPTA seldom highlighted gender issues separately either at the theoretical level or at the level of cultural practice. And neither the male leaders nor the women activists could break away from all gender (just like class) prejudices common to people in their station of life. Hence little fundamental change could be achieved in this connection.

Another aspect of the movement that did draw my attention but that I felt too unsavoury to deal with is problems of interpersonal relationships and the resultant factionalism. Particularly after the end of the Second World War, the movement became beset with individual rivalries and petty politicking. Subrata Bandyopadhyay in his essay on the Communist artist Chittaprosad, included in Prakash Das edited *Chittaprasad*, Kolkata, 2011, talks about the slandering campaign based on sheer lies that alienated and ruined many comrades during the ultra-leftist phase of 1948–50. Indeed, this was too glaring a problem with the movement, and more often than not it took the appearance of ideological struggles. I have addressed this problem in ideological terms. Addressing this at an ethno-sociological level would have enriched our knowledge and understanding of Bengali society and culture. I leave it to some young scholar to analyse this problem and thus enrich us in the near future.

1

Communist Cultural Organizations in their Historical Context

Rise of Fascism and Anti-fascist Resistance

Electric lights adorning the sky above.
Beneath the extremely barbarous and the
deepest black.

At the night of the netherworld,
A terrible conflict between the hungry
and the glutton

Has spread the fire of sin.
The booty of plunder has accumulated
in the hell called Civilization.

—RABINDRANATH TAGORE
The poem 'Prayashchitta' (The Penance), 1937

PRAMATHANATH BISI ONCE wrote a story entitled 'Chitragupter Report' (The Report of Chitragupta, the head assistant of the God of death, Yama). Chitragupta visited the earth and found men introducing themselves by different names—leftist, rightist, left-leftist, Communist, fascist, republican, etc. Suddenly he saw some people running and asked them the reason. They replied, 'But running is our creed, we are progressive.' Then, somebody from his side told Chitragupta, 'Creed cannot make a man run so fast. Look behind, Sir, there is a mad dog chasing them.'

We do not know whether Bisi, while writing this story, had in his mind the 'progressives' of the 1930s and 1940s. But there was actually a mad dog acting as the principal factor in bringing out the progressive elements of these men. It was fascism.[1]

The post-First World War years saw the rise of fascism in different parts of the world. Mussolini came to power in Italy in 1922. Fascism posed a grave threat to mankind and its culture. Some leading intellectuals like Romain Rolland and Henri Barbusse tried to unite all conscientious and cultured men of Europe and the world in an anti-fascist resistance. A big anti-fascist conference of intellectuals was held in Paris on 23 February 1927, presided over by Einstein, Barbusse and Rolland. An international committee was formed to enlighten people about fascism, to encourage them to resist it and to hold out their hands to its victims. Barbusse addressed a copy of his 'Appeal to the Freed Spirits' to Rabindranath Tagore, who signed the Appeal and sent a sympathetic reply.[2] In 1928, Tagore sent a message to the *Golden Book of Peace* to be published by the World League of Peace under the initiative of Rolland and Barbusse.

But the fascist threat continued to increase. The Japanese aggression on China in the early 1930s shocked the world. In 1932, a Peace Conference was held in Amsterdam and on the eve of this conference Rolland sent a personal appeal to many intellectuals. A copy of it was sent to Ramananda Chattopadhyay, editor of the reputed periodical *Modern Review*, in order to publicize it in India. According to a resolution accepted at Amsterdam, 1 August was observed as International Anti-War Day. In Calcutta too some progressive intellectuals took part in this observance.

In 1932, Hitler became the Chancellor of Germany. On 10 May, there was a bonfire of books written by world-famous writers at Berlin Square. Even Rabindranath Tagore was not spared (a few of Tagore's paintings that he had gifted to Germany were burnt too, as 'degenerate art'. Soumyendranath Tagore who was in Germany at that time was arrested in connection with the burning of the Reichstag, the German Parliament—an incident known to have been masterminded by Hitler himself trying to trap his opponents. After detention for a few months, Soumyendranath was released. His book *Hitlerism or The Aryan Rule in Germany* was published from Calcutta in December 1933.

On 21 June 1935, in Paris, Rolland, Gorky and Barbusse convened an assembly of progressive writers in defence of culture. Other sponsors and speakers were Andre Malraux, Thomas Mann, Waldo Frank, Andre Gide, E.M. Forster, Aldous Huxley, Julien Benda, Michael Gold and John Strachey. They condemned both fascism and the fear of fascism, warned mankind against the prospect of a war, demanded from the writers an awareness about the reality, as also moral responsibility and mass contact. They paid tribute to Soviet Russia where human civilization had taken a great leap forward.

In the meantime, Italy's preparation for an all-out attack on Abyssinia had advanced and this was condemned in a meeting at the Albert Hall in Calcutta on 26 July 1935.[3] The Association against the Italian invasion of Abyssinia was constituted at a meeting[4] on 27 October, joined by 60 political parties and trade union organizations including the Congress Socialist Party of Bengal, Labour Party of Bengal, Calcutta Tramway Workers' Union, etc. Prominent Indian doctors including Nilratan Sarkar, K.S. Roy and others from Calcutta appealed to people to raise funds and offer themselves as volunteers to nurse the wounded in Abyssinia.[5] The Lucknow session of the Indian National Congress, April 1936, condemned the assault on Abyssinia and responded to Rolland's appeal to send delegates to the Peace Conference to be held in Geneva in September.

India thus became integrated into the international movement against fascism and war. The League against Fascism and War sent an appeal to the Faizpur session of the Indian National Congress (December 1935) to spread the movement in India. The India Civil Liberties Union, of which Tagore was the President, maintained a link with the League against Fascism and War. A Bengal branch of the latter was soon established. It observed Anti-War Day on 1 August 1936. It sent a message to the Brussels World Peace Congress (3 September 1936) condemning not only the fascist war efforts but also the proscription of foreign literature by the Government of India.[6] It was signed by distingushed intellectuals and writers like Rabindranath Tagore, Sarat Chandra Chattopadhyay, Ramananda Chattopadhyay, Naresh Chandra Sengupta, Jawaharlal Nehru, Prafulla Chandra Ray, Pramatha Chowdhury, Nandalal Bose, Premchand and others. On 6 September, Peace Day was observed throughout India.

On 18 July 1936, General Franco rebelled against the lawful Government of the Spanish Republic and plunged the country in a bloody Civil War. An International Brigade, 40,000 strong, fought in defence of Spain. It included many artists, writers and other idealists who knew nothing about the art of warfare. Andre Malraux, Ernest Hemingway and other prominent names could be found on the list. There were even some Indian members of the International Brigade. Among them, only Gopal Mukund Hudder survived the Civil War. Felicia Brown, an English sculptor, Ralph Fox, a noted English writer and Christopher Caudwell, another Marxist writer of England, laid down their lives on the battlefields of Spain. Talented men like Frederice Garcia Lorca, the famous Spanish poet, were killed by the fascists.

H.G. Wells, Norman Angell, G.D.H. Cole, E.M. Forster, Julian Huxley, Gilbert Murray, Virginia Woolf, Stephen Spender and many others made spirited appeals on behalf of the Spanish Republican government. Rolland's ardent appeal issued on 20 November 1936 was published in the *Ananda Bazar Patrika* in Bengal (17 January 1937).

This was a time when writers and artists not only confronted reality, but became deeply involved in it as determined fighters in the cause of humanity and its progress. They would fight with their pens and brushes, and some of them with machine-guns too. Spain and the International Brigade greatly helped them to make up their minds. Thus, the famous singer Paul Robeson gave a call through a radio broadcast from the continent to a big London rally in defence of Spain:

Every artist, every scientist, must decide *now* (italic in original) where he stands. He has no alternative. There is no standing above the conflict on Olympian heights. There are no impartial observers. Through the destruction in certain countries, of the greatest of man's literary heritage, through the propagation of false ideas of racial and national superiority, the artist, the scientist, the writers is challenged. The struggle invades the formerly cloistered halls of our universities and other seats of learning. The battle front is everywhere. There is no sheltered rear.[7]

In June 1937, a group of writers, including Heinrich Mann, Aragon, Neruda, Auden and Spender, appealed to fellow-writers to support the Spanish cause: 'It is clear to many of us throughout the whole world that now, as certainly never before, we are determined or compelled, to take sides. The equivocal attitude, the Ivory Tower, the paradoxical, the ironic detachment, will no longer do.'[8] Writers and artists took sides on the question of survival and progress of human civilization. In India and Bengal also, they did not lag behind and showed a similar spirit of resistance and commitment.

Early in 1937, an All-India Committee of League Against Fascism and War was formed with Tagore as its President. The Chairman and the General Secretary were Professor K.T. Shah and Soumyendranath Tagore respectively. Other office-bearers were Acharya Prafulla Chandra Ray, Sarojini Naidu, S. Brelvi (Editor, *Chronicle*), K. Santaram (Editor, *Madras Daily Express*), R.S. Ruikar (Assistant President of AITUC), Tushar Kanti Ghosh (Editor, *Amrita Bazar Patrika*), Dhiren Sen (Editor, *Advance*), Surendranath Goswami (Secretary, Bengal Progressive Writers' Association), Sajjad Zaheer (General Secretary, All-India Progressive Writers' Association), Swami Sahajananda (Secretary, All-India Kisan Sabha), S.A. Dange, Jayaprakash Narayan, Indulal Jajnik (Secretary, All-India Kisan Sabha)[9] and others. The Committee published a booklet titled *Spain* which included an appeal from Tagore to the conscience of humanity to stand by the Spanish people in the hour of their trial and sufferings. This appeal was published in *The Statesman*, 3 March 1937.

On 11 March 1937, the League Against Fascism and War convened a public meeting at Albert Hall, and appealed for help. It was presided over by Sarojini Naidu. Soumyendranath Tagore, Surendranath Goswami, Hiren Mukherjee, Gunada Majumdar, Ram Manohar Lohia and other members of the organization were present. A Spain Aid Fund was launched at this meeting.[10] The Bengal Committee of the League took up a week-long programme of organizing meetings and processions in Calcutta to apprise the public of the frightful situation in Spain. On 12 April, the first day of Spain Week, a big public meeting was held at College Square, with Surendranath Goswami as the President. The second day's session was held at Wellington Square.

Hitler became bolder, grabbed Austria in March 1938, and set his covetous eyes on Czechoslovakia. The League of Nations and the Big Powers had already bowed before him. Now in 29 September 1938, England and France conceded a large part of Czechoslovakia to Hitler through the infamous Munich Pact. Within a few months, the whole of Czechoslovakia was occupied by Hitler. In a radio broadcast on the Christmas eve of 1937, Carel Chapek, the noted dramatist and novelist of that country now facing an endangered and uncertain future, had sought courage from Rabindranath Tagore, a symbol of peace. The poet had readily responded. On receipt of the news of the rape of Czechoslovakia, Tagore sent a letter to his Czech friend Professor Lesny saying how keenly he felt about the sufferings of the people of that country (9 November 1938).[11]

During 1937–8, the Japanese aggression in China created a grave situation and the Indian National Congress condemned it repeatedly. (The Working Committee, Allahabad, 26–9 April 1937 and Calcutta AICC, 29–31 October 1937). Responding to the call of Jawaharlal Nehru, the Congress President, China Day was observed on 26 September 1937, throughout the country. Demonstrations were held at the Japanese Embassies in Bombay and Calcutta and a call was issued to boycott goods from Japan. Funds were raised for China. When Rasbehari Bose sent a telegram to Tagore requesting the latter, on behalf of the Indians residing in Japan, to help stop the 'anti-Japanese activities of Jawaharlal Nehru and the Congress', the poet sent a strongly worded letter of refusal (10 October 1937).

Towards the end of 1937, the Chinese situation became desperate and the need to help China was felt intensely. Nehru appealed to his countrymen to observe 9 January 1938 as China Day. Tagore, who had expressed deep sympathy for the struggling China a number of times even from his sickbed, asked everyone to contribute liberally to the China Aid Fund on that day. He himself contributed Rs. 500.[12] He sent an encouraging message to the Chinese people through Professor Tan Yun-Zhan.[13] About this time, he also got involved in a controversy with his one-time friend Yone Noguchi, a Japanese poet, who wrote to him justifying the Japanese aggrandizement. Tagore decried the massacre carried out by the Japanese in China. He thus ended his letter, 'Wishing your People whom I love not success, but remorse'[14] (September 1938).

The Indian National Congress continued to do whatever it could for China. In response to Chu Teh's appeal for help, it sent an Indian Medical Mission headed by Dr Atal and consisting of Dr Kotnis, Dr Bijoy Basu, Dr Debes Mukherjee and a few others. They set out for China in September 1938, with greetings from the then Congress President Subhas Chandra Bose, Tagore and many others. The Tripuri Congress, 10–12 March 1939, expressed its deepest sympathy for the Chinese and recorded its disapproval of the British foreign policy culminating in the Munich Pact, the Anglo-Italian Agreement, and the recognition of rebel Spain.

This is a sketchy overview of how fascism provoked collective resistance from all righteous men of the world and thus created an international bond among intellectuals. This internationalism was an important characteristic of the progressive culture that developed in the 1930s and 1940s. A sort of 'progressive' culture had been taking shape for quite some time under the pressure of structural wrongs. Now the conjuncture of fascism hastened the process. It also brought home the need for a body of culture that would become the basis of a new united cultural front participating in the world cultural movement not only intellectually but organizationally as well. The All India Progressive Writers' Association was thus born in 1936.

The threat of fascism led the Communists to take up the strategy of a United Front which increased their influence among writers, artists and the general public throughout the world. Communist ideas and activities played a notable role in the progressive culture of this period.

Rabindranath's untiring protest against fascism became a source of great inspiration to the intellectuals of India and Bengal who forged the progressive culture movement. Though the poet was a very old and sick man, the way he stood up against the fascist threat through his numerous writings and also by sending messages and lending his name to various anti-fascist efforts made a deep impact on the political and cultural scene of India.

Strengthening of Socialism

> At last I have come to Russia. What I see here strikes me with wonder. It is not like any other country. The difference is fundamental. They have equally awakened all men from top to bottom. Had I not come here, the pilgrimage of this life of mine would have remained very much incomplete.
>
> —RABINDRANATH TAGORE
> *Russiar Chithi* (*Letters from Russia*), 1931

Since the Bolshevik Revolution, the influence of Russia, Lenin and socialism had started making itself felt in the Bengali intellectual world despite every attempt by the British to censor news from that country.[15] Numerous articles in different periodicals[16] expressed admiration for the Russian experiment, though the admiration was generally based on the emotion of a people forcibly kept backward, and not on any rigorous analysis. Among these discourses only a few are mentioned here—Pramatha Chowdhury's *Rayater Katha* (About the peasantry, 1926), Sibram Chakravarty's *Moscow Banam Pondicherry* (Moscow vs. Pondicherry,1929), Sushobhan Sarkar's 'Rusbiplaber Itibritta' (History of Russian Revolution, *Parichay*,1931–2), and above all Rabindranath Tagore's *Russiar Chithi* (*Letters from Russia*, 1931).[17] The practice and the theory of socialism was becoming a subject of lively interest, as a reader's letter in response to Pramatha Chowdhury's article on Marxian Dialectics in the journal *Parichay* shows.[18] The letter-writer Debkumar Chowdhury in his enlightening discussion called Dialectical Materialism 'D-Materialism', not only for the sake of convenience, but because, 'As you know, after the discovery of Vitamins, this age can rightly be called the Vitamin Age. And you also know, Vitamin D not only makes us strong and healthy, but also straightens rickety crooked bones. As Dialectical Materialism intends to impart health to the old Mechanistic Materialism and also to straighten the idealism bent on an opposite direction, nobody will object if I call it D-Materialism.'

Sympathy for the poor, condemnation of an exploitative social system and the longing for a better society were expressed in Najrul's verse-books like *Agnibina* (1922), Rabindranath's symbolic plays *Muktadhara* (1922) and *Raktakarabi* (1926), Sarat Chandra Chattopadhyay's short stories 'Mahesh' (1922) and 'Abhagir Swarga' (1922). But it must be admitted that the interest of writers in the lives of poor people was not wholly due to the influence of socialism.[19] Only Najrul had come under the ideological influence of the international project of socialism and was associated with one of the earliest socialist parties in this country, the Peasants' and Workers' Party. The experiment of the young writers associated with the famous literary magazine *Kallol*–Premendra Mitra's novel *Pank* (1926), Achintya Kumar Sengupta's *Bede* (1926), Manish Ghatak's *Pataldangar Panchali* (the stories written in 1920s, though published as a book in 1956), Sailajananda Mukherjee's stories on the coal-mine workers—all depicting the life of the poor,[20] were not based on any systematic understanding of socialism, but a vague kind of protest against the social and economic inequalities of life. In fact, these writers were trying to pursue not socialism but 'realism' in literature, largely under the influence of modern Western literature. For them, this meant writng on sexual themes as well as the lives of the poor and the lower middle-class. The first was a protest against the patriarchal orthodoxy and the second a response to the worsening economic difficulties of the time. Moreover, the Indian national movement was drawing the writers' attention to the lower strata of society. Of course, *Kallol* published commendatory reviews of Gopal Lal Sanyal's *Samajtantrabad* (Socialism), Bertrand Russell's *Bolshevism*, Soumyendranath Tagore's translation (Bengali) of the *Communist Manifesto* and so on. But the magazine maintained a neutral attitude in politics and never really professed socialism.[21]

There emerged a fairly strong left alternative in politics during the 1930s. During the 1920s the political formation of the left had emerged as a number of small parties. The Meerut Conspiracy Case, though fabricated in order to cripple the newborn Communist Party of India, gave the left an unprecedented prominence. The ultra-leftist line taken up at the sixth congress of the Comintern in 1928 alienated the Communists from mainstream nationalism. But by the mid-1930s, leftism found a space both within and outside the Congress. Though the CPI was banned in 1934 following some labour disturbances, the Communists were working from within the Congress which had leaned leftward itself. The large-scale conversion of revolutionary terrorists to Marxism in the detention camps during the mid-1930s through intense reading and ideological debates strengthened the left too.[22] Indeed, this period saw an overall consolidation and advance of socialism. The failure of the Civil Disobedience Movement disillusioned many about the Gandhian path. The Congress Socialist Party was formally launched in 1934. The ideology of its founders ranged from vague radical nationalism to Marxian 'scientific socialism'. Though the right-leaning Congress leaders disliked the new trend, this socialist ginger-group became quite powerful. Historians today can clearly see that the group's power lay mostly in words and actually it failed to prevent the consolidation of the right wing of the Congress.[23] But on international issues, in sharp contrast, the left clearly set the tone, thanks in large part to the dynamic leadership of Jawaharlal Nehru. This explains the consistent support that Congress rendered to the victims of fascism.

In art and literature, a further change took place during the 1930s. As the reality was becoming increasingly starker, the artists tried to face it boldly and positively. Thus, a concern for exploitation and oppression, hope in man's positive possibilities—attitudes that should be inseparable parts of a socialist view of life—gained ground in the cultural life of Bengal, not necessarily as a result of any close familiarity with socialist thought, but mostly as a result of the circumstances of the time. The broad difference between the 1920s and the 1930s in this respect is traceable in the subtle difference between the two fiction-writers Jagadish Gupta and Manik Bandopadhyay. Gupta in his writings of the 1920s, had excelled in his disenchanted observation of the cruellest reality of slums and barracks. His characters always sank in abysmal misery and frustration.[24] Manik Banerjee too probed the life of the poorest people and the decaying middle-class in his novels *Padmanadir Majhi* (The Boatman of the River Padma, 1936) and *Putul Nacher Itikatha* (The History of Puppet Dance, 1936).[25] But his protagonists would not capitulate to their fate even after being defeated. There was an element of hope somewhere, which was yet to turn socialist. (Banerjee did not become a Communist until the next decade.) Poetry too underwent a change from a negative attitude to a positive one. One notable instance is the way the poet Bishnu Dey overcame his bitter helplessness of the 1930s and developed a positive attitude of commitment to humanity at the turn of the decade—an intellectual and spiritual quest largely associated with his conversion to Marxism and reflected in his transition from his first book of poems *Urvasi O Artemis* (1933) to *Purbalekh* (1941).[26] The more direct influence of socialism can also be identifiable in some cases. Naresh Chandra Sengupta, founder-president of the Peasants' and Workers' Party, was a very good writer as well. Already in the late 1920s he had written a story 'Robin Master' where the title-hero becomes a socialist in the end. In 1933, Manoranjan Hajra wrote two novels—*Pali Matir Phasal* (Harvest of Alluvial Soil) and *Nongorhin Nauka* (Boat without an Anchor), which were analyses of a critical reality with a professed socialist outlook. The writer was deeply involved in the leftist political movement.[27]

The formulation of the United Front theory by the Comintern greatly contributed to the growth of socialist consciousness and of the socialist movement. In the face of the fascist threat the World Communist Movement had been undergoing a process of reorientation culminating in this theory, presented by Dimitrov at the seventh congress of the Communist International (Moscow, 25 July–21 August 1935). Now the Communists were to forge a broad unity of democratic forces against fascism and imperialism. This would naturally brighten the image of the Communist parties in the eyes of the common people and increase their strength. The Communists were to develop big mass national parties which together would comprise an international force. The Dutt-Bradley Thesis was accordingly formulated for India.[28] The illegal CPI carried on mass activities by working within the CSP and in fact provided many of its effective mass leaders (Namboodiripad, Krishna Pillai, etc.)

In that 'Indian Summer' of socialism, at the historic Lucknow session of the Indian National Congress (April 1936), its President, Jawaharlal Nehru, pledged his support for socialism 'not in a vague humanitarian way, but in the scientific, economic sense'. On the occasion of this Lucknow Congress Session some major developments took place. The All-India Students' Federation, All-India Kisan Sabha and All-India Progressive Writers' Association were founded. The Communists, working along the line of United Front, took the initiative in the formation of these organizations which became very useful mass fronts for them. These bodies were all vehicles of a broad-based movement, and by no means restricted to Communists. The AIPWA, for instance, was able to draw into its fold almost all prominent writers of Bengal over the next decade or so—Communist Party members like Gopal Haldar, Manik Banerjee or Sukanta Bhattacharya; those who broadly sympathized with socialism, but were distant from the Party, e.g. Tarasankar Banerjee and Buddhadev Bose (many other writers of Bengal passed through such a stage in the 1930s and 1940s) and even some of those who were strongly opposed not only to the Communist Party but also to Communist ideology as it was understood during those days, e.g. Sajanikanta Das.

Not that Bengali art and literature could be called 'socialist' or 'leftist' or 'Marxist' from now on, but the epithet 'progressive' found wide acceptance. The idea that civilization would have to progress leaving behind the dark fascist phase and towards a better future gained popularity among writers and intellectuals.[29] Also, a number of writers were more or less attracted by socialism during this period whose spirit almost confirms Sartre's saying: 'Marxism is the one philosophy of our time which we cannot go beyond'. Bishnu Dey thus describes the cultural ambience of the time:

> What is more important, the economic and political atmosphere we lived in was getting more and more heart-rendingly complex and linked up by the very nature of the unavoidable and fast-moving complexity with the rest of the world, of the ruthlessly wily phase of the forces of capitalism and facism with their various political instruments. We found that these forces were capable of dissecting and then using some of the unrelated strands of the fundamental concepts which are really bound together in one philosophy of life and one programme for the whole of human civilization against capitalism. But history is on this side and the active mind of men has patience and arduous hope. . . . A poet or an artist realises, however dimly and even in a self-contradictory manner, the laws of development which his particular talent and his social affiliations—his whole being—demand from him, with their own logic of foresight and discipline. . . . Marx and Engels made it possible for this foresight—which is not prediction but an active state of preparedness of the mind, to be sought after and nurtured, even in the sphere of aesthetic activity.[30]

The All-India Progressive Writers' Association and the Bengal Progressive Writers' Association

Their flaming swords
Scatter the inky darkness into shreds.
They have made their pen
A mighty sword.
They are determined
that their days of dancing attendance
on Uttara—the princess—are over,
And Brihannala,
long shorn of manliness,
must get metamorphosed
into Arjuna—
the great wielder of the Gandiva.

—SAROJ DUTTA
Agrani, February 1939

[It was recited by him at the Second Conference of the AIPWA, Calcutta, December 1938 (translator unknown)]

The Paris Conference of June 1935, was the first attempt to organize the writers of the world in the cause of anti-fascist resistance in particular and human progress in general. The International Association of Writers for the Defence of Culture against Fascism was formed here. All this brought to writers a new awareness of the role they could play in the contemporary world. Now they knew that they should come out of their Ivory Tower and respond collectively to socio-political problems. At the second conference of this Association in London, 19–23 June 1936, Mulk Raj Anand represented India. The conference tried to work out practicable ways for the defence of culture and an encyclopaedia of world culture was planned. In the summer of 1937 a special conference of the Association was held in shell-torn Madrid—a magnificent gesture of solidarity with the people of Spain.

Soon after the Paris Conference some Indian students residing in England decided to take part, organizationally, in this emerging international literary movement. They all had a taste for literature though not all of them were litterateurs and they were drifting towards socialism. As Mulk Raj Anand describes it: 'It is almost uncanny to look back upon those dark foggy November days of the year 1935 in London when after the disillusionment and disintegration of years of suffering in India and conscious of the destruction of most of our values through the capitalist crisis of 1931, a few of us emerged from the slough of despondence of the cafes and garrets of Bloomsbury and formed the nucleus of the Indian Progressive Writers' Association.'[31]

In fact, the preparation had been going on for quite some time. We learn from Sajjad Zaheer's account[32] that a regular meeting had already been held in his room in London, a committee constituted to organize the Indian Progressive Writers' Association and a manifesto drafted to formulate its aims and objects. A cellar at the back of a Chinese restaurant in London had provided the venue for another meeting starting a Progressive Writers' Association with Mulk Raj Anand as the President and an Executive Committee of four or five. They collected about thirty to thirty-five Indians in London within a short time and the meetings of the PWA used to be held once or twice a month in London. All this was prior to the Paris Conference which encouraged then to make their organization stronger, so that it could get itself affiliated to the international literary centre. They regretted that in Paris, India was inadequately represented. This is the short history of the beginning of the Progressive Writers' Association. Among its first members were M.R. Anand, Sajjad Zaheer, Hiren Mukherjee, Bhabani Bhattacharya, Iqbal Singh, Raja Rao, Muhammed Asraf, Bhabani Dutta, Jyotish Chandra Ghosh and Promode Sengupta.[33] An early draft of their objectives appeared in the *Left Review* in London and the *Hans* in India under the initiative of Munshi Premchand.[34]

Though the founders of the PWA were staying abroad, the Indian situation worried them no less than the Spanish Civil War and other crises of the West: 'We saw the ugly face of fascism in our country earlier than the writers of the European country, for it was (the) British imperialism which perfected the method of the concentration camp, torture and bombing for police purposes which Hitler, Mussolini and the Japanese militarists have used so effectively later on.'[35] And though they knew little about the current state of vernacular literature in India, they realized: 'a few exiled Indians could do little more than draw up plans among themselves and produce an orphan-like literature under the influence of European culture.' They felt the movement could bear fruits only when it was propagated in various languages in India and an organization in India proper was formed. And then they would maintain this affiliation as a foreign branch of the central organization in India to keep contact with the progressive literary movement abroad, to represent Indian literature in the West and to interpret for India the thoughts of the Western writers.[36]

II

Their hope was fulfilled in no time. On returning to India they found the Indian situation propitious with the writers becoming increasingly sensitive to man's predicament. Some eminent devotees of literature in India collaborated with them to form the All India Progressive Writers' Association in Lucknow on 10 April 1936. It was a grand show facilitated by the session of the Indian National Congress being held in Lucknow at the same time. This first All India Progressive Writers' Conference was presided over by Munshi Premchand. Among the north Indian writers were present Yashpal, Sumitranandan Pant, Rashida Jehan, Faiz Ahmed Faiz and Sajjad Zaheer. From south India came the famous Telegu poet Abburi Ramakrishna Rau, Sarojini Naidu and Maulana Hasrat Mohani, the noted politician and Urdu poet respectively, gave speeches. From Bengal, Rabindranath and Sarat Chandra, the two stalwarts of the old generation, sent their blessings. Four Bengali representatives were present at the conference. Surendranath Goswami was supposed to attend, but failed ultimately. His essay 'Towards Progressive Literature' was read out by Hiren Mukherjee and was highly appreciated.[37] Hiren Mukherjee wrote a letter[38] to S. Zaheer a few days before the Conference saying that Asit Mukherjee, M.D. (London), editor of *Bishan*, Surendranath Goswami, Lecturer of Calcutta University and writer of philosophical subjects, A.K. Bhattacharya, Bar-at-Law, associate editor of a Bengali monthly *Rageshree* and himself would be attending. Two of Bengal's leading young writers, Buddhadev Bose and Premendra Mitra, Mukherjee noted, would not be coming, but they had every sympathy for the

Conference. In the list of the members of the AIPWA, prepared by the police soon after the Conference, three Bengali names occur—Asit Mukherjee, Surendranath Goswami and Debendranath Mukherjee of Calcutta.[39]

What sort of literature did these people want to cultivate? The manifesto of the AIPW[40] solemnly resolved to 'develop an attitude of literary criticism that would discourage the general reactionary and revivalist tendencies on the question(s) like family, religion, sex, war and society', and decried 'the literary trends reflecting communalism, racial antagonism, sexual libertinism and exploitation of man by man'; it pledged to 'rescue literature and other arts from the conservative classes in whose hands they have been degenerating so long, to bring into closest touch with the people'. As for the definition of 'progressive literature', it said, 'we believe that the new literature of India must deal with the basic problem of our existence today—the problem of hunger and poverty, social backwardness and political subjugation. All that drags us down to passivity, inaction and unreason, we reject as reactionary. All that arouses in us the critical spirit, which examines institutions and customs in the light of reason, which helps us to act, to organize ourselves, to transform, we accept as a progressive'.

In his presidential address to the First All India Progressive Writers' Congress, the great Hindi litterateur Munshi Premchand said that writers should stop writing unrealistic tales for entertainment or for merely gratifying the sense of wonder. They should take upon themselves the task of striving after man's spiritual and moral betterment. 'Are we then to give up our ideals (brotherhood and equality)?', said Premchand,

> If that were so, the human race might as well perish. The ideal which we have cherished since the dawn of civilization; for which man has made, God knows, how many sacrifices; which gave birth to religion—the history of human society is a history of the struggle for the fulfilment of this ideal. We too have to place that ideal before ourselves; we have to accept it as an unalterable reality and then see the vulgar pride, ostentation and lack of sensibility in the one, the strength of modesty, faith and endeavour in the other.

He wanted the writers not to sit inane after doing a little bit of creative work on a piece of paper—they should acquaint themselves with the general condition of society and actively participate in building the new order which is not opposed to beauty, good taste and self-respect. He also said that the literature of the masses should speak their language and not that of the privileged classes.[41]

The AIPWA thus provided a minimum basis of unity for all writers who might differ in many ways. The original manifesto also intended to establish organizations corresponding to various linguistic zones, to coordinate these branches by holding conferences, to produce and translate literature of a progressive nature and thus to further the cause of India's freedom and social regeneration, and also to protect the interest of progressive authors. An English publication entitled *New Indian Literature* was planned. Its editorial board consisted of Sumitranandan Pant, Sajjad Zaheer, Krishan Chander representing Hindi and Hindustani, Umashankar Joshi Gujarati, Hiren Mukherjee Bengali and so on.

The progressive writers' movement in India was clearly a response to an Indian reality and not an attempt to introduce a outlandish fashion in India, though some foreign-returned Indians played a prominent role in the formation of the AIPWA and the idea had been first mooted in London. 'Progressive' literature, consistent with the idea propounded in the manifesto and the speech of Premchand, had already been existent in India and Bengal by the middle of the 1930s. And as we will later see, the movement went from strength to strength not due to any foreign influence but to the persistent will of Indian writers and intellectuals to stand up to crises in their own country such as the impact of the Second World War, the Japanese attack and the Bengal Famine. Branches were opened in a number of major cities of north India—Bombay, Calcutta, Allahabad, Delhi, Kanpur, Ahmedabad, Lucknow, Bhopal, Agra, Hyderabad, Lahore, Amritsar and Patna (south India was left rather untouched by the movement)—and by 1947 it grew to over 50 branches.[42]

III

We now need to examine another question—how far was the AIPWA a Communist organization? Within a few days of the publication of the AIPWA manifesto, *The Statesman*'s representative at Simla blatantly abused the Communist Party in the following words:

> That (the aims of the AIPWA) sounds innocuous enough, and even praiseworthy. But it lacks candour to the extent that it is not the whole or most important part of the story, and the manifesto might have attracted more attention if it had said something about the progressive writers' antecedents. One important point is that a large majority of the manifesto's signatories came from well-to-do middle-class families, who had their higher education in England, where for several years the Communist Party has been trying hard to attract just this type of Indian students.[43]

M.G. Hallet, Home Secretary, Government of India, warned the regional governments against the AIPWA on the same grounds within a few months. The Hallet circular abused the Communist Party for having founded the AIPWA, which was 'a typical example of the methods, now being pursued by Communists in all countries—in accordance with the current policy of the Communist International'.[44]

Files kept at the Intelligence Branch of the West Bengal Police contain such comments in abundance. In 'Extract from the 49th Plenary Session of the Indian National Congress' we find the following comment about the inaugural session of the AIPWA: 'A manifesto was issued, but it carefully concealed the Communist origin and proclivities of the association. The proceedings were of no interest except for some outspoken criticism of Government by R.S. Pandit (J.L. Nehru's brother-in-law) for hampering the press, customs and Criminal Law Amendment Acts, production and distribution of seditious literature.' The report said that the speeches of Kirloskar of Poona, M. Hasrat Mohani of Cawnpore, Raghupati Sahai Firaq of Allahabad University and Faiz Ahmed Faiz of Punjab 'contained touches of utilitarianism, atheism and mild Communism'.

An Uttar Pradesh (UP) Criminal Intelligence Department (CID) report dated 10 July 1937 said:

> In the guise of literary propagandists, the members of the IPWA are consciously or unconsciously stimulating the cult of class hatred and disrespect for law and authority. Their platform is being used to disseminate quasi-socialist propaganda among intelligentsia. The association appears to have been conducted in close conjunction with the British Movement on similar lines and gives the budding Indian litterateurs access to the office of such publishing houses as Messrs Martin Lawrence & Company whose main business is the production of Communist publication and books of 'progressive' kind.

There was an element of truth in these allegations, though naturally the Communists did not like the vein of the accusation,[45] and sometimes the allegations were a bit over-extended. It is undeniable that Communists played a notable part in the formation of the AIPWA. It was not intended to be a political organization, but many of the founders were conscious that 'we have to align ourselves with the vanguard of the Indian struggle for political and economic emancipation'. On the other hand, it is true that the organization included writers of all kinds—apolitical and of various political leanings, some of them even vehemently anti-Communist. It was creditable of the Communists and their United Front theory to have united them under a single banner. Hallet suggested that, 'suitable opportunities may be taken to convey, preferably in conversation, friendly warnings about this Association to journalists, educationists and others who might be attracted by its ostensible programme'. But there was really nothing secretive about the Communist involvement in the Association, and yet it succeeded in attracting a host of writers and intellectuals, thanks to the patient and friendly attitude of the Communists and above all of P.C. Joshi, the accomplished and open-hearted secretary of the Indian Communist Party.

As Hiren Mukherjee, one of the founder members of the AIPWA, told me in an interview later, the CPI had naturally expected that the culturally enthusiastic people associated with it would build up the AIPWA as a broad united front and that extensiveness would be the measure of the AIPWA's success. Otherwise, the CPI could have founded a Red Writers' Organization as in France. The AIPWA's task was to prepare the soil, so that it would be possible to build upon it.

IV

The Bengal Progressive Writers' Association

The Progressive Writers' Movement found in Bengal wide and active response. On 11 July 1936, the Organizing Committee of the Bengal Progressive Writers' Association arranged a meeting at Albert Hall in memory of Maxim Gorky who had died the previous month. The convenors were men of letters—Satyendranath Majumdar, Najrul Islam, Hiren Mukherjee, Surendranath Goswami, Vivekananda Mukherjee, Dr Dhirendranath Sen, and Khagendranath Sen. Naresh Chandra Sengupta was supposed to preside over the meeting. Due to his inability to attend, Satyendranath Majumdar presided. The formal inauguration of the Bengal Progressive Writers' Association took place at this meeting, with Naresh Chandra Sengupta as its President and Surendranath Goswami as the Secretary.[46]

On 16 August 1936, the Bengal PWA convened a Gorky Memorial meeting at Ashutosh Hall in response to a call given by S. Zaheer, Secretary of the AIPWA. Tagore sent a message for the meeting. On 30 January 1937, the AIPWA arranged a meeting to pay homage to the memory of Ralph Fox, at Mahat Ashram. The speakers were Satyendranath Majumdar, Hiren Mukherjee, Arun Mitra and Probodh Kumar Sanyal.

How widely the organizers of the AIPWA tried to draw sympathy from intellectuals and writers would be evident from the list of persons to whom S. Zaheer addressed the AIPWA circular no. 1.[47] The police intercepted all these book-posts and passed them on after copying the names of the addressees. They were prominent members of the Bengali (a few were non-Bengali) literati and of various political (also apolitical) orientations (Appendix III).[48] From circular no. 2 of the AIPWA (dated January 1937) intercepted and copied by the police, we can form an idea about the activities of the Bengal Branch in its early phase. Here it was reported that five district branches had already been opened and six more would be opened shortly.

Appeals and reports of the PWA, published frequently by the Calcutta press, particularly the *Ananda Bazar Patrika* and very often the *Prabasi*, had received an encouraging response from young writers and students of Bengal and Assam.

The All Bengal Students' Conference and other district student conferences adopted resolutions welcoming the PWA. The Secretary of the BPWA and Hiren Mukherjee extended greetings to the Kisan Sabha Conference. The Secretary also spoke at the meeting organized by the League Against Fascism and War, on 4 September, which was presided over by Ramananda Chatterjee. A marked feature of the PWA conferences and meetings were debates on topics like 'Literature as a factor in the transformation and reconstruction of society' or 'Economic and social factors in the formation of the ideas of the East and the West'. Large number of young men participated in these debates. Medals were awarded to the successful debaters. A public meeting was held under the auspices of the PWA on 22 November 1936, in the '33 club. Bijoylal Chatterjee of the literary journal *Desh* read a paper on 'Democratic literature and national life'. Naresh Chandra Sengupta chaired the meeting. Other speakers were Premendra Mitra, Editor, *Navashakti*, Satyendranath Majumdar and Hiren Mukherjee. The circular also reported that the translation of 'Theses on Feurbach' was ready with an introduction and would soon be published in the monthly journal *Parichay*.[49]

Another source of information for the BPWA activities about this time is Surendranath Goswami's letter to S. Zaheer (dated 15 December 1936, intercepted by the police).[50] Here he reported a meeting of the PWA study circle held on 6 December 1936. In this meeting Sudhindranath Dutta spoke on literature. Other speakers were Hiren Mukherjee, Vivekananda Mukherjee and Shyamal Krishna Ghosh. Their speeches were to be published in *Parichay*. Goswami also reported that he had been invited by the students and members of the Radical Party to speak on 'Society and individual' at their study circle to be held on 11 December 1936. He also noted the publication of a preliminary discussion on Dialectical Materialism in the Paus issue of *Parichay*. It was in fact, a long review of Sidney Hook's *From Hegel to Marx* and T.A. Jackson's 'Dialectics', and was based on the *Theses on Feurbach*. Other articles on this subject were shortly to be published as a special number of the journal *Sahityika*.

The BPWA's involvement in linguistic areas other than Bengal was also revealed in this letter. According to the letter, at the next meeting of the BPWA, Professor Jha of the Hindi Department, Bangabasi College, would deliver a lecture on Premchand and Hindi Literature, and Satyendranath Majumdar would speak on Jawaharlal Nehru's *Autobiography*. They were hopeful about holding weekly meetings of the study circle from the next month. It is also learnt from this letter that Goswami, on behalf of the BPWA, was helping Ananta Patnaik, Editor, *Adhunik* (Cuttack), to organize the Orissa PWA. This is corroborated by another letter intercepted by the police. This one was from Sachi Routroy of Cuttack asking Goswami to help form the 'All Orissa Progressive Writers' Association'.[51] Nava Yuga Sahitya Sansad, a local progressive literary organization was expected to get incorporated in it.

However, despite these activities of the BPWA, the AIPWA, on the whole, seems to have suffered from serious organizational weaknesses. A letter written by Mahmud Zaffar to Mulk Raj Anand in December 1937,[52] expressed a grave concern: 'But the PWA as a whole is dying, If not dead. [This sentence was originally underlined.] It is a terrible thing to admit at the stage of our general movement. The fact has to be admitted that there are no progressive writers themselves willing or capable of running the show and the others are upto the neck in political work. There is a tragic dearth of cadres.' The letter-writer appealed to Anand to return to India in order to reorganize this cultural front. But it seems that things in Bengal were not so discouraging. Here the organization was working satisfactorily.[53]

A report from District Intelligence Officer of Tipperah informed the Superintendent, Special Branch, Calcutta (dated 31 March 1938)[54] that at the Students' Conference at Comilla, it had been decided to start branches of Pragati Sangha (the Intelligence official described it as an international organization having a branch in England and wondered whether it was a 'Left Book Club') all over the District. The source of information was Sudhir Brahmo, who himself was active in this respect. Brahmo had approached the boys at the Bagichapara playground. They were to be given lectures and training in different subjects. Just now there would be no politics, but the organizers would have no objection to politicizing these boys. Brahmo had further confided to the DIO that even Muslim students were interested in this movement which they considered to be an antidote to communalism, racism and political subjugation. Brahmo thought that the government was then in an embarrassing position owing to its internal and international troubles, and hence had to allow all sorts of political activities to avoid further troubles. The DIO concluded the report on a pessimistic note by saying that the situation was 'Undoubtedly changing very fast towards the worst' and that the move by the Anushilan and the Jugantar terrorists after their release to associate with the youth would lead to further chaos.

Another report on the PWA of Tipperah about this time is included in a police file, under the heading of 'Communism'. According to this report, a secret meeting of the PWA had been held on 15 August 1938 in the bookshop of an ex-detenue Ranajit Roy Chowdhury. It had been attended among others by ex-detenues Bankim Chakrabarty, Rabindra Goswami and Purnendu Sen. Ranajit Roy Chowdhury ordered books on Communism from England to the value of Rs. 200.

How widely the Progressive Writers' Movement had pervaded the cultural field of Bengal was revealed in the BPWA publication *Pragati* (*Progress*,

1937) edited by Surendranath Goswami and Hiren Mukherjee.[55] Tagore sent his blessings. The introduction was written by Naresh Chandra Sengupta. The contributors were reputed Bengali writers like Bhupendranath Dutta, Dhurjati Prasad Mukherjee, Bibhuti Bhushan Banerjee, Sudhindranath Dutta, Sajanikanta Das, Buddhadev Bose, Premendra Mitra, Probodh Kumar Sanyal, Manik Banerjee, Bijoylal Chatterjee, Bidhayak Bhattacharya and Samar Sen, Among the foreign writers who found place in this collection were Karl Marx, Andre Gide, E.M. Forster, T.S. Eliot, Alexander Block, Gulam Gafur and Karabiyev. The translators were Abu Sayeed Ayub, Nirendranath Ray, Soumyendranath Tagore, Abdul Kadir, Bishnu Dey and Arun Mitra. The writings of Sailajananda Mukherjee, Pabitra Ganguly and Tarasankar Banerjee were received too late to be included.

Several articles in this book attempted to define 'progressive art and literature'. While specific traditions and requirements of art were taken into account, an emphasis was put on its connection with the real life. There was, of course, a conformity to the avowed aims and objectives of the AIPWA. Tagore wrote to Surendranath Goswami after reading *Pragati*: 'A storm wind of thoughts and ideas, of spirit and practice is sweeping over the whole world. Our minds have not been spared from its forceful shove. You have collected descriptions of this phenomenon in your book Pragati.... In your book is reflected the stir created by this phenomenon. This stir has blurred the distinction between our own country and foreign lands. This also has been recognized in your collection' (6 October 1937).[56]

Many of the writers contributing to *Pragati* never claimed to be socialist or even progressive. Sajanikanta Das, editor of *Shanibarer Chithi*, even ridiculed the Progressive Writers' Movement more than once in his journal. Sudhindranath Dutta had his reservations about the socialist view of the world. Yet all of them rallied around the cause of resistance against fascism. Their socialist and progressive friends influenced them to do so. Hiren Mukherjee was perhaps right when he said that though all did not welcome the movement whole-heartedly, every devotee of Bengali literature accepted it somehow, except only two—Mohitlal Majumdar and Banaphul (pen-name of Balaichand Mukherjee).[57] Buddhadev Bose became rather over-enthusiastic about progressive culture and went so far as to attack Tagore in his speech at the second annual conference of the AIPWA, Calcutta, 1938 (of which more shortly).

Sarat Chandra, while sending a message to the inaugural conference of the AIPWA admitted the nobility of the cause it upheld, but disapproved of the idea of group literature.[58] To him, literature was primarily an individual's creation. But this view was also expressed by Naresh Chandra Sengupta who was closely associated with the movement from the beginning: 'Formation of a group does not create literature' (*Pragati*). And yet Sengupta stressed the need for unity among litterateurs to save human civilization from the imminent disaster. The report of the second AIPWA conference (Calcutta 1938) in the leftist journal *Agrani* expressed the same view: 'Few writers today would directly deny that the crisis of literature is part of the wider social crisis. Yet from the way reactionary forces have penetrated each pore of the body of society it is clear that mere personal efforts of progressive writers would not be enough for a cultural revolution. Unity is necessary. And the Progressive Writers' Association has been born out of a sense of this need.' It was felt that such an organization as the AIPWA could be a symbol of the united conscience of the writers and at the same time could actively create a climate of protest which in its turn would revitalize literature.[59]

V

The Second AIPWA Conference

Bengal hosted the second AIPWA conference in December 1938,[60] at Ashutosh Memorial Hall, Calcutta.[61] A Presidium was elected at the beginning of the two-day conference. It consisted of writers Mulk Raj Anand, Sailajananda Mukherjee, Sudhindranath Dutta, Buddhadev Bose and Pandit Sudarshan. Hiren Mukherjee says, 'As far as I remember, due to Umashankar Joshi's inability to come, the assembly elected Buddhadev Bose in his place'.[62] Among those present were Premendra Mitra, Hiran Kumar Sanyal, Ahmad Ali, Balraj Sahni, Abdul Aleem, Shahid Suhrawardy, Nirmal Kumar Siddhanta et al. Two Urdu poets—Mazaj Ali and Ali Sardar Jafri became the centre of attraction. Naresh Chandra Sengupta was the President of the Reception Committee. Surendranath Goswami and Satyendranath Majumdar worked hard for the success of the Conference. It was inaugurated with the reading of Tagore's message. Atul Chandra Gupta, Rajsekhar Basu and other prominent writers read out welcome addresses. Saroj Dutta recited his own poem.

Here many non-leftist intellectuals rallied to the cause of progressive culture. Sudhindranath Dutta said, 'Not the introspecting intellectuals but the enduring masses are the guardians of tradition and dictators of progress, and whatever be the calibre of the experiment or unless he passes the pragmatic test of his people, the facts he would fondly establish are febrile dreams and the truths he would loudly proclaim are feeble fancies'. Buddhadev Bose attacked Tagore for being a representative of the bourgeois culture, saying that Tagore's genius had absorbed and nearly exhausted all the creative and progressive forces of the bourgeois culture and that time had come for a new culture for which the writers needed mass contact and thoughts about a new social system.[63] Mulk Raj Anand, however, paid tribute to the great poet at the same conference—'And from the beginning we had the guidance, the goodwill and active help of the oldest and youngest poet of Bengal, Rabindranath Tagore, who came out boldly in defence of the civil liberties campaign and who was the first writer to sign the statement sent by the Indian intellectuals to the Peace Congress at Brussels.'

It is a fact that during the last days of his life Tagore was becoming more and more outspoken against the evils in human order. It is also a fact that the organizers of the 'progressive' cultural movement sought and did get Tagore's support several times and he did not leave the camp of progress till his death (1941). But on the whole he had a love-hate relationship with the progressives. His feelings were naturally hurt at comments such as those made by Buddhadev Bose and he made some tart remarks about progressive literature in a letter to Amiya Chakravarty.[64]

At this conference emphasis was laid on freedom. The president Naresh Chandra Sengupta, said, 'Progress of man, as I understand it, and I hope you understand it, means a widening of his freedom. The history of civilization is the history of expanding freedom.' Freedom was indeed a vital issue in the context of imperialism, fascism and every kind of restrictive thought and exploitation. The first resolution adopted by the Conference was to help those who were fighting for India's political freedom. The second resolution sympathized with the victims of fascism and supported those who were fighting against it. The third one demanded expansion of individual freedom, protested against proscription of foreign literature and so on.

Mulk Raj Anand said at this conference:

> We have to align ourselves with the vanguard of the Indian struggle for political and economic emancipation as ordinary persons, in (the) day to day work. In this capacity our technical skill can be mobilized in the vigorous journalism that has grown and is growing in the wake of the national movement; because this training in journalism will not only improve our skill through the short crisp sentences of ready speech, thus refashioning our language overweighted by ornate metaphor and imagery, but it will bring us into daily contact with the actual national and social problems and with the people whose lives make these problems (the) urgent necessity of the hour quite apart from speculative interest.

During the next ten to fifteen years, journalism actually entered the field of literature, and brought about a welcome change in the latter. In the leftist papers like *Janayuddha*, *Swadhinata*, *Parichay*, *Arani*, *Agrani* and *Natun Sahitya*, gifted literatteurs like Tarasankar Banerjee, Manik Banerjee, Subhas Mukherjee, Nani Bhowmik, Gopal Haldar and Ghulam Quddus practised journalism dealing with a variety of topical problems. To give only a few examples, Gopal Haldar arguing in favour of reducing the production of jute (*Janayuddha*, 1943), Tarasankar demanding the release of political prisoners (*Swadhinata*, 13 April 1946), Subhas Mukherjee covering the Post and Telegraph strike (*Swadhinata*, 24 July 1946, and 3 August 1946), Manik Banerjee reporting on the worker–owner conflict at some printing presses (*Swadhinata*, June 1947), etc. This is an indication of how the leftist cultural movement under discussion contributed to a major field of literary activity and also brought writers and artists close to life.

VI

Branches of the BPWA: The Dhaka Branch

During 1937–8, the BPWA spread its network in Bengal. Among the district branches, the most prominent was the Dhaka branch.[65] At South Maishandi, Dhaka, some young Communists had opened a Pragati Pathagar (Progressive Library) and a Communist Study Circle with Satish Pakrashi, a one-time revolutionary terrorist, as the teacher. The place was near the office of the Communist Party at Jorpul Lane. These young Communists soon set up a Progressive Writers' Association. They were Somen Chanda, Kiransankar Sengupta, Amrita Dutta, Saralananda Sen, Ranesh Dasgupta and Jyotirmoy Sen. In the second half of 1939, they got affiliated to the BPWA. Soon they met Achyut Goswami and the latter lent a room of his house (21 Court House Street) for their weekly *Baithak* (meeting). In these meetings, they used to read out their own creative writings. In one of these meetings, Somen Chanda read his excellent story 'Danga' (Riot) on the recent Dhaka riots.

The Dhaka PWA was inspired by the Calcutta PWA's publication *Pragati* and published another such compilation entitled *Kranti* (Revolution) in 1940. The twenty contributors were all local writers. But they created a sensation. The learned circle in Calcutta welcomed them. After this, their contact with the progressive writers of Calcutta broadened. Benoy Ghosh, Subhas Mukherjee, Abdul Odud, Buddhadev Bose, Manik Banerjee, Gopal Haldar, Manoranjan Bhattacharya and others visited Dhaka and attended some big meetings of the Dhaka PWA. This in turn attracted the learned men of Dhaka. Many more people such as Jiban Chakrabarty and Ranen Majumdar joined the Association.

The Youth Cultural Institute

> Men and women are so deeply influenced by the circumstances which surround them through their adolescence, that during times of rapid change, like the present, generations divided by completely different views of life succeed to

each other in less than ten years, instead of thirty. The attitude of young men at the Universities is a good test of this.

—STEPHEN SPENDER, reviewing a book on John Conford,
a Cambridge student and poet, who had been killed
in the Spanish Civil War

By the end of 1939, some Calcutta University students planned to organize a Research Group to enlighten the public about the various socio-economic and political problems of the world, the main problem being fascism. Somehow or the other, this plan did not materialize. A few months later they seriously contemplated forming an organization to create a new cultural movement, primarily designed to arouse anti-fascist consciousness amongst people.

Among the first members of the Youth Cultural Institute[66] were Jyoti Basu, Nikhil Chakrabarty, Renu Roy (later Chakrabarty), Shyama Nath Sinha, Sunil Chatterjee (Paltu), Chinmohan Sehanabis, and some of the best students of the University—Jolly Mohan Kaul, Subrata Banerjee, Sunil Sen (two persons of the same name), Harkumar Chaturvedi, Ramkrishna Mukherjee, Sujata Mukherjee (later Davies), Rama Goswami, Uma Chakrabarty (later Sehanabis), Neville Campbell, Kamal Bose, Debabrata Bose (Bablu), Dilip Roy, Chitra Majumdar, Mohit Banerjee and Tarun Mukherjee.

Their first meeting was held at the house of Sunil Jana, a renowned photographer, with the painter Chintamani Kar, who had just returned from Spain, as the President. Shahid Suhrawardy (not the later Chief Minister of Bengal) was chosen as the President of the organization, and A.K.M. Zackeria, ex-Mayor of Calcutta and Professor Niharranjan Ray as Vice-Presidents. The university professors were attracted by the YCI activities and Dr Radhakrishnan, Georgé the Fifth Professor of Philosophy, was one of their patrons. The formal inauguration took place at the Students' Hall. Here Jolly Kaul was elected the General Secretary. A room was rented at Kent House, P-33, Mission Row Extension. Here they would hold regular discussions, debates, lectures, play-acting and other cultural activities. Later, the office was shifted to 46, Dharmatala Street.

These young enthusiasts were generally well-off and upper class. A good many number of them had been educated at English schools. They had a liberal outlook and were inclined towards Communist ideas. But because of their family and educational backgrounds, they knew more about Western culture than about the culture of their own land. This was revealed in their first poster exhibition that centred round the theme of 'Crisis of Culture'. The artists of this exhibition belonged mostly to the YCI itself. Among the guest artists was Satyajit Ray. The students' posters criticized stalwarts like T.S. Eliot, Ezra Pound, Andre Gide and Bernard Shaw saying 'They are not the remedy, they are the disease'. Though Rabindranath was quoted once, on the whole, an ignorance of Indian culture was evident. This prompted some adverse comments from distinguished visitors. Still, this was probably the first poster exhibition in Calcutta and the young YCI members were keen on overcoming whatever limitations they had.

The themes of the debates they held were often significant. Once the motion was 'Gandhism is out-of-date'. Priyaranjan Sen and Humayun Kabir spoke against the motion and the speakers for the motion were Hiren Mukherjee and Surendranath Goswami.

On another occasion, the motion of debate was: 'C.K. Naidu, the cricketer, Ramananda Chatterjee, the journalist and Leela Desai, the film star are marooned in an island. The rescue boat has room for only one. Who of these three should be rescued in the best interest of the nation?' Leela Desai's cause was valiantly upheld by the majority of the speakers. With their political consciousness and seriousness about forging a new cultural movement they exuded a sort of carefree joviality. They often arranged picnics for entertainment.

The YCI was a pioneer in the field of the People's Theatre and the People's Song Movements. They introduced contemporary reality in their dramas and songs, and though they were distant from the masses, they wanted to overcome this isolation and forge links with them. We will discuss this later in the chapters on music and theatre.

The YCI was short-lived. Following the bombing of Calcutta and the mass evacuation, YCI activities declined sharply. The Institute disappeared by the middle of 1942.

The Second World War and the People's War of the Communists

Few loiter in the streets today,
Middle-class lamp-posts are dim in fear,
No smoke from the evacuees' kitchens
obscures the sharp moonlight!
The blue light spreads endlessly,
the aweful light of the moon in the dark blue!
They say the enemy's wings receive aid in this light
which flows into our homes
Yet flows without rest in deadly glory. Oh! On life's peak,
let me have the glory of death,
No blind accident! Why in this worldwide war
Middle-class Calcutta seeks pity from blood-red battlefields!
Vacant is the seat of the leader of the people, fill it, our heroes!
Let foxes confer in secret; yet China and the USSR,

The farmers and workers of all lands pour their manhood,
To redeem the wages of selfishness,
into the foundations of the established.
Desperately, restlessly, war stalks on land and water and air—
India too is shaken—in the dark days of her life!
Calcutta's full moon spreads out her Jatayu wings
over USSR and far-off China.

—BISHNU DEY
'22 June 1941', A Sonnet
(The first poem of his book *Baishe June*
published by the AIPWA, translator unknown)

In September 1939, the much dreaded Second World War finally broke out. The British government unilaterally associated India with the British declaration of war on Germany, without caring to consult even a single Indian leader. The Congress provincial ministries resigned in protest. However, Congress hostility to fascist aggression continued and it was prepared to back the British war efforts provided some minimum conditions were met: a post-war independence pledge and an immediate National Government at the centre. But the British did not pay heed to them. During the years 1940–1 the Congress was forced (to some extent due to leftist pressure from within) to take up a programme of Satyagraha with prominent individuals, starting from Gandhi and Nehru, courting arrest.

The left was more militantly anti-war and anti-government.[67] The Communist Party raised the slogan, 'Na ek pai, na ek bhai', i.e. not a single paisa and not a single brother for the British war efforts. The reversal of the Comintern policy after the Nazi-Soviet Pact of August 1939 was a serious embarrassment for Communists in Europe, but a blessing for their comrades in India, allowing an easy synchronization of 'internationalist' support to Soviet policies with nationalist hostility to Britain's war. According to Hiren Mukherjee, the Communists even debated among themselves the desirability of a tactical friendship with the fascists, for, after all, the latter were the 'enemy's enemy'. Even the detenues at different camps and the Andaman Islands sent their opinions. Ultimately, the consensus was against such a move.[68] Since its rigid anti-war stand the Party lost whatever little legality it had been previously enjoying and became a prominent target of the 'Ordinance Raj's' policy of repression.

All this, however, changed on 22 June 1941—the day Hitler attacked Russia. The Communists felt obliged to render full support to the world's only socialist state engaged in a life-and-death struggle for survival. They suddenly realized that victory of fascism would delay Indian Independence and an isolationist attitude on India's part in the war would be a blunder. So they decided to back the British, an ally of Russia, while reiterating the standard Congress demands for an independence pledge and for an immediate National Government. But these were no longer regarded as indispensable preconditions for support. The War, they now argued, had so long been an imperialist one, with imperialist powers fighting each other, but now it had turned into a People's War with patriotic people fighting against fascist aggrandizement. However, it took six months of hesitation and internal debate before the Party officially announced the new line at the All Students' Conference in Patna, in January 1942. A number of individual Communists felt bad about it and yet had to accept the decision. The commitment, though a source of enormous difficulties for the Party later, paid off immediately. The ban on the Party was lifted on 22 July 1942.

Concern and sympathy for Russia was widespread. Soon after Hitler's attack on that country, a manifesto admiring Soviet achievements and wishing them victory was issued by the Bengali intellectuals. The signatories included many prominent professors, barristers, artists and writers of Bengal, not all of them Communist.[69] But the Communists soon faced practical difficulties in combining anti-imperialist and anti-fascist sentiments, and the People's War theory proved to be utterly problematic.

In the Congress, Nehru had a deep internationalist and anti-fascist commitment and concern for Russia. He tried hard for a compromise to secure Indian support for the war during the Cripps negotiation (February–March 1942). Such a compromise, he argued, had now become urgent, as the Japanese conquest of Singapore, Rangoon and the Andamans had brought the war near India's frontier. But the British were not really ready to make any concession. The bulk of the Congress leadership was probably from the beginning unenthusiastic about the Cripps Mission. Things, in fact, were now rapidly moving towards a total confrontation. The majority of the Congress leaders lacked the global perspective that Nehru and the Communists had. British obstinancy was unendurably provocative to them. Moreover, they felt that the British was going to be defeated and the time had come for a bold strike for achieving freedom. This perhaps explains the uncharacteristic militancy of the famous 8 August Resolution of the AICC and Gandhi's 'do or die' speech the same day. Though the Resolution called for 'mass struggle on non-violent lines', it had a significant rider that if the leadership was removed by arrest, 'every Indian who desires freedom and strives for it must be his own guide'.

Yet the calculations and plans of the Congress leaders can only partially explain the largely spontaneous outburst that took place after the leaders had been arrested on 9 August 1942. The Quit India Resolution had not given much detailed instruction regarding struggle and the insurgent millions certainly went beyond whatever little it had suggested. While the resolution had called for stopping of trains 'by pulling chains only', the people blew up railway bridges. Whatever the August Resolution had meant, the struggle that actually took place was a violent and determined people's war for national literation. The colonial police had much difficulty in quelling it. Midnapore and Satara saw the setting-up of even National Governments, though temporarily.

But this also meant disruption of the British war efforts and was naturally disliked by people like Nehru and of course, the Communists. And in their opposition to an all-out anti British struggle they found themselves in the strange company of a few right-wing Congress leaders like Rajagopalachari and Bhulabhai Desai. Nehru accepted the August Resolution and even moved it, as often before, against his very wishes. CPI members of the All-India Congress Committee (AICC) voted against the Quit India Resolution claiming that it was premature.[70] It is true that the Party also condemned the government repeatedly for not caring a fig for Indian nationalist sentiment and demanded the release of the imprisoned leaders. However, their stand 'to place themselves between the police and people' and the mere suggestion of ensuring national unity as the only prudent course of action, while the patriotic people were fighting with their back to the wall, made them unpopular.

The Communists became unpopular also because of their open denunciation of Subhas Chandra Bose's activities. Bose went to Germany and then to Japan to fight for India's freedom with the latter's help, on the same 'enemy's enemy' tactic that had been considered by the Communists not very long ago. But now the Communists called Bose a 'Quisling' and a 'Fifth Columnist' and derided him in the Party papers. Later, they admitted that despite their tactical differences with Bose, they should have recognized his patriotism and courage. Anybody who was ready to welcome the Japanese out of sheer grudge against the British, anyone who would oppose the British in the smallest way appeared to the Communists as a Fifth Columnist. 'The way the word "Fifth Column was misused is ridiculous"', says the devoted Party worker Manikuntala Sen in her reminiscences,

> A small *bhukha michhil* (hunger procession) was being led by some workers of the Socialist Party. It consisted of a few students, children and poor people. We knew that if they proceeded further the police would flog them and hence we tried to obstruct their way. They got angry and beat us. We called them Fifth Column. Later on I came to know that a socialist friend of mine was in the procession. He did not accept our Party line, but definitely did not deserve to be called Fifth Column. He reproached me later. 'You did this?'[71]

Later, the Communists generally agreed that while the line of People's War had been correct, the way they implemented it had been erroneous. About their opposition to the Quit India Movement, they say that it was later vindicated when Hitler's plan of 'Operation Orient' came to light. When the Quit India Movement was talking place, Hitler was proceeding quickly towards Stalingrad and a breakthrough there would have brought the Nazi forces to India, via Iran and Afghanistan, his plan being the coincidence of his advance from the West with the Japanese advance from Burma to Chittagong and from there to Calcutta—an eventuality frustrated by the heroic Red Army.[72] But some Communists have expressed doubts as to whether they were right in opposing the August Movement. Manikuntala Sen asks, 'Could we do everything according to the Party line? When the bourgeois owners closed down their factories, could our trade unions prevent it? Could we prevent the uprooting of rail lines? Should we not have rather sided with this struggle? Would that have much harmed the Soviet?'[73] Hiren Mukherjee once heard P.C. Joshi telling Tripurari Chakravarty that had the Communists joined the August Movement, it would have succeeded. Mukherjee wondered, if this was so, then would not participation in the movement have been a more sensible decision on the part of the Communist Party?[74]

The Communists have been branded as British agents for their role during the War. However, contrary to a widespread impression, they did not have any secret agreement with the British during the People's War period. In fact, the government was angry at their biting criticisms, and considered banning the Party once again. A secret circular (dated 20 September 1943) from R. Tottenham, Additional Secretary to the Government of India, to the provincial governments, throws light on the attitude of the government towards the Communists during that time:

> They [the Communists] have vociferously condemned the arrests of Mr Gandhi and the Working Committee and have persistently demanded their release. . . . The attacks on Government which have accompanied this propaganda in the Communist press, have undoubtedly at times been embarrassing and we are aware of the disquiet felt by some provincial governments on this score. . . . The Party's pro-war propaganda has almost invariably been heavily interlaced with attacks on bureaucratic inefficiency, the effect of which must have detracted from the value of its condemnation of sabotage and fifth column.

Tottenham made a distinction between the 'short-term' and the 'long-term' policies of the Party: 'The long-term view must be taken as embracing the probable course of events after the war and from this point of view the fundamentally opportunist character of the Party must not be lost sight of'. He calls the Party opportunist, because, 'It is a nationalist party working for Indian independence notwithstanding its lip service to internationalism.'[75]

The Communists certainly did an injustice to Subhas Bose and to many others by calling them Fifth Columnists, which came in the way of the

Communist cause too. A sad result of the People's War policy was the total rift with the Congress Socialist Party (CSP), with former comrades calling each other 'traitors'. This did immeasurable harm to the left movement as well as to the national movement. Ironically, when the Communists were following the policy of a United Front at the theoretical level, in practice their policy led to splits within the national movement. Another sad result was the Communist Party's coming closer to the Muslim League now that the relations with the Congress were strained. The Communists now abandoned their condemnation of the League as unrepresentative of Indian Muslims and gradually yielded to its 'Two Nations' theory. Above all, the charge that they were marionettes, if not paid agents, of the British, has become a permanent blot on the career of the Indian Communists.

It is quite natural that the Communists have had to pay dearly for their opposition to a huge patriotic uprising like the Quit India Movement. But strangely, during the People's War period iself, the progressive cultural movement grew in strength. It seems that even non-Communist writers and artists somehow realized that the Communists had not quite given up their nationalist concerns and they also sympathized with the international perspective of the Communists.

The Friends of the Soviet Union

Serpents are breathing out poison all around.
The pleasant message of peace sounds like a hollow joke.
So before I leave, I call you all—
You who are getting ready at every home to fight the monster.

—Rabindranath's poem, quoted on the cover of *Soviet Desh*, a collection of essays, ed. Gopal Haldar and Sukumar Mitra, and published by Punthighar on behalf of the FSU

The Friends of the Soviet Union (FSU)[76] was part of the development that took place as a result of Hitler's attack on Soviet Russia. A press statement issued by Gopal Haldar, Pramatha Bhaumik and Prasanta Sanyal on 4 July 1941 first mooted the idea of this organization. Its purpose was to mobilize the Indian public opinion in favour of Russia. On 21 July, a big meeting at the Town Hall observed 'Soviet Day'. An organizing committee was formed with Dr Bhupendranath Dutta as the Chairman and Hiren Mukherjee and Snehangshu Acharya as Joint Secretaries. Its office was at 27, Baker Road, Alipore (the house of Acharya). The office of the FSU, when it was formed, was 46, Dharmatala Street, the house that was the venue for a variety of Communist cultural activities.

Surendranath Goswami went to Santiniketan and got the blessings of the ailing Rabindranath for this newly-formed organization. Tagore became a patron of the FSU and approved of the new Party line, while warning them that the British were assuring the Soviet of their help because of their own interest: 'but don't you trust them. You Communists don't get lax in your struggle against the British'. The Communists would have been well-advised to listen to this piece of wisdom.

The FSU was primarily an organization of the Communists working on the basis of the United Front theory. The Party entrusted the work of this organization to Jyoti Basu, S. Acharya, Bhupesh Gupta, Hiren Mukherjee and Mohit Banerjee. An Intelligence Bureau (IB) report (prepared in the early 1950s) from which much information about the FSU could be obtained, says, 'In fact, however, the Friends of the Soviet Union afforded the Communists an open forum to carry on open activities under cover of FSU for the propagation of Communism in addition to the secret and underground work which the CPI was hitherto indulging in'. It is to be kept in mind that at the time of foundation of the FSU, the Party was still debating its People's War policy and the ban on it was yet to be lifted.

According to the draft constitution, the aims of the organization were (a) to study and publicize the conditions of life and the work of reconstruction in the USSR, particularly among its backward people; (b) to enlighten the Indian public regarding the nature of the war started by the fascist powers against the Soviet Union; (c) to give to the fighting Soviet people all practical aid that Indian condition and interest allowed; and (d) to facilitate, maintain and develop by all practical means friendly contacts between India and the Soviet Union.

Soon after the formation of the organization, probably in July 1941, an All-India Friends of the Soviet Conference was arranged at the University Institute Hall, Calcutta. They invited D.D. Kosambi, a famous historian, to preside over the conference. When he regretted his inability to come to Calcutta at that time, Mian Iftiqaruddin, President of the Punjab Provincial Committee of the Congress, was selected. The two Joint Secretaries for the Conference were Hiren Mukherjee and Jagjit Singh who later became a Kisan Sabha leader. A separate assemblage of workers was arranged. A procession of a thousand workers ('literally', says Hiren Mukherjee)[77] attended it.

Numerous meetings followed. Hiren Mukherjee specially remembered the huge conference at the Town Hall on 7 November 1941, on the occasion of the anniversary of the Bolshevik Revolution. The period 7–14 November was observed as 'Soviet Week' with meetings, processions and poster-exhibitions. At this conference there was a proposal to send an Indian leader to Russia. However, the British government did not permit it.

The Indo-Soviet Journal, the fortnightly organ of the all India unit of the FSU, was mainly looked after by Hiren Mukherjee, though the first few issues had the name of Jyoti Basu as the editor. Basu was also the secretary of the provincial committee of the FSU. They had more publications to their credit—*The Land of the Soviet* edited by Snehangshu Acharya and Hiren Mukherjee, *Soviet Desh* in Bengali by Sukumar Mitra and Gopal Haldar, *Soviet Juddher Tin Mas* by Gopal Haldar, and many more books and pamphlets in Bengali, English, Hindi and Urdu. They were even able to send some money to Russia in order to help the Soviet war efforts. The first instalment was sent through Chiranjilal, a member of the FSU.

Among those who worked for the FSU were Bhabani Sen, the Bengal Provincial Secretary of the CPI, who took classes at the FSU study circle; Satyabrata Chatterjee, who worked for the organization diligently; Girin Chakravarty, a writer mainly for children and his friend Amal Bose, the owner of the Gupta Press (famous for its almanac) which printed the *Indo-Soviet Journal* and many other books and journals for the leftists; Kshitin Roy Chowdhury, a prominent Party member and Ramkrishna Mukherjee, a bright student who was involved in the students' movement. Among those who patronized the FSU were the scientist Meghnad Saha; Satyendranath Majumdar, Editor, *Anandabazar*; Kshitis Prasad Chattopadhyay, a learned Congress man, a friend of Subhas Bose and an enthusiast about all progressive activities; Pandit Rahul Sankrityayan; D.D. Kosambi; Sarojini Naidu and also Jawaharlal Nehru, at least in its early phase.

Very soon organizational units of the FSU were started in almost all districts and even in remote villages. Among them the Dhaka FSU thrived with Kiransankar Sengupta and Debaprasad Mukherjee as Joint Secretaries. They arranged a week-long art exhibition at the Baptist Mission Hall near Sadarghat. There were about hundred pictures on the new civilization in the Soviet Union and on its multifarious achievements. This 'Soviet Mela' was inaugurated by Dr Muhammad Sahidullah. After the grand success of this exhibition, they arranged a few more outside Dhaka.

But after some time, the activities of the FSU seem to have slackened. The IB report mentioned previously says,

> Since 1945 no activity of these units have come to notice. After 1945 the Provincial Unit with its headquarters at 46, Dharmatala street was the only unit that was functioning in the whole of Bengal. In a circular issued by the Bengal Committee of the FSU on 20 May 1947, District Committees were called upon to set up organizing committees of the FSU where no unit existed before and to revive the units that have gone defunct. This circular, however, appears to have met with very little response.

Actually, the centre of activities of the FSU shifted from Calcutta to Bombay in 1944. Just after the FSU Provincial Conference in Calcutta in 1944, an all India conference was held at Bombay. Sarojini Naidu helped them considerably to arrange it. Vijaya Lakshmi Pandit was made the President.

Hiren Mukherjee remembers that he had a slight altercation with Mrs Pundit who while admiring Soviet Russia made some adverse remarks too.[78] At this conference it was decided that the head office of the FSU would be shifted to Bombay and that the *Indo-Soviet Journal* would be published from there.

The Intelligence Report of the early Independence era noted some correspondence between the FSU on the one hand and the USSR Embassy in New Delhi and the USSR Society for Cultural Relations with Foreign Countries (known as Voks) on the other. Since such connections and due to the Anglo-Soviet Agreement, Russian books, journals, pictures, posters and films were coming to India in large quantities. The *International Literature* (renamed *Soviet Literature*) became available again. Alexander Block, Mayakovski, Pasternak, the Ujbek Poet Gafur Gulam, the Kajak writer Karabiyev were widely read. The illiterate bard Jambul of Kazakhstan came to the limelight in India. Ostrovsky's novel *How the Steel was Tempered* moved many a reader.

Among the films shown were *Suvorov*, a remarkable wartime picture, *Childhood of Maxim Gorky*, *Kuban Cossaks*, *Tale of Siberia*, *Peter the Great*, *Ivan the Terrible* and *Battleship Potemkin*. Once, Satu Roy financed and arranged a few film shows at Chhabi Ghar near Sealdah Station. On another occasion, the FSU collaborated with the newly-established Calcutta Film Society (1948) to show some Soviet films. The IB report says that these shows were mostly meant for propaganda and that even during show intervals, appeals were made to the audience to enlist themselves as members of the FSU. The report further says, 'It may be of interest to note that the FSU raised a great row when the film "Iron Curtain" which according to Communists was anti-Soviet was exhibited in Calcutta. They even threatened to attack and destroy the cinema house which exhibited the film.'

Several exhibitions of Soviet posters and photographs were also organized by the FSU. Newspaper reports too corroborate this. The most important of the series was the one held in November 1947, at the Indian Art School, 139, Dharmatala Street, in connection with the observance of the anniversary of the Bolshevik Revolution. Another such exhibition was held at 46, Dharmatala Street on 26 March 1949, all this 'drawing a rosy picture of the Soviet Union' (in the words of the IB Report).

At the time when the IB report was prepared, the office-bearers of the FSU were:

President	Satyendranath Majumdar, editor, *Swaraj*
Secretary	Hiren Mukherjee
Joint Secretaries	Birendra Ghosh and M.A. Latiff, Bar-at-Law

Finally the report says: 'Secret information has been received through different sources that the office of the Friends of the Soviet Union at

46, Dharmatala Street, Calcutta, is being utilized with advantage as a contact place for open and underground Communist workers'. The reference is to the illegal phase of the Communist Party during 1948–50.

ISCUS or the Indo-Soviet Cultural Society later inherited the tradition of the FSU.

Murder of Somen Chanda and the Anti-Fascist Writers' and Artists' Association

> The go-between dies out. The starved and the unemployed, the workers and the beggars multiply as the days pass by. Flies of red-faced soldiers march towards the huge gates of hell. What is this journey for, from one day to another, from one death to another? Where is the end of it? A harrowing pestilence, a deathless hell?
>
> The sultry sky speaks after a long silence: Brave inheritors of ancestral selfishness, listen! With what last straw will you build your home now that a primordial flood sweeps across your world? Tell me, who will light the spark of wisdom in this all-conquering darkness?
>
> —SAMAR SEN
> 'New Year's Resolution' (In memory of Somen Chanda)
> (Translator unknown)

Murder of Somen Chanda

Somen Chanda, a promising 19-year-old writer of Dhaka, Secretary of the Dhaka Progressive Writers' Association, a close associate of the Communist Party and Secretary of the Dhaka Railway Workers' Union, was brutally murdered on 8 March 1942, while leading a procession of railway workers to an anti-fascist meeting organized by the FSU.

The murder was condemned by *Arani*, *Ananda Bazar*, *Parichay* and many other journals. The FSU and the AISF expressed their profound shock. 'Somen Day' was observed at various places. Somen was likened to the artists who had laid down their lives in the battlefields of Spain. Reputed Bengali writers issued a statement on 23 March 1942, paying their homage to Somen as a fighter for people's right, a martyr of Marxist and anti-fascist struggles:

> It is difficult for us to understand the complexities of Bengal politics, particularly the vicious vapour of reprisal that has polluted the communal and political sky of Dhaka. We are unable to follow the psychology behind all this. With our hearts aggrieved at the death of our courageous colleague, we appeal to our countrymen to voice their strong hatred unanimously against this thirst for blood and the poisonous sin. It was signed by Pramatha Chowdhury, Atul Chandra Gupta, Indira Devi, Abu Sayeed Ayub, Pramatha Bisi, Subodh Ghosh, Jyotirmoy Ghosh, Nirendranath

Roy, Kiransankar Sengupta, Bimalaprasad Mukherjee, Abdul Kader, Kamakshi Prasad Chatterjee, Hiran Kumar Sanyal, Subhas Mukherjee, Samar Sen, Benoy Ghosh, Swarnakamal Bhattacharya, Arun Mitra, Amiya Chakravarty, Saroj Dutta, Buddhadev Bose, Ajit Dutta, Bishnu Dey and others.[79]

The murderers of Somen Chanda were never tracked down. But the leftist journals suspected rival political parties, particularly the Forward Block and the Revolutionary Socialist Party which were supporting the fascists. Fascism thus no longer seemed a distant threat. According to these journals, such political murders had become rampant in Dhaka and elsewhere. *Agrani*, while reporting Somen Chanda's murder, also carried the news of another such incident a week before—on 21 February, at the town of Comilla, a Communist student named Sudarsan Lal had been stabbed and seriously injured. Pradyot Sarkar, a student of Jagannath College, had been stabbed to death a few days earlier. Such crimes against Communists seem to have continued till 1944–5. Kochi Nag, a Communist student, Ranesh Dasgupta and many others were badly injured by assailants in Narayanganj 1944.

Somen Memorial Libraries were founded in Dhaka and Calcutta. Every year, 8 March was observed as the Somen Memorial Day. The South Calcutta Students' Federation dedicated an anthology of anti-fascist poems—*Prachir* (Barrier)—to Somen's memory (April 1942).

Anti-Fascist Writers' and Artists' Association

Somen Chanda's murder was the proximate cause of the formation of the AFWAA.[80] The Bengal branch of the Progressive Writers' Association which had almost become defunct for quite some time due to organizational weaknesses, was now revived with a new name and much wider scope, admitting as members not only writers, but also practitioners of other art forms.

The Bengal Provincial Students' Federation convened a meeting of anti-fascist writers on 28 March 1942, at the University Institute Hall, to mourn Somen's death. Ramananda Chatterjee presided. Buddhadev Bose recited his poem written on Somen. Sujata Mukherjee recited Tagore's poem. The music of the Central and the South Calcutta branches of the Bengal Provincial Students' Federation was reported to have been of a high quality. Niharranjan Ray, Surendranath Goswami, Hiran Kumar Sanyal, Gopal Haldar, the poet Abdul Kadir and Dev Banerjee, a student leader, unequivocally condemned in their speeches the murder of Somen Chanda which showed 'our own people how fascism was stalking inside our dear country, how we must be on our guard to root it out'. In conclusion, Atul Chandra Gupta called for awareness and unity. A resolution mourning the death of Somen Chanda was passed.

An Organizing Committee consisting of Atul Gupta, Gopal Haldar, Surendranath Goswami, Subhas Mukherjee and Bishnu Dey (Convenor) was constituted, with a view to forming the Anti-Fascist Writers' and Artists' Associatior. The newly formed organization had its office at 1/10, Prince Golam Mohammad Road (Bishnu Dey's house). In September 1942 the office shifted to 46, Dharmatala Street. Ramananda Chatterjee was the President of the Association, Bishnu Dey and Subhas Mukherjee were the two Joint Secretaries.

The AFWAA Conference, December 1942

An All-Bengal AFWAA Conference was held at the University Institute Hall on 19–20 December 1942.[81] The Chairman of the Presidium was Tarasankar Banerjee, who read out his article 'Responsibility of Artists'. The Associate Presidents were Habibullah Bahar, Abu Sayeed Ayub, Buddhadev Bose and Vivekananda Mukherjee, who was elected because of the unavoidable absence of Jamini Roy. Hiran Kumar Sanyal was the President of the Reception Committee. The conference was inaugurated by Atul Chandra Gupta.

Writers and artists came from Dhaka, Nadia, Mymensingh, Behrampore, Khulna and other districts and Punjab sent delegates. Amiya Chakravarty, Niharranjan Ray, Subhas Mukherjee and many others participated. Among those who sent message wishing the conference success were Rahul Sankrityayan, Jamini Ray, Sajjad Zaheer, Gertrude Emerson Sen (editor, *Asia*), the Telegu poet and dramatist Abburi Ramakrishna Rau, Prakash Chandra Gupta, a prominent name in the UP Progressive Writers' Movement, Nandalal Ray (editor, *Dunia*, published from Benares), Amrit Rai (editor, *Hans*, Benares), the Muslim Writers' Association, Jaigopal Narang (Punjab Friends of the Soviet Union), Surendranath Goswami (AIPWA), Achyut Goswami (Dhaka PWA), Muhammad Ismail (Bengal Provincial Trade Union Congress), Abdullah Rasul (Bengal Provincial Kisan Sabha) and Sadhan Gupta (Bengal Provincial Students' Federation). Abdul Aleem, General Secretary, AIPWA, Lucknow, sent greetings dated 18 December 1942.[82]

Hiren Mukherjee observed in his report on this conference in *People's War* (10 January 1943) that despite the attendance of only a limited number of intellectuals from chosen circles and despite factionalism, the conference represented the widest possible agreement among writers. 'Anami' (pen-name of Swarnakamal Bhattacharya) wrote in 'Kathaprasange' (*Arani,* 15 January 1943):

> It is at this conference that the aim and ideology of the Writers' Association have been explicitly stated after a long time; the community of artists and writers is not only anti-Axis like Ameri, Churchill and Linlithgow; they are anti-fascist because

they are anti-imperialist, they are against all kinds of anti-social falsehood; they do not agree with the idea that the inner world and the outer world are two self-contained and isolated currents flowing and ought to be flowing parallelly. Briefly, they are against everything that is against life.

The principal resolution of the conference pledged support for the anti-fascist struggle. Another resolution condemned the government for throttling freedom (harassment of journalists and so on) and thus helping none but the fascists. On the occasion of this conference the AFWAA brought out an anthology of poems (*Ek Sutre*) by 50 noted Bengali poets.

Ironically enough, a few hours after the conference, the very night of 20 December 1942, there was a Japanese air-attack on Calcutta.

Japanese Air-raids

Since the middle of 1942, different areas of eastern India—Assam and Chittagong—had been subjected to occasional Japanese bombardments. The Communists had come to the rescue of the affected people and stepped up anti-fascist propaganda. The moving experience of devastation and death made many artists and musicians of the Communist Party aware of the effectiveness of their respective art-forms in their struggle against such evils. This was the beginning of the career of Somnath Hore and Chittaprosad Bhattacharya as artists and of Benoy Roy as a composer and singer. The Communists also took great pains to explain to the people that it would be short-sighted of them to be led by sheer anti-British sentiment to welcome the Japanese, since the Japanese were aggressors and not liberators. However, while resisting the Japanese, the Communists tended to ignore the anti-British struggle. Many of them admitted this later in self-criticism.

The Bengal Famine and the Relief-Work of the Communists

'Poet, tell me what you intend to do now.'
'Maharaj, listen to that noise of wailing outside your door. We will have to run through it now.'
'But that is a task meant for men of action. What can you do in this Famine?'
'Men of action often make the work discordant. So we have to come running to tune it up.'
'Oh poet, what do you think I could do?'
'I ask you to get up, Maharaj, I ask you to move. That lamentation yonder is a call from soul to soul. Whether we will be able to do anything is a different matter—

> *but if our hearts do not respond to this call, if our souls do not move, then we should be worried not so much because we shirk our duty, as because we are already dead.'*
>
> —RABINDRANATH TAGORE
> The play *Phalguni*

The event that most stirred the cultural soul of twentieth-century Bengal, next perhaps to the partition of 1905, was the devastating Bengal Famine of 1943.[83] Men died like insects and humanity suffered a terrible degradation, and the Famine was found all the more abominable because it was man-made. How the war needs of the British and the profiteering of wily grain-traders caused the Famine was not quite clear to contemporaries. That it was man-made, however, quite evident and they could guess who the culprits were. Kalicharan Ghosh's *Famines in Bengal (1770–1943)*, Shyamaprasad Mukherjee's *Panchaser Manwantar* and *Maladministration in Bengal*, a compilation of editorials, illustrations and correspondence of *The Statesman* between March and October 1943, and of course the literature and other arts reflecting on the Famine, all show an awareness of the fact.

During 1942–3, food production in Greater Bengal (Bengal, Bihar and Orissa), the main rice-producing area of India and the Greater Punjab, the principal supplier of wheat, was much more than that of the previous years.[84] And it was a modern state ruled by a supposedly civilized government from which one could expect an efficient transport system ensuring the necessary food supply. Yet the gruesome Famine took place.

A long-term decay in Bengal's agrarian sector had already created a chronic insufficiency of food supply in the state and it had started depending heavily on supply from outside. In 1943, there was an absolute deficiency of supply. Rice imports from Burma and South-East Asia had stopped. Bengal was forced to export more food crop than it could import during 1942–3.[85] Ceylon, for instance, because of its importance as a big naval base of the Allied Powers, received a large supply of rice from Bengal during these two years, when the Bengalis were already starving.[86] We must also mention the ruthless 'Denial Policy' of the government that took away from the people of a vast area the crop that the latter badly needed for their own consumption. This policy allowed the British to seize thousands of boats, thus throttling rural commerce and particularly ruining the fishermen. Also, a large part of whatever crop remained in Bengal villages was continually drained away to Calcutta to feed the 3 million soldiers stationed there, the numerous people engaged in the war industries and the railway workers. So, the rural Bengal had to suffer terribly.

All this was done without any consultation with Fazlul Huq, the Chief Minister of Bengal. The Herbert-Huq disagreement resulted in Huq's replacement by the Muslim League leader Nazimuddin. After this, Ispahani, the agent through whom the government procured rice, became ruthless. He made a profit of 4 million British pounds in this business and his close associate was Hanuman Baksh. But they were not the only greedy persons between the exacting government and the helpless peasant. It was a big racketeering process. There were thousands of hoarders and blackmarketeers to aggravate the situation. These people artificially inflated the prices of paddy with the support of the government. B.M. Bhatia, a historian of the Famine, has commented, 'It was for the first time in the Bengal Famine that the part played by speculation in regulating process of foodgrains in a period of drought and scarcity was officially recognized.'[87] On the whole, it was a picture of gross mismanagement and widespread corruption.

The abnormally high prices of foodgrains became increasingly unaffordable by the people who had helped grow them. These rural people started perishing from 1942, though it was not noticed so early. The months July–December 1943 saw the worst phase of the Famine. A large number of hapless villagers walked to Calcutta to starve to death on its streets, begging no longer for rice, but just for the water in which it had been cooked. The mortality rate was admittedly heavy. Later, a commission chaired by the noted anthropologist K.P. Chattopadhyay found that about three-and-a-half million people had perished. And there is really no account of how many girls became prostitutes, how much of cattle-wealth was lost, how many peasants lost their holdings, and so on. Malnutrition leading to epidemic continued to take a heavy toll even after the worst months were over. And now victims had to face a scarcity of medicines, cloth and other necessities. Not only the poor, but the middle-class suffered too. The district of Midnapore was one of the worst sufferers, for it had already been subjected to terrible police repression due to its deep involvement in the Quit India Movement, and then even while the Famine was raging, the district was devastated by a terrible cyclone on 16 October 1942. The government suppressed the news of the cyclone as long as possible and did not lift a finger to help its refractory subjects of Midnapore.

The government was extremely reluctant to admit the existence of a famine situation in general. So it did not take up the 'Basic Food Plan' that had already been formulated for the equal distribution of food between 'shortage provinces' and 'surplus provinces'. The rationing measures were belated, and when they were introduced at last, were inadequate and confined to a few cities. The procurement schemes of the government were conducted half-heartedly and with little success. The government's indifference to the food problem was tragically reflected in its statement issued in May 1943, stressing the danger of over-eating and asking people to eat less.

II

The government was indifferent to the sufferings of millions of people. But their countrymen tried hard to help them. The Congress leaders were mostly in jail. But the Communist Party with all its mass fronts—the Kisan Sabha, the Students' Federation, the Mahila Atmaraksha Samity (the women's front), etc., became deeply involved in the relief work. Theirs was indeed a very energetic drive to ameliorate the peoples' sufferings. The efforts of the Muslim League, the Hindu Mahasabha and private individuals and groups were also considerable.

Apart from continually urging the government through the columns of their newspapers *People's War* and *Janayuddha* to introduce a proper rationing system and adopt other relief measures, the Communists mobilized public opinion in Calcutta, Howrah and Hooghly to support the famished people. They opened controlled price shops of food and canteens to feed them. They formed the People's Relief Committee (PRC)[88] to organize relief work. Its formal inauguration took place at the Town Hall, Calcutta. The central office of the PRC had Snehangshu Acharya as its Secretary and Bhupesh Gupta as an active member. Its branches were formed in Dhaka, Chittagong, Khulna, Jessore, Mymensingh, Dinajpur, Rangpur, etc. The medical aspect of the relief work was very important. The doctors' cell of the PRC was led by Satish Pakrashi. Some other organizations also offered medical help and all these were organized into a broad body—the Bengal Medical Relief Coordination Committee—under the leadership of Dr Bidhan Chandra Roy.[89]

The Communists naturally wanted to resist hoarders and blackmarketeers. But here they faced a problem. Resistance against such anti-socials was likely to have created a law and order problem and this would be incompatible with the people's war policy that required all possible cooperation with the British. Gopal Haldar, then associated with the Kisan Sabha, was later asked in an interview whether this presented a dilemma to the Communists. Haldar denied this and observed that at that time the people were not keen on collectively resisting the blackmarketeers. Perhaps they lacked the courage—with huge armed forces surrounding them, they were too frightened to try and tame the greedy hoarders. So with no pressure from the people, the Communists did not face much of a dilemma. Haldar adds proudly that whatever little opposition the hoarders and the blackmarketeers faced at that time came from the Communists and none else.[90]

Indeed, we have come across stray instances of how different mass fronts of the CPI—the People's Relief Committee, the Mahila Atmaraksha Samity and even Kishore Bahini (the teenagers' front)—forced hoarders and blackmarketeers to give people rice at a fair price. Such militancy was more noticeable in the border areas. In Chittagong, for example, the people were not very timid, and the Communist volunteers of the PRC retrieved tons of rice from the greedy grip of hoarders. Kalpataru Sengupta, a local Communist leader of that time, later reminisced[91] that they had had friends among the British soldiers camping in Chittagong. There was a whole brigade from Lancashire, consisting of left-minded people who were willing to cooperate with the Indian leftists. Thus, the local Communists had a supply of tommyguns, etc., which they used on quite a few occasions, e.g. during a conflict at a tea-garden. The owners had been depriving the coolies of their rationing quota. The coolies, furious at this, murdered the manager of the tea-garden. Sengupta said that the Communists used to get supplies of arms even from the Japanese army and the Indian National Army camping on the opposite bank of the river Nuf.

One thing is certain that the Communists sympathized with the suffering millions and the latter found their sympathy genuine. Gopal Haldar thus accounted for the increase in the membership of the Kisan Sabha during 1944–5, 'The people and the peasants realized that the Kisan Sabha belonged to the ordinary people and did not leave them in the lurch. Once this is realized, much is achieved. This is the essence of politics. This understanding is a heart-felt understanding. What will be or will not be the political line is a separate thing.'

The genuine concern of the Communists for the Famine-stricken, their sustained relief work, the constraints imposed on their efforts by the Party policy in regard to the British war efforts and yet their honest attempts to get over those limitations—all this was reflected in the cultural movement of the period. Of course, it was not Communism but sheer humanitarianism that moved the artists and litterateurs. But the Communists were playing an important role in the cultural field during those days. It was to aid the PRC that the Bengal branch of the Indian People's Theatre Association staged *Nabanna*, thus starting the People's Theatre Movement in this country. The 'Voice of Bengal Squad' that toured the whole of northern India and moved the people everywhere by its song recitals and dances, had been formed to raise funds for the PRC. The Famine was also a major motivation behind the formation of the Calcutta Group of Artists who ushered in a new age in pictorial art in this country. Men from the cultural field came nearer the masses of people while participating in the relief work of the CPI.

The art and literature of the Famine are surely its best documentation. Apart from anguish, the works also throb with anger at the man-made character of the Famine. Amartya Sen has put forward his theory of FEE (Failure of Exchange Entitlement) in place of FAD (Food Availability Decline) to explain the Bengal Famine.[92] To contemporaries, however, much more important than any economic theory was the responsibility of wily humans including the British government. They could not fully understand the complex process behind the man-made Famine, more particularly so because the government was trying its best to suppress facts. Yet they unmistakably condemned the culprits in many cases. In Tarasankar's novel *Manwantar*[93] (that highlighted the relief work done by the Communist volunteers, as the Gandhian author had recently become close to the Communists), an important character Bijoyda (who, by the way, was a Gandhian) thus accused the British government for the Famine—'Had it been a free country, there would have been another impeachment just like the impeachment of Warren Hastings.' 'Bijoyda's eyes glowed: Hoarders? Who created the hoarders?' Amartya Sen did admit in a later piece of writing that for an understanding of individual sufferings behind the aggregate statistics of the famine and of the misinformed callousness and cruelty of the rulers, which an economic analysis of the famine cannot easily generate, one must turn to its arts. This feeling is vital 'for our ability to direct our critical wrath on the governance of the country and the respective states'.[94]

The Anti-Facist Writers' and Artists' Association and the Indian People's Theatre Association

> *It [the People's Theatre Movement] is a movement which seeks to make our arts the expression and the organizer of our people's struggles for freedom, economic justice and a democratic culture.—It stands for the defence of culture against imperialism and fascism and for enlightening the masses about the causes and solution of the problems facing them. It tries to quicken their awareness of unity and their passion for creating a better and just world.*
>
> —From the IPTA Bulletin No. I

The AFWAA was part of the cultural front of the battle against Fascism and the famine. The weapons in its armoury were prose, poetry, drama, song and pictorial art. The movement made rapid strides. The number of books that the Association brought out testifies to this—apart from the anthology *Ek Sutre* (In One String) published on the occasion of the 1942 Conference, there were Buddhadev Bose's *Fascism O Sabhyata* (Fascism and Civilization), Pratibha Bose's *Fascism O Nari* (Fascism and Women), Bijon Roy's (Professor Sushobhan Sarkar' pen name) *Japani Shasaner Asal Rup* (The True Nature of Japanese Rule), *Janayuddher Gaan* (a collection of songs on the People's War), etc. Even the local branches published periodicals—*Pragati* from Jessore, *Balaka* and *Samhati* from Sylhet, *Nabayug* from Comilla, *Adhikar* from Chittagong, *Jagaran* from Bankura, *Pratirodh* from Dhaka and so on.

Part of our information about the AFWAA activities before 1944, particularly outside Calcutta, is derived from newspaper reports like the *Janayuddha* report entitled 'Samskritir Masal Jalo' (Light the Torch of Culture) dated 2 May 1943, describing a cultural gathering at the Public Library Hall of Sibpur, Howrah, arranged by the local Students' Federation and the journal *Abhibadan* (Salutation) and presided over by Gopal Haldar, where a committee to organize a local branch of the AFWAA had been formed (25 April). It also reported on the AFWAA conference at Naihati, where Benoy Roy, Dilip Roy and Supriya Mukherjee had presented 'people's songs' (18 April); the conference at the Bankura Brahma Samaj Hall—a local AFWAA affair (2 May); the conference at Rajbari, arranged by the local Krisi Kendra (27 April); the conference at Dinajpur, arranged by the Student's Federation and chaired by Sukumar Sen (28–9 April); and also the inaugural ceremony of the local branch of the AFWAA at Rangpur. A report in *Janayuddha*, 28 April 1943, wrote particularly of how the People's Song Movement had spread like wildfire all over Bengal. According to the reporter, the movement owed its immense popularity mainly to the untiring efforts of Benoy Roy. These songs had become popular even amongst backward tribals like the Hajongs. And yet the report admitted that a lot more had yet to be done. A report prepared in the beginning of 1943 by Chinmohan Sehanabis pointed out the shortage of competent workers.

The session of the AIPWA and the inauguration of the Indian People's Theatre Association in May 1943, at Bombay, greatly stimulated the cultural movement. The AFWAA which had already been acting as the Bengal branch of the AIPWA, now became an affiliate of the IPTA as well.

Fourth All-India Progressive Writers' Conference

The Conference[95] along with the IPTA inaugural session took place simultaneously with the first Communist Party Congress in Bombay. The literary conference was conducted by a Presidium consisting of S.A. Dange (Communist leader), Josh Malihabadi (Urdu poet), Tapi Dharma Rao (Telegu writer), Jitubhai (eminent Gujrati writer and critic), Satyendranath Majumdar (Editor, *Arani*) and Professor Jagirdar (Kanarese scholar). Dange's address was particularly enlightening because of a masterly socio-economic analysis of the growth of Marathi literature from its very inception, apart from a reaffirmation of the ideals of the progressive writers' movement.

The Conference passed a resolution demanding the release of the national leaders and sent its greetings to the Soviet and Chinese writers. Other resolutions demanded the release of progressive writers in jail; expansion of civil liberties; better distribution of subsidized paper; and affirmed the rights of writers in regard to payment by publishers. There was also a resolution asking progressive writers to try to influence the film industry in a progressive direction. The Conference unanimously adopted a manifesto which was to serve as a guide to all progressive writers.

A new All-India Executive was elected. Sajjad Zaheer became the new General Secretary, Bishnu Dey and K.A. Abbas Joint Secretaries, Mama Warekar the Treasurer—other members included representatives of all linguistic zones. The central office of the AIPWA was shifted from Lucknow to Bombay.

The members pledged to reorganize the PWA and put it on a firmer basis. At that time it was working properly only in Bengal, Andhra and Bombay. They wanted other linguistic zones to be as active.

The IPTA Inaugural Conference

The IPTA Conference[96] took place on 25 June 1943, at the Marwari Vidyalay Hall, Bombay. Professor Hiren Mukherjee, elected to the chair, read out all the provincial reports of the work done so far. Bombay was represented by Anil de Silva, Bengal by Snehangshu Acharya, Punjab by Eric Cyprian, Andhra by Dr Gopalan; UP by Begum Rashida Jehan and Malabar by K.P. Namboodiri. The main resolution was proposed by Anil de Silva (a lady of Ceylonese origin): 'This conference held under the auspices of the Indian People's Theatre Association recognizes the urgency of organizing a People's Theatre Movement throughout India as the means of revitalizing the stage and the traditional arts and making them at once the expression and organizer of our people's struggle for freedom, cultural progress and economic justice.'

There followed the election of an all-India Committee and Organizing Committees for various provinces. The former consisted of the following:

President	N.M. Joshi (General Secretary, AITUC)
General Secretary	Anil de Silva
Jt. Secretaries	Benoy Roy (Bengal) K.T. Chandy (Bombay)
Treasurer	K. Ahmad Abbas

For representatives of different provinces see Appendix III.

The Bengal Organizing Comitte had as its members Sunil Chatterjee, Dilip Roy, Sambhu Mitra, Bijan Bhattacharya, Sujata Mukherjee, Manoranjan Bhattacharya, Snehangshu Acharya, Bishnu Dey and Benoy Roy.

Cultural programmes were an integral part of the schedule of those busy days of May 1943. The PWA Conference of 22 May, the Communist Party Congress at Kamgar Maidan in the afternoon of 23 May and all other sessions resounded with songs by the Bengal Squad. On 24 May, at Damodar

Hall, a National Cultural Festival was held. The Bengal Squad, particularly its *panchali*-singer Nibaran Pandit, won the greatest appreciation. Panchali was a popular folk form of Bengal and Pandit was a peasant poet. But the most important cultural show was presented on 25 May, at the same auditorium. Squads from different provinces participated. The Bengal Group presented Benoy Ghosh's play *Laboratory*, apart from Tagore songs and IPTA songs. The performance was acclaimed by critics. On 28 May, the Bengal squad staged another drama—*Agun* (Fire).

The IPTA in Bengal

After the inaugural conference of the IPTA, the members from Bengal got busy in organizing the movement in this province. It seems that the General Secretary of IPTA took a personal interest in this matter. In a letter from Calcutta (29 July 1943),[97] Anil de Silva urged Benoy Roy to help Chinmohan Sehanabis compile a collection of songs, choose kisan boys for forming kisan units in different zones and enlist the help of the Kisan Sabha leader Rasul in this matter. She informed Roy that a Calcutta Committee had been formed with three Secretaries—Sudhi Pradhan (Organization Secretary), Sambhu Mitra (Production Secretary) and Hemanta Mukherjee (Music Secretary) and also with Chinmohan Sehanabis as Treasurer, Manoranjan Bhattacharya as President and several comrades from Trade Unions and Kisan Sabhas. Benoy Roy was also a member of the committee.

The report[98] prepared by Benoy Roy on his return to Calcutta tells us about the plan of the IPTA to arrange several benefit shows, with Bishnu Dey getting the artists of Calcutta to participate. We also know from the report that the IPTA workers were contacting workers' unions to form workers' troupes, particularly in Howrah, creating interest among amateur dramatic clubs about the new theatrical tendencies emerging all over the world; that they had got the consent of the His Master's Voice Company to record four of their songs; that Comrade Rasul had told them of the possibility of forming cultural units on a zonal basis, for which district kisan workers needed to be trained up, and that they were writing plays and doing translation work too.

Thus the IPTA had a good start and went from strength to strength. During 1943–4, a squad from Bengal toured northern India to collect money toward helping the victims of the Famine in Bengal and in the course of its journey captivated a huge audience including the famous dancer Uday Shankar who lent them a few artists of his own troupe and helped them form a Central Cultural Squad at Bombay. Santi Kumar Bardhan, Abani Dasgupta, Sachin Shankar, Ravi Shankar—all of them from Uday Shankar's cultural centre at Almorah and Benoy Roy, Reba Roy, Usha Dutta, Bhupati

Nandi, Priti Sarkar, Dasrathlal, Rekha Jain, Prem Dhawan were important members of this Central Troupe. We will discuss all this in detail in the chapters on 'people's songs' and 'people's theatre'.

The ideological basis of the IPTA was the same as that of the AIPWA. But it was supposed to be closer to the masses of people, because of the directness of appeal of the art-forms it dealt with—music and drama. It was expected that the organization would reach out to a wider and poorer audience, discover and highlight talents from among folk artists and also in the process reinvigorate various forms of folk art. As in the case of the AIPWA, Communist ideology and initiative were the moving force behind the IPTA as well, but there was no question of an imposition of Party politics.

Of course, difficulties did appear in the way of the implementation of the United Front theory. But on the whole, a democratic atmosphere prevailed, *Nabanna* (New Harvest) by Bijan Bhattacharya, the drama that is said to have started the people's theatre movement in this country in October 1944, opened with a scene paying tribute to Matangini Hajra, a heroine of the Quit India Movement, which the Communist Party had not supported. This created some confusion. Some were opposed to the staging of the play. But P.C. Joshi intervened and saved the situation. *Nabanna* was staged with an astounding success. Joshi was for the independence of artists within the structure of the IPTA. He argued that the correction of any mistake made by an artist should be left to the masses and the future, and not to any immediate intervention by the Communist Party. Bijan Bhattacharya writes, 'We took *Nabanna* to various places. Our policy was not to talk about the Party, but about our country and countrymen. We prepare the soil, you sow the seeds. We wanted to prepare men from a humanist viewpoint.'[99] It is notable that while talking about the objective of the AIPWA Hiren Mukherjee uses the same analogy—preparation of the soil.[100] This was what the leftist cultural movement intended to do. Sowing the seeds and reaping the harvest were, of course, the cherished dreams. But materializing these dreams could not possibly be the immediate task of the cultural fronts.

The Second Annual Conference of the AFWAA, January 1944

The second annual conference of the AFWAA[101] took place in Calcutta on 15 January 1944. Tarasankar Banerjee, Chairman of the Reception Committee, welcomed the delegates. He negated the charge that the term 'anti-Fascist' implied a negative conception. It connoted, he said, a positive fight for the country's freedom. A Presidum of seven conducted the proceedings of the Conference: Premendra Mitra (Chairman), Manik Banerjee, Gopal Haldar, Atul Bose, one of India's leading artists, Manoranjan Bhattacharya, a front-ranking thespian, Abdul Mansur Ahmed, journalist and satirist, and the reputed musician Sachin Dev Barman. Premendra Mitra called on his fellow-artists to shed their pride and join hands with the people fighting against fascism, a new appellation for the malice and cruelty that had continued through the ages, but that had now at its disposal the deadliest of weapons.

The main resolution called for a gallant fight on the part of writers and artists against fascism, famine and a self-centred imperialist bureaucracy that had kept the national leaders behind bars.[102] The organizational resolution proposed the formation of a mobile cultural squad that would tour different districts; it also stressed the need for more publications and for district libraries helped by a central library. It promised the publication of a bulletin and the formation of a Translation Section to keep contact with other Indian regional languages.[103] Other resolutions urged film, stage and radio authorities to assist men fighting to keep up the immortal tradition of humanism.[104] The conference also mourned the death of the noted journalist Ramananda Chatterjee, Ajit Ghosh, a worker of the Association, the great actor Durgadas Banerjee, the poet Mankumari Basu, the poet Ajoy Bhattacharya and the potter Gopeswar Pal.[105] A central cultural bureau consisting of Gopal Haldar, Hiren Mukherjee, Manoranjan Bhattacharya, Bishnu Dey, Sunil Bose, Benoy Roy, Moni Roy, Niren Roy and Chinmohan Sehanabis (convenor) was formed.

On 16 January 1944 morning, a cultural festival took place at Sraddhananda Park before an audience of 6,000. Nibaran Pandit, a folk poet of Mymensingh, Nirmal Chowdhuri, Hemanga Biswas and other singers from Sylhet, Amulya Sen, a *Kirtania* of Rangpur, Satish Mondal leading a group of *Gambhira* singers from Maldah, Himangshu Chakrabarty from Khulna, Nepal Sarkar, a *Kavi* from Jessore, Dayal Kumar, a *Panchali*-singer from Hooghly, Benoy Roy, Haripada Kusari and many others participated in music and dance programmes. The conference concluded on 17 January with another cultural show at the Minerva Theatre. It was inaugurated by the leading dramatist Sachin Sengupta. The highlight of this evening was Bijan Bhattacharya's play *Jabanbandi*.

Arani ('Katha Prasange') gave a detailed report of the Conference and concluded that it was a great success despite many organizational limitations, of which the gravest was the absence of many prominent writers and artists. The newspaper said that the absence of writers from the mofussil might be excused, but wondered why several artists residing in Calcutta did not attend the conference.

The Work of the AFWAA

Before 1944, the AFWAA did not keep a regular record of the work done. Just before the Conference of January 1944, Sajjad Zaheer wrote to Chinmohan

Sehanabis that ever since the Bombay Conference he had not received any report from the Bengal AFWAA, 'supposed to be our strongest and best branch'. He asked for a report covering activities such as meetings and creative writings, names of office-bearers, actual membership and the way the office of the AFWAA had been functioning. He also wanted information about the forthcoming cultural conference.

The first comprehensive report of the works of the organization was available in mid-1944. It was the *Half-Yearly Report*, January–June 1944. It said that after the Conference in January, the AFWAA had toned up its office work, started keeping audited accounts, chalked out monthly programmes and executed them more or less punctually. Its efficiency had increased by the opening of three subcommittees—the IPTA Subcommittee headed by Chitta Banerjee, the Fine Arts Subcommittee headed by Rathin Moitra and the Publication Subcommittee under Prafulla Roy.

In the last six months, the Central AFWAA arranged thirteen meetings on different occasions. Among these were the reading of the play *Nabanna* by the playwright Bijan Bhattacharya, birthday celebration of Rabindranath and Nazrul, discussions on subjects like the Soviet Art and the People's Theatre. They mourned the death of Acharya P.C. Roy and donated Rs. 100 toward the medical treatment of Nazrul Islam who was ill at the time. Jointly with the FSU they founded a library and a reading room—Somen Chanda Memorial Library and Reading Room—on 18 April and 26 March, respectively.

Several meetings were held outside Calcutta—at Bali, Beleghata and Naihati. District Conferences were held in Bankura (25 March), Howrah (22 April) and Murshidabad (16 May), presided over by Gopal Haldar, Manik Banerjee and Tarasankar Banerjee, respectively. Literary Conferences were arranged at Sylhet, Jalpaiguri and Lalmonirhat. The first one was chaired by Manik Banerjee and the others by Vivekananda Mukherjee. While at the beginning of the year there had been only two branches, now they had—Murshidabad, Jalpaiguri, Dhaka, Jessore, Howrah, Beleghata, Koligaon and Bali. Branches were to be opened shortly in Sylhet, Dinajpur, Bogura, Nadia and Rangpur.[106]

The report also pointed out the limitations of the AFWAA. It ought to have been more particular about maintaining links with the local branches. It should bring out a monthly bulletin. It should boost up its publication department that had published only two books in the past six months—*Keno Likhi* (Why Do I Write), an anthology that collected a number of writers' answers to the question and Gorky's *Problems of Soviet Literature*: the first editions of the already published books—*Fascism O Nari* (Fascism and Women) by Pratibha Bose, *Baishe June* (22 June) by Bishnu Dey and *Japani Shasaner Asal Rup* (The True Nature of the Japanese Rule) by Bijon Roy (pen-name of Sushobhan Sarkar) having long been sold out. And above all, it should find more workers; for 'when the field is prepared, organization can help the movement crystallize like sugar-candy'.

Attached to this report prepared by Jyotirindra Moitra and Gholam Quddus, Joint Secretaries of AFWAA, there were separate subcommittee reports. The IPTA report talked about the popularity of its plays and songs in towns and villages and even outside Bengal. Benoy Roy's songs, Jyotirindra Moitra's poem 'Madhubanshir Goli' (The Lane Named Madhubanshi) recited by Sambhu Mitra and the play *Jabanbandi* were specially admired. It proudly remembered the tremendous success of the 'Voice of Bengal Squad' that had toured northern India the year before. The report informed that *Nabajibaner Gan* (The Song of New Life), a dance drama by Jyotirindra Moitra and the play *Nabanna* were being rehearsed at that time. By way of self-criticism, it stressed the need for more workers and also for more sympathizers from amongst noted writers and artists. So far only Manoranjan Bhattacharya and Sachin Dev Burman had come so close to them as to advise them and participate in their programmes.[107]

Finally, the report contained the names of the office-bearers—the Presidium consisting of Premendra Mitra (the Chairman), Manik Banerjee, Atul Bose, Sachin Dev Burman, Abdul Mansur Ahmed, Gopal Haldar, Manoranjan Bhattacharya and Satyendranath Majumdar; the two Joint Secretaries were Gulam Quddus and Jyotirindra Moitra, the Office Secretary Dev Kumar Gupta; the members of the Executive Committee—Tarasankar Banerjee, Prabhabati Devi Saraswati, Mujibur Rahman Khan, Subhas Mukherjee, Moni Roy, Chinmohan Sehanabis, Sudhi Pradhan, Hiran Sanyal, Arun Mitra, Swarnakamal Bhattacharya, Surya Roy, Benoy Roy and Sambhu Mitra; the Subcommittee Secretaries—Chitta Banerjee (IPTA), Rathindra Moitra (Fine Art) and Prafulla Roy (Publication).

The *Annual Report* published on the occasion of the AFWAA Conference of March 1945, says that the membership of the Central AFWAA that had been only 75 at the beginning of 1944 and 284 at the time of publication of the *Half-yearly Report*, was now 442. The number of branches had increased to 14.[108] The new branches were at Mymensingh, Dhakuria, Gobordanga, Bankura, Kalimpong and Naihati. In one year the number of workers had increased from 15 to 50.

Then the report spoke of the Central AFWAA meetings, of its new publications—*Madhubanshir Goli* and *Tinti Natika* (Three Playlets), of its plays *Jabanbandi* and *Nabanna* and of the art exhibition entitled *Bhukha Bangla* (Hungry Bengal).

The activities of the fourteen branches were described in detail. The reports of functions arranged, plays staged, songs composed and books published by them, seemed very encouraging. We will use these details in the chapters on music and theatre. The Murshidabad branch seemed particularly active. They had regularly offered felicitation to local artists and given on these occasions the local poet Sourindra Bhattacharya Rs. 100, Ustad Qader Baksh Rs. 100 and the actor Radhakanta Sarkar Rs. 50. The members of the Central AFWAA participated in the conference organized by the local branches.

With the purpose of coordinating the sporadic efforts of different districts, two Progressive Writers' and Artists' Conferences were planned in Eastern and Western Bengal and two organizing committees were formed for this purpose. Dhaka, Mymensingh, Chittagong and Noakhali sent delegates to the Eastern Conference; Murshidabad, Howrah, Jessore, Calcutta, Nadia and 24-Parganas attended the Western one. Two training classes were held in Calcutta to teach songs, acting, etc., and to give an idea about the nature of their cultural movement to members from different parts of Bengal—one class was held just after the 1944 conference and the other in November.

Then there were subcommittee reports. The IPTA report talked about *Nabanna* and *Nabajibaner Gan* in particular. The Fine Arts Subcommittee reported a number of art exhibitions among other things. The Publication Subcommittee introduced three more publications, brought out on the occasion of the 1945 Conference, *Kayekjan Lok-Kabi* (Some Folk Poets) edited by Sudhi Pradhan, *Jatiya Sangeet* (National Songs) and *Akal* (Poems of Famine). The IPTA Subcommittee stressed the need for more time to organize the movement all over Bengal and for a fixed place of rehearsal. Among the other needs that were stressed were organizing the artists oppressed by the radio authorities, gramophone companies and film producers, and drawing more folk artists from rural areas to the movement.

About the end of 1944 and the beginning of 1945 there was a spate of activities, evident from numerous letters kept in the police archives. This was because of the huge AFWAA Conference held at Behrampore, Murshidabad, on 30 November and 1 December, followed by the grand affair at Calcutta in March 1945. Dev Kumar Gupta, Office Secretary, wrote to Secretary PWA, Murshidabad, about the arrangements for the Behrampore conference (8 November 1944). Nani Gopal Chakrabarty, Secretary, Reception Committee, Behrampore, wrote to Nirmal Sen, Secretary, Dhakuria Branch, asking for his cooperation in arranging the coming conference (November 1944). Nirmal Sen replied giving his consent. The SP, DIB, 24-Parganas later informed the DIB, Murshidabad that Nirmal Sen, Salil Chakrabarty and Pijus Banerjee had actually attended the conference. He also reported that the Dhakuria Branch had 23 members, including Birendra Chatterjee and Narendra Sen. He gave details about their professions and about their families. Then there is the letter of one Anil Biswas to Nani Gopal Chakrabarty saying that it would not be possible for them to send a squad, at best one delegate could be sent (25 November 1944). Santosh Biswas,

Secretary, Jessore District PWA, wrote to Secretary, Murshidabad District PWA, Khagra, stating that their representatives would be Sadhan Bhattacharya, Santimoy Roy, Swaraj Ghosh, Ram Ganguly and himself. They would take the local musician Amar Majumdar with them and if possible, would take a whole squad of folk singers.

There are a couple of letters from Anil Sinha, Secretary, Reception Committee, to Secretary, PWA, Behrampore (January 1945) and to Babu Keshablal Bose of Rangpur, asking for reports on local activities and requesting delegation for the conference to be held in Calcutta in March (February 1945).

The Cultural Festival of the AFWAA, March 1945

Bengal's Anti-Fascist Writers and Artists met in their third annual conference on 3 March 1945, at Muhammad Ali Park.[109] Their pavilion was named Rabindra Nagar and the main gate leading to it was 'Somen Chanda Memorial Toran'. Nearly 200 delegates came from different districts. The composition of the Presidium reflected the AFWAA's attempt to unite urban intellectuals and folk artists. The Chairman was Sailajananda Mukherjee. His colleagues were Manik Banerjee, Tarasankar Banerjee, Prabhabati Devi Saraswati, Dhiren Sen, Sheikh Gomhani, a gifted *Kavi* (village bard) from Murshidabad and Pasupati Bhattacharya, a village potter. Among the participants in the various sessions of the conference were Bhupendranath Dutta (Vice-President, FSU), Bankim Mukherjee (General Secretary, AIKS), Satyendranath Majumdar (editor, *Arani*), Moulavi Abdul Karim Sahitya Bisarad, a scholar and an authority on the legendary Muslim poet Alaol; Congress leaders like Professor K.P. Chatterjee, Nalinaksha Sanyal and Daulatunnesa Khatun; the poets Amiya Chakravarty, Bishnu Dey and Bimal Chandra Ghosh; writers like Narayan Ganguly, Ashok Bejoy Raha and Radhika Ranjan Ganguly; literary critics like Abu Sayeed Ayub and Hiran Kumar Sanyal; Jyotirmoy Roy, Director of the famous film *Udayer Pathe* (On the Road to Sunrise) and Professor Ahmad Ali, author of *Twilight in Delhi*. Fraternal greetings were sent by Sean O'Casey, the Irish playwright, Sajjad Zaheer (Secretary, AIPWA), Raja Rao (Andhra Provincial Unit of the IPTA), Professor Dhurjati Prasad Mukherjee from Lucknow, Irwat Singh, leader of the freedom movement in Manipur and the poet Kumud Ranjan Mallik.

Among the resolutions passed by the conference was one affirming the duty of writers and artists to join hands with all patriots to reinvigorate the crumbling economic life of Bengal. By another resolution it was decided to change the name of the Association to Progressive Writers' and Artists' Association, in anticipation of an imminent fascist defeat. Other resolutions referred to the collection of money for the Tagore Memorial Fund, to the need for a better type of children's literature and for a drastic improvement in the standards of the radio and the cinema.

At the six-day long cultural festival in which squads from different districts participated before an audience of 5,000, the most remarkable thing was the large-scale participation of folk-artists—Saheb Ali, the foremost *Baul*-singer of Agartala and Tagar Adhikari, the blind *dotara* (a two-stringed instrument) player of Coochbehar, to name only two. The highlight of the festival was the *Kavi* contest between Sheikh Gomhani Dewan (from Murshidabad) and Ramesh Seal (from Chittagong). The staging of *Nabanna* provided a fitting finale to the celebration. An art exhibition entitled 'My Country' was arranged on the occasion. Manik Banerjee and Swarnakamal Bhattacharya were elected Joint Secretaries of the Association for the ensuing year.

It is pertinent here to note that it is the leftists who introduced the notion of cultural conference or cultural festival to the cultural life of India and Bengal during the period of our study. Niharranjan Ray says,

> In fact, it is since 1935 that cultural conferences were rapidly popularized in Calcutta and in the then Bengal, as an adjunct of a political mass movement. This continued till the late 1940s and during the whole of the '50s. Every political party used to arrange occasional cultural conferences. I think, they learnt this practice from the political parties of socialist and Communist Europe. Anyway, some political groups also started following their examples by arranging cultural shows.... Today such conferences and functions are in vogue all over India and these are known as cultural conferences.[110]

Now, did such a cultural conference mean just a passing excitement for 2–3 days or did it leave any deep impact on culture? These conferences certainly provided platforms for deliberation amongst intellectuals and artists and thus enriched them. Salil Chowdhury nostalgically remembered later how at the all-India conferences one could meet musicians from all over India and learn musical forms of different provinces by visiting them in their camps. At least Chowdhury himself was immensely benefitted by these conferences. When he commented, 'The IPTA was our university of music', he particularly had in his mind the memories of these conferences.[111]

The Artiste Association

> *An art can only be learned in the workshop*
> *of those who are winning their bread by it.*
>
> —SAMUEL BUTLER, *Erewhon*

One of the avowed aims of the progressive cultural movement was to look after the material interest of artists. This object was fulfilled by the formation in 1942 of the Bengal Artiste Association,[112] the first trade union of performing artists in this country. It became affiliated to the AITUC in 1945.

For some time, the ideal of amateurism had been giving way to that of professionalism in the world of art. Art was becoming the livelihood of its practitioners. The need was being felt for an organization to fight against differents categories of employers of artists. At the same time, the progressive cultural movement was making the ideal of ivory-tower artists irrelevant in a broader sense.

The initiative in this matter was taken by some non-Left persons who resented the way artists were being exploited and formed a committee of which the President was Nalini Ranjan Sarkar (a member of what was known as the Big Five of Bengal politics); Associate Presidents Nirmal Chandra Chunder (another member of the Big Five, a reputed lawyer and the father of Pratap Chandra Chunder who too was interested in this Association); Bidhubhusan Sengupta (owner of the United Press) and Tushar Kanti Ghosh (editor, *Jugantar*); Organization Secretary Phani Mondal (known to be related to the rich and famous Laha family) and Treasurer Durga Prasad Chakrabarty (owner of Mohini Mill). Their office was 23 Wellington Street, the house of Nirmal Chandra Chunder.

'They were moved more by family heritage and a youth-like humanism than by socialism that was pervading the young minds at that time' (Sudhi Pradhan). But some of them had a personal acquaintance with some members of the AFWAA and the latter were naturally drawn to the Artiste Association. Its first annual ceremony on 22 April 1943, was attended by Tarasankar Banerjee, the President of AFWAA and Sadhan Gupta, President of the Students' Federation. Sachin Dev Burman, Kamal Dasgupta, Kanak Das, Santosh Sengupta sang in chorus together with Benoy Roy, the star artist of AFWAA. These were generally AFWAA songs. Despite requests from the audience, they refused to give solo performances and sang together to stress the need for unity among artists and to underline their identification with the masses. Sudhi Pradhan said in his report on this function to *Janayuddha*,[113] that this testified to the influence of the ideology and organization of the AFWAA.

The War and the Famine worsened the plight of artists. A need to strengthen the organization was urgently felt. At the request of the artists connected with both the Artiste Association and the AFWAA (like Santosh Sengupta and Hemanta Mukherjee), Sudhi Pradhan was appointed the Organization Secretary at the annual conference of 10 March 1945. His association with the CPI and the IPTA had made him an experienced organizer and as a whole-timer of the IPTA, he was not in danger of losing his job while fighting against the exploiters of artists. Along with Pradhan a big Executive Committee was elected which included many significant names. The names are available from the Report of 1945–6, which is presented in Appendix III. The list of names include almost all the eminent artists of Bengal, particularly from the world of music, most of them known to be apolitical; and some non-artist organizers like Pratap Chandra Chunder who was a Congressman and Sudhi Pradhan who was a Communist and an organizer of the IPTA. But the report says that all the artists mentioned were not really active in politics.

The report also said that at that time their activities were limited to Calcutta, Howrah and 24-Parganas; the number of members was 747, though many of them had not paid their subscriptions. During that year they arranged a number of shows to raise funds; condoled the deaths of artists; held regular functions ('Silpi Parichay') to bring into the limelight new artists and improve their standard through constructive criticism; got the Association registered (No. 699) to give it legal status in its struggle against employers of artists; brought about an orderliness in their office activities and account-keeping and successfully organized a radio strike. The radio authorities were forced to concede their demands, of which the main one was an end to the shift system which prevented artists from working with other companies. Many reputed artists participated in this strike and its success gave the Association considerable prominence. After this, they took up the demands of gramophone artists for an increase in royalty, dearness allowance, etc. But before anything came out of their negotiations, they got involved in some specific disputes—taking the side of Satyadev Chowdhury in his dispute with Bharatlakshmi Pictures[114] and supporting the artists of the Pioneer Company in their conflict with the foreign-controlled Gramophone Company.[115]

The report of 1946–7 wrote of the improved state of organization of the Artiste Association. Though the number of members had not increased, it was considered a hopeful sign that all 400 members had already contributed their subscriptions. The Association felt the need for an office at south Calcutta and hoped to become an all-India organization very soon. They had largely succeeded in convincing the Gramophone Company about the justification of their general demands, but their fight in support of the right of recording of the Pioneer and the Bharat Recording Companies had been without success. The radio authorities had partly accepted their demands regarding the grades of radio artists. But the report admitted that nothing much could be done about the theatrical artists.

During that year they staged another successful radio strike. This was part of the post-War popular upsurge that had been rocking the country since the winter of 1945–6. The people were in a militant mood and keen about waging a last battle against the Raj. Strikes were taking place everywhere.

The Communist Party called a general strike on 29 July 1946, in support of the Post and Telegraph employees who were on strike. On that day, some girl students of the Party (including Geeta Mukherjee and Alaka Majumdar) were picketing in front of the radio station. The police assaulted them, while the Station Director and some other workers looked on. A unanimous decision in favour of a strike was taken at a meeting of the Association. Leading artists along with ladies and students of different organizations participated in the picketing from 11 August. Pankaj Mallick, Kamal Dasgupta, Sukhendu Goswami, Mustak Ali Khan, Abbasuddin Ahmed, Santosh Sengupta, Dilip Roy, Jahar Ganguli, Suchitra Mukherjee, Jaganmoy Mitra and Bimal Bhusan were amongst the picketers. The public support behind them was evident from a huge meeting at the University Institute Hall. Lakshmanan, the Deputy Director General of AIR, came all the way from Delhi to talk with them and removed a couple of officers whose behaviour they had resented. The strike ended abruptly due to the outbreak of communal riots on 16 August. But it ended on honourable terms for the artists.[116] It is interesting that the nationalist leaders often showed a lukewarm and even hostile attitude to the people's militancy at this phase of the national movement, as they found it inconvenient vis-à-vis the policy of negotiations with the British. The radio strike was condemned by Sardar Patel, whose opinion was voiced by his secretary P.C. Chowdhury. Subsequently, the Association's demands regarding grades of artists were partially conceded. But its report admitted the failure to do much for film and theatre artists.

According to this report, the Executive Committee for 1947–8 consisted of Nirmal Chandra Chunder (President), Sachindranath Sengupta, Sailen Roy and Jnanprakash Ghosh (Associated Presidents), and many other distinguished people, particularly performing artists. During the years 1947–8, they forced the owner of the Kalika Theatre to pay bonus to its artists. But after this, those artists became indifferent to the Association. The report of 1947–8 complained that this attitude of callousness was common amongst theatre workers. Even those on the Executive Committee shared this attitude. At a meeting convened by the Association to discuss the condition of theatre and theatre artists, only Ahindra Chowdhury and Jahar Roy were present amongst the reputed artists. The Association started a movement against film censorship also. They demanded a democratic board at Radio to fix grades of artists, to restrain the wilful bureaucracy and to prevent injustice to the staff artists. They also did relief work and other public works during communal riots and flood, helped poor artists, and secured the re-appointment of Sunil Dasgupta, who had been sacked during the radio strike.

From this report we know of the composition of the Executive Committee for 1948–9, which included Nirmal Chandra Chunder (President), Jnanprakash Ghosh, Sailen Roy, Manoranjan Bhattacharya

(Associate Presidents), Hemanta Mukherjee (Secretary), and many other performing artists (Appendix III).

But from 1948, due to the left sectarian policy adopted at the second Congress of the Communist Party (February–March 1948), an atmosphere of hatred and suspicion was created in the United Front centred around the Party, and in the Artiste Association as well.[117] The organization formally existed till the early 1950s. But towards the end it was but a shadow of its former self. We will discuss the last phase of the Artiste Association in a later section titled 'The Disintegration of the Cultural Front'.

Other Mass-Fronts of the CPI

The new world asks for the artist's assurance
At this auspicious moment of creation.
Come unto the equality of unity and association,
Come unto the friendship of the masses.
Come piercing the darkness of sorrows,
Destroying the cruel fear of destruction.
Come, fill up the citadel of life.

—From a popular song of JYOTIRINDRA MOITRA

All the mass fronts of the CPI worked hand-in-hand and each of them did their bit to forge a leftist cultural movement in this country. The contribution of the Kisan Sabha, the trade unions, the All-India Students' Federation, the Mahila Atmaraksha Samity and the Kishore Bahini in this respect was no less important. Perhaps it was greater than that of the organizations more directly concerned with the cultural movement—the AIPWA, the IPTA, etc. For a number of artists, cultural activities were just extension of political activities in one of these fronts.

The Kisan Sabha, the trade unions and the Students' Federation were engaged in manifold activities and each had a long and eventful history which we cannot deal with at length here. Since monographic studies on these organizations are available, we will just touch upon them in order to indicate their role in the leftist cultural movement. Their cultural activities will be discussed in detail in the chapters on music, theatre and visual arts.

The Mahila Atmaraksha Samity and the Kishore Bahini are less known organizations. Particularly the latter seems to have been a forgotten episode. So we will discuss these two in greater detail.

All-India Kisan Sabha

The Kisan Sabhas sponsored the leftist cultural movement in rural areas. It discovered many talents from amongst folk poets and artists and arranged cultural shows of the AFWAA in villages. The significant role of the Kisan Sabha in the field of culture is evident from the fact that a prominent artist like Nirad Majumdar decorated the pavilion of the ninth All-India Kisan Conference at Netrokona (Mymensingh) in May 1945. Gopal Haldar, even after he had been established as a leading prose-writer of Bengal, continued to be a worker of the Kisan Sabha.

The greatest contribution of the Kisan Sabha to the leftist culture resulted from a realization that it was to strengthen the Kisan Sabha Movement that the cultural elements of folk life should be helped to flourish. This was stressed in the Krisak Council meeting of May 1944:

> In many a district of Bengal, music, *Jananatya*,[118] dances, songs and other cultural activities are being organized as an integral part of the peasants' movement.... The Krisak Samities should take the lead in this work, under their supervision a cultural body should be organized. Dances and songs prevalent in the countryside should be supplemented, revised or rewritten; artists should be recruited from among the peasants to form cultural squads; and this will really strengthen the peasants' movement.[119]

In Chapter 2 entitled 'The Music of Politics and the Politics of Music' we shall see how strikingly successful the Kisan Sabhas were in this respect, in the field of music; though, in contrast, they could hardly do anything to promote the People's Theatre Movement. Whatever success the leftist achieved in the latter field was mostly due to the efforts of the Indian People's Theatre Association. And this success was largely confined to the middle-class layer of society.

Trade Unions

Leftist trade unions were responsible for fostering the cultural movement among the industrial workers. The labour movement had split into three national centres and consequently substantially weakened. Unity in the movement and its reinvigoration were badly needed. In 1935, the Red Trade Union Congress dissolved and merged with the All India Trade Union Congress. Efforts were also made for the merger of the National Trade Union Federation, which occurred in 1940. There was a considerable organizational growth (in 1933–4, the number of trade unions in Bengal was 54; in 1937–8, it was 172) and a rise in the militancy of the workers. The historic general strike of jute workers in 1937[120] made the Communists very popular among those workers. They were also influential among the tramway workers, the employees of the Calcutta Corporation and workers of many other industries. The IPTA singers used to go and teach songs to the workers and organize cultural squads among the latter. The percussionist Dasrathlal, who was to become a prized possession of the IPTA, was a member of the tramway workers' cultural squad. Gurudas Pal, a worker of Metiabruz, and a talented *Tarja*-composer, was another product of the trade union movement. We will talk about these workers-artists in the chapter on music. But again, though the success of the trade union movement was quite remarkable in the field of music, it was not so in theatre.

Many a talent from among the middle-class also flourished in association with the trade union movement. It is the trade union movement that produced the golden-voiced Benoy Roy, a pioneer in the People's Song Movement, 'who had so long, it seems, hidden his musical talent under a bushel'. Manoranjan Hajra, said to be the writer of the first 'socialist novels' in Bengali, was a product of the jute workers' movement, of which he had intimate experience.

The Students' Federation

The Bengal Provincial Students' Federation (BPSP),[121] which was entirely dominated by the Communists, provided hundreds of middle-class youths a forum for conscious politics and produced a galaxy of creative personalities during the 1940s and the early 1950s. The study circles arranged by the Students' Federation attracted many talented young men and helped their political thinking and creative ability flourish simultaneously. Thus, Bengali culture should acknowledge its debt to the Beleghata Study Circle for one of the most popular poets of Bengal—Sukanta Bhattacharya. On the occasion of its fortieth anniversary (1976) the Students' Federation approached five prominent personalities of Bengali culture, with the following questions: (1) Why did you join the Students' Federation? (2) How did the students' movement and the Students' Federation nourish your art and intellect? Mrinal Sen, a reputed film director, answered as follows: (1) 'Because only a fool could possibly remain outside the Students' Federation'. He explained that at that time he urgently felt the need to be a partisan. He also realized that to sharpen this partisanship he needed a spiritual and organizational relationship with a body like the Students' Federation which was inspired by a particular political ideal. Moreover, the country was fighting its last battle for independence, so he did not have any hesitation or doubt whatsoever. (2) When Sen was actively involved in the Students' Federation, he did not really think of making films. Of course, he used to read literature and do some creative writing himself. But because of his association with the Students' Federation, 'I could see my surroundings from a particular angle of view, I could learn to see with much warmth, I could love the collective strongly and hate the enemy intensely. These were to prove very valuable in my art life; this was my nourishment.' The four others who were asked the same questions—the famous thespian Ajitesh Bandyopadhyay, poets

Abanti Kumar Sanyal, Ram Basu and Amitabha Dasgupta—replied in the same vein.[122]

The Students' Federation also played a more direct role in fostering the leftist cultural movement, particularly in its early phase, when the leftist cultural organizations were either non-existent or inactive. At this stage, the BPSF used to send cultural brigades to various districts of Bengal. It is also the BPSF that took the initiative in the formation of the AFWAA. *Bengal Painters' Testimony* (1944), the best documentation of the visual arts of Bengal of the period, was published by the BPSF. The meetings and conferences arranged by the Students' Federation provided platforms to singers, thespians and artists.

Mahila Atmaraksha Samity

An idea had been there for quite some time that the girl students of the Students' Front of the CPI should be organized into a Ladies' Front. On Sarojini Naidu's advice, student leaders like Renu Chakravarty and Manikuntala Sen had joined the All-India Women's Conference which provided both Congress and Communist-minded women with a scope for social work. But the latter soon felt the need for a separate organization for themselves. The AIWC, they felt, was meant for women from well-off families, and they wanted poor women to participate in their movement. So in 1943, the plan of the Mahila Atmaraksha Samity (Women's Self-protection Committee)[123] was chalked out at the house of Ela Reed, who became the Secretary of the organization.

The workers of this Ladies Front, Manikuntala Sen, Kamala Chatterjee, Latika Sen, Suhasini Ganguly, Renu Chakravarty, Juiphul Ray, Bela Lahiri, most of them sisters and wives of Communist leaders, started travelling all over Bengal and opened branches in different districts. Of course, some women who were Communist continued to work from within the AIWC.

Even before its formal inauguration, the Mahila Atmaraksha Samity had started working informally when, following the Japanese air-raid, the Communist women went from door to door apprising the women of the situation, telling them not to panic, explaining the need to defend themselves and the need for national unity and national government. Of course, they had to overcome considerable patriarchal resistance in doing this. And they often used music and cultural programmes in their campaign. Branches thus had already spread all over Bengal before the formal foundation of MAS.

When the Famine hit the province, the work of the Mahila Atmaraksha Samity increased manifold. Its workers worked day and night in the slum areas of Calcutta and also in villages providing Famine relief. And they also held numerous meetings at the local and district levels. They arranged a number of hunger-processions. One such procession in Bankura consisted of 400 peasant women. A procession in Calcutta went to the Legislative Assembly and despite his initial reluctance, Fajlul Haq, the then Chief Minister, distributed 100 bags of rice amongst them. At some places in North Bengal, they forced (sometimes jointly with the PRC) black marketeers to sell rice at a fair price.

In the meantime, in March 1943, when the number of members was about 20,000–22,000, they held their first conference at the Overtoon Hall, Calcutta. Indira Devi Chowdhurani was the President. The second conference was a bigger affair. It was held at Barisal in May 1944. Snehalata Das, Headmistress of the local girls' school, became the President of the Reception Committee. Her inclusion was a very good example of how the United Front theory worked. She was reluctant at first to get involved in the work of the Communists. So the latter showed her their pamphlets, handbills and reports, discussed their objectives with her and then asked, 'We may be Communists. But do you find any of our works objectionable?' Das gave her consent at last. The President of the conference was a local Congress lady. Nelly Sengupta, the reputed Congress leader, was elected the President of the Samity at this Conference.

Apart from doing reconstruction work in the wake of the Bengal Famine, particularly amongst poor women, the members of the Samity were also concerned with problems like polygamy, prostitution, etc. The United Front policy of the Communists seemed most successful on the Party's women's front. Women of different political parties and even apolitical women had little difficulty in reaching out to each other and collaborating to serve society.

In 1944, the Mahila Atmaraksha Samity, jointly with other relief organizations, formed the Nari Seva Sangha of which Shyamaprasad Mukherjee became the President and Professor K.P. Chattopadhyay and Sita Chowdhury the Secretaries. This organization helped poor village girls return home from the city after the Famine, opened a number of *Asrams* and work-centres. On 28 December 1944, the Samity and the Nari Seva Sangha jointly arranged an art exhibition at Presidency College. Their own handiworks and the touching Famine sketches of Zainul Abedin were exhibited. Indeed, the leftist cultural movement of the period was indebted to the Samity in many ways.

The third conference of the Atmaraksha Samity was held at the University Institute Hall, Calcutta. It was just after the end of the War. The membership had reached the figure of 50,000 by the time. The conference was presided over by Jyotirmoyee Ganguly, a prominent Congress leader. Her participation was remarkable at that time of vehement anti-Communist propaganda by the Congress. The monthly organ of the Samity was *Ghare Baire*, edited by Manjusri Devi (wife of Professor K.P. Chattopadhyay). Later, Kanak Mukherjee became the Editor. Accomplished writers like Leela Majumdar, Ashapurna Devi, Mira Devi, Asha Ganguly and Maitrayee Devi used to contribute to this journal. The Samity continued to work during the communal riots and the Tebhaga Movement, though not as extensively as before. Then it merged with the All-India Womens' Coordination Committee, formed at a conference in Copenhagen in 1953 and got affiliated to the Women's International Democratic Federation.

Kishore Bahini

A Kishore Bahini or Teenagers' Band (1943–8)[124] was formed in Bengal under the initiative of the Communist Party. The leftists started organizing children at local levels to encourage them to develop a socially and politically conscious and constructive way of life. In April 1943, these local efforts were given organized shape by the Party. A number of letters and reports in *Janayuddha*, March–April 1943, and an interview with Nripen Banerjee, the first Secretary of the Kishore Bahini, help us reconstruct the history of the formation of this organization.

By way of explaining the origins of the Kishore Bahini, Nripen Banerjee says:

> Joshi might have made mistakes in politics, but he undeniably had a very broad idea about Communism. To him Communism was a way of life and one could not practise Communism by oneself; so not individual Communists, but Communist families should be units of the Communist movement. As the Ladies' Front was formed for the women of such Communist families, the Kishore Bahini was formed for the children—for their proper mental and physical development.[125]

On the one hand, the formation of the Kishore Bahini was designed to counter the prevalent trend of keeping children detached from reality and of disseminating amongst them ideals devoid of any social relevance—a trend, which, according to them, 'Moumachhi' (pen-name of Bimal Ghosh) of the *Ananda Bazar Patrika* and the Monimala Clubs was nurturing with a great zeal. In the words of Nripen Banerjee, theirs was 'a line more conservative than that of the Congress'. On the other hand, an aim of the Kishore Bahini was to inspire the children to serve their country. Stories about the children of Russia and China were a source of inspiration. Maybe they did not know much about the Little Red Devils of China at that time. But the role played by the Pioneers (age limit 10–16 years) and Young Communist League (age limit 14–20 years) in the post-Revolution reconstruction of Russia was well-known to them. At a more practical level, the Kishore Bahini (the upper age limit of which was probably 16) was planned as a stepping stone for membership of the Students' Federation. In fact, there was an overlap and complementarity between the two bodies. A number of youths belonged to both.

The central office of the Kishore Bahini was 8/2, Bhabani Dutta Lane, which was also the office of the Students' Federation. Anandasankar Bhattacharya, a prominent BPSF leader, was the main spirit of this newly-formed organization. He was fondly called 'Chhorda' (the little elder brother) by its members. In 1944, he became the secretary of the BPSF, thereby handing over all responsibilities of the Kishore Bahini to Sukanta Bhattacharya, and the young poet proved himself extremely competent in the somewhat prosaic task of organization.

The Kishore Bahini increasingly prospered. Branches were established in several areas of Calcutta and in far-off villages. Ultimately it reached a strength of 30,000 in 600 centres. Many members came from peasant families. Girls were drawn from conservative Muslim families. The most prominent branch was at the house of Kamal Bose, 13/1, Balaram Ghosh Street. This Shyambazar Branch excelled in sports and games, cultural pursuit and social services. Sukanta himself looked after its activities and he was helped by Arati Pakrashi (later Ganguly).

The motto of this children's organization was 'Education, health, service and independence' (vide *Janayuddha*, 19 May 1943). They held weekly assemblies, where they had discussions on subjects like the lives of great men, current politics, problems of physics, etc. Sometimes some reputed scholars were invited to give lectures. At the same time, the elders tried to instill political consciousness in them. Some of the educational activities undertaken included publishing magazines, both printed and handwritten, founding libraries and organizing night schools for the poor children. Cultural pursuit was considered part of education. The children practised dance, music, *antakshari* (war of poems) and acquainted themselves with other forms of culture. They often held cultural functions. They practised various sports and games including *lathikhela* (playing with sticks) which was inspired by the tradition of the Rashtriya Swayamsevak Sangh. They worked for the welfare of their own localities and villages. The Bengal Famine called for a widening of the scope of their work. They helped the poor, nursed the sick, controlled queues at ration shops, ran *langarkhanas* (where food was offered on charity), distributed the milk supplied by the Red Cross Society and so on. Arati Pakrashi[126] and her brother Amulya Pakrashi,[127] who was a member of the Students' Federation and a patron of Bagbazar Kishore Bahini at that time, remember interesting details about the activities of the Kishore Bahini.

The children tried to help their *dadas* (the elders who were mostly members of the Students' Federation) in many ways. During 1942–3, when anti-Communist feelings were running high among common people because of the CPI's opposition to the Quit India Movement, the Communists often ran the risk of getting beaten up in certain areas. Bagbazar was one such place. Amulya Pakrashi remembers that whenever he happened to visit Bagbazar, members of the Bagbazar Kishore Bahini escorted him out of danger. He also remembers what an admirable role the Kishore Bahini of his own locality Fariapukur had played in building up anti-communal resistance during 1946–7.

The leftist elders—Hemanga Biswas, Subhas Mukherjee, Kanak Mukherjee, Bishnu Dey, Jyotirindra Moitra, Nani Bhowmik, Khagendranath Mitra, Girin Chakravarty and many others—used to write songs, poems, stories and essays for the Kishore Bahini. Many of these were published in the section 'Kishore Sabha' of *Swadhinata*—a section edited by Sukanta. During the late 1940s Khagendranath Mitra, a well known children's writer, edited the daily *Kishore* for these children. Sukanta himself wrote a number of poems and stories. His drama *Abhijan* (which was published by the Kishore Bahini, along with Anandasankar Bhattacharya's *Bijayee*, in April 1944) was very popular among the kishores who enacted it many a time. *Abhijan* was about the noble efforts of a girl Sankalita to raise funds for her Famine-stricken countrymen by visiting a neighbouring land and impressing the people there by singing songs. But the *kotwal* (chief of police) of that land opposed Sankalita. The *kotwal's* sin brought Famine to that land too, whereupon the people there revolted and imprisoned the *kotwal*. Anandasankar Bhattacharya reminisced about this play: 'In the original play the *kotwal* was killed by the oppressed people in the last scene, which seemed quite natural to the revolutionary consciousness of the playwright. The play was read out to our friends and patrons. On their advice, the *kotwal* was saved from death and was just arrested at the hands of the people. Today I cannot but feel sad and angry at this undesiarable change.'[128]

After the War, the Communists became busy in leading the popular struggles such as the INA (Indian National Army). Release Movement and the Tebhaga Movement, and started neglecting the Kishore Bahini. The death of Sukanta Bhattacharya in early 1947 almost broke the link between the Communist elders and the teenagers. After the second congress of the Party (1948) the Kishore Bahini was practically wound up. The Party was going through an ultra-leftist phase. Asoke Bhattacharya, a brother of Sukanta, was a member of the Kishore Bahini at that time and edited *Natun Din*. He remembers that a Communist elder once came and told them, 'First Revolution, then Kishore Bahini, etc.'[129] Nobody seems to have considered the possibility that the Kishore Bahini could play an important role in the Revolution too.

After the War

How long will you get your drinking water from the lake?
The billowy ocean yonder calls you.
To which group do you belong?—
rushes the impetuous query.
Haven't you yet enrolled yourself in the ranks of the 'ruffians'?

—SUKANTA BHATTACHARYA
'The call', *Swadhinata*, 23 February 1946,
A reply to Patel's condemnation of the
RIN mutineers as 'ruffians'
(Later included in his book of poems *Chharpatra*)

The end of the War in 1945 was naturally an occasion for rejoicement of all those involved in the progressive cultural movement. But the movement also faced a crisis at about the same time. The cultural activities, broad-based as they had been, were generally regarded as Communist activities all the same. Gopal Haldar says: 'This is precisely what became fatal for the movement, this Communist mark. How was it fatal? The moment the Congress leaders came out of jail in 1945, they started campaigning against us; although we had tried for their release and had done it earnestly.' As a result of this Congress *jihad,* the Communist Party and its mass-fronts suffered badly.[130] This included the cultural fronts. The loyalty of many members and patronizers was shaken and existing goodwill was largely lost.

What discredited the Party was the lapses of its people's war theory and its bitter opposition to Subhas Chandra Bose during the War. Besides these, there was the Adhikari Thesis (adopted in August–September 1942), 'which came perilously near to accepting the Pakistan demand' of the Muslim League 'in what was perhaps an opportunistic bid to draw close to the other big national force, now that relations with the Congress were so strained'.[131]

Slander against the Communists went on at meeting after meeting. Chinmohan Sehanabis recalled[132] one such meeting at Desapriya Park. Nehru, who had once done much sabre-rattling against Subhas Bose, now stood in front of a huge portrait of the latter at this meeting and directly instigated the public against the Communists. The microphone was not working. A man, marked off as a Communist, was blamed for putting it out of order and beaten up ruthlessly. Ultimately, however, it was found that this man was rather close to the Congress. There were attacks on Party Offices in Calcutta and elsewhere (including the Party Headquarters at Bombay). The CPI members had to resign from the Congress on 5 October and the Communist AICC members were formally expelled in December.

The concerted campaign against the Communists lessened their chances in the 1946 elections. Only three of their candidates in Bengal got elected—Jyoti Basu, Ratanlal Brahman and Rupnarayan Roy.

The Indian National Congress now opened a cultural front of its own—Congress Sahitya Sangha, attracting a number of writers and artists and thus further weakening the Communist cultural fronts. Its President was Atul Chandra Gupta, Vice-Presidents Kiransankar Roy, Sajanikanta Das, Priyaranjan Sen and Humayun Kabir, Joint Secretaries Sachindranath Mitra and Subodh Ghosh, amongst the members were Akhil Niyogi, Amal Home, Nirupama Devi, Pratap Chandra Chunder, Pramathanath Bisi, Bijoylal Chatterjee, Bimal Ghosh, Monoj Bose, Rani Chanda, Sagarmoy Ghosh, and so on. Many of them had once fallen in line with the idea of the progressive cultural movement and had come close to it. Even now, on issues like communal riots or celebration of Independence, the PWAA and the Congress Sahitya Sangha worked unitedly.[133] Yet, the formation of the former meant a rift in the latter. But the Congress Sahitya Sangha was never able to attract the galaxy of talents that was the pride of the progressive writers' and artists' movement; and its achievement was nothing compared to that of the latter. Only the dance drama *Abhyuday* (The Advent) put up by this organization is worth mention. It was based on the theme of a united and nationally-motivated India.[134]

The Post-War Popular Upsurge

Despite considerable unpopularity, the post-War years were by no means a totally negative experience for the Communists.[135] The organizational advantages that they had enjoyed during the War now made them fit to lead the popular upheaval that marked the last days of the British Raj. There were uprisings against multilayered oppression in the country, particularly against the Raj itself. The prose, poetry, drama and art of the period documented them faithfully and reflected the militant mood in general. The popular upsurge that Calcutta witnessed during the winter of 1945–6, for example, was documented in Tarasankar Bandyopadhyay's novel *Jhar O Jharapata* (The Storm and the Fallen Leaves) and Manik Banerjee's *Chihna* (The Sign), and the documentation was so close to life that, according to Chinmohan Sehanabis, the leftist activists associated with No. 46, Dharmatala Street used to identify themselves with different characters of these novels.

The first explosion took place in the winter of 1945–6, the months that have been described as 'the edge of a volcano'. The British inflamed patriotic Indians by putting up on trial three prisoners of the INA of Subhas Bose. They included a Hindu, a Muslim and a Sikh. An Intelligence Bureau note admitted, 'There has seldom been a matter which had attracted so much

Indian public opinion, it is safe to say sympathy—this particular brand of sympathy cuts across communal barriers.' On 21 November, hundreds of students carrying flags of the Forward Block, the Students' Federation and the Muslim League squatted on Dharmatala Street, Calcutta, face-to-face with armed troops, demanding the release of the INA prisoners. The police firing killed two students and during the next two days the trouble spread as Sikh taxi-drivers, Communist-led tramwaymen and workers of several factories went on strike. Cars and lorries were burnt, trains stopped and barricades put up on important thoroughfares. Thirty-three were killed and several others suffered injuries.

Order was restored, but only temporarily. The people were in a rebellious mood. The British were very nervous about the INA spirit spreading to the Indian army. People were unhappy about the use of Indian army units to restore French and Dutch colonial rule in Vietnam and Indonesia. The usual post-war problems of unemployment and high prices were aggravated by crop failures in different parts of India. The all-India organizations of railway workers and postal employees were threatening strikes in the context of rising prices and ration cuts. The Communists identified themselves with the militant masses and came to the forefront of all struggles.

The second major outburst took place again in Calcutta, in February 1946, on the same INA issue.[136] On 11 February the students rose in protest against a court judgement sentencing Abdul Rashid of the INA to 7 years rigorous imprisonment. Again there was a perfect unity between students and workers, Muslims and Hindus. On 12 February, a Communist-led general strike paralysed the industrial life of Calcutta and there was a massive rally at Wellington Square addressed by Congress, League and Communist leaders. The police restored order only after there were 84 deaths (according to an official estimate).

Within a few days the ratings of the Royal Indian Navy revolted at Bombay (18–23 February). The tricolour, crescent and hammer-and-sickle were raised jointly on the mastheads of the rebel fleet. Their demands included the improvement of service conditions as well as the release of the INA and other political prisoners and the withdrawal of Indian troops from Indonesia. The Royal Indian Navy was renamed the Indian National Navy. In their support, the Bombay CPI called a general strike, which was supported by Congress Socialist leaders like Aruna Asaf Ali. 'For the first time the blood of men in the service and in the streets flowed together in a common cause.' But stalwarts like Gandhi and Patel condemned the strike. On failing to get the support of the national leaders, the mutinous ratings were at a loss and surrendered ultimately.[137] Not only on this particular occasion, but throughout this period when the country was in a battle readiness, the support of the national leadership for the insurgent people was either lukewarm or totally absent. Militancy was found extremely inconvenient in the context of negotiations with the Raj.

But there was no respite for the British. The strike wave of 1946 surpassed all previous records with 1,629 stoppages. The journal *Swadhinata* vividly documented the agitated mood of the time. Since April, the idea of Tebhaga (demanding two-thirds of the crop, instead of the usual half or even less, for the sharecroppers of Bengal) floated in the air. In that month, there were widespread police strikes (though not in Bengal) and there was even a report of a strike by hangmen in different central jails of Bengal, causing stoppage of execution of death sentences. Throughout the summer, there was a threat of an all-India railway stoppage. A postal strike took place in July and on 29 July the Communists called a total bandh in sympathy with the postal employees. All this testified to the fighting spirit of the people, which was however, to be marred very soon by communal holocaust. The *Swadhinata* of 7 August reported mounting tension all around, it reported a besiegement of the Assembly House by jute workers and a strike by the workers of the Imperial Bank. On 9 August the paper announced that the Calcutta District Communist Party would hold a public meeting that day to pay tribute to the martyrs of the Quit India Movement and to pledge a final fight for complete independence in tune with the tradition of the Quit India. From 11 August there were reports on the radio strike in which many eminent radio artists took part. But on 16 August, a diabolic Communalist outrage broke out in Calcutta and for a few days this prevented the paper from being published at all.

Communal Riots

A terrible fratricidal war started on 16 August with the Great Calcutta Killing. It contaminated Bombay from 1 September, spreading to Noakhali in East Bengal (10 October), Bihar (25 October), Garmukteswar in UP (November) and the Punjab (from March 1947 onwards). In Calcutta, it started after a Maidan Rally addressed by Chief Minister Suhrawardy on the Direct Action Day declared by the League Ministry. Hindus and Muslims fought each other violently in what has been called 'a pogrom between two rival armies of (the) Calcutta underworld'. A madness seized the people. By 19 August, there were at least 4,000 killed and 10,000 injured. This was followed by chronic disturbances. The British, with all their might, made very few attempts to check this communal frenzy.

The Communists tried individually and organizationally to resist the tide of communalism and to provide relief to the distressed people. The Mahila Atmaraksha Samity, for example, sent a team of workers to the troubled areas of Chowmuhani and Noakhali. Some Communist ladies went to Chandpur on behalf of the All-India Women's Conference.[138] The greatest credit in this respect should go to the Kisan Sabha of Hasanabad (near the border of Comilla). A terrible communal war had broken out in neighbouring Ramnagar. The peasants of 11 villages of Hasanabad, of whom 80 per cent were Muslims, rescued and provided shelter to almost 3,000 Hindus of Ramnagar, under the leadership of the Kisan Sabha[139]—an incident that was immortalized in Bishnu Dey's poem 'Hasanabadei'.[140] All the writers and artists of Bengal strongly denounced the communal frenzy, some with deep despair and others with profound hope for the future.

In a statement issued by the progressive writers of Bengali, Urdu, Hindi, Marathi, Gujarati and English, the responsibility for communal disturbances was laid at the door of the British and their 'divide and rule policy'. They also reproached the leaders of the main political parties, who 'instead of seeing through the imperialist game, are preparing to carry out this fratricidal policy'. These writers called upon everyone to help to turn the tide from fratricidal hatred to the struggle against imperialism.[141] The most remarkable achievement on the part of the writers and artists of Bengal was to forget all differences and to present a common front against this evil phenomenon. The members of the PWAA, the Artist Association and even the Congress Sahitya Sangha jointly brought out a procession of writers and artists preaching brotherhood and singing songs on the bloody streets of Calcutta. Sajanikanta Das was one of the main organizers. This was a bit later—in October 1947. But Calcutta was still writhing under communal bitterness. The murder of Sachindranath Mitra, Secretary of the Congress Sahitya Sangha, was the proximate reason behind organizing this united procession.[142]

Popular Movements Continued

The communal riots naturally disrupted the mass struggle against imperialism and its allies, but not for long. Five months after the August riots students of Calcutta came out on the streets again in a 'Hands off Vietnam' demonstration, against the use of the Dum Dum Airport by French planes (21 January 1947). The same day saw the beginning of a victorious 85-day tram strike under Communist leadership. Port employees, Howrah engineering workers and many others went on strike. In fact, there was a new strike wave at the beginning of 1947—strikes in Kanpur textiles, in Coimbatore, Karachi and elsewhere, a threat of coal stoppage, due 'largely to Communist agitation'. The *Swadhinata* of 26 April 1947, reported a strike by primary teachers on economic demands. And in all these, Hindus and Muslims fought unitedly.

Then the Communists led a number of rural movements in different parts of India. There were a series of successful revolts by the Warli tribals of Maharashtra against forest contractors, merchant-moneylenders and outsider landlords (from 1945). In the Travancore State, from September 1946 there was a massive campaign against Dewan Ramaswami Iyer's plan of an 'American-model' constitution and this bloody Punnapra-Vayalar rising helped to bring about the integration of the state with India the following year. But the most notable uprising was that of Telengana between July 1946 and October 1951—a peasant guerilla war against the regime of the Nizam of Hyderabad which had retained the most atrocious forms of feudal exploitation and was now trying to set up an independent Muslim-dominated state in the interior of India. The Telengana Movement had the character of a national liberation struggle till September 1948 when the army of Independent India marched in. Now the state was integrated with India. And this was the end of the Telengana Movement too.

The Tebhaga Movement

After 16 August 1946, the Communist Party realized that to fight communalism they needed to embark upon a positive programme and in a country where the majority were peasants, it had to be a peasants' movement. So a new development in Bengal in 1946–7 was the Tebhaga Movement[143] led by the Kisan Sabha. The idea of Tebhaga had been floating in the air for quite some time and isolated movements had been led here and there on this issue. Now Joshi's article in the *People's Age* calling for a peasants' movement to resist communalism, made the position of the Party in regard to this matter more definite. In September 1946 the Bengal Provincial Kisan Sabha gave a call to implement through peasants' struggle the Floud Commission's (1940) recommendation of Tebhaga. Communist cadres, student militants and even writers and artists went out into villages to organize the bargadars (sharecroppers) and participate in the latter's struggle against the jotedars. In November, when the harvesting time came, the bargadars of Dinajpur, Rangpur, Jalpaiguri, Maldah, Midnapore, Jessore, Khulna and Mymensingh, led by the volunteers of village Tebhaga Committees, started taking paddy to their own *kholan* (farmyard) instead of the jotedar's house as before, so as to enforce Tebhaga. Their battlecry was 'Jan dibo, tobu dhan dibo na' (We shall sacrifice our lives, but not surrender the paddy). North Bengal was the stronghold of the movement. These were the same sharecroppers who had helplessly resigned themselves to their gruesome fate during the Famine of 1943–4. The Famine had increased their number (60 per cent of villagers in some cases) by causing loss of their lands and made them wise enough to try and win their rights by hard struggle. And indeed, it was a valiant struggle of almost unarmed peasants against the resourceful jotedars and the ruffians hired by them.

The struggle intensified as the League Ministry published in January 1947 a draft bill to enact Tebhaga and to protect the bargadar's right on the land he cultivated. This gave the bargadars renewed confidence. The jotedars were on the other hand determined to nullify the bill. More skirmishes took place. The movement spread to hitherto unorganized areas, where the Kisans took the initiative and contacted the 'Red Flag'. Hundreds of villages in 19 districts became 'strongly guarded forts of Red Flag. Sharecroppers were now supported by small peasants and landless labourers. The League Ministry stopped 'unnecessary police intervention'. Thus, the middle of February was the peak period of the Tebhaga Movement.

On 20 February, Attlee declared June 1948 as a deadline for Transfer of Power. The prospect of power made both Congressmen and League leaders demand the withdrawal of the Bargadar Bill, for they feared that it would strengthen the Communists and enable them to create trouble. From the end of February, the peasants faced a brutal police offensive. They were arrested and killed in hundreds. Their crops were taken away and girls raped, though even about this time there took place a remarkable incident like the refusal of the police to open fire on peasants of Narail (Jessore).

The Tebhaga Movement shows how the Communists sharpened the consciousness of the people about their rights, led their struggle against the exploiters and yet bungled as leaders by failing to formulate proper political tactics and military strategy. First, even as late as May 1946, at the Mowbhog Kisan Conference, there had been no proposal for starting a Tebhaga Movement. The Communists called for the movement almost without any preparation. They did not have any idea about how to proceed and how far. The way the peasants responded to their call was beyond their wildest imagination and they were at a loss about how to tackle the situation. This became crucial when the police launched a brutal offensive in February 1947. The peasants were determined and demanded arms. The Communists did not have arms, and in any case, could not envisage an all-out armed struggle for economic and political emancipation. So they 'decided not to take any decision' about a counter-attack. The peasants had to admit defeat helplessly and this did irreparable harm to their self-confidence. Only in Mymensingh could the Hajongs escape to forests and put up a last-ditch fight. And when Abani Lahiri and Krishnabinode Roy, two top leaders, went to Kakdwip to talk to the peasants there, the latter directly refused to retreat. They actually kept fighting with *lathis* and *bontis* (a sort of knife to cut vegetables) thus creating a heroic but tragic saga in the history of Bengal.

It may also be pointed out that the Communists kept the movement confined to a very narrow economic demand of only a section of peasants. They did not even try to include the agricultural labourers, a no less-aggrieved section, in the struggle. They did not raise the slogan 'Langal jar jami tar' (Land to the Tiller), the dream of every poor peasant that had been nurtured by the Kisan Sabha too for quite some time. When Bhabani Sen at last realized the need to raise other demands along with that of

Tebhaga and thus broaden the struggle, it was too late and the movement was already on the decline. The bulk of the agrarian population was left outside the movement and this made it easy for the jotedars to suppress it. It goes to the credit of the villagers themselves and not the Communist leadership that in some cases a number of non-bargadar peasants did join the struggle (Chiar Shai Shaikh of Khanpur, Dinajpur, an agricultural labourer who was killed in police firing is one example) and the movement was turned into a broad-based struggle for power in the countryside.

Another vital failure of the Communists was to organize the middle and the poor peasants, the workers and the urban midle-class to take effective action in support of the sharecroppers. Again, in the Dooars, the tea-coolies did join the movement. But they did so on the basis of their tribal solidarity with the peasants (both workers and peasants were Santal and Oraon) and not inspired by the Communists.

Later, quite a few researchers[144] have blamed the Communists for not combining economic and political demands and for thus wrecking the Tebhaga Movement. Indeed, the lack of a political vision made the Tebhaga Movement irrelevant to the cause of nationalism on the eve of Independence. Thus, though hundreds of peasants and middle-class Communists fought dedicatedly against the jotedars, though masterpieces like Manik Banerjee's story 'Chhoto Bakulpurer Jatri' (Visitors to Chhoto Bakulpur) were occasioned by the movement, though a talented student artist like Somnath Hore filled up his diary with sketches of the fighting peasants of Rangpur, the movement failed due to the myopic leadership of the Communist Party. Some other historians are of the opinion that the organizational strength of the Communists was negligible at that time and that a decision in favour of an all-out armed struggle would thus have been suicidal.[145] But one cannot help feel that even if the charge of betrayal of the peasants by the Communists is a bit far-fetched, the leadership they provided was definitely inadequate and this was not just the inadequacy of organization and physical strength. The Communist leaders showed a miserable lack of preparation, planning and purpose. They launched the movment not so much to better the conditions of the peasants, but to counter communalism.[146] Then, the Bargadar Bill made them complacent. They thought that the battle was almost won. Their post-Bill leadership was by no means effective.

The inadequacy of Communist leadership is true not only with respect to the Tebhaga Movement, but the entire post-War popular militancy. Since the days of the People's War, the Communists had been vague about the anti-imperialist struggle. Even when the defeat of the Axis powers seemed imminent, they could not formulate an anti-imperialist programme for India. The only political demand that they raised was that of unity between the Congress and the Muslim League. This shows that they wanted independence from above were not really serious about building up an anti-imperialist struggle from below.[147] The INA Release Movements, the RIN Movement, etc., were not really part of a well-formulated anti-imperialist programme of the Communists, but rather showed how the Communists responded to the sponteneous anti-British sentiment of the masses. And the Communists could not sustain this militant anti-imperialist spirit for long. In the words of a prominent Communist leader, E.M.S. Namboodiripad: 'Each of these streams passed through little channels and finally petered out.... The leftist parties including the Communist Party were not strong enough to unify and comprehend [*sic*] them into a single comprehensive revolutionary upsurge.'[148]

Independence and the Communists

Gratifying all my thorns
will bloom the flower.
All my agonies will get coloured
To become a rose.

—An oft-quoted verse by Tagore. The line '*To become a rose*' (Golap Hoye Uthbe) was chosen by Saroj Bandyopadhyay for the title of a novel of his—which is perhaps the best documentation of the Communist movement of 1948–50—story of a dedicated young Communist carrying out a disastrous party policy at the cost of his own life. The author himself had intimate experiences of the Communist activities of the period. The novel was serially published in *Parichay*, 1962–3.

Communal riots combined with the unworkability of the Congress-League coalition at the Centre led to an Independence that was accompanied by Partition of the country. So from this section onwards the history we are narrating is disrupted by geography. We will now confine our narrative to the western part of Bengal, leaving out the eastern part which than became part of Pakistan. There was a sense of betrayal in both the countries though and the progressive cultural activists found themselves at loggerheads with the new governments in both cases.

Partition meant a grave human tragedy—thousands were torn from their age-old roots and turned nearly overnight into hapless refugees. Yet the country rejoiced on getting the long-cherished Independence, and so did the Communists. Chinmohan Sehanabis described how enthusiastically No. 46, Dharmatala Street celebrated Independence jointly with the Congress Sahitya Sangha. But this sense of joy was only temporary. The Communists had hard times ahead, partly due to the hostility of the ruling government and partly due to their own follies. The Congress hostility towards the Communists continued unabated after Independence. In early

1948, a World Youth Congress was held in Calcutta. A reception was arranged for foreign delegates at the Dixon Lane house of Charuprakash Ghosh of IPTA. Some armed hooligans (who according to the Communists, belonged to Congress) attacked the place killing Sushil Mukherjee, a IPTA member and Bhabamadhav Ghosh, a relative of the host. This was the last straw on the camel's back. After this, Congress-Communist reconciliation seemed practically unattainable.

But the tension that prevailed after Independence was largely the CPI's own making. Strangely enough, ignoring the most traumatic problem of the time, the plight of the uprooted (perhaps they were reluctant to give due importance to the problem, for after all, they had supported Partiton), the Communists soon plunged into an imaginary revolution. The Soviet Russia got caught up in the Cold War and trying to reassert its control of local Communist movements was fomenting agitations and even guerrilla wars against governments in many parts of Asia. The Indian Communists too became suspicious and started nurturing theoretical reservations about Independence. At first they had called it a step forward and a weapon in the hands of the people, but not complete Independence. Their attitude towards Independence and the government of independent India increasingly hardened and they ended up by saying at the Second Party Congress, Calcutta, February–March 1948, 'Yeh Azadi Jhuta Hai' (This is a sham independence).[149] Now they said that the Independence was nothing but a 'deal struck with imperialism'. This naturally antagonized the Indian government which banned the CPI promptly enough (26 March). But what was more serious for the CPI was that this curious slogan made them lose the popular support that had been their mainstay.

At the Central Committee meeting held at Bombay in December 1947 it was the comrades from Bengal who had for the first time formally demanded a change in the Party line. Now at the Second Party Congress, B.T. Ranadive endorsed this change in the political thesis presented by him. He criticized the 'Reformist Deviation' carried on for long by P.C. Joshi in the name of national unity, and called for a line of struggle. At this meeting, Joshi was removed, Ranadive was elected the new General Secretary and his thesis was adopted.

The new line meant abandonment of the United Front policy that had paid rich dividends for over a decade. The United Front had stood for an anti-fascist and anti-imperialist alliance with the bourgeoisie. But now fascism was not a threat any longer and imperialism had made the bourgeoisie its 'junior partner' in a bid to extend its base. Very soon, this 'junior partner' was found to be the 'senior partner' at the helm of the imperialist-bourgeois-feudal conspiracy. The Communists further said that in India the Bourgeois-Democratic Revolution would no longer need to precede the Socialist-Proletarian one. They quoted Lenin to prove that in colonial countries capitalism is weak and hence the bourgeoisie cannot play a progressive role and carry out the task of the democratic revolution. 'The proletariat, on the other hand, had taken up a position to carry on the anti-imperialist struggle to the final phase of democratic revolution, the transitional point to the dictatorship of the proletariat'—'the democratic dictatorship of workers and peasants'. And they also quoted from Stalin, 'According to this theory (theory of Lenin) the hegemony of the proletariat in the bourgeois revolution, the proletariat being in alliance with the peasantry, would grow into the hegemony of the proletariat in the socialist revolution, the proletariat now being in alliance with the other labouring and exploited masses.'[150]

Having formulated this theory, the General Secretary assisted by one or two politburo members ruled the Party in a most undemocratic way, which was perhaps the only way possible during the illegal phase. A suffocating atmosphere of suspicion, intrigue and fear was created in the Party. Suspension of entire district committees, a spate of expulsions, a drastic fall in the membership—this was the picture of the functioning of the Party during the months that followed the Second Congress. If the picture within the Party was such, that of the United Front created by the Party was much worse. The United Front was found to be full of 'opportunistic bourgeoisie' who were ruthlessly attacked and alienated. So far as the 'proletariat' and their allies were concerned, the Party leaders found them already prepared for revolution but did not have any concrete programme for bringing it about.

On 27 January 1950, the Cominform in the editorial of its organ *For a Lasting Peace. For a People's Democracy*,[151] stressed imperialism and feudalism as the real reactionary forces and mooted the idea of uniting with the national bourgeoisie against these forces. But what had been lost was never to be retrieved, and the fundamental error remained—the error of formulating theories 'not on the basis of a concrete study of the concrete situation but on the basis of quotations from Lenin and Stalin and later from Mao and Chinese leaders.' *The Lasting Peace* editorial just changed the Russian path into the Chinese path.

The above criticism has been made by M.B. Rao who edited *Documents of the History of Communist Party of India* (*Volume VII—1948–50*), the CPI's own publication. Rao further says,

> Problems were solved with historical parallels. In the first period Nehru was Kerensky, 15 August was February revolution, insurrection maturing, hey presto! we march to socialism. After the Lasting Peace editorial Nehru was Chiang Kai-Shek, 15 August was China's 1927, the peasant army was marching with steady steps to liberate the cities and establish a new democracy. But this second appearance of historical personage, as Marx once said, ended as a farce.

The limitations of this 'revolution on paper' were manifest in the fiasco of the railway strike on 9 March 1948, which had been intended to be the pivot of a single all-India general strike. The people were just not ready for it and the only result was the arrest of all effective cadres. Then a jail front was opened and the Communist prisoners were instructed to 'fight militantly for each and every footling demand'. Prolonged hunger-strikes were forced on them. Outside the jail many of them died in clashes with the police. 'The ranks were hypnotized into believing what the party leaders were asking them to do was pure Bolshevism. Sometimes the ranks in their enthusiasm went far ahead of even what the leaders wanted.' Isolation from the mainstream of the national life might have bred a sense of heroism, self-sacrifice and idealism.

In June 1950, at the Central Committee meeting, the members from Andhra suggested another change of line in accordance with the Cominform instruction of January. Now the banner was taken over by a new Central Committee headed by Rajeswar Rao. But the illusion of Revolution continued for some time. The new leadership gave a call for enacting Telengana all over the country in the name of the Chinese path when the very existence of the Telengana Movement was in grave danger. With the entry of the Indian troops in September 1948, the struggling people of Telengana had hoped that they would get a better deal from the Indian government and yet the Communist leadership gave the command to continue the struggle, now against the Indian government. The Indian Army was much more powerful than the Nizam's Razakars. From a broad agrarian movement, Telengana became a losing battle of isolated peasant squads retreating into the forests for sheer survival, until the movement was withdrawn in October 1951. The Communists reflected later that it would have been wiser to limit their aims to agrarian reforms alone after 1948. A Telengana hero like Ravi Narayan Reddi even commented that continuing the guerilla struggle itself had been a mistake once the Indian Army had marched in.

Since the end of the Second World War the Indian populace had been in a militant mood. But once their main enemy, the British, was removed from the scene, their militancy considerably diminished. In any case, the Communists never seriously set themselves the task of preparing for a revolution. Instead their leaders kept talking of Revolution and a handful of cadres risked their lives in a valiant but Quixotic struggle. The people 'turned their back thinking that the leaders had gone delirious'. The inevitable result was the total abandonment of the path of struggle very soon. From 1951, the Communists became more interested in the World Peace Movement than in the dream of Revolution. They went to the masses not through a revolutionary struggle, but through the general elections of 1952. That Ravi Narayan Reddi returned to the Parliament by a majority even bigger than Nehru's testifies to the glory that the 1948–50 period achieved for the Communists despite all their errors.

The 'Party Program' and the 'Tactical Line' of 1951[152] made a departure from 'Revolution by Analogy' and stressed the need for understanding the specifics of the Indian situation, maintaining the unity of the Party and pushing it back to the masses. Of course, talks about Revolution continued. The document 'Tactical line' opened with the declaration—'Not Peaceful, but Revolutionary Path'. It suggested 'combining two basic factors of the revolution—the partisan war of the peasants and workers rising in the cities'. But the actual passivity of its policy would be revealed in the section where, questioned about the details of the partisan war, the leadership answered more than once: 'It does not depend on us. If the masses are ready and eager we should assist them'.[153] And while they declared 'Not peaceful, but Revolutionary Path', their only concrete suggestion for mobilizing the masses was a peace movement.

The Disintegration of the Cultural Front

The lapses of the political line of 1948–50 were reflected in the cultural front of the Party with disastrous effects. Intolerance towards writers and artists of the past and the present had been shown by some so-called Marxian critics even in the 1930s. During the war period, the attitude was apparently abandoned in the interest of the United Front. After the War and particularly after the Second Party Congress this attitude returned with a vengeance. In 1947 the Aragon-Garaudi controversy in France raised a storm in the Indian literary world as well. The former recommended a definite Party line for the writers and the latter denied it. Towards the end of 1947, a meeting was held in Calcutta under the chairmanship of Tarasankar Bandyopadhyay to consider this French debate. According to the instructions of the cultural subcommittee of the Party, Tarasankar, Jyotirmoy Roy, Bishnu Dey and other defenders of Garaudi's view were allowed to have the last word. Officially, the Party did not have a definite cultural policy at that time, and at any rate, did not want to disturb the spirit of unity. But this did not allay the undercurrent of tension.[154]

After the second Congress, however, the Party evolved a definite cultural policy, though a highly repressive one. In April 1949 fourth conference of AIPWA was held. Its manifesto said that while bourgeois literature had once been progressive, as reflected in the writings of Rammohan, Michael and Rabindranath, now this literature was in the last stage of degeneration, it was dealing with the self-conceit, petty politicking, despair, sentimentalism and confusion of the decaying middle-class, it was supporting imperialist America and even fascism and denigrating the Soviet Union. A few of these writers belonged to the 'Third Power', they sympathized with the rights of workers and peasants verbally, but they claimed 'freedom of creation' for themselves, paid too much attention to forms of writing, wanted literature to be apolitical and based on an 'absolute value'. Actually, they were paid agents of the capitalists. The manifesto said that the glorious struggle of the proletariat should be the only theme of progressive literature, and to be able to create such a literature the writers should go and participate in these struggles and merge with the communities of workers and peasants. Chinmohan Sehanabis in his address to the conference stressed that all the writers should go to the 'front', even at the cost of their writing.[155]

Unqualified hatred for 'bourgeois' artists was expressed in the volumes of *Marxbadi*, the theoretical journal of the Party from October 1948 to September 1949. This vicious trend just destroyed the united cultural front. A talented and sympathetic writer like Tarasankar who had come very close to the AIPWA was vehemently condemned; Bishnu Dey, a sincere fellow traveller of the Party, was called 'a Trojan horses in the camp of progress'; even Manik Banerjee, a devoted Party member, was criticized for not being sufficiently 'proletarian' in attitude, not to speak of the denigration of the great literary figures of the past, including Rabindranath Tagore. After all this, whatever remained of the writers' front was a shadow of its former self.

The same thing happened to the IPTA. Sajal Roy Chowdhury,[156] the Secretary, West Bengal IPTA, condemned popular IPTA productions like the drama *Nabanna* or the ballet *India Immortal* as reactionary bourgeois affairs, confined to 'rehearsal-show-rehearsal'. Devoted artists were denigraded and alienated. The People's Theatre Movement broke up and gave way to the Group Theatre Movement. But we shall discuss the history of the decline of the leftist cultural movement later, in detail.

The fate of the Artiste Association too can be touched upon briefly in this connection. Hemanta Mukherjee, the Secretary of the organization at this time, told us how the new Party leadership (Sudhi Pradhan had gone underground) had fomented tensions and divisions among artists. A number of members were branded a 'opportunist' without any valid grounds. Mukherjee blamed the autocratic attitude of the Party leaders for ruining the Artiste Association.[157]

The Fifth IPTA Conference had been held in Ahmedabad in December 1947. No major change of outlook had been noticeable there. But the Sixth Conference at Allahabad from 4–9 February 1949,[158] which elected a new Executive Committee of which the president was Anna Bhau Sathe, the folk poet of Maharashtra and the general secretary Niranjan Sen, blamed the policy of compromise accepted at Ahmedabad, for creating an atmosphere of frustration and confusion and letting incidents like the Dixon Lane Murder occur. The Sixth Conference tried to work out 'the correct ideological stand of the People's Theatre Movement in the current political situation and the correct organizational structure necessary to implement its programme'. The resolution that was unanimously accepted here pledged to build the People's Theatre Movement among the revolutionary masses of the country. But no concrete steps were suggested to achieve the goal.[159]

Revolution and participation in revolutionary struggles on the part of writers and artists and thus building a revolutionary People's Theatre Movement was just wishful thinking. Some isolated struggles going on in a few Tebhaga villages and some other pockets were enough to delude the middle-class leftists that the Revolution was round the corner. However, we should admit that some cultural activists, charged by a vision of Revolution, embarked upon a period of guerrilla-style cultural exploits amongst the peasants and workers of the disturbed areas, often risking confrontation with the police, though they were not really ushering in any Revolution or acting through any definite guidance from above.

Anyway, very soon at a meeting of fourteen representatives and the All-India General Secretary, at Bombay, on 14 May 1951, it was decided to withdraw the Allahabad manifesto, 'since it contained a number of serious errors', to 'unite all progressive cultural forces, take the message of peace to the people, and create works of art reflecting the real needs and desires of the people'.[160]

Similarly, the Calcutta Young Writers' Conference in October 1950, adopted a manifesto that sounds much toned down, though still polemical and quite vague. It said that the writers were responsible to society, particularly as society was still burdened with problems such as imperialist oppression, starvation and unemployment. The writers should support peace against the threat of a nuclear war, they should wage a war against feudal tendencies, decaying and reactionary bourgeois thinking and against imposition of languages other than Bengali on the Bengali-speaking people; they should study folk forms deeply to have a feel of the folk life. The Conference recognized the positive achievements of the old 'bourgeois' literature of Michael, Bankim and Rabindranath, and stressed the need to befriend 'honest' writers who had been alienated by the talks about slogan-mongering literature.[161]

Sectarianism was much less rigid now, and the dogmatic attack on writers and artists much less intemperate. But it did not disappear altogether. While political understanding remained rather poor, the aesthetic debate continued in political terms. The Party leaders continued suspecting a number of artists of helping the bourgeois cause. Even as late as 1954, the attitude of the Party was not very encouraging in this respect. Surama Ghatak, wife of Ritwik Ghatak, the famous film director, who was then a member of the Party and the IPTA, recollects how,[162] her aunt Sadhana Roychowdhury used to tell her that Ritwik Ghatak, Salil Chowdhury and Utpal Dutta were intellectuals, but Trotskyites (which in this case probably meant those who claimed autonomy for artistic practices), and so she forbade her to mix with Ritwik. The Party actually tried to prevent Ritwik from staging his play *Nicher Mahal.* A one-man commission comprising Promod Dasgupta was set up to censor him. The commission found him 'not guilty'. Yet *Nicher Mahal* could not be staged due to difficulties created by the Party, and well-wishers continued to ask Surama not to mix with Ritwik. Ultimately, Ritwik Ghatak had to leave the IPTA (we will see how Salil Chowdhury and Utpal Dutta had to leave too).[163] This is only one example of the attitude of the Party as regards its cultural front—an attitude that was not very helpful either to the cause of culture or to that of political advancement.

The Peace Movement

> *The deliberate aim at Peace very easily passes into its bastard substitute, Anaesthesia.*
>
> —A.N. WHITEHEAD
> *Adventures of Ideas*

After the end of the second world war, a cold war developed among the great powers, much to the anxiety of the war-weary people. A Peace Movement was started on a worldwide scale. India was an enthusiastic participant. Left-minded people took a leading part in this Movement. They thought that a collective and organized effort could prevent the war-mongers from setting the world ablaze. The Peace Movement was apparently directed not only against the economic interests and imperialist aggression pushing the world to the brink of another devastating World War, but against all kinds of social oppression as well.

The exponents of the Peace Movement were most worried about the way people were being conditioned for war through the propagation of prejudice, fear, hatred and enmity amongst themselves. Radio, press, film and television were all being used to poison the minds of people and make them accept the inevitability of war. Culture had become the worst weapon of war propaganda. Literature and art were obssessed with sadism and sex, particularly in capitalist countries, and India was not immune to all this. Thus there was an attempt to link the struggle for peace with the struggle for a new culture. The united front of progressive writers and artists were called upon to head the movement for peace through their particular art forms by insisting upon the people's birthright to life and peace and by discovering the dynamism that lies in the collective strength of humanity.

A World Peace Congress was held at Breslau, Poland. It was organized by some famous pro-left intellectuals such as the scientists J.D. Bernal and

Joliot-Curie and the writer Ehrenburg. After this, Communists all over the world became enthusiastic about the Peace Movement. The Indian Peace Council thrived under the dynamic leadership of Ramesh Chandra. The Paschim Banga Shanti Samskriti Parishad was an affiliate of the international and national organizations for peace. The Communist Party entrusted two of its workers—Narahari Kaviraj (a member of the Progressive Writers' Cell of the Party) and Niranjan Sen (the General Secretary of the IPTA)—with the task of organizing a broad-based Peace Movement in Bengal. Kaviraj was to formulate the ideological side of the movement and the cultural side was to be looked after by Sen.

Numerous peace meetings were held. Kaviraj told me in an interview later[164] that he himself had addressed at least a hundred such meetings. There was a drive to collect signatures in support of peace. A large number of poems, stories, plays and songs were written on the theme. We would get an idea about this Peace Movement, its achievements and shortcomings, from the discussion of the two big peace conventions held in India in the early 1950s.

The All-India Peace Convention (Bombay, 1951)[165] was held at the Sunderbai Hall on 11 May. Dr Saifuddin Kitchlew, a leading Congressman was the President. Prithviraj Kapoor, the celebrated actor, welcomed the 400 delegates. Messages of greetings poured in. The journal *People's China* of Peking and the great singer Paul Robeson sent massages. People from all walks of life, Congress leaders Dr Atal and Sunderlal, Z.A. Ahmed of the CPI, famous mathematician D.D. Kosambi, renowned writer Mulk Raj Anand, film producer Phani Majumdar, R.K. Karanjia (editor of *Blitz*), Sardar Gurbaksh Singh, novelist from the Punjab and many others attended the Conference. Speeches by the businessman Sohanlal Dugger and Sadhu Mohan Jairam Das, representative of 5,60,000 sadhus, were found especially significant. Of special interest was the report by Niranjan Sen, the delegate from West Bengal where the movement had already made rapid strides by gathering hundreds of prominent artists and many organizations in the Shanti Sanskriti Parishad, an affiliated body of the World Peace Congress and by holding two highly successful peace cultural festivals.

The Convention urged the Indian Parliament to 'take the initiative to call a conference of the five great powers to discuss all outstanding issues', called for the withdrawl of all foreign troops from the Asian soil, urged the Parliament to declare that Indian soldiers, Indian bases, Indian raw materials and war materials would be denied to foreign powers.

The following decisions on cultural work in connection with the Peace Movement were taken: (1) to organize a National Commission for cultural exchanges with other countries, with its office at Bombay; (2) to encourage cultural exchanges between different states of India; (3) to plan a writers' and artists' conference in October; and (4) to consider a proposal that an Asian cultural festival be held in India. K.A. Abbas announced at the cultural session that a number of films would be produced on the theme of peace by famous producers. The Commission considered issuing a pledge for peace to be signed by all lovers of art and culture in the country.

In April 1952, the All-India Cultural Conference and Festival for Peace was held in Calcutta.[166] This big affair was arranged at the Park Circus Ground from 2–6 April. Just before the conference started, posters of an organization calling itself the Young Socialist League branded it as a Communist conspiracy. According to the Communists, this organization was a paid agent of the Americans. The following complaints too were made by the Communists in this connection. The national newspapers tried their best to blackout all news of this conference. Howard Fast and Paul Robeson were refused passports by the American government and hence could not attend the conference. The Indian government refused visas to the Soviet and Chinese delegates, Nazim Hikmat of Turkey and many others. On the first day of the conference there was an attempt to set fire to the pavilion, though not much harm was done due to the efficiency of the Fire Brigade.

The theme of the conference was 'the present tension in Indian culture arising from the threat of an international war'. The conference divided up in five commissions to study the implication of the threat of war. Their themes were: (1) Living conditions of men of culture as they are affected by the present tension; (2) The growing propaganda for war; (3) Culture and the Indian tradition of peace; (4) Cultural exchanges between the various language groups of India and the various cultural zones, as a basis for our contribution to cultural exchange among nations of the world; and (5) The implications for our culture of penetration and spread of racialist, imperialist and other corrupt ideas.

The conference expressed concern at the deepening of the colonial crisis due to the preparations for a Third World War. Korea, Iran, Egypt, Tunisia, etc., were cited as examples. They felt that constant attempts were being made by some powers, particularly the USA, to intensify their control over India. In the economic sphere British capital still dominated India and the increasing integration of the Indian and American economies was manifest in the Four Point Programme, the World Bank loans and other private US investments. In the political sphere, part of this foreign conspiracy was to foment disunity between India and Pakistan in order to tighten control over both these countries, the most brazen interference being that over the issue of Kashmir which was intended to be converted into a base against India's great neighbour China. The conspirators were also fomenting racialism to further the belief that the colonial people belonged to inferior races and to justify the theory of the white man's burden. They were also fanning Hindu–Muslim tension to accentuate the disunity between India and Pakistan.

Seven hundred delegates from all over India attended the conference. Delegation came from East Pakistan, West Pakistan, Nepal, Kashmir and Ceylon. Many eminent people were among them (Appendix III). About 10,000 people attended the conference daily. It closed with a 10,000 strong rally at the Calcutta Maidan. More than Rs. 25,000 was collected as contribution to the conference fund.

Different provinces participated in the 6-day long festival—Andhra with its Burrakatha (bardic recital); Maharashtra with its singing squad led by Omar Sheikh, Anna Bhau Sathe and Gavankar; Kerala with its Kathakali group directed by Vallathol and so on. A Mushaira was arranged. Bengal presented a ballet entitled *Atom and Man.* Among other presentations were the Bahurupi theatre group's production *Chhenra Taar* (The Broken Strings) and a new drama *Janak* (Father) based on a story by Sushil Jana about a family in the Midnapore district affected by the last war. The festival presented both 'culture on peace' directly campaigning against war and 'culture of peace' depicting peaceful life. By subordinating all other issues to the basic issues of peace and national independence, the conference succeeded in achieving a broad unity of intellectuals irrespective of their political opinions and artistic standpoints.

Since they were getting over their ultra-leftist line and avoided raising the issues of class-conflict openly, the Communists immensely benefitted from the peace movement. Kaviraj told me that people like Tarasankar Banerjee and Manoranjan Bhattacharya who had been alienated by the sectarian policy of the Party responded favourably when the Communists appealed to them to support the cause of peace. The Peace Movement regained for the Communists the popularity they had lost during 1948–50. An IB report dated 5 May 1952 expressed concern about the way the Communist Party was gaining popularity through this movement. Yet, in the opinion of Kaviraj, if the Communists had been more clear-sighted, this convention could have been larger and the Peace Movement much broader. Even after the Party had officially changed the sectarian line, many members still remained under its influence. Some of them attempted to shut the door of the Conference against the Gandhians and other non-left pacifists. According to Kaviraj, this frustrated the aim of building up a broadbased movement. A Peace Movement, according to him, should have been conducted as a democratic struggle and issues of class-struggle should not have obscured this basic orientation.[167]

Kaviraj told me this in the 1980s. It is interesting to note that 30 years back he had attributed the shortcomings of the Conference to a very opposite reason. He wrote an article on this Conference in *Unity,* July 1952, where he had criticized the organizers' tendency to avoid class conflict (indeed, as we have seen, even big businessmen (and sadhus) attended the Peace Conference!). At that time Kaviraj argued that the Peace Convention had not been able to mobilize the masses on a large scale because in a country like India where the people had not directly faced the horror of war, mere anti-war propaganda would not do. Here, the peace campaign should be more of an anti-exploitative nature. They needed to make people conscious of the desirability of peace in the context of all kinds of exploitation that the latter faced everyday, which, of course, meant the sharpening of class conflict.

The change in Kaviraj's emphasis was not unexpected. A changed situation and changed political stand do change one's view of the past. I pointed out this shift or contradiction to Kaviraj and he responded saying that the Communists should carry on two struggles simultaneously—a democratic struggle and a class-struggle and that they should try to combine the two, which they failed to do at that time.

Anyway, it is clear that at the time of the Peace Movement there was very little emphasis on class-struggle, perhaps to counter the sectarian rashness of the last couple of years (though there was an undercurrent of tension due to the persisting sectarian mentality of some Party members). It seems that in history one extreme always feeds the other. Campaigning for peace in general terms appealed to the intellectuals of the literary and artistic world, but not to the masses as a whole. So the Peace Movement of the early 1950s could not become a mass movement.

By the mid-1950s, Soviet Russia began to use India and other newly-independent states as political allies in its opposition to America and to encourage the Communists to take a friendly attitude once more to the new regimes. In this swing back, the Communists found their aspirations to a great extent corresponding to the current of Nehruvian socialism. The progressive writers and artists did not want to remain marginalized and gradually became part of the wider and state-sponsored mainstream culture. This was perhaps the logical conclusion of the Peace Movement.

Appendices

The progressive cultural movement had many internal problems based on relationships at the individual as well as group levels. Though it was a national-level movement, regional sentiments did not always go well with pan-Indian solidarity and aspirations. Within Bengal too, the movement was beset with problems of petty individual and factional rivalries. This has been occasionally hinted at in the present book, but not elaborated. The appendixes below give a glimpse of Bengal-versus-India tensions, which may be viewed to some extent as individual-level tensions too.

Appendix I

Before the second AIPWA conference, an interesting correspondence took place between the BPWA and the AIPWA. First, D. Aleem, Acting General Secretary, AIPWA, wrote a letter to Surendranath Goswami (Lucknow, 27 July 1937) saying that at the All-India Committee meeting in Delhi it had been decided to hold the up coming All-India Conference in Delhi. But then, Soumendranath Tagore had given them to understand that Calcutta would be the most suitable venue and that they also thought so, for Calcutta was the most active branch of the AIPWA. Then Aleem asked Goswami to request Rabindranath Tagore on their behalf to inaugurate the conference.

It seems that Rabindranath was not available, probably due to his illness. Sometime later, Hiren Mukherjee wrote to S. Zaheer that the Bengali members were unanimous on the point that Jawaharlal Nehru would be the best person to preside over the coming conference. But they also felt that if Nehru was not available, there should be a Bengali President. It seems that there was a proposal from the AIPWA to make Mulk Raj Anand the President. Hiren Mukherjee raised objections to this arguing that Anand did not write in an Indian language; he did not want Sumitranandan Pant, Kirloskar or any writer of south India too, because they were little known in Bengal. He added in this connection, 'And you fellows must not think that Bengal claims to be India's premier literary province. (We are not really provincially-minded. You ought to hear us self-criticizing!) But if the Association is to function effectively, we must not alienate Bengali litterateurs, some of whom like Buddhadev Bose and Premendra Mitra are really "progressive"!' And finally 'After all, you had an U.P. President at Lucknow'. Undoubtedly the AIPWA facilitated fraternal exchanges amongst Indian writers of various provinces on a larger scale than was ever possible either before or after it. But even then, such a letter was written asserting the claim of a particular province, though disclaiming provincialism.

But another letter written just about this time by Surendranath Goswami to Mulk Raj Anand (dated 2 January 1938) confirm our suspicion that the central body of the PWA did hurt the pride of the Bengalis. The letter expressed appreciation of 'our friends in other provinces (including you)' and yet said: 'But Bengali writers do not get the same catholicity of treatment there'. It complained that in an advertisement in the *New Indian Literature*, the organ of the AIPWA, the list of contributors included only two Bengali writers. The Bengal PWA had not even been consulted in this matter. All this was creating misunderstanding, and also difficulty in the way of securing subscribers.

APPENDIX II

In 1937, the AIPWA undertook to publish a volume of Indian short stories, Messrs Harrops of London having made them an offer. It was to be edited by Mulk Raj Anand. Hiren Mukherjee in his autobiography blames Anand for having been irresponsible about the task and failing to bring out the symposium, though the required stories had been sent to him.

A number of letters kept in the police files throw light on the matter. Some of the letters were written in connection with the drive to get contributions of short stories from different provinces: Mahmud Zaffar's (a Communist suspect, according to the police) letter to Harindranath Chatterjee, his old Oxford acquaintance, asking for stories from the Andhra Branch (20 November 1937); S. Zaheer's letter to Gurdial Mallick of Santiniketan, saying that the latter's story had been received and asking him to contact any of the three members of the committee for the publication of the volume—Akhtar Husain, Delhi; Ahmed Ali, Lucknow and Hiren Mukherjee, Calcutta; and Zaheer's letter to a Lalit Shankar of Upper Circular Road, to the same effect (according to the information with the police, this Lalit Shankar, originally belonging to Bolepur, had come to Calcutta to appear in his B.A. exams).

In a letter dated 3 December 1937 to S. Zaheer, Hiren Mukherjee expressed his annoyance with M.R. Anand. First, Anand had ignored the BPWA and written to Bengali writers personally. Second, 'a youngster (one of the younger Tagores) (the reference was possibly to Soumyendranath Tagore, who was a communst but refused to conform to the line of the Communist International and the CPI) who is notorious for a curious type of ludicrous writing' kept on telling people that Anand was dissatisfied about the work of the BPWA and was going to authorize him to open a branch. Naturally, Mukherjee did not like it.

Mahmud Zaffar in a letter to Anand tried to set right the misunderstanding between the latter and the BPWA, particularly Mukherjee. Then there was S.N. Goswami's letter to Mahmud Zaffar of Bombay asking for more freedom for the BPWA in selecting and translating, saying that he did not mind his writing directly to Bengali writers, though the letter alleged at the same time that the Bengalis did not get 'the same catholicity of treatment' from the central authorities. We have talked about this letter in Appendix I. It seems that what offended some members of the BPWA at that time was not so much the central authority of the AIPWA as the 'dictatorship of a single individual'—M.R. Anand. Anand returned to India in 1938 and in the matter of administration of the AIPWA he was gradually replacing Zaheer who was a great friend of many Bengalis. Perhaps there was some problem also in the personal relationship between Mulk Raj Anand and Hiren Mukherjee.

APPENDIX III

Many names have occurred in the main body of the first chapter, which perhaps do not convey much to the reader except showing how broad-based the leftist cultural organizations and their programmes were. There are many Bengali names, with which the Bengalis are perhaps familiar, but not the non-Bengali reader. Readers are not expected to know about all the non-Bengali persons mentioned either. Here, I give short bio-notes to make the names a little more meaningful. I have made separate lists of bio-notes first for the non-Bengali (Indian) persons and then for those based in Bengal. But even for me, some names are just names. I have not been able to unearth any detail related to them and writing bio-notes has not been possible in such cases. But we want to keep a record of as many such participants as possible, which will also prove more clearly how extensive the appeal of the movement was—how Communists and non-Communists, cultural and political activists, Bengalis and non-Bengalis worked together in this cultural movement (though all the persons named were not equally active). Apart from the strictly cultural bodies, the participants in the activities of the Mahila Atmaraksha Samity and the Kishore Bahini too have bio-notes to their names, for these two organizations often engaged in cultural activites. At the end of these bio-notes, the reader will find some more lists of names, which were too long to have been included in the main body of the chapter. We refrain from giving bio-notes related to these names. We also do not engage in such an exercise for the names occurring in the next three chapters. But in those chapters the names are at least contextualized in concrete creative activities like music, theatre and pictorial art. Needless to say, many of the names that we deal with here in relation to the organizations and their functions will occur in the next three chapters as well.

APPENDIX IV

Bio-Notes (Non-Bengali Persons)

Abburi Ramakrishna Rao: noted Telegu writer

Abdul Aleem (Dr): of Lucknow University and a leading member of PWA at Lucknow—General Secretary, AIPWA at one point of time

Ahmed Ali: belonged to the *Angare* group of young writers who initiated a socially conscious and realistic mode in the Urdu literature by publishing a volume of short stories and later became initiators of Progressive Writers' Movement—had contact with the cultural activists of Bengal—later had problems with his relationship with PWA

Akhtar Hussain: we don't know who he was—we can just mention that Kaifi Azmi was born as Akhtar Hussain Rizvi into a family of landlords in Azamgarh, Uttar Pradesh

Ali Sardar Jafri: Urdu writer, poet and critic

Amrit Rai: Editor, *Hans*, Benares

Ananta Patnaik: Editor, *Adhunik*, Cuttack, initiator of PWA in Orissa

Anil de Silva: a lady of Ceylonese origin, the first General Secretary, IPTA

Anna Bhau Sathe: Maharashtrian folk artist, along with Gavankar and Omar Sheikh, revived folk-forms like *tamasha* under the aegis of the IPTA

B.T. Ranadive: Secretary of CPI during 1948–50, an ultra-leftist phase

Balraj Sahni: famous actor and writer

D.D. Kosambi: mathematician and historian, came close to FSU, participated in the Peace Movement

Eric Cyprian: journalist and a Communist Party worker of Punjab, participant in the inaugural programme of IPTA in Bombay

Faiz Ahmed Faiz: famous Urdu poet, a left-wing intellectual and a notable member of PWA

Gavankar: along with Omar Sheikh and Annabhau Sathe, constituted the famous trio of Maharashtra IPTA that adapted folk forms like *Tamasha* to progressive purposes

Gertrude Emerson Sen: Editor of *Asia* magazine in the USA—eventually settled in a village of north-eastern India and married Basiswar Sen—occasionally responded to the cultural efforts of the Communists

Gopalan: from Andhra, attended the IPTA inaugural conference, maybe the same person as noted CPI(M) leader A.K. Gopalan

Indulal Yajnik: a freedom fighter and Kishan Sabha leader from Gujarat

Irawat Singh: a Manipur freedom fighter—attended an AFWAA conference

Jagirdar (Professor): Kanarese scholar, attended an AIPWA conference

Jaigopal Narang (Punjab FSU): Punjab Congress leader, sent message to an AFWAA conference

Jayaprakash Narayan: prominent political activist, made a transition from Marxism to Gandhism, member of CSP, later became famous for leading the opposition to the Emegency regime of Indira Gandhi

Jitubhai: Gujarati writer—came close to AIPWA

Josh Malihabadi: writer and poet in Urdu, freedom fighter, very actively involved in the Progressive Writers' Movement

Jawaharlal Nehru: because of his internationalist perspective and socialist sympathies, sometimes found common ground with the Communists

K. Shantaram: Editor, *Madras Daily Express*

K.A. (Khwaja Ahmad) Abbas: a leading leftist intellectual, a novelist, screenwriter, and journalist in Hindi, Urdu and English—best known as a film-maker—leading figure in the progressive cultural movement

K.M. Ashraf: Nehru's trusted lieutenant, asked to head the mass contact programme of the Congress

K.P. Namboodiri: from Malabar, attended the inaugural function of IPTA

K.T. Shah (Professor): a scholar in economics, a member of the Constituent Assembly, founding president of the All-India Labour Congress (1949)

Kishan Chander: famous fiction-writer in Hindi and English

Mahmud Zaffar: together with Sajjad Zaheer, Ahmed Ali and Rashid Jehan, was responsible for the famous collection of short stories *Angare*, considered a landmark in Urdu literature, and was one of the initiators of the progressive movement in Urdu literature—also actively involved in the organization PWA

Mama Warekar: reputed Marathi writer, worked closely with the AIPWA

Maulana Hasrat Mohani: a romantic poet of Urdu language, journalist, freedom fighter, came close to PWA

Mazaj Ali: Urdu poet

Mian Iftiqaruddin: President of Punjab Congress, a liberal Muslim politician, his name has occurred in connection with FSU

Mulk Raj Anand: a famous Indian English fiction writer, very active in AIPWA

N.M. Joshi: a moderate labour leader—General Secretary of AITUC, attended the inaugural conference of the IPTA

Nandalal Ray: Editor, *Dunia*, Benares—collaborated with AFWAA, Bengal

Nemichand Jain: talented performing artist, member of Central Squad of IPTA along with his wife Rekha

Omar Sheikh: Marathi folk poet, a prized asset of IPTA

P.C. Joshi: General Secretary of CPI for the most part of the period of our study, aesthetically inclined and of a liberal disposition, the gathering of hundreds of brilliant artists and writers under the banner of AIPWA and IPTA goes largely to his credit

Prakash Chandra: taught English literature in St. John's College, Agra and then at Allahabad University from 1941, dabbled in both critical and creative writings in English as well as Hindi, came close to PWA and IPTA

Prem Dhawan: a left-oriented and talented performing artist, a member of IPTA Central Squad in Bombay

Premchand: famous Hindi fiction-writer: enthusiastically involved in the foundation of AIPWA

Prithviraj Kapoor: famous actor, had a leftist orientation and was close to the Communist cultural movement

R.S. Pandit: Nehru's brother-in-law, husband of Vijaya Lakshmi Pandit, collaborated with Communist cultural efforts

R.S. Ruikar: a pioneer of the Indian labour movement, became President of the All-India Trade Union Congress in 1938, he joined the All-India Forward Bloc and soon became general secretary of that party

Raghupati Sahai Firaq: Urdu poet, particularly of ghazal, professor at Allahabad University

Rahul Sankrityayan: known as 'Mahapandit', well-versed in many languages and wrote on a wide spectrum of subjects—particularly famous as a Hindi writer—wrote novels, dramas, travel accounts, biographies, philosophy, history and science, a patron of FSU

Raja Rao: a well-known writer of Indian English novels with deep philosophical concerns, on Presidium of AFWAA Conference in Calcutta 1945

Ram Manohar Lohia: freedom fighter and socialist thinker, one of the founders of the Congress Socialist Party

Rashida Jehan: famous Urdu writer, one of those who put together the path-breaking collection of short stories *Angare*—deeply involved in the AIPWA

Romesh Chandra: freedom fighter, spent years in British prisons, the founder of the All-India Peace Council and its General Secretary for many years

Rekha Jain: a talented actress, wife of Nemichand Jain, both of them were in the Central Squad of IPTA, Bombay

S.A. (Syed Abdullah) Brelvi: Editor, *Bombay Chronicle* that promoted India's struggle for freedom

S.A. Dange: a well known pioneer of the Communist movement in India, on the Presidium of the Fourth AIPWA conference in Bombay

Sachi Routroy: a prolific writer in Oriya, belonged to the group of poets who called themselves, 'poets of the people', took the initiative in founding PWA in Orissa

Sahajananda (Swami): an ascetic and a nationalist peasant leader, founded Bihar Provincial Kisan Sabha and in 1936 became the first President of All-India Kisan Sabha

Saifuddin Kitchlew: freedom fighter, barrister and a Muslim nationalist leader of Congress from Punjab, his name has occurred in connection with the peace movement

Sajjad Zaheer: renowned Urdu writer—belonged to the path-breaking *Angare* group—an early Communist and a founder-leader of the AIPWA

Sarojini Naidu: famous Congress leader and poetess, patron of FSU, collaborated with the Communist women in women's movement

Sudarshan (Pandit): reputed writer in Hindi—particularly famous as a lyricist

Sumitranandan Pant: reputed writer, the foremost proponent of *Chhayabad* (romantic) Movement in Hindi poetry, was close to PWA

Sundarlal: Congress leader, involved in the Peace Movement

Tapi Dharma Rao: noted Telegu writer, on Presidium of the Fourth AIPWA Conference in Bombay

Umashankar Joshi: a front-ranking poet of modern Gujarati literature, responded to the Communists' cultural efforts

Vallathol: known as Mahakavi in Kerala, a celebrity poet, he performed at a peace conference

Vijaya Lakshmi Pandit: sister of Jawaharlal Nehru, wife of R.S. Pandit, presided over the FSU conference in Bombay in 1944

Yashpal: as a rising Hindi writer, participated in the stream of militant nationalism—he too came into contact with Communist cultural activists

Z.A. Ahmad: CPI leader

Bio-Notes (Persons Based in Bengal)

A.K.M. Zackeria: ex-Mayor, Calcutta, Vice-President of YCI

Abani Dasgupta: a dancer in Udayshankar's troupe—joined IPTA Central Squad on Udayshankar's instruction

Abanti Kumar Sanyal: Student Federation activist and poet—went on to become a well known leftist intellectual

Abbasuddin Ahmed: famous exponent of folk music from Cooch Behar—contributed a lot to popularizing folk music among upper and middle classes—participated in the radio strike of 1946

Abdul Qadir: an exponent of the *Buddhir Mukti Andolan* of liberal-minded Muslims that was built up around the journal *Sikha*—a well-known poet of the pre-Independence period, influenced by Nazrul Islam—occasionally collaborated with Communist cultural activists

Abdul Odud (Kaji): a pioneering exponent of liberal thoughts among Bengali Muslims (that flourished around the journal *Sikha*)—a reputed scholar

Abdullah Rasul: began his career in Congress and Khilafat politics, but later became a member of the Communist Party and General Secretary of Kisan Sabha—collaborated with cultural activists

Abu Sayeed Ayub: a non-Bengali intellectual, having a deep grounding in philosophy, who made Bengal his home and became a well-known Bengali writer—he was interested in Marxism, though not dogmatic about it and was also close to the *Parichay* group of intellectuals

Abul Mansur Ahmad: journalist and satirist, politician close to Fazlul Haq of Krishak Praja Party—occasionally responded to the Communist cultural efforts

Abdul Karim Sahitya Bisharad (Moulavi): a distinguished scholar, famous as collector of old Bengali manuscripts (*punthis*)—collaborated with AFWAA occasionally

Achintya Kumar Sengupta: well-known fiction-writer who first appeared on the Bengali literary scene as a member of the group that ran the journal *Kallol*

Achyut Goswami: noted Marxist critic of Dhaka—a novelist too—Editor, *Pratirodh*

Ahindra Chowdhury: famous thespian of the Bengali stage, popularly know as 'Natasurya' (the thespian sun)—also acted in films—actively participated in Artiste Association

Ajit Dutta: a member of *Kallol* group—distinguished poet of Dhaka during the 1930s and 1940s—later came to Calcutta and became an educationist—occasionally responded to Communist cultural movement

Ajit Ghosh: a worker of AFWAA—came close to the CPI in Mymensingh, then got involved in the students' movement in Calcutta—untimely death in 1943

Ajitesh Bandyopadhyay: a member of AISF—later became a noted thespian of Group Theatre

Alaka Majumdar: prominent leader of AISF—later married Debiprasad Chatterjee, the left-minded philosopher—herself became an educationist

Amal Bose: of Gupta Press, where a lot of Communist literature was printed—associated with FSU

Amar Majumdar: musician of Jessore, who probably attended Behrampore AFWAA conference

Amitabha Dasgupta: at that time a member of Students' Federation—a leftist poet

Amiya Chakravarty: famous poet, scholar and literary secretary to Rabindranath—worked closely with the Communist cultural front during the 1940s

Amulya Pakrashi: came from the family of Satish Pakrashi and brother of Arati Pakrashi—associated with both Kishore Sabha and Students' Federation

Amulya Sen: a *kirtan*-singer from Rangpur singer—associated with AFWAA

Anil Sinha: on the reception committee for Behrampore AFWAA conference—probably, the Editor of the leftist journal *Natun Sahitya*

Anandashankar Bhattacharya—dedicated leader of Students' Federation and Kishore Sabha

Arati Pakrashi: sister of Amulya Pakrashi, active in Kishore Sabha

Arun Mitra: well known leftist poet, literary critic, professor of French literature—associated with Satyendranath Majumdar's journal *Arani*—closely involved in AFWAA

Asha Ganguly: wife of the noted writer Narayan Ganguly—herself a writer too—wrote for the organ of Mahila Atmaraksha Samity

Ashapurna Devi: famous writer—wrote for the organ of Mahila Atmaraksha Samiti

Asit Mukherjee: MD, London—Editor of *Bishan*

Asok Bhattacharya: younger brother of Sukanta Bhattacharya—Editor of *Natun Din*, journal of Kishore Sabha—later became an art historian of repute

Ashok Bejoy Raha: origin in Sylhet—poet and educationist—came into contact with AFWAA

Atul Bose: an artist who specialized in portraiture, landscapes and idyllic scenes in the realistic tradition and was widely acclaimed—came into contact with AFWAA—referred in the chapter on art

Atul Chandra Gupta: writer—his relationship with the Communist cultural front became distant after the end of the War—a noted lawyer and scholar

Bhavani Bhattacharya: a widely acclaimed Indo-Anglian novelist—his novel *So Many Hungers* (1947) was set in the background of Bengal Famine—a founder-member of AIPWA

Bhabani Dutta: an initiator of AIPWA in London

Bhabani Sen—a very prominent CPI leader during the period of our study—occasionally participated in cultural activites (e.g. FSU)—became the Party's foremost theoretician in the ultra-leftist phase

Bhabamadhav Ghosh: relative of Charuprakash Ghosh, who was a leading figure in IPTA—killed at IPTA conference of Dixon Lane

Bhupati Nandi: musician—member of IPTA Central Squad—close to Salil Chowdhury

Bhupendranath Dutta: younger brother of the famous monk Vivekananda—made his way to Communism from militant nationalism—later became a noted sociologist—Vice-President of FSU

Bhupesh Gupta (FSU): started his political career in militant nationalism—later became a noted CPI leader—was involved in FSU—later a noted parliamentarian

Benoy Ghosh: a leftist scholar, journalist and writer of many research-based books—particularly interested in social and cultural history of Bengal—close to IPTA—his play 'Laboratory' was staged by AFWAA even before the birth of IPTA

Benoy Roy: made his way from Communism from militant nationalism—singer and composer from Rangpur—deeply involved in the creative and organizational activities of AFWAA and IPTA—will features prominently when we discuss the People's Song Movement in the next chapter

Bela Lahiri: a worker of MAS—wife of the prominent CPI activist Somnath Lahiri

Bibhuti Bhushan Banerjee: famous novelist—along with Tarasankar and Manik, dominated the literary scene of Bengal for many years in late-colonial and early-Independence era

Bidhan Chandra Ray: famous doctor and Congress leader, who went on to become the Chief Minister of Bengal after Independence—collaborated with the Communists in providing medical relief during the Famine—uncle of Renu Chakrabarty

Bidhayak Bhattacharya: reputed playwright, not known as a leftist though

Bidhubhushan Sengupta: owner of United Press—active in Artiste Association

Bijan Bhattacharya: famous playwright (writer of the play *Nabanna*) and thespian—a pioneer of the IPTA movement—features prominently in the chapter on theatre

Bimal Bhushan: a well-known singer—participated in the radio strike led by Artiste Association in 1946

Bijoylal Chatterjee: a poet—Gandhian in his political views—his socialistic leaning sometimes found compatibility with Communism—but when Congress Sahitya Sangha was formed, he joined it

Bimal Chandra Ghosh: a prolific leftist poet—naturally involved in the Communist cultural movement

Bishnu Dey: famous poet and intellectual—belonged to the original *Parichay* group—a close fellow traveller of the Communist Party—deeply involved in various cultural activities of the Communists

Buddhadev Bose: famous litterateur—came close to the Communists during the war period along with wife Pratibha

Chinmohan Sehanabis: intellectual and writer, particularly interested in history and literature—an early Communist—a chief organizer of the Bengal PWA—also involved in YCI and AFWAA—treasurer, Calcutta Committee of IPTA

Chintamani Kar: a reputed artist and sculptor—trained in Calcutta, Paris, London and Brussels. Began his career as a teacher in school, lecturer in art and sculpture at University of Calcutta—realized the importance of social consciousness for artists and sympathized with the Communist cultural efforts at a point—involved in YCI—designed its logo

Chittaprosad Bhattacharya: talented artist and a Communist—will feature prominently in the chapter on art—used to compose songs too—we will talk about his musical experimentations in the chapter on music

Chitra Majumdar: involved in YCI

Dasrathlal: percussionist with Calcutta Tramways trade union—became a member of IPTA Central Squad—a prized possession of IPTA

Daulatunnesa Khatun: devoted to social work and creative writing—prolific writer whose works appeared in different literary journals—worked for the Krishak Praja Party—also close to Congress movement and militant nationalism—on the Presidium of the AFWAA conference in 1945

Dayal Kumar: *panchali*-singer of Hooghly—got involved in the Communist cultural movement

Deb Banerjee: a student leader—got close to AFWAA

Debabrata Bose (Bablu): son of the scientist D.M. Bose—involved in YCI

Debaprasad Mukherjee: Jt. Secretary, Dhaka FSU

Deb Kumar Gupta: associated with *Agrani*, a journal for Marxist intellectuals—Office Secretary, AFWAA

Dhiren Sen: Editor *Advance*—came in contact with AFWAA

Dhurjati Prasad Mukherjee: leftist intellectual and writer—taught at Lucknow University—wrote on economics, sociology and music apart from some widely acclaimed novels—involved in Communist cultural movement in many ways

Dilip Roy: member of YCI—used to sing songs for AFWAA—involved in the Bengal IPTA from the very beginning—actively participated in radio strike led by Artiste Association in 1946

Durgaprasad Chakrabarty: owner of Mohini Mill—involved in Artiste Association

Dwijen Chowdhury: musician, music teacher—husband of Suchitra Mukherjee (later Mitra)—involved in radio strike led by Artiste Association in 1946

Geeta Mukherjee: from a Congress-minded family, became a prominent leader of CPI—wife of Biswanath Mukherjee—picketed in front of All India Radio during the 1946 srike

Ghulam Quddus: journalist and poet associated with the Communist Party—later became editor of *Parichay*

Girin Chakrabarty: a writer for children—wrote for Kishore Sabha—involved in FSU

Gopal Haldar: made his way to Communism from militant nationalism—journalist, novelist and a prominent intellectual of the CPI—also worked for Kisan Sabha—edited *Soviet Desh* for FSU along with Sukumar Mitra

Gopal Lal Sanyal: freedom fighter close to Subhas Chandra Bose

Gunada Majumdar: a prominent member of the Congress Socialist Party

Gurdial Mallik: a writer and translator, a favourite disciple of Gandhi and Rabindranath: came in touch with AIPWA

Gurudas Pal: a talented composer-singer, who was a worker in a factory at Metiabruz (Calcutta) and a trade unionist—he was discovered and brought to the limelight by IPTA—feature prominently in the chapter on music

Habibullah Bahar: a well-known figure in political, social and literary arena, a prominent member of Muslim League—involved in AFWAA

Haripada Kusari: a composer of songs, deeply involved in the activities of AFWAA and IPTA—referred to in the chapter on music

Harkumar Chaturvedi: involved in YCI—later became a jute industry specialist and worked in Indian Statistical Institute (National Sample Survey Section)

Hemanta Mukherjee: famous singer—Music Secretary of the Calcutta Committee of IPTA—Secretary of Artiste Association during 1948–50—referred to in the chapter on music

Hemanga Biswas: a talented composer-singer form Sylhet—became Communist and an enthusiastic member of IPTA—feature prominently in the chapter on music

Himangshu Chakrabarty: a folk-singer from Khulna, discovered by IPTA

Hiran Kumar Sanyal: an intellectual and writer, who belonged to the *Parichay* group and later wrote his reminiscences about it

Hiren Mukherjee: a professor of history, distinguished writer and orator, an early Communist—later became a famous Parliamentarian—played a leading role in the Communist cultural movement under discussion—in PWA, FSU and so on

Humayun Kabir: a brilliant student, involved in trade union movement and one of the chief founders of the Krishak Praja Party, he joined the Indian National Congress—edited the journal *Chaturanga* which was a vehicle of socialist thoughts of a kind different from the mainstream Communism—a debater at YCI

Indira Devi: associated with Akashbani, contributed a lot to its women's and children's programmes—a writer too—protested against Somen Chanda's murder

Indira Devi Chowdhurani: Rabindranath's niece—married to the well-known intellectual and writer Pramatha Chowdhury—well-versed in music—President of first MAS conference 1943

Jagadish Gupta: fiction writer and a major exponent of modern Bengali literature—associated with the change towards realism that the Kallol group introduced in Bengali literature—known for his strange character portrayal and unique narrative style

Jaganmoy Mitra: a well-known singer of modern Bengali songs—actively participated in the radio strike of 1946

Jahar Ganguli: noted actor in Bengali films, a singer too—actively participated in the radio strike 1946

Jahar Ray: noted comedian of Bengali theatre and films—involved in Artiste Association

Jamini Ray: famous artist—friends of Communists like Bishnu Dey and hence came into contact with Communist cultural activities—will feature prominently in the chapter on art

Jnanprakash Ghosh: famous classically trained musician—came in touch with AFWAA

Jolly Mohan Kaul: General Secretary, YCI—creatively involved in its musical and theatrical activities—joined the CPI at the age of 19 in 1941 and remained there till the Party split up in 1963—husband of Manikuntala Sen

Juiphul Roy: a Communist worker of Barishal—particularly active in MAS—wife of Khoka Roy, another Communist activist

Jyoti Basu: an early Communist—converted to Communism in London—involved in YCI and FSU—later Chief Minister of West Bengal

Jyotirindra Moitra: poet and musician—a Communist and a star contributor to IPTA cultural activities—features in the chapter on music

Jyotirmoy Ghosh: a mathematician and litterateur—pen name Bhaskar—taught at Presidency College—protested against the murder of Somen Chanda

Jyotirmoy Roy: director of the famous film *Udayer Pathe*—on the Presidium of AFWAA conference 1945

Jyotirmoy Sen: of Dhaka PWA

Jyotirmoyee Ganguli: daughter of the famous Brahmo couple Dwarakanath Gangopadhyay and Kadambini—educationist—Congress leader—became close to Communist women while working for women's uplift—injured by the army while participating in the Azad Hind Release movement in 1945 and died

Jyotish Chandra Ghosh: one of the initiators of AIPWA in London

Kalpataru Sengupta: a Communist activist of Chittagong deeply involved in the relief work during the Japanese air raid and Famine—later became known as a leftist writer

Kamakshi Prasad Chatterjee: a well-known poet and prose-writer, particularly famous for children's literature—a good photographer—came in touch with the Communist cultural activists

Kamal Bose: coming from a prosperous and educated family, became a Communist—involved in YCI—his home on Balaram Ghosh Street in North Calcutta became the venue of many activities of the Party and its cultural fronts—later became the mayor of Calcutta

Kamal Dasgupta: a well known exponent of Nazrul songs and modern Bengali songs—a talented and creative musician—involved in Artiste Association

Kamala Chatterjee: of MAS

Kanak Das: an noted exponent of Rabindra Sangeet—involved in Artiste Association

Kanak Mukherjee: a prominent leader of CPI (later CPI-M)—wife of Saroj Mukherjee—particularly involved in the women's movement—later became Editor of MAS

Khagendranath Mitra: once active in militant nationalism and then in Congress movement—later became involved in leftist politics—made a mark as a children's writer—wrote for Kishore Sabha

Khagendranath Sen: journalist and educationist—professor of political science—Assistant Editor, *The Advance*, then joined *Hindustan Standard* and *The Nationalist*—founder Editor of the children's magazine *Rangmashal* and also conducted 'Galpadadur Asar', a popular radio pragramme for teenagers during the 1940s and 1950s

Khitin Raychowdhury: prominent Party member and involved in FSU

Kshitish Prasad Chattopadhyay: a very good student and noted researcher—contributed a lot as the Education Officer of Swaraj Party—Congressman—friend of Subhas Bose—sympathetic to progressive cultural movement—got involved in FSU and the Communist women's movement (along with wife Manjushri)

Kiran Sankar Sengupta: Jt. Secretary, Dhaka, FSU—a young enthusiastic Communist—a writer and a friend of Somen Chanda—Editor, *Pratirodh*

Kumud Ranjan Mallik: a well-known poet of rural romance in Bengali literature—on the Presidium of AFWAA conference 1945

Latika Sen: a student of Dhaka Eden College—involved in militant nationalism—then a teacher of Beltala Girls' High School, Kolkata—wife of a veteran Communist Ranen Sen—a dedicated Communist worker herself—was killed in 1949 in police firing on a women's procession

Leela Majumdar: noted writer, particularly known for her unique writings for children—contributed to *Ghare Baire*, MAS organ

M.A. Latif: Bar-at-law—Jt. Secretary, FSU

Maitrayee Devi: close to Rabindranath and noted writer herself—contributed to MAS

Manik Bandyopadhyay: famous novelist—a major figure in modern Bengali literature—became a Communist in the early 1940s

Manikuntala Sen: a prominent leader of the CPI, who joined the Party in its illegal phase and remained there till 1963—particularly active in the women's front—acted in the famous drama *Nabanna*—married Jolly Kaul

Manish Ghatak: a noted litterateur—known for his realistic writings on the life of the poor—belonged to the same family as Ritwik Ghatak, the film-maker

Manoranjan Bhattacharya: noted thespian—came close to the IPTA and later acted as a mentor to the theatre group Bahurupi—features in the chapter on theatre—his name comes up in connection with Artiste Association and the Peace Movement

Manoranjan Hajra: a trade union worker and novelist who wrote on the basis of his experience of the workers' life

Manjushri Devi: wife of K.P. Chattopadhyay—related to the famous Tagore family—Editor of *Ghare Baire*, organ of MAS

Manoj Bose: freedom fighter, school teacher and litterateur—joined Congress Sahitya Sangha—involved in Peace Movement

Meghnad Saha: eminent scientist—patron of FSU

Mira Devi: a writer for MAS—probably the same person as Mira Dutta Gupta—a noted social worker, close to CPI

Mohit Banerjee involved in YCI and FSU; composer of songs—translated the *Internationale* into Bengali

Moni Ray: artist—leading member of AFWAA Cultural Bureau and Executive Committee

Mrinal Sen: member of AISF—later became famous film director

Muhammad Ismail: leader of Bengal Trade Union Congress—sometimes collaborated on the cultural front

Muhammad Shahidullah: graduated from the Sorbonne in Paris in 1928 and was awarded a Ph.D. for his research on the *Charyapada*, the earliest extant specimens of Bangla language, became the Head of he Bangla Department, Dhaka University—patronized Dhaka FSU

Mustaq Ali Khan: a famous sitar, surbahar and pakhwaj player—participated in the radio strike led by Artiste Association

Nabendu Ghosh: progressive fiction writer—later wrote screen-plays for movies—involved in the Peace Movement

Najrul Islam (Kaji): a revolutionary poet—a source of tremendous inspiration for the Bengali youth since the 1920s, particularly for those engaged in militant nationalism and socialist politics—a composer of music too

Nalinaksha Sanyal: economist, professor, deeply involved in the Congress movement—a Congress MLA during 1937–45—on the Presidium AFWAA conference

Nandalal Bose: famous artist based in Kala Bhavan, Santiniketan—referred in the chapter on art

Nani Bhowmik: noted leftist fiction-writer

Narahari Kaviraj: a Communist intellectual, a scholar and professor of history—a leader of the Peace Movement

Narayan Ganguly: intellectual, a scholar, professor of Bengali literature and a noted fiction-writer—involved in the AFWAA and the peace movement

Naren Dev: once member of a revolutionary group, dedicated most of his life to learning and literature—involved in the Peace Movement

Nareshchandra Sengupta: a reputed lawyer, professor of law and involved in progressive politics—also a progressive writer—made substantial contributions to Bengali literature through his excellent essays, short stories, plays and novels—a pioneer in writing naturalistic Bangla novels, analysing the psyche of criminals and the role of sex in the commission of crime—close to the Communist cultural front

Nelly Sengupta: Congress leader—wife of Jatindramohan Sengupta—made President of MAS at Barishal conference in 1944

Nibaran Pundit: folk composer-singer of Mymensingh—prominent in IPTA

Niharranjan Ray (Professor): a freedom fighter and noted historian, well-known for his works on history of art and Buddhism—in 1946, appointed *Bagishwari Professor of Fine Arts* in Calcutta University—Vice-President, YCI

Nikhil Chakravarty: taught history at Calcutta University in the 1930s before taking to journalism—later joined the CPI—involved in YCI—husband of Renu Chakravarty—went on to become a top Indian political columnist—founder-editor of the weekly journal *Mainstream*.

Nirad Majumdar: noted artist belonging to Calcutta group—came close to the Communists too—features prominently in the chapter on art

Niranjan Sen: General Secreary, IPTA, in its ultra-leftist phase—later joined CPI(M)

Nirendranath Ray: Communist intellectual and aesthetician—in AFWAA Cultural Bureau

Nirmal Bhattacharya: economist, political scientist and professor at Scottish Church College and Calcutta University—a Congressman—involved in Peace Movemnet

Nirmal Chandra Chunder: a Congressman, lawyer and one of the leaders known as the Big Five of Swaraj Party—involved in working class movements—but a Congressman throughout—played a leading role in Artiste Association—later Mayor of Calcutta

Nirmal Kumar Siddhanta: a distinguished scholar, taught at Lucknow University—later became Vice-Chancellor of Calcutta and Delhi Universties—occasionally involved in Communist cultural activities

Nirmalendu Chowdhury—belonged to Sylhet IPTA—famous exponent of Begali folk music

Nripen Banerjee: of Kishore Bahini—an academic

Pabitra Ganguly: associated with the *Kallol* group—noted translator of European literature—a distinguished personality in the field of literature—involved in Peace Movement

Pankaj Mallik: famous musician and singer—actively involved in Artiste Association

Pasupati Bhattacharya: a village potter—on the Presidium of AFWAA conference 1945

Phani Majumdar: film producer—involved in Peace Movement

Phani Mondal: related to the famous Laha family—involved in Artiste Association

Prabhabati Devi Saraswati: a Calcutta Corporation schoolteacher, labour leader, and above all, prolific writer—member of Executive Committee, AFWAA

Prabodh Kumar Sanyal: noted fiction writer—the turbulent times of the 1930s and 1940s were reflected in his writings, though not known as a leftist—noted writer of travelogues—occasionally involved in the leftist cultural movement

Prafulla Ray: associated with the journal *Agrani*—headed the publication subcommittee of AFWAA

Prafulla Chandra Ray (Acharya): famous scientist, teacher, thinker, social worker and patriot

Pramatha Bhowmik: initiator of FSU

Pramatha Chowdhury: close to Rabindranath and married his niece Indira—a barrister—contributed considerably to Bengali literature—Editor *Sabujpatra*—noted for his intellectual temperament—occasionally responded to Communist cultural efforts

Prasanta Sanyal: initiator of FSU—involved in trade union activities and students' movement—sent to Assam in 1941 to start a Communist Party—then worked as General Secretary AISF in Bombay—later made a brilliant career in advertisement, public relations and management

Pratap Chandra Chunder: Nirmal Chandra's son—historian and educationist—Union Minister of Education—involved in Artiste Association

Pratibha Bose—Buddhadev Bose's wife and a writer of fiction herself—involved in AFWAA—wrote *Fascism o Nari*

Premendra Mitra: noted litterateur who originally belonged to *Kallol* group—delved into the life of the lower middle-class and the poor—had socialist leanings—showed a versatility in different genres of literature—came close to AFWAA

Priti Sarkar (later Banerjee): a very good singer—member IPTA Central Squad

Promode Sengupta: involved in labour movement—came close to the Communists abroad—one of the initiators of PWA in London—came close to Subhas Bose too

Radhika Ranjan Ganguly: writer—on the Presidium AFWAA conference

Rajshekhar Basu: a scientist by profession—became a noted Bengali writer—particularly famous for his unique humorous stories—compiler of a popular Bengali dictionary

Ram Basu: member of AISF—leftist poet

Ramesh Seal: a folk-poet from Chittagong—deeply involved in AFWAA and IPTA

Ramesh Sen: leftist fiction-writer of repute—wrote realistic novels and stories, generally about poor people's lives

Ramkrishna Mukherjee: associated with YCI, AISF and FSU—professor and author of many books on sociology

Ranesh Dasgupta: of Dhaka PWA—intellectual and writer known in both Bangladesh and West Bengal

Rathin Moitra: heading Fine Arts Subcommittee of AFWAA—a socially conscious artist, belonged to the Calcutta Group—brother of Jyotirindra Moitra, the IPTA musician

Ravi Shankar: talented musician and sitarist—joined the Central Squad of IPTA in Bombay on his elder brother Uday Shankar's instruction

Reba Roy: talented singer, dancer and actress—Benoy Roy's sister—member of IPTA Central Squad

Renu Roy: niece of Bidhan Chandra Roy—married Nikhil Chakravarty—involved in YCI—very active in MAS

Ritwik Ghatak: writer—interested in theatre and films—famous film director—belonged to the family of the noted fiction-writer Manish Ghatak—was deeply involved in IPTA towards the end of the 1940s

Sachin Dev Burman: famous musician and singer—later made a mark in Bombay film industry—came close to AFWAA

Sachin Shankar: brother of Uday Shankar and Ravi Shankar—joined the Central Squad of IPTA on Uday Shankar's instruction

Sachin Sengupta: a socially conscious playwright—came close to AFWAA

Sadhan Gupta—a leader of AISF and a good singer—involved in AFWAA and Artiste Association—later became a lawyer and the Advocate General of West Bengal

Sadhana Raychowdhury: performing artist of IPTA—made a mark in Bengali theatre

Saheb Ali: baul-singer of Agartala—participated in the cultural festival of AFWAA conference in 1945

Sailajananda Mukherjee: noted fiction writer—associated with the *Kallol* group—his stories on the life of coal mine workers had made him famous—responded to Communist cultural movement occasionally

Sailen Roy: composer of romantic music—involved in Artiste Association

Sajal Raychaudhury: actor and cultural activist—Secretary, WB IPTA during its illegal phase

Sajanikanta Das: writer, journalist, editor of the journal *Shanibarer Chithi*—anti-Communist, but collaborated with the Communists occasionally (e.g. to resist communalism)

Salil Chowdhury: brilliant and famous musician—deeply involved in the Communist movement and greatly contributed to IPTA song movement—referred repeatedly in this book

Samar Sen: a left-minded poet, but often criticized by his leftist colleagues for his cynical views on life—later edited the famous leftist journal *Frontier*

Sambhu Mitra: famous thespian—a pioneer of the People's Theatre Movement—features prominently in the chapter on theatre

Santi Kumar Bardhan: a dancer and choreographer who belonged to Uday Shankar's troupe and then played a leading role in the Central Squad of IPTA on Uday Shankar's instruction

Santimoy Ray: an acitivist in militant nationalism—joined the Communist Party in 1936—a professor of history—close to the Communist cultural movement

Santosh Sengupta: noted exponent of Rabindra Sangeet—involved in Artiste Association

Saratachandra Chattopadhyay: famous Bengali novelist

Saroj Dutta: a Communist poet and literary critic—deeply involved in the progressive writers' movement—known for his intolerant views on literature and litterateurs—later became involved in the Naxalite Movement

Satish Mondal: folk-singer of Malda—came in touch with AFWAA

Satish Pakrashi: prominent Communist leader, made his way from militant nationalism to Communism—headed the PRC's doctors' cell—Amulya and Arati Pakrashi of Kishore Bahini came from the same family

Satya Chowdhury: an exponent of Najrul and post-Najrul modern Bengali song

Satyajit Ray: a person of great creative talent—participated in a poster exhibition of YCI—a world-famous film-maker

Satyendranath Majumdar: a prominent journalist–writer of the leftist circle—editor, *Ananda Bazar*—also edited *Arani*—close to FSU and other cultural bodies of the Communists

Sibram Chakrabarty: a creative writer with special talent for humorous writing and with Communist sympathies—later became renowned as children's writer

Shahid Suhrawardy—a well known educationist, writer and art critic—close to the *Parichay* group—President, YCI, when he was Curator of Victoria Memorial

Sheikh Gumhani Dewan: a folk musician of Murshidabad, who drew the attention of Rabindranath and then came close to the Communists during the Famine—features prominently in the chapter of music

Shyamal Krishna Ghosh: a distinguished member of the literary circle that was formed around the journal *Parichay*

Shyamaprasad Mukherjee: famous educationist and political leader—belonged to a different politics altogether—a Congress MLA representing the Calcutta University early in his career—after the elections of 1937, founded a non-Congress and non-Muslim League coalition ministry with Fazlul Haq of Krishak Praja Party as Chief Minister and himself as the Finance Minister—resigned in protest against repressive measures of the British during War and Famine—later became a leader of the politics of Hindutva and was the founder of Bharatiya Jana Sangh—even he collaborated with the Communist women in the latter's social work

Sita Chowdhury: daughter of the famous journalist Ramananda Chattopadhyay—noted writer herself—involved in MAS and then Nari Seva Sangha (which was formed with help from MAS)

Snehangshu Acharya: belonged to a zamindar family of Mymensingh—a barrister of Calcutta High Court—deeply involved in the Communist movement along with wife Sujata (nee Mukherjee)—Secretary, FSU

Snehalata Das: belonged to a distinguished Brahmo family of Barishal and an accomplished educationist, particularly so far as female education is concerned—hostess, Barishal MAS conference 1944

Somen Chanda: a talented writer and a CPI worker of Dhaka, who was killed at a very young age during the Peoples' War period

Somnath Hore: a talented artist from Chittagong who was a Party worker too—went on to become a front-ranking artist of Bengal—will feature prominently in the chapter on pictorial art

Soumyendranath Tagore: born of the famous Tagore family of Jorasanko and held in affection by Rabindranath Tagore, he was close to the international Communist movement—but ultimately he defied the Soviet-controlled Communist line and formed his own Revolutionary Communist Party of India

Subhas Mukherjee: famous Communist poet—a major poet of modern Bengali literature—deeply involved in the Communist cultural efforts—later became disillusioned with the Communist movement

Subodh Ghosh: a well-known fiction-writer in Bengali—came close to the Communist cultural activities—his play 'Fossil' played an important role in initiating the People's Theatre Movement—soon he became bitter about the Communists—joined Congress Sahitya Sangha

Subrata Banerjee: of YCI—became involved in the Naval Mutiny of 1946

Suchitra Mukherjee: talented singer—along with sisters Sujata and Supriya, became very close to the Communist cultural movement—involved in the radio strike of 1946—later became a famous exponent of Rabindra Sangeet as Suchitra Mitra—referred to in the chapter on music

Sudhi Pradhan: made his way from militant nationalism to Communism—an important organizer of the Bengal IPTA—played a leading role in Artiste Association—associated with the Communist journals *Janayuddha* and *Swadhinata*

Sudhindranath Dutta: reputed poet and intellectual—Founder-editor of the prominent journal *Parichay* since 1931—later handed it over to his leftist friends

Suhasini Ganguly: made her way from militant nationalism to the women's movement sponsored by the CPI—involved in the women's front in particular

Sujata Mukherjee (later Acharya): involved in the cultural, particularly musical activities of the Communists, along with sisters Supriya and Suchitra

Sukumar Mitra: made his way from the Congress movement to the left movement—started a Communist organization in Jessore—journalist and writer—involved in FSU and edited *Soviet Desh* jointly with Gopal Haldar—received Soviet Land Nehru Award

Sukanta Bhattacharya: a famous poet who emerged from within the Communist movement—member of AISF and looked after Kishore Sabha—died untimely of TB in 1946

Sukhendu Goswami: a classically trained musician of repute—involved in Artiste Association

Sunil Bose: member of AFWAA cultural bureau—ran the publishing house National Book Agency

Sunil Chatterjee (Paltu): associated with the editing of *Agrani*—dramatized Subodh Ghosh's story 'Fossil' for YCI—wrote plays—a pioneer of IPTA movement in Bengal

Sunil Jana: of YCI—a noted photographer—documented the Famine and other events of the 1940s with great social consciousness and competence

Sunil Sen: reputed scholar—was involved in Tebhaga Movement—later made a mark as a historian (Jolly Kaul in his memoirs speak of two other Sunil Sens associated with YCI: one of Lakkhi Babu Jewellers and another who was probably a student of English Department of the University)

Surama Ghatak: involved with IPTA—later wife of Ritwik Ghatak

Surendranath Goswami: reputed Professor (attached to Bangabasi, Bethune and Sanskrit colleges at different times), orator and intellectual—trained in Indian philosophy, then attracted to Marxism—was deeply involved in PWA, intellectually and organizationally—untimely death in 1945

Surya Roy: artist—involved in AFWAA Fine Arts Subcommittee

Sushobhan Sarkar: legendary professor of history at Presidency College since 1932—inspired generations of students by his Marxist interpretation of history—a fellow traveller of CPI—particularly close to its cultural front—wrote *Japani Shasaner Asal Rup* using the pen-name Bijon Roy

Sushil Jana: well-known left-oriented fiction-writer—close to the Communist cultural movement

Sushil Mukherjee: IPTA member killed in Dixon Lane murder

Swarnakamal Bhattacharya: involved in the Communist cultural movement and wrote a lot, particularly in *Arani*

Tagar Adhikari: talented *dotara*-player of Cooch Behar—spotted by the IPTA—Bijan Bhattacharya later wrote and staged a play *Marachand* based on Tagar's life

Tarasankar Banerjee: famous fiction-writer—the three Banerjees, Tarasankar, Bibhuti Bhushan and Manik, were the foremost novel-writers of Bengal during the period of the study—came close to the Communists during the War period, but then parted ways

Tarun Kanti Ghosh: Editor, *Jugantar*

Tripurari Chakrabarty: a reputed scholar—had a socialist leaning with spiritual overtones

Tushar Kanti Ghosh: Editor, *Amrita Bazar Patrika*—wrote quite a lot himself

Uma Chakravarty: sister of Nikhil Chakravarty, later married Chinmohan Sehanabis—went on to become a noted educationist

Usha Dutta: talented performing artist—member of Central Squad of IPTA

Utpal Dutta: talnted actor and intellectual—was involved in the IPTA towards the end of the 1940s

Vivekananda Mukherjee: distinguished journalist, attached to *Ananda Bazar* during the 1920s, and then to *Jugantar* from the 1930s—his *Dwitiya Mahajuddher Itihas* (History of World War II) is a well known book

Zainul Abedin: the most famous artist of the Bengal Famine—came close to the Communist cultural movement—will feature prominently in the chapter on pictorial art

A List of Persons in Calcutta to whom AIPWA Circular No. I (addressed by Sajjad Zaheer) was posted can be found from a police file. We are giving the list here exactly as it was

Radharani Devi; K. Chatterji, Hathkhola; Hiran Kumar Sanyal; Sufian Raut; Hirendra Kumar Roy, Editor, *Chhanda*; Shahid Ahmed, Editor, *Saki*, Delhi; Nirode Chowdhury, Shyambazar; Secretary, Students' Union, F.C. College, Lahore; A.S.M. Ayion, Calcutta; Bibhuti Bhusan Banerjee, Mirzapur Street; K.C. Mukherji, High Court; Satyendranath Mukherji (Majumdar?); Vivekananda Mukherjee, c/o *Ananda Bazar Patrika*; Sajanikanta Das, Editor, *Shanibarer Chithi*; Ramananda Chatterji; Nirendranath Roy, Bangabasi College; B.C. Gupta, University College of Science; Bimal Chandra Ghosh, Hindustan Buildings; Humayun Katra (Kabir?);

Atul Chandra Gupta; Kalidas Nag; Shahid Suhrawardy; Nripendra Krisna Chatterji; Nandagopal Sen; Jiten Sen, c/o Dhiren Sen, Behala; K.C. Bhattacharya, Philosophy Department, Calcutta University; Premendra Mitra; Arun Mitra, c/o *Ananda Bazar Patrika*; Sudhindranath Dutta; P.C. Ghosh, Presidency College; Probodh Sanyal, Cossipore; Sarat Chandra Bose, Woodburn Park; Anil Kumar Chandra, Santiniketan; Pramatha Chowdhury, c/o Editor, *Parichay*; Sarat Chandra Chatterji; Nibaran Chandra Mukherji, c/o Hiren Mukherji; Mohitlal Majumdar; Sushil Kumar Mitra, Philosophy Department, Calcutta University; Sushovan Sarkar; A. Hornphry (Humphry?), Presidency College; Sailendra Kishore Gupta; Surendranath Moitra; Sailajananda Mukherji.

Representatives of Different Provinces in the Organizing Committees of the IPTA, Selected at its Inaugural Conference

Mama Warekar (Bombay), Snehangshu Acharya and Manoranjan Bhattacharya (Bengal), Eric Cyprian (Punjab), Sarala Gupta (Delhi), Dr Rashida Jehan (UP), K.P.C. Namboodiri (Malabar), Kesari Kesavan (Mysore), Kulukund Shiva Rao (Mangalore), Makhdoom Mahoiuddeen (Hyderabad), Dr Raja Rao (Andhra), S.C. Jog (C.P. and Behar), K. Ramanathan (Tamil Nadu), Bankim Mukherjee (President, AIKS), S.A. Dange (President, AITUC), Sajjad Zaheer (General Secretary, AIPWA), and Arun Bose (AISF).

Members of Executive Committee of Artiste Association for 1946–7 as Listed in the Organization's *Annual Report of 1945–6*

Patrons—Nalini Ranjan Sarkar, Tushar Kanti Ghosh, Bidhubhusan Sengupta, Girijasankar Chakrabarty, Krisna Chandra Dey; Executive Committee—Nirmal Chandra Chunder (President); Sachindranath Sengupta, Sailen Roy (Poet); Ahindra Chowdhury and Sajanikanta Das (Associated Presidents); Jnanprakash Ghosh (General Secretary); Dilip Roy and Abbasuddin Ahmed (Assistant Secretaries); Sudhi Pradhan (Organizing Secretary); Aditya Mukherjee (Office Secretary); Pratap Chandra Chunder (Treasurer); Nirmal Bose (Publicity Secretary); also Pankaj Kumar Mallik, Kamal Dasgupta, Rajen Sarkar, Sukhendu Goswami, Mustak Ali Khan, Paritosh Seal, Malina Devi, Ranjit Roy, Birendra Krishna Bhadra, Hemanta Mukherjee, Jaganmoy Mitra, Santosh Sengupta, Satyadev Chowdhury, Ajit Chatterjee, Phani Pal, Gour Ghosh, Tarakanath Dey, Pabitra Chatterjee; Subcommittees—Theatre Section—Prabhat Sinha, Santosh Sinha, Kanu Banerjiee, Panchanan Banerjee, Mihir Bhattacharya, Jiben Bose; Radio—Bani Kumar, Biren Bhadra, Taraknath Dey, Amiya Adhikari, Suren Pal, Ardhendu Ghosh; Film—Niren Lahiri, Khagen Roy, Hiren Bose, Pashupati Chatterjee, Sunanda Devi, Kanan Devi; Instruments—Newman, Basanta Gupta, Barada Gupta, Biren Bal, Ajit Bose, Moni Chatterjee, Amar Dutta, Bidhu Chakrabarty, Paritosh Seal; Record—Dilip Roy, Durga Sen, Dhananjay Bhattacharya, Rabin Majumdar, Kamal Dasgupta, Pankaj Mallik, Satyadev Chowdhury, and Satya Chowdhury.

Members of Executive Committee of
Artiste Association for 1947–8 as Listed in the
Annual Report of 1946–7

Pankaj Kumar Mallik (General Secretary); Sudhi Pradhan (Organization Secretary); Mustak Ali Khan and Dilip Kumar Roy (Assistant Secretary); Pratap Chandra Chunder (Treasurer); also Chhabi Biswas, Kamal Mitra, Rabi Roy, Ajit Chatterji, Bimal Prasad Chatterji, Sukhendu Goswami, Nanigopal Banerjee, Hemanta Mukherjee, Santosh Sengupta, Dwijen Chowdhury, Suchitra Mukherjee, Dhananjay Bhattacharya, Rajen Sarkar, Satyadev Chowdhury, Ardhendu Ghosh, Amar Roy Chowdhury, Jatin Das, and Nirmal Bose.

Members of Executive Committee of
Artiste Association for 1948–9 as Listed in the
Annual Report of 1947–8

Dwijen Chowdhury and Benoy Roy (Assistant Secretary); Sudhi Pradhan (Organization Secretary); Pratap Chandra Chunder (Treasurer); other members Santosh Sengupta, Pankaj Mallick, Sukhendu Goswami, Kumaresh Bose, Nanigopal Banerji, Rathin Chowdhury, Bimalaprasad Chatterjee, Ajit Bose, Ajit Chatterji, Rajen Sarkar, Savita Dutta, Nirmal Bose, Suchitra Mitra, Radhamohan Bhattacharya, Dilip Roy, Taraknath Dey, Amar Roy Chowdhury, Amiya Adhikari; Office Secretary Nirmalendu Ghosh.

Delegates to the All-India Peace Conference and
Festival in Calcutta Park Circus Ground in
April 1952

Vallathol, the great poet of Kerala, Mulk Raj Anand, Prithviraj Kapoor, Krisan Chunder, Ram Bilas Sharma, K.A. Abbas, S. Kitchlew, Raghunath Chowdhury, Kaifi Azmi, Anna Bhau Sathe, Makhdum Mahiuddin, Ali Sardar Jaffri, Omar Seikh, Niaz Hyder, Majru Sultanpuri, Manmohan Misra, Amrit Rai, Prithwi Singh Azad, N.S. Krisnan, Sardar Gurbax Singh, people from all walks of life attended the conference. Among local participants were Sachin Sengupta, Naren Dev, Manik Banerjee, Manoj Bose, Pabitra Ganguly, Manoranjan Bhattacharya, Gopal Haldar, Nabendu Ghosh, Narayan Ganguly, Ramesh Chandra Sen, Sushil Jana, Narahari Kaviraj, Kaji Abdul Odud, Nirmal Bhattacharya, Hiren Mukherjee, Benoy Ghosh, etc.

Notes and References

1. In reconstructing the history of the anti-fascist resistance at the international and the national levels, I have been immensely helped by the following works:
   (a) The files of *Ananda Bazar Patrika*, at the office of this periodical in Kolkata.

(b) *Banglar Fascist Birodhi Aitijhya*, published on the occasion of the 30th anniversary of victory over fascism, by Manisha in collaboration with the Indo-GDR Friendship Society, Kolkata, 1975.

(c) *Anti-Fascist Traditions of Bengal: An Anthology in Celebration of the 20th Anniversary of the Foundation of the GDR*, compiled and published by Indo-GDR Friendship Society.

(d) Nepal Majumdar, *Bharate Jatiyata O Antarjatikata Ebang Rabindranath*, vol. IV, nos. 5 and 6. Distributor Chatuskon Private Limited, Kolkata, 1971.

(e) Arabinda Poddar, *Rabindranath: Rajnaitik Byaktitwa*, Uchcharan, Kolkata, 1982.

(f) A Bengali anthology entitled *Pratirodh Pratidin* (Resistance Everyday), dedicated to International Anti-Fascist Conference, Patna, 4–7 December 1975, Manisha, 1975. This is an elaborated version of *Parichay, Fascist Birodhi Sankhya*, May–July 1975, edited by Dipendranath Bandyopadhyay and Tarun Sanyal. It shows how intellectuals from all over the world including Bengal joined hands in their protest against fascism during the 1930s and the 1940s. It is a collection of essays, poems and stories by more than 70 writers including Romain Rolland, Henri Barbusse, Maxim Gorky, Andre Gide, S.M. Forster, Dolores Ibarruri (the Communist lady who gave a heroic call to defend Spain the day the Civil War started. She later became the General Secretary of the Communist Party of Spain), Ted Allan and Sydney Gordon (who were members of Dr Norman Bethune's medical unit doing relief work in Spain), Rafael Alberti (a Communist friend of Lorca, the poet who laid down his life in the Spanish Civil War), Ernest Hemingway, Bernard Shaw, Bertrand Russell, Jean Paul Sartre, Charlie Chaplin, Georgi Dimitrov (a Communist leader of Bulgaria, who had been imprisoned in connection with Reichtag arsenal), Vercors (an unknown French writer whose *The Silence of the Sea* was translated into Bengali by Bishnu Dey in the 1940s), Aragon, Ehrenburg, Gabriel Peri (a Communist member of the French Parliament, who was killed by the Nazis), Ernest Toller (the German poet and dramatist, who too was killed by the Nazis), Julius Fuchik (who was killed in Czechoslovakia), Thomas Mann, Konstantin Simonov, John Conford, Brecht, Neruda, Hernandez, Ho Chi Minh. From Bengal there are Buddhadev Bose, Sudhi Pradhan, Surendranath Goswami, Susobhan Sarkar, Kiransankar Sengupta, Narahari Kaviraj, Mohit Sen and others. The Foreword is written by Augustina Fuchik, wife of Julius Fuchik, herself an anti-fascist fighter and later a member of the Central Committee of the Czech Communist Party.

(g) *The Penguin Book of Spanish Civil War Verse*, edited by Valentine Cunningham, 1980, shows how the conscience of humanity spoke out during those traumatic days through the poetry of numerous poets, many of them actually fighting in the battlefield, some of them this century's best-known literary figures—Auden, Spender, MacNeice and Orwell, but also several neglected poets such as Charles Donnelly, Clive Branson and Miles Tomalin.

(h) Also *International solidarity with the Spanish Republic*, Soviet War Veterans' Committee, Moscow: Progress Publishers, 2nd edn., 1976.

(i) Susnata Das, *Fasci-birodhi Sangrame Abibhakta Bangla*, Kolkata: Prima, 1989.

2. Published in *Visva-Bharati Quarterly*, July 1927.
3. Report of *Ananda Bazar Patrika*, 27 July 1935.
4. Ibid., 29 October 1935.
5. Ibid., 28 November 1935.
6. The message condemned the proscription of a number of books on Russia—Tagore's *Letters from Russia*, the Webbs' *Soviet Communism*, Low's *Russian Sketch Book*. It also condemned the suppression of 348 Indian newspapers by the British. These details are known from Intelligence Branch record.
7. From his autobiography *Here I stand*, p. 60.
8. It was actually a letter 'To the writers and poets of England, Scotland, Ireland and Wales', asking them the questions: 'Are you for, or against, the legal Government and the people of Republican Spain?' and 'Are you for, or against, Franco and Fascism?' The answers, mostly anti-fascist, were printed in a pamphlet by *Left Review*.
9. Report of *Amrita Bazar Patrika*, 3 March 1937.
10. Ibid., 12 March 1937.
11. Published in *Hindusthan Standard*, 10 November 1938.
12. Tagore protested against the Japanese aggression in China and against fascism in general also in *Prabasi*, Magh, 1344; *Amrita Bazar*, 17 October 1937; in his letter to Amiya Chakravarty, Baisakh, 1345; *Modern Review*, October 1939; and of course, in numerous poems.
13. See *Ananda Bazar Patrika*, 28 June 1938.
14. Published in *Ananda Bazar Patrika*, 3 September 1938.
15. Abinash Dasgupta, *Lenin, Rushbiplab O Bangla Sambad Sahitya*, Calcutta Book House, published on the occasion of Lenin Birth Centenary. Also the articles of Gautam Chattopadhyay and Ashis Sanyal in *October Revolution: Impact on Indian Literature*, ed. Qamar Rais, New Delhi: Sterling Publishers Pvt. Ltd., 1978.
16. Some such periodicals were published by ex-terrorists trying to find a new and more meaningful mode of action (e.g. *Atmashakti*, *Bijali*), some were connected with peasants' and workers' movements (e.g. *Langal*, *Ganabani*), some were mainly concerned with the Muslims (e.g. *Masik Mohammadi*, *Samyabadi*), some were for the ordinary *bhadralok* (e.g. *Basumati*, *Anandabazar*), to give just a few examples. The anthology *Bangalir Samyabad Charcha* compiled by Sipra Sarkar and Anamitra Das (Kolkata: Ananda Publishers, 1998) contains a good selection of socialistic writings from the Bengali periodicals of the late colonial period.
17. *Moscow Banam Pundicherry*, included in *Sibram Chakravartyr Granthabali*, Basumati Sahitya Mandir (n.d.); *Rushbiplaber Itibritta* serially published in

Parichay, October 1931–January 1932; *Rayater Katha*, Biswa-Bidya Samgraha Series, Viswa-Bharati Granthalay, 1351/1944; *Russiar Chithi*, included in *Rabindra Rachanabali*, vol. 20, Viswa Bharati, 1966. A very rich collection of such writings is to be found in *Bangalir Samyabad Charcha*, ibid.

18. The letter was published in Kartik, 1343/1936. Chowdhury's article had been published in Sraban, 1943.
19. Nazrul Islam, *Agnibina*, Kolkata: D.M. Library, 1337/1931 (21st edn.).
 Jatindranath Sengupta, *Kabita Sankalan*, ed. Sunilkanti Sen, West Bengal State Book Board, 1981.
 Muktadhara, included in *Rabindra Rachanabali*, vol. 14, Viswa-Bharati, 1968.
 Raktakarabi, included in *Rabindra Rachanabali*, vol. 15, Visva-Bharati, 1968.
 'Mahesh' and 'Abhagir Swarga', included in *Sarat Sahitya Sangraha*, 3rd edn., vols. XII & XIII, Kolkata: M.C. Sarkar & Sons Pvt. Ltd.
20. *Pank*, 2nd edn., 1947.
 Pataldangar Panchali (the writer's pen-name was Yubanaswa), Kolkata: Karuna Prakashani, 1981.
 Shailajananda Mukhopadhyay, *Kayla-Kuthi*, Kolkata: Baroda Agency, Kolkata, 1336/1929.
21. Jibendra Sinha Roy, *Kalloler Kal: Bangla Sahitya Palabadal*, Kolkata: Kathasilpa, 1380/1973. Also see Achintya Kumar Sengupta, *Kallol Yug*, Kolkata: M.C. Sarkar & Sons, 6th edn., 1387/1980.
22. About this time the Royists were active too in the Indian political scene. They were the followers of M.N. Roy, a Communist leader of international reputation. In 1928, he was expelled from the Comintern for his 'decolonization thesis'. After this, he returned to India and started working here, still professing Communism.
23. Sumit Sarkar, *Modern India*, Macmillan India Ltd., 1983, pp. 338, 370–1.
24. *Jagadish Gupta Rachanabali*, vol. I, Kolkata: Granthalay, 1385.
25. *Manik Granthabali*, vols. I and III, Kolkata: Granthalay, 1982.
26. Asru Kumar Sikdar has drawn our attention to this transition of Bishnu Dey, see Sikdar's article 'Bishnu Dey-r Anwesan: Bar khunje Fere Sattwa' in his book *Adhunik Kabitar Digbalay*, Kolkata, 1381/1974.
27. Robin Master, Manoranjan.
28. This thesis was published in *International Press Correspondence*, 29 February 1936. Seen through the courtesy of Sudhi Pradhan.
29. While reminiscing about the foundation of this progressive cultural movement, Hiren Mukherjee stressed that progress was the most vital need of human civilization—life is an endless motion, lack of motion means death. Mukherjee quoted the famous line 'Charaibeti' (Move on and on) of the *Aitareya Brahman* to drive home this point; 'Pragati Lekhak Sangha: Smriti Satta Bhabishyat, *Parcichay, Sharadiya*, 1393/1986.
30. Bishnu Dey, 'Marx and Bengali', *In the Sun and the Rain*, Delhi: PPH, 1972, pp. 187–9.
31. Mulk Raj Anand, 'On the Progressive Writers' Movement', 1939, included in Sudhi Pradhan's *Marxist Cultural Movement in India*, vol. I (1936–47),

published by Sudhi Pradhan from Kolkata, Distributor National Book Agency, 1979.

32. Sajjad Zaheer, 'Reminiscences', 1940, included in Sudhi Pradha, ed., ibid.
33. These names were known from an interview of mine with Hiren Mukherjee.
34. Talat Ahmed, *Literature and Politics in the Age of Nationalism: The Progressive Episode in South Asia, 1932–56*, New Delhi: Routledge, 2009.
35. Mulk Raj Anand's article, included in *Marxist Cultural Movement*, op. cit., p. 17.
36. Sajjad Zaheer's article, ibid., pp. 39–40.
37. See Hiren Mukherjee's *Tori Hote Teer: Paribesh, Pratyaksha o Pratyayer Brittanta*, Kolkata: Manisha, 1974, p. 301. The book gives interesting details about the organizational and other activities of the AIPWA. Mukherjee's book *Chakshusa Kanah* too furnishes significant facts about the initial stage of the Indian Progressive Writers' Movement. Relevant extracts from this book have been included in *Somen Chanda O Tar Rachana Sangraha*, vol. II, ed. Dilip Majumdar, Kolkata: Nabajatak Prakashan, 1977. But while in *Tori Hote Teer*, Mukherjee says, Abburi Ramakrisna Rao could not attend the first AIPWA conference, in the latter book he says Rao actually attended the conference.
38. Intercepted by the police. The copy of this letter is kept in a file of IB, WB Police.
39. Seen at the library of IB, WB Police.
40. The manifesto is included in Sudhi Pradhan's *Marxist Cultural Movement*, vol. I, op. cit., pp. 20–1. It is, in fact, the amended manifesto adopted by the Second AIPWA conference held at Calcutta, December 1938.
41. Munshi Premchand, 'The Nature and Purpose of Literature', his Presidential address delivered to the first conference of the AIPWA, included in Sudhi Pradhan's *Marxist Cultural Movement*, vol. I, ibid.
42. Talat Ahmed, op. cit.
43. 'Communist Propaganda: Moscow Changes Tactics', *The Statesman*, 7 July 1936.
44. The Hallet Circular (File No. 7/9/36, Home Political, 1936) has been included in Sudhi Pradhan's *Marxist Cultural Movement*, vol. I, op. cit., pp. 344–5.
45. See the protest of Sajjad Zaheer, General Secretary, AIPWA against the 'False Campaigning of the Statesman'. The Bengali version was published in *Ananda Bazar*, 27 Asar 1343.
46. Report, *Ananda Bazar Patrika*, 30 Asar 1343/1936.
47. All these letters and reports have been seen at the library of IB, WB Police.
48. All these were names of prominent intellectuals of Bengal, most of whom were known to be apolitical or at least non-left. Some were even anti-left, e.g. Sajanikanta and Mohitlal Majumdar. Among the names enlisted many became attracted to Communism in the course of time—Arun Mitra,

Nirendranath Ray, Sushobhan Sarkar. Some never professed Communism, e.g. Ramananda Chatterjee and Sarat Chandra Bose.

49. All the sources have been seen at the library of IB, WB Police, unfortunately I was not allowed to note down the number of the IB files.
50. This letter has been seen at the library of IB, WB Police.
51. All these letters have been seen at the library of IB, WB Police.
52. Seen at the library of IB, WB Police.
53. In Bengal the Progressive Writers' Movement found a wide response. Some intercepted letters in the police files bear testimony to this. For example, there is a letter written by Bibhuti Bhusan Lahiri (c/o Asutosh Lahiri, B.E. Retd. Dist. Engineer, Rangpur), dated 13 April 1938, to the PWA headquarters, Allahabad, expressing his willingness to join along with his friends. We do not know what personal reason he had for ignoring Calcutta and writing to Allahabad.
54. Seen at the library of IB, WB Police.
55. Hiren Mukherjee has furnished many interesting facts about *Pragati* in his *Tori Hote Teer*, pp. 312–14. Chinmohan Sehanabis possessed a copy of *Pragati*, which he let me go through.
56. Quoted by Nepal Majumdar, 'Pragati Lakhak Sangha: Rabindranath O Suren Goswami', *Nandan*, Sharadiya, 1390.
57. *Tori Hote Teer*, p. 379.
58. Ibid.
59. The journals that sponsored progressive literature initially nurtured an atmosphere of unity too. The foremost among them was the monthly *Parichay* (1931). The Founder-Editor of this monthly was the reputed poet Sudhindranath Dutta, who was not a Marxist. But he had many Marxist friends who contributed book reviews, articles, poems, stories and novels to *Parichay.* The weekly 'adda' of Parichay was a lively meeting of Marxist and non-Marxist intellectuals and facilitated exchange of views. However, in 1943, Sudhindranath Dutta handed over *Parichay* to his Marxist friends. The character of the journal gradually changed.

    Agrani was launched in 1939 as the monthly journal of Marxist intellectuals in Bengal. The editor Prafulla Roy and all others associated with it—Devkumar Gupta, Advaita Dutta, Birendra Majumdar, Chinmoahn Sehanabis, Saroj Dutta, Sunil Chattopadhyay, Sudhi Pradhan, Anil Kanjilal and others—were confirmed Marxists. Some of them were of liberal views compatible with the spirit of the United Front, but quite a few nurtured extremely mechanical views on aesthetics. Gradually such mechanical views began to predominate in the cultural field and led to a sort of intolerance and sectarianism. This was evident in the weekly *Arani* that replaced *Agrani* as the cultural journal of the Bengali Marxists in 1941. It was backed by the Communist Party itself and was run by a group of Marxist intellectuals many of whom had once been associated with the journal *Anandabazar* but then broke away from it during the late 1930s. Satyendranath Majumder, editor of *Anandabazar,* became the editor of *Arani*. However, the journal did encourage liberal aesthetic views too. After all, it was the period of the United Front. And after the establishment of the Anti-Fascist Writers' and Artists' Association, *Arani* became the organ of this organization. Whereas *Agrani* had not published a single piece of writing by Bishnu Dey, a powerful poet and fellow traveller but denounced by many Marxists, a number of his poems appeared in *Arani*.

60. An interesting correspondence between the BPWA and the AIPWA preceded this conference. Copies of these letters are in a file of IB, WB Police. For a summary of this correspondence see Appendix I.
61. Nepal Majumdar's book, op. cit., covers the conference extensively.
62. Hiren Mukherjee, *Chakshusa Kanah*, an extract from which is included in *Somen Chanda O Tar Rachana Sangraha*, vol. II, op. cit.
63. A copy of the full speech of Buddhadev Bose was in the possession by Nepal Majumdar who let me see it. Parts of this speech have been quoted in Majumdar's *Jatiyata O Antarjatikata Ebang Rabindranath*.
64. See the letter dated 30 December 1938, referring directly to Buddhadev's criticism, also the letter dated 17 March 1939 in *Chithipatra*, vol. 11, Viswa-Bharati, 1974.
65. *Somen Chanda O Tar Rachana Sangraha*, vol. I, ed. Dilip Majumdar, contains a number of essays written by different people in memory of Somen Chanda. From these one can form an idea about the activities of the Dhaka PWA at its initial stage. The articles are: Satish Pakrashi, 'Somen Chanda', *Parichay*, Phalgun 1349; Saralananda Sen, *Pratirodh*, Somen Memorial Number, 1350; Jnan Chakravarty, 'Somen Chanda', *Ekata* (10 March 1973); I also interviewed Ranesh Dasgupta who was closely associated with the Dhaka Progressive Writers' Movement at this stage and also in subsequent years. At the time of the interview he was residing at Park Circus, Calcutta.
66. Sources for the YCI activities:
    (a) Subrata Bandopadhyay, 'YCI-er Dinguli', *Bahurupi*, Nabanna Smarak Sankhya, no. 2.
    (b) Jolly Kaul, 'YCI—Smriti', *Bahurupi*, Nabanna Smarak Sankhya no. 2.
    (c) Amarendra Mukherjee, 'The Youth Cultural Institute (1940–2)', *Unity*, December 1953.
    (d) Interview, Chinmohan Sehanabis and Uma Sehanabis.
67. With the exception of M.N. Roy's group which felt that the anti-fascist side should be supported unconditionally.
68. Hirendranath Mukhopadhyay, 'Ardhashatak', *Communist* (published by the CPI on the occasion of its golden jubilee), p. 37.
69. Published in *The Land of the Soviets*, published by the Friends of the Soviet Union, September 1941.
70. Dilip Bose, *1942 August Struggle and the Communist Party of India*, a booklet published by the CPI, June 1984 (in reply to Arun Shourie's four articles published in the *Illustrated Weekly of India* alleging that there had been a truce between the British government and the Communists during the War period), p. 17.

71. Manikuntala Sen, *Sediner Katha*, Kolkata: Nabapatra Prakashan, 1982, p. 61.
72. Dilip Bose, *1942 August Struggle and the Communist Party of India*, op. cit., p. 13.
73. *Sediner Katha*, op. cit., p. 65.
74. *Tori Hote Teer*, p. 431.
75. For details of how the British Government viewed at the Communists during the 'people's war' period, see Dilip Bose, *1942 August Struggle*, op. cit., pp. 28–31.

    Also see in this connection Sumit Sarkar, 'The Communists and 1942', *Turbulent Times*, ed. Biswamoy Pati, Bombay: Popular Prakashan, 1998, responding to Arun Shourie's articles. Sarkar counters Shourie's charge, even after admitting that there was much that was dubious and perhaps wrong-headed about the Communist line of People's War (as well as in their near-support to Pakistan). He stresses that the wrong came not from any softness towards British rule, but rather from a misguided international perspective, something they shared with Congressmen like Nehru. (Certainly, opposition to the Quit India movement did not prevent others like Nehru and Rajagopalachari from becoming national heroes.) Sarkar wants only the timing and the question of immediate strategy to be considered while trying to understand the People's War policy.

    In 'An Extremely Troubled Relationship: The British Colonial State and the Communist Party of India, 1942–4', in *Turbulent Times*, Sanjoy Bhattacharya tells us that by lifting the ban on the Party, the British tried to utilize its assistance to counter the perceived Congress threat during a period of extreme military crisis, that the government wanted the Communists to come out doing propaganda against the Congress, to support the British in all aspects of the latter's war-efforts as well as the post-war constitutional questions. However, as Bhattacharya shows, all these aims were dashed. The CPI leadership became progressively hostile to the British and never quite lost sight of national imperatives. The mutual suspicion of the British officials and the Communists remained.
76. In writing this history of the FSU, I have heavily depended on an IB report prepared sometimes during the early 1950s, Hiren Mukherjee's *Tori Hote Teer*, Snehangsu Acharya's article on the FSU in *Janayuddha*, 28 April 1943 and Hiren Mukherjee's article in *Janayuddha,* 17 June 1942.
77. *Tori Hote Teer*, p. 422.
78. *Tori Hote Teer*, pp. 476–7.
79. *Ananda Bazar Patrika*, 23 March 1942.
80. *Amrita Bazar Patrika*, 28 March 1942 and *Ananda Bazar Patrika*, 29 March 1942.
81. Hiren Mukherjee's report in *People's War*, 10 January 1943; and *Janayuddha*, 23 December 1942.
82. It was intercepted by the Bengal Police.
83. The causes of the Bengal Famine have been analysed in:
    (a) *Samskriti O Samaj*, 1st year, 1st issue, April 1983, ed. Baudhayan Chattopadhyay, Niharranjan Ray Jatiya Samhati Charcha Kendra. The

whole of it deals with the Bengal Famine. Baudhayan Chattopadhyay's article, 'Panchaser Manwantarer Karyakaran Sandhane' (and its continuation in the next two issues of the same journal) is particularly helpful.

(b) Niranjan Sengupta, 'Panchaser Manwantar; Ganahatyar Dalil', *Baromas*, Sharadiya, 1981.

(c) *Shyama Prosad Mukhopadhyay, Panchaser Manwantar*, a collection of speeches and writings, Bengal Publishers, 2nd edn., 1351 (1st edn., 1350/1943). Mukherjee as a member of the Legislative Council fought hard to make people conscious and the government ashamed of the man-made character of the Famine.

(d) *Maladministration in Bengal*, a collection of editorials, illustrations and correspondence which appeared in *The Statesman* between March and October 1943, *The Statesman*, ed. Ian Melville Stephens.

(e) Somnath Lahiri, *Kapar Chai* (We Want Clothes), July 1945, republished in 2009 by Sutradhar, Kolkata.

(f) Amartya Sen, *Poverty and Famines: An Essay on Entitlement and Deprivation*, first published, New York: OUP, 1981, Oxford India Paperbacks, 1991.

(g) Paul R. Greenough, *Prosperity and Misery in Modern Bengal: The Famine of 1943–1944*, New Delhi: OUP, 1982.

(h) Two recently published books are important for understanding the man-made character of the Famine, particularly the responsibility of the British for it—Srimanjari, *Through War and Femine: Bengal 1939–45*, Hyderabad: Orient BlackSwan, 2009; and Madhusree Mukerjee, *Churchill's Secret War: The British Empire and the Ravaging of India during World War II*, New York: Basic Books, 2010.

84. George Blyn's statistics, quoted by Baudhayan Chatterjee, ibid.
85. The Department of Commercial Intelligence and Statistics, Government of India, quoted by Baudhayan Chatterjee.
86. P.G. Salvey, Memorandum on the Trade between India and Ceylon quoted by Baudhayan Chatterjee
87. Bhatia, *Famines in India (1860–1952)*, 1st edn., Bombay: Asia Publishing House, 1963, 2nd edn., 1967, p. 324.
88. See Ranen Sen, *Banglay Communist Party Gathaner Pratham Yug* (1930–48), Kolkata: Bingsha Satabdi, 1388/1981, pp. 130–2.
89. This famous doctor was another right-wing Congress man who had been averse to the Quit India Movement and now collaborated with the Communists in the work of famine-relief.
90. 'Prasanga Panchaser Manwantar', an interview with Gopal Haldar (The interview conducted by Maitreya Ghatak in June 1982), *Samskriti O Samaj*, 1st year, 1st issue.
91. Interview, Kalpataru Sengupta at his Salt Lake residence.
92. Amartya Sen, *Poverty and Famines*, op. cit.

    Another interesting theory by way of explaining the Bengal Famine is found in Paul R. Greenogh, *Prosperity and Misery in Modern Bengal: The Famine of 1843–1944*, New Delhi: OUP, 1982. He explains the Famine in terms of abandonment of the clients by the patrons and notices this abandonment at three levels: (1) abandonment of the people by the government, (2) abandonment of the rural poor by the rural rich, and (3) abandonment of wives and children by men at the familial level. According to Greenough, these three processes together led to the Famine: 'In a direct, political sense, the epithet "man-made" was an accusation, a shaft directed at the officials, politicians and merchants popularly held responsible for the Famine. But the fuller implications of calling the Famine "man-made" were that it was not a result of natural disasters or organic pathologies; that it was shaped by purposeful human conduct, and that the chief actors were—literally—Bengali men, whose actions reflected Bengali values and Bengali conceptions of what was ultimately at risk. In short, the epithet "man-made" Famine was culturally patterned in its onset, crisis and denouement.' Greenough attributes equal responsibility for the Famine to the British government, the greedy big hoarder, the helpless raiyat who wanted to keep a little stock of rice in his house with a view to the future requirement of the family as well as the hapless victim of the Famine who abandoned his wife and children in a dire situation. Greenough thus cleverly confuses the cause and symptoms of the Famine. I have argued at length with Greenough (as well as Amartya Sen) in an article on the Arts and Literature of the Bengal Famine in my book *Sekaler Marxiya Samskriti Andolan*, Kolkata, 2000. Here I refrain from doing so. The point I want to make is that the contemporary artists and writers had a clearer and more humane perception of the matter.

93. *Manwantar* was published in *Sharadiya Anand Bazar*, 1943 and as a book in 1944. Available in *Tarashankar Granthabali*, vol. 5, Kolkata: Mitra and Ghosh, p. 318.
94. Amartya Sen's 'Introduction', in Nikhil Sarkar, *A Matter of Conscience* (*Artists bear witness to the Great Bengal Famine*), a Punashcha Publication, Kolkata, 1998. This volume is a collection of sketches and paintings on the Famine. Sen recommends viewing these pictures on this ground.
95. *People's War*, 6 June 1943. Chinmohan Sehanabis, 'Samskriti Sammelan', *Arani*, 2 and 9 July 1943.
96. *The IPTA Bulletin No. I.*
97. Included in Sudhi Pradhan, ed., *Marxist Cultural Movement*, vol. I, op. cit., pp. 176–9.
98. Included in Sudhi Pradhan, ed., ibid., pp. 176–9.
99. Bijan Bhattacharya, 'Abhijnatar Theatre', *Gandharva* (Speical issue on *Bijan Bhattacharya: Banglar Theatre Andolan)*, 30th issue, ed. Nripendra Saha, p. 15; also see Chittaranjan Ghosh, 'Natak Nabanna', in the same magazine, pp. 22–3.
100. See the section 'The All-India Progressive Writers' Association and the Bengal Progressive Writers' Association' in the present chapter.
101. Hiren Mukherjee, *People's War*, 13 February 1944; *Janayuddha*, 26 January 1944; and *Arani*, 4 February 1944.
102. Proposed by Hiren Mukherjee and seconded by Hiran Sanyal.

103. Proposed by Ranesh Dasgupta and seconded by Susanta Pathak.
104. Proposed by Nihar Sarkar and seconded by Swarnakamal Bhattacharya.
105. Proposed by Abdul Mansur Ahmed.
106. That attempts were made to establish branches in other places would be borne out by a letter written by Dev Kumar Gupta, the Office Secretary, to Himangshu Chakravarty of the Communist Party Office, Khulna. The letter was intercepted by the police.
107. The details of this IPTA Subcommittee report and of the report of the Fine Arts Subcommittee would be discussed later.
108. The AFWAA continued to expand even after the date of this Report. For example, a new branch was established in Asansol in 1946. For details see Ramshankar Chowdhury, 'Assansol-e Gananatya Sangha O Pragati Lekhak O Silpi Sangher Andolan', *Gananatya*, October 1975.
109. Hiren Mukherjee, *People's War*, 1 April 1945; Arani, 23 March 1945.
110. Niharranjan Ray, *Kristi Culture Samskriti*, Bichitrabidya Granthamala, Jijnasa, December 1979.
111. Interview, Salil Chowdhury.
112. Information about this organization has been obtained from:

    (a) *Artiste Association, Bengal, Annual Report (1945–6)*, (1946–7) and (1947–8).

    All the three reports were published by Sudhi Pradhan on behalf of the Association from 23, Wellington Street.

    (b) My interview with Sudhi Pradhan (May 1984) and relevant newspaper clippings, letters, etc., in his collection.

    (c) Sudhi Pradhan, 'Artiste Association, Bengal', *Bangladesh*, special number, 3rd tr., 20th issue, Calcutta, 14 September 1973.

    (d) Sudhi Pradhan, 'Nirmal Chandra Chunder o shilpi Sangha', *Chitrabani*, Chaitra, 1359/1953, Hajra Lane.

    (e) Sudhi Pradhan's article in *Shilpi* ('The only organ of the radio, record, theatre and film artists. Run by the members of the Artiste Association, Bengal'), 1st year, 1st issue, 1 Magh 1355/1949; ed. Nirmal Bose.

    In Bengali, sometimes the organization was called 'Shilpi Sangha'. I wrote an article on this organization in more detail, which has been included in my book *Sekaler Marxiya Samskrii Andolan*, Kolkata, 2000.
113. 28 April 1943.
114. The Company had made Chowdhury work hard for the music of their film *Grihalakshmi*. Then they most ungratefully replaced him at the time of recording the songs for gramophone discs.
115. The latter was creating obstructions in the way of release of discs by some recording companies, including the former.
116. The 3rd annual report of Artiste Association and a few issues of *Swadhinata* since 11 August 1946, cover this historic radio strike.
117. A minute-book of the Artiste Association, which was in possession of Sudhi Pradhan, shows how squabbles among its members wrecked the

organization in 1948. These generally seem to be personal squabbles, sometimes with political tensions. Hemanta Mukherjee, the secretary of the Artiste Association during this crucial last phase, in an interview, also threw much light on its decline and winding up.

118. At the initial stage of the *Gananatya Andolan* (People's Theatre Movement), *Gananatya* was often called *Jananatya*. But before long 'Gananatya' was finally chosen.
119. Organizational Document, 1 June 1944—included in Abdullah Rasul, *Krisak Sabhar Itihas*, Kolkata: Nabajatak Prakashan, 3rd edn., 1982, pp. 147–8.
120. Which made even Rabindranath Tagore express his support for the struggling workers and urge his countrymen to come forward to their aid—*Amrita Bazar Patrika*, 30 April 1937; referred to by Sukomal Sen, *Working Class of India*, Calcutta: K.P. Bagchi and Company, 1979.
121. Amarendranath Roy, 'Students Fight for Freedom', *Ananda Bazar Patrika*, 1967.
122. *Chhatra Abhijan*, published on the occasion of the 40th anniversary of the Students' Federation.
123. Interesting details about the activities of the Mahila Atmaraksha Samity are given in Renu Chakravarty, *Communists in Indian Women's Movement*, Delhi: PPH and its Bengali translation by Pushpamayee Bose and Manikuntala Sen, Kolkata: Manisha, 1980. Also see, Manikuntala Sen, *Sediner Katha*, Kolkata: Nabapatra Prakashan, 1982.
124. A much more detailed study of this little known mass-front of the CPI and its cultural activities is my article 'Banglar Kishore Bahini', in *Sekaler Marxiya Samskriti Andolan*, op. cit.
125. Interview, Nripen Banerjee. At that time he was a professor at Centre for Studies in Social Sciences, Calcutta.
126. Interview, Arati Ganguly, 3 July 1984.
127. Interview, Amulya Pakrashi, 12 December 84.
128. Cited in Sarojmohan Mitra, *Sukanter Jiban o Kabya*, 2nd edn., Kolkata: Granthalay, 1976, p. 126.
129. Interview, Asoke Bhattacharya, 3 May 1985.
130. Gopal Haldar, 'Prasanga Manwantar', *Samskriti O Samaj*, 1st year, 1st issue, op. cit., p. 95.
131. Sumit Sarkar, *Modern India*, p. 412. But, again, some leading Congress right-wingers from the South also pleaded for negotiation on the Pakistan demand.
132. Interview, Chinmohan Sehanabis.
133. *Shahid Sachindranath Mitra o Anya Ek Swadhinata* (compil. and ed. Anuradha Roy), Kolkata: Sutradhar, 2009, throws some light on the Congress Sahitya Sangha in which Sachindranath was deeply involved.
134. *Abhyuday*, published by Subal Chandra Bandyopadhyay on behalf of the Congress Sahitya Sangha, provides the names of the members of the Sangha.

135. The account of the post-War mass-struggle is largely based on Sumit Sarkar's *Modern India*.
136. See Gautam Chattopadhyay, 'The Almost Revolution: A Case Study of India in 1946', in *Essays in Honour of Prof. S.C. Sarkar*, Delhi: PPH, 1976.
137. B.C. Dutta, 'Revolt of the Ratings of the Royal Indian Navy', *Challenge*, Delhi: PPH, 1984.
138. Renu Chakravarty, *Communists in Indian Women's Movement* (the chapter entitled 'Communal Riots'), op. cit.
139. Abdullah Rasul, *Krisak Sabhar Itihas*, pp. 165–6.
140. Included in his book of poems *Sandwiper Char*.
141. Statement on Communal Disturbances 1946, Sudhi Pradhan, ed., *Marxist Cultural Movement*, vol. I, op. cit., pp. 336–41.
142. Chinmohan Sehanabis reminisced about this memorable procession in *No. 46*. Details are known from Sudhi Pradhan, one of the organizers. They also held a big meeting of writers and journalists at the University Institute Hall under the Chairmanship of Tarasankar Banerjee, as the *Swadhinata*, 18 September 1947, informs us. See *Shahid Sachindranath Mitra o Anya Ek Swadhinata*, op. cit., for details.
143. Sources for Tebhaga Movement are—*Tebhaga Rajat Jayanti Smarak Grantha*, published by the CPI from the Office of *Kalantar*. Two articles are particularly informative—Bhabani Sen's 'Banglay Tebhaga Andolan' (originally published in the monthly journal *Communist* in September 1947) and Krishnabinode Roy's 'Tebhagar Sangram'; Sunil Sen, *Agrarian Relations in India (1793–1947)*, Delhi: PPH, 1979; also *Agrarian Struggle in Bengal, 1946–47*, Delhi: PPH, 1972; Kunal Chattopadhyay (pen-name Amitabha Basu), 'Banglay Tebhaga Andolan', published serially in the weekly *Janasakti*, 16 February–16 November 1978; Binay Bhusan Chaudhuri, 'Organized Politics and Peasant Insurgency', *The Calcutta Historical Journal*, July 1988–9, University of Calcutta; Peter Custers, *Women in the Tebhaga Uprising*, Kolkata: Naya Prakash, 1987; Adrienne Cooper, Sharecropping and Sharecroppers' Struggle in Bengal, 1930–50, Kolkata: K.P. Bagchi, 1988.
144. For example, Kunal Chattopadhyay, Peter Custers and Adrienne Cooper. According to some participants of the Tebhaga Movement too (including Krishabinode Roy, the then Secretary of the Kisan Sabha), it was the half-heartedness of the CPI and its failure to supply arms to the peasants that brought about such a disappointing end to the Movement.
145. For example B.B. Chaudhuri and Sunil Sen, the latter had been a participant too.
146. Even if one does not agree with Sugata Bose who says in *Agrarian Bengal: Economy, Social Structure and Politics 1919–1947* (Part II, Chapter VIII), Cambridge University Press, 1986, that the Communist Party launched the Tebhaga Movement to serve their own interests, to retrieve the ground lost due to its opposition to Quit India Movement.
147. It is pertinent to quote Gopal Haldar in this context: 'Our main slogan was 'Unite, Congress, League and Communists!' How impractical this slogan

was, would be revealed from the following example. Once Jinnah came to Calcutta. A few of our friends tried to meet him. At that time, there was a club called the Pakistan Renaissance Club in Calcutta. We contacted them. They fixed two minutes for us for meeting Jinnah. Anil Kanjilal was one of those who called on Jinnah. He requested Jinnah to meet Gandhi. Jinnah asked, 'Who are you?' Our delegates tried to explain that they were members of the Communist Party and that they had come to him to suggest that he should meet Gandhi and take up a united programme for India's Independence. Jinnah instantaneously retorted, 'Who are you to say that? If Gandhi wants to meet me, he should approach. Go. . . .' Another example relates to R.I.N. Mutiny. We were driven away by both Liyakat Ali and Patel. On the other hand, the opposition of the Muslim League made the Muslim workers retreat. I am still of the opinion that we should have given a call for seizure of Bombay.' [Quoted in Souri Ghatak, 'Banglar Pragati Sahitya O, Gananatya Andolan Keno Byartha Holo', *Shiladitya*, February 1982.]

148. *A History of Indian Freedom Struggle*, Trivandrum, 1986, pp. 185–6.
149. For the Political Thesis adopted at the second Congress and other documents relating to the new line of the Party see *Documents of the Communist Party of India (Vol. VII) 1948–50*, ed. M.B. Rao, Delhi: PPH, 1976.
150. From 'On People's Democracy', Document adopted by the December 1948 Politbureau meeting—included in *Documents of the History of the Communist Party of India (1948–1950)*, op. cit., p. 452.
151. Ibid., pp. 609–13.
152. Included in *Documents of the History of the Communist Party of India, Vol. VIII, 1951–1956*, ed. Mohit Sen, Delhi: PPH.
153. Ibid., p. 35.
154. Interview, Chinmohan Sehanabis.
155. Both the manifesto and Sehanabis's speech were printed in *Parichay*, Jaistha–Asar, 1356/1949.
156. In *Loknatya*, 1st year, 1st issue, Magh, 1355. Here his pen-name was Mritunjay Adhikari.
157. The Artiste Association demanded proper celebration of Subhas Bose's birthday (23 January 1949) on the radio. The radio authorities were impervious to this demand. So the artists decided to boycott all radio programmes on that day. On 14 January, however, the police opened fire on the refugees at Sealdah Station killing three. On 18 January, some students protesting against this incident at the gate of University of Calcutta clashed with the police. These incidents scared a number of artists and they retreated from the decision of boycott, though some courageous ones like Jnanprakash Ghosh and Pankaj Mallik did stick to the decision and did not participate in their scheduled programmes on that day. This is the version of Sudhi Pradhan. Hemanta Mukherjee, however, says that a number of artists felt that dedicating all the programmes of the day to Netaji would be a bit too much. After all, it was All India Radio. Moreover, these very people had called Netaji a traitor not very long ago. Anyway, following this, Party leaders started blaming a

number of artists as 'opportunist' and very soon the organization ceased to exist. I have tried to understand the end of the Artiste Association in more depth in my article included in *Sekaler Marxiya Samskriti Andolan*, op. cit.

158. Reports on this Conference are included in Sudhi Pradhan, ed., *Marxist Cultural Movement,* vol. II, p. 49.

159. Of the writings that have come to my notice, only a review report written after the Allahabad Conference (Printed in *Loknatya*, the second issue, included in Sudhi Pradhan, ed., *Marxist Cultural Movement*, vol. II, p. 55) approached the problem of mass-contact in more precise terms on the basis of this resolution. It suggested developing IPTA units inside organizations of militant workers, peasants and youths, to participate in their day-to-day struggles and to carry the mass movement forward by supplying it with cultural weapons. The comrades-in-arms of IPTA were to be deputed to work in mass organizations, would become both soldiers of the cultural front and of the greater struggle. They would not consider themselves as short-term instructors or outsiders, but as part of those mass organizations. They should make all their decisions known to the workers and leaders of the mass organization and seek the latter's consent.

In view of the predominantly middle-class character that the IPTA had retained so far, the report suggested that while the able and leading workers of the IPTA would go to participate in mass movements, the rest who might, because of their middle-class connection, be incapable of building up organizations with a changed outlook would conduct middle-class squads as local IPTA branches. But the middle-class branches would not constitute the major part of the People's Theatre Movement. The branches within the different mass organizations would be its main strength. And if exodus from the middle-class branches to the working-class branches affected the formers' strength and the remaining members failed to carry on IPTA activities locally, it could not be helped. Eventually and gradually, the regional branches would merge with the branches grown inside the organizations.

Finally, the report asked the question whether the IPTA needed to exist as an independent front at all and answered in the affirmative. The independent existence of the IPTA was vital for uniting conscious 'art-soldiers' and developing a forceful leadership to direct the People's Theatre Movement on the basis of People's struggle.

But all this was suggested on an assumption that the mass struggle had spread far and wide. And this was an illusion. Because of this basic fault, the programme could not be worked out in more practical details.

160. Sudhi Pradhan's *Marxist Cultural Movement*, vol. II, op. cit., pp. 59–61.

161. See the report of this conference in *Parichay*, Kartik, 1357/1950 (Under the heading 'Samskriti Sambad').

162. Surama Ghatak, *Ritwik*, Kolkata: Asha Prakashani, 1384/1977.

163. Though, ironically, it is rumoured that Ritwik Ghatak engineered Utpal Dutta's expulsion from the IPTA on the charge of 'Trotskyite deviation'. See Arup Mukhopadhyay, *Utpal Dutta: Jiban o Srishti*, Delhi: NBT, 2010, p. 72.

164. Interview Narahari Kaviraj.
165. Report in *Unity*, June 1951.
166. Mangala Charan Chattopadhyay, 'Eso Shantir Janya', *Parichay*, Baisakh, 1359/1952 (With illustrations by Debabrata Mukherjee), and Nibaran Chakrabarty, 'Shantir Dake Samskriti Karmider Samabesh', *Natun Sahitya*, Baisakh, 1359/1952.
167. Interview, Narahari Kaviraj.

2

The Music of Politics and the Politics of Music

The People's Song: An Heir to the Swadeshi Song

IN HIS PREFACE to the book *Salil Chowdhuryr Gan* (Salil Chowdhury's Songs).[1] Hemanga Biswas, another composer-singer of the period of our study, said, 'the People's Song (*Ganasangeet in* Bengali) is born at the confluence, where the stream of patriotism flows into the ocean of internationalism of the proletariat'. So far as the educated class of Bengal was concerned, the People's Song was indeed a successor to the patriotic or swadeshi songs. There was a time when the political and social thoughts of the Bengalis generally revolved around the problem of national subjugation. The agony of a subordinated nation produced numerous swadeshi songs from the days of the Hindu Mela.[2] The largest number of such songs was composed during the Anti-Partition or Swadeshi Agitation in the first decade of the twentieth century. The songs of Rabindranath, Rajanikanta, Atul Prasad, Dwijendralal, Nazrul, Govinda Das and Mukunda Das[3] captivated the minds of the patriotic Bengalis. Then from about the 1920s, a new dimension of social consciousness was added to patriotism, in which elements of Aryanism and Hindu revivalism were largely absent.

As far back as 1872, a journal entitled *Bharat Sramajibi* (Indian Workers) published a song by Sibnath Sastri—'Get up, wake up, brother workers'. But this is only a stray example of the *bhadralok* concern for the workers and it did not allow much initiative to the workers as a moving force of history.[4] Just before the beginning of the period of our study, Kaji Nazrul Islam broke away from the confines of narrow anti-British sentiments and expressed in his songs an urge for the liberation of peasants and workers. His 'Song of the Worker' and 'Song of the Peasant' (1926), his tribute to the Russian Revolution—'Behold, the norwester is blowing the banner of the new', his translation of the 'Internationale'[5] and of the song of the British workers—'People's flag is deepest red'—all these[6] and many more set a trend which undoubtedly influenced the later People's Song Movement. Since the mid-1930s, with the strengthening of the political left, socialistic ideas made themselves more markedly felt in all spheres of cultural activities, including the composition of songs.

Hemanga Biswas later recollected that around 1929, as a boy living in the village Hobigunge of Sylhet, he used to sing in procession Hari Moktar's song:

> *Mother Chhinnamasta!*[7]
> *Be incarnated in your formidable appearance.*
> *We shall flush your scarlet feet with our blood.*[8]

Hindu religious symbols, including the concept of Mother Goddess as supreme principle of *shakti* or prowess, abounded in swadeshi songs.

Among Biswas's other favourite songs of that time were Najrul's 'Say "Ma Bhoi" (Shed fear), brother', Kaliprasanna Kabyavisarad's 'You try to make us forget our mother by caning us! Are we such sons of the mother?', Tagore's 'Cry out "Mother" but once', and, the *Jatra* songs of Mukunda Das. Another song he liked very much was by Gobinda Das:

> *You call this your own country,*
> *But this country is not yours.*
> *The field yonder, full of crops,*
> *Does not belong to you at all.*
> *You are just entitled to its cultivation*
> *And not to its consumption.*

We know how later, under the influence of Marxian ideology, Biswas' thoughts about labour and consumption broadened beyond a mere desire for political independence.

Priti Banerjee (née Sarkar), the golden-voiced singer of the Central Squad of the IPTA, said in an interview[9] that it was the natonalist movement that had launched her on her music career. While a student at her school at Rajshahi, she used to join the *Prabhat Pheri* (morning procession) singing D.L. Roy's famous song: 'The earth of ours is full of riches, crops and flowers/ And one country here is the best of all countries'. Then, one day, she came across a CPI pamphlet containing Benoy Roy's song: 'Wake up, Indians! How long will you go on sleeping?' Thus started a new phase of her life.

The composer Benoy Roy himself was a convert from revolutionary terrorism to Communism. He, along with his brother, used to work for the Jugantar Party, while their father was a Congress leader. Then he joined the trade union movement from where he enrolled himself as a member of the CPI and became one of its most enthusiastic cultural activists. The history of People's Songs succeeding swadeshi songs runs parallel to the history of nationalism broadening into socialism.[10]

This is true of some folk-singers as well. Ramesh Seal, a barber's son from a Chittagong village, wrote during the Assam-Bengal Railway strike of 1921:

We can't keep quiet any more
Under Jatindrababu's leadership[11]
The wheels of the trains
Will be stopped.
The United strength of the workers
Will make the rail tracks gather rust
You fill your stomach with our blood
And dare to call us 'Damn bloody'!

Likewise he responded to the Khilafat Movement, the Chittagong Armoury Raid and other political events of the 1920s and 1930s. Then in the 1940s, he came to the forefront of the People's Song Movement singing ovations to workers and peasants and mourning the death of thousands of famished people. Such examples can be multiplied.

II

But even after conversion to the new ideology, the composers carried on many features of the swadeshi songs into the People's Song Movement: the longing for a golden past, bemoaning the present plight, the urge to fight for salvation and a call for unity. Even in language, symbols, imagery and tune, some of the People's Songs testified to the powerful influence of the swadeshi songs. The urge for freedom was no less powerful in People's Songs, though here the concept often acquired a social dimension. Many instances of such resemblances can be cited; for example the 'Song of the Independence Day' starting with the line 'Dukher rater ghor tamasa bhedi swadhinata dibas elo je phire' (the Independence Day has come once again piercing the dark night of sorrows) written by Hemanga Biswas on the occasion of 26 January, which used to be celebrated as Independence Day at that time:

Wake up, citizens, wake up.
Mother India is crying in her shackles
Longing for emancipation.[12]

Then the song said that as long as the famished people cried from hunger, the sacrifices of the martyrs of the freedom movement would go to waste. It was the first song of Biswas's verse book *Bishan* (The Bugle, 1944) on the front cover of which a bracket contained the words 'Swadhinatar Gan' (Songs of Independence). This particular song was based on *Iman Rag*, which was very popular with the composers of swadeshi songs. In fact, it very much reminds us of Tagore's popular swadesi song 'Aji Bangladesher hriday hote kakhan apani'.

Another song by Biswas in the context of the distress caused by the War and the Famine:

Where is that Bengal,
Profusely watered and abounding in crops,
With clouds hanging like her hair,
Mountains, fields and rivers girdling her like ornaments,
Bengal, the mother of heroes,
Bengal with her incandescent smile?
Doels and shyamas[13] *sing no longer,*
No more heard are pastoral songs.
Nor is the Bhatiali of the boatmen.
Only the roaring laughter of ghosts!
Your country is still being ruled by foreigners.
In your sky are thundering the Japanese aeroplanes.
Black-marketeers, greedy and wicked,
Are cheating their own country.
Hey patriots, can't you hear the dead
Souls crying fie upon you?
Hold aloft the sword of unity
And remove this stigma.[14]

It strongly resembles the old swadeshi songs in its passion for the flora and fauna of the motherland, the use of rhetoric, the metre-composition, etc.

Then again, the call for women's awakening that had marked the swadeshi songs, featured in People's Songs. Sometimes even the language is nearly identical. For instance, Ramesh Seal's:

Wake up, Indian women!
With your awakening India will be independent.
Awake yourself, mother, and wake everyone up!
You incarnation of power!

In his introduction to *Janayuddher Gan* (Songs of People's War)[15] Benoy Roy traded the development of People's Songs to the history of the swadeshi songs. The book was an Anti Fascist Writers' and Artists' Association (AFWAA) publication. The organization published another book *Jatiya Sangeet* (Songs of the Nation),[16] a collection of patriotic songs by Rangalal, Bankim Chandra, Rabindranath, Nazrul and also People's

Songs by younger poets like Jyotirindra Moitra and Subhas Mukherjee. In the preface to this book and in his review of it in *Janayuddha*, Hiren Mukherjee described People's Songs as a vector of the tradition of the swadeshi songs in enriched and more coherent idiom, with an added resolve to resist fascism and express the multifarious sufferings and the hard struggle of the masses of people.[17]

A New Generation of Composers and Singers

From 1937, the branches of the Bengal Progressive Writers' Association started operating all over Bengal. Its local branches used to encourage the singing of progressive songs at their meetings and functions, songs mostly of Tagore and Najrul. According to Sudhi Pradhan, Apurba Mukherji of Calcutta and Rabi Majumdar of Jessore used to sing inspiring Najrul songs (e.g. 'Wake up, peasants all over the world, hold your ploughs tight') at meetings of peasants and workers during the late 1930s.[18] About this time, many composers started composing new songs with an urge to reach peasants and workers. Particularly those inclined to leftist politics and residing in the mofussil felt a close affinity with the peasants. Benoy Roy of Rangpur and Hemanga Biswas of Sylhet are good examples. 'By 1938–9, *kisan-majur* had already figured in my songs', says Biswas, 'It is with a marked influence of Nazrul in language and tune that I wrote':

March forward, workers and peasants!
Listen, bugles are sounding in the battle-field.[19]

It is the Youth Cultural Institute (YCI) that for the first time consciously tried to forge a People's Song Movement.[20] The young members of the organization started this movement with a small stock of patriotic songs by Tagore and Nazrul. The two other songs that they sang very often were 'Jhanda uncha rahe hamara' (Our flag is flying aloft) and 'Hindustan hamara hai' (Hindustan is ours). Soon they started composing songs for themselves. Of these, the most famous was Jolly Kaul's:

Mazdoor, mazdoor, mazdoor hai ham
Sari duniaki raja hai ham.

(We are workers,
We are the monarch of the whole world).

It was set to music by Nikhil Sen.

The boys and girls of the YCI drew inspiration from the anti-Japanese song movement led by Ni-Eh-Erh in China, about which Epstein had spoken eloquently in his book *People's War*.

The roof of a house at Ballygunge Place, belonging to Arpita Das, a table tennis champion, was the place for their rehearsal. Among those who used to come were Debabrata Biswas, Dilip Roy, Sadhana Bose (later Roy Chowdhuri), Nivedita Bose (later Das), Binata Bose (later Roy), Uma Chakravarty (later Sehenabis), Nikhil Sen, and Dwijen Chowdhuri. The themes of their songs were generally based on current problems, and tunes were forceful and easy to learn. They contributed considerably towards popularizing community songs in Bengal. All this and excellent team-work won them rapid popularity. At functions they used to ask the audience to join them. Once, at the Ashutosh Memorial Hall, Pahari Sanyal, the renowned film artist, got so enthused, that he mounted the dais to sing 'Mazdoor, mazdoor, mazdoor, hai ham' with them.

Calcutta, the cultural nerve of Bengal, was naturally the meeting place of artistic talents from all over Bengal. Thus, this metropolis brought together Benoy Roy, Hemanga Biswas, Jyotirindra Moitra, Debabrata Biswas and a host of other exponents of People's Songs. The growing intimacy among them created in them a sense of purpose and stimulated their creative urge. The interest of the young Marxist Jyotirindra had till then been confined to Indian and Western classical music and he himself used to sing songs of Tagore in the main. Then, as he recollects,

> One morning, I was at home, 5, S.R. Das Road, arguing sharply about Christopher Caudwell, with my younger brother Rathin Moitra and a young friend of his. Suddenly a resonant and powerful voice rang out from the neighbouring house. I must admit, I had never heard such a voice before. The song was—'Hoi, hoi, hoi'. Our debate stopped abruptly. We listened intently to the song. This was followed by another song from that marvellous voice—'Sharpen your sickle well, O Kisan brother'. I got a feel of the direction that our songs could take, of the road lying ahead.[21]

Then Jyotirindra Moitra came to know Benoy Roy, who had been singing those songs—the first one composed by Roy himself and the second one by Hemanga Biswas. Together they proceeded along the same melodious path.

When the CPI became legal in 1942, there was a spate of activities. Of all anti-fascist meetings, festivals, fairs and processions arranged by Friends of the Soviet Union, Mahila Atmaraksha Samity, All-India Student's Federation, All-India Kisan Sabha, Anti-Fascist Writers' and Artists' Association and other leftist organizations, People's Songs were an essential part. Leftist journals like *Janayuddha* and *People's War* carried reports of these meetings. Above all, there was the IPTA, founded in 1943. One of its principal tasks was to forge a People's Song Movement in this country.

The young enthusiasts sang songs everywhere—on roads and in buses. A popular song was Subhas Mukherjee's 'Raise your voice of thunder'. But the poet himself was utterly unable to follow the right tunes, and Bijan Bhattacharya writes,

> But his out-of-tune voice always encouraged us with its hearty intrusion. We used to return home by the last tram after finishing the day's work of the Association (IPTA), singing militant IPTA songs. Arun Mitra, Swarnakamal Bhattacharya, Jyotirindra Moitra, and of course, Subhas, and a host of others would join us. Sometimes even the tram conductors would join in. Everybody had a right to participate in the chorus.[22]

Bijan Bhattacharya himself was a talented composer. We will talk later about his songs such as 'Amla Jamlar Gan' and 'Damukdiar Chachar Gan'.

In those days, No. 46 Dharmatala Street used to vibrate with such songs. Benoy Roy, Hemanga Biswas, Jyotirindra Moitra, composers and singers from the mofussil, and accomplished musicians like Jananprakash Ghosh, Sachin Dev Barman and Sukhendu Goswami used to frequent this place. Jnanprakash Ghosh was the leading musician at many musical demonstrations at No. 46. Harindranath Chatterjee, the celebrated brother of Sarojini Naidu, taught here many of his own songs: 'Surya ast ho gaya' (The Sun has Set), 'Ab nabhme pataka nachta hai' (The Flag is Dancing in the Sky), etc. Harindranath had been arrested for his song 'Suru hui hai jang hamara' (Our War has Started) during the Civil Disobedience Movement. This song too was now sung with its last line slightly altered. Earlier it had been, 'We shall save India, we shall place her high in the universe, / We shall make the venomous white snake dance to our own tune'. Now in the place of 'white snake' they sang 'fascist snake'.[23]

Jyotirindra Moitra's 'Nabajibaner Gan' (The Song of a New Life), a grand musical drama of thirty-three songs, was perhaps the most famous composition on the Famine of 1943. It was a beautiful blend of folk and classical music. Many used to claim proudly that since Tagore, no one had shown such great musical talent. It gives a panoramic view of a society gripped by a terrible Famine. There are seven groups of singers appearing one by one in the drama. The first group believes in life. They defy death. The second group consists of political activists whose attention is drawn to the third group—starving peasants. The next group is full of life. They are eager to work hard in order to remove all miseries. The fifth group comes as a contrast to the others. They are dissociated from reality and engaged in day-dreams. Then come factory workers and coolies as representatives of the people. They want to face and fight the reality. The last is the group of doctors giving new assurance of life. In the end, 'there will be the sharp sound of the breaking of shackles—the notation of thunder acquired through the newly-won right of the people deprived for long.'[24]

Jyotirindra's 'Come, open the door of darkness', a song of lasting popularity, is a good example of how immediate need gave birth to songs of a high quality. Sitting in a damp room of the Gupta Press of Beniatola Street, Jyotirindra extemporized an inaugural song for a meeting due to be held at the University Institute Hall that evening. It unmistakably reveals the creative passion of the leftist youths of the time:

We have raised the Lakshmi of life
By churning the ocean of death.
The new world asks for the artist's assurance
At this auspicious moment of creation.
Come unto the equality and unity of Association.
Come unto the friendship of the masses.
Come piercing the darkness of sorrows,
Destroying the cruel fear of destruction.
Come, fill up the citadel of life.

Hiren Mukherjee has recollected the history of this song in his autobiographical *Tari Hote Teer* (*From the Boat to the Beach*) and said that this was probably the first People's Song to be recorded by any Gramophone Company. Jyotirindra's other compositions—the 'Song of the Soil', the 'Song of the Procession', the 'Song of the Storm', etc., also testify to his musical talent.

Another name that was on the lips of everyone connected with the Communist cultural movement was George (Debabrata) Biswas. He has been compared to Paul Robeson as a mass-singer. A devout leftist, he charmed the audience everywhere with his passionate and barytone voice. Hemanga Biswas thus paid tribute to him after his death:

> His music was a 'declaration of faith'. The red flag actually fluttered in his voice, when he sang Harindranath Chattopadhyay's 'Ab nabhme pataka nachta hai, bahre uska rang'. His rendering of 'Karbate badalta hua jamana', set to tune by Pankaj Mallik, stirred the huge audience at the Ahmedabad IPTA conference in 1947. Sukanta's 'Abak Prithibi' (The strange world), set to music by Salil Chowdhury, seemed to have been composed for none else than Georgeda. Nobody else could utter 'abak' in the manner he did. Georgeda used to sing 'I'm at the front of these masses' instead of 'I'm behind these masses', and thus drew the poet to the forefront of the struggle.[25]

Debabrata Biswas' autobiography *Bratyajaner Ruddha Sangeet* (The Suppressed Song of an Outcast), particularly the chapter entitled 'Banyer

Rasta' (The Leftward Road) throws considerable light on the People's Song Movement.[26]

Among other exponents of People's Songs were Haripada Kusari, Paresh Dhar, Sujata, Supriya and Suchitra Mukherjee—the three sisters, the Nandi brothers—Bhupati and Surapati, Dilip Roy, Tripti Bhaduri who later preferred dramma as her medium and during the late 1940s, Salil Chowdhury, admittedly the greatest musical genius of the period. Many of the composers and singers of People's Songs did not belong to the CPI, did not even give much thought to Communism. But all of them must have been convinced of the sincerity of the Communist efforts and hence joined hands with them. Hiren Mukherjee as well as Sudhi Pradha gratefully remembered how Hemanta Mukherjee had taken great risks in participating in their functions even when the Party was illegal.

Among composers and singers who had their base outside Calcutta were Jiten Sen, a leader of the Krishak Sabha of Mymensingh; Himangshu Roy of Khulna, competent in both music and dance; Hemanga Biswas, Nirmalendu Chowdhury, Gopal Nandi, Shanta Sen (Roy) Barun, Lakshmi, Hena, Sundhya and many others forming a big musical squad in Sylhet, Sadhan Dasgupta and Satyen Sen of Dhaka composing People's Songs and even Ranesh Dasgupta, known more as a learned leader of the Dhaka PWA, composed songs occasionally: The singers of Dhaka included Kanu Laskar, Gour Basak, Beni Chakravarty, Sudha Roy, Harakali Acharya and Pratyaksha Dutta. Priti Banerjee and Alpana Gupta were two songstresses of Rajshahi. Bankim Sen, a leader of the Peasants' League in Chittagong, and Chittaprosad Bhattacharya of that district, better known for his contributions to pictorial art, composed songs in the local dialect. This is to name only a few of the middle-class exponents of People's Songs.[27] The genuine folk-singers are dealt with in a later section.

Gradually the Movement spread beyond the confines of a few talented leftist youths and reached the masses. Great efforts were made to spread the People's Song Movement throughout the length and breadth of Bengal. Middle-class men and women, students, workers and peasants alike contributed to the spread. But more about this later.

The Bengal Squad and the Central Squad of the IPTA

In May 1943, a select group of musicians and dramatists led by Benoy Roy went to Bombay in order to attend the inaugural conference of the IPTA. This event occasioned a cultural festival on 25 May at the

Damodar Hall. One of its main items was songs presented by the Bengal Squad. These songs enthralled the audience.

Bombay also hosted the first congress of the CPI about the same time. At the Red Flag Fair arranged by the Party on this occasion on 29 May, the Bengal Squad presented Benoy Roy's 'Guerrilla Song' (Hoi, hoi, hoi) and the 'Kisan's Call' in chorus. There was also a Hindi ballad on the theme of People's War. It had been composed by Rahaman, a tramway worker of Calcutta. This too was highly appreciated. The inaugural songs were all Tagore's and their lead singer was Debabrata Biswas. In the Red Flag Cultural Contest, Bengal came second in order of merit, with Andhra winning the first position.[28]

Towards the end of 1943, the 'Voice of Bengal' Squad (originally named 'Punjab Squad') went on a tour of Punjab to rouse the conscience of the people there in regard to the Famine-stricken people of Bengal. Benoy Roy was the squad leader. Harindranath Chatterjee was in charge of its cultural activities. Other members were Bhupati Nandi, Dasarathlal, Sadhana Guha (later Sen), Naren Bhattacharya and Usha Dutta (later Singh). They arranged shows at several places in Punjab, Delhi and Agra from 17 November to 27 December. Sudhi Pradhan possessed a detailed report prepared by Benoy Roy about the venues and dates of these functions, the class-composition and the size of the audience in each case, and also about the amount of collection and the organizing agencies. This report in the form of a table is appended to this chapter. According to Roy, they were able to raise Rs. 32,472, 30 maunds of grain, 25 pieces of ivory bangles, a pair of silver bangles and lots of gold ornaments in all. More than 10,000 people were claimed to have attended these shows.

The squad singing 'Ham tumhari purab duari Bangalka insan' (We are the people of your eastern gateway—Bengal) and appealing to every 'Hindke rahnewale' (Indian) to stand by the Bengalis in their distress,[29] was indeed richly rewarded not so much by money, as by the warm love of a large number of people. Their songs moved some peasant women of Punjab to throw on to the dais the ornaments they had been wearing. An old peasant handed them Rs. 2, his only provision for the next day. The feeble-looking little girl Sadhana Guha (Sen) singing 'Bhukha hai Bangal' so moved some peasant women that they took her to their hut and persuaded her to drink a potful of milk. A tailor's wife of Punjab gave away her precious conch bangles (the last mark borne on her person to indicate that her husband was alive) and the auction of these bangles fetched Rs. 1,100. Soldiers attending their open-air performances requested their commanders to organize shows at army camps.[30]

Another achievement of the squad was to impress the famous dancer Uday Shankar and this was to benefit them a great deal in the near future. Shankar was staying in Delhi and on 24 December 1943, Benoy Roy and some other squad members called on him. Roy wrote to Sudhi Pradhan about this memorable meeting. Uday Shankar liked the nature of their work. His eyes lit up when they introduced to him their gifted percussionist Dasarathlal, a tram conductor of Calcutta. He told them of his eagerness to get to the masses, but confessed that he could not do it on account of his constant worry about money needed to run his Almorah Institute. He asked them to keep in touch, and to write in detail to Rajen, his younger brother, who was in charge of the Institute. He proposed a sort of cultural exchange between his own troupe and the Bengal Squad.[31]

In January 1944, the IPTA organized a couple of Uday Shankar's shows at the famous Parel Maidan, Bombay. Tickets were sold at a cheap rate (4 annas), mainly to the working population of the city and Shankar handed over the entire collection (Rs. 3,700) to the People's Relief Committee.[32] At Ahmedabad, at a felicitation given to him by the Friends of the Soviet Union, he expressed his admiration for the work and the spirit of the IPTA.[33]

In the meantime the Voice of Bengal Squad had returned to Calcutta and attended the AFWAA conference, 15–16 January 1944. Benoy Roy's dance-drama 'Main Bhukha Hun', songs of Nirmalendu Chowdhury, a recruit of the Sylhet IPTA, Panu Pal's '*Hunger Dance*' and the songs of Reba, Benoy Roy's sister, were greatly applauded.[34]

Next, the Bengal Squad went to attend the All-India Kisan Conference at Bezwada. Here also they were successful. Again Andhra and Bengal were placed first and second, respectively, in the Cultural contest. Usha Dutta of Bengal stood first personally.[35]

The Voice of Bengal Squad then toured Bombay, Gujarat and Maharashtra. Benoy Roy led the music section and Sambhu Mitra the drama section. This time, the members were Bhupati Nandi, Satyajiban Bhattacharya, Usha Dutta, Panu Pal, Reba Roy and Dasrathlal. As usual, praises were showered on them. Hindi and Gujarati versions of Bijan Bhattacharya's drama *Jabanbandi*, a number of songs and dances, particularly the '*Mahabubhuksha Dance*' (Great Hunger Dance) constituted their programme.

The appreciative audience included Bhulabhai Desai, Sarojini Naidu, Vijaya Lakshmi Pandit, Prithviraj Kapoor and other prominent personalities. Reba Roy Chowdhury recalled later that during a public performance at the Maratha Centenary Hall (near Charni Station, Bombay) the famous film star Prithviraj Kapoor had said in an impassioned voice

'Brothers, I too want to do something for Bhukha Bengal'. Then he went to the audience with his hat in his hand and collected Rs. 17,000.[36] Khwaja Ahmed Abbas used to write the last page of the *Bombay Chronicle* under the pen-name of 'Chronicler'. There he admired the above-mentioned show at the Maratha Centenary Hall and another at the Cowasji Jahangir Hall for a perfect merger of art and propaganda.[37]

II

The journey terminated at Bombay. Uday Shankar's Almorah Centre had closed down and he had moved over to this city. The Bengal Squad, some members of Uday Shankar's Troupe and the Bombay IPTA jointly produced a ballet *Save Bengal*. It was directed by Shanti Kumar Bardhan, the famous Tipra Dance specialist, and the musician Abani Dasgupta, both from Uday Shankar's Troupe. This was the beginning of a long-term cooperation. The encouragement of Shankar and the initiative of the IPTA led to the formation of the Central Squad of the IPTA. Abani Dasgupta and Shanti Kumar Burdhan became the squad's dance and music teachers respectively at Shankar's behest. A number of artists of the Bengal Squad stayed back to work for the new squad. Benoy Roy became its Secretary. Other artists from Bengal were Usha Dutta, Reba Roy, Bhupati Nandi, Gouri Dutta (Chittagong) and Dasrathlal. There were also Prem Dhawan (Punjab), Nemi Chand Jain, Rekha Jain (UP), Appuni, Gangadharan (Malabar), Reddi (Andhra—he was a student of Visva-Bharati), Santa Gandhi, Dina Pathak, Guniel Hasan (Gujarat) and others. The CPI entrusted the work of liaison to Parvati Krishnan.

Within a few months, Sachin Shankar, a cousin and student of Uday Shankar, came to Bombay in order to try his luck in the cine world. He too was attracted by the Central Squad and joined it. Talented artists like the sitarist Ravi Shankar, a brother of Uday Shankar, Balraj Sahni, Naren Sharma and Kaifi Azmi joined the squad. Abani Dasgupta's brother Sushil, drummer and flutist, came soon. Priti Sarkar was brought over from Rajshahi and a girl named Ruby Dutta from Chittagong.

A large garden house was located at Andheri, sixteen miles from Bombay. Their commune life there has been compared to the collective and austere training that the students of ancient India received at their masters' houses. The food, which they cooked themselves, was simple. Everyone had to sweep the floor and wash the utensils in turn. Along with the rigorous artistic training they had to undergo political training as well, hawking *People's War* on the streets and participating in public meetings and processions.

And above all, it was a festival of creativity. They produced two excellent ballets—first, *Spirit of India*, directed by Shanti Bardhan (1944), then after Ravi Shankar came, *India Immortal*, under the latter's direction (1946). Many more songs and dances were produced. Among them a famous one was Iqbal's 'Sare jahanse achha' (The best of all lands) set to tune by Ravi Shankar. In his reminiscences *Rag Anurag* Ravi Shankar complained that the fanaticism of the Party members had caused him discomfort at Andheri, but in the same breath he said, 'On the whole, I spent that time delightfully. It presented a great opportunity for me to experiment with tunes to my heart's content.'[38] Later they produced three more ballets—*Gandhi Jinnah, Phir Mile* (Gandhi Jinna, Meet Again), *The New Village* (related to the peasant movements) and another on the RIN Mutiny. All of these became popular in and around the city of Bombay. The Bombay government banned the last one soon after it had been produced.[39]

Artists from Calcutta used to visit the place frequently. Jyotirindra Moitra often went there to teach his 'Nabajibaner Gan; as a 'visiting professor'. Debabrata Biswas too stayed as a guest for some time.[40]

In 1947, when the whole Communist cultural movement was facing a crisis, attacked from outside and undermined from within, the Central Squad was wound up. It has been alleged that the socialist Mayor, Minoo Masani, did not like them and that the local Congress workers harassed them. That there was a tension within the Central Squad is evident from the complaint of some artists about the attempt of the Party to impose its political line on them[41] and from some Partymen's allegation that some artists were opportunistic, devoid of political awareness and lacking the firmness of character needed to lead a commune life, particularly with girls.[42] The immediate reason for the dissolution of the Central Squad was its huge expenses which the Party was unable to meet. Moreover, by that time, some Party members had became impatient with any kind of meticulous care for music as an art form, which, they thought, would alienate the artists from the people, and the Central Squad seemed to them to be gradually moving away from the people. So the Party did not need it any more.[43]

Themes of the War-Time Songs

One of the major themes of the People's Songs of the war period, till about the Famine, was resistance to the Japanese. Benoy Roy's guerrilla song, 'Hoi hoi hoi', though written in the dialect of Rangpur, northern Bengal, became popular all over the province:

Hark, hark, hark!
The Japs are coming to our village
Come out, you young guerrillas,

Come Rahim, come Rahaman,
Come Jogesh, Come Paran,
Come out Hindus and Muslims all.

Subhas Mukherjee's:

Raise your thunder voice
We shall resist the dacoits today.
The Japanese aeroplanes
Would not throw Swaraj as a gift to India.

A number of songs were composed by Dayal Kumar, a *Panchali*-singer of Hooghly: 'Listen, soldiers! The drum of the war of freedom is sounding/ it is good that the soil of Bengal has been stained with the blood of the Bengalees', 'Come running, if you want to resist the Japanese wild boar' (a song to be sung to the accompaniment of *Madal*) or 'Hey workers and peasants! the banner of the war has been hoisted' (an imitation of Najrul's 'Break and destroy the iron gate of the prison'); then a song popular among the workers of the Narayangunj textile mills: 'Bugles are sounding/Soldiers, get ready!' or a favourite song of the Rangpur comrades: 'Let us go to the anti-Jap war together'. Many more such instances may be cited.

Then came the ghastly Famine. Human skeletons lying everywhere, corpses holding a feast for vultures, parents selling their children, women's modesty being outraged, exodus from villages to the city, people begging pathetically for a little *phen* (the water in which the rice had been cooked), the ripe crop rotting on the field in the absence of able-bodied men to harvest it—such painful experiences gave birth to a rich crop of songs.

We have already referred to Jyotirindra Moitra's musical drama *Nabajibaner Gan*. The poet's compunction at the sight of God's children dying like ants made him protest vigorously:

Nay! Never shall we accept this.
Millions of death we shall buy
with the price of our lives.
Live we won't in the kingdom of fear.

This was the central theme of the music drama.

Haripada Kusari's 'How do you expect to live by indulging in factionalism,/When death is knocking at your door' was another popular one. Among locally popular songs on the Famine were Hemanga Biswas's 'Song of the Epidemic of Baniachang' and Chittaprosad's account of the sufferings of a peasant's wife in a typical Chittagong dialect. The latter starts with a recollection of her happy past:

I had my home at Satkania,
My husband was a peasant.
I had four oxen for ploughing the field
And a barnful of paddy.
Listen, mothers and sisters

While analysing the sufferings of the Famine victims, the composers generally blamed the blackmarketeers, hoarders and money-lenders. They blamed the British in some cases. But this seems to have lacked the force of conviction. At that time the People's War policy of the CPI called for cooperation with the government.

The Japanese aggrandizement was described most of the time as a bid to wrest the freedom of an independent country. Some times the composers went a roundabout way asking the people to win freedom by defeating the Japanese. The last stanzas of Benoy Roy's famous 'Hoi hoi hoi' and Subhas Mukherjee's 'Raise your voice of thunder' were respectively:

Let any son of a bitch come
We shall chop him fine
And we shall be independent,
We, kisans all.

And

We are not a race of cowards,
We shan't allow our country to pass into
Another's hand.
If we fail to strike today
Never shall the posterity forgive us.

It was always difficult to reason out the connection between driving out the Japanese and acquiring independence. Yet the songs were on the whole forceful. There must have been some earnestness in the patriotism of the composers. And at least the Famine songs were based on the immediate experience of a gruesome reality.

Except for the call to resist the Japanese, there was not much militancy in the war-time songs. Some of them, of course, tried to incite the anger of the masses against hoarders and money-lenders. For instance:

They thrive on the country's woes,
Yet they smile,
Seize these disguised devils
Of the blackmarket.
Listen, ye Indians![44]

Only in a handful of songs were the hoarders, the government and the Japanese blamed alike:

When the country is bewailing
The hoarders are profiteering
The government is sleeping unperturbed
The government is betraying the country
The Jap dacoits have taken this opportunity
to make a raid upon us
We are between the crocodile in the water
and the tiger on land.[45]

But even in this song there was just a suggestion that mere unity could provide the way out of the impasse. In fact, almost all the songs of the period could think of unity alone as a redress. Pradyot Guha wrote:

Your freedom struggle starts today
Take up arms.
You don't have bombs and bullets,
Your weapon is unity.

By unity they meant Hindu-Muslim unity, Congress-League unity and even unity between the *amir* and the *fakir.*[46] Class struggle was put off for the time being. Satyen Sen's 'Unite Congress and League/ Join hands' became popular in quite a few districts. Benoy Ray called upon all to unite and thwart the enemies:

Suno Hindke Rahnewals, suno, suno
Tum Hindu ho, ya Muslim ho
Aorat marad, amir fakir,
Sabhi tum suno suno.

(Listen, all inhabitants of Hindustan,
Be ye Hindu, be ye Muslim,
Man, woman, well-off or beggar,
Listen, all of you.)

Apart from unity in general terms, formation of People's Relief Committees, (Women's) Self-Defence Committees, Peasants' Committees and Cooperative Food Committees were also suggested. Peasants were asked to produce more crops, workers to produce more goods, railway workers to run the trains properly, in order to help the British war efforts and to ameliorate their own conditions. The songs of *Janayuddher Gan* and *Bishan* were full of such suggestions.

Many songs appealed to the public to help the victims of the Famine—for example, Benoy Roy's 'Take upon your shoulder the responsibility of feeding the hungry' or Kanak Mukherjee's 'Song of Begging for a Handful of Rice'. But, except for providing relief to the victims, they could not think of any effective solution to the Famine situation. Jyotirindra Moitra advised the peasants to go back to their villages. In his opinion, this would bring about happy days for both the city and the village. Hemanga Biswas even wrote the 'Song of the Spinning Wheel' about this time, upholding the Gandhian solution to India's problems.

Along with Japan, they also denounced Italy and Germany, and extolled Russia and China. For instance, in *Bishan*, 'Bravo, bravo, Great China/Your resolute struggle for freedom is without a parallel' and the 'Song of the Soviet Red Army', Satyen Sen's 'Bravo Russia, a chip of the old block' and 'The skilled boatman Soviet is steering the boat' or Benoy Roy's 'Bravo, brother China', composed on the occasion of China Day.

Sadhan Dasgupta poked fun at Hitler after the latter's discomfiture at Stalingrad:

O let go, brother Stalin!
I touch your feet,
Let me go,
I—the Aryan Hitler—am dying of shame.

This song set to the roof-ramming tune of Dhaka, became very popular.

Subhas Chandra Bose and as a matter of fact, all Indians ready to welcome the Japanese directly or indirectly, were branded as the Fifth Column. One of the songs based on the theme of such denouncement was by Tarapada Bhowmick:

I was the much esteemed Subhasbabu in my country,
So I took the opportunity to betray her.

There were songs specially meant for teenagers, students and women. Kanak Mukherjee wrote many such songs—I found quite a few of them in an old exercise book belonging to Hemanga Biswas and some were collected in Mukherjee's own book *Desrakshar Dak*. Biswas wrote a few songs for students and march songs too. One of them was set to the tune of a popular film song of that time—'Proceed, young heroes'. He wrote some songs specially for women, to be sung to the rhythm of *Dhamail* dance of Sylhet. His exercise book also contains Nazrul's 'Awake women, the burning flame'.

Then there was applause for workers and peasants and for the ideology of Communism. Kshetra Chatterjee wrote: 'Wake up, people almighty' (*Malkosh*). A Kirtan song of Dulal Chand of Hooghly: 'Come to this assembly of Marx and Engels'.

Some specific events were documented in songs. Four young Kisan leaders of the village Kayyur of Malabar were hanged on 29 March 1943, on a false charge of murder (which shows that even during the People's War period all was not well with the relationship between the Communists and the British government). A number of songs were dedicated to these martyrs. The most famous of them was Benoy Roy's: 'Give back, O give back, our Kayyur friends'. The song ended on an angry note: 'In exchange of four Kayyurs, we want thousands of them'[47] Dayal Kumar composed a *Panchali* on Kayyur brothers. Sadhan Dasgupta's 'Peasant, give your red salute to the red flag' was on the same theme.

Sadhan Dasgupta addressed the martyr Somen Chanda in another song: 'Alas, who floods the street with the blood of your heart?' [48]

Old Swadeshi Songs and Foreign Songs

Along with the recently-composed People's Songs, old swadeshi songs too were heard at the processions and meetings of the leftists. From *Jatiya Sangeet* published by AFWAA, we can form an idea about the kind of swadeshi songs that they preferred. Among the forty songs compiled here only eleven were recently composed People's Songs by Benoy Roy, Jyotirindra Moitra and others, twenty-nine were old patriotic songs: Rangalal's 'Who cares to live without freedom?', Hemchandra's 'Bharat Sangeet', Govinda Chandra Roy's 'How long will you take, India, to cross the ocean of sorrows?', songs by Satyendranath Tagore, Manomohan Bose, Rajanikanta Sen, Kamini Kumar Bhattacharya, Kaliprasanna Kavyabisarad, Bipin Chandra Pal, Sarala Devi Chaudhurani, Debabrata Bose, Dwijendralal Roy, Kamini Roy, Atul Prasad Sen, Sabitri Prasanna Chattopadhyay and Najrul Islam. There was also the 'Momin' song of the Mymensingh Suhrid Samity and of course, songs of Rabindranath—'Fear I won't', 'My golden Bengal, I love thee', 'The tighter they will bind us, the looser will be our bondage', 'The soil of Bengal, the water of Bengal'. These songs, eulogizing India, bemoaning her present condition and expressing a determination to obliterate all miseries, had been extremely popular in Bengal for quite some time. And even the new generation in a new situation and with a new outlook found them enchanting.

Among other Tagore songs patronized by them were 'Break the shackles', 'The bewilderment of hesitation is an insult to oneself', 'If you thwart us, we shall fight back', etc. On the cover of *Janayuddher Gan* was quoted Tagore's 'We have strung together thousand souls with one thread' and on the inside cover 'Oh my heart, wake up at this place of pilgrimage'. At a Sino-Indian Anti-Japanese Friendship meeting was heard: 'Delighting every country',[49] in a procession of writers and artists in a city devastated by communal riots—'A violence-torn world, gone berserk'[50] and also a solo from the melodious voice of Suchitra Mitra standing on a truck—'I feel gratified, mother, that I've been born in this country'.[51] 'For through famine or invasion, imperialist oppression or proletarian upsurge, the voice of Tagore remains the VOICE OF BENGAL, consoling, exhorting, the people of that great though unhappy land', commented K.A. Abbas on watching a show put up by the Voice of Bengal Squad in Bombay.[52] The show ended with Tagore's 'We have strung together thousand souls'. The popularity of Tagore songs among the leftists is evident from the fact that even their friends from abroad learnt some of these songs. In March 1942, at the MCA of College Street the performance of Tagore's '*Rather Rashi*' was followed by the rendering of Tagore's 'Do not fear, win we will, this door will open' in the voice of Arnold Bake, a Dutch friend.[53]

Even during 1948–50, when hostility to Rabindranath in the leftist circles had reached its peak, some Communist prisoners at the Dum Dum Jail proposed to sing a Tagore song to overcome despondency immediately after decrying Tagore. Chinmohan Sehanabis, who was being tormented at that time by an inner conflict between love for Tagore and allegiance to the Party, found it outrageously hypocritical and flew into a rage.[54]

Most of the times they altered the musical time, tempo, etc., of the old songs, thus giving them freshness and vigour. Jyotirindra Moitra recalls how Benoy Roy once told him: 'You know, what now goes on in the name of Rabindranath—a sort of namby-pamby expression, actually distorting Rabindranath . . . Come, let us choose a few vigorous Tagore songs and popularize them.' And they actually did it.[55] Debabrata Biswas also noted how some high-brow foreign-returned friends of his, who used to consider all Tagore songs dull and lifeless, had changed their opinion after hearing him at a function arranged by the Mahila Atmaraksha Samity. That very day Hemanga Biswas too came to him and admitted that never before had he experienced this intoxicating quality of Tagore songs.[56]

Swadeshi songs other than those of Rabindranath were also similarly adapted. At the inaugural conference of the IPTA, held in Damodar Hall, Bombay, on 25 May 1943, Bankimchandra's 'Bande Mataram' (I Salute Thee, Mother) was rendered in a novel tune. A critic asked, 'Is it an accident that a new and stirring version of 'Bande Mataram' is being sung; not like a nation weeping over and lamenting its fate, but like a nation girding itself for battle?'[57] Rangalal's 'Who cares to live without freedom' was set to tune afresh by Jyotirindra Moitra.[58] There are many more such examples.

II

Translations or adaptations of foreign songs were sometimes very popular.[59] Najrul's 'Internationale' was not based on the original tune. So Mohit Banerjee of the FSU translated it anew. There was a Hindi version too, composed by Harindranath Chatterjee and an Urdu version as well. At all their functions the leftists used to sing 'Internationale', sometimes in all the three languages.

Mohit Banerjee also translated the English song 'Soviet Land'. Benoy Roy composed a song based on Najrul's translation of 'People's flag is deepest red'. Harindranath Chatterjee translated in Hindi the famous 'La Marseillaise' of the French Revolution, keeping the original tune intact: 'Ab komar bandh, taiyar ho/Laksha koti bhaio'.

The YCI members used to sing English songs: the 'Red Army Song of Russia'—'Whirlwinds of danger are raging around us', the 'Red Cavalry Song'—'When the white Guards invaded' and the 'Song of the Partisans—'Through the winter's Cold and Famine'[60] (which was translated by Hemanga Biswas later in 1949). There were also 'At the call of Comrade Lenin' and 'Our engine rolls'. All these songs were originally in Russian.

There were Chinese songs as well. In the *People's War*, 15 November 1942, Hiren Mukherjee wrote of a cultural exchange evening that had given the Indians opportunity to learn a few guerrilla songs of China. Some of these were translated into Bengali.

The Post-War Period

A great awakening convulsed the country in the post-War period and the people rose in a last bid to liquidate the British Raj. The People's Songs reflected this militancy.

Hemanga Biswas wrote in memory of the martyrs of the INA Release Movement:

There they call—
Rameswar and Manoranjan
Kadam Rasul and Dhirranjan—
Don't you forget
The message written in blood
on the thoroughfares.[61]

The mutinous ratings of the Indian Navy too were eulogized in this song:

The streams of the sailors' blood
Has turned the blue ocean red.
They too have heard our call
And responded.

The song ends as follows:

Who wants a compromise with murderers?
We are a race wakeful,
Not faint-hearted.
The accumulated anger of thousands of souls
Surges for the last grim battle.

On 13 February 1946, the Rashid Ali Day,[62] the journal *Swadhinata* carried a message from Benoy Roy, 'A Victory Worth the Name' (to be sung in the style of Mukunda Das):

Workers, students and middle classes,
Millions of hearts turned into one,
Will snatch away the precious treasure,
Fighting shoulder to shoulder.
Let's solemnly resolve not to
be embroiled in fratricidal feuds.
Not to bear any longer
the unbearable agony of slavery.
Red, Green and Tricolour will march on together,
Subjugation and oppression will end.
The enormity of divisions will erode.
That will be a victory worth the name.

It is largely the threat of a massive and militant movement in India that prompted the British government to send three of its cabinet members to discuss with the Indian leaders the question of setting up an interim government and of the eventual transfer of power. A number of songs were written on the Cabinet Mission: 'Aya tin madari' (Three Jugglers Have Arrived) and many others. Benoy Roy lamented the prospect of secession of Kashmir from India as plotted by the Cabinet Mission:

Oh, Kashmir!
Where do you go leaving us behind?
We, who fight among ourselves
And flatter the rajah—

A letter written by Sachin Dev Barman from Bombay to Sudhi Pradhan (4 April 1947), informs us that three of Benoy Roy's songs were banned by the British, and according to Pradhan, this song was one of them.[63] Of course, that was a time when even Tagore songs could not be sung without permission from the police.

In the early months of 1946 the composers of People's Songs were busy campaigning in favour of the Communist candidates in the context of the coming elections to the provincial legislative assemblies; for instance Jiban Banerjee's call to establish a Majur-Kisan Raj in a song based on the roof-ramming tune.[64] But the best of these was perhaps Bijan Bhattacharya's 'Amla Jamlar Gan', where he ridiculed, most hilariously, the British Raj and its three courtiers—the bureaucrats, the zamindars and the mahajans, and also criticized the Congress and the Muslim League.[65]

But the call for a greater and the final battle had already been given. On 29 July 1946, a general strike was observed in sympathy with the strikers of the Post and Telegraph Department. Salil Chowdhury's memorable song written on that occasion was as follows:

Waves surge, jails break, the morning
dawns and souls awaken
Wheels of oppression will move no more, no more,
Black smoke will emanate from the Chimney,
no more, no more,
The funeral pyre will burn in the boiler
no more, no more
Thousands of hands are clapping strike,
Strike, strike, strike!
Strike today! Today the wheels have stopped![66]

It is true that very soon (from 16 August 1946 onwards) the terrible communal riot was to engage the attention of composers, and some of them tried to find a solution to the communal problem by demanding an agreement between Gandhi and Jinnah rather than through a united struggle from below. Still, it is the militancy and solidarity of popular struggle from the winter of 1945 onwards that led to the most glorious phase of the People's Song Movement.

From September 1946 started the Tebhaga Movement. Already in 1945, a peasant movement in his native village Sonarpur (24-Parganas)[67] had inspired Salil Chowdhury to write: 'Raise the red banner of freedom with your firm and alert hands'. Now he gave a call for Tebhaga:

On your guard! Guard your paddy,
Sharpen your sickle,
Upon our life and our honour

We are not going to surrender the paddy
Sown with our own blood.
We've recognized thee aright,
We know thee well.
Ain't you the black mahout of the white elephant?
Thousands of lives we've sacrificed in 1350,
Also the honour of our mothers and sisters.
Ain't you the one who illuminates the black market?

And also a call to follow the instances of 'Kamlapur Bara' and 'Kakdwip Dongajora':[68]

Let's go, brothers and friends,
Sons of Ram and Rahim,
On a mission of self-defence.
Let's harvest our crop. Whom do we care?
Let's fill up our own granary and sharpen our sickles.
If the enemy comes to raid at all,
We'll see that he meets a humiliating fate
And his greed for plunder is extinguished once for all.

Hemanga Biswas paid tribute to the martyrs of the Tebhaga Movement—

Many Sibrams and Samiruddins[69] *have sacrificed their*
Lives for their country.
Countless peasants have lost their sons.
Their deaths have enlivened this dead land.
They have united peasants and workers
with their blood.

Benoy Roy's call to avenge the killing of Sarojini and Ahalya of Chandanpniri[70]—'How long, Oh, how long shall we bear this death and insult?' It ends like this—

Mother Ahalya, your child remained unborn,
Today, every home suffers labour pain
for the unborn child.
On every field, there are talks
about the child
That will be born to kill hundred of Kamsa[71]

Ahalya a peasant's wife, who was pregnant at the time of her death, inspired a number of composers.

Kali Sarkar, a leader of the Tebhaga Movement in Dinajpur, composed a *Jang* song, while in the Rajshahi Jail in 1950. Later it was sung and appreciated at the Nanking Triumph Festival at Khapra. The militant style of *Jang*, which was sung by the Muslims during the Muharram and had as its theme the War of Karbala, eminently suited this Tebhaga song describing the heroic fight of Chiarsai against British police.[72]

Hemanga Biswas lamented the death of the Kisan comrade Madhavinath who had been imprisoned in the Silchar Jail (Biswas, being a son of Sylhet, was close to the cultural movement of north-east India)—

Oh martyr, we will never forget him
Who stained the dark jail with the blood of your heart!

But this was composed slightly later—in 1950. By that time, many changes had taken place. India had achieved Independence. The CPI rejected this independence as a false one and got itself banned. Hemanga Biswas wrote—

There comes the command from
Jalinabag and Jalalabad
Come here, wear your soldiers' uniform.
Your freedom struggle is not over yet.

Another one set to the tune of a *Jayantiya* song, was on the same theme and ended as follows—

This is a trap set by Imperialism,
A foundation laid by capitalism
Break it with all your might,
Here is the message for you
From Great China.

Sometimes, instead of 'Great China' they used to sing 'Telengana'.

The most popular song by Hemanga Biswas during this period was 'Mountbatten Mangalkavya'. He had heard a folksong sarcastically expressing the joy of the villagers at the death of their zamindar, and he parodied this song:

Oh Mountbatten Sahib!
To whom did you leave your precious baton?
Where have you gone, darkening your golden palace?
Sardar weeps, so do Pundit and Maulana,[73] *(Alack)*
Delhi is submerged in tears
Away drifts the broken Bengal

This long song with *Panchali*, *Kirtan*, satirical use of *Ramdhun*[74] and many other tunes was a highly effective one, particularly when it was sung by Debabrata Biswas at the sixth IPTA Conference of Allahabad, February 1949. The composer says: 'In 1951, the police arrested me and took me to their office in Lord Sinha Road. There a detective introduced me to an officer by saying, 'Sir this is the composer of Mountbatten.'

Even after the Party changed its line, became legal once again and started preparations for the coming elections, the dissatisfaction with the new regime continued. Bijan Bhattacharya's 'Chaturanga', a very long song published in *Natun Sahitya*,[75] was on this very theme.

The name that would be written in red letters in the history of this golden age of People's Songs is Salil Chowdhury. 'The language of protest, the fire of resistance' glowed in his song:

Take up arms in your robust hands
Raise the banner of blood.
The fate of Chiang's collaborators is sealed
Mao is ready at every home.

He called patriots to pay off the debts of Bhagat Singh, Surya Sen, Kadam Rasul and Rameswar—

Break the prison gate
Break it with a collective blow.

He was very good at sarcasms as well. A pot-bellied political leader says in one of his songs—

Who will remain there
To serve the motherland?
Considering this question,
I always tell people to die,
But have not died myself.

Or

My father was a fool
And I'm the son of my father
He was imprisoned for setting fire to
English piecegoods.
And you presented us with
An indigenous cord,
One end of which
Is tied with the gown.
We made a noose of the other end
And hanged ourselves from it.

One more instance of his sarcasm skill is the description of his visit to the 'Land of Spades' where cows live in multistoreyed buildings and men sleep in cowsheds.

His other famous songs tell us of the shattered dreams of the village housewife (Ganyer Badhu); of 'Kaviguru's (Rabindranath's) 'Krishnakali', the dark-complexioned charming girl roaming about and crying in hunger; or they simply express the ecstatic joy at the coming of the cherished new age, 'Dhitang dhitang bole'.

In tonal composition Salil Chowdhury was perhaps matchless. He composed 'On your guard! Guard your paddy' in a folk style. He divested *Kirtan* of its religious and lyrical quality to use it for a totally different type of song—'Hey justice, those who will put you on trial have awakened—this mass of people'. He used different regional musical forms and also adapted western music with great virtuosity. So far, even songs showing Western influence (like those of Rabindranath Tagore) had retained the 'modal' nature of Indian tradition highlighting a basic melody based on a cerain combination of notes. Chowdhury moved away from the modal structures by using a series of melodies each with its given combination of notes and accompanied by harmonic orchestration. Chowdhury's greatest achievement was the introduction of harmony in chorus. Hitherto, chorus had been sung in unison. The extraordinary effect that harmonization now produced is examplified by the song: 'Waves surging, jails breaking down'. Easy harmonization along with an excellent orchestration and an amazing control of metro and tempo makes the song resound with footfalls of countless marching people. His description of the course of the journey of the *Palkee* (palanquin)(the original poem by Satyendranath Dutta), the way he makes the *Abak Prithibi* (Confounded World) rise in *bidroha aaj, bidroha charidike* (insurrection today, insurrection everywhere) (the original poem by Sukanta Bhattacharya) by skilful handling of rhythm and tune is extra-ordinary.

The post-War popular struggle was, however, interrupted by communal riots, which were a rude shock to the human conscience. Paresh Dhar wrote:

Could you tell me, my brother, my friend,
Why you stained your hand with my blood?
Was it my fault?
Had you any gain to expect
by setting fire to your neighbour's house?

Many composers pointed to the divisive policy of the British as the root cause of communalism. Bijan Bhattacharya told 'Damukdiar Chacha':

Don't run after the golden deer
Don't get misled by their talks
Let your good sense prevail.
Never talk about your home to a stranger.

Salil Chowdhury's call to build 'a bridge of unity across the river of dissensions':

This is the river of our blood
This is the river of our tears
Our rib-bones make the riverbed.
In the silt of the river hides a crocodile
Intending to break our happy home.
We stretch out our friendly hands from two opposite banks
Heave ho! Work hard! Let us build the bridge.
Let us build the bridge from heart to heart
With the passion of our souls.

And whenever the composers gave calls for class-struggle, they never forgot to address both Ram and Rahim, Paran and Hossain. They always stressed class-war instead of communal war as a solution for all problems.

But the post-war mass militancy gradually cooled. The People's Songs became quite subdued in their mood. The most militant and glorious phase of the People's Song movement ended in the quietism of songs that had world peace as their theme and had nothing more to do than flying white doves in the sky. The most popular of these songs was 'A bright flock of doves', written by Bimal Chandra Ghosh, set to tune by Salil Chowdhury and recorded in the voice of the reputed songstress Sandhya Mukherjee. Another one was Paresh Dhar's 'The flag of peace, bearing the emblem of white dove/We will kill the war monster with this flag in our hands'. Some songs could indeed rouse the ardent passion of peace loving humanity. Salil Chowdhury's:

The sun takes on colour on account of
our dream of liberation
The Himalayas rise on account of the
advent of our youth
The sea surges in our peace procession
Take care, you war-mongers, the
enemies of civilization!

Or his song that was applauded at the Peace Conference in Calcutta, 1951:

When the choice is between
destruction and creation
Our eyes sparkle
Our Answer is—
'Creation, creation, creation!'
When the choice is between
War and peace
We make no mistake
We shout—'Peace, peace, peace!'

This noble assertion, with its relevance to the war-weary world still threatened by the Cold War, touched the hearts of hundreds of people. Yet an important question remained to be answered by the leftists—a question later framed by Salil Chowdhury himself: 'Where did the Revolution, that had been round the corner in the recent past, vanish?'[76]

Dances and Ballets

Music was often accompanied by its sister art, dance. 'Action songs' appealed to man's eyes as well as ears, so that the appeal became doubly strong. Gradually, dance became important in its own right. Uday Shankar's example was found greatly inspiring.[77]

Jyotirindra Moitra says in his reminiscences:

> And there was dance. Those days Bijan, Hemanga and I did dancing along with and no less than singing. Those ballets or dances based on folk styles must have helped to some extent to awaken people's minds against the Famine and Fascism. When Japan attacked Kohima, I wrote a poem-cum-song with the refrain 'We are not to give away our golden Manipur any longer'. It was rendered into dance for a function at the Minerva. Hemanga was one of my intimate friends at that time. I can remember his:
>
> *What is this that we hear, friend, what do we hear?*
> *The Japanese have come to steal the honour of women!*
>
> —Sadhana singing the song in a tune based on *Dhamail*; Hemanga, myself, an extremely lean Nirmalendu Chowdhury and a bare-bodied Bhupati or Surapati with a *gamchha* tied around his waist dancing and at the same time singing with Sadhana.[78]

Towards the end of 1943 or the beginning of 1944 was formed the Calcutta District Party Cultural Cell, which used to work in the name of the IPTA. It consisted of Nihar Dasgupta (Secretary), Sajal Roy Chowdhury, Sambhu Bhattacharya, Ranjit Basu, Anu Dasgupta, Bishnu Mukherjee and Haripada Kusari. They put up *Chuallisher Bangla* (Bengal of 1944) at the house of Kamal Basu for the first time. The plot was as follows. An idealist teacher became very poor and had to hire a room in a slum. The residents of the slum helped him overcome his despair. He started a school for the children of the slum. The play used to end with an impressive dance by Sambhu Bhattacharya and Anu Dasgupta. They enacted the play at several meetings and in the slums of Calcutta.[79] Mention may also be made of the musical drama *Abhijan* (The Expedition) written by Sukanta Bhattacharya and enacted by Kishore Bahini, which also involved dance.

The Voice of Bengal Squad earned a reputation for some of its dance items—*The Epidemic Dance* (Tune and dance created by Panu Pal, performed by Panu Pal and Usha Dutta), *Mai Bhukha Hun* (Partly pantomime and partly dance, composed by Benoy Roy and rendered by Reba Roy Chowdhury), Benoy Roy's *Hoi Hoi Hoi*, etc. Another dance item was *The Curd-seller* performed by Harindranath Chatterjee. The Bengal Squad performed a dance-drama, *Save Bengal* in Bombay with the assistance of some members of Uday Shankar's troupe.

The Central Squad formed with the blessing of Uday Shankar, excelled in dances and ballets. Shanti Bardhan, Ravi Shankar, Naren Sharma, Reba Roy Chowdhury, Usha Dutta, Dina Pathak (Sanghavi), Santa Gandhi, Leela Sundaraiya, Rubi Joshi, Rekha Jain, Prem Dhawan, Nagesh Gangadharan, Appuni Reddi—all were talented dancers, though many of them were only novices at that time.

The first ballet produced by the Central Squad was the *Spirit of India*, choreographed and directed by Shanti Bardhan in 1944. The theme was the coming of the British to India and the subsequent history of exploitation, warfare, black-market and famine, and of course, the resistance put up by the people. After Santi Bardhan's *Call of Drum* there was a Rajasthani *Sword Dance* sending out the meassage of a heroic struggle, then there was *Dhobi Dance*, based on a story of 'Ramlila' written by Dasrathlal in a rural dialect of Bihar. Next, there was the *Dance of Cooperative Farming* in the particular form of the Lambardi tribals of Hyderabad. In the middle of that mirthful dance a man would come running and tell them that the Mahajans and other exploiters were taking away their produce. Then they would resume dancing to ridicule those exploiters. There were also a *Boat Dance* with a *Bhatiali* song, *Dance of Fishermen*, Manipuri Dance and *Holi*[80] *Dance*. All of these were about the joys and sorrows of Indian folk life and based on folk forms. The script was written jointly by Dasrathlal, Prem Dhawan, Benoy Roy and P.C. Joshi. Parvati Krisnan used to give the commentary.

A critic of the *Tribune* of London saw a show of the *Spirit of India* in Bombay and was deeply impressed. He wrote that this play of the IPTA was a living newspaper and going to have a great impact on the illiterate peasant masses of India, in whom long exploitation had awakened a spontaneous desire for freedom and progress. He also said that in this way the Indian Peoples Theatre Movement would become much more important than the similar movements going on in England.[81]

Only a small section of the vast mass of Indian peasantry had the opportunity to see the ballet and get inspired by it. But it was admired by a sizeable section of intellectuals. K.A. Abbas saw it at Cowasji Jahangir Hall in Bombay and showered praises on the performers.[82]

According to Reba Roy Chowdhury, once during a show at the Elite Cinema in Calcutta the famous singer Dilip Roy came to the green room and congratulated them, particularly Priti Banerjee and Benoy Roy.

Their next ballet, *India Immortal* (directed by Ravi Shankar) too was admired by Dilip Roy.[83] Here too was a pledge of resistance against imperialism and it was expressed through *Gajan Dance* of Bengal, *Kharau Dance* of Tripura and *Chaturanga Dance* based on classical forms (Raga Durga, Tala Teora). Roy was amazed at the very difficult success that the ballet had achieved. It assured him that 'even if the sun of Uday Shankar's genius sets, a dark night would not fall on the world of dance'. According to him, Uday Shankar used to steal the spectator's mind in such a way that the latter could never get an opportunity to watch the performance of others on the stage; and thus in Uday Shankar's case, even a collective dance used to become a solo dance. Dilip Roy found it encouraging that though the IPTA could not claim a genius like Uday Shankar, it could, by sheer team work, provide spectators with as good an entertainment.[84]

Uday Shankar himself graced many of the IPTA's functions by putting up shows of his *Ramlila. The Worker and the Machine, The Rhythm of Life*, etc. He inaugurated the Seventh All India People's Theatre Conference in 1953.

During the end-game of the Empire, the following were some of the dance items put up by the Central Squad—*Aye Tin Madari* (ridiculing the Cabinet Mission), *Gandhi Jinnah Phir Mile*, *Kashmir* and *The New Village* (the Tebhaga Village).

The Central Squad put up its *Spirit of India* in Calcutta and it became very popular in the city. This inspired the West Bengal IPTA that founded a ballet squad. Abani Dasgupta of the Central Squad introduced the West Bengal IPTA members to the dancer Bulbul Chowdhury and the musician Jnan Majumdar and these two took the lead in this matter.[85] The Ballet Squad put up *Lest We Forget*. Narayan Ganguly helped it to write the script. Bhupati Nandi, Kalim Sharafi, Khaled Chowdhury, Debabrata Biswas, Priti Banerjee, Benoy Roy and many others participated. The commentary was given by Amitava Ghosh, and Satya Banerjee. According to Sajal Roy Chowdhury, not many collective art works of such a high quality, having a political perspective and involving so little cost, were produced on the platform of the IPTA.[86]

Just before Independence, the West Bengal IPTA produced a shadow play *Shahider Dak* (The Call of Martyrs), based solely on dance forms. Anadiprasad was the dance-director and Jnan Majumdar was in charge of the music. The whole thing was planned by Niranjan Sen. The play was a protest against communalism and the imminent partition of the country. (It seems that though the Communists had supported the Muslim League's Two-Nation theory, they found the actual Partition unsavoury.) The play tried to expose the helpless misery of the Indian and the diabolical conspiracy of the imperialists. The different scenes of the shadow play portrayed the lives of the different classes of Indians—the peasants, the workers and the unemployed middle-class, and at the beginning of each scene they used to show the heavy boot of the British coming down to trample these classes.

In June 1947, a select group of about fifteen or sixteen including Salil Chowdhury, Nirmalendu Chowdhury, Sambhu Bhattacharya, Reba and Sajal Roy Chowdhury and Benoy Roy went on a two-month tour to Assam and East Bengal and put up numerous shows of *Shahider Dak*. They often included fresh political or other relevant occurrences in this play. When everyone except Sarat Bose and Shyama Prasad Mukherjee had accepted the Mountbatten Plan, they voiced a strong protest against it. But ironically, soon after the squad returned to Calcutta. India was partitioned. Another irony is that Sushil, the young actor, who used to play the role of Rameswar Banerjee, a martyr of the INA Release Movement, himself became a martyr very soon during the infamous Dixon Lane shooting. Others who participated in the play on different occasions included Atul Chowdhury, Kalyani Chowdhury, Chitta Hore, Baby Hore, Amitabha Ghosh, Bhupati Nandi, Surapati Nandi, Debabrata Biswas, Haripada Kusari and Ajit Sanyal. Sajal Roy Chowdhury used to give the commentary.[87]

Besides the above-mentioned items, we have come across many more names of dances and ballets produced by the IPTA—Sadhan Dasgupta's popular song '*Oh brother Stalin! Leave me. I beseech you*' rendered into dance (1943); Sachin Shankar's '*Bhukha Dance*' (Hunger Dance); Reba Roy Chowdhury's *Chinese Folk Dance*; Bulbul Chowdhury's '*Quit India*' (1945–6); Sukanta Bhattacharya's poem 'Runner' (The Postal Runner) set to music by Salil Chowdhury and choreographed by Sambhu Bhattacharya; Benoy Roy's '*Give back, O give back Our Kayyur friends*' choreographed by Shanti Bardhan; *Kolkata Jindabad* (Long Live Calcutta) enacted by the West Bengal Squad at the Ahmedabad IPTA conference (1947–8); *Ahalya* (directed by Sakti Nag) and *Sonar Bangla*, performed many times in different districts and Calcutta towards the end of 1951, as a IPTA news letter informs us; the IPTA's *Atom Dance* at the All-India Peace and Culture convention in April 1952 at the Park Circus Ground; a ballet on the *Awakening of Korea* at the Youth Festival in Calcutta, 1951.[88]

The *Unity* (July 1952) reported that a ballet troupe had been formed in North Calcutta and under the able direction of Paresh Dhar it was rehearsing two ballets composed by Samar Chatterjee. The Central Ballet Troupe that had already prepared the *Atom and Man* for the All-India Cultural Conference was now rehearsing another ballet named *Shapath* (The Pledge) on the theme of Famine. It had been composed by Sambhu Bhattacharya and Sakti Nag and the dance-directors were Kesto Basu and Salil Roy. *Ahalya* still retained its popularity and was in heavy demand. *Runner* and the *Sword Dance* too were still popular.

A Movement for and of the People

The fact that the best singers and composers of Bengal assembled in the IPTA is sufficient to prove the strength of the People's Song Movement. Yet the real strength of the Movement perhaps lay in the way it spread amongst the masses of people.

Hemanga Biswas wrote in his introduction to *Bishan*:

> A process of transformation has started in the field of culture—not revival, but transformation. The two isolated and thin streams of rural and urban culture have reached a confluence and are about to flow into the ocean. One can hear the uproar of the ocean of the masses. The increasing political consciousness has brought about a high tide in the dried-up river of mass culture. On the other hand, the uprooted, self-centred and decadent urban writers and artists are being irresistibly convulsed by a new social consciousness. The artists of this country have turned their faces towards the masses.

The spontaneous music movement amongst peasants and workers inspired by a new political consciousness will be discussed in the next section. Here we will see how the middle-class composers and singers associated with IPTA, tried to give a mass-orientation to their own music.

From some reports[89] of leftist papers we come to know that as early as 1943, big music squads were organized to spread the People's Song Movement. In Calcutta alone, there were at least two squads—one consisting of 60 members, led by Benoy Roy and another having 300 members. Women did not lag behind and they had three separate squads in the city. These squads and many more brought the new music to the common people—students, office-going middle-class and factory workers. They deeply touched hundreds of hearts in meetings and processions and the audience would frequently join in with unsophisticated voices and not-true-to-the-scale tunes. On one occasion, even the police entrusted with the task of keeping a watch over the meeting broke into their songs.[90]

The IPTA also organized song bands amongst tramway and jute mill workers. Benoy Roy, Debabrata Biswas, Jyotirindra Moitra,

Bhupati Nandi, Surapati Nandi and others would teach IPTA songs to these workers. In one case, even the officers and gate-keepers of a jute-mill learnt these songs. Jyotirindra Moitra remembered having taught songs to the railway workers of the Howrah Maidan and the jute-workers of Chapdan.[91] The workers themselves contributed to the stock of IPTA songs too. The IPTA even taught songs to the little children eating at free food kitchen—very simple songs like—

> *We children take our bath*
> *And go to the canteen to eat hot* Khichri.[92]

Janayuddha, 4 August 1943, reported a training class taken by Benoy Roy in Hooghly, 13–15 July 1943, and commented that this was the first such school in Bengal. Music classes used to be held at Party offices in Calcutta, Howrah, Hooghly and 24-Parganas. Mohit Banerjee used to take classes at the office of the FSU. At Amta, Howrah, a training class was held for peasant volunteers who were organized into a singing group.

The untiring Benoy Roy was the moving spirit behind the People's Song Movement. He gave music lessons in Calcutta as well as in the mofussil areas. In 1943 he toured ten districts of northern and north-eastern Bengal, taught songs to ninety people at thirteen centres and organized a number of music squads among peasants. Often the peasants would not let him go and would insist on his singing over and over again. They would sit through pouring rain patiently awaiting his arrival. Even tribals like the Garos and the Hajongs of Mymensingh, considered to be the least acculturate section of the Bengali population, were extremely enthusiastic about these songs. The songs soon became a regular feature of all Kisan meetings and they were sung and heard by hundreds even in village *haat*s (weekly markets).

Numerous stories are current about the astounding response of the common people to People's Songs. Here are a few from Priti Banerjee's memories: At a small station in Gujarat the train was to stop only for one minute. But the admiring signalman delayed its departure by quite a few minutes to enable all the members of the squad to board with their luggage. The station was Godra. The name cannot but strike us with the irony of history. A station that saw a warm expression of humanity that day, was to witness a horrendous act of cruelty many years later.

On another occasion, while they were making a box collection on a steamer bound for Barishal, a gentleman accused them of doing business in this way and forbade others to contribute. Then they broke into 'Maranshiyare daladali kore kemone banchibi bal' ('How do you expect to live disunited, when death knocks at your door', a Famine song composed by Haripada Kushari). The gentleman was so moved that he apologised profusely and donated his mite to their box.[93]

Yet another story of Priti Banerjee: she was facing difficulty in organizing a women's movement in Howrah where the conservative menfolk did not encourage women's participation in outdoor work. It was then that she learnt some songs from 'Benoyda' and approaching the women and their guardians now became a much easier task. Many middle-class women of Howrah did join the Mahila Atmaraksha Samity.[94]

Professor Gautam Chattopadhyay, then a student leader, recollected later:[95]

> In 1943, the provincial SF Conference was being held in Rajshahi. Not even a hundred copies of our English organ *The Student* had been sold by then. The acting organizer, my friend Sunil Munshi, felt despondent. Benoyda was walking past. He looked at our crest-fallen faces, heard our problems, took a copy of *The Student*, leafed through its pages and hummed some tune for a few moments. Then he said, 'Sunil, let us get into the conference pandal. I will sing and you will sell *The Student*. This is exactly what happened. As we entered the pandal, we heard Benoyda's battle-cry. 'We want *The Student*, the organ of our Federation,/ Arun Bose, leader of the student's movement, is its editor,/ This paper shows the path forward to the students of our country,/ It is their organization,/ We want The Student.' There was a sensation inside the pandal. All copies of *The Student* were sold within half an hour.

The Party leaders were aware of how deeply songs could move the masses. Songs were indispensable in every meeting arranged by the Party or any of its mass-fronts. Speeches would be interspersed with songs sung either by some real peasant or by some middle-class singer, often bare-bodied and clad only in a few metres of dhoti, looking every inch a peasant. The *Janayuddha* (23 May 1942) published an instruction from the Communist Party to the organizers of the anti-Japanese meetings stressing the need for the rehearsal of songs beforehand. Music was a strategy of the people's war.

Music also became the most effective weapon for mobilizing the share-croppers during the Tebhaga Movement, when gentlemen from urban areas went into the interior of villages rousing the peasant's militancy with fiery songs. Jyotirindra Moitra's 'The Soldier of the Field' rendered by Bhupati and Surapati Nandi enthused many a peasant, as did Akhil Chakravarty's *Baul* songs that he used to sing during his hurricane tours of the villages of Mymensingh.[96]

The Party leaders Somnath Lahiri and Nripen Chakrabarty sent the artist Somnath Hore to participate in the Tebhaga Movement in Rangpur. From Hore's diary written during those days[97] we learn how much the People's Songs meant to the rebel peasants. They used to go to the field and harvest paddy with songs on their lips, defying the jotedars. And even at night when they would assemble at a particular place to rest their tired limbs and discuss strategy,

> a Kisan comrade started with one of our Kisan songs. Next he sang 'Dhenar badhua tui'[98] an ancient song of the Rangpur region. The audience did not respond much enthusiastically. The next song was 'Piercing the dark night of sorrow'. I noticed the aged Nilkant Panchayet and his friend Durgababu beating the musical time by clapping their hands. Soon they started humming the tune. A number of swadeshi songs followed. Young and old alike kept humming them. If they found a song difficult to comprehend, they would learn its meaning and sing once again. The entranced old men could only say, 'Bravo! Excellent!' As soon as a song ended they would request, 'One more, please'. Election songs, songs on oil, salt and kerosene, swadeshi songs—none was omitted. It occurred to me anew that the songs that had entered our life as a temporary excitement was becoming the culture of the normal life of the peasants.

II

Even before the formation of the IPTA, composers residing in villages had composed songs about peasants' life, their joys and sorrows, using folk tunes and dictions. Their examples naturally inspired the IPTA. In an article in *Janayuddha* (25 January 1945) Sudhi Pradhan talked about one such composer from Chittagong—Asutosh Chowdhury. The composer was already dead.[99] But the songs collected in his book *Geetika* were still popular among the local people. Their themes were practical problems of the peasants' life; they tipped off the boatmen about the details of the waterway telling them how to avoid shallows and eddies; the songs also drew a picture of perfect amity between local Hindus and Muslims. The selection of words in his songs reflected his closeness to both Hindu and Muslim cultures of his village.[100]

The IPTA composers followed this tradition when in their urge to 'connect life with life' they adapted their music to folk elements—both tonal and linguistic. For this they had first to collect folk songs. Benoy Roy was an assiduous collector. His extensive tours of villages were richly rewarded in this respect. It is he who made the Calcuttans familier with the famous 'Allah! Megh de, pani de' (God Give Us Clouds, Give Us Rain). When he first sang it at No. 46 Dharmatala Street, it greatly delighted the audience including Sachin Dev Buman, one of the greatest exponents of folk music of Bengal.[101] The earlier-mentioned 'Dhener badhua tui' of Rangpur too was in Roy's collection. There was an advertisement on the back cover of Kanak Mukherjee's *Desrakshar Dak* of a book to be published shortly by the National Book Agency.

The name of the book was to be 'Benoy Rayer Ganer Jhuli' (Songs collected by Benoy Roy), containing numerous songs collected from Mymensingh, Dhaka and Rangpur. But we have not come across the book.

The Santal songs always smell strongly of the soil. Many such songs were collected during this period—simple and touching songs welling from the Santal's feeling of identification with the soil, from his agony caused by commercialization, urbanization and other evils. *Parichay* (Phalgun 1359), for example, published quite a number of Santal songs. To quote only one of them:

City! City!
Darling, my heart palpitates!!
City! City!
No, we won't dance!
City! City!
Our son died at the rice-mill!
We won't dance!!
City City!!

The composers who had been born in the mofussil, could, because of their nearness to villagers, imbibe folk tradition in greater depth. Benoy Roy had such a folk background. He had spent his childhood in a Rangpur village. Another such composer was Hemanga Biswas, son of a zamindar of a Sylhet village. He had been intiated into music by his mother's *Parban* and *Brata* songs, by the annual *Manasa Mangal* festival with *Mirdha*, the local hut builder, as its lead singer, and by the 'Song of Bhawal Sannyasi' of Hari Acharya, a *Kabiyal* of Dhaka.

Naturally, the songs of such composers often spoke the language of the peasants, were set to the peasants' tunes and expressed the sufferings and struggles of the peasants. Hemanga Biswas' maternal uncle Jaynath Nandi Majumdar (Bejura village, Sylhet) had no connection with the Communist Party and yet, already in the 1930s, he had composed a *Kavigan*, 'The distressed peasants of India'. Another gentleman, Abdul Gaffar of Sylhet, composed in 1943–4 a song that soon became very popular among peasants: 'Oh sweet heart! The areca-nut tree has been taxed'. Its tune was *Dhamail*. Then, instructed by the Party, Hemanga Biswas started composing songs for the peasants of his locality and he recollected later how the acceptance of his songs by the peasants had thrilled him. But the success was perhaps not very surprising for someone who always found a feel of the voice of Subal Majhi of his childhood, whenever he himself sang *Bhatiali*.[102]

In Hemanga Biswas' *Bishan*, almost all the songs were set to folk tunes. In some cases, tunes of particular folk songs were kept intact and changes were made only in their thematic content. He heard a *Sari* song from a boatman on the river Lula: 'Sadhubhai, utter the name of the Guruji with caution', and he set his own 'Sharpen your sickle, kisan brother' to exactly the same tune.[103] Similarly his 'The darkest Kaliyug[104] has descended on the Golden Bengal' was set to the tune of a song of Sharatnath of Mymensingh—'Chaitanya's chariot has entered Golden Nadia', and the 'Pestilence Song of Baniachang' set to the tune of 'What charming game of Kali in the district Mymensingh!'

Besides these, the book contained songs based on *Baul*, *Bhatiali*, *Santali*, *Sari Gan*, *Kavi Gan*, *Dhamail* and other folk tunes. There was an anti-hoarder song set to a tune of Mukunda Das, the famous nationalist bard. A *Santali* song was written jointly by Hemanga Biswas and Sudhangshu Ghosh: The 'Harvest Song of the Majurs of Tea-gardens', and another by Sudhangshu Ghosh alone: 'Song of Increasing Production by the Majurs of Tea-gardens'. Surath Pal Chowdhury and Hemanga Biswas jointly composed a long song in the form of a dialogue between a kisan and a kisani. It was set to the tune of the popular 'Bede Song' (Gypsy Song) of Syhlet and Mymensingh.

The songs of *Bishan* were sung over a wide area and widely acclaimed, thanks to the dedicated efforts of the IPTA cultural Squad of Sylhet, consisting of Hemanga Biswas, Nirmalendu Chowdhury, Khaled Chowdhury, Hemanta Das, Gopal Nandi, Barun, Lakshmi, Hena, Sandhya and many others. Shanti Sen choreographed the dances accompanying the dance-songs. A special attraction of *Bishan* was a *Bhat* song composed by a peasant, Rajendra Nandi.

We have already quoted a song by Chittaprosad, where a peasant's wife of the village Satkania of Chittagong narrates her sad tale of losing everything and everyone during the Famine. It was set to the tune used by the boatmen of the river Sankha flowing past Satkania—a very touching tune that seems to have sprung out of the vast expanse of the desolated land on the riverside and perfectly suited to Chittaprosad's theme. Chittaprosad carefully studied the different folk-tunes of his region. For example, the town Chittagong where he lived had two rivers—the Karnafuli and the Halda—girdling it on two sides. There was a difference between the boatsongs of these two rivers. The Karnafuli songs would move fast, full of vigour. The 'Halda-fata Gan' was much slower. All these tunes left their imprint on Chittaprosad's songs. A collection of his songs was published during the People's War period. But unfortunately, it is not traceable now.[105]

The most widely circulated song book of that period was *Janayuddher Gan* that ran into three editions between July and September 1942. In the first edition, most songs, composed by urban gentlemen, only marginally borrowed folk forms. However, the very first song was Benoy

Roy's 'Hoi, hoi, hoi' bearing the stamp of a north Bengal dialect and a regional tune—a song that had created a sensation at the Provincial Kisan Conference held at Domar. Besides this, there were 'We are not scared of Japan', to be sung in *Ramprasadi* tune[106] and another anti-Japanese *Bhatiali* song. There was also a song by Haldharji, a tramway worker of Calcutta.

The third edition included quite a few songs based on folk-forms—one anti-Japanese song by Dayal Kumar and another by Satyen Sen. The latter became popular among the textile mill workers of Narayangunj. The book also contained a *Baul* song by Satyen Sen on the theme of the food problem. There was also Hemanga Biswas's song on the Famine, set to a particular tune used by the Muslim Fakirs[107] of the Surma Valley.

A Hindi section was added to this edition with a view to reaching out to the workers of Calcutta who were mostly Hindi-speaking. It included two songs by Rahman, a tramway worker of Calcutta—'Get up, awake, you poor! The Red Flag beseeches you' and 'My beloved. Hindustan', an anonymous composer's 'We forty crores of Indians, ready to defend our country and die for her' and Shashi Bakaya's 'The people's war has started'.

People's Songs of Bengal included many Hindi songs. Benoy Roy learnt many Hindi songs from the Bihta Peasants' Conference, Bihar. It was he who brought from Bombay Bharat Bhusan Agarwal's 'March forward, you meek peasant! March forward, you militant worker! (viewing the peasant as meek and the worker as militant of course conformed to classical Marxism!). He himself wrote a number of Hindi songs. Many Hindi songs were written by Harindranath Chatterjee. We have already quoted some of them. In addition there were Harindranath's 'Song of Fishermen', 'Song of Boatmen', 'No food, no God', 'The day of independence has come;/ March forward', etc. Songs by Kamala Bakaya, Makdum Mahiuddin, Omar Sheikh, and other composers of People's Songs from all over India used to be sung in Bengal. Many of these were translated into Bengali as well.

A Movement by the People—Composers from the Ranks of Peasants and Workers

The People's Song Movement justified its name by drawing a large number of composers and singers from the ranks of the peasantry and the working class. We have already referred to a few of them. But they were in fact more numerous than the middle-class composers and singers. The Communist cultural movement, which was a middle-class movement in the main, thus acquired a new dimension in the field of music and became to some extent a real people's movement.

The people of the soil have always had a rich tradition of folk-music as an integral part of their life. This music partly represents the stream of folk-consciousness down the ages—consisting of their oral tradition of religious, mythological and folklores, of their day-to-day experiences, joys, sorrows and struggle for existence, the combination of which has been called 'Mother's Milk Ideology' by George Rude.[108] A number of such folk songs represent their spiritual quest. Spirituality has always been an important component of human life, and folk songs are usually overlaid with a very earthy kind of spirituality. Sometime, we only need to divest them of their supernatural form to discover their mundane content. Their God is hardly a God of cosmic forces, but one having an unmistakable human personality. Also, from time to time, folk music has been pitched in a loud key to protest directly against the oppression of moneylenders, landowners and the like. The Battle of Plassey, the Sepoy Mutiny, the Santal Rebellion and the Indigo Revolt—all enriched the treasury of Bengali folk-songs. The mass-awakening of the twentieth century made the folk-singers lament the death-sentence passed on Khudiram and pledge their support to Gandhi's Non-Cooperation Movement.[109] Needless to say, in such songs, their 'Mother's Milk Ideology' merged with what Rude has called 'Derived Ideas'. The process of this merger in folk psychology is, of course, complicated.

In the period of our study, a particular set of externally-derived ideas constituted an important element in folk-consciousness, i.e. ideas preached by the Communists. During this period, the Communists came very close to the masses of people while resisting the Japanese, providing Famine-relief and leading the Tebhaga Movement. All their mass-fronts—kisan sabhas, trade unions, the IPTA, etc.—were deeply engaged in this task.

The IPTA was particularly entrusted with the task of carrying the leftist ideas to the masses through music and theatre. We have seen in the last section that with regard to music, this organization was largely successful. The gentlemen of IPTA not only taught their own songs to workers and peasants, they even spotted musical talents from among the latter and inspired them to compose People's Songs in their turn. But the People's Song Movement was, in fact, much wider in scope than the IPTA. Most of the peasant and working class composers flourished through kisan sabhas and trade union. Only a few of them came to the notice of the IPTA that lent them its own platform and brought them to the limelight. Others were lost in the oblivion of history. The People's Song Movement was largely a spontaneous development at the grassroots level—the result of a blending of 'Mother's Milk Ideology' and a particular category of 'Derived Ideas'.

The book *Kayekjan Lok-Kavi* (Some Folk Poets)[110] edited by Sudhi Pradhan and published by the AFWAA in 1945 discussed how folk-music was being regenerated all over Bengal consistent with the spirit of the new age. Sudhi Pradhan wrote an article on Ramesh Seal of Chittagong to show how the Communist influence perfectly fitted in with the humanitarian and protestant spirit that had always been an important characteristic of this poet. Another article by Pradhan was on Sheikh Gumhani Dewan of Murshidabad, though the latter was yet to come under the Communist influence. Hemanga Biswas showed how in Sylhet, Hari Acharya, Ramanimohan Das and later Phani Das had purged all elements of obscenity and vulgarity from the local folkform *Lal* and infused in it patriotism and a refreshing vigour. Anil Majumdar and Panchanan Das discussed how the *Kavigans* of Noakhali and Nadia were being transformed in the same way. This process of revival, the contributors to the volume argued, could gradually lead to the development of altogether new themes in folk music—a possibility that the Communists should clearly realize. The introduction was written by Tarasankar Banerjee. There he said, 'I have written about these people in my novel *Kavi*—but that was by no means such a sacred historical feat. This book is an invaluable record for the cultural chapter of our national history.'

II

On the basis of this book and other sources we intend to make some case-studies to show how a combination of continuity and change gave birth to the People's Song. Ramesh Seal will be our first example.[111] Son of a barber of the village Gomdandi in Chittagong, Seal responded to the Anti-Partition Agitation, the death of Khudiram, the Satyagraha of Patuakhali and other political events by composing songs on them. His songs also protested against casteism and supported widow-remarriage. Here is a song on the Khilafat Movement:

Our eyes have opened, and our mouths too.
We have awakened to the loot carried out by the
British in our country.
We are no longer going to look on helplessly,
while the dog eats away the cream of the milk.
We defy your angry eyes.
We are not scared by the hissing of a non-venomous snake
Do you think, we are meek tadpoles?

Either you will hand over the gadi (seat of power) to the Khalifa,
or you are going back to England.
The Hindus and the Muslims are not going to allow
you any escape.

After this the poet became a devotee of the *Pir* of the Majhbhandar Sarif[112] (under the police station Phatikchhara) and there came a spiritual phase in his composing career. But at the same time events like the Chittagong Armoury Raid inspired him to write songs of a different type:

I've been born in a land of heroes,
My desire is fulfilled.
Jalalabad, red with the blood of martyrs!

The Japanese aggression on Chittagong closely followed by the Famine shocked and bewildered the poet. Just about this time, he chanced upon a copy of *Janayuddha* which showed him the way out of this impasse. He first made friends with the local CPI workers who used to sell the paper and in due course came into the fold of the Party. His verse-books—*Changing Times, Songs of the Country, The Election Mystery* (occasioned by the 1946 general election), *Verses of Storm, Verses on the Murder of Gandhi*, etc.—bear testimony to his new outlook.

Not only Ramesh Seal, but his associate *Kavis* too were subject to a similar influence. The Chittagong Armoury Raid had created a political fervour among a large number of *Kavis* of this district and yet just about that time another section of *Kavis* started singing *Phulgan*, a loose and lascivious expression of a low level of morality. This crude kind of *Kavi-gan* was designed at that time to keep people away from the current political awakening and it was patronized by jotedars, police-officers and the like. Ramesh Seal and some other *Kavis* of the region took upon themselves the task of refining *Kavi-gan*. With this purpose, they founded the Ramesh Udbodhani *Kavi* Samity in 1938. Phani Barua, a clock mechanic, was one of its founder-members. But the Samity was short-lived, because of adverse circumstances.

After some time Ramesh Seal came close to the Communists through his contact with the local *Janayuddha*-sellers and Phani Barua through his involvement in the peasant movement in the area under the Raujan Police Station. Now, instructed by P.C. Joshi, the Communist Party leaders took the initiative in forming the Chittagong District *Kavi* Samity. The formal inauguration took place on 7 and 8 February 1944, on the occasion of the District Peasant Conference. Ramesh Seal was its president, Govinda Chandra De the Secretary, the other members being Phani Barua, Maulavi Hedayet Ali, Ejahar Mian, Taracharan Das and two Party men—Bankim Sen and Nirmal Das (Assiastant Secretary). They aimed at refining *Kavi-gan* and making it responsive to socio-political problems, and they largely succeeded in doing so.

'It is a new kind of *Kavi*-contest', said Subhas Mukherjee on hearing *Tarja* songs sung by these Chittagong *Kavis*.

There is no personal attack, no mere bandying of words—only a relentless struggle between two opposite ideologies. Picture after picture is being screened before our mind's eyes! On the Arakan road, a procession of thousands of blood-stained feet returning home; Rangamati and Patenga being bombarded; bombs being dropped on the hills of Kachhari; paddy selling at the price of gold; lives selling at the price of paddy; human skulls and bones being heaped up by the roadside; souls too starting to rot.

The themes of these Kavis were not much different from those of the middle-class composers. Apart from lamenting the death and decay all around, they decried the Fifth Column and made a strong plea for unity:

There was a Bibhisan in the Treta Yug
He gave unto Rama the kingdom of Ravana.
He destroyed his own family that had held sway
all over the world.
The Fifth column comprises of the kindred of this Rakshasa.

—RAMESH CHANDRA SEAL

or

Look, the ants stay together during a crisis
And they don't drown in flood water.
We are inferior to them, we don't unite even for
a single day,
Despite our human conscience and judgement.
To prevent the unity of the Congress and the League
The conspiratorial bureaucracy has imprisoned both.
Unite Hindus and Muslims, get the leaders released!
Jinnah will sign an agreement.
National unity will come, difference between friends
and foes will no longer be there
Once the leaders are free.
We will attain swaraj, the Japanese will run away
All miseries will be dispelled.[113]

—PHANINDRALAL BARUA, 2.3.43.

Even after the days of the Japanese attack and the Famine were over, these *Kavis* continued to be productive. Ramesh Seal in particular went a long way to achieve a lot of fame. Seal had written in 1943:

Had the zamindar realized the distress,
He would have remitted the unrealized tax,
The peasant would have been happy
And would have produced much more crop.

He sounded much more militant during the Tebhaga Movement in 1946:

The oppressive zamindar—
Not jamidar, but Jam-duar (gateway to hell).
The peasants demand land for those who plough it.
Hindus and Muslims, shout together—
'Abolish zamindari, save life'!

His song on the Simla Conference shows his mature political judgement:

Brothers and sisters, haven't you heard the news from Simla?
I'm feeling feverish on hearing of the failure of the Conference.
The Congress thought it could do without the Muslims.
And the Muslims would not proceed a single step without Pakistan.

Ramesh Seal became a prized asset of the Communist Party and the IPTA.

III

Another pride of the IPTA was Sheikh Gumhani Dewan.[114] He was a peasant with some lands at the village Jindighi of Mursidabad. As the Hindu Ramesh Seal used to sing the glory of Muslim *Pir*, the Muslim Gumhani used to compose ballads on themes from the *Ramayana*, the *Mahabharata*, the *Harivamsha*, etc. In his ballads, there was an inversion of these Hindu religious stories. He used to side with the characters traditionally branded as 'sinners' such as Ravana and Duryodhan. The poet was also aware of the current socio-political problems. He led the Banyeswar Union of the Peasants' League. Themes like Hindu-Muslim unity, untouchability, irrigation problems and rural development figured in his songs. In his ballads entitled 'The Past and the Present', 'The Young and the Old', 'Lakshmi and Saraswati' and 'Workers and

Capitalists', he supported the suffering and forward-looking common people. He used to start his *Palas* with tribute to men and not with the customary worship of gods. Rabindranath Tagore is said to have been affectionate towards Gumhani, whose songs became a regular item of all festivals held at Santiniketan.

Then came the terrible Famine. The poet himself was badly affected. He suffered from a difficult disease and saw his closest disciple Kavi Lambodar Chakrabarty starving along with his wife and children. He raised his voice of protest against injustice and oppression. Gumhani and Lambodar Chakrabarty participated in rural ballad contests over a wide area of Murshidabad. Gouricharan Bhattacharya, a Party worker of Behrampore, found him and helped Sudhi Pradhan to bring him to the AFWAA Conference, Calcutta, in March 1945. Gumhani was on the Presidium along with prominent personalities like Manik Banerjee, Tarasankar Banerjee and Sailajananda Mukherjee.

Those who attended the conference remembered for a long time the night-long *Kavi*-contest between Ramesh Seal and Gumhani Dewan as a rare treat. Ramesh started the *Pala*. His theme was 'Congress, League and Communist' and he supported the Communist policy in his song. Gumhani knew much less about politics than Seal. He was hesitating to reply to the latter's *Chapan*.[115] Then on the request of the organizers, he got up and just expressed the extreme distress of the common people, greatly impressing the audience.

His familiarity with world politics gradually increased and he came under the influence of the Communist ideology. Gouricharan Bhattacharya and Sudhi Pradhan helped him considerably in this respect.[116] Two entire political booklets written by Bhavani Sen—*Bengal on the Way to Liberation* and *Bengal on the Way to Destruction*—were versified by Gumhani. He faced Ramesh Seal in a tournament once again in Calcutta, in 1946, when the city was writhing under communal bitterness. Their songs about united Hindu–Muslim struggle were extremely touching. Ramesh Seal played the role of a Muslim and Gumhani that of a Hindu. Only one example of Gumhani's composition is cited below—a song expressing his disappointment after Independence:

Oh lifeless Indians! The crematorium is your only glory.
Your 'Asoka'-branded flag has earned you fame all over the world.
Everyone in America, Australia, Britain, Japan and Spain knows that you are independent.
You alone have no such knowledge.
Rama has rescued Sita and is enthroned in the kingdom of heaven.

He had left behind Hanuman, Nal, Nil, Jambuban and
other apes.
They are filling their tummies, looting the crops of our
field and the trees of our garden.
Where can we lead a carefree life in this jaundiced
land?

IV

Another discovery of the IPTA was Nibaran Pandit of Mymensingh.[117] Born of a very poor family, he had to earn his living while still a child by making *biris*.[118] At that time, he used to complain to God about his unbearable poverty and against the swindling mahajans of the *biri* business. Later as the leader of the local music party, he composed songs on Radha-Krishna on the one hand; and on incidents like the communal riots of Dhaka, 1926, on the other:

Hari, inscrutable are your intentions.
Man is killing man and setting fire to houses
In broad daylight in the city of Dhaka.

Nibaran Pandit became the Secretary of the Latifabad Union of the Kisan Sabha. During a visit to Mymensingh, Sambhu Mitra discovered this folk poet and made him attend the first congress of the CPI in Bombay, May 1943. The influence of Tagore was perhaps as decisive at this stage of the poet's life as the Communist influence. Hiran Kumar Sanyal, Editor of *Parichay*, presented him with a copy of *Sanchayita*, a collection of Tagore's poems, and Sambhu Mitra recited some of these poems to him. He was so moved that he wrote an ode to Tagore on the latter's birth anniversary. It described the peasants' sufferings during the Famine and sought inspiration from Tagore to get over the crisis. Even the language and the metre clearly showed Tagore's influence. But soon Nibaran Pandit reverted to his own natural style.

Local folk-forms like *Punthipara*, *Ghosa-pat*, *Jari*, *Sari*, etc., were rejuvenated in Nibaran Pandit's songs. A sad song in the background of the Famine set to the tune of *Bhatiali* was as follows:

Oh boatman!
My beloved precious jewel lies under the tree yonder.
I've bid him farewell for want of a handful of rice.
Oh boatman!
Don't bring your boat to the bank.
Keep it at the turn of the river.
I don't want to show my wretched face to anyone.

Oh boatman!
I'll just have a last look at my village and take my
leave for good.

Nibaran Pandit also mocked at the middle-class *babus* who were misusing the newly introduced systems like 'Control' and 'Contract' during the War:[119]

My Manju's mother doesn't understand Control.
Whenever she cooks, she starts crying.
She can't cook without salt.
I fell at so many babus' feet
I was shoved and pushed so many times.
(Alas) My broken hut is barely thatched.
It rains there even without clouds.
(My) pitter-patter never ceases.

This was a *Ghosa* song.

Among the songs on People's War, the most widely-sung one was probably Nibaran Pandit's *Rhyme of Janayuddha*, 70,000 copies of which are said to have been published by the Mymensingh Kisan Sabha and circulated all over Bengal. We quote here a portion of this long poem, taunting those who were eager to welcome the Japanese:

A rumour has spread. Some people hope that the Japanese
will make Indians extremely happy.
The benevolent Japan will gift India Independence.
They will gift every Indian a beautiful woman.
They will fill up all godowns with swaraj.

The communal riots horrified the poet:

What is this going on in this country?
Mutual fight between the Hindus and the Muslims!
All those who have died are poor coolies and mazdurs
The leaders never die.

After Independence, Pakistan became his home. He wrote two verse-books censuring the League Government there—*The Conspiracy* and *The New Law*. Then he escaped to Alipore Duar hoodwinking the Pakistani Police. Here, he had to earn his living by selling his new verse book *The Dying Song of a Refugee* in weekly *Haats*[120] and on trains.

V

Now we shall list some less-known composers. Our main sources of information are an article by Benoy Roy in *Janayuddha* (1943)[121] and the reminiscences of Sadhan Dasgupta in the *Communist* (1975).[122]

In Rangpur there was a blind dotara[123] player named Tagar Adhikari. He came to Calcutta on the occasion of the AFWAA Festival held in 1945. There he captivated a huge audience with his song—

The sun is the beauty of day
The moon is the beauty of night
Plough is the beauty of the peasant
Paddy is the beauty of the soil.

Bijan Bhattacharya's play *Marachand* written some years later was based on the life of Tagar Adhikari.

Purna Adhikari's music party had been famous in Rangpur for its rendering of *Padma Purna*—a ballad based on the old folk tale of Behula and Lakhindar.[124] Now he composed a new *Padma Puran* describing the peasants' life and calling for more production in accordance with the Communist Party line.

Jamshed Ali Chati, a peasant of Rangpur was barely literate before joining the Kisan Sabha. But after this his knowledge increased and was reflected in his songs. During the Tebhaga Movement, he continuously travelled from village to village to inspire the peasants through his songs.

Among other folk composers of the Tebhaga were Bipin Burman of Gayabari and Rajendra Sadhu of Ga Bharan. Two Muslim *Baul* singers—Jamshed and Rasiuddin—became involved in the People's Song Movement in Mymensingh. They used to to sing with Nibaran Pandit. The Hajong tribe of Mymensingh produced a number of composers and singers—Dhaneswar Chowhan, Chandra Sarkar, Kangal Das and others.

Dulal Roy was a reputed *Kirtania* of Hooghly. He was a member of the Kisan Sabha as well. Bijay Modak and Dayal Kumar encouraged him to use *Kirtan* and *Tarja* for new themes. Harindranath Chattopadhyay once came to Hooghly and was so impressed by Dulal Roy's heroic postures and style of presentation that he advised him to sing *Ganakirtan*. His songs like the 'Eulogy of Russia' or 'Produce More Crop' are said to have become as popular as the traditional 'Mathur'[125] or the 'Song of Nimai Sanyasi'.[126]

Hemanga Biswas's exercise book already mentioned contains a song composed by Manik Das, a peasant of Koepara, Chittagong:

Look, brother, look out,
The Jap dacoit is plundering country after country.
They have bombarded Rangumat and Patenga (Chattia)
And consigned the Indians to utter misery.
When they go to China yonder
The Chinese serve them right.

Now they have set their covetous eyes on our Chattia.
We shall fling them to the ground with our collective force.

We know very little about these composers hailing from poor families of rural Bengal. In many cases, they have left only names and not even a single song. In the *Third Annual Report of the AFWAA* (*1944–5*), for example, there is the mention of a Gosaipada Sadhu who had composed three *Tarja* songs for the Gobardanga branch. Nothing more is known about this composer.

Janayuddha, 22 March 1945, reported the Provincial Peasant Conference held at Hatgobindapur, Burdwan. Here a local peasant-poet Manmatha Das sang before an audience of 30,000:

Let me narrate our history—
Our ploughing bullocks have floated away
We can no longer till the land.
All our wrappers and pillows are lying on the top
of bamboos.
The Ajoy and the Damodar have overflown,
So have the Khari, the Kunur and the Banka.

The sufferings of the people of that area due to the recent floods, mismanagement of the irrigation system and the fresh taxes imposed by the zamindars, were described in this song.

Here are some instances cited in the *Swadhinata*. On 21 January 1946, the paper reported an election meeting held among the peasants of Panjia as part of the campaign for the Communist candidate Krishna Benode Roy (17 January). Here, Pulin Sarkar of Abhayanagar and Bishnu Das of Sobhana expressed through songs the suffering and struggles of the peasantry. *Swadhinata*, 24 January 1946, reported a *Kavi* tournament between Janakinath and Rohit Dutta, two textile workers of Narayangunj, in support of the Communist candidate Brajen Das. On 15 December 1946, a Tebhaga song was published by a Namasudra peasant, Panchanan Das. The long song spoke of the multifarious grievances of peasants, welcomed the Tebhaga Movement which was being led at Narail by Chandra Basu and Nur Jalal and lastly articulated fervent hopes for the future.[127] *Swadhinata*, 29 June 1947, published a *Santal* poem collected from Midnapore (Sadar):

We cleared the forests
Drinking only phen and amani.[128]
We levelled the ground
The crop smiled.
We don't any longer own the land.
Our appetite is still there
The only thing we have is nothing.

The distress of the tillers of the soil was simply but touchingly expressed in this poem, particularly in the context of the Tebhaga Movement.

Lal Sukra Oraon was a tea-coolie of Jalpaiguri. He was expelled from the tea-garden and took shelter at Burma Dhura of Mathachakla, where he came into contact with Communists and started composing People's Songs in the Sadri language. During the Tebhaga Movement, he, along with his sister Poko Oraon toured a number of villages in this area singing such songs.[129]

Bhotan Yatra, a folk song of Rangpur, had a sad theme—a description of how the peasant, who is hopelessly indebted to the zamindar and the mahajan, is forced to leave his village and go to the hilly area:

Holding his wife's hand
And with a broken tumbler on his head
He goes Bhotanat.

During the Tebhaga Movement, a reversed *Bhotan Yatra* was composed.[130] Ramesh, the jotedar, is running away. His servant Gana is thrilled. For so long Gana has been forced to remain a *Dhyana*[131] (unable to get married) for financial reasons. But now with his master gone, he dreams of a happy family life:

Holding his wife's hand
Ramesh goes Bhotanat
Now Gana Dhyana
Wants a male-child.

(Patriarchal values privileging the male child were of course true in even such a sorry state of povety!)

Most of the songs written by peasant and working class poets are lost to us. We know even less about the tunes they were set to. But practically all these songs were based on folk-tunes, for these composers discovered their music in their own indigenous tradition which was rich in numerous musical forms. In his article in *Janayuddha* (1943), Benoy Ray gave a very encouraging account of how folk forms that had been dying out for quite some time were being revived and transformed by hundreds of unknown and little-known composers. The examples that he gave were *Kavi Gan, Baul, Kirtan, Jari, Sari, Bhatiali, Bhawaia*, etc. He said that in Dhaka alone, the gypsy music, the *Sardar Bari* music, the roof-ramming music and the morning music of *Bairagis* were undergoing a process of rejuvenation. The *Santals* of the district of Rangpur were adapting their dance-music—*Dang* and *Ringjheng*—to call for unity against the Japanese aggressors and the Italian padre. They had been holding competitions among different music parties of their villages to foster these new types of song.

VI

The folk form that should be specially discussed in this respect is *Gambhira*[132] of Malda. Though its original content was the glory of Siva (a Hindu God) it started showing a pronounced social awareness from a very early period. During British rule, this popular musical form degenerated into a sort of vulgar entertainment. But the twentieth century produced Gambhira singers like Gopal Das, Sharat Chandra, Dr Satish Chandra Das and Sufi Rahaman who rescued Gambhira from bad taste and vulgarity. They were inspired by the social reform movement of the nineteenth century and the freedom movement of the twentieth. Gopal Das wrote:

> *You called us low and became low yourself.*
> *We died and you died alongside.*
> *The infernal Kali Yug came and India remained subservient.*
> *It is all because of the caste system.*

and also 'We shall resort to *lathi* (cudgel) to shake the earth', the song that became popular during the Anti-Partition Agitation of 1905.

Most of these progressive *Gambhira*-composers were town-bred middle-class people. But soon the villagers followed their example, and as the new *Gambhira* music took the shape of a mass movement, it antagonized the British Government. In 1928, the Indian National Congress invited some *Gambhira* singers, Gopal Das, Satish Doctor, Sufi Rahaman and Dr Dharanindra Saha, to attend its Calcutta session. The government prevented them from going there and started repressing the *Gambhira* composers with a heavy hand.

But at least Dharani Doctor was undaunted and his example encouraged many others—Govinda Seth, Fajlur Rahaman and Soleman Doctor among them. During the Bengal Famine, they expressed the sufferings of the people and attacked the unscrupulous bureaucracy and black-marketeers. One popular song was as follows:

> *Our paddy was taken away by the blackmarketeering mahajans*
> *And Bhola (Siva)! You made them kings.*
> *You know everything and yet having smoked ganja*
> *You snore in your sleep.*[133]

The District Magistrate, Maldah, was prompt in taking action. He banned all songs by Govinda Seth and some by Dharani Doctor. His order also forbade Seth to sing publicly in future. This news was published in the *Janayuddha*, 5 July 1945, and it prompted Subhas Mukherjee to write an essay on the valorous tradition of *Gambhira*. Towards the end of this essay, he expressed surprise that not much protest had been made against this prohibitory order.

Despite all odds, *Gambhira* thrived. More composers took up this medium—Bishu Pandit, Abdul Majid, Satish Mondal and many others. A report appeared in *Swadhinata* (May 1946):

> On 12 May, the District Magistrate (Maldah) announced through the beating of *Dhol* that *Gambhira* was to be banned in the whole district. When the reputed composer and singer Fajlul Haq was exposing the British imperialist conspiracy, he was stopped and arrested and his song-book snatched away. The poet Banamali Kundu's songs too have been banned on the pretext that they were propagating class-hatred and communalism. As the composer Ramkrishna Das was singing at Basukitala his song 'Preservation of the Empire by the Cabinet Mission on a Divide and Rule Policy', he too was stopped. Govinda Seth's song on the historic Santal Rebellion was banned.
>
> 'The people have become furious at this repressive attitude of the Government towards their favourite *Gambhira* music. At a huge public meeting presided over by Sri Prafulladhan Mukherjee a deep contempt for this repressive policy has been expressed and a demand has been raised to revoke with immediate effect all prohibitory orders'.

The people were evidently in a much more militant mood in 1946 than a year earlier.

The *Gambhira* singers continued their tradition even after Independence. At the Peace Convention held in Calcutta in 1951, the *Gambhira* music party from Maldah made a sarcastic use of Ramdhun, known to be Gandhi's favourite:

> *Raghupati Raghaba Raja Ram*
> *A pair of loin-cloths costs thirty rupees!*[134]

VII

Folk-forms of Bihar and UP too were rejuvenated in Bengal during this period. Most of the workers of industrial Calcutta came from the villages of these provinces. So *Kajri*, *Chaiti*, *Rasia*, etc., were their favourite mediums, and their language was, of course, Hindi and its regional variations.[135]

Tramway workers showed considerable musical talent. We have already spoken of Dasrathlal. Then there was Haldharji who contributed to the very first edition of *Janayuddher Gan*. His song 'Kekra Kekra nam bataun' (Let us name all our exploiters) had become popular not only amongst his own colleagues, but also amongst middle-class Communists.[136] In the next edition, there were two songs by Rahaman, another tramway worker. Chaturali was yet another composer among them. He sang in *Kajri* tune:

The Red Flag asks you, brother workers,
Sacrifice everything to defend your country.

The audience too used to join him to the accompaniment of *Dholak*[137] and *Khanjani*.[138]

A jute worker, Bipad, could compose *Kavi Gan* extemporaneously. He used to visit factories and slums in the jute area to expose the mismanagement inside the factories, to inspire the workers to join unions and also to produce more goods, as required by the People's War policy of the CPI. His colleagues were immensely proud of him.

A port worker, Rajkumar, wrote: 'The Red Army has started the war of the Red Revolution'.

Ali Hussain, a worker-poet of Howrah, gave a call to produce more (in *Kawali*):

Our flowr-bed is in danger
The Japanese dacoit is at the door.
We shall sacrifice our bodies, souls and
properties to produce more.

Muhammad Ershad, a worker of Barrackpore, used *Kajri* to derive inspiration from Stalingrad:

Everyone knows the tale of Stalingrad—
They are living on sheer water to defend the country.
We shall join hands with Stalingrad to finish off
the devils.
And we resolve to become independent in this way.

Asgar,[139] a biri-worker of Rajabazar, used to sing electrifying songs for his co-workers in *Kajri* style to the accompaniment of a harmonium. He belonged to a cultural squad of biri-workers, organized by Basir.

During the communal riots, *Swadhinata* published a poem sent by a worker of Batanagar, Muhammed Islamuddin:[140]

Come Hindu! Let us go to the temple
folding our hands.
Come Muslim! Let us go to the mosque
to do Monazat.
Oh, the master of the sun and the moon,
the earth, the sky, days and nights!
Remove this weariness.
Oh Lord! Why has man been possessed by a monster?
Oh, the Ocean of Kindness! Man needs your compassion today.

We fold our hands as a gesture of obeisance—
Settle this fratricidal feud.
We lift our hands to do Monazat—
Stop this deadly game.

A very simple verse. But reading it side by side with the reports on bloody communal riots in the paper, one can feel its great humanitarian value.

We have found references to songs composed by the workers of Maheshtala Cotton Mill, Kushtia Cotton Mill and also songs as well as a play of the workers of Bangalakshmi Cotton Mill on the theme of strike, in *Janajuddha*, 21 June 1944.

Suren Naskar, a worker of Raiganj Jute Mill, Howrah, was a skilled singer of *Ghentu Gan*. After he got involved in the workers' movement, 'he would sing the song of *Ghentu Raja* (a folk god) while working at the loom and this song would constantly include new lines which no one had heard or composed before. This was *Ghentu Rajar Gan* and yet not exactly *Ghentu Rajar Gan*. This was the song of the new age.'[141]

In 1946, a branch of the IPTA was established in Asansol, and the only trade union of the town, a union of sweepers, founded their own Majdur Gananatya. They excelled in both musical and theatrical activities. This was one of the very rare instances where the workers got creatively involved in the leftist theatre movement, which, as we will see in the next chapter, was an almost exclusively middle-class movement. They often did not have any written script. 'At any time and any place, they would enact a play about their own life, lighting a hurricane-lamp on a make-shift stage. Their troupe consisted of singers and instrumentalists. They used to compose their own songs and set them to tunes.'[142]

Bengali workers included Gurudas Pal (alias Sanatan Pandit),[143] a factory worker at Metiaburuz. He started his composing career with spiritual songs and was freed from this trend only after joining the trade union movement. But his songs continued to have a religious colour even after this:

If you need liberation,
Worship the Mother Goddess of Power
Awaken the primordial and supreme Goddess of life.
Let the Great Power invigorate your soul.
Let the fire set the world ablaze.
Let the worker awaken, let the peasant awaken.
Let the universe quake.

—Set to a tune of MUKUNDA DAS

In 1945, Gurudas Pal had the opportunity to hear a *Kavi* contest between Ramesh Seal and Gumhani Dewan and from then he accepted the style of *Tarja* as his own medium. Only one example will suffice to show how powerful this musical form became in Gurudas Pal's hand:

Alas, how to save our faces?
We have got into the clutches of a cheat.
The crow always caws and never can say Krishna.
However hard you teach it.
Can rose-water make a mole smell nice?

During the late 1940s and the early 1950s, Gurudas Pal was among the front-ranking composers of the IPTA. He was one of the first persons to use the *Jatra* form as a vehicle of politics. The name of the *pala* was *Sanghat* (The Conflict) and it was performed by the Badartala Workers' Unit in 1954.[144]

These songs were transmitted orally over a wide area of Calcutta and its suburbs, sometimes in revised and enlarged forms. Liaqut, a paint-factory worker, added a few lines to Haldharji's 'Kekra kekra naam bataun' to make it up-to-date. This was reported in the *People's War* with the comment that these people treated the songs as their very own and never felt any 'bourgeois' inhibition about their amendation.[145]

VIII

All these natural poets, whether worker or peasant, Bengali or non-Bengali, owed both their thematic and tonal compositions largely to their own native tradition. This tradition meant a musical richness as well as a social awareness. The direct or indirect influence of the Communist ideology and organizations helped and intensified traditional social consciousness, and in some cases, restricted it also. Muhammed Ershad's song quoted above ends with a hope of achieving Independence by driving out the Japanese—not a very logical hope. As we have already seen, the middle-class composers too suffered from the same kind of irrationality. This was the flaw of the People's War policy of the CPI. In 'Kekra Kekra nam bataun', the folk composer marked off scores of enemies—mill-owners, hoarders, moneylenders, Germany, Japan, Italy, etc. But he seemed to have been completely ignorant of the existence of the British, a foreign power, reigning in India for their own interest. The People's War policy involved cooperation with the British Government. The CPI increased the political and social knowledge of these composers, brought them into a mass movement and got them fame in some cases, but also tied them down to their own political policy and strategy.

The Communist endeavour to secularize folk culture perhaps created some tension too. At least Ramesh Seal later told Hemanga Biswas that his touching Maijbhandari spiritual lyrics had been written from an 'inner urge' and Communist songs composed for an 'outer movement'. Seal found the latter much inferior to the former.

IX

Our study is based on Communist Party documents and we have concentrated on the history of folk music only insofar as it was inspired and used by the Communists. But it is a safe guess that during the period of our study there were many folk poets who had no Communist connection whatsoever and yet the pressure of the socio-political situation made them write 'protest songs'. Some such examples may be cited.

Tona Mian of Chittagong used to work sometimes as a farm-hand and sometimes as a hut-builder. But in his heart, he was a poet and used to sing *Panchali* on themes such as the Chittagong Armoury Raid, its heroine Kalpana Dutta and the Famine as well as the traditionally popular romantic stories like the *Kechchha of Bhelua* or the *Kechchha of Shaher Banu*.[146] In a long ballad entitled *Golapjaner Kechchha*, he vividly described the plight of Chittagong during the War and the Famine. With amazingly clear insight, he marked off those who were responsible for it. Then he narrated how Ramjan Ali, an upstart rich, cast his covetous eyes on Golapjan, the beautiful young wife of poor Daulat Majhi. When Golapjan refused to leave her husband and come with him, Ramjan sought the help of his foreigner friends in the army, then camping in Chittagong. They kidnapped Golapjan. But she tried to escape and was shot dead in the process. Thus, the ballad ended in touching pathos.

This ballad has been collected by a Communist—Kalpataru Sengupta, a leader of the local Communist movement. But according to Sengupta, Tona Mia had nothing to do with the Communists, and the Communists could do nothing for him when within a few days after writing this ballad he died of starvation. Sengupta could remember many such natural poets singing songs on the streets and at the market-places of Chittagong at that time.

Chittaranjan Deb in his valuable book *Palligeeti O Purba Banga Kathakata* (Folk Songs and Narration of Mythological Stories in East Bengal)[147] has included some *Akasmat Geeti* (accidental songs) some of which were written in response to social and political problems. His collection includes quite a few songs on the Famine of 1943, written by anonymous rural poets of unknown backgrounds. Most probably, these composers had no connection with any political party. Deb says in the introduction to his book that while travelling in East Bengal he came across these songs composed and sung spontaneously by local people. Another such 'spontaneous' song in his collection was composed by some villagers of Barisal in July or August 1945. The corruption of the President of the local Food Committee enraged these people and they took the initiative to punish him. The song thus goes:

Listen, Uncle, Listen to the great news from Barisal:
They've put a garland of shoes on the neck
of the president of the Food Committee
In an open street.
More news has come!
They've tied around his neck a ration card,
And put a bit of sugar in his hand
And oil on his head.
They've made a leash of a new cloth
With which they've dragged him from street to street.
They've served him right, uncle, served him right
After so long!

The Decline of the Peoples' Song Movement

The People's Song Movement declined gradually from the early 1950s, despite the fact that it had been rich in talent, enthusiasm and the dedication of individuals and that it had grown to the stature of a mass movement. It was the time when the whole leftist cultural movement went out of gear and post-War popular militancy gradually faded. The policies of the Communist Party that had played an important role in fostering both the socio-political and the cultural movements had m uch to do with this decline.

The shortcomings of Communist politics were reflected in its cultural fronts. During the period 1942–52 the Party alternated between inaction, ultra-leftist rashness (mainly in words, the practice hardly being consistent with them) and inaction once again (while the ultra-leftist grandiloquence continued). Hemanga Biswas, in his long self-criticism in *Prastutiparba* 1383 (1976), has vividly portrayed these phases, particularly the first and the third, with special reference to the People's Song Movement.[148]

The first phase was the period of the People's War, which turned the leftists, in Biswas's words, 'into a tail affixed to the British war-efforts'. The composers expressed hopes of achieving Independence by defeating the Japanese. They unfairly abused many people as 'Fifth

Columnists'. They underestimated the patriotism of Subhas Chandra Bose. Naturally these songs hurt the strong nationalist sentiment sweeping the country at that time.

The Party leaders used to demand from the composers 'way-out', i.e. suggestion for the way out of the Famine situation and 'link-up', i.e. relating every problem with Fascism and the Japanese aggression. Biswas ended a song with the following lines:

> *The peasants of this country are starving to death.*
> *On top of it, have come the Japanese to undo us.*
> *And still the foreign Government*
> *Denies us freedom of action.*

But the leaders did not quite like it. They complained, 'You haven't given a way-out, comrade!' So Biswas added: 'Organize People's Relief Committees today', etc. The emphasis of the song thus changed, the protest against the government was toned down.[149]

The value of such songs was naturally ephemeral. Furthermore, they often sounded very mechanical. Biswas has drawn a distinction between these two. In his opinion, 'momentary' songs can at least serve some immediate needs of the Party and the people, and on this ground he defends Kanak Mukherjee's song, 'Fill the quota'—part of the drive to increase Party membership—which was once severely criticized for being too crude. The songs that pretended to deal with graver human problems but did so mechanically, had much less appeal and could even estrange the people.

Not that all the People's Songs were mechanical. Many of them overcame the limitations imposed by the Party and were able to move the listeners. *Nabajibaner Gan* touched the feelings of many because of the sheer humanitarian sympathy expressed in it for the suffering millions and of the fervour for a happier future. Despite the Party policy leading to inaction and compromise, some songs of *Bishan* could not help being militant in spirit.

The post-War period witnessed a rising militancy among the people and the Communists led popular movements everywhere. But the Party did not really have a clear view of its own objective and the popular upsurge soon began to ebb. Even the post-Independence slogan 'Ye azadi jhuta hai' could not instill a revolutionary spirit in the people. Hence the revolutionary cultural activities of the period 1948–50 proved meaningless. Hemanga Biswas said at a general body meeting of the IPTA about this time: 'So long we have tried to make nice flowers blossom in the paddy field. Now we will have to sow paddy.'[150] Unfortunately, however, the soil had not been prepared. Of course, excellent pieces of musical creation can be credited to this phase of militancy (a number of songs by Salil Chowdhury or a few by Biswas himself may be cited).

In 1950, the Party line changed. All creations of the past two years were brushed aside as mere 'foolhardiness'. The composers started composing peace songs for the 'Peace Movement of the Upanisad type, with no tooth and claw' (in a self-critical Hemanga Biswas's words). In 1952, the Communist Party contested the general elections, and songs of election were composed.

II

Moveover, the phase of militant leftist culture soon took an unfortunate turn. Both in the AIPWA and the IPTA friendly artists and successful art-works were cried down as 'reactionary'. Some Party men seemed keen on bringing culture to the people. But they could never really reach the people and in the bargain just alieneated talented artists who had for so long worked with the leftist cultural fronts. The Party decided to expel Hemanta Mukherjee and many others from the IPTA and when Benoy Roy tried to prevent it he was branded a 'Trotskyite'.[151] After a few days, Roy who had played a remarkable role in forging links with the masses of people, was removed from the country and sent away to Russia as the Bengali announcer of the Moscow Radio.

Salil Chowdhury was another target of the attack. His song 'Rush in, Rains!' had a line: 'Alas! Cruel Providence! The scorched earth sheds tears in vain, no crop is produced'. The words 'Cruel Providence' was taken as a religious statement and the song was decried. His highly popular song 'The village housewife' was condemned as reactionary and even proscribed. Salil Chowdhury says in an interview that the clash started on the issue of 'Ganyer Badhu' (The Village Housewife). The Party wanted to ban it on the ground that while the peasant women of 24-Parganas were fighting off the police with chilli dust, how could one say that their dreams had been shattered. And Chowdhury defends himself:

> But I was an eye-witness to the fate of the peasant women. I used to work in villages. Did you ever work in villages? I used to walk all the way from Sonarpur to Panchghara to teach in a night school. Haridhan and Khepuda (two local comrades) used to accompany me. On our way, there was an old banyan tree called 'Jiren Bat' (The Resting Banyan). At the foot of which people used to rest a while on their way to the crematorium. It was just after the Famine. At moonlit nights the place used to look absolutely white from a distance. It was because of the piled-up skeletons. There were not enough people in the villages to cremate dead bodies.

So they just dumped those bodies at the place and it used to look brilliantly white in moonlight. I saw all this. I used to walk from village to village. There was not a single soul—not even a dog or a crow. After all, I did not concoct 'Ganyer Badhu'. I was not engaged in drawing room politics,You who were sitting in your drawing rooms in Calcutta were throwing Chilli dust from there. You instigated thousands of peasants and then backed out. The peasants suffered terribly and you shed crocodile tears for Ahalya. The leaders were not affected even slightly.

Chowdhury concludes that the Party just proved its isolation from the masses by banning 'Ganyer Badhu' the disc of which had sold like hot cakes. Even much later, the audience would not let Hemanta Mukherjee get up unless he sang 'Ganyer Badhu'.[152]

A commission was formed to censor Chowdhury. In his autobiography *Jiban Ujjiban*, Salil Chowdhury has burst out in an old rage:

My heart revolted. I was not going to sing before them. I was not going to submit to an ordeal conducted by some monsters. These people were the standard-bearer of the Party culture! Since the age of six, I had wholly concentrated on my music, I had spent hundreds of hours to perfect it. I had spent invaluable years of my life running amok like a rabid dog chased by the police with the sole purpose of serving my country with my music. Why had I done it, for what ideology? And these were the faces of those carrying the banner of that ideology?[153]

When, thus alienated, Salil Chowdhury entered the cine-world of Bombay and became a great commercial success there, many leftists, of course, said that it was because of his inherent opportunistic tendency.

III

The decline of the People's Song Movement is often attributed to the failure of the IPTA to draw enough talent to its fold from among folk-poets, which in its turn was attributed to its negligence of folk-forms. The organization undertook a laudable venture in these two directions and yet its members were always dissatisfied that they had not achieved enough. The Bengal Squad that attended the IPTA inaugural conference was described by the *People's War*[154] as 'composed overwhelmingly of middle-class youths from Calcutta, most of whom knew English, a distinct contrast to the squads that came from Andhra and Kerala'. Amongst twenty squad members, there were only two folk-poets—Dasrathlal and Nibaran Pandit, and this was considered a shortcoming. This perhaps made the judges rank Bengal second to Andhra in the Contest for the Red Banner.

And their self-criticism in reagard to the inadequacy of their use of folk-forms was brought forth in the following report on the work done by the Bengal IPTA till 1945:

But, strange to say, even when we went to the masses, I mean rural masses who form the bulk of the population of Bengal, it is always with forms of art that had come to stay in Bengal after our contact with the West. No doubt, they composed and wrote in the language of the folk, and the songs and plays touched their life as they did never before in recent history. But what was not utilised to the fullest extent were the folk-forms of art which would have taken us deep down to the masses. This is where the work of the Bengal of IPTA differs from the work of the Andhra branch.

This was found particularly unfortunate, for 'having no big temples as in the South or big royal courts like those of the Mughals and Rajput princes as in the North, before the coming of the British, where classical dance and music grew to its full stature under the patronage of princes and priests, Bengal developed its folk forms of art almost to a perfection' and was 'the foremost among the provinces for richness and colour, variety and vigour of folk art in general'. The report ended with the suggestion: 'IPTA in Bengal can become a widespread movement only when local talent in the districts is tapped and all folk forms of art given as much prominence as other forms so far taken up by IPTA'.[155] The question of using more folk forms and drawing more folk-poets to the IPTA surely needed careful attention. But at least the folk-poets cannot be accused of neglecting folk-forms and it is pertinent to ask why the folk-poets who had been flourishing outside the IPTA gradually moved away from the People's Song Movement, why the trend of peace songs and election songs of the early 1950s failed to inspire them much. The question cannot be answered with reference to musical forms alone.

Moreover, when within the IPTA the question of form came to preoccupy the cultural activists, there was no constructive criticism, but just personal attacks. Many IPTA composers were accused of 'formalism', which meant any experimentation outside the area of pure folk-forms. Salil Chowdhury became a favourite target on this count as well. Hemanga Biswas attacked Salil Chowdhury for neglecting folk-forms. Here is a piece of candid self-criticism penned by Hemanga Biswas many years later:

To argue exclusively on folk form without giving the first consideration to content is another kind of formalism and trying to criticize Salil's formalism I myself fell a victim to the latter kind of formalism. The battle took place on the issue of forms. While criticizing Salil's 'Oh brother boatmen' I said that a rebel boatman never sings this 'boatman song'. This song used to be sung in a 'harmonized' form those days. I missed the real difference between this one and the chorus Salil had composed earlier: 'Waves surging, jails breaking down', a striking example of successful harmony. Under Salil's able direction the latter song, a harmonized chorus, could successfully reflect the multifarious dimension of the consciousness of revolutionary masses on the move. But the song 'Oh boatman brother' had nothing but an abstract musical escapism. I failed to approach the question in this way. So the debate just got centred around the question—folk-form or urban-form.

Biswas added:

And, after all, folk-tradition and folk-music are not the same thing. Band party was introduced in our village life many years ago. Gagan *Dhuli* of our village formed a band party. Trumpets, trombones and clarionets were introduced in our *Jatra* concert. So in the present age, even if we accept the predominance of *Ektara* and *Dotara*, we need not be shocked to see Spanish guitars or accordions alongside them in a revolutionary chorus. But the fact remains that while we stay away from the masses and their struggle, all debates and experimentations are sure to go astray.[156]

So according to Biswas, ultimately it was the failure of Communist politics that led to the failure of the People's Song Movement.

So far as the form was concerned, it was not possible for Salil Chowdhury's innovative genius to just repeat some old folk forms. Moreover, his musical background too was different from that of Hemanga Biswas. His father had a very good collection of records of symphony orchestra as well as of Western folk songs like negro spirituals. So he, from his childhood, could make an in-depth study of Western music, of chord accompaniment, counter-point, scale-modulation, etc. At the same time he loved attending conferences of Indian classical music. The IPTA added a new dimension to this rich musical background, when it introduced Chowdhury to folk music from all over India. But he could not get over the influence of Western music, and thanks to this influence, the music of Bengal was enriched with a brilliant vocal orchestra like 'Waves surging, jails breaking down' and tremendously appealing songs like 'Ganyer Bandhu', 'Runner' and Palkee Chale'—songs introducing a new genre in Indian music. It is interesting to note that while the movement of 'Ganyer Bandhu' is influenced by Western music, at places it has overtones of Indian classical *Ragas* like *Bhairabi*. And according to Salil Chowdhury, such novel experimentation was necessitated not by any formalistic urge, but by the content itself. He just tried to express the new requirement of a new age.[157]

Apart from Salil Chowdhury's harmonization and other experiments, Jyotirindra Moitra's *Nabajibaner Gan* may also be cited as an example of the meaningful assimilation of Western music. Here, he followed the movements of Beethoven's Ninth Symphony to describe a valorous struggle against the Famine. At the same time, Moitra was trained in Indian classical music. In this composition, classical music, both Western and Indian, blended nicely with folk-forms.[158] Such music was inevitably complex.

Furthermore, even folk-music needs to be perfected and cannot just be reproduced in the raw. Dilip Kumar Roy thus commented on the ballad *India Immortal* of the IPTA: 'The heart is entranced with a peculiar feeling on hearing 'Alas, what is the remedy'—a feeling of aesthetic joy and creative talent, but they do not involve the leisure of art endeavour. Without this endeavour art cannot flourish to the full.' In the *Gajan* dance of *India Immortal*, according to Roy, this endeavour had been added to the folk tradition and perfection had been achieved, thereby winning his admiration.[159] The Party members did not give any thought to these finer points when they cried down the famous IPTA productions including *India Immortal* as reactionary.

Even so far as the common people are concerned, because folk music has emerged from their lives and they are familiar with and even appreciative of it, it does not automatically follow that it will inevitably inspire them in an ideological struggle. Even while recognizing the simplicity and directness of the folk idiom, both in form and content, and its possible appeal to the people, one may need to consciously work on the structure of folk music to use it for popular struggles. Sumangala Damodaran tells us that in Kerala, the activists of KPAC (Kerala People's Art Club aligned with the IPTA) had to mould folk tunes and craft a 'new folk' idiom, for it was felt that the Malayalam tradition consisted of forms that were rather monotonous and repetitive.[160] In Bengal the idea was to keep the folk tunes intact and just insert new words in them. Musicians like Salil Chowdhury were rare exceptions in this respect. Chowdhury dared to experiment with folk tunes in the most innovative ways to enhance their appeal. And on the other hand, the fact that he used the tune of a peasants' song from Andhra Pradesh for one of his popular songs 'We won't accept this bondage' shows the universality of the appeal of folk forms that can reach out even to people of other lands. Khaled Chowdhury has pointed out yet another problem in this connection. Though he was deeply involved in the People's Song Movement during the 1940s, he later found those songs greatly deviating from the authentic tradition of folk music, largely due to the artificiality of their lyrics. And hence, according to him, their appeal to the folk was limited too (we will discuss Khaled Chowdhury's point in some detail in the conclusion of this book).

Ultimately, as we have already seen, Hemanga Biswas blames it all on the narrow political line of the Party. And he is probably right.

Folk-forms, even highly successful ones, are bound to be futile, if the Party fails to provide leadership to the struggling masses. Hemanga Biswas took up the tune of a popular folksong of his region. 'Shyam has come/Go, decorate the bower' and put in it the new theme of anti-Japanese resistance. This *Dhamail* song became popular and used to be sung by rural people over a wide area. But then the people forgot the Japanese and 'Shyam has come' came back stealthily.[161] Direct products of Party politics are naturally short-lived. If the mass-movement ceases, mass-culture simply dies out.

IV

In late 1951, the *Swadhinata* published 'Songs of Ferrying the River of Vote' by Ramesh Seal and Hemanga Biswas with a view to the coming general elections. On reading these, Hadi Harish Burman, an obscure folk-poet from Jalpaiguri, wrote to the editor a letter entitled 'Oh poet! Why doesn't your show the way to liberation?'[162] He said, 'In the "Songs of Ferrying the River of Vote" your poet has given a call':

Oh my precious jewel!
Make the crumbled boat of the Congress sink.
It is overloaded with the sinful purchases of the last five years.
Oh, make it sink!

After this he describes the sinful activities of the Congress during these years and then said:

We are not going to vote for Congress
We will never forget the Congress highhandedness.

Such a campaign is being made by all the parties other than Congress. Many of them are your contestants. So where does your campaign differ from theirs?

The only difference was in the last four lines. But this was too subtle for the rural people to understand:

The way to liberation has opened up in
Burma, Malay, China and Korea.
We shall harvest the crop with the power
of sickle and corn.
We won't give away our paddy
to the herdsman of the British oxen.

(We haven't understood the meaning of the words 'with the strength of sickle and corn'. But we can see that these are your election symbols. Maybe that is what you tried to convey.)

The writer of this letter tried to open the eyes of the readers to the mechanical side of People's Songs. And this mechanicalness was so unmistakable that it made people doubt the sincerity of the composers. The letter-writer thus said,

> The Congress had already disillusioned the people. Today your talks remind us of the promises that the Congress leaders had formerly made. Who knows whether you too are bluffing us as adroitly and as convincingly as those leaders!
>
> 'Oh poet! Where do the conscious and organized peasants and workers exist in your election songs? Without their conscious and organized existence, your election songs will be futile. The people of India live consciously. They have struggled, are still struggling and are ready to struggle in the future. The elections may at best be a single step of this continuous struggle. In our region, there is a commonplace rhyme:
>
> *Fluke is your name—*
> *You have cast your net on the land,*
> *Do you expect the fish to jump on to the land?*
> *First of all, you'll have to stir the water of the lake.*

Liberation will not be achieved without struggle.

> *You will have to explain to the rural people in a simple way, but not in a one-sided and imperfect way. They are simple, but not simpletons. If you try to deceive them, you will be deceived yourself.*

The writer of the letter realized at that time what Hemanga Biswas was to realize much later. The mechanical superficiality and the apathy to struggle that had always impeded the People's Song Movement ultimately became the reason for its decline and failure.

APPENDIX I

Statistical Chart

Bengal Cultural Squad Tour (a table prepared by Benoy Roy)

Place	*Shows*	*Date*	*Classes*	*Attendance*	*Collection*	*Organizers*
1. Lyalpur Dt.	1. Ramlila Hall	17. 11. 43	All classes	1200	Rs. 487★ some clothes	Party
.	2. Mundi Ground	18. 11. 43	–	5000		
	3. Conf. 1st night	20. 11. 43	Mainly peasants + artisans	2000	Rs. 201★ 25 ivory bangles	K. S.
2. Huveli (Peasantry Conf. Montgomery District)	4. '2nd'	21. 11. 42		2500		Bengal Relief Committee★ all soc. polt. leaders
3. Ferozpur	5. Cant. Show	22. 11. 43	P. B. + other classes	1500	Rs. 3,500	
	6. Women's show	23. 11. 43	All classes	2000		
	7. General show	23. 11. 43	—	5000		
	8. Girls' school	23. 11. 43	Principals + teachers	300		
.	9. Women's show	24. 11. 43	Mainly peasants	600	Rs. 3,500★	Bengal Relief

(*contd.*)

Appendix I (*contd.*)

Place	*Shows*	*Date*	*Classes*	*Attendance*	*Collection*	*Organizers*
	10. General show	24.11.43	Townfolk incl. merchants + peasants	1500	20 md. Wheat	Committee with strong peasant influence
4. Ludhiana	11. Cinema Hall	25.11.43	All cases	1000	Rs. 1,500	Party
	12. Women's Medical College	25.11.43	Principal + teachers + students	500	Rs. 600	College staff* one woman comrade
5. Jullundhar	13. Night show	26.11.43	All cases	500	Rs. 450	Party
6. Hoshiarpur	14. City show	27.11.43	Town folk	500	Rs. 200	Party
	15. Bahnwal K.S. Conf.	28.11.43	Peasants	8000	Rs. 300 + 10 md. maize	K.S.
7. Jullundhar	16. Jhandelwala K.S. Conf.	29.11.43	—	6000	Rs. 6,000 collection by D.K.S. Rs. 1,800	K.S.
8. Amritsar	17. Lit. Circle	30.11.43	P.B. + intellectual	300	Rs. 3,500 auction of bangles	Lt. circle
	18. Temperance Hall	1.12.43	W.C. + P.B.	250	Rs. 600	Bengal Relief

(*contd.*)

Appendix I (*contd.*)

Place	*Shows*	*Date*	*Classes*	*Attendance*	*Collection*	*Organizers*
9. Lahore	19. Y.M.C.A. Hall F.C. College	5.12.43	P.B. + upper intell. + students	300	Rs. 7,000, auction of many articles	—
10. Gujranwala	20. D.A.V. College ground	6.12.43	Students + teachers Town folk	700 6000	Rs. 1,500 Rs. 273	S.F. Party
11. Rawalpindi	21. Women's show	8.12.43	Girl students + women	150	Rs. 2,000 + auction of some articles	Girl S.F. + M.S.L. + T.U. + Party
	22. Bourg. Show at Cinema	8.12.43	Bourg. + intell.	150		
	23. General show at D.A.V College Hall	8.12.43	Town folk	500		
12. Municipal Native State (Naya State)	24. Women's show	11.12.43	Peasants + town women	2000	Rs. 800 + some ornaments	Bengal Relief Committee
	25. Public show	11.12.43	Peasants + town folk	6000		
13. Bhatinda	26. Rly. Inst. Show	12.12.43	All Classes	1000	Rs. 3,000	Bengal Relief

(*contd.*)

Appendix I (*contd.*)

Place	*Shows*	*Date*	*Classes*	*Attendance*	*Collection*	*Organizers*
14. Lahore Ramgarh W.C.	27. Y.M.C.A. Hall	16.12.43	Students P.B. + intellgentsia	300	Rs. 800	S.P. + M.S.L. + Party + TU
	28. Ramgarh	15.12.43	W.C.	4000	Rs. 72	Party + T.U.
15. Agra Show	29. College Hall	22.12.43	Town folk	400	Rs. 200	Leading people of town + party
16. Delhi	30. Saraswati Bhutan	23.12.43	P.B. + intelligentsia	250	Rs. 200 (promise of Rs. 800 appr.)	Cult. Society
	31. Delhi Cloth (Pahargunj)	24.12.43	W.C.	2500	Rs. 20	I.P.T.A. + Party
	32. Gandhi Ground	25.12.43	P.B. + shop	6000	Rs. 100	—
	33. Sabji Mundi	27.12.43	W.C.	8000		—
	34. Party show	19.12.43	Party + sympathizers	60		Party
17. Nakodra	35. Jain Mandir	13.12.43	Town folk + Kisan	2500	Rs. 100	Party + Bengal Relief

P. B. – Petite Bourgeoisie and, W. C. – Working Class

In 10 districts of Punjab, 2 native states, Delhi and Agra there were 35 shows among which 3 were mainly attended by working class, 6 by peasants and 6 by women and girls. The total number of people who attended the shows was 1,00,750 and the collection amounted to Rs. 32,472.00 + 30 maunds grain + 25 ivory bangles + 1 pair of silver bangles + gold ornaments.

There are a number of inaccuracies in this report. First, serial mumber 10 is missing. Then, if we follow the table exactly, the amount of money collected comes to Rs. 32,654.00 and not Rs. 32,472.00, and the total number of people attending the shows comes to 79,472 and not 1,00,750. But on the whole the table shows how wide their mass contact was.

APPENDIX II

Chronology of the Performances of the Bengal Squad and the Central Troupe of the IPTA, prepared on the Basis of the *First Bulletin* of the IPTA published in 1946

Bengal Squad

- The tour of Punjab in 1943—raising funds for the People's Relief Committee
- On 15–17 January 1944, participation in the second conference of the AFWAA in Calcutta
- In the first week of February, attending the Peasants' Conference in the district of 24-Parganas.
- In March, performing at the All India Kisan Conference at Bezwada.
- The tour of Bombay, Gujarat and Maharashtra—under the leadership of Sambhu Mitra and Benoy Roy.
- Seven members staying back at Bombay as members of the newly formed Central Squad of the IPTA and the others returning to Calcutta in June 1944.
- Several shows in Calcutta and its neighbourhood (at least 16).
- In July, attending the Bengal provincial Kisan Conference held in 24-Parganas.

Central Squad

- They were not prepared to perform before the public until December 1944—in that month their first show was arranged in Bombay, at a meeting of the Students' Union.
- Performance at the Cowasji Jehangir Hall, Bombay, at the annual conference of the Bombay IPTA.
- Two or three more shows in Bombay.
- Participated in the AFWAA ceremony of January 1945, held at Muhammad Ali Park, Calcutta.
- Returned to Bombay—more shows.
- From April 1945, preparation for the next year and for more performances. By that time the Central squad had become a powerful and permanent part of the IPTA.

APPENDIX III

Short notes on some folk-forms referred to in this chapter

Baul: Songs of a sect of recluse singers. Though recluse, they are not really isolated from the people. They do not conform to any religious rites, either Hindu or Muslim. Human life, human body and soul constitute the main theme of their songs.

Beder Gan: The professional song of *Bede*s or Gypsies.

Bhatiali: A solo song by a lonely boatman on the river. Its birth place is East Bengal which is full of rivers. Big rivers and the vast expanse of lands on the river-bank facilitated its development. Its theme is usually love, separation from the beloved and despair.

Bhawaia: A kind of song sung in North Bengal where there are rivers with strong currents amidst deep forests. The main theme is love and separation from the beloved. The hero of the song is either a *Maisal* (cowherd) who always wanders from one place to another or a boatman of a highland river. The sigh of his beloved, who is away from him, is heard in this song.

Chhad Petanor Gan or roof-ramming song: A kind of work song. Its theme is love, particularly the love of Radha-Krisna. 'But the love of Radha-Krisna turned into a sort of mental perversion' in this folk song, which became of obscenity. The beat of this song is more important than its tune.

Dhamail: A kind of folk-dance and accompanying song, performed by women. It is prevalent over a wide area of Sylhet, Cachhar and Tipperah. While singing, the women dance also by clapping their hands and tapping their fact on the ground, thus maintaining the musical rhythm.

Gambhira: A speciality of Malda, it originated in the *Gajan* festival of Siva, held in the month of Chaitra. Originally, it used to be accompanied by a mask-dance. The songs were not exactly sung in praise of Siva. Rather, the singers used to scold Siva for the wrongs in their society and ask remedies of him. *Gambhira* has always been based on current events and marked for biting satire. Today, *Gambhira* is sung independent of the *Gajan* festival and it is popular in its own right. The transformation from a mere festival song to a popular social song has been a big step in history—a historical process that has taken place in the twentieth century on account of the two World Wars, Indian Independence and other events. The mask-dance associated with *Gambhira* is fast disappearing.

Gajaner Gan: In the month of Chaitra, rural Bengal celebrates the *Gajan* festival which is worship of Siva, in the main. *Gajan Gan* means hymns praising Siva.

Ghosa: Sometimes long narrative songs are punctuated with short songs on totally different themes, thus providing a diversion. These short songs are called *Ghosa*. Their themes vary from religion and mythology to everyday domestic life.

Jari: A kind of Muslim folk song sung on the occasion of Muharram, it is particularly famous in the district of Mymensingh. It is accompanied by dancing by men and is full of manliness and valour and also sadness. The usual theme is the famous War of Karbala.

Kavi Gan: To an educated city-bred Bengali, *Kavi* means poet. But in rural Bengal, *Kavi* and composer-singer are synonymous terms. In a narrower sense *Kavi* means *Kaviyal*, a particular category of composers specializing in *Tarja*. *Tarja* is a kind of song-tournament where two parties of singers are engaged in a dialogue in songs composed extempore. Each party has its leader and *Dohars* who help the leader or just repeat some lines sung by him. One party throws a challenge (*Chapan*) to the other which then gives a reply (*Utor*). The contest goes on in this process.

This Kavi contest originated in villages. But since the mid-eighteenth century, on account of the British occupation of Bengal and then the Permanent Settlement (1793), absentee zamindars and other newly-rich classes of Calcutta started patronizing the *Kavis*. To suit their taste, the singers made *Kavi* songs crude and often obscene. It became dissociated from contemporary reality. During the time when *Kavi Gan* was thriving in Calcutta, the rural *Kavis* somehow managed to survive despite the strong pull of the city and the influence of the crude urban *Kavi Gan*.

About the mid-nineteenth century, the newly-enlightened middle class of Calcutta rejected this crude type of songs. While the urban *Kavi Gan* started dying out, it gradually revived in villages. The new generation of *Kavis* made their songs a powerful medium of expression of social and political discontent. It is this revival that has been discussed in the book *Kayekjan Lok Kavi*.

Kirtan: During the medieval period, the florescence of Neo-Vaisnavism gave birth to this popular musical form. Originally it was based on folk-tunes, but gradually got dissociated from folk music and became a class by itself. It is very popular all over Bengal and even outside Bengal.

Kissar Gan or *Kechchhar Gan*: Long narrative prose of Muslim composers is sometimes interrupted by short songs, associated with the main story. These solo songs are called *Kissar gan*.

Pala: The subject (or part of the subject) of a narrative song.

Panchali: A kind of narrative song usually singing the glory of gods and goddesses.

Phulgan: Nothing much is known about *Phulgan*. But a kind of narrative song called *Phulpat* is commonly heard in rural Chittagong. Because it is narrative in nature, it is usually set to the tune of *Panchali*. It has no connection whatsoever with '*Pat*', the common folk pictorical art of Bengal.

Parban: Songs sung on particular lunar days occasioning particular rituals, like the worship of the snake goddess Manasa in the month of Sravan (in English, these are called 'calendric songs').

Sari: A kind of group songs sung by boatmen while rowing. It is different from *Bhatiali* which is sung by a lone boatman who just keeps his scull still in the water, while the boat proceeds on its own in a downstream direction. *Sari* is 'action song'. The singing boatmen together propel the boat with their sculls. When they drop their sculls in the water, they hit the edge of the boat and make a sound. This sound helps the boatmen maintain the rhythm of the song.

For these short notes I have heavily depended upon Asutosh Bhattacharya, *Bangiya Loksangeet Ratnakar* (4 vols.), Paschim Banga Lok Sanskriti Gabesana Parisad, 32 Becharam Chatterji Street, Calcutta-34, 1966–7.

Notes and References

1. *Salil Chowdhuryr Gan*, collected by Dipa Mukhopadhyay and Subas Chowdhury, Kolkata: Saraswat Library, 1975.
2. Hindu Mela—a nationalist organization run for some years from 1867 by Nabagopal Mitra with the backing of the Tagore family. For the patriotic songs of the nineteenth century with a detailed discussion of their nature see my (compiled and edited) book *Swaseshprem o Swajatyabodher Gan o Kabita: Unabingsha Shatabdi*, published by Pashchim Banga Bangla Akademi, Kolkata, 2012.
3. Mukunda Das flourished during the Anti-Partition Agitation. His impact was felt even in the remotest villages of East Bengal. For the nationalist songs of the twentieth century see my (compiled and edited) *Swadhinata Sangramer Gan o Kabita: Bingsha Shatabdi*, Sahitya Akademi, New Delhi, 2001. Also see Geeta Chattopadhyay, ed., *Bangla Swadeshi Gan*, Dehi: University of Delhi, 1983. The first collection of Bengali patriotic songs is probably *Jatiya Sangeet* edited by Dwarakanath Gangopadhyay (1876) (42 pages, 29 songs). Such song books proliferated during the Swadeshi Movement.
4. Quoted by Hiren Bhattacharya, 'Sramajibi Manusher Andolan o Bangla Gan', *Sangeet Barta*, published by Rajya Sangeet Akademi, Department of Information and Culture, West Bengal Government, 1 March 1984.
5. Composed by a French worker-poet in 1871 as a tribute to the Paris Commune.
6. Interesting facts about these songs are known from Muzaffar Ahmad's *Kaji Nazrul Islam-Smritikatha*, Kolkata: National Book Agency, 1975 (4th edn.). Also Narayan Chowdhury, 'Rush Biplab O Kaji Najrul', *Sahitya Bhabna*, Kolkata: Popular Library, 1978.
7. A truncated manifestation of Goddess Durga.
8. From Hemanga Biswas's 'Gananatya Andolane Amar Gan', *Prastutiparba*, 1383/1976.
9. Interview, Priti Banerjee, in January 1983.

10. Jaya Roy, 'Life Sketch of Benoy Roy', *Benoy Roy—A Tribute,* Delhi: PPH, 1984.
11. Jatindramohan Sengupta. He called a railway and steamer strike during the Non-Cooperation Movement. Quoted in Pulak Chanda, *Ganakabiyal Ramesh Seal o Tar Gan*, Kolkata, 1978.
12. *Bishan* was published from Assam, 2nd edn., May Day, 1944.
13. Doel and Shyama are common birds of rural Bengal.
14. This song by Hemanga Biswas was included in *Bihsan*.
15. *Janayuddher Gan*, 3rd edn., AFWAA, May 1943.
16. *Jatiya Sangeet*, AFWAA, February 1945.
17. *Janayuddha*, 15 March 1945.
18. Interview, Sudhi Pradhan.
19. Hemanga Biswas's article in *Prastutiparba*, op. cit.
20. We learn about the YCI activities from many sources and these have been enumerated in the first chapter. So far as the musical activities of the YCI are concerned, 'The Youth Cultural Institute (1940–2)', an article by Amarendra Mukherjee, in *Unity*, December 1953, is very illuminating.
21 .Jyotirindra Moitra, 'Amader Nabajibaner Gan', *Sharadiya Kalantar*, 1972. It is, in fact, an interview conducted by Dipendranath Bandyopadhyay.
22. Bijan Bhattacharya, 'Gananatya Andolane Sekal O Ekal', *Bahurupi—Bijan Bhattacharya and Jyotirindra Mitra Memorial Number*, 1 May 1978.
23. Chinmohan Sahanabis, *No. 46* and Hiren Mukherji's *Tori Hote Teer* give delightful accounts of the musical activities of No. 46, Dharmatala Street, the centre of leftist cultural activities those days.
24. *Nabajibaner Gan*, Words and tunes—Jyotirindra Moitra, Notation—Jnanprakash Ghosh, Published by Progressive Writer's and Artists' Association, on behalf of the IPTA, 1945. On the front cover was published Sarojini Naidu's compliments (dated 12 January 1945). In his Introduction, Moitra acknowledged his debt to Jnanprakash Ghosh, Debabrata Biswas, Santosh Kumar Mitra, Pankaj Kumar Mallik and Hemanta Mukherjee—all of them closely associated with the IPTA. The book was reprinted in 1978 by Indira Shilpi Gosthi, Kolkata.
25. Hemanga Biswas, 'Shraddhanjali: Debabrata Biswas', *Baromas*, Sharadiya, 1980.
26. Debabrata Biswas, *Bratyajaner Ruddha Sangeet*, Kolkata: Karuna Prakashani, 1385.
27. The names listed in these two paragraphs are known from different sources—reminiscences of and interviews with different people. Sadhan Dasgupta's 'Purba Banglar Ganashilpi' in *Communist*, published by the CPI on its 50th anniversary in 1975, is particularly valuable, for it provides the names of a number of little-known artists of East Bengal.
28. *The IPTA Bulletin*, no. I.
29. Quoted from Benoy Roy's famous 'Suno Hindke rahnewale, suno, suno', rendered by Sadhana Guha and later Reba Roy; it became popular in Bengal too.

30. *Janayuddha* of 15 December 1943, 21 December 1943, 26 January 1944, 16 February 1944 and many other issues reported the sensation created by the Voice of Bengal Squad.
31. This letter was seen through the courtesy of Sudhi Pradhan.
32. *Janayuddha*, 31 January 1944.
33. Ibid., 22 March 1944.
34. The sources for this conference have been listed in Chapter I.
35. *Janayuddha*, 22 March 1944.
36. Reba Roy Chowdhury, 'Gananatya Sangher Ek Adhyay', *Gananatya*, Sharadiya, 1985.
37. Sajal Roy Chowdhury, 'Gananatyakatha (Part I)', *Gananatya*, Sharadiya, 1985.
38. Ravi Shankar, *Rag Anurag*, Kolkata: Ananda Publishers, 1980, p. 125.
39. We have come to know about the Central Squad's daily life and creative activities from various sources—interview with Priti Banerjee; Ravi Sahankar's *Rag Anurag*, pp. 123–8, *Benoy Roy: A Tribute*; Sajal Roy Chowdhury, 'Gananatya Katha' in *Gananatya*, Saradiya, 1985; also his book *Gananatya Katha*, Kolkata: Ganaman Prakashan, 1990; Reba Roy Chowdhury, 'Gananatya Sangher Ek Adhyay', *Gananatya*, Sharadiya, 1985; also her book *Jibaner Tane Shilper Tane*, Thema, Kolkata, 1999.
40. Jyotirindra Moitra, 'Amader Nabajibaner Gan', Sharadiya *Kalantar*, 1972.
41. Ravi Shankar, *Rag Anurag*.
42. Interview, Sudhi *Pradhan*. Ravi Shankar in particular has been blamed by Reba Roy Chowdhury in this connection, *Jibaner Tane Shilper Tane*, op. cit., pp. 21–2. She has talked about Ravi Shankar's ambition and extravagance (with a hint at his alcoholic habit), the expenses for which had to be met by the Party.
43. Interview, Reba Roy Chowdhury.
44. By Hemanga Biswas.
45. The last line is, in fact, a Bengali proverb which is similar in meaning to the English proverb 'Between Scylla and Charybdis'. The song is by Hemanga Biswas.
46. The rich and the poor.
47. This song by Benoy Roy was later used by Sambhu Mitra in his *Chand Baniker Pala* in a slightly altered form and with an acknowledgement to Roy.
48. The sources from which I have found the war-time songs are listed in the Bibliography.
49. The report of this meeting held on 7 July 1942, came out in *Janayuddha*, 15 July 1942.
50. The procession was arranged on the occasion of Id, October 1947. The *Swadhinata* reported the event on 21 October 1947.
51. Recollected by Chinmohan Sehanabis in his *No. 46*.

52. Quoted by Sajal Roy Chowdhury in his article in *Gananatya*, Sharadiya, 1985. K.A. Abbas' comment was originally published in the *Bombay Chronicle*.
53. Hiren Mukhopadhyay, *Tori Hote Teer*, pp. 439–40.
54. Interview, Chinmohan Sehanabis.
55. Jyotirindra Moitra, 'Amader Nabajibaner Gan'.
56. Debabrata Biswas, *Bratyajaner Ruddha Sangeet.*
57. *The IPTA Bulletin No. 1.*
58. Jyotirindra Moitra, 'Amader Nabajibaner Gan'.
59. Priti Banerjee and Hemanga Biswas possessed copies of many such songs, which they allowed me to see. Professor Gautam Chattopadhyay too recited many of them for me.
60. A brochure published by the YCI on the occasion of a function in August 1941 contained these songs. It has been included in Sudhi Pradhan's *Marxist Cultural Movement,* vol. I.
61. This song by Hemanga Biswas as well as his other songs quoted in this section has been included in *Hemanga Biswaser Gan*, published by Mass Singers, Kolkata, September 1980.
62. See Chapter I, the section entitled 'Post-War Popular Upsurge'.
63. Interview, Sudhi Pradhan. It seems that the song had two versions—Hindi and Bengali,
64. *Swadhinata*, 16 January 1946.
65. Ibid., 24 January 1946.
66. The People's Songs composed by Salil Chowdhury during this period, including this one, were compiled in a book *Ghum Bhangar Gan,* Kolkata: Naya Samskriti Prakashani, 1358/1951. Later, they were included in *Salil Chowdhuryr Gan*.
67. The river Vidyadhari had silted up and hundreds of acres of arable lands had been flooded with the salty water of the Bay of Bengal. The Peasants' Movement was in demand of the dredging of the Vidyadhari. Interview, Salil Chowdhury.
68. These two villages, Bara Kamlapur in the district of Hooghly and Dongajora in Kakdwip (24-Parganas), put up a tough fight during the Tebhaga Movement.
69. These two peasants of Chirir Port (Dinajpur) were killed in a clash with the police on 4 January 1947.
70. In Chandanpniri (South Kakdwip), eight villagers including Ahalya Das were killed on 6 November 1948, during a clash with the police.
71. A tyrannical king of the Hindu Mythology. He was ultimately killed by his nephew *Krishna*.
72. From *Tebhaga Sangram—Rajat Jayanti Smarak Grantha.*
73. Sardar Vallabhbhai Patel, Pundit Jawaharlal Nehru, and Maulana Abul Kalam Azad.
74. 'Raghupati Raghaba Raja Ram', a song in glory of Rama. It was a favourite song of Gandhi.

75. Election Number, December 1951.
76. Salil Chowdhury, 'Jiban Ujjiban', *Pratikshan*, 17 August 1983. Having been serialized in the journal *Pratikshan*, it was later published as a book.
77. Significant aspects of such dances and ballets are known from the following articles and books—Sajal Roy Chowdhury, 'Gananatya Katha' in *Gananatya*, Saradiya 1985; also his book *Gananatya Katha*; Reba Roy Chowdhury, 'Gananatya Sangher Ek Adhyay', *Gananatya*, Sharadiya, 1985, also her book *Jibaner Tane Shilper Tane*.
78. Jyorindra Moitra, 'Amader Nabajibaner Gan'.
79. Sajal Roy Chowdhury's article in *Gananatya*, Sharadiya 1985.
80. A Hindu festival where participants throw red powder at each other.
81. London, 21 December 1945, quoted in *Swadhinata*, 28 December 1945.
82. Translated in the *Janayuddha*, I February 1945.
83. *Parichay*, Phalgun, 1351/1945. Reba Roy Chowdhury, however, says in *Jibaner Tane Shilper Tane* (pp. 21–2) that *India Immortal*, which was largely based on classical music, thanks to Ravi Shankar's direction, failed to be as popular as the folk-based and much simpler *Spirit of India*.
84. Of course, the dance efforts of the IPTA had to face opposition as well. Santidev Ghosh complained in the *Anandabazar* (4 Chaitra, 1351/1945) that while Rabindranath had tried to popularize dance as a source of spontaneous and pure joy, Shankar had introduced hundred percent professionalism in it, followed by the IPTA using it for the entertainment of soldiers and shamelessly putting aside all social inhibitions about young men and women dancing together on the IPTA platform, mostly in erotic movements. Ghosh also did not like the use of the *Dhobi Dance* of rural Andhra in the *Spirit of India* to depict the defeat of the Nazis at the hands of the Red Army in Moscow. He found such adaptation inappropriate and unnecessary. Nibaran Chakrabarty penned a sharp protest against Santidev's views in *Arani* ('Gananritya Banam Santidev Ghosh', *Arani*, 6 and 13 April 1945).
85. Article by Sajal Roy Chowdhury in *Jibandharmi Natya Prayojanar Rup Rekha*, Kolkata: Jatiya Sahitya Parishad, ed. Sunil Dutta, p. 162.
86. C.P. Ghosh's report entitled '*Crisis in Bengal IPTA*', 1946, Sudhi Pradhan, ed., *Marxist Cultural Movement*, vol. I, pp. 295–6.
87. Those pieces of information about *Shahider Dak* have been provided by Sajal Roy Chowdhury and Reba Roy Chowdhury.
88. Source: *Parichay*, Bhadra, 1358/1951.
89. Two reports are particularly informative—'Singing They Go Into Battle Inspired by Bengal's Anti-Fascist Bards' by an anonymous writer, *People's War*, 7 February 1943. Chinmohan Sehanabis, 'Samskriti Anodolaner Natun Dhara '*Janayuddha*, 28 April 1943. Also a report in *Janayuddha*, 6 June 1943. The next few pages are largely based on these reports.
90. The above-mentioned article of *People's War*.

91. 'Amader Nabajibaner Gan'.
92. Quoted by Benoy Roy, 'Deshpremik Loksamskritir Pataka Janasadharaner Hate' *Janayuddha*, 6 October 1943.
93. Interview, Priti Banerjee.
94. Priti Banerjee, 'Benoy Roy's Role in Atma Raksha Samity', *Benoy Roy: A Tribute*.
95. Gautam Chattopadhyay, 'Benoyda', in the same book.
96. Sadhan Dasgupta's reminiscences in *Communist*.
97. Somnath Hore, 'Tebhaga Diary', *Ekshan*, Sharadiya, 1981.
98. A locally popular song describing how a young wife makes fun of her old husband.
99. He died in 1943.
100. This distinguished native of Chittagong assisted Dinesh Chandra Sen, one of the pioneering folklorists of Bengal, in the latter's study of the folk-culture of Chittagong (Interview, Kalpataru Sengupta, the Chittagong District Communist Party Secretary during the 1940s).
101. Hiren Mukherjee, *Tori Hote Teer*, p. 456.
102. The background of Hemanga Biswas's music career is known from his interview published in *Kalantar* (Autumn Issue 1982), his article in *Prastutiparba* (October 1976) and my interview with him.
103. This song and Sachin Dev Burman's famous romantic song 'Nishithe jaiyo phulobonere bhramara' (Oh Bumble-bee, go to the flower garden at night) have a striking tonal similarity.
104. The last age of creation, according to Hindu scripture—an age full of sins.
105. Interview, Kalpataru Sengupta.
106. This particular style was developed in the eighteenth century by Ramprasad, the famous composer of devotional songs addressed to the goddess Kali.
107. Mendicant ascetics.
108. George Rude, *Ideology and Popular Protest* (First Chapter), London: Lawrence and Wishart, 1980.
109. This aspect of Bengali folk songs has been discussed in Hemanga Biswas, 'A Glorious Heritage', *Folk Music and Folklores* (An Anthology), vol. I, Kolkata: Folk Music and Folklore Research Institute, 1 October 1967; and Hemanga Biswas, *Lokasangeet Samiksha: Bangla O Assam* (Two Chapters, both entitled 'Palli Samajer Sangeet O Sanghat'), A. Mukherjee and Company Private Limited, 1385/1978.
110. In rural Bengal, *Kavi* or 'poet' and 'composer-singer' are synonymous. In a narrower sense *Kavi* means *Kaviyal*, a particular category of composers specializing in *Tarja*, a kind of song tournament where two parties of singers are engaged in a dialogue in songs composed extempore. Also see Appendix III.
111. Sources for Ramesh Seal and his associate *Kavis* of Chittagong:
    (a) Subhas Mukhopadhyay, 'Chatganyer Kaviyala', *Janayuddha*, 22 September 1944.

(b) Sudhi Pradhan, 'Banglar Pallikavi', *Janayuddha*, 25 January 1945 (it was about Ramesh Seal and Asutosh Chowdhury).

(c) Pulak Chanda, *Ganakaviyal Ramesh Seal O Tahar Gan*, Kolkata: Kathasilpa, April 1978.

(d) Atul Chandra Bandyopadhyay, ed., *Chetanik* (Ramesh Seal Centenary Special Number), Lalbag, Mushidabad, 1976–7. The article by Kalpataru Sengupta is particularly informative.

(e) Interview, Kalpataru Sengupta.

(f) Interview, Sudhi Pradhan.

(g) Sunil Chakravarty, 'Kavi-gan O Kaviyal Ramesh Seal', *Gananatya*, Sravan, 1374/1967.

(h) For the verse-books of Ramesh Seal and his associate Kavis, see Bibliography.

112. A *Pir* is a Muslim saint. *Sarif* means sacred as in Macca *Sarif.*

113. These two songs are from *Kavir Gan* published by Ramesh Seal from Chittagong soon after the inauguration of the Chittagong Jila Kavi Samity. The other contributors were Raigopal Das, Govinda Chandra De, Muhammad Hedayet Islam Khan, Sailen Sen, Bankim Sen and Dhiren Kanu.

114. Sources for Sheikh Gumhani Dewan:

(a) Sudhi Pradhan, 'Kavi Sheikh Gumani Dewan', *Janayuddha*, 1 March 1945.

(b) Atul Chandra Bandyopadhya, ed., *Chetanik* (Gumhani Dewan Memorial Special Number) 4th year, 3rd issue, Murshidabad, n.d., probably it was mid-1970s.

(c) Samarendra Sengupta, *Desh*, 'Charansamrat Gumani Dewan', *Desh*, Kartik, 1383/1976.

115. The challenge thrown by a party of singers to the opponent party in a Kavi contest.

116. In several letters, the poet acknowledged his debt to them. Here is an extract from one such letter (addressed to Gouricharan, dated 3.9. 51): 'Accept my sincere regards. I've received all the papers and journals sent by you. These are indeed food to me. I've seen the songs of mine which you revised. You have done it excellently. I'll compose some more very soon.'

117. Sources for Nibaran Pandit:

(a) Hemanga Biswas, 'Lok-Kavi Nibaran Pandit, *Gananatya*, January 1976.

(b) A copy of Nibaran Pandit's verse-book *Lok-Sangeet* was owned by Sudhi Pradhan (for details see Bibliography). Some songs by this composer are in an exercise book belonging to Hemanga Biswas. Other songs are probably lost. *The IPTA Bulletin*, 1 July 1943, informs us of two *Panchalis* by Nibaran Pandit. Their themes were anti-Japanese resistance and national crisis. Five thousand copies were sold, according to the Bulletin.

118. A kind of cigarette made of tree-leaf.
119. Food Control and War Contract.
120. Weekly markets held in rural Bengal.
121. Benoy Roy, 'Desapremik Lok Samskritir Pataka Janasadharaner Hate' (The People Hold Aloft the Banner of Patriotic Mass Culture), *Janayuddha*, 6 October 1943.
122. Sadhan Dasgupta, 'Purba Banglar Ganashilpi', *Communist*, 1975.
123. A two-stringed musical instrument common in rural Bengal.
124. A popular Bengali folk tale that describes how Behula, whose husband had died of snake-bite during their wedding night owing to a curse of the snake-goddess Manasa, pluckily went all the way to heaven, pleased the gods there by dancing and got her husband back. This story constitutes the theme of the popular folk ballad *Manasa Mangal* which is sometimes called *Padma Puran*.
125. Songs on Radha-Krisna. The theme is their separation from each other, when Krisna, as the ruler of Mathura, stays away from Radha who is a resident of Vrindaban.
126. Nimai Sannyasi is Sri Chaitanya, the founder of Neo-Vaishnavism in sixteenth Century Bengal.
127. This particular issue of *Swadhinata* is not available anywhere. I have found this song in the form of a clipping kept at the archives of the Intelligence Branch of the West Bengal police.
128. *Phen*, is the water in which rice has been cooked. *Amani* is the water in which the cooked rice has been soaked overnight.
129. Jagat Saha, 'Lal Sukra Oraon o Tar Katha' in *Jalpaiguri Loksamsriti Utsav Smaranika* (n.d., probably sometime in the 1970s or 1980s).
130. Manikrisna Sen, 'Tebhaga Andolane Rangpur', *Tebhagar Sangram Rajat Jayanti Smarak Grantha*.
131. Manikrishna Sen says that the *Dhyana*s were a social problem in Rangpur at that time.
132. For details about *Gambhira* I have seen an Interview with Biswanath Pandit (taken by Ratna Bhattacharya), *Gananatya*, Sharadiya, 1985. Pradyot Ghosh, *Gambhira Loksangeet O Utsav*, Kolkata: Chakra and Company, 1376/1969.
133. Quoted by Hiren Bhattacharya, 'Sramajibi Manuser Andolan O Bangla Gan', *Sangeet Barta*, 1 March 1984.
134. Report of *Parichay*, Bhadra 1358/1951.
135. Songs of these worker-poets have been obtained mainly from Hemanga Biswas's collection.
136. This song was translated into Bengali by Benoy Roy.
137. A kind of tomtom.
138. Tambourine.
139. Information about Asgar has been obtained from Sajal Roy Chowdhury.
140. *Swadhinata*, 24 October 1946.

141. Jaykesh Mukherjee, 'Howrah Jelar Gananatya Sangha: Pratham Jug', *Gananatya*, January 1986.
142. Ramshankar Chowdhury, Asansol Gananatya Sangha o Pragati Lekhak o Shilpi Sangher Andolan', *Gananatya*, October 1975.
143. See Hemanga Biswas, *Loksangeet Samiksha—Bangla O Assam*, p. 142.
144. Sudhi Pradhan, ed., *Marxist Cultural Movement*, vol. II, p. 219. In his reminiscences he said that in 1942 he had written a *Jatra Pala* named *Muktir Dak* in response to the People's War line and that this had been enacted at Badartala Rathtalar Math in front of about 1,000 spectators, and also that in 1948 he wrote another *Jatra Pala* ('Jiban o Shilpa', *Gananatya*, January 1969).
145. 'Singing they Go into the Battle. . . .', *People's War*, 7 February 1943. According to Sudhi Pradhan, the lines added were probably 'Singapore luta, Rangoon jwalaya, Hindpar keya dhabaiya ho' and there were further additions yet later—'Soviet jita, German hara/ Japan lute, Chinne roka'.
146. See Appendix III.
147. The book was published in 1360/1953. The third chapter consists of songs that have been called '*Akasmat Geeti*' or 'accidental songs' by the author. Their themes are topical incidents and they give us glimpses into society, politics and history. This part has been subdivided into three sections: 'Nationalist songs', 'Songs on contemporary events' and 'Songs composed during the period from the Japanese attack and Food Control to the Partition'.
148. Also 'Apasamskritir Biruddhe Samskritik Jukta Fronter Swarup O Samasya' by Hemanga Biswas (under the pen-name Mohan Murmu), *Anik*, September–October–November 1973 and December 1973, Berhampore. Here he has discussed the political problems of People's Songs, not only with reference to the period of our study, but in a broader context.
149. Though when I requested Hemanga Biswas to sing the song, he sang it up to the line 'Still the foreign government denies us freedom of action' and could not remember the rest. The same thing happened with Sudhi Pradhan and Saroj Hajra. It seems the last part artificially added failed to become popular.
150. Cited by Reba Roy Chowdhury, *Jeebaner Tane Shilper Tane*, Kolkata: Thema, 1999, p. 34.
151. Dipendranath Bandyopadhyay, 'Benoy: A Tribute', *Benoy Roy—A Tribute*, p. 67.
152. Interview, Salil Chowdhury
153. Salil Chowdhury, 'Jiban Ujjiban' (*Life Brought to Life*) published in *Pratikshan*, 2 July 1983–17 June 1984. Later published as a book.
154. 6 June 1943.
155. Included in Sudhi Pradhan's *Marxist Cultural Movement*, vol. I.
156. Hemanga Biswas's article in *Prastutiparba*, op. cit.

157. Interview, Salil Chowdhury. Salil Chowdhury remembers having crossed swords with Hemanga Biswas on the issue of folk-form at a conference in Bombay. His arguments in reply to Hemanga Biswas's allegation that by disregarding folk music and using Western forms he was distorting Indian culture and getting alienated from the Indian people were similar to Biswas's later-day realization. Chowdhury asked Biswas if every field of Indian culture borrows from the West to become up-to-date (he gave the examples of the novel, the sonnet and the blank verse in literature), why music alone should remain in the Middle Ages. He told Biswas 'You have come from Calcutta by plane. If you are so fond of Indian culture, you should have started from Calcutta three months back in a bullock-cart to reach here'. Chowdhury argued that after all a good chorus cannot be based on *Kirtan* or *Bhajan*, and that long back the nationalist urge had made Tagore use a marching rhythm in his songs, e.g. 'Eka sutre bandhiachi sahasrati man'. Chowdhury believes that if one wants to survive, one must keep on moving ahead. Exact reproduction of folk forms cannot live long. One has to experiment.
158. For a good discussion on the musicological aspect of *Nabajibaner Gan*, see Padmanabha Dasgupta, 'Bajrer Swaralipi', *Parichay*, Criticism Number, 1387 (1980)
159. *Parichay*, Phalgun, 1352.
160. Sumangala Damodaran, 'Protest through Music', www.india-seminar.com/2008/588/588_sumangala-damdaran.htm
161. Hemanga Biswas, 'Jibaner Madhye Sur Chhariye Achhe', Sharadiya *Kalantar*, 1982. (It is, in fact, an interview taken by Dipa Mukherjee).
162. Published on 18 November 1951.

3

The Theatre of Politics and the Politics of Theatre

The Background

THEATRE, A 'DIRECT' art of a perceptible and even tactile quality and so a very powerful art, is at the same time a people's art more than any other art-form. This claim is justified by the fact that it turns a great number of people into actors even as they watch the actors portray life before them. It makes all of them share intense feelings at one time and place, thus creating at least for the time being a bond of fellowship. Theatre appeals to the social minds of individuals and arouses collective thoughts bypassing all individual variations.

But what happens if the theatre becomes just a market place where producers sell entertainment to a faceless audience sitting in a dark auditorium? If money-making is the only motive in the whole process of production—the writing of the play, the acting and so on? If those who watch the drama are alienated from society and from their own social selves? All this means a negation of the very nature of theatre.

And this was exactly the state of the Bengali theatre in the early 1940s when some people thought of building up a People's Theatre, which would be distinguishable from the usual run of commercial theatre. One of the advocates of the new theatre described the contemporary commercial theatre in the following words:[1]

> Theatre? What does it stand for, to the average people? It is just glamour—a well-lit stage—din and bustle in the auditorium—indifferent music—actors and actresses only to be seen and applauded on the stage but shunned off it—queer scenes badly painted and wrongly arranged. This is about all. And what about the plays? Vague themes and forgotten gods—historical events twisted and turned into fantastic, unrecognisable forms—social sketches which are just as unreal as the stories of Jules Verne—musical comedies which are neither musical nor comedies. . . . The Bengali theatre caters for a certain section of people who have nothing better to do and are just bored.

This was the Bengali middle-class whose patronage made commercial theatre thrive in Calcutta. The War had caused a sharp increase in the urban middle-class population, often suddenly made rich, and seeking cheap entertainment. Five theatre-halls in the city continued to be packed to capacity and a new one had just come up in Dhaka at a time when competition from the film world kept the theatre at bay in other parts of India and when a disastrous Famine was devastating Bengal. 'Thanks to that class for whom the disaster was not something absolute, the class that kept its eyes shut to the misfortune. This class always looks upward and never downward. As they are engaged in the difficult task of denying the internal rift caused by a downward pull from outside, their life is full of contradictions and these contradictions are reflected in their theatre.' This was the observation of Manoranjan Bhattacharya, a renowned actor who was once associated with the commercial theatre and then became a votary of the People's Theatre.[2]

Mythological, pseudo-historical and domestic plays were all that were produced to help the alienated audience of the middle-class simultaneously escape from reality and fill their vacuity. At best, these dramas were an indiscriminate glorification of old hierarchical values, attempts to rouse the nationalist spirit through distorted history, often smacking of communalism, or so-called 'social' plays which were nothing but stories of domestic quarrels or cheap love, intended to arouse maudlin sentimentality and with no social perspective at all.

It is true that during the 1930s the quality of commercial theatre improved considerably, primarily due to the efforts of Sisir Kumar Bhaduri, the talented actor and producer. He brought aesthetics to the staging of plays. His acting, though of a romantic nature, was superb. Backdrop, music, dance, lighting—everything was given proper care for a harmonized effect heightening the appeal of the play. Moreover, about this time, Satu Sen introduced into the Bengali theatre new ideas about stage-craft (e.g. revolving stage) and lighting (e.g. mood-light). But despite all this, theatre lagged far behind the contemporary reality which was strewn with numerous social and political problems. Sisir Kumar mostly enacted plays written by playwrights of earlier generations, having little contemporary relevance—Kshirod Prosad Vidyabinod, Dinabandhu Mitra, Girish Chandra Ghosh, Dwijendralal Roy, and also some plays from Tagore and Sharat Chandra. His famous plays were *Alamgir*, *Sita*, *Chandragupta*, *Shah Jehan*, *Naranarayan* (Man-God, standing for Krishna), *Pandab-Gourav* (The Glory of the Pandavas), etc.,—the very names indicate how dated they were.

It is interesting that Srikumar Bandyopadhyay, a well known literary critic (and not known as a leftist), had serious reservations about Bhaduri's contribution to the Bengali theatre:

Though his reform of the stage and his art of production reached an unthinkable height, he failed to give inspiration to the writing of entirely modern plays suitable for his age. Even those of his plays, which were not mythological or historical and were based on modern society and were written under his own custody, were not of any high standard. They were no match for the superb quality of his acting. His unique talent for acting has been applied to second and third-rate plays loaded with irrelevant matters and this shows that the life of theatre is not exactly dependent upon stage application and the improvement in one does not necessarily bring about an improvement in the other. A great drama does not depend on talented actors and skilful production; it springs from the source of an invisible emotional swelling of the national life.[3]

At the time when Sisir Kumar was staging *Bandanar Biye* (Bandana's Wedding) and Ahindra Chowdhury, another notable personality in the commercial theatre, was repeating dramas written a quarter of a century ago. The 'emotional swelling' caused by the Bengal Famine of 1943 produced the famous drama *Nabanna* (New Harvest), having as its characters some peasants ruined by the Famine. It was put up by the IPTA in October 1944, at the Srirangam, Sisir Kumar's own theatre hall. But the IPTA's very starting-point was different from that of any commercial producer. The IPTA enthusiasts felt outraged by some grave social wrongs and wanted to protest against them. To provide theatrical entertainment was not their primary concern. The way they confronted live social issues had been unthinkable in the commercial theatre. So far as the theatrical form was concerned, *Nabanna* was a worthy succesor to and in fact much bolder and more innovative than Sisir Kumar's theatre. Thus, a new theatre movement started in Bengal.

While pointing out the newness of the new theatre movement ushered in by *Nabanna*, I would like to stress that it was not really *sui generis*. For one thing, the politics of nationalism had been permeating the theatre space of Bengal for quite some time, Dinabandhu Mitra's play *Nildarpan* being a very early example. Though its impact could not be sustained for a number of reasons, different phases of the freedom movement in the twentieth century did make their marks in the field of theatre. Two of the most famous exponents of the IPTA-introduced theatre—Sambhu Mitra and Utpal Dutta—both acknowledged Sisir Bhaduri as a great source of inspiration. Utpal Dutta said that never had he let go of any opportunity to watch Sisir Bhaduri's theatre and was aggrieved that the new theatre movement never acknowledged its debt to the glorious past of the Bengali theatre.[4] Sambhu Mitra used to watch Bhaduri's acting from beside the wings and admired its terrific power and lifelines. He was keen to act in Bhaduri's theatre too. Mitra comments: 'He was our first theatre director who visualized the stage holistically, with light, backdrop and acting.' Still

Sisir Bhaduri could not fully satisfy Mitra's quest for theatre, and ultimately the latter joined the IPTA.[5]

The Idea of the People's Theatre

Where did the idea of the People's Theatre come from? What exactly was meant by the People's Theatre?

A theatre movement with a view to challenging commercial theatre and presenting something serious to the audience, had been crystallizing in Europe since the late nineteenth century. In 1887 Andre Antoine established the Theatre Libre in France, probably the oldest attempt at a new theatre movement. Between 1887 and 1911, the movement spread to France, Belgium, Germany, Sweden, Hungary, Russia, England and Ireland. From 1911 onwards, America was included in the movement. This alternative theatre wanted to highlight contemporary issues on the one hand and on the other, carry out formalistic experiments in order to get the spectators involved in the theatre in a profound way.[6]

The exponents of the People's Theatre in India had heard of the Theatre Libre of France, Thomas Grain's Independent Theatre of England and so on. But not many books on this new kind of theatre were available to them. About the theatre movement in Germany, for example, Hauptmann's[7] books were all that they had read. They had not read much about Brecht, though his talent was attaining its full bloom during the 1930s and 1940s, to be more precise, during 1933–48, when he was in exile.[8] They had read Romain Rolland's book *People's Theatre* and were inspired by its content. Whatever they knew about the People's Theatre Movement of Soviet Russia (Stanislavski's Moscow Art Theatre, for example) and China strongly influenced them. They had read Stanislavsky's book on the Russian Theatre and the writings of Edgar Snow, Anna Louis Strong and Epstein on the Chinese People's Theatre.

But the Indian People's Theatre was not just an imitation of these foreign experiments. Rather, it was born out of the socio-political matrix of India. It was but one aspect of the total programme of widening ties with the people and moving towards a better society, an ideal dearly held by a section of the intellectuals at the time. In other countries too, the new theatre had more or less a political context. Particularly in Russia, which was busy building up a post-Revolutionary society and in China, which was in the throes of a Revolution, the theatre movement was considered as part of the political movement. Hence, of all People's Theatres, those of Russia and China were found to be the ideal models for the Indians to emulate. It seemed that without a strong political affiliation, the ideal of the People's Theatre could not be fully realized. And by politics, they meant Communist politics.

The front cover of the first IPTA Bulletin[9] proudly declared: 'People's Theatre stars the People'. By people they primarily meant the workers and the peasants. No doubt, they also intended to wean away a large number of middle-class people from the lure of the commercial theatre, though it was not articulated in that bulletin. They wanted their theatre to communicate to the audience their perception of the social reality of the time and thus heighten the sensibility of the audience. In Bishnu Dey's words, 'Not only does a dramatic production work upon already-known association, but it must create new powers of understanding; it must, as it were, renew the self-consciousness of the people and stimulate their power of association and integration,' which, according to Dey, was the teaching of the Soviet Theatre.[10]

With this intention, they thought of new themes for their plays, preferably rooted in contemporary reality. Indeed, to them contemporaneity meant a shocking eventfulness. The fascist brutality manifest in the Japanese assault on East Bengal, the benumbing Bengal Famine, etc., represented to them significant themes. The new theatre would also mean exploration of folk forms like the *Krishna Jatra*, *Manasa Panchali*, etc. In fact, the whole cultural heritage of India received their regardful attention. 'Nor is it (the People's Theatre Movement) a movement which discards our rich cultural heritage, but one which seeks to revive the lost in that heritage by re-interpreting, adopting and integrating it with the most significant facts of our people's lives and aspiration in the present epoch.' said the above-mentioned bulletin.

This, roughly, was the idea of the People's Theatre. This central notion was elaborated by different people on different occasions. For Manoranjan Bhattacharya, for example, reaching the poor and the lowly meant reaching the Muslim community that had so far been excluded from all thoughts of the dramaturges. Indeed, popular themes like patriotic Hindus fighting oppressive Muslim rulers tended to encourage the impression that the Bengali theatre was not meant for the Muslims. Yet the patronage of this large section of the Bengali population would be vital for the theatre. Bhattacharya said, 'If the theatre wants a healthy contact with the mainstream of national life, it must give up the bias towards a particular religion and talk about delights and sorrows, hopes and aspirations of the universal man. People inspired by nationalism and a new humanism would have to join the theatre as dramatists, actors, directors and producers.' He also wanted changes in stage-craft, acting and play-writing:

Stage-craft is expensive at present—more an attempt at pomp and grandeur than beauty. The stage-designer needs to change his angle of vision. He should show that beauty can be created at a small cost. The actor would have to follow the styles and dictions of common people, both Hindus and Muslim. The playwright would have to write about the sufferings, hopes and strength of the masses. The compassionate businessman must resist his greed in order to help reach the people.[11]

But, despite the optimism of Manoranjan Bhattacharya, 'compassionate businessmen' could not be expected to produce the People's Theatre, for that was not a sound commercial proposition for them, and anyway the IPTA had been formed to act as the producer. The IPTA was to fight simultaneously on two fronts to achieve its end—first, to fight the economic system of a society that treats culture as a commodity—by developing a new kind of relationship with the consumers of culture; and second, to fight the cultural limitations of the audience, to develop a new cultural taste in them by overpowering their characteristic lightmindedness.

The Beginning

The beginning of the People's Theatre Movement in Bengal is usually dated from the staging of *Nabanna* in Calcutta in October 1944. However, this performance was preceded by a series of one-act plays based on topical issues and organized by the Students' Federation, the Youth Cultural Institute, the Anti-fascist Writers' and Artists' Association and the IPTA itself.

BPSF

It is not surprising that the People's Theatre in Bengal was first undertaken by a group whose concern was not so much the theatre as the people. From 1938, the Bengal Provincial Students' Federation (BPSF)[12] started organizing cultural conferences where progressive plays, often written by students themselves, were staged. At the Patna Students' Congress of 1941, the BPSF presented Clifford Odets' drama *Waiting for Lefty*. It was about a taxi drivers' strike in New York at the height of the Depression. The BPSF used to send cultural brigades to different districts. After the Japanese attack on the eastern frontier, they sent out one such brigade to tour six districts of East Bengal, presenting two plays—*Japanke Rukhte Hobe* (Resist Japan) and *Rajbandider Mukti Chai* (Set the Political Prisoners Free). The first one, written by the young poet Sukanta Bhattacharya, was later edited and named *Manipur*[13] and had at least one show in Calcutta—on China Day, 7 July 1942, at the University Institute Hall.

On 16 May 1942, an advertisement appeared in *Janayuddha* inviting more anti-Japanese plays and offering a prize of Rs. 10 for the best one. The conditions were: (1) The play should be suitable for open-air performance and should require minimum scenes and costumes; (2) The language should be easy and comprehensible to uneducated people; (3) It should be able to arouse anti-Japanese feelings and a spirit of resistance among the audience.;

and (4) The performance should be completed within an hour-and-a-half. The plays were to reach the *Janayuddha* office by 31 May 1942 and to be judged by Satyendranath Majumder, Professor Hiren Mukherjee and Gopal Haldar, Later the deadline was extended to 31 June, because the plays that had been received were not found up to expectations and a prize of Rs. 30 was offered.[14] Eventually, *Desrakshar Dak* (A Call to Defend the Country) written by Banaspati Gupta was declared the prize-winning play and the editor promised to publish it shortly, though the promise was never kept.

Once again, on 3 November 1943, plays for pamphleteering purpose were invited through *Janayuddha.* The notice said that it was time to reap the *aman* crop (autumn paddy) and the peasants should be kept informed of the evil intention of the black-marketeers and hoarders. New songs and plays were needed for this purpose and they were to be sent to the cultural division, *Janayuddha.*

YCI

When political workers were staging plays of a new kind for sheer propaganda, the members of the YCI,[15] mostly Calcutta University students, were engaged in theatrical experimentations mainly to invent a new cultural form. They were left-minded, of course, but had little connection with the common people. Their isolation is evident in the fact that they started by staging plays in English.

The first play they selected was *Politicians Take to Rowing* written by Jolly Mohan Kaul, who was one of them.[16] It was a satire on the eminent political leaders of the world as well as India. Hitler is challenged to a boat race by India. He is advised in this respect by Mussolini and the British. The captain of the Indian team is Linlithgow, but Indian leaders like Gandhi, Rajagopalachari and Jinnah are in the team too. The play exposes the hollowness of fascist politcs and also the fractured world of Indian politics. There was a suggestion that healthy politics needed the participation of common people. The actors were Dilip Bose, Subrata Banerjee, Prasanta Sanyal, Kamal Bose, Jolly Kaul, Sunil Kanti Sengupta and others. The first performance was at the annual function of the Calcutta University Rowing Club. It was presided over by Shyama Prasad Mukherjee, Vice-Chancellor of the University. Soon they received invitations from different places including Scottish Church College, where they staged two shows.

Then there was Jolly Kaul's *The Boy Grows Up*, based on an anti-fascist German play. Debabrata Bose (Bablu Bose) helped him in the work of adaptation. Debabrata Bose himself wrote *In the Heart of China.* The theme was China's struggle for unity, particularly the famous Marco Polo

Bridge incident.[17] The cast was composed of Renu Roy, Uma Chakravarty, Rama Goswami, Kamal Bose, and others. Another play by Bose—*The Shopkeepers*—on the plight of petty shop-keepers in fascist Germany, was enacted at YWCA. He wrote yet another play on Dnieper Dam, but that was never staged.[18]

After some time, the YCI thought of staging Bengali plays. *Anjangarh*, the dramatized version of 'Fossil'[19] written by Subodh Ghosh, the story that had been published in *Agrani* and created quite a sensation, was their next venture. The story told the misery of the poor 'Kurmi' subjects of the Anjangarh estate. They were oppressed by the feudal Maharajah on the one hand and the British capitalists on the other. The dramatization was done by Sunil Chatterjee who was also the director. The actors were Sanat Lahiri, Subrata Banerjee, Kamal Bose, Sunil Sen, Sabitasundar Bose and others. This, along with *In the Heart of China*, was staged at the Overtoon Hall (at the junction of College Street and Harrison Road) towards the end of 1940. Among those present was Sarojini Naidu.

Kerani (Clerk) written by Sunil Chatterjee was another drama staged by the YCI. It analysed the awakening of the lower middle-class clerks of a merchant office into political radicalism and yet their inability to overcome hesitation. It projects the working class as superior in terms of radicalism and unity. Shows were held at the Muslim Institute Hall and the YWCA. Sarojini Naidu and Suniti Kumar Chatterjee, among others, watched the play. There was some novelty in the stage-craft. The stage was bicameral and the spectators could see two scenes at the same time. The cast included Samar Gupta, Dhiren Gupta, Jolly Kaul, Barun Mukherjee and Ardhendu Mukherjee. Ardhendu Mukherjee, later to become a renowned film director, directed the play.

AFWAA

In the meantime, some theatre-enthusiasts such as Bijan Bhattacharya and Sambhu Mitra had gathered around the newly formed AFWAA.[20] Sunil Chatterjee was appointed Secretary of the Drama Division of AFWAA. A full-fledged theatre movement was to start soon.

Among the first dramas staged by the AFWAA was Tagore's *Rather Rashi* (The Rope of the Chariot). The all-powerful Brahmanas, Khatriyas and Vaisyas pulled the rope of the chariot of *Mahakal* (Eternal Time) with all their strength and yet could not move it. It was the outcast Sudras who were able to pull the carriage at last. The actors were Hiren Kumar Sanyal, Buddhadev Bose, Kamakshi Prasad Chatterjee, Chanchal Kumar Chatterjee and others, i.e. mostly men of letters.[21]

Numerous plays were staged by local branches of the AFWAA. In the *Third Annual Report* of the organization[22] the list is as follows: *Dui*

Purush (Two Generations) written by Tarasankar Banerjee, staged by the Murshidabad branch; *Namaiba Kebalam* (The Name Only) written by Sanjib Bhattacharya, produced by the Jessore branch; *Amader Vidyatan* (Our School) put up by the Mymensingh branch with the help of a local theatrical group; the Gobardanga branch's *Bir Kisan* (The Heroic Peasant) presented at the peasant conference at Badarhat, Khantura and Banagram sub-divisions. According to the report, two plays had been written for the Jalpaiguri branch. The report also points out that Subodh Ghosh wrote a play, *Karnaphulir Dak* (Call of the River Karnaphuli), specially for the AFWAA (according to Sudhi Pradhan, this was not the well-known playwright Subodh Ghosh of Calcutta, but a local writer of Chittagong), which staged the play in Chittagong.[23] A 'timely people's play' was written by Harindranath Chatterjee and was staged at Srirangam on 23 March 1943 under the auspices of the AFWAA and the FSU. Among the actors was the writer himself. This is known from a notice in *Arani*, 19 March 1943.

Meanwhile a terrible Famine had gripped Bengal. Bijan Bhattacharya wrote a one-act play *Agun* (Fire) about some famished people queueing up in front of a rice control shop. Under the playwright's direction it was staged at Natyabharati (later named Grace Cinema, on Mahatma Gandhi Road) in May 1943.[24]

On the same night at Natyabharati, *Laboratory* written by Benoy Ghosh was also staged.[25] The theme was social use or misuse of science. A dedicated scientist engaged in the pursuit of 'pure science' was brought to his senses by his own children who had a keen social consciousness and were involved in leftist politics. The play was heavily influenced by the film *Professor Mamlock* (1938), shown a year before in Globe Cinema Hall.[26] *Laboratory* was staged on the occasion of the inaugural ceremony of the IPTA in Bombay in May 1943. It was enacted by the Bengal Squad and directed by Sambhu Mitra.

After the IPTA came into being, the performing artists of the AFWAA set up the Bengal branch of the IPTA. They staged *Homeopathy* written by Manoranjan Bhattacharya, President, Bengal IPTA.[27] It protested against religious superstitions and communal feelings in a plague situation in rural Bengal, then showed how in the face of the brutal Japanese air-raids, the Hindus and the Muslims of a village felt the need for unity. The director was Sambhu Mitra. The play somehow failed to be popular and was not staged more than twice. The first show was held at Star on 3 January 1944, along with another play, *Jabanbandi*.

Jabanbandi (The Attestation) produced by the IPTA was important in many ways. Written by Bijan Bhattacharya,[28] it was the first play in Bengal since *Nil Darpan* (written in the nineteenth century) to give importance to peasant issues, presenting the story of a Famine-striken peasant family migrating to an indifferent city, vying with dogs there in their scramble for food in garbage bins, and dying on the street dreaming of golden crops. It presented a stark contrast between the harsh reality of the rural world and the affluence of city life. This story was later to be elaborated on in *Nabanna*.

Under the direction of Sambhu Mitra, *Jabanbandi* was staged on 3 and 7 January 1944, at Star and Minerva respectively and was highly successful. The whole team of actors consisting of Gangapada Basu, Bijan Bhattacharya, Tripti Bhaduri (later Mitra), Rabin Majumdar, Amal Bhattacharya, Sudhi Pradhan, Monika Bhattacharya, Jalad Chatterjee, Anu Dasgupta, Rani Chakravarty and others, was greatly admired. They proved to be a determined and disciplined team, inspired by patriotism, spirit of experimentation and courage to give shape to 'Socialist Realism' (a term popular among the leftists at that time, though it was not without problems) by responding to current social problems. The future of Bijan Bhattacharya as a playwright and of Sambhu Mitra as a director was decided. The critics of *Ananda Bazar Patrika*, *Arani*, Manujendra Bhanja who was the film and theatre critic of the English journal *Dipali*, playwright Sachin Sengupta, actor Naresh Mitra and Biswanath Bhaduri, left-minded intellectual D.P. Mukherjee, all unhesitatingly applauded this effort of the IPTA.

Jabanbandi was also presented at the peasant conference held in Dinajpur in March 1944 and in 24-Parganas in July 1944, at the invitation of the Bengal Kisan Sabha before thousands of peasants. In Bengal, 16 shows were performed before an aggregate audience of 50,000, which collected Rs. 15,000 in aid of different relief organizations.[29] The play was translated into Hindi by Nemichand Jain. The Hindi version *Antim Abhilash* (The Last Will) was put up by the 'Voice of Bengal Squad' in Bombay and other parts of India under Sambhu Mitra's direction. The translator and his wife Rekha acted in these shows. In Guajrat they put up a Gujarati version of *Jabanbandi*.

These shows raised Rs. 100,000 for the People's Relief Fund, a considerable part of which was spent on providing relief to the Famine-stricken, and this won all-India fame for the Bengal IPTA. *Jabanbandi* also laid a firm organizational basis for the IPTA, for the People's Relief Committee gave back to the IPTA part of the donation towards forming a team on a wholetime basis on condition that this cultural team would collect more money for relief work. A Drama Squad was set up within the Bengal IPTA as distinct from the singing section of the organization. This facilitated the production of *Nabanna*.

It is known from the *Half-Yearly Report* (*January to June, 1944*)[30] of the AFWAA that the shows of *Antim Abhilash* were appreciated by all Bombay newspapers (*Bombay Chronicle*, *Bombay Sentinel*, *Inqilab*, *Janambhumi* and even *Times of India*) and also by Sarojini Naidu, Bhulabhai Desai, the film director Santaram, actor Motilal, Soviet film distributor Sayadiyants, actor Balgandharva, poet Sumitranandan Pant and many others.

In Bengal, also all the shows of *Jabanbandi* in different parts of the province were warmly received. A report to the IPTA Headquarters from the Bengal branch informs us that in the first week of February, under the auspices of the Kisan Conference held in 24-Parganas, an open-air performance of the play took place before a huge assembly of kisans. In February, they organized five more performances of the same play at different places: at the ARP Headquarters, at Minerva Theater and three shows at Jamshedpur. In March 1944, the play was enacted before the huge gathering of the Bengal Provincial Kisan Conference held in the district of Dinajpur. In March 1944, they also staged the play at the Friends of the Soviet Union Conference at Jessore where they impressed amongst others the well known actor Naresh Chandra Mitra, who presented a silver medal to Tripti Bhaduri.

This, in short, is the story of the beginning of the People's Theatre Movement in Bengal. There is a controversy, about the pioneering role of *Jabanbandi* (and *Nabanna*) in this respect. Some people claim that Manoj Basu's *Natun Prabhat* (The New Dawn) written in 1939 and staged a few times, started the New Theatre Movement. The theme was peasant life—particularly a conflict between the progressive and conservative attitudes of peasants.[31.] But the plays written by the student-writers of the YCI and *Fossil* and *Kerani* were almost contemporaneous with *Natun Prabhat* and had wider impact.

In this connection, mention may also be made of the play *Bhanga Chaka* (The Broken Wheel) written in jail in 1939 by a prisoner, Jyotirmoy Sengupta, who had been a revolutionary terrorist.[32] The story of the play revolved around a conflict between the workers and the owner of a factory. According to Sudhi Pradhan, it was the first Bengali play thoroughly influenced by Marxism. Sengupta wrote in 1943 another one-act play—*Chaler Dar* (The Price of Rice).

Digindra Chandra Bandyopadhyay's *Dipsikha* (The Flaming Lamp—an extended form of his earlier play *Abhijan*)[33] and *Antaral* (Screened from the View)[34] were written before *Jabanbandi* and *Nabanna*. The girls of the Rabindra Sangeet Vidyalaya staged *Dipsikha* on 22 October 1943, i.e. one year before *Nabanna* was staged. *Antaral* was about the problem of illegitimate children. A character of the play, a leftist youth, was himself an illegitimate child. The problem of illegitimacy was attributed to the economic system of the present society and it was suggested that the solution lay in a restructuring of the economic order, which, it was believed, would surely come about. Shows of *Dipsikha* were stopped by the British government in Delhi. *Antaral* too was stopped by the Calcutta Police in 1944.

Later, it was staged after a thorough censorship.[35] But these plays by Digin Banerjee did not even get the chance of creating any impact, while the stir created by *Jabanbandi* and *Nabanna* was unprecedented. Of course, all these plays together indicate that a big change was taking place in the world of theatre during the late 1930s and early 1940s.[36]

NABANNA

Nabanna[37] was the high-water-mark of the new theatre movement that revolutionized the Bengali theatre in content and form. Written by Bijan Bhattacharya, this four-act play, exposing the grimness and the man-made character of the Bengal Famine, was serially published in *Arani* from 12 May 1944. The first show was on 24 October 1944, at Srirangam Theatre, followed by many more. The first few shows were an extraordinary success and earned a lot of praise for the two directors, Bijan Bhattacharya and Sambhu Mitra and the whole team of actors and actresses. The idea of the People's Theatre, conceived by the IPTA and partially realized in its earlier performances, particularly *Jabanbandi*, seemed to have been most successfully embodied in *Nabanna*. All the critics hailed it as having started a new theatre movement in Bengal.

The cast consisted of Bijan Bhattacharya, Sambhu Mitra, Gangapada Basu, Sobha Sen, Tripti Bhaduri (Mitra), Charu Prakash Ghosh, Sudhi Pradhan, Sajal Roy Chowdhury, Manikuntala Sen, Kalyani Kumarmangalam, Jalad Chatterjee, Monika Bhattacharya, Bibha Sen, Lalita Biswas. Ranjit Basu, Nihar Dasgupta, Manoranjan Boral, Chitta Hor, Gopal Haldar, Sambhu Bhattacharya, Robin Majumdar, Amal Bhattacharya; music director: Gour Ghosh; stage-manager: Chitta Banerjee and advisor: Manoranjan Bhattacharya.

The ideological commitment of actors and actresses was the most important factor in the production of *Nabanna*. What made Bijan Bhattacharya write the play, first of all? In his own words,

> Everyday I used to pass by the D.N. Mallik Square on my way to office. Every day I used to watch the domestic life of hungry villagers—families of men, women and children. Sometimes there were dead bodies covered with dirty cloth. The dead bodies used to look much smaller than living men. Adults and children could not be distinguished. Sometimes there were different scenes. A young boy about to cut the telegraph wire was shot by the police and dropped to the ground like a ripe fruit. One day I was myself beaten heavily by the police. Everyday on my way back from the office I used to think of writing something on all this. But how to write? I was afraid that whatever I write would become too whiningly sentimental. One day I overheard a conversation between a man and a woman. They were chatting about the village they had left, about *Nabanna* and other rituals. They were trying to

imagine what was happening in the village in their absence. I got my form. These people would speak for themselves in a play.[38]

All other participants in this theatrical event had similar experiences which they wanted to share with the audience. They also wanted to communicate to the audience their intense yearning for an end to this degradation of humanity. Manikuntala Sen, a political activist who had a role to play in *Nabanna*, said: 'Persons who had normally turned away their faces on seeing corpses, cried when they watched *Nabanna*; this was our credit.'[39]

Nabanna, like *Jabanbandi*, is the story of a family wrecked by the Famine of 1943–4. But it gives us a panoramic view, wide in time and space. The story starts with the Quit India Movement of 1942, the first of a series of crises that upset the rural life of Bengal. The locale of the story—Aminpur village—really stands for every Famine-stricken village of Bengal; and though the focus is on the Samaddar family, many other similarly distressd families meet the Samaddars on the roadside in the course of the story. The head of the family is Pradhan Samaddar whose wife and two sons have been killed during the Quit India Movement. The character of his wife Panchanani was modelled on Matangini Hazra, the famous old lady of Midnapur, who had been shot dead by the police while leading a procession during the August Movement (this was despite the Communist opposition to the August Movement—though some Party men did find the scene objectionable, the intervention of P.C. Joshi, the liberal-minded General Secretary of the Party, saved the situation). So, in fact, it is the family of his brother's sons—Kunja and Niranjan—a joint family. Gradually, food becomes scarce in their village, Kunja's son dies of malnutrition and they leave for the city with death encircling them. There they get separated from each other. But, one by one, they return to their village along with other neighbours. On the advice of Dayal, an elderly peasant, they resort to cooperative farming (*Gantaye Khata* and *Dharma Gola*). The play ends with the scene of the *Nabanna* festival and the echo of their united utterance: 'Strong resistance!'. Thus, perhaps it reduced the problem of exploitation to one of merely protecting the harvest and ended up with a mere message of unity. The role of the peasants' exploiters became diluted.

However, *Nabanna* was more than a domestic tragedy. It had the stretch of an epic drama. The different aspects of the Famine situation was sought to be presented in a comprehensive manner. The grievous Bengal Famine was presented in its varied aspects—the starved and homeless peasants, the typical money-lender on the look out for any opportunity to grab more peasant holdings, the urban hoarder with an enormous quantity of paddy and rice, and also trafficking in helpless girls from villages, the photographer who is delighted by the sight of skeletal beggers who would be good subjects for photography and earn him praise from the newspaper editor, the distressed urban *babu* who is not able to afford rice in the black market—*Nabanna* was a big canvas strewn with typical characters.

And the character of Pradhan Samaddar (personized by the playwright himself) adds a new dimension to the play. His is not a typical character. He behaves like an eccentric. He is always excited. His words are full of biting satire and sometimes he repeats the same words again and again, as if in a trance, and the words betray a mood of elation as if the truth has been discovered. Pradhan's powerful insight is the cause of his eccentricity. In the first scene, he points his finger at the crimson-coloured morning sky and says to Kunja, 'After all, a day will come, Kunja, and my Sripati-Bhupati have predicted that its complexion will be, O Kunja, just look, like that, beautiful like that, terribly beautiful like that!' When Kunja's son Makhan is on the point of death, Pradhan says, 'I'll never forget that the boy died of hunger. Nobody can make me forget that the boy died of hunger. Nobody can make me forget that the boy died of hunger. . . .' In Calcutta, he goes to a charitable hospital and complains of an ache in his body. But he cannot locate the ache, and says to the doctor: 'It was here just now, then it ran away—ran away, crossed rivers, waded through canals, traversed jungles and shrubs. There, look, it runs like a car. . . .' The doctor gets annoyed and says, 'Forget your pain. You don't have any pain.' Pradhan leaves the hospital repeating the doctor's words in bewilderment—'Forget your pain, you don't have any pain. Forget your pain . . .', thus expressing many thoughts at the same time: (1) The pain is imagined, so better forget it; (2) The doctor is a learned and knowledgable person. So I must listen to him.; (3) Rather sarcastically—'How can this man or anyone for that matter understand the pain I'm suffering from!'

Sambhu Mitra says that Pradhan Samaddar's utterings were poetical. According to Mitra, *Nabanna* was full of 'poetry of moments'.[40] Poetry sometimes emerged out of touching scenes—side-by-side with the house of some rich people hosting an extravagant wedding reception, men and dogs scramble for food around a garbage-bin. A dog bites Kunja. The wound bleeds profusely. Kunja's wife bandages it tearing a part of her already-torn sari, shouts wildly at the dog and the next moment asks her husband softly, 'Are you thirsty? Shall I get you some water?' While watching the scene, Manoranjan Bhattacharya felt: 'This is eternal.'[41] Thus *Nabanna* was more than a faithful documentation of history, it was a great drama.

The People's Theatre Movement introduced real social drama in Bengal. The prevalent trend on the commercial stage had been to produce, in Sambhu Mitra's words, 'social' plays with dhoti-clad characters as distinct from 'historical' plays where the actors would wear silk and velvet.

Indeed, this was the only difference.[42] There was no social consciousness at all in the 'social' drama of the commercial stage, and whatever they meant by society was confined to the bounds of the middle-class. In this state of affairs, the IPTA showed great courage in taking up burning social issues and presenting unsophisticated and shabbily-dressed peasant characters on the stage. That is why many critics applauded *Nabanna* for having revived the tradition of *Nildarpan*. It was the first peasant drama since *Nildarpan* (consideringing *Jabanbandi* as a rehearsal for *Nabanna*) and like the latter, showed a strong awarness of the grim social reality.[43]

Nabanna also broke away from the convention of drama centring around a hero and a heroine and gradually rising to a climax. Sushil Jana wrote after watching the first show:

> In *Nabanna* all the characters play the distinguished role of a hero to depict the harsh reality of life. Every one of them translates a sense of reality into a strong shout—no one is inferior to the other in this respect, no one is superior. One's sorrows have not concealed others' affliction for the sake of dramatic effect. *Nabanna* has an episodic character. Each of the scenes seems self-contained and ends in a climax. This hampers the sequence of the play.[44]

To Jana this was not a drawback of the play, but only a depiction of the reality—different crises, apparently isolated, yet together affecting a collective mass of people. In his opinion, the uniform attention paid to all these disasters gave a wholeness to the play. To Jyotirindra Moitra too, *Nabanna* was a 'great symphony connecting too many apparently unconnected events with a singular skill.'

But the episodic character seemed a shortcoming to some other critics. Hiran Kumar Sanyal observed, '*Nabanna* is not at all an able writing. A number of events more than the wholeness of the story and varieties more than the intensity of dramatic emotion are noticeable here.' The writer tried to string so many occurrences of the recent past into one single play, but has failed. After all, it is impossible for one single family to go through this vast range of misfortunes. The high quality of acting, however, according to Sanyal, concealed this serious limitation.[45]

The playwright's allegiance to reality can explain to a large extent what Hiran Kumar Sanyal considered to be drawbacks of the play. Aminpur was in fact Midnapur and during the early 1940s this district had suffered exactly in the same way as described in *Nabanna*. The reality was greater in magnitude than the knowledge and imagination of critics like Sanyal could conceive. Sanyal commented: 'Not being content with the sufferings caused by epidemic and Famine, the writer has made a cyclone devastate the village.' But this was actually the reality of Midnapur. Many years later, the drama critic Samik Banerjee was to show that in the history of the Bengal Famine, as reconstructed by researchers like Paul Greenough, the sequence of events correspond perfectly to that of *Nabanna*: first, a brutal police action in the context of the Quit India Movement, then a devastating cyclone, these factors along with others culminating in an irreversible Famine situation. Samik Banerjee also says that no one, living amid the horrors of the Famine, could at that time possibly view the Famine wholly; particularly because the government was trying consciously to conceal the causes, the sequence and the extent of the Famine. So the playwright could only see isolated scenes of terrible human degradation and he was perhaps afraid that any attempt to set his experience in a holistic logic, i.e. to follow the familiar path of writing plays, would curb the terribleness of the reality.[46] So *Nabanna* had to be episodic in character. Amongst contemporary critics, Sushil Jana realized this, though Hiran Kumar Sanyal, accustomed to the conventional pattern of play writing, did not. Manoranjan Bhattacharya said, 'You cannot judge the dramatic quality of *Jabanbandi* or *Nabanna* by applying the formula of other dramas. They are a new creation. Their rules will be formulated later on.'[47]

However, all the critics admired the acting in *Nabanna*. The performance did not centre around one or two individual actors, but the whole lot of them, determined to make the play a success. This was demanded by the very nature of the play and was possible because the actors' ideology gave them great zeal and confidence to overcome the handicap of inexperience. Most of them were not actors at all, but political activists. But this was perhaps an advantage to them. Because of their close contact with the masses, they could represent the distressed peasant characters very credibly and movingly. Leave aside the major characters, even the minor ones like the old beggar (played by Gopal Haldar) or Panchanani (played by Manikuntala Sen) were excellent on the stage.

The team-spirit with which the actors of *Nabanna* worked had scarcely been seen in the commercial theatre of that time and was another hallmark of the People's Theatre. The commercial stage was a field of competition, and not of cooperation. A year before, in the Puja issue of *Arani*, Manoranjan Bhattacharya had written an article 'Mere Deoa' (To Beat).[48] Here he said that the phrase 'Mere Deoa' was very common among the theatre-goers and was used to describe an actor beating all others on the stage by the sheer force of his acting. Bhattacharya said that such acting, usually considered to be something creditable on the part of the actor, was in fact a symptom of the vicious competitive trend in the theatre and could even ruin the play at times. 'Suppose a mere messanger beats His Majesty the Emperor in a scene to draw attention to himself and thus beats the play itself!' *Nabanna* showed for the first time what comradeship instead of competition can achieve for the theatre.

Moreover, for the first time, girls from 'respectable' middle-class families appeared on the public stage. They had acted before in Tagore's plays, but the audience was a select one, and even then Tagore had to face the wrath of the orthodox section of society on this count. The IPTA had to overcome many inhibitions in this respect. Even in the days of the YCI, such inhibitions had been very strong. Two girl students of the YCI agreed to act in *Anjangarh*, but refused to appear in scenes where boys too would be present. Hence, the scene of a hospital presented two female nurses, but there was no patient in the bed which was just covered with a white sheet.[49] The IPTA productions like *Nabanna* thus pioneered a radically new trend risking much social harassment.

Not only the spirit of acting, but its mode too, along with costumes, make-up, stage-craft, lighting, etc., was carefully worked out and these were all remarkable deviations from the usual norms of the commercial stage. Briefly speaking, everything was as realistic as possible.

Acting in Bengali theatre had so far been 'theatrical', one that seemed to be excessively stylyzed in powerful actors and 'ham acting' in weak ones. *Nabanna* introduced naturalistic acting for the first time. Moreover, the actors wore tattered rags that almost stank.[50] They used the rugged language of the peasantry. Manik Bandopadhyay thus complimented the playwright after the latter had finished reading the script at No. 46 Dharmatala Street: 'Sir, you seem to be a born peasant.'[51] Their mode of speaking too could easily pass as that of real peasants. Sambhu Mitra says that the fact that they were all novices was a point of advantage in this respect. They had untrained voices like peasants and were asked by the directors to talk loudly which the real peasants naturally do. On the whole, it came out well. Those having clean voices were given roles of gentlemen—ARP, civic guards, etc.[52] Sobha Sen remembers that the first thing Bijanbabu did was to teach them the dialogue. It was a local dialect and the pronunciation had to be like that of Jessore, Bhattacharya's own district (though the locale of the play was Midnapore). Bijan Bhattacharya was careful about maintaining a uniformity of pronunciation among different actors.[53]

The stage-craft was most skilled and artful, and a break away from the hitherto prevalent naturalistic style which meant 'painting a house for a house and a room for a room'. For all the four acts of *Nabanna* there was simply a jute curtain as the backdrop. For the park scene, a railing was put up in front, for the hospital scene, a red *shalu* was hung with the words 'Charitable Hospital' written on it.[54]

The directors also resorted to two different layers of occurrences: a pantomime in the background, on a raised platform, symbolizing a social revolution, with no direct link to the characters of the play and yet rendering all the latters' activities inevitable. Thus, the play did not remain just a story of some individuals. It became part of a kaleidoscopic social history.[55]

In practical terms too, the use of two planes considerably helped them, for example in presenting the very first scene of the play. Here Panchanani, a lady resembling Matangini Hazra, the great heroine of the Quit India Movement, would lead a procession and shout all the while, 'Go ahead, go ahead!' Ultimately, she would be shot dead by the police. But the directors were at a loss about how to present this scene on the stage. The huge crowd would always be moving and Panchanani as a part of that moving crowd could not remain on the stage for long. Yet she would have to be there for quite some time shouting and inspiring the crowd till she drops dead, and all this time she would have to be amongst a moving stream of people. The problem was solved by using two platforms. In the front, the procession moved fast and at the back on a higher plane was Panchanani, who, while her changing postures made her look like a part of that moving crowd, remained on the stage at the same time.[56]

Some more interesting details about the stage-craft and lighting of *Nabanna* are available. There was a scene of a heavy storm with no elaborate arrangement and modern equipment for its audio-visual presentation. Sambhu Mitra narrates how the directors planned the scene. The sound of the flood rushing in was captured by a piano, which was later joined by other instruments (the use of piano was a compromise with their principle of avoiding Western instruments, but in this case they could find no alternative). The stage was plunged in darkness, and the cries of imperilled people could be heard. Bijan Bhattacharya having been drenched in a bucket of water came on the stage and was lighted by a carbon arc (those days, the carbon arc was the only means available for spotlight). He cried out, 'The road has now entered the home.' Then came Sambhu Mitra, thoroughly dabbed in oil which, lighted by spot, looked like water. On Maharshi's (Manoranjan Bhattacharya) instruction, they had made an apperture in the backdrop by removing a flap. A part of the back section of the revolving stage and a grey curtain could be seen through it. But it looked like a grey void in the dark, a grey, ugly and lifeless wreckage. Along with the flap some iron rods were also removed to give the roof of the hut a slanting look.[57]

Sambhu Mitra also remembers that there was a scene with girls passing by with lamps on their heads and singing a song. Instead of lighting these girls they used floodlight on the backdrop. The girls looked silhouetted. The weak and flickering flames on their heads looked superb. This was the first time that silhouette was used in Bengali theatre. Sambhu Mitra later recollected[58] the surprised exclamation of the stage-worker on being asked to throw floodlight on the background from the side of the wings: 'What are you saying? I won't have to throw light on the characters?'

All this shows how a new and noble ideal profoundly affected the whole thought-process of those people, and how new content ushered in new forms. And they did everything with minimum facilities at their disposal. The new theatre meant a sea-change from the prevalent commercial theatre. The Srirangam theatre-hall was packed to capacity for all the seven initial shows of *Nabanna*. And among the audience was Sisir Kumar Bhaduri, who got completely absorbed in the play. Bijan Bhattacharya says,

> He looked at Pradhan Samaddar absent-mindedly, touched the shoulder of his brother Biswanath who was sitting next to him and said, 'Bishe, that washerman of ours. . . . Don't you remember him? Only Sisir Kumar knows who that washerman was of whom Pradhan Samaddar of *Nabanna* reminded him. But from his momentary illusion I could not but feel that Ramachandra was trying to gratify himself by playing the role of Guhak Chandal—in this case, a washerman.[59]

Of course, the audience did include persons to whom the frisking and shouting of some rustics wearing loin-cloth seemed indecent and some did not like the jute curtain, devoid of the usual glamour of the commercial stage.

After Nabanna

The IPTA's efforts to follow up the success of *Nabanna* were not up to expectation. For months and even years to come, nothing attractive came up.

Perhaps stimulated by the success of *Nabanna*, the AFWAA staged *Punarujjiban* in 1945. It was an adaptation from Yeats' *Resurrection* by Sudhindranath Dutta, first published in *Parichay*, Bhadra 1343/1936. This drama was enacted by the literary section of the AFWAA and not by its Drama Squad. Bishnu Dey was the director and among those who participated were Debiprasad Chatterjee, his brother Kamakshi Prasad and their friend Sudhir Gupta. Hemanta Mukherjee was the music director, and besides him Sujata Mukherjee, her sister Supriya and Abha Chatterjee did the singing. The purpose was to raise money, particularly for the treatment of the ailing poet Sukanta.

The play was based on the story of the Resurrection of Jesus Christ. Profound spiritual questions were raised in the course of the play. The mystic incident helped the dramatic aspect. The play also brought out the significance of the incident in the context of the progress of human civilization, as is evident from the final chorus:

> *Dark thoughts! Man erring and torn by hesitation!*
> *On the thoroughfare where anarchy rules*
> *Scream archaeological beasts.*
> *So compassionate God has descended on Galilee.*

The producers wanted the stage to be like that of a *Jatra*, i.e. no stage at all. Their intention was to remove the distance between the audience and the actors. The floor of a huge room at the Asutosh College provided the auditorium. There was only a heavy screen to be drawn by the chorus-girls. A dramatic character in fact made his way to the stage from amidst the audience. But whatever the success or failure of *Punarujjiban*, the play was watched by a small and restricted audience.[60]

The IPTA was invited by the Rabindra Smriti Sahitya Samity to take part in the celebration of *Rabindra Saptaha* (the week celebrating Tagore's birthday) in May 1946 and the Drama Squad took the initiative in putting up Tagore's *Muktadhara* (The Unobstructed Stream). It was a symbolic drama expressing repulsion for machines, that had done incalculable harm to humanity, and calling for a heroic struggle to resist this evil force. The plot was as follows. Jantraraj Bibhuti has constructed a machine to check the river Muktadhara. In this he has been encouraged by the King of Uttarkut, who thus intends to deprive his subjects of Shivtarai of drinking water and to harass them, simply because they belong to a foreign race. Abhijit, the Crown Prince, has been appointed the ruler of Shivtarai some time back and has loved those people. So he hates the idea of denying drinking water to them. He finds a flaw in the machine, damages it, sets the Muktadhara free, but himself gets drowned in the process.[61]

The cast included Charuprakash Ghosh, Satyajivan Bhattacharya, Bijan Bhattacharya, Sudhi Pradhan, Tripti Bhaduri and Sadhana Bose. The directors were Sambhu Mitra and Gangapada Bose, the music directors Hemanta Mukherjee and Debabrata Biswas. Suchitra Mukherjee (later Mitra) was among the singers and the stage was done by Nirad Majumder. But this play too had little impact, at least quantitatively. Sambhu Mitra describes the production as 'organizationally and aesthetically an ignominious failure.'[62]

On one occasion the IPTA Drama Squad staged a playlet written by Sambhu Mitra. But the writer was away at Bombay and his approval was not sought. On his return to Calcutta, Mitra was greatly surprised to see the drama being staged. He did not like the performance at all.[63]

These were the only new productions. Of course, they continued to repeat *Nabanna* now and then. But even this seemed to be having too many difficulties. A report of 1946 says,

> Nearly forty performances of *Nabanna* were given in Calcutta where the opposition of the proprietors of the public stage was a serious hindrance in the matter of securing stages. We also gave performances in Behrampur, Jessore, Chandennagar and Hatgobindapur (Burdwan) before the provincial Kisan Sabha Conference where 15,000 witnessed the show. Invitations from all over Bengal and outside poured in, but these could not be fulfilled as all the artists were not in a position to leave Calcutta for more than a day or two at the most. Altogether the play was performed to an aggregate audience of 40,000 people.[64]

Gradually the IPTA became paralysed and continued to be so for quite some time. This is often attributed to the opportunism of some members, factional squabbles and so on. However, the factor that seems to have proved eventually crucial was that the theoretical shortcomings of the Communist Party had begun to impinge on the cultural front. We will discuss this in detail a little later.

At the time when the IPTA was lying virtually inactive, the commercial theatre had to its credit a dramatic exploit, done in the spirit of the IPTA. *Duhkhir Iman* (Honour of the Poor) written by Tulsi Lahiri, was staged by the doyen of the then Bengali commercial theatre, Sisir Kumar Bhaduri, at Srirangam. Tulsi Lahiri and Manoranjan Bhattacharya were the two directors. The first show was on 12 December 1946. The cast included Kali Sarkar, Durgadas Sanyal, Nitish Mukherjee, Manoranjan Bhattacharya, Kanu Banerjee, Durgadas Banerjee, and many others.[65] This was a story of the Famine—how it devasted the poor Bahe-speaking people of North Bengal. While such a theme had hitherto been unthinkable in the commercial theatre, the performance was a success. Kanu Banerjee, who played a leading role in this drama, later said that he could never have imagined that the reaction of the audience could be so overwhelming and encouraging. One night, a spectator came to Sisir Kumar and donated Rs. 10, which was a lot of money in those days.[66] *Duhkhir Iman* was the greatest tribute paid to *Nabanna*. It meant that even the commercial stage had recognized the power of the People's Theater and tried to follow it, however partially.[67]

After some time, the IPTA took up a play of Digin Banerjee for performance, *Bastubhita* (The Homestead). Written in August 1947, it was about a Hindu family in East Pakistan—a poor *pathshala*-teacher, his wife and daughter, their attachment to their homeland, village and homestead and affection for their neighbours, generally Muslims. Yet some Hindu friends insist that they should leave their homeland and go to Calcutta, a *terra incognita* to them. The wicked behaviour of some Muslim neighbours convinces them of the necessity of leaving. But when they are all set to go, some Muslim neighbours come and prevent them. Thus, the play stressed the social bonds between the Hindus and the Muslims who had for long been living together amicably. It wished that the friendship between Mahendra Master and Amin Munshi would prove imperishable.[68]

The play was first staged by a small group Dipayan Sangha at the University Institute Hall on 15 October 1947. This show impressed some IPTA members who staged it themselves soon after. Different people acted in different shows put up by the IPTA—Manoranjan Bhattacharya, Kali Sarkar, Satya Ray, Priti Ray, Gangapada Basu, Anu Banerjee, Sobha Sen, Amitabha Ghosh, Phani Gupta, Mumtaj Ahmed, Santi Mukherjee, Nakuleswar Chakrabarty, Swaraj Basu, Asit Chakrabarty, Ajit Mitra, Sunil Ghosh, Sajal Roy Chowdhury, and others. A show was also held at the Jagabandhu Institution in which Manoranjan Bhattacharya, Kali Sarkar, Sambhu Mitra, and others acted. The play became popular and was later staged by a number of local amateur clubs.[69]

After *Nabanna*, the IPTA toyed with the idea of staging *Jiyankanya* (A Girl Brought Back to life),[70] written by Bijan Bhattacharya, but at that time it did not materialize. However, on the day of Independence it was broadcast by the All India Radio. Then, in November 1947, the play was staged at Rangmahal on Bijan Bhattacharya's private initiative. Bhattacharya directed the play. The actors were Mahasweta Devi, Sunanda Roy, Gouri Ghosh, Ira Roy, Arun Bhattacharya, Salil Sen, Manisha and Monika Sen, Muhammad Israil and Bijan Bhattacharya himself.[71]

Jiyankanya was a symbolic drama. On the backdrop there was a map of India. The story was about Nandanpur, a village of gypsies who are born snake-charmers. And yet, Ulupi the beautiful and only daughter of their Sardar Prabir dies of snake-bite. Her parents and all the gypsies lament her death, for she was loved by all. Then some veteran sorcerers amongst them volunteer to bring her back to life. But all their incantations and occult tricks of enchantment fail, the body of Ulupi lies still. Then Badar Ali, a sorcerer from a neighbouring place suggests that they should all utter their mantras together, for this will be the invocation nearest to the original *Dhanwantari Mantra*. The suggestion worked wonders, the *Kalnagini* (a fatally poisonous snake) is defeated, sucks the poison from Ulupi's body and withdraws. The gypsies become aggressive and strike it hard. Ulupi opens her eyes, full of vivacity. The map of India in the background becomes prominent, as the 'dimmer' light on it increases in units. The song of life is echoed everywhere. The bite of the *Kalnagini* and its ultimate withdrawal stand for British aggrandizement and the achievement of Independence respectively. Some took the incident of the snake-bite as a symbol for communal fury. But the play had been written before the bloody riots of 1946–7 took place. Of course, the play's plea for communal unity is unmistakable.

On the whole, the performance was not a success, though the play was admired by many. The poet Sudhindranath Dutta realized its potential and wished to produce it a second time with more care. But the matter rested there.

1948–50

The period to be discussed, i.e. 1948–50 is interesting.[72] In February 1948, the second congress of the Communist Party was held. The Allahabad Conference of the IPTA was held a year later. We have noted how the Party took up a revolutionary line in these conferences, though in practice it could not judiciously follow that line. But at least the IPTA entered a phase of renewed activities.

It was not through any thoughtful guidance from above that some drama enthusiasts of IPTA, moved by the vision of Revolution, embarked on a period of hyper activities. The revival of activities resulted in the production of a number of short dramas, generally performed amongst the peasants and workers, often involving risks of confrontation with the police. Though the Communist Party hesitated to lead the mass uprisings of the time, the cultural activists did whatever they could on their own. The IPTA split into a number of local groups and started functioning under different names to deceive the vigilant police. First, there came into being the North Calcutta Squad and the South Calcutta Squad.

But the most popular play of this period was *Nayanpur* performed in several villages of the Sundarbans area, the hot-bed of the Tebhaga Movement. Written in 1948 by Anil Ghosh, the Secretary of the IPTA branch of 24-Parganas, it described the peasant-police clash that had taken place in Donagajora village earlier that year. The play describes events full of tension leading to the last scene where the police fire on the peasants' gathering. The volunteers used to burst a few crackers to create the required sound effects. This often used to alarm the real police who had come to keep a watch on the show and made them fire blanks.

During 1949–50 several shows were held in villages. Anil Ghosh himself was the director. The actors were generally the local members of the CPI. Raghu Chakrabarty, Sachin Sen, Radhakanta Dutta and other actors too participated. Later, it was staged in Calcutta by Sajal and Reba Roy Chowdhury, Sadhana Roy Chowdhury, Usha Dutta, Dipali Ganguly, Kali Banerjee, Ajit Mitra, Arun Choudhury, Suresh Haldar and others. They also presented this play at the open session of the Allahabad Congress of the IPTA (February 1949) on behalf of the Bengal Branch and earned praises.

Lekhak (The Writer) written by Salil Chowdhury, was performed by the South Calcutta Drama Squad of the IPTA around 1948. The actors were Kali Banerjee, Sajal Roychowdhury, Reba Roy Chowdhury, Karuna Banerjee and others. It was the story of a writer who believes in pure art and would by no means connect art with life. And yet when he sits down to write a play, he cannot write a single line. His circumstances—poverty and social injustice affecting him as well as his near and dear ones—make him unable to write anything. But gradually those very circumstances take the shape of a drama. The writer realizes that this is the best drama possible now.

Sanket (The Signal) written by Salil Chowdhury towards the end of 1949 opens with the scene of a little girl practising Bengali handwriting. She exclaims suddenly, 'Oh no! I've written "Kangsa" (a tyrannical king of

Hindu Mythology) in place of "Congress".' She is the youngest daughter of a middle-class family. One of her elder brothers is involved in leftist politics, and the other members of the family resent this. The drama is about the resultant conflicts in the family. Gradually the crises all around envelope all of them. The father realizes the need to protest against injustice. He agrees to participate in a strike against his office authorities. Then he returns home to hear the news of his son's death. The boy died as the police fired on a precession demanding the release of political prisoners. The role of the mother was superbly personized by Sadhana Roy Chowdhury. Though in many shows were forcibly stopped by the police, they continued to stage it under different names.

1949 was a fruitful year for the IPTA drama movement. Numerous dramas were written and enacted in that year. But we know very little about them. The theatre workers of an illegal political party could not manage to preserve the scripts, nor could they store much in their memories about the themes and productions, for they were always in a great hurry and very busy all the time, keeping the police at bay and overcoming all kinds of difficulties.

Salil Chowdhury's *Janantik* (Aside) was staged in that year by Sajal Roy Chowdhury, Sadhana Roy Chowdhury, Mamtaj Ahmed, and others.[73] *Dak* (Call) by an unknown writer was another contribution of the IPTA in 1949. The actors were Reba Roy Chowdhury, Sajal Roy Chowdhury, Mamtaj Ahmed, Niranjan Sen and others. A show was held at the Muslim Institute for an assemblage of railway-workers. Kamal Sarkar, a fugitive at that time, organized it. The police besieged the place on that occasion. *Sab Payechir Desh* (El Dorado) written by Arun Chowdhury was staged many times. During a show at Manohar Pukur there was a brawl with the police. The same thing happened during a show at Hindustan Park. Kali Banerjee, Karuna Banerjee, Sajal Roy Chowdhury and others comprised the cast. The story was about an underground press and the revolutionary activities around it.

Taranga (Wave)[74] written by Digin Banerjee was staged by the North Calcutta squad at Srirangam. It was about a wave of protests sweeping through national life and stirring even a remote village of Bengal. The villagers are protesting against all kinds of oppressors—the Hindu zamindar exacting 'tola' (tax) on their produce sold at the village 'hat', the Muslim jotedar and the British police—all cooperating with each other. In the end, the army enters the village and massacres innocent people in order to suppress the nationalist upsurge which is evidently a part of the Quit India Movement. Sajal Roy Chowdhury remembers at least one show dated 15 February 1949.

Moni Majumdar's *Mrityu Nai* (No Death) deals with the labour movement. It was staged at the Hillary Institute, Rammohan Mancha and other places. Not many shows could be arranged because of interference by the police. *Luthtaraj* (Plunder and Pillage) written by Sunil Dutta in 1950, was an anti-imperialist play based on the life of workers. On Sambhu Mitra's suggestion, some tramworkers put up a show at the Wellington Square and created a stir.[75] Sajal Roy Chowdhury says that about this time some tramworkers of a mess-house at Dover Lane enacted an adaptation from Clifford Odets' play *Waiting for Lefty*. Roy Chowdhury also remembers that a play *Purnagras* (Total Eclipse) written by Jyoti Roy on the slum life of Calcutta, was prepared for staging.[76]

The theatre-workers were working under the spell of a revolutionary vision during this period. Some of them had just been released from jail. Others were working underground, constantly hoodwinking the police. Friends and sympathizers would lend them houses for rehearsals and procure them halls for shows. The house of a film actor at Ballygunj Place was the venue of the rehearsal for *Janantik*. In north Calcutta, Dhiren Ray's house and Bangiya Kalalay (near Fariapukur) were their haunts. They staged many shows at YMCA and Minerva. Sometimes, local clubs would invite them to give shows. Sajal Roy Chowdhury later remembered having accepted invitations from Chetla Rakhi Sangha which had a member named Sudhir Pakira committed to the Communist cause.

Soon, the Calcutta-based activists started visiting villages in Howrah, Hooghly and 24-Parganas, singing songs, enacting dramas and selling the illegal Party newspaper *Swadhinata*. They organized District Committees with the help of local people for cultural work. Roy Chowdhury remembers having organized a District Committee in Murshidabad with the help of Sudhir Sen, a local comrade with influence. During 1948–50, the cultural workers risked everything to fight shoulder to shoulder with the peasants and workers.

Sunil Dutta and Sajal Roy Chowdhury later recollected incidents relating to the staging of *Nayanpur*. Sajal Roy Chowdhury acting as an oppressive *nayeb* was often attacked by the peasant audience after the show and his colleagues had to be careful about his safety. Once in the village Kalnar Dutta and Mamtaj Ahmed Khan were asked to prepare a stage with scarcely any equipment. The first thing they noticed on reaching the village in the morning was a hillock and they promptly turned it into a stage. The proscenium and the wings were made of palm leaves. In the evening, the show started in the light of hurricane lanterns with which they even created the effect of spotlights by using cardboard and cellophane paper. According to them, the whole set-up was excellent and unforgettable. After some time, hooligans hired by the local jotedars tried to foil the show. But the villagers put up a successful resistance. On the latter's request, another show had to be held and this time it was heavily guarded by members of the local kisan sabha. 'This show was more lively, for two dramas were going on simultaneously', and the drama *Nayanpur* was interrupted for a while by the real drama of peasants chasing away the hooligans. Then it started again with renewed vitality.[77]

From such reminiscences, one gets a feel of that period. The accounts of Sunil Dutta and Sajal Roy Chowdhury would be corroborated by many other activists of that time. According to Kali Banerjee, for instance, at that time he used to work amongst the workers day and night. In the process he met the folk-poet Gurudas of Badartala (Metiabruz), and brought him into the fold of the movement. Everyday there were incidents at some place or the other. They used to prepare short dramas on these conflicts and put them up after a rehearsal of four or five days.

In Banerjee's words:

> These were guerrilla-style performances. After the selection of the area, news would be passed on orally to everyone there. After the show is over, the organizers would collect things and run to another area for another performance. Sometimes in the middle of the show news would come that the police is coming and there will be a row. We would disperse and hide ourselves in the locality. The police would come and find not a single man. This was the mode of performance and after the performance we used to stick posters the whole night. Sometimes I would return home at day-break, and sometimes not at all. But I never felt tired. There was only one dream—to make the earth habitable.[78]

Kali Banerjee, one of the finest actors of the Bengali film world, later admitted that this phase of his life had significantly contributed to his making as an artist. Working amongst common men, he saw their real selves. He used to study every reaction of theirs in detail—the dark-skinned peasants who provided him with flattened rice, their children looking like lion cubs, varieties of men with varieties of callings. This was his training ground for character-acting later.

Indeed, this phase of the IPTA with stubborn drama-warriors reaching the grass-roots, studying life in the raw and at close quarters and largely successful in bringing about an identification between themselves and the audience, is a short, forgetten, but remarkable period in the theatre history of Bengal.[77]

From 1950 Onward

A peculiar combination of inactivity and ultra-leftism at the Party level, however, put an end to the outburst of revolutionary excitement. From January 1950, the Party officially followed a policy of moderation and the revolutionary spirit was dying down. This was reflected in the theatre movement. About this time, besides the North Calcutta and the South Calcutta Squads, the Central Calcutta Squad came into being.

The Peace Movement was in full swing by then. At the Peace and Culture Festival held at Smarta Ground, Bhawanipur, the IPTA presented a play on the theme of peace—*Itibritta* (History). Here a writer, opposed to the idea of peace, turns a peace-lover at the end of the play and delivers a lecture commending peace. Organizations other than the IPTA presented *Shantir Prahari Jage* (The Watchman of Peace is on Guard), *Shanti Chai* (We Want Peace) and *Jabab* (The Reply). All these plays were just crude propaganda.[79]

In the changed situation the IPTA once again started staging full-length plays. *Bhanga Bandar* (The Eroded Port), the first of them, was presented by the Central Drama Squad. Written by Purnendu Pal, it was a story of a refugee family of fishermen uprooted from their native village of Pabna (East Bengal). The two brothers Gagan and Paban, struggle hard against black-marketeers and other exploiters. Paban is gradually drawn into leftist politics. But it seems that the play failed to have much impact.[80]

In 1951, the IPTA staged more full-length plays and each had a number of shows. An IPTA Newsletter[81] from early 1952 notes that the West Bengal Branch of the IPTA had staged a record number of musical dramas and ballet performances during the months of November and December. The song groups had given their performances before thousands of people in the Bengal districts almost every day during these two months and the Calcutta Drama Squad staged the full-length dramas, *Nagpash*, *Bichar*, *Bisarjan*, *Officer*, and the ballets, *Ahalya* and *Sonar Bangla,* at 36 shows arranged in the districts of Midnapore, Murshidabad, Burdwan and 24-Parganas as well as in various localities of Calcutta, covering an audience of nearly 100,000 people.

This newsletter particularly talks about a recent success of the Drama Squad: the new short drama *Bhoter Bhet* (The Gift of the Elections) by Purnendu Pal—an agitational sketch exposing the hypocrisy of the Congress regime. The play was claimed to have been greatly appreciated at a rally of over 100,000 people in Calcutta. The newsletter also informs us that in addition a whole-time Calcutta Squad toured Cooch Behar and Jalpaiguri for twelve days, performing a number of dramas and folk-song recitals and covering an audience of about 28,000 people.

Utpal Dutta, who got involved in the People's Theatre Movement about this time, later remembered the following about *Bhoter Bhet*—a small temporary group was formed within the IPTA under Panu Pal's leadership and the play was a contribution of this group. Re-election was to be held at Maheshtala, due to the capricious insistence of the Congress candidate, Niharendu Dutta Majumdar. The group including Utpal Dutta himself, went there to campaign for the eventually victorious Communist candidate Sudhir Bhandari. 'In the fields, on roads, at public-meetings and street-meetings of Maheshtala, it was proved how successful a drama can be in the work of propaganda.'[82] Bhandari did win this time too.

Bisarjan (Sacrifice), a famous play by Tagore, was selected by Utpal Dutta for the Central Squad of the IPTA. The very selection of a classical play, evincing deep human sympathy and dealing with problems of social irrationality and yet far away from contemporary reality, suggests that the IPTA and the new theatre movement as a whole had reached a sort of crossroads and had started doing some rethink.[83] The cast of *Bisarjan* included Utpal Dutta, Sobha Sen, Kali Banerjee, Nibedita Das and others. Ritwik Ghatak directed this play.

Dalil (The Document), written by Ritwik Ghatak, was staged by the Central Squad during 1951–2. The actors were Ritwik Ghatak himself, Mamtaj Ahmed, Umanath Bhattacharya, Sobha Sen, Sita Mukherjee, Kali Banerjee, and others. Mamata Chaterjee, Anil Ghosh, Tripti Mitra, Utpal Dutta too acted in many a show. The play was about the refugees. At the seventh All-India conference of IPTA at Bombay, this play was awarded the shield for the best production on the theme of peace by the All-India Peace Council.[84]

Nagpash (A Snake-rope) written by Moni Majumdar, was based on the life of the middle-class and dealt with the problems of unemployment. It was a production of the North Drama Squad.[85]

Unity, July 1952[86] reported that during the last five months, the Calcutta IPTA had staged about 84 shows in the city and suburbs to an audience of about 200,000. Besides *Nagpash* and *Dalil*, a number of plays staged by different local squads of the IPTA were listed in this report. These are *Julius Fuchik*, a dramatization of Fuchik's *Notes from the Gallows* by Umanath Bhattacharya, staged by the Central Squad; *Agni* (Fire) a social drama by Umanath Bhattacharya,[87] staged by the Central Squad; *Anna* (Food), a poster drama on the current food problem, performed by the Central Squad; *Abad* (Tillage) by Govinda Chakrabarty, based on the problems of peasants and caste-riots after the Partition, a production of the South Drama Squad; *Natak Noy* (Not a Play) by Biru Mukherjee, dealing with the problems of the city-based middle-class, a production of the South Drama Squad; *Arati* (Enemies) an adaptation from Gorkey's *Enemies* by Nirmal Ghosh, at that time being rehearsed by the North Drama Squad; *Mukti Yuddha* (Struggle for Liberation) depicting the Malayan people's struggles and the confusion inside the imperialist camp, written by Nirmal Ghosh and staged by the North Drama Squad; *Aguner Phul* (Flowers of Fire), about the terrorist activities of the 1930s and of a patriotic spirit, written by Jyoti Roy, being rehearsed by the North Drama Squad. This report in *Unity* also said that in Budge Budge, Haren Chandra Dalui, Secretary of the local IPTA Branch, had written a full-length drama which inspired the jute and petroleum workers. This drama was based on the actual struggle of the workers of the Standard Vacuum Oil Company.

A rich theatrical performance was staged during the West Bengal IPTA Convention at Naihati (August–September 1952) the highlight of which was a drama on the life of factory workers, written by a railway worker.

Sajal and Reba Roy Chowdhury remembered that *Suryagras* (Solar Eclipse) written by Sushil Jana had been enacted several times during the early 1950s in a number of villages. Apart from themselves, the cast included Anil Ghosh, Raghu Chakrabarty and others. They also remembered the performance of two dramas by Tulsi Lahiri—*Natyakar* (The Playwright) and *Naba-Varsa* (New Year). These were performed by Nibedita Das, Kali Sarkar, Sadhana Roy Chowdhury, etc.[88]

Digin Banerjee's *Mokabila* (Confrontation) was first staged by the Dum Dum IPTA Branch, then by the Sibpur IPTA quite a few times in 1951, though the central IPTA tried to prevent them. It was about the plight of the middle and the working classes of independent India.[89]

From People's Theatre to Group Theatre: Continuity and Change

In the meantime, like-minded theatre groups other than the IPTA had come into being. After *Nabanna*, the IPTA had proved unable to hold fast a unified theatre movement and dissensions grew. In 1948, Bahurupi was formed under Sambhu Mitra's leadership. Manoranjan Bhattacharya, Tulsi Lahiri, Kali Sarkar, Gangapada Basu and Muhammad Israil belonged to this group. But Bahurupi could not achieve anything substantial before 1950 (it acquired the name Bahurupi too only in that year).[90] In the early 1950s, several other groups came into existance. Utpal Dutta, while an active member of the IPTA, founded another group—Little Theatre Group. Some members of the IPTA, Bijan Bhattacharya, Gangapada Basu, Sudhi Pradhan, Ritwik Ghatak, Sobha Sen and others formed a separate group Natyacharka with the single purpose of staging *Nildarpan* which had been criticized as reformist by some ultra-leftist members of IPTA. Within a few months, Bijan Bhattacharya formed Calcutta Theater. Kranti Silpi Sangha had been formed at Baharampur by some members of the Revolutionary Socialist Party as early as 1946. Atin Majumdar, a member of the AFWAA and Debu Chatterjee were among its founders. In the early 1950s, some RSP workers and a few others—Kanu Banerjee, Bhanu Banerjee, Bolin Som, Salil Sen, Nepal Nag, and so on—organized Uttar Sarathi. Then there was David Cohen's Unity Theatre, another off-shoot of the IPTA.[91] Thus started the Group Theatre Movement. Subsequently, many more groups came up and many of them disappeared too before long. The process still goes on. The IPTA itself started admitting in its fold many local groups, particularly during times of elections when the need was felt for its organizational growth. But we will restrict ourselves to the contribution of the Group Theater till 1952 only.

The Group Theatre Movement carried on the tradition of the People's Theatre, above all the latter's motto of starring the people. In the place of a single organization now we had quite a few—Bahurupi, LTG, etc. The IPTA itself was functioning under several names. But there was no sharp break in the nature of the theatre. This explains why all the left-minded journals of that time, including the Party organ *Swadhinata*, were all praises for all these theatrical groups and why all of them were closely watched by the police.

The themes of the plays continued as before, to depict and dissect the hard reality of the life of the poor and the middle-class under an exploitative social system. The Hindu-Muslim tension and the refugee influx were current problems and a number of plays were based on them, e.g. *Natun Ihudi* (The New Jew) staged by Uttar Sarathi and *Banglar Mati* (The Soil of Bengal), a production of Kranti Silpi Sangha. The former tried to analyse what made the innocent Pundit ofVikrampur and his wife, the Namahsudra peasant Kesto Das and his wife, Pari, Duikhya, Mohan and hundreds of other residents of East Bengal leave their beautiful native land and come to Calcutta. The latter was about a Hindu family of East Pakistan. It showed how in a mixed village of Hindus and Muslims, doubts and tensions were created by conspiring vested interests and how amity prevailed in the long run. Bahurupi's *Chhenra Taar* (Broken String) showed how poor peasants were ruined during the Famine which had occurred only a few years back and was still a nightmare to many. The powerful jotedar Hakimuddi harasses Rahim, an honest peasant, in every possible way and also covets the latter's wife Phuljan. During the Famine, he refuses to give food to Phuljan and her son at the *langarkhana* opened at his house. Rahim gives *talak* to Phuljan so that she can eat and survive. Phuljan, divorced by her husband, becomes a servant of Hakimuddi who uses the pretext of the Muslim religious law to prevent her from visiting her son when the latter is ill. Rahim commits suicide to remove the obstacle in the way of the mother–son reunion. Bahurupi's *Pathik* (The Passer-by) was a story about the helpless workers of a coal-mine area, the powerful anti-social elements backed by the unscrupulous owners, and the conflict between the two sides.[92]

But the character of the peasant in distress was gradually becoming rather monotonous and stale. The flesh-and-blood reality of the peasants of *Nabanna*, who had been regarded as true representatives of the famished rural Bengal, seemed missing. Moreover, the characters seemed to have been dragged, rather machanically, towards a premeditated development along a single track; political or social conclusions were superimposed, particularly because after Independence the leftists were not sure whom to fight, whom to befriend and also about the way class alignment should be determined. Experiences of the Communist movement of the period 1948–50 had caused much confusion and bitterness. New themes were sought in the changed situation.

Bahurupi was one of the pioneers in this respect. The first three plays staged by this group had been in perfect congruity with the IPTA's thematic preference. *Pathik* and *Chhenra Tar* written by Tulsi Lahiri (*Pathik* was in fact an adaptation from Robert Sherwood's *The Petrified Forest* and we have already summarized the plot of *Chhenra Taar*) were about the hard life of poor people and *Ulukhagra* (the name taken from the Bengali proverb 'While the kings fight, the reeds in the marsh are trampled to death') written by Sambhu Mitra under the pen-name of Sri Sanjay was a story of a decaying middle-class family. These three plays, presented at the drama festival of Bahurupi in 1950, were generally acclaimed by leftist critics.[93] The play *Bibhav* staged in 1951 was to the liking of the leftists too, for it was about the ongoing food movement and documented the firing on a hunger procession by the police. But their next venture *Char Adhyay* (Four Chapters) put up in that very year created controversy. The theme of the play was how impetuous leaders, in their obsession with abstract political ideas, ignore basic human responsibilities and thus cause serious calamity. The very bitter experience of the rash leftist politics of the post-Independence years formed the background to the staging of this play which was actually about the revolutionary terrorist activities of pre-Independence days. Tagore's controversial novel, published and severely condemned in the mid-1930s for belittling the terrorist heroes of Bengal, became the subject of a renewed controversy in the early 1950s, when it was staged. Many considered it to be a deviation on the part of Sambhu Mitra from the ideal of the People's Theatre.[94]

But whether some people liked it or not, the theatre movement was to explore new themes from now on. Bahurupi's next production *Dasachakra* (An Intrigue by Many, an adaptation from Ibsen's *The Enemy of the People*) exposed those who pursue their own selfish interests under the cover of their rhetorical propaganda and false slogans in the name of the people. It was 1952, the year of the first general elections in independent India. Yet Bahurupi dared to raise its voice against the sacred concept of 'majority'. Then came *Raktakarabi* (Red Oleanders, 1954) in which the idea of ending exploitation had the flourish of a richer sense of humanity. The choice of this classic play by a classic writer, hitherto thought to be too abstract and intellectual to be a stage-play, meant a new direction for the theatre movement. Sambhu Mitra writes about its selection, 'We thought that Rabindranath's prowess is as vast as an ocean and it is bound to stir one and all. We just tried to promote this appreciation. We tried as best as we could.'[95] Classics, though not having strictly contemporary relevance, have a universality of appeal and this discovery led many producers to try their hands at such plays. Utpal Dutta, staged *Bisarjan* of Tagore (IPTA) and *Othello* and *Macbeth* of Shakespeare (LTG).

In the context of a situation, too confusing and baffling to be analysed, the thespians sometimes looked beyond that situation to classics which could take them to the very roots of human problems. There was a hue and cry in the Communist circles that this was a deviation from the ideal of People's Theatre. For example, the production of *Macbeth* at Srirangam in 1951 on the birth anniversary of Shakespeare made the critic of *Swadhinata* comment that all the enthusiasm, discipline, dedication and artistic skill of LTG would be in vain if they did not strike roots in the hard and dirty soil of the working class, and that there would be disappointment, weariness and a poisonous reaction. In the critic's opinion, so much labour and endeavour just for the aesthetic luxury of some aristocratic audience was not consistent with the purpose of the Little Theatre which had emerged from the People's Theatre Movement.[96] *Othello* too faced a similar criticism in the journal *Theatre*[97] and from other quarters.

However, the Little Theatre Group of Utpal Dutta also presented American progressive playwright Clifford Odets' *Waiting for Lefty* on a taxi drivers' strike in New York as its first production in 1950. It also staged Odets' *Till the Day I Die* in 1950 at the Festival of Peace and Culture held at Bhawanipur Smarta Ground. The latter's theme was the struggle and sacrifices of a banned Communist party, a theme very close to the IPTA spirit. And the leftists did like these plays. It is also interesting that in 1949, Dutta had staged *Romeo and Juliet* and did not find it contradictory to bring out on that occasion an article protesting against the ban imposed on the CPI. In the same year, he had also staged *Julius Caesar* as a modern political play interrogating fascism. But soon he realized that such plays appealed to a minority audience in the present state of society and turned more and more to directly 'socio-political' and, of course, Bengali plays.[98]

On the other hand, Sambhu Mitra believed that honesty to himself, to the audience and to humanity was all that a thespian needed, and this encompassed socio-political awarness also. Even when he did *Nabanna*, a play on contemporary reality, staged under the banner of the Communist Party, he just tried to be honest. Mitra told me in an interview that Mr Jyoti Basu had once been sent to the theatre group of the IPTA to impart political training. Basu said, 'One should stage plays on current problems. Take for example, the present crisis of scarcity of salt. You should pick up this problem for staging a play.' Mitra said to Basu, 'Tell us then whether we are to put up plays on salt or on man. Salt may be a starting point. But we have to proceed further—along the line of humanity.' Mitra never shirked current problems, but to him they were never be-all and end-all.[99]

Other major achievements of the Group Theatre during the early 1950s are listed below:

Natyachakra staged *Nildarpan* on 27 August 1950 at the IIR Mansion Institute (now called Netaji Mansion, at Sealdah). The actors were Bijan Bhattacharya, Ritwik Ghatak, Nakuleswar Chakrabarty, Moni Mukherjee, Bolin Som, Nabendu Ghosh, Digin Banerjee, Gangapada Basu, Sudhi Pradhan, Gita Som, Sobha Sen, and others. The manager was Jnan Majumdar, music director Dhananjay Mullick and the lighting was looked after by Tapas Sen. The play was also presented at the Peace Festival at the Bhawanipur Ground under the direction of Bijan Bhattacharya. After the inaugural show at the IIR Institute, four more shows were held at Kalika and one at Bhawanipur Ground. There could be no more shows on account of a disagreement between Bijan Bhattacharya and Sudhi Pradhan about the script.[100]

Bijan Bhattacharya's Calcutta Theatre started its career in 1951 with two one-act plays *Mara Chand* (The Dead Moon) and *Kalanka* (Disgrace), presented at IIR Mansion on 13 May. *Mara Chand* was a story based on the Famine of 1943–4; it ruined a happy family and in the end Paban, the baul (a class of singer devotees of Bengal) protagonist, rediscovered his lost tunes in the call of a political party. In depicting the character of Paban, the playwright Bijan Bhattacharya had in mind the blind singer Tagar Adhikari whom the IPTA had discovered in Dinajpur.[101] *Kalanka* was a story of atrocities of American soldiers in a Santal village of Bankura.

The Kranti Silpi Sangha, the drama front of RSP staged *Banglar Mati* (Soil of Bengal) written by Tulsi Lahiri.[102] It was a play on the problem of the Hindus in East Pakistan. The West Bengal Government objected to its staging. It was finally staged after some time, heavily censored. On 3 October 1953, it was staged at the All-India Kranti Silpi Sammelan Mandap.

The Amateur Theatrical Club of Behala created a sensation by staging *Ma* (*Mother* by Gorky) at Minerva on 6 February 1953. Many professional actors like Nitish Mukherjee, Asha Devi of Rangmahal and Malina Devi comprised the cast. Malina Devi playing the title role and earned warm tributes. The critic of *Parichay* (Phalgun, 1359/1953) was all praises for this performance of *Mother* in Bengali Theatre.[103]

Natun Ihudi (The New Jew), written by Salil Sen, was another drama on the refugee problem (we have already given a summary of the plot). It was staged by the Uttar Sarathi for the first time on 21 June 1951, at Kalika Stage, on an experimental basis. It had regular shows at Rangmahal from 23 July 1952. The director was Manoj Bhattacharya, and the actors were Sushil Majumdar, Kanu Banerjee Shyam Laha, Bhanu Banerjee,

Sunil Dasgupta, Bolin Som, Gautam Mukherjee, Sabitri Chatterjee and others.[104]

Masal (The Flambeau) written by Digin Banerjee was enacted on the occasion of the All-India Youth Peace Festival at the Park Circus Ground by the theatre group Asani Chakra. In 1950, there were renewed communal disturbances in both parts of Bengal. The playwright had seen with his own eyes how brutally the Muslims were tortured at Jagaddal. The play, set in the background of a mill area, tried to analyse the psychology of the workers in this respect, exposed how the owners instigated communalism in their own interests and ultimately, of course, how good triumphed over evil. Apart from Asani Chakra, Chandanagar Abhijatri Sangha, which was a branch of the IPTA, Bhadrakali Natyachakra and many local theatre groups staged this play at different places and it became particularly popular with the working class.[105]

The IPTA's tradition of bold and imaginative experiments in production technicalities was continued by the group theatre. Much attention was paid to stage-craft in order to make it most appealing with a minimal cost, and the usual histrionic pyrotechnics were discarded. A report by Sambhu Mitra[106] shows how simple properties made their plays—*Pathik*, *Ulukhagra*, *Chhenra Tar* and *Char Adhyay*, highly successful. *Pathik*, for example, was just one set—a tea-cum-grocery shop. For this, they completely covered three sides of the stage with sack-cloth in which were cut doors and windows. Some tea-chests, one dirty tea-table, three iron chairs and a few typical groceries were all the stage apparatus they used.

Khaled Chowdhury, who had once belonged to the IPTA and then joined Bahurupi and helped them produce their historical *Raktakarabi*, the man who was perhaps most responsible for uplifting the standard of stage-craft in Bengal at that time, has discussed in detail how careful attention was increasingly given to every inch of the stage in order to convey the message of the play. The articles on the platform were no longer mere decorations. At the same time, one had to bear in mind that stage-craft cannot play an autonomous role, but only a functional one. It should not be too emphatic and become an obstacle between the spectators and the play.[107]

As regards lighting effects too, the legacy of *Nabanna* was unmistakable. While on the commercial stage, lighting still meant 'follow-focusing' of the arc lamps and intensifying the effects of melodramatic scenes, Tapas Sen and others tried consciously to realize all the dynamic possibilities of lighting—to help the play glide from one scene to another or to change scenes abruptly, as the need may be, to make selective use of spot lights using various amounts of white light, thus intensifying the effect of acting, to plan subtle psychological applications of light and so forth. This was not only true of Bahurupi's productions, *Nildarpan* of Natyachakra too was highly successful in this respect. And all this was achieved despite economic handicaps and a lack of technical facilities.[108]

Similar attention was paid to background music and of course, acting—pronunciation, style and over-all composition. All these specialized efforts blended with the one objective—to make the performance effective. A whole team had to put in disciplined and hard labour to meet this high theatrical standard. And this became a proud tradition for the Bengali theatre.

But howsoever carefully the theatre groups chose their plays and looked after their productions, they were moving farther and farther away from the ideal of the people's theatre. The IPTA had been formed by a political party organizing and leading a mass movement. But now we had isolated theatrical groups with little means to address people outside a small elitist urban audience. With the mass movement dying down and the Party abandoning its revolutionary stand, even the IPTA did not find the situation very encouraging in this respect.

Contrary to what some people try to establish, it is not true that the 'right deviation' of the groups other than the IPTA dismantled the ideal of the People's Theatre. The groups that preferred themes other than the peasant, working class or lower middle-class life and did not try to mechanically pack their plays with contemporary meanings and excelled in technicalities of production, have been particular targets of the attack. But the responsibility rather lies with the original IPTA that could not sustain a big and potent theatre movement. When, after *Nabanna* the IPTA found itself in the doldrums and broke up into several groups, the fate of the People's Theatre Movement was sealed. So now we turn to the story of the decline of the IPTA.

The IPTA on the Decline and the People's Theatre Movement Dismantled: The Causes

The decline of the IPTA is often attributed to personal factors. No doubt, there were tensions between different persons in the IPTA right from the staging of *Nabanna*. But the story of this tension, as it is presented to us, deserves careful scrutiny.

The nature of the tension that prevailed immediately after the staging of *Nabanna*, was analysed in a report by the Cell Secretary, Charu Prakash Ghosh, dated 18 August 1946 and entitled 'A Crisis in the Bengal IPTA'. Here, the responsibility is laid largely at the door of some 'cultural leaders' of the Drama Squad, particularly Sambhu Mitra and Bijan Bhattacharya.[109]

First, according to Mr Ghosh's report, these cultural leaders were intolerant towards the non-artist members acting as liaison between the IPTA and the Communist Party. Sudhi Pradhan, the organizational Secretary of the Bengal IPTA, headed the latter group, while Sambhu Mitra usually voiced the opinion of the former. The cultural leaders had an attitude which amounted to saying: 'Leave us alone where art is concerned.'

The cultural leaders 'put a great emphasis on the importance of technique in any production. They would rather put up nothing to staging any technically imperfect show.' The other group seems

> to think that since the justification of IPTA lies in building up a wide-spread people's art movement, activity in the service of the people, in close contact with the masses, will by itself attain a satisfactory form. They (the group opposed to the cultural leaders) tend therefore to make the pursuit of technique as such secondary, perhaps they also consider such pursuit as a remnant of bourgeois ideas.

To Charuprakash Ghosh, Sambhu Mitra's undue insistence on technique was evident in his refusal to stage *Nabanna* on fixed types of boards. 'He insisted on the revolving type stage, as otherwise, he feared, it would not be possible for us to maintain the tempo of the drama. The result was that we had to suspend all activities.'

Having been requested by the PRC to organize a charity performance for the benefit of the flood-stricken people, most members of the IPTA wanted to revive *Nabanna*. But Sambhu Mitra opposed the idea on the ground that in view of the high standard of the previous performances of the IPTA, preparation for a month or so would not be enough to produce *Nabanna,* particularly because of the characteristic unpunctuality and irregularity of the members of the Drama Squad in attending rehearsals. 'Most of the members present, however, insisted on taking up *Nabanna* in spite of Com. Sambhu Mitra's invective. This made him furious and caused him to leave the meeting in a huff, with this remark that as far as he was concerned he would accept the decision to show *Nabanna* provided each and every member of the Drama Squad solemnly promised to attend rehearsals everyday from 6 p.m. to 10 p.m. without fail.'

Mr Ghosh mostly blamed Sambhu Mitra and other cultural leaders. But in summing up, Ghosh criticized the other group also: 'They tend to subordinate the artists to directions from above, parading their loyalty to the Party and in their rigid loyalty to the Party they refuse to face the special problems of the artistic and cultural front in which regimentation without persuasion does not work so well.'

However, the most serious charge levelled against the cultural leaders does not relate to theoretical or aesthetic differences, but to personal pettiness. 'From these theoretical premises they tend to take up a position in which personal factors enter. They feel impatient with Party leaders and with other groups within the IPTA, e.g. the Ballet Group.' A considerable part of Mr Ghosh's report dwells upon the apparently unreasonable resentment of the drama leaders at the formation of a Ballet Squad under the leadership of Bulbul Chowdhury and Jnan Mazumdar. The subsequent non-cooperative attitude taken by the drama leaders towards the Ballet Section, at least the way it is described in the report, seems to suggest that it was sheer personal grudge and that the likely motive was that as they themselves were doing nothing they should not allow the Ballet Group to do anything creative either.

Labouring these charges, Sudhi Pradhan, in his later writings, goes so far as to call these leaders' 'opportunist dictators' and 'soap-bubble socialists'. In fact, in an essay[110] included in his book *Samskritir Pragati*, he blames the Party, which in pursuit of the United Front theory, gave too much indulgence to men of artistic talent vis-à-vis political organizers in cultural fronts. He calls the former 'professional, half-professional and would-be professional men, ignorant of or indifferent to the Party's political line and yet trying to obtain a platform through the Party'.

He says that personal pettiness strained relations amongst the cultural leaders themselves. Sambhu Mitra was not enthusiastic about staging Bijan Bhattacharya's plays—*Jiyankanya* and *Abarodh*—because they were jealous of each other and did not want to share the credit for *Nabanna*. Pradhan says that those cultural leaders were handsomely paid by the IPTA and yet not satisfied. So when the IPTA film, *Dharti ke Lal* offered a better prospect for the future, Sambhu Mitra and Tripti Mitra left for Bombay. He says, 'Moreover we knew that enthusiasm of the general workers of the IPTA knew no bounds. They used to come for rehearsals or functions after spending the whole day in offices or in household work, without expecting any pay and used to work till late at night on two pieces of bread with jelly, a banana and a cup of tea provided by the IPTA.' Then he goes so far as to blame the cultural leaders for having once asked for a particular food, and thus causing trouble.

That Sambhu Mitra happened to be absent during the sten gun attack made on the IPTA workers at the house of Charu Prakash Ghosh seemed to Sudhi Pradhan an evidence of Mitra's escapist selfishness. Pradhan regards it as an instance of how the eminent cultural leaders of the IPTA left the organization once the Party was banned in 1948 and the Congress workers started attacking the Communists, sometimes violently.

In another article, Pradhan blames the egoistic attitude of Manoranjan Bhattacharya and Sambhu Mitra in presenting an alternative script of *Nildarpan* edited by the latter, when Digin Banerjee's script was already under consideration, thus foiling the staging of the play. Digin Banerjee had kept the original play more or less intact, for he felt that classics should not be altered significantly to suit present-day needs and that the audience themselves, would reinterpret it in their own terms. Sambhu Mitra had made a lot of changes to modernize the play. The changes were appreciated by many, but at the same time many felt that classics should not be distorted to that extent.[111]

It is clear that tension was building up in the organization, resulting from clashes of personalities. It is difficult to judge what exactly went wrong without knowing the other point of view. But when I did my research during the 1980s, Bijan Bhattacharya was dead and Sambhu Mitra found it beneath his dignity to relate his side of the story, answering his critics point by point. He, however, expressed his grievances in general terms about the way the Party had treated the question of building up a theatre movement; for instance, the Party tended to altogether ignore the question of having a theatre hall of its own. Non-existence of this facility, he argued, hindered the growth and consolidation of a stable theatre movement designed to create a new culture. He said, 'The best I can say of the Party leaders is that they were fools.' Sometimes his bitterness was articulated in stronger personal tone, 'The Party used to treat the artists as court-jesters. We were not supposed to have any freedom.'[112] And even Charu Prakash Ghosh admitted this at least once in his report: 'They (the Party leaders) tend to subordinate the artists to directions from above, parading their loyalty to the Party. From this point they also tend to take up a personal attitude and are drifting into a position in which they face with unconcern the prospect of dropping out from the IPTA of comrades with undoubted artistic excellence.'

Here I present my views regarding the matter. That *Nabanna* had not many repeat shows cannot be just Sambhu Mitra's failing. This particular play required a remarkably large cast of actors and actresses, and it was very difficult to mobilize the whole team, particularly when the show was outside Calcutta. This, of course, was no one's fault. Second, because of its episodic character, *Nabanna* required a revolving stage to make quick shifts of scenes. This would have enabled the audience to shift quickly from one episode to another—from the wedding feast to the beggars fighting for food near the dustbin, from the child dying of malnutrition to the peasant's wife being approached by a city tout and so on. Thus, different segments of the reality could be linked up and could make the audience think in a holisitic way. Otherwise, the abrupt ending of each scene would have impeded the involvement of the audience in the flow of the story. Without a revolving stage, the play would have lost all appeal. In fact, this actually happened. Despite Sambhu Mitra's initial objection, they did organize a few shows at different Calcutta theatres, only one of which had a revolving stage. The purpose was a laudable one—to raise funds for the PRC. But the play seems to have lost popularity. Sudhi Pradhan himself admits, 'Because *Nabanna* was not attractive without a revolving stage, it lost its popularity towards the end.'[113]

So Sambhu Mitra was not just being unnecessarily fastidious when he insisted upon a revolving stage. It was not just a question of technical perfection, but of communicating the message of the play to the audience. We have seen that the producers of *Nabanna* discarded the naturalistic stage-craft of the commercial stage requiring a multiplicity of paraphernelia in favour of a low-cost production making the best use of the available resources, and yet succeeded in preparing a stage better and more expressive than a naturalistic one. The gunny back-cloth can be cited as an example. So the charge of lack of flexibility and consideration does not hold good. And after all, an artist cannot be blamed for his keenness on perfection. If Sambhu Mitra insisted on a rare technical facility for making a particular play effective or criticized his colleagues for not attending rehearsals regularly, it only showed his earnestness about the job.

About the indecision in regard to staging of plays other than *Nabanna*, the alleged pettiness of the cultural leaders cannot explain away things. Sambhu Mitra says that he liked *Jiyankanya* and was keen on staging it.[114] But, as Charu Prakash Ghosh informs us, they needed to produce something very quickly to help the PRC, and *Jiyankanya* required long preparation. As to Mr Pradhan's charge that Sambhu Mitra did not stage Bijan Bhattacharya's *Abarodh* out of jealousy, it can perhaps be argued that this play was not of a good quality and that no one, not even Mr Pradhan, tried to stage it on behalf of the IPTA, even subsequently.[115] So far as *Nildarpan* is concerned, Sambhu Mitra's alternative script may have aggrieved Digin Banerjee whose script had already been accepted by some IPTA members. But it was certainly not the reason why the idea of staging it was dropped altogether. The play was not staged because some ultra-leftist members branded it as 'reformist'. This is admitted by both Sudhi Pradhan and Digin Banerjee. After the controversy between Digin Banerjee and Sambhu Mitra (and Manoranjan Bhattacharya), the Ballet Group of IPTA tried to render *Nildarpan* into a shadow play under the leadership of Jnan Majumdar. But the ultra-leftists discarded it outright.[116]

Even after the ultra-leftist trend was officially reversed in 1950, some members still considered the play to be 'reformist'. Sudhi Pradhan himself says that he and a few others had to form a separate group, Natyachakra, to stage this play. And if Sambhu Mitra's theoretical disagreement with Digin Banerjee as to the editing of the play stood in the way of staging it the first time, Sudhi Pradhan's disagreement with Bijan Bhattacharya, the director, explains why the play actually staged in 1950 could not be continued. Sudhi Pradhan says that he intended no personal opposition to Bhattacharya, but the latter had not been able to catch the contemporary relevance of *Nildarpan*, whereas he himself wanted to make it relevant to the Tebhaga fighters of the time.

The ultra-leftism of some Party members was responsible for the rejection of yet another play after *Nabanna*. Digin Banerjee informs us that just after *Nabanna*, the IPTA considered and then rejected one of his plays, alleging that it indulged 'reformism'. This was *Taranga* (Wave), the theme of which was some poor villagers' resistance against a Hindu zamindar, a Muslim jotedar and also the British police. Their leader is a member of the zamindar family itself—a Gandhiite believing in non-violence. But his son who takes over the leadership thinks that non-violence is useless and there is also a faint hint that he considers class-conflict to be the only way to solve socio-political problems.[117] Ultimately, the father–son conflict remains unresolved, and the whole village is subjected to a fearful police repression in the wake of the Quit India Movement. Some Party members disliked the play for not resolving the conflict definitely in the son's favour and for portraying the Quit India Movement. Digin Banerjee says that Gopal Sen, Treasurer of the IPTA, even gave him money to book the Rangmahal for 5 nights in order to stage *Taranga*. But then some members of the IPTA started threatening him and hence he backed out.[118]

Thus, each and every point against the cultural leaders is easily refuted. And there are some points that require no refutation at all. Censuring the cultural leaders for asking on some occasion for some special food sounds too uncharitable. Then *Dharti Ke Lal* was a film produced by the IPTA and as IPTA whole-timers, Sambhu Mitra and Tripti Mitra were duty-bound to work for it.[119] And if Sambhu Mitra can be blamed for being absent at a particular place during a sten gun attack, one can even blame those who were present during that attack and yet were not injured or killed. Sudhi Pradhan himself says that in 1948, after the Party was banned and association with the Communists was very risky, Sambhu Mitra staged *Nabanna* at least once.[120] Examining specific personal charges is perhaps useless. A People's Theatre Movement cannot be undermined by a couple of individuals, however unacceptable their points of view may be. In fact, this tendency of personal fault-finding can itself be held responsible for the decline of the movement. The tendency persisted and even affected the judgement of those interested in the history of the IPTA and the subsequent theatre movement. Even some apparently academic discourses, heavily influenced by Sudhi Pradhan's views, hold a few 'opportunistic' individuals almost solely responsible for the decline of the IPTA.[121] Criticizing others and absolving oneself became the most unfortunate tradition in the left movement and its cultural front.

II

It is, in fact, the lack of pragmatic thoughts and proper organizational efforts that created so much of personal tension which gradually ruined the IPTA as an organization. The alternative notion of theatre as conceived by the IPTA could not be realized overnight. An organization would have to move progressively towards that idea with a judicious sense of practical requirements. These requirements would, of course, be determined by a given time and place. The exponents of the People's Theatre in different countries worked out different strategies to achieve the common goal of establishing performing arts on an economic basis, very different from that of the commercial theatre, and of developing a new kind of audience. The full realization of the idea, of course, could be possible only when the economic structure of a country undergoes a basic change.

During the period of our study, such a change had taken place only in Russia. It has been said (maybe a bit wishfully) that the Soviet stage was increasingly concerned with the exciting drama of an entire people engaged in making a historic transition—a struggle not only to live better, but to be better human beings. With the solid support of the Communist government, the new cultural efforts were slowly transforming the culture of the vast land, the most inconspicuous mountain hamlets, isolated desert settlements as well as the towns and cities. There were no box office barriers and tickets were within the reach of all. The actors enjoyed multifarious facilities and great honour as well.[122] One remembers the enchanting description by George Thomson of the Soviet Theatre in his book *Aeschylus and Athens*. He felt that the theatre there was a ritual of the whole community, where both the actors and the audience participated. Even accounts which are rather critical of the way the Soviet government forced the artists to follow its policy, speak highly of the production system of the Soviet theatre.

To the men associated with the IPTA, the Russian Theatre was naturally a source of inspiration. Bishnu Dey, while writing on *Nabanna*, quoted a passage describing how Meyerhold's Theatre in Moscow had galvanized an intensity of emotion by introducing into the performance reports of the progress of the Civil War as the news arrived in Moscow—the glorious achievements of the partisan bands of Chapayev and his army and so on. The play thus became a living thing, a struggle between life and death of those very people sitting in the theatre and acted as a stimulus to action. Then added Bishnu Dey: 'But that is Meyerhold's theatre in Moscow, after the Revolution.' 'If—yes, we all said that', continued Dey,

> If only the conditions were different, the theatrical conditions and the social climate. And what a tribute it was to the year-old Indian People's Theatre Association that

we could have such thoughts, sitting in a crowded and dingy hall with miserable stage, hired for the evening after much persuasion at an exorbitant rate, the imperial squalor of Calcutta all around us. Not after, but very much before the Revolution. The crowded and deeply moved audience, the hostility of the professional theatres, the very great demand for repeat performance, all these prove the IPTA's revolutionary role in the art of the Bengali Theater, especially with their third production *Nabanna*.[123]

But how to transform this almost-revolutionary illusion into a real Revolution? Nobody seemed to know the answer. They would just sit and wait for the Revolution to come. Manoranjan Bhattacharya said,

> If a day comes when exploitation ends, the system of production and distribution becomes fair and inequality disappears, the people themselves would come forward to extend the boundaries of the theatre and make it a real People's Theatre. But till that day comes, an attempt should be made on the part of the theatre to reach the people. However, the avaricious theatre-companies do not dare to make the slightest movement away from the routine and safe path. What is the way then?[124]

Bhattacharya did not suggest any concrete means, but placed his faith on the IPTA. Unfortunately, however, even the IPTA was very vague on this matter.

What can be done to advance the cause of the People's Theatre in a country that had not undergone a socio-economic revolution? Romain Rolland wrote *The People's Theater* at the beginning of the twentieth century having in mind the contemporary French situation, one of his objectives being to make the new theatre accessible to the working class. So far as the organizational side of theatre was concerned, he borrowed the fertile ideas of Eugene Morel's P*roject de Theatres Popularises*.

Morel had placed his People's Theatre on a reasonably sound financial basis through subscriptions for weekly performances. This would help the theatre survive and the audience form the right attitude and habit, for, according to Morel, education requires repetition. Morel also suggested the price of tickets and methods of easy payment. He reduced expenses by reducing the author's royalties and suggested a reform in the Public Charities Taxes, which was making a People's Theatre almost impossible to run. And finally, he concluded. 'We are not establishing a charitable institution; but must have a system whereby very few families would be too poor to go to the theatre; and consequently, the theatre, far from being a luxury, would actually develop a sense of thrift and economy.'

Morel also suggested that once a People's Theatre became a financial success, the profits must go to the founding of another theatre, in a different neighbourhood. In this way, the play would no longer be performed only seven days, but fourteen, and the capital spent on the foundation of the original theatre would be replaced out of the profits of the second. The second, then making use of the material as well as the actors of the first, would have no difficulty to start, and would indeed be enriched by the experience of its predecessor. Thus theatres would be organized not only throughout Paris, but in every province of France, and they would be closely allied under the administration of a central committee.

Rolland only indicated the principal features of Morel's project and suggested that Morel's book should be read from cover to cover. But this was enough to remind the readers that the exponents of People's Theatre should be conscious about the physical conditions of the People's Theatre. Rolland's book had many readers in India. Sudhi Pradhan writes.[125] 'Forty years back, when I was entrusted with the task of organizing the Marxist Cultural Movement, I did not know of any better book pointing out the relationship of socialism with the theatre.' But the few pages containing the above discussion seem to have been missed by all the readers in Bengal. Of course, here they could not exactly follow Morel or Rolland. The situation was different. Here the main emphasis was on the peasantry and not so much on the workers. Still they could have learnt something useful from the book.

And recruiting subscribers at a cheap rate as a method of bringing theatre to the people is not just a theory confined to Rolland's book. It had actually been practised by exponents of the People's Theatre in different countries. In Germany, for example, the *Freie Volksbuhne* set up in 1890 used to function on such a basis. In 1914, this organization split into two factions, one close to the Social Democratic Party (SPD) and the other not so close. The latter faction alone had 70,000 members and was able to build its own theatre hall. After some years the two reunited. But without proper political guidance, the method of subscription could not represent the interests of the working masses, and the membership became middle-class enough for the organization to become in effect a huge cooperative ticket agency rather than a political force. This led the famous dramatist Erwin Piscator to break away from it and found the *Piscatorbuhne*. But when he did so, he too invited subscription. He started with 16,000 members (mostly, according to him, young workers) who committed themselves to five forthcoming productions.[126]

But here in India the IPTA organizers had no such thinking, no thinking at all about founding the People's Theatre on a sound economic basis.

There could be another method for the People's Theatre Movement—the agitprop (agitation propaganda) method as was then being tried by the Chinese. The valorous Chinese efforts captivated the imagination of the cultural activists here and numerous essays extolled them. A booklet[127] published by the Progressive People's Press of Bombay contained what Anna Louis Strong and Edgar Snow had said about the drama soldiers of

China, who, grouped in 200 mobile troupes, were working behind the lines with the guerrilla fighters. They used to have open-air performances—democratic gatherings with no tickets sold, no dress-circle, no preferred seats, the scantiest properties and minimum preparation. What they lacked in subtlety and refinement was made up by their robust vitality, sparkling humour and a sort of direct rapport between the actors and the audience. They used to work as a 'living newspaper' through the constant shifting of programmes according to newly-rising military, political, economic and social requirements. When the Reds occupied new areas, it was the Red Theater that allayed the fear of the local people. Their theater was indigent (possessing perhaps only a square box or a silk curtain with the words 'People's Anti-Japanese Dramatic Society' written on it), so were their theatre workers. They used to walk long distances from one village to another and the local peasants arranged their food and transport. They got small living allowances, slept anywhere and ate cheerfully whatever was provided for them. Sometimes, they would put up a show after overnight rehearsal and they often depended on local recruits.

And saying all this, the Indian votary of the Chiness-type People's Theatre said,

> Is India not in such a state now as to demand all that we can give to help her? The scope of development of our People's Theatre is tremendous. We need plays, plays and more plays—written directly and simply on subjects dealing with our urgent problems—food, unity, national freedom, national defence. Is it too much to ask of our writers and dramatists that they should help us by writing suitable playlets and dramas for our People's Theater?[128]

As if the situations of India and China were not different and it was only the lack of suitable plays that prevented them from running a full-fledged agitprop theatre movement!

Not only the Chinese style theatre, but Noel Coward's Phoenix Theatre fighting on the side of the British army on the battle-fields of Arakan using an improvised stage and with makeshift arrangements which was a striking contrast to the great facilities it had enjoyed in London, also appealed to the People's Theatre enthusiasts of Bengal.[129] They found all these very heroic, but they did not seem to have realized that such efforts needed a war-time situation.

Agitprop theatre can also develop in less revolutionary situations than that of China. During the years between the two World Wars, the widespread working class discontent in a number of countries in the West had led to such a development. The exponents of the Indian People's Theatre were perhaps not aware of this. In Germany, side by side with the experimental theatre of Piscator and other recognized dramatists who had broken away to a large extent and yet not fully from the conventional theatre, there emerged several agitprop theatre groups of workers. Plays were written and enacted by the workers themselves who innovated simple and novel dramatic forms which constituted a direct challenge to the norms of the conventional theatre. Piscator, Brecht and other progressive thespians increasingly cooperated with these 'Agitprop Truppen' as the rise of fascism made it difficult for the former to express their views within the legitimate theatre.[130]

In England, the powerful Workers' Theatre Movement (1928–36) was a similar kind of development. Even in America, seemingly prosperous and secure, there was an undercurrent of class tension and thus during the late 1920s and early 1930s, there was a proliferation of agitprop groups, together known as the *proletbuehne*. The agitprop theatres of these countries were heavily influenced by the German agitprop movement.[131]

The agitprop theatre is evidently quite different from the other type of People's Theatre.[132] It exchanges indoor performances for a theatre of the street. Its forms are sketch, cabaret and revue. The agitprop group would mount a sketch on some important current event with minimum delay, put up a quick show at a street corner, and then move on to the next street, perhaps collecting relief funds for some strikers. Portability is its essence and the greater the number of such portable groups, the more successful the agitprop theatre. The same play can hardly be used for both the agitprop theatre and the other kind of People's Theatre, nor the same actors. The actors in the former are generally political activists interested in theatre and in the latter they are progressive and yet professional thespians. Agitprop does not want so much as to raise the cultural level of the workers by bringing them into great dramatic art, which may be the aim of other type of People's Theatre; its task is to conduct mass working class propaganda through the particular method of dramatic representation and indeed, the agitprop proved to be a splendid weapon for this purpose.

But agitprop is very suceptible to changes in the political atmosphere. In 1936, when the Communists professed the United Front theory and there was a radical realignment of political forces, agitprop theatre nearly died out in no time in all the countries where it had recently flourished. The earlier revolutionary exuberance disappeared. The success of the United Front thus cost the agitprop a great deal. There is perhaps a considerable element of truth in the following comment of a historian of the American agitprop theatre: 'Agitprop was a less suitable form in which to discuss anti-fascist politics than it had been with the more clear-cut issues of class-conflict'.[133]

This perhaps explains why in Bengal where the People's Theatre Movement was born during the United Front period itself, its exponents did not really think in terms of agitprop theatre during the first few years. They found the agitprop method of the Chinese People's Theatre very romantic and even thought that India was ready to use it, but there was not a single move to use this method in practice till 1948.

What did the organizers of the IPTA do? They produced *Nabanna*, a novel experiment in content and form, a play that dealt with the distress of the Famine-stricken peasants and expressed their aspirations. But the play was staged on the commercial stages of Calcutta where it had no chance at all of addressing the peasant audience, and not even the city workers, for the tickets were naturally out of the reach of the poor. And, in any case, the urban workers could not even dream of entering the theatre halls meant for the *babus*. Then, when the owners of the commercial theatres refused to lend their boards to the IPTA because they saw a threat to their own type of theatre, the IPTA organizers were at a loss as to how to reach any audience at all. But even then they did not try to find some means of self-support.

The only alternative they could think of was to stage the play in the trail of meetings organized by the Communist Party and its mass fronts all over Bengal. But for a Calcutta-based organization consisting of only a handful of whole-timers it was very difficult to attend meetings in remote parts of the province, particularly because a drama like *Nabanna* required thorough preparations, elaborate arrangements and a huge team of actors and actresses. Sudhi Pradhan says that *Nabanna* was not performed at more than five places outside Calcutta.[134] So, unlike the People's Song Movement, the People's Theatre could not flourish through political meetings, not with a drama like *Nabanna*. And the political activists generally blamed the artist-leaders of the drama squad for this.

According to Sambhu Mitra,[135] after *Nabanna*, some admirers came forward and offered to raise funds for the purpose of founding a theatre hall.[136] Mitra said that he had felt immensely encouraged. After all, in his words, one cannot forge a theatre movement without a hall of one's own. If it is your own stage, you can make a hole in the platform and make the actors appear from beneath, which you can never do in a hired hall. Varieties of experiments with form are possible in one's own theatre. But the greatest advantage of such a theatre is that a repertoire and a permanent group of actors and actresses can be formed around it. This will even make it possible for the group to go to the districts regularly and perform there. Sambhu Mitra chalked out a long programme regarding all this and sent it to Bhabani Sen. But the Party did not approve of it. The Party leaders thought that it would turn out to be a bourgeois affair without having much to do with the People's Theatre. Sambhu Mitra was very sore about this dream of his, which remained unfulfilled till his death.

But what seems to have been even more unwise on the part of the IPTA organizers is that while rejecting Mitra's plan they did not try any alternative. They could have formed a large number of local theatrical groups all over the province and encouraged the enacting of plays suitable for such small groups and small-scale performances. Thus, there could be a decentralized People's Theatre Movement, if not an agitprop movement. But the IPTA just sat idle and kept blaming a few artists of the drama squad for not being able to build up a widespread theatre movement.

In the beginning, the local branches of the AFWAA had been very active in putting up plays, as the *Third Annual Report* of the organization informs us. Then, an article by Benoy Roy in *Janayuddha* (6 October 1943) says that at a workers' conference the tramway workers of Calcutta had enacted a play written by Manoranjan Bhattacharya on the Hindu-Muslim problem, and a play by Gurudas Pal had been staged by some local workers of Metiabruz. An advertisement on the back cover of Kanak Mukherjee's *Desrakshar Dak* informs us that some playlets and tableaux written by Manikuntala Sen, Kanak Mukherjee and other workers of the women's movement (e.g. *Food Queue* and *Call for Self Defence*) will be compiled and published shortly. But after some time, such small-scale efforts were no longer encouraged. At least, we do not have evidence that they were. The Party organizers say that the success of *Nabanna* turned the heads of the cultural leaders. But it seems that the success rather turned the heads of the Party men whose expectations from now on were wholly to be centred on the lone Drama Squad of Calcutta and its only production *Nabanna*.

And because of this imprudence of the organizers, the drama squad really became a burden to the IPTA. The IPTA was constantly facing a financial crisis. Their expenses on wages, house rent, etc., amounted to approximately Rs. 800 per month, while they had no fixed source of income. They had to reduce the number of whole-timers to three (Bijan Bhattacharya, Sambhu Mitra and Tripti Mitra) and put the IPTA on a part-time basis to straighten out their financial difficulties. But even these three had to be paid and as a part-time organization, the IPTA further lost its mobility and became seriously handicapped in producing anything on a large scale.[137] The Party leaders, of course, thought that this was due to the reluctance of Sambhu Mitra and others to produce anything that could fetch money, and the Party leaders also wanted the IPTA to give financial help to the PRC without thinking of its own economic viability.

While the IPTA organizers cherished the success of *Nabanna* they admonished the cultural leaders for being much too insistent about its technical aspects, which, according to them, made it impossible to repeat the drama anytime and anywhere. It did not occur to them that without this 'fuss' this play would simply flop. They seemed to have been impervious to any argument in favour of meticulous attention to dramatic forms on the part of the artists. But famous exponents of the People's Theatre—Meyerhold, Brecht and others—are all famous for their attention to and innovations in forms. They even made use of complicated machineries sometimes. In his drama 'Petroleum', Brecht had to show how oil was drilled and treated. Of course, there can be plays the production of which requires less cost and shorter preparations—plays useful for another kind of People's Theatre Movement—agitprop or almost agitprop theatre movement. But even agitprop demands attention to forms.

The IPTA organizers also accused the artists of 'professionalism'. The Party organizers of the IPTA denounced 'professionalism', though after the first shows of *Nabanna*, many critics rather admired the 'professional seriousness'[138] of the team that had made the play successful. To the Party leaders, professionalism did not connote any virtue, but was associated with self-seeking. They forgot that this might be necessarily true in a society dominated by capitalist values, but might not be so in a different idealistic frame.

The Party Leaders used to glorify the idea embodied in the Bengali proverb—'Eating at home and tending wild buffaloes',[139] which means, at best, love's labour. But an objective like the People's Theatre Movement needed sustained activities and normally required a number of whole-timers whose means of livelihood (though not of luxury) must be ensured, and only then can their love's labour produce the ideal People's Theatre—professional and yet non-commercial. If the sustenance for the workers of the People's Theatre does not come this way, it would have to come from some other source—a massive movement submerging all personal needs and presenting the prospect of an alternative society in the near future. But this prospect never seemed very bright in India, except perhaps for a few months in 1948–50, when agitprop theatre flourished. But even then there was no proper planning to build up a theatre movement and anyway, this period was too short and the forced revolutionism petered out very soon. The political party supposed to be working for this cherished future did not have a clear view of its own objective and seems to have been not very serious either about its end.

The whole left movement in India thus suffered from a deep theoretical flaw and this was reflected in the cultural front. As there was no sound theory to generate solid organizational activities and sustain the fighting spirit of individuals, artists and non-artists—disruptive forces crept into the organization and it was unable to withstand the onslaught of the establishment.

III

The second phase of the IPTA's activities (from 1948 onwards) would corroborate this conclusion, for the second phase of its activities was also the second phase of its decline. During the period 1948–50, precisely when the IPTA was engaged in vigorous agitprop activities, forces of disintegration were at work. Lack of well-thought-out organizational efforts was made up this time by the angry snarling of some instant revolutionaries denouncing a large section of the members and sympathizers of the Party as rank opportunists. This denunciation was very similar to that of Sudhi Pradhan. But this time it was more sweeping. Earlier the party leaders would at least outwardly go by the 'United Front' theory. Now, after the second congress of the Party, the theory itself was openly denounced.

Bedevilled by an adventurous ultra-leftism, Sajal Roy Chowdhury (using the penname Mrityunjay Adhikari) wrote an essay in *Loknatya.*[140] The writer was the Secretary, West Bengal IPTA. He presented an extremely distorted view of the role of the reputed artists of the IPTA:

> Professional artists, acquainted with urban culture, naturally came bringing their talents with them—and with their arduous efficiency in artistic forms. Along with that they also brought a deep-rooted distorted idea about art—successful artistic creation has no connection with common man's happiness and grief, hopes and aspirations, art's is an impalpable world of *rasa*—Disassociate yourself from the struggle for existence of common man and sit in a solitary room and you will create effective art.
>
> Look, propaganda and art are not the same thing. Yes, you have started a new kind of artistic creation—but you have not yet attained a reasonable success. If you are engaged in peasants' and workers' movements day and night—go around shouting slogans—how would you learn to create successful art? So, come, we will give you lessons in successful art. You hire rooms, raise funds and organize group. And look, we are accepting the framework of your movement, but exclude the word 'struggle'. For, if you try to talk directly about struggle, art will become propaganda.

He not only inveighed against the 'cultural leaders' of the IPTA, but completely ignored the past achievements of IPTA and even denigrated them. *Nabanna*, *Spirit of India*, *India Immortal*—all of them were denounced, because they had been performed on the commercial stage and in a professional style and had been products of 'rehearsal-hall-show, show-hall-rehearsal'.

He further criticized the cultural leaders for neglecting folk-forms, for taking up a dictatorial attitude in matters of artistic forms, for their insistence on the exclusion of politics, for demanding the profit for their own comforts, for realizing their own interests using the name of the IPTA and for deserting it as soon as the IPTA was in danger.

And all this came from a man holding a top position in the organization. Sajal Roy Chowdhury was supported by Pradyot Guha (under the pen name Prakash Roy)[141] in the Party's theoretical journal *Marxbadi*. And this negative tongue-lashing is all that they did—no positive steps were taken to reach the peasants and workers.

Many members and sympathizers of the IPTA were shocked. Surapati Nandi, an active singer of IPTA, said[142] in protest that Adhikari had not only insulted the cultural leaders, but also by exaggerating their importance and by suggesting that other members were helpless against these leaders, he had showed disrespect for all of them. Nandi pointed out that *Nabanna*, *Nabajibaner Gan*, etc., constituted a glorious heritage of the IPTA.

He was also critical of Adhikari's voluble programme for future:

> About planning for future he (Roy Chowdhury alias Adhikari) says, 'we will have to go to peasants and workers'; 'we will have to develop leadership of peasants and workers in the IPTA'; 'The culture that is being created, signed by blood, will have to be valued most'; 'Give shape to the life and struggle of the exploited and stand courageously to face reactionary forces'; 'Take part in every political struggle,' etc. These words are very vague and have been heard several times before.

This reviling of a large number of artists inside the IPTA together with the repression of the government led to its fragmentation. In the 1950 Puja issue of *Natun Sahitya*[143] Digin Bandyopadhyay, the playwright, reviewed the situation. By that time the political line of the party had been changed. Banerjee condemned the ultra-leftist 'Sab Jhuta Hai' (Everything is false) cry that had caused irreparable damage to the IPTA:

> The hope of keeping IPTA as a democratic organization was extirpated by roots. The workers and leaders not believing in ultra-leftism withdrew with honour seeing no other alternative. It became clear that the cause of the disease was lying elsewhere.
>
> It is funny that those who had dreamt of an overnight Revolution refused to realize that the way the People's Theatre Movement could be carried on in villages was not suitable for urban areas, with a predominantly middle-class population, particularly in a metropolis like Calcutta. There were differences between rural and urban environments, and between rural and urban tastes. Hence the People's Theatre Movement would have to be run along two different lines in villages and cities. Denying this reality the ultra-leftists advocated a kind of movement that had been possible only in the 'free zones' of China and Vietnam.

Digin Banerjee also noted that taking advantage of the weakness of the IPTA, the government had stepped up repressive measures. The 1876 Dramatic Performance Act had been revived. Over the past one-and-a-half years, the Police Commissioner had banned a number plays such as *Mrityu Nai* (No Death), *Manjil* (Palace), *Sanket* (Signal), *Taranga* (Wave), etc. The police had asked different hall owners for information about the IPTA and copies of their contracts with this organization, i.e. to spy for the police—an idea that would have put even the British police to shame.

III

Digin Banerjee was also worried at the plight of the commercial stage. The owners were making fortunes, but the workers were denied a share. Discontent was growing amongst the workers of Srirangam, Rangmahal, Minerva and Kalika. Rangmahal had been lying locked out for quite some time. On the other hand, new cinema halls were coming up, old theatres were being transformed into cinema halls. The only new theatre was Kalika. The owners kept on running old plays—even Sisir Kumar was guilty of doing it. He was not giving new dramas and new dramatic groups a chance. These theatre-owners were reluctant to take any risk. Those who had fought for progressive drama were gradually losing ground because of the avarice of producers, directors and renowned actors.

Finally, Banerjee expressed hopes about the future. Many dedicated workers of the IPTA had realised the mistake of ultra-leftism and were already trying to rectify it. The organization might be reinvigorated through an external stimulus. The IPTA would therefore have to establish close contact with the other progressive dramatic societies. Whatever the difference of opinion among them regarding the means, they could be unified as fellow-travellers with one destination in their mind. A new culture would arise in the process of fighting the feudal economy still prevalent in India and its ally imperialism now working from behind the screen.

But these hopes were belied. First, contrary to Banerjee's belief, locating the enemies had become very difficult after Independence. Second, Banerjee, while deploring the degeneration of the commercial stage and linking up the fate of the People's Theatre Movement with it to some extent, had implicitly assumed that the new theatre was depending on the commercial stage and was unable to nurture any reasonable hope for an alternative economic basis. In fact, it was the time when the popular upsurge was dying down and agitprop theatre was fading out. Third, despite much talk about what was to be done, the Party and its cultural front did not really know what to do. Last, the Party had not yet been rid of ultra-leftism. The tension was not over, the attacks on artists continued.

This period has been interestingly described in the reminiscences of Kali Banerjee.[144] It was a time when the urge for open-air performances in both factory areas and the countryside was abating. The enthusiasm of the audience and the actors declined fast. Under such circumstances, some theatre enthusiasts started thinking of a long-term planning for People's Theatre in place of participation in day-to-day mass movements which were also then non-existent. They felt the need for a theatre academy for research and training, for producing good theatre workers with good reasoning and skills. The Moscow Art Theatre was such an academy. China too could boast of her Lu Tsun Academy besides her open-air theatres.[145] Kali Banerjee and a few others managed to obtain detailed information from the Moscow Art Theatre about the latter's course. A study circle was set up at Utpal Dutta's house.

But their dream did not materialize. The viable economic basis needed for such an academy was not easy to achieve under the existing social system. Nor could the Communist Party be convinced of its need. The artists intending to fight a long-drawn battle demanded a suitable pay, and many from within the IPTA objected. In Kali Banerjee's words, 'Today I realize that none of them wanted to take up drama as a profession, hence this opposition. I was broken-hearted.'[146]

Yet another case in point is Utpal Dutta. A talented but anglicized thespian, he got attracted to Bengali theatre towards the late 1940s alongside his continued involvement in Shakespearean theatre. The motivation was obvious—to reach a wider audience. And though he founded his own Little Theatre Group, he was deeply involved with the IPTA too. But he could not stay in the IPTA for more than ten months, on account of his differences with the Party bosses regarding the content and presentation of plays. Also, he found the IPTA workers lacking discipline and dedication, particularly when he contrasted this with Jeffry Kendal's theatre group Shakespeareana with which he had worked. [147]

The struggle for the People's Theatre just petered out. There remained a theatre movement avowedly to carry on the ideal of the People's Theatre, but the initial intention was not fulfilled. A man or a small theatrical group cannot conduct the struggle for People's Theatre all alone. Bijan Bhattacharya, one of the architects of the IPTA, who later broke away and formed a separate group, was once asked what exactly had caused the break-up of the IPTA despite the dedication of its members. Bhattacharya answered in a mood of self-criticism: 'That is a foolish question! The struggle for existence tired them out. There was no real dedication. They remained earnest for sometime. When the situation became a difficult one, they just petered out, pulled out, because they were opportunists.' [148] But could some individuals alone on their own can achieve the end? Soon afterwards, Bijan Bhattacharya said in a huff: 'One can not do anything by staging dramas all alone and here we want a strong party leadership. The Party must take the lead, must create an ideal situation.'

When the People's Theatre Movement gave way to the Group Theatre or New Theatre Movement, there was nothing very new in its character. All the groups including the IPTA were inspired by the People's Theatre Movement started by *Nabanna*, though they differed in matters of details about the means of realizing the ideal. Yet even in the early 1950s they expressed the desire to unite on a common platform and work together, if a good leadership could be found. Some attempts at unification were actually made. But this was not found feasible. And the small theatrical groups found the original task of People's Theatre increasingly difficult.

Gradually the drama groups realized that they lacked the right means to attain their ideal—communicating with and inspiring the masses for a better society. Some of the groups started deviating even from the ideal. They proved susceptible to various types of compromise. And the phrase 'smearing of lines', used to mean the vanishing gap between the Broadway and the off-Broadway theatre in America, could apply to the difference between Bengal's commercial and non-commercial theatre as well. Even the so-called progressive groups claiming lineage from the IPTA became quite commercial in their attitude. The ideological conflicts also continued. As the disillusionment of these groups about achieving the objective of People's Theatre increased, their differences regarding political persuasions and modes of experimentations became sharper. In the words of Sambhu Mitra, they entered the field of theatre each carrying a banner and then throwing away the banners, they started fighting each other with the sticks.[149] But this is a story that lies beyond the scope of our study.[150]

IV

The organizers of the IPTA neglected not only the material basis of the People's Theatre, but also another vital aspect of it—the remoulding of the taste of the audience. They wanted to win over middle-class theatre-goers from the unwholesome influence of the commercial theatre—a hard task at the time when commercial theatre was running more or less satisfactorily. But what was even harder was to form a new audience amongst the workers and the peasants who had been accustomed for a long time to watch pompous *Jatras* dishing out banal values. The IPTA was surely wrong in considering peasants and workers as being culturally equipped to respond to its message. Romantic revolutionary thoughts made the political activists think that these were the very revolutionary classes and hence more culturally conscious than the decaying middle-class. But experiences repeatedly contradicted this assumption.

Nabanna was first put up on a Calcutta stage and was able to captivate the audience, which was exclusively middle-class in character. Some members of the intelligentsia felt overwhelmed. The IPTA organizers inferred the success of *Nabanna* from the opinions of this small elite group and felt extremely happy. Even much later they used to say boastfully that after seven shows of Nabanna, Bidhayak Bhattacharya's *Tai To*, a so-called 'social play' typical of the commercial theatre, was enacted in a miserably empty hall of Srirangam. But the fact remains that *Nabanna* soon ceased to be a box-office success. Perhaps, as time passed by, Calcuttans found the theme of the Famine less and less appealing. Moreover, without a revolving stage, its performances were not effective.

What happened on the few occasions when the IPTA took *Nabanna* outside Calcutta? Sajal Roy Chowdhury frankly admits[151] that at Hatgovindapur, peasants watched the show in large numbers, but left unimpressed. The IPTA members felt extremely disheartened when Lalita Biswas,[152] a local recruit playing the role of Panchanani as a substitute for Manikuntala Sen, informed them of the poor response of the audience. Perhaps, in a dull village life, the very arrival of some *babus* from the city to stage a show was exciting. But that did not necessarily mean that the villagers would like the play, dealing as it did with their own lives. But at the same time, Roy Chowdhury happily remembers that at Berhampore where anti-Communist feeling was running high and the hostile local people were throwing stones at them, their show of *Nabanna* created quite a stir and a profound impact on the people. Roy Chowdhury says from his general experience that when the people were in a militant mood they reacted favourably to the shows of IPTA, but not otherwise. I have heard similar comments from quite a few activists in regard to the People's Song Movement too.

Kali Banerjee's experience is worth recounting in this connection. He recollects that during the early 1950s when the popular militancy was subsiding, the IPTA went to a certain working class area for a show of *Bisarjan*. Heavily-drunk people arriving with lanterns in their hands boisterously demanded after some time: 'Make the girl dance', i.e. Aparna, a young female character in the play, would have to dance to entertain the audience. At last Panu Pal tried to please them by performing his famous 'Famine Dance'. But that was obviously not the thing the audience had asked for. The actors somehow managed to complete the show and hurriedly left. Later on they came to know that the villagers had been told by the Party that the IPTA would put up a *Jatra* there and expected one of the typical *Jatras* that they were used to see.[153] And yet 'if in the theatre there is no interaction between the stage and the audience, the play is dead, bad or non-existent: the audience like customer is always right'.[154] Socially conscious theatre activists like Brecht have always regarded the spectator as a 'co-author'.

Ultimately, the People's Theatre Movement reached a stage a ppropriately described by the playwright Sachin Sengupta in 1952 in the following words:

> Those for whom the People's Theatre has been created (workers and peasants) find greater pleasure in witnessing dramas that have been staged for the last 80 years rather than *Gananatya*. That is because those dramas are more colourful in costumes and décor, dialogue and acting.... On the other hand, city-dwellers are tired of

witnessing plays written in the old style and are delighted to see a reflection of rural life on the stage. This pleasure in witnessing a reflection of rural life does not mean that they desire to live that rural life or have any interest in improving the conditions of rural life. It is the appeal of novelty that pleased them.[155]

We may not wholly agree with Sengupta's diagnosis of the ills of the new theatre. But his appraisal of the situation seems to be basically correct. His forecast that soon the new theatre would lose its novelty for the urban audience, who would then revert to the old type of drama, did not come true. During the course of the next few decades, the new theatre, originally intended to be the People's Theatre, remained somewhat distant from the poor people, but definitely won over a section of the urban middle-class. And yet this new theatre was unable to shake the complacency of the middle-class spectators. Watching such plays just made them feel 'progressive' and committed to an egalitarian political ideology, i.e. feel good on the whole.

The votaries of the People's Theatre would perhaps recall what Brecht said about Epic Theatre: 'The point is not to leave the spectator purged by a cathartic but to leave him a changed man; or rather to sow within him seeds of changes which must be completed outside the theatre.' But if conditions outside the theatre are not favourable, a play, despite its firm commitment to bringing about a change in the values and attitudes of the audience, and despite its competent enactment, fails to produce the effect of which Brecht writes. So ultimately the failure of the People's Theatre Movement that dates from *Nabanna* has to be explained in terms of factors lying outside the theatre, just as the failure of the People's Song Movement has been explained in our last chapter in terms of extra-musical factors.

Folk Forms

One important aspect of the People's Theatre was the adaptation of folk forms. The IPTA papers repeatedly pledged to 'restore old folk forms that grow luxuriously like neglected weeds on the roadside'.[156] In fact, since they could not find any viable economic or organizational means for reaching out to the masses, they continued to stress the revival of folk forms as the only solution. And they indeed pioneered the revival process. We have seen this also in the case of music. But in the case of theatre, revival of folk forms was not that easy. And just as in the case of music, the revival of folk forms alone was not likely to help them achieve their goal.

The theatre-workers of Bengal faced difficulties in adapting folk forms. The forms of folk music were rich and lively and they could of course be used for the purpose of the theatre. But as for folk-drama proper, Bengal had only *Jatra*. Here too, music dominated and the effect was operatic. By the period of our study, however, this form had already degenerated and nearly died out. *Jatra* had become just an imitation of theatre. Mukunda Das temporarily revived it by infusing in it the spirit of patriotism, but this experiment could not outlast his death (1934). Though dating from the sixteenth century, this form had not acquired enough vitality and dynamism to keep pace with the changing times. So the few *Jatras* still staged in villages and sometimes even in cities, were about gods and goddesses and had little to do with popular progressive thoughts. The form was slowly becoming obsolate.[157]

Thus, revitalizing *Jatra* was not an easy task. The adaptation of musical folk forms was not much of a problem. Folk poets themselves came up with their own creation to enrich the People's Song Movement. A healthy give-and-take relationship developed between them and the *babus* of the IPTA. But nothing of that kind happened in the field of theatre (we have come across two to three stray cases of workers putting up small theatrical performances on their own, but nothing is known about their forms). With all its talks about the assimilation of folk forms, the IPTA could not put up a single *Jatra* during the first decade of its existence. It was in 1954 that Biru Dutta's *Rahumukta* staged by the IPTA showed for the first time that even the *Jatra* form could be adapted to the need of People's Theatre. An IPTA newsletter of 1953[158] announced that at the coming provincial convention at Naihati a team from 24-Parganas would present a *Jatra*. But from subsequent newsletters, it appears that the *Jatra* was not put up at all.

Here in Bengal there was nothing compared to the historic turn of the drama-form *Tamasha*[159] of Maharashtra. *Tamasha* comprising both music and acting had always been a strong cultural medium of the poor people there. Inside the IPTA a whole-time *Tamasha* Troupe of eight people was set up, with D.N. Gavankar (an untouchable), Anna Bhau Sathe (a landless peasant) and Omar Sheikh as the nucleus. They used to prepare *Tamasha*s along with *Powada*s and other types of folk music. We learn from an IPTA newsletter of 1952 that the efforts of the last eight years in this direction had 'led to the formation of nearly 300 squads drawing professional *Tamashawala*s too, as the old *Tamasha* is more or less obsolete now. These squads prepare programme on the pattern of the main troupe.'[160]

In Bengal they could, of course, use the musical quality that dominated the *Jatra*. *Jatra* had a tradition of *Juri* songs—a kind of concert analysing the story in music at moments of emotional intensity. In fact, the whole rural life of Bengal is marked by a fondness for music. Perhaps the village folks are highly lyrical and poetic all over the world. In the words of Rolland, 'It is the poem of earth impregnated with the odor of the field and overflowing with peasant humour and rich language.' So the folk forms 'preserve what is poetic in the life of the small communities and records for posterity their vanishing individuality'.[161] Sambhu Mitra says, 'A poetry was created through the performance of *Nabanna*—the poetry of emotion, the poetry of helplessness, the poetry of love.'[162] Actually perhaps it was the poetry of folk-life, composed of all these elements. The grippingly lyrical quality of the emotional speeches of Pradhan (Bijan Bhattacharya) enriched the dramatic richness of the play *Nabanna*. It is this imperishable tradition of poetry that links up a drama with the never-ending vitality of the folk. In the musical drama *Jiyankanya*, this lyricism was far more prominent. Of course, all this does not show any direct influence of the *Jatra* form, but perhaps an affinity with it.

The theatre-workers could also use some other qualities of *Jatra* to their advantage. 'Our mental habits and social structure made the theatre the vehicle for more certain ideas',[163] said Mulk Raj Anand and he cited *Ramlila*, *Nautanki*, *Ras* and *Jatra* as examples. Perhaps Sambhu Mitra expanded Anand's idea when he claimed[164] that *Jatra* was a vehicle of education and culture: 'I have seen Duryodhon come onto the stage and with the utterance 'Janami Dharman Na Cha Me Prabritti'[165] start a theoretical lecture trying to prove his point by way of self-defence. Such polemics and discourses mean veritable intellectualism. The peasants of villages are more intellectual than the urban *babus*. When some debate on moral laws is going on, they are all ears!' In this respect too, the *Jatra* form was suitable for the People's Theatre and Mitra thought that it could thus rescue Bengali theatre from its state of excessive emotionalism, devoid of any intellectual base.

Sambhu Mitra has drawn our attention to another quality of Indian or rather Asian theatre, if not of *Jatra* in particular. That is symbolism affecting the play, the stage-craft, the acting and so on, and making the whole thing profoundly realistic. In old Sanskrit plays we would find: 'Raja Rathena Natayati' (The King simulates at charioteering). It seems that neither the chariot nor the horse had a physical presence on the stage. The acting was sufficient to create an illusion of charioteering by the King. Sambhu Mitra himself used the Japanese *Kabuki* method in his play *Bibhav* a few years later, and *kabuki* is similar to the above method of 'Natayati'.[166] In *Bibhav*, the actors would create the illusion of a tramway by holding a picture of tram-car in their hand and would make a 'ting-ting' noise with their mouth to indicate its ringing bells. This method, because it involves least cost and demands of the audience more imagination, concentration and hence a greater involvement in the play, is surely suitable for the People's Theatre.

The Indian theatrical tradition including *Jatra* also 'created a oneness between the actors and the audience and the illusion of drama would perhaps be created by a strip of cloth behind which the actors come on to the stage'.[167] The physical approximation would perhaps help the audience identify itself with the performance and this is vital for the People's Theatre. The open-air performances of the IPTA sometimes resembled the *Jatra* in this respect. Salil Chowdhury even went so far as to attempt a new experiment to create a more intense physical nearness in his play *Janantik*. An actor (Sajal Roy Chowdhury) would come on to the stage making his way through the audience saying 'What is this going on in the name of drama?' while members of the audience would pull his shirt and try to make him sit down.[168]

So much thought was given during the period of our study to bring to the theatre indigenousness, if not indigenous forms in the raw. Folk forms were blended with European techniques. But form is form and can never compensate for the lack of proper spirit. Folk forms are just sites on which political and cultural struggles are forged. Thus, they can be good or bad, imprisoning or liberating, backward-looking or progressive. But some Party leaders constantly criticized the artists for neglecting folk forms and for their unwillingness to discard the proscenium stage. The idea remained for a long time that this failure on the part of thespians had doomed the People's Theatre Movement. Sambhu Mitra's reply is that it is naïve to think that the masses of people can be reached just through folk forms. What is really important is to catch the Indianness, so that the people find in it something which is their very own. He cites the examples of Hindi films which are so popular today. Do they use folk forms? But there is indeed a certain indigenous element in Hindi films—the heroes and heroines singing out every now and then—a practice that many of our cultured people find detestable.[169]

Mitra also asked—how is it possible to use 'pure' folk forms? After all, everything is changing so rapidly in this country, and so is folk culture. Take the local dialects, for example. Once, a play written in a dialect of 24-Parganas was to be staged in Mymensingh. The IPTA people asked Nibaran Pandit, the famous folk poet of Mymensingh, if they should rewrite the play in the dialect of his area. Pandit answered that this was not necessary at all. Rather they should draw the language closer to the refined language of the city. For the rural people had come to understand it well and liked it better than their own local dialect.[170]

'Discarding the proscenium' also should not become a cliche. Even Bijan Bhattacharya, who imbibed folk culture more than anyone else in theatre, warned against this:[171] 'What is wrong in taking advantage of and respecting the convention of the proscenium, where it exists?' In cities, for example, one might very well carry on the People's Theatre Movement with the help of the proscenium. In villages, of course, it might not be available. Cities and villages are different in circumstances and needs. They require different types of plays and preferably different teams (not one or two, but many teams, as the demand rises), and open-air theatre would gradually develop its own style. But, of course, cities and villages are coming closer to each other too. Ultimately, perhaps, we have to keep in mind that the folk always appropriates modernity and is itself appropriated by modernity, and that a creative synthesis of the traditional and the modern may be the best solution.

G.P. Deshpande, an activist in the progressive cultural movement himself, has criticized the IPTA for posing a false and irreconcilable contradiction between the classical and the folk. For one thing, says he, in celebrating folk forms, it never worked out its relationship with the classical language and traditions and thus handed them over to the orthodoxy (e.g. the error of identifying Sanskrit with Brahmin priests or Urdu with Muslims). Also, according to Deshpande, in promoting the folk, the progressives nurtured a kind of populism, which gradually permeated even the new bourgeoisie. The city-bred and exclusivist middle-class people want to escape the boredom of urban life and nurture a pride in tradition by appreciating folk culure, and today the progressives' position can hardly be distinguished from this.[172]

And of course, as we pointed out before, so far as the original social objectives of the progressives are concerned, folk form or for that matter, any experimentation with theatrical form, can be meaningful only when there is the spirit of the People's Theatre (or music) and when the condition outside the theatre is conducive to that spirit.

APPENDIX I

Plays found Objectionable by the Police

In 1949, a secret circular issued by the West Bengal Government against IPTA and PWA to the district and police authorities, said: 'Should any attempt be made by them to stage drama or other performances in public places, that should be stopped by the District Magistrates as far as possible by the use of the Dramatic Performances Act 1876 (XIX 1876) or any other law which may be applicable.' According to the circular, such performances would spread Communist propaganda.[173]

The Dramatic Performances Act had been passed in 1876 when the patriotic theatre of Bengal was becoming extremely troublesome to the British. Plays like *Nildarpan* (The Mirror of Indigo), *Chakar Darpan* (The Mirror of Tea), *Trial of Gaekwar, Gajadananda and the Prince* and *Surendra Binodini* were found damagingly seditious. The act empowered the government to prohibit any play performed or about to be performed, if found defamatory, seditious or obscene in character. This enabled the British government to throttle many a play. And the government of independent India tried to revive the Act with renewed vigour to repress various theatre groups.

During the early 1950s, the police became particularly active in harrassing the theatre groups. They often asked these groups to submit handwritten manuscripts and printed manuscripts of their plays, and sometimes their zeal in this matter appeared quite ridiculous, as when they asked the IPTA to submit the manuscripts of *Raktakarabi* (Tagore's well-known play, and easily available too), *The Goat* (a piece of imagination, perhaps) and *Tulsi Lahiri* (not a play, but a playwright). Once, in the context of the performance of *Nildarpan*, they asked the playwright Dinabandhu Mitra, who had long been dead, to present himself at the Police Station, Lalbazar.

Fifty-nine plays performed by the IPTA and other groups were demanded on another occasion: *Sab-Payechhir Desh* (El-Dorado), *Jadu Ka Kursi* (Magic Chair), *Rail ka Kanth* (Voice of the Rail) *Kantowala*, *We Want Light*, *Suk-Sari* (The Papinjay Couple), *Mrityu Nai* (No Death), *Atlantic Chukti* (The Atlantic Treaty), *Haspatal* (Hospital), *Dak* (Call), *Sanket* (Signal), *Manjil* (Palace), *Juddha Chai Na* (We Do Not Want War), *Itibritta* (History), *Till the day I Die*, *Nildarpan*, *Padadhwani* (Footfall), *Mahesh*, *Arunodayer Pathe* (On the Way to the Sunrise—an adaptation from a play by Lady Gregory), *Hangover*, *Dheu* (Waves), *Chhenra Taar* (Broken String). *Ulukhagra* (Reedy Grass), *Avarta* (Vortex), *Lest You Forget*, *Nabanna* (New Harvest), *Kanchrapara*, *India Immortal* (actually, this was a ballet), *Shahider Dak* (Call of the Martyrs), *Janatar Dak* (Call of the Masses), *Disahara* (Nonplussed), *Bisarjan* (Sacrifice), *Officer*, *Bichar* (Justice), *Ahalya Uddhar* (Rescuing Ahalya), *Char Adhyay* (Four Chapters), *Abad* (Cultivation), *Charge-sheet*, *Nagpas* (A Snake-like Rope), *Durbhiksher Panchali* (Poem of the Famine), *Natak Noy* (Not a Drama), *Janak* (Father), *Malayer Mukti Juddha* (The Liberation War of Malay), *Bhua Swadhinata* (False Independence). *Dharti Ke Lal* (Petted Children of the Earth), *Chasar Baromasi* (Twelve Months of the Peasant), *Kantak* (Thorn), *Dalil* (Document), *Path* (Path), *Bhanga Bandar* (Eroded Port),

Pathik (Passer-by), *Udayasta* (From Dawn to Dusk), *Jabanbandi* (Attestation), *Sanghabadhhata* (Unity), *Gora*, *Mountbatten Mangalkavya* (this is actually a song), *Nicher Talar Manush* (People of Lower Strata).

In 1954, according to a verdict by the Allahabad High Court, the 1876 Act was withdrawn. But the harrassment continued under other pretexts.[174]

APPENDIX II

Attempts at Unification of Theatrical Groups

As early as 1940[175] an amateur dramatic club was formed at the house of Nirmal Chandra Chunder (23 Wellington Street). This group named the 'Shanibarer Baithak' (Saturday Club) staged a few rather informal shows. Niren Bhanja was one of them. The actor Bireswar Sen and a film director Salil Dutta were products of this group. After achieving success inside their own limited circle, they thought of forming a larger body consisting of all such amateur theatre groups with the purpose of building up a theatre movement outside the conventional theatre. This institute named the 'Bharat Natya Parishad' (The Indian Stage Academy) had as its ideal England's New Drama Movement. Sudhi Pradhan, one of the organizers of the IPTA, that had recently acquired fame for the production of *Jabanbandi*, joined Bharat Natya Parishad as its director. The contact with Sudhi Pradhan had been made through the Artiste Association of which he was a leader. But Bharat Natya Parishad did not last long. First, its constituents had no ideological understanding. While the IPTA was motivated by Communism, Shanibarer Baithak had no such ideology; rather in the later years, many members of the latter group turned anti-Communist. Second, Sudhi Pradhan became too busy with the thriving IPTA to pay much attention to the Parishad.[176]

The above attempt at unification is not very important from our point of view. But in the early 1950s, when several theatrical groups were working with the ideal of the People's Theatre carrying on the tradition of the IPTA and yet did not really know how to realize that ideal through isolated efforts, there was again an attempt to unite them and build up a powerful theatre movement. From that very address—23 Wellington Street—a circular dated 5 April 1951 was issued to various people associated with the progressive theatre. The crisis of the Bengali theatre world was discussed here. The commercial stage was not accommodating modern scientific thoughts and was nurturing old values. The non-commercial groups were smarting under pressure from the police. In this situation, a large-scale theatre movement was needed to give shape to modern thoughts and ideologies. No one person or group could do it. Hence, as the first step of united efforts, they felt the need for a theater conference and a theater festival in West Bengal. All theatre-loving and democratic individuals and institutions would be able to express their views there, and present to the public their advanced artistic feats. To decide what was to be done in this respect and to form a committee to prepare for the proposed theatre conference and theatre festival they were to arrange a meeting on the coming 24 April, Tuesday, at 5 p.m., at the Commercial Museum Hall (College Street Market, Calcutta). The conveners were Sachin Sengupta, Narayan Gangopadhyay, Tarasankar Bandyopadhyay, Manoranjan Bhattacharya, Hemendranath Dasgupta, Manoj Bose, Digin Bandyopadhyay, Pratap Chandra Chunder, Utpal Dutta (LTG), Gangapada Basu (Bahurupi), Jnan

Majumdar (Natyachakra), Sailen Ray (Dipayan Sanskriti Sangha), Niranjan Sen (IPTA), David Cohen (Unity Theatre), Chinmoy Ghosh Dastidar (Bhawanipur Art and Culture), Debdas Bandyopadhyay (Natyachakra, Bhadrakali), Mamtaj Ahmed Khan (Swastika Sangha), and Ramanath Sengupta (Ananda Sangha).[177] These names show how broad-based they wanted the movement to be. Pratap Chandra Chunder was a Congress member. Tarasankar Bandyopadhyay had once been closely associated with the Communist cultural movement, but at that time he sympathized more with the Congress. Niranjan Sen represented the Communist-led IPTA. Utpal Dutta was a Communist and used to work for the IPTA, but he also had a separate theatre group of his own. Gangapada Basu was one of those who had broken away from the IPTA to form Bahurupi.

Accordingly, talks were held on the scheduled day with a view to uniting for a common ideal. Many eyes were turned to Sisir Kumar Bhaduri, who, they thought, could provide them with a platform, because he had tremendous weight in the world of theatre and had progressive views at the same time. But there were people who would not accept his leadership. After he had left, Utpal Dutta criticized the idea of uniting under a man belonging to the commercial theatre.

Anyway, preparations for the theatre festival and theatre conference went ahead. On the basis of the discussion held in the above meeting, a draft was prepared containing its purposes and programmes. In this draft the main proposal was to found a public theatre to make up for the inadequacy of the commercial theatre that did 'not have the confidence to help progressive efforts partially due to economic reasons, partially bound by the established system and to some extent to fulfil the demand of a particular kind of audience'. Then there was an approximate estimate of the income and expenditure of the proposed conference and a ten day-long festival. In addition to the persons whose names had been included in the above mentioned circular, now we have many more names—men belonging to different theatre groups including the IPTA, and also big names from the world of commercial theatre—Ahindra Chowdhury, Ardhendu Kumar Gangopadhyay, Naresh Mitra, Prabha Devi, and others. Utpal Dutta too lent his name.[178]

But the plan did not fructify. Sudhi Pradhan gives the following reasons. The IPTA was the only organization having the strength to give shape to this big idea. But as the general elections drew nearer, the IPTA thought of devoting all its resources to the propaganda on behalf of the Communist candidates and for this purpose, developing its own organization was considered more desirable than forging a unified drama movement. Moreover, the men holding top positions in the IPTA were afraid that they would lose their prominence in a unified organization. So their's was only a half-hearted effort for unification.

A few years later, another such attempt was made and again without success. Just before the Durga Puja of 1953, on the appeal of three drama groups, Ashanichakra, Lokmancha (at that time known as Lok O Natak) and Lok Samskriti Sangha, a committee was formed by some drama enthusiasts with a view to organizing Bangiya Natya Parishad amalgating all theatre and *Jatra* groups. The immediate purpose was to demand a few reforms—the withdrawal of the 1876 Dramatic

Performance Act, abolition of the pre-censor system and exemption of all groups from entertainment tax. And they were ready to accept the equal right of everyone in the proposed National Theatre, irrespective of affiliations and opinions.[179]

A committee of seven directors was formed. This included Narayan Gangopadhyay, Tulsi Lahiri, Sudhi Pradhan, Sulalita Goswami, Nirmal Ghosh (IPTA), Arun Majumdar (Kranti Silpi Sangha) and Charu Prakash Ghosh (Convenor). They thought of spreading the new theatre movement in towns and far-off villages. They published a theatre magazine with which were associated Ahindra Chowdhury, Debiprasad Bhattacharya and Sadhan Kumar Bhattacharya. But ultimately, nothing resulted from this.[180]

APPENDIX III

Cinema inheriting the IPTA spirit

While keeping in mind theatre's capacity for transforming society, the progressive cultural activists soon realized that cinema was perhaps becoming a more powerful popular medium and did try to experiment with it. Here is a short history of the beginning of their venture.[181]

The movie that needs to be mentioned first in this connection is *Udayer Pathye* (Towards the Light,1944) directed by Bimal Roy. It was about a highly-educated idealistic lower-middle class youth joining the side of the workers of the factory owned by his employer and demanding justice for them, while the employer's daughter falls in love with him. The first and the only IPTA film was *Dharti ke Lal* (Children of the Earth, 1946) directed by Khwaja Ahmed Abbas, a progressive writer and close sympathizer of the CPI. This was about the 1943 Bengal Famine, based on Bijan Bhattacharya's *Nabanna* (The New Harvest) written in 1944, an IPTA short play *Antim abhilash* (The Last Desire) and a short story by Krishan Chunder—*Annadata* (The Giver of Food) written in 1943. Abbas adopted all three of them together for this new and powerful medium. He also wrote the script for *Neecha Nagar* (The World Down Below), another film made in 1946, partly funded by IPTA and directed by Chetan Anand. Here, the battlelines were clearly drawn between the rich and the poor. Both films were widely acclaimed. The next Bengali movie that has to be mentioned is *Chhinnamul* made by Nemai Ghosh in 1950, about the trauma of the refugees. This is often considered as a movie in the neo-realistic mode and in this sense as a predecessor to Satyajit Ray's *Pather Panchali*. Two other films of the 1950s bore the progressive movement's hallmark—the 1951 film *Hum Log* directed by Zia Sarhadi and the 1953 film *Do Bigha Zamin* (Two Acres of Land) directed by Bimal Roy. This film by Roy too stressed the exploitation of the poor by rich landlords and starred Balraj Sahni as a poor farmer, on whose two acres of land the zamindar wants to build a factory. Sambhu, the farmer, migrates to the city and becomes a rikshaw-puller. This was a depiction of Nehru's India where corrupt officials, unscrupulous landlords, moneylenders and businessmen made life very difficult for the poor people. Then came Raj Kapoor, defining formulaic Bollywood cinema, populist with a concern for the poor and yet ultimately its progressive message was hijacked by the nationalist fervour of the newly independent state. In his movies, we find kind-hearted policemen, reformed gangsters and poor men making good and marrying rich girls. However, the progressive cultural tradition partly survived in this way. Bollywood achieved another success too in terms of the IPTA objectives. It firmly established Hindustani as a popular language. The progressives of North India had fought a long battle for this, but failed to make it the official language.

Notes and References

1. Snehangshu Kumar Acharya, 'Theatre and the People', *US*, August 1943, included in Sudhi Pradhan, ed., *Marxist Cultural Movement*, vol. I, 1936–47, Kolkata, 1979, p. 199.
2. Manoranjan Bhattacharya, *Theatre Prasange*, published by Progressive Writers' and Artists' Association, Kolkata, sometime in the mid-1940s.
3. Moni Bagchi, *Sisir Kumar O Bangla Theatre*, Kolkata: Jijnasa, 1960, introduced by Srikumar Bandyopadhyay.
4. Arup Mukhopadhyay, *Utpal Dutta: Jiban o Srishti*, Delhi: National Book Trust, 2010, pp. 13, 65, 73.
5. *Saonli Mitra, Sambhu Mitra: Bichitra Jiban Parikrama*, Delhi: NBT, 2010, p. 19.
6. Zola, whose short story was to provide Antoine with the play to start a new theatre movement in France in 1887, commented: 'Theatre needs fresh life instead of fairy tales, imaginary worlds and fabricated plots' ('Naturalism in Theatre', an article written in 1881). Later, Piscator in Germany began his theatre movement 'by causing complete theatrical chaos. While they turned the stage into a machine-room, the auditorium became a public meeting. Piscator saw the theatre as a parliament, the audience was a legislative body. To this parliament were submitted in public form all the great public questions that needed an answer.' (Brecht, 'On Experimental Theatre', from John Willett, ed., *Brecht on Theatre*, 3rd revd edn., London: Methuen, 1964).
7. Hauptmann (1862–1946), famous for his pioneering naturalistic drama, in which sociological problems often overshadowed the personal.
8. A translation from Brecht in one of the early issues of *Arani* (1941) may be regarded as an exception. He became popular in India from the 1960s to the 1980s, which has been called the Brechtian season in Indian theatre.
9. *The IPTA Bulletin*, no. I, July 1943. Sudhi Pradhan possessed a copy of this bulletin and included it in his *Marxist Cultural Movement*, vol. I.
10. Bishnu Dey, 'Navanna': After Twenty-five Years', *Bahurupi, Nabanna Smarak Sankhya*, no. 2, June 1970.
11. Manoranjan Bhattacharya, 'Janagan O Theatre', *Janayuddha*, 28 April 1943.
12. Sources of information about the cultural activities of the BPSF:
    (a) 'Bengal Report' (A report from Bengal Branch to Central IPTA), in *Marxist Cultural Movement*, vol. I, Sudhi Pradhan, ed., p. 151.
    (b) Interview, Sajal Roy Chowdhury.
13. Sajal Roy Chowdhury's information.
14. *Janayuddha*, 17 June 1942.
15. Sources of information about the YCI activities:
    (a) A. Mukherjee, 'The Youth Cultural Institute', 1953, included in Sudhi Pradhan, ed., *Marxist Cultural Movement*, vol. I, p. 23.
    (b) Chinmohan Sehanabis, 'Nabanner Pristhapat', *Bahurupi, Nabanna Smarak Sankhya*, vol. I.
    (c) Sunil Chattopadhyay, 'Anjangarh O Keranir Bhumika', *Bahurupi*, ibid.
    (d) Subrata Bandyopadhyay, 'YCI-er Dinguli', *Bahurupi, Nabanna Smarak Sankhya*, vol. II.

(e) Jolly Kaul, 'YCI—Smriti', *Bahurupi*, ibid.
(f) Sudhi Pradhan, 'Nabanatya Andolan Prasange', *Samskritir Pragati*, Kolkata: Pustak Bipani, 1982, pp. 177–9.
(g) Interview, Uma Sehanabis.

16. Aishwarj Kumar has obtained the script of the play from Natya Shodh Sanstha in Calcutta.
17. A battle between the Republic of China's National Revolutionary Army and the Imperial Japanese Army, often regarded as the beginning of the Second Sino-Japanese War (1937–45)
18. The Dnieper Dam was built between 1927 and 1932 by Stalin in order to provide hydroelectricity to industrialize the country. Once it was considered one of his great achievements. Later, however, the terrible harshness of his measures in building the dam came to light. In any case, the dam was destroyed by Stalin to cover his Ukranian retreat in August 1941, for he feared that the Germans would use it to their advantage.
19.. Published in *Agrani*, May 1940.
20. Sources of information about the AFWAA and pre-Nabanna IPTA activities:
(a) *Bahurupi, Nabanna Smarak Sankhya,* nos. 33 and 34, vols. I and II, October 1969 and June 1970 respectively.
(b) Sudhi Pradhan, 'Nabanatya Andolan Prasange', *Samskritir Pragati*, pp. 180–2.
21. Chinmohan Sehanabis provided this information about the staging of *Rather Rashi*.
22. *Fasci-Birodhi Lekhak O Silpi Sangher Tritiya Barsik Sammelane Grihita Karyabibarani* (a report on the year starting from 17 January 1944).
23. Interview, Sudhi Pradhan.
24. The play was first published in *Arani*, 23 April 1943. It was translated into English by Amal Bhattacharya, an M.A. student.
25. Published in *Arani*, 14 May 1943.
26. Niranjan Sen asked in his review of the play in *Arani* (7 April 1944) why the writer had not admitted it. But perhaps the influence was too obvious to have to be admitted at all.
27. Published in *Arani*, 5 November 1943.
28. Published in *Arani*, 29 October 1943. Along with two other one-act plays—*Laboratory* and *Homeopathy*, it was published later by the AFWAA in the book *Tinti Natika* (Three Playlets) (Paush 1350/1944).
29. Sudhi Pradhan, *Marxist Cultural Movement*, vol. 1.
30. The Annual Report mentioned before and this Half-yearly Report were obtained from Sudhi Pradhan.
31. The play was published by Bengal Publishers (Kolkata) and won the approval of the reviewer of *Arani*, 18 February 1944.
32. Ramprasad De, 'Gananatyer Pratham Lekhak Jyotirmoy Sengupta, *Gananatya*, Sharadiya 1392/1985, claims that Jyotirmoy was the first playwright of the People's Theatre.

33. Published by Bengal Publishers, Kolkata, 1944.
34. Published by Bengal Publishers, Kolkata, 1945.
35. I am grateful to Digin Banerjee for giving me detailed information about the staging of his plays and for letting me read them.
36. Digin Banerjee, a left-minded playwright and a good playwright, was very close to the Communists (his wife was a Party Member). Yet he did not join the IPTA before 1946. He says that he had found the IPTA limited to the Party periphery, while he himself was thinking in terms of a broad and democratic theatre movement. He had close connections with the commercial theatre on the one hand, and on the other, he was popular among numerous local amateur clubs, and both were imbibing progressive ideas at that time. As a journalist in the *Ananda Bazar*, he used to write about this general progressive trend. Of course, the focus of his writings was on the IPTA.
37. Many facts are known from *Bahurupi, Nabanna Smarak Sankhya*, vols. I and II, op. cit., and the Souvenir published on the occasion of the first show (or one of the first few shows), a copy of which was owned by Chinmohan Sehanabis.

    I saw the manuscript edited by Sambhu Mitra, which was used for staging the play in the private collection of Sudhi Pradhan. Sambhu Mitra told me that even this manuscript would not help much to give a feel of the staged drama. There was a vast difference between the play and its performance.

    Nabanna was published in book-form several times. In the early 1980s, Prama Publication, Kolkata, published an edition with an Introduction by Samik Banerjee. This is the edition I have mostly used.
38. Interview of Bijan Bhattacharya, *Sharadiya Kalantar*, 1374.
39. Manikuntala Sen, 'Nabanna', *Epic Theatre*, May 1977.
40. Sambhu Mitra, 'Rajar Kathay', *Prasanga Natya*, Kolkata: Samskrita Pustak Bhandar, 1971, p. 163. Also see his article 'Bijan' (written in 1978) in the book *Sanmarga-Saparya*, Kolkata: M.C. Sarkar and Sons, 3rd edn., 1408/2001 for some interesting insights into Pradhan Samaddar's character.
41. Sambhu Mitra's talk to Samik Bandyopadhyay, quoted by the latter in his Introduction to the latest edition of *Nabanna*, Kolkata: Prama, 1984.
42. Sambhu Mitra, 'Banglar Nabanatya Andolan', *Prasanga Natya*, p. 128
43. For example, reviews in the *Amrita Bazar Patrika*, 28 October 1944, and *Arani*, 29 October 1944. The latter review was written by Sushil Jana (pen-name Suja). In fact, Jana had said this in regard to *Jabanbandi* too (*Arani*, 23 June 1944).
44. The above-mentioned review by Suja.
45. Hiran Kumar Sanyal, 'Natyakala: Nabanna', *Parichay*, Kartik, 1351/1944.
46. Samik Bandyopadhyay using Paul Greenough's *Prosperity and Misery in Modern Bengal: The Famine of 1943–44*, Amartya K. Sen's *Poverty and Famines: An Essay on Entitlement and Deprivation* and Boudhayan Chattopadhya's article in *Transactions*, 1981, in his Introduction to *Nabanna*'s Prama edition.

47. Quoted by Samik Banerjee in his introduction to *Nabanna*, Prama Edition.
48. Manoranjan Bhattacharya, 'Mere Deoa', *Arani*, Sharadiya, 1943.
49. Sudhi Pradhan, 'Nabanatya Prasanga', *Sanskritir Pragati*, p. 178.
50. Sambhu Mitra, *Prasanga Natya*.
51. Bijan Bhattacharya's talk to Samik Bandyopadhyay, quoted by the latter in his article entitled 'Nabannar Dhara Theke Anya Dhara: Ekti Asampurna Alochana', *Bahurupi Nabanna Smarak Sankhya*, vol. 2.
52. Sambhu Mitra, 'Prasner Uttare', Interviewed by Chittaranjan Ghosh, *Bahurupi Nabanna Smarak Sankhya*, vol. 2.
53. Sobha Sen's reminiscences in *Bahurupi Nabanna Smarak Sankhya*, vol. 1.
54. Sambhu Mitra, 'Banglar Nabanatya Andolan' *Prasanga Natya*.
55. Ibid.
56. Chittaranjan Ghosh, 'Natyasamalochana', *Bahurupi, Nabanna Smarak Sankhya*, vol. 2, written on the basis of his talk with Sambhu Mitra.
57. Sambhu Mitra, 'Prashner Uttare', *Bahurupi Nabanna Smarak Sankhya*, vol. 2.
58. Ibid.
59. Bijan Bhattacharya's introduction to the fourth edition of *Nabanna* (1962), reprinted in the Prama edition.
60. Debiprasad Chattopadhyay's reminiscences in *Bahurupi Nabanna Smarak Sankhya*, vol. 2, p. 53. The play was reprinted in this issue of *Bahurupi*.

    The quotation we have given in the text is a translation from Bishnu Dey's adoptation. In Yeats' original play it thus ran:

    In pity for man's darkening thought
    He walked that room and issued thence
    In Galilean turbulence;
    The Babylonian starlight brought
    A fabulous formless darkness in;
    Odour of blood when Christ was stain
    Made all Platonic tolerance vain
    And vain all Doric discipline . . .
61. *Muktadhara, Rabindra Rachanabali*, Visva-Bharati, vol. 14.
62. Sambhu Mitra interviewed by Samik Bandyopadhyay, quoted in the latter's article in *Bahurupi Nabanna Smarak Sankhya*, vol. 2, p. 100.
63. My talk with Sambhu Mitra, December 1984.
64. Included in Sudhi Pradhan, ed., *Marxist Cultural Movement*, vol. I, p. 256.
65. The book was published in Jyaistha, 1354/1947 by Bimal Basu, Chhotoder Asar, 16A, Duff Street, Calcutta.
66. Kanu Banerjee's interview in *Bahurupi Nabanna Smarak Sankhya*, vol. I.
67. Under Sushil Majumdar's direction this play was later adapted for a film named *Sarbahara* (Completely Ruined). But the film was not as popular as the play.
68. *Bastubhita* (2nd edn); published by Kalipada Bandyopadhyay, Deshbandhu Nagar, 1954. I have seen it through the courtesy of Digin Bandyopadhyay.
69. The Janakalyan Sangha of Hajra Road did it during the Festival of Peace and Progressive Culture held on the occasion of Saraswati Puja in February

1951, as we are informed by the *Swadhinata*. Digin Banerjee can remember many more shows put up by local clubs. Even theatre enthusiasts belonging to the Congress and the Rashtriya Swayam Sevak Sangha enacted *Bastubhita*.

70. The play has been reprinted in *Bahurupi Nabanna Smarak Sankhya*, vol. I.
71. Mahasweta Devi, 'Manche Jiyankanya', *Bijan Bhattacharya Smarak Grantha*, published by Nabarun Bhattacharya, 1978. I came to know a lot about *Jiyankanya* also from my talk with Chinmohan Sehanabis.
72. Although this period saw an unprecedented efflorescence of dramatic activities, there was almost no documentation due to political reasons. Still, we have learnt a great deal about the plays and their productions from Sunil Dutta, *Jibandharmi Natya Prayojanar Rup O Rekha*, Jatiya Sahitya Parishad, n.d., published sometime during the 1980s, and interviews with Sajal Roy Chowdhury, November 1985 as well as Salil Chowdhury, November 1985.
73. According to Salil Chowdhury, *Lekhak* and *Janantik* were really the same play with different names.
74. This is probably the only play of the period that has survived. I have read the second edition published by Pustakalay, Kolkata, 1954, through the courtesy of the playwright.
75. But Sambhu Mitra did not remember anything about it, when I talked to him.
76. Sajal Roy Chowdhury was probably confused about the name of the author. We have come across a play of the same name and on the same theme written by Digin Banerjee in July 1948. It was published by Pustakalay and stated to have been 'Sanctioned by the IPTA'.
77. Sunil Dutta, *Jibandharmi Natya Prajojanar Rup o Rekha*,
78. Kali Bandyopadhyay, 'Theatre-Cinemay Anekdin', Sharadiya *Baromas*, 1981.
79. That is why the critic of *Natun Sahitya*, November 1950 found them disappointing.
80. Reviews in *Swadhinata*, 19 April 1951, and *Natun Sahitya*, April 1951, create such an impression.
81. Included in Sudhi Pradhan, ed., *Marxist Cultural Movement*, vol. II.
82. Utpal Dutta, 'Samaj Biplab O Gananatak', Ajker Natak O Nabanatya Andolan, ed. Sunil Dutta, Kolkata: Jatiya Sahitya Parishad, n.d.
83. The play was about the determination of the King of Tipperah to stop the tradition of animal sacrifice before the goddess Kali, thus generating conflicts involving deep human ego, reason and love.
84. Jointly with *Call of the Valley*, a dance-drama from Kashmir.
85. A show was held at the Rammohan Library Hall on 23 December 1952, in a function arranged specially for the members and sympathizers of the IPTA.
86. Seen through the courtesy of Sudhi Pradhan.
87. It seems Umanath Bhattacharya also wrote *Chargesheet* which was enacted as a street play in 1952, Arup Mukhopadhyay, *Utpal Dutta: Jiban o Srishti*, p. 78.
88. Interview, Sajal Roy Chowdhury and Reba Roy Chowdhury.

89. The play was written in 1949, first published in January 1950, and first staged by a local club, Shibpur Shilpi Sangha, in December 1950.
90. According to Saonli Mitra, Bahurupi's first production was a repeat show of *Nabanna*, Saonli Mitra, *Sambhu Mitra: Bichitra Jiban Parikrama*, Delhi: NBT, 2010.
91. *Unity*, the organ of Unity Theatre, shortly became the organ of IPTA.
92. These three plays were written by Tulsi Lahiri and have recently been compiled in a book entitled Tulsi Lahirir Nirbachita Natyasangraha, Jatiya Sahitya Parishad, 1388.
93. See *Natun Sahitya*, December 1950 and *Parichay*, Paush, 1357/1951.
94. See *Natun Sahitya*, August 1951. We get to know from Saonli Mitra's book, op. cit., that even Sambhu Mitra's close friend Chinmohan Sehanabis disapproved of the play on seeing it for the first time. But later Sehanabis admitted: 'Sambhu staged it at the right moment', p. 70.
95. 'Raktakarabi Prasange', *Bahurupi*, vol. 55, p. 13.
96. Swadhinata, 24 November 1951.
97. First issue, 1952.
98. See Rustam Bharucha, *Rehearsals of Revolution*, Calcutta: Seagull Books 1984, the chapter on Utpal Dutta. Also Arup Mukhpadhyay, *Utpal Dutta,* op. cit.
99. Interview, Sambhu Mitra.
100. For details see the following section of this chapter.
101. The dialect used in the play was that of Faridpur and not of Dinajpur. Faridpur was the birthplace of Mr Bhattacharya.
102. First published by D.M. Library, Kolkata, Baisakh, 1361/1954. This edition has been seen through the courtesy of Sudhi Pradhan.
103. *Parichay*, Jyaistha, 1360/1953, published a letter by Gouri Chatterjee of Chinsura. According to her, the Behrampore Kranti Silpi Sangha had already in September 1952, staged this play, on the occasion of a literary conference. The play was translated by a local writer.
104. The play was first published on May Day, 1953, by Indiana Limited. This edition has been seen through the courtesy of Sudhi Pradhan.
105. The play was published by Kalipada Bandyopadhyay (Deshbandhunagar, 1954). Commendatory Reviews were published in *Swadhinata*, 31 August 1951 and Parichay, Bhadra 1358/1951.
106. Included in Sudhi Pradhan, ed., *Marxist Cultural Movement*, vol. I, p. 88.
107. Khaled Chowdhury, 'Manchasajja: Prathamik Dayitva' *Parichay*, Paush 1372/1965.
108. Tapas Sen, 'Theatre-enhancement Notun Alo', *Parichay*, Paush 1372.
109. The report has been included in Sudhi Pradhan's *Marxist Cultural Movement in India*, vol. I.
110. Entitled 'Sangha Banam Andolan, Na Andolan Banam Subidhabadi Eknayaktantra' (reply to an article by Sobha Sen).
111. Sudhi Pradhan, 'Nildarpan Natak Punahprayojanar Aitihasik Tatparya', *Natun Theatre*, vol. 2, 15 March 1973. Pradhan was supported by Digin Banerjee in the latter's essay 'Nildarpan Punarujjibaner Nepathya Kahini',

Bangarangamancha Satavarsapurti Smarak Grantha, ed. Azaharuddin Khan; Studies, Kolkata: Mahatma Gandhi Road, 1380/1973.

112. Interview, Sambhu Mitra.
113. Samskritir Pragati, p. 239.
114. *Prasanga Natya*, p. 162.
115. As regards Sambhu Mitra's disapproval of the Ballet Squad, Saonli Mitra says that her father was indeed skeptical about the quality of the Ballet Squad, that he suspected that the latter was trying to get cheap popularity by staging variety programmes and also by inviting commercially established artists to perform on such occasions. Sambhu Mitra raised objection to the proposal to invite Kanan Devi, the matinee idol, to an IPTA show, and in this he was supported by the ultra-leftist Sajal Roy Chowdhury. See Saonli Mitra, *Sambhu Mita*, op. cit., p. 47.
116. See the above-mentioned articles of Sudhi Pradhan and Digin Banerjee about the staging of *Nildarpan*.
117. As the father abuses the son: 'I shiver when I think of your politics. You incite one class against another, you want to conquer violence with the help of violence. . . .'
118. Interview, Digin Banerjee.
119. Tripti Mitra told me in regard to this particular charge (that it was opportunistic of them to go to Bombay to work in *Dharti Ke Lal*): 'If that is so, then why did I turn down the offer to work in a commercial film in Bombay for sixty thousand rupees and return to Calcutta to do *Muktadhara*?'
120. *Samskritir Pragati*, p. 241.
121. For example, Darsan Chowdhury, *Gananatya Andolaner Pratham Paryay*, Kolkata: Anustup, May 1948. Sasipada Bandyopadhyay, 'Rabindrottar Yuger Natya Andolan Banam Kartripaksha Sreni', *Prasanga: Gananatya*, published by Krisna Bandyopadhyay, 33A /1A, Harekrisna Seth Lane, Calcutta—50, March 1981. Even a much more sophisticated and at places very enlightening article like Malini Bhattacharya's 'The IPTA in Bengali' in *Journal of Arts and Ideas*, January–March 1983, has such a bias.
122. See Mike Davidow, *The Soviet Theatre from Box Office to Stage*, Moscow: Progress Publishers, 1977. Also, M. Slonium, *Russian Theatre: From the Empire to the Soviets*, The World Publishing Company, Cleveland and New York, 1961—the last 3 chapters cover the post-revolutionary era. There are numerous other books and essays on the subject, some very eloquent in their admiration of the Russian theatre and others having some reservations. But even the latter praise the production system of theatre in the post-revolutionary Soviet Russia. See, for instance, the relevant chapter in Elmer Rice, *The Living Theatre*, New York: Harper and Brothers, 1959.
123. Bishnu Dey, 'Nabanna' *Bahurupi—Nabanna Smarak Sankhya*, vol. 2.
124. Manoranjan Bhattacharya, *Theatre Prasange*.
125. Romain Rolland, *The People's Theatre*, ed. Sudhi Pradhan, Kolkata: G.A.E. Publishers, 1980. Introduction by the Editor.

126. See John Willett, *The Theatre of Erwin Piscator: Half a Century of Politics in the Theatre,* Eyre Methuen, London, 1978.
127. Included in Sudhi Pradhan, ed., *Marxist Cultural Movement*, vol. I.
128. *Marxist Cultural Movement*, vol. I, p. 175. Numerous articles were published in leftist periodicals about the Chinese theatre movement, e.g. Ambika Ghosh, 'Chiner Natun Sanskriti', *Arani*, 20 March 1942.
129. Ramyangshu Sekhar Das, 'Gananatya', *Arani*, 21 July 1944.
130. See John Willett, *The Theatre of Erwin Piscator: Half a Century of Politics in the Theatre*, Eyre Methuen, London, 1978; Martin Esslin, *Brecht: The Man and his Work*, Columbia University Press, 1969, Satya Bandyopadhyay, *Brecht O Tar Theatre*, Kolkata: Asha Prakashani, 1977. The Introduction is by Utpal Dutta.
131. See the following essays in *Performance and Politics in Popular Drama*, ed. David Bradby, Louis James and Bernard Sherratt, the Cambridge University Press, 1980: Martin Kane, 'Erwin Piscator's 1927 Production of *Hoppla, We're Alive*'; Rapheel Samuel, 'Workers' Theatre (1926–36)'; Stuart Corgrove, 'Prolet Buehne: Agit-prop in America'.
132. Stuart Cosgrove's essay mentioned earlier.
133. Perhaps the only exception during this period was the French agitprop theatre which developed parallel to the theatre patronized by the Front Populaire Government (June 1936—January 1938). While the government-sponsored theatre tried to cover up all conflicts and give out a call for peace, agitprop groups like the 'October Group' staged plays on every topical issue like the Reichstag Arson Trial, the strike by the workers of the Citroen Company and other problems of workers and peasants. This small-scale agitprop theatre developed in a direct clash with the mass spectacular theatre commissioned by the government and was very short-lived. See David Bradby's 'The October Group and Theatre under the Front Populaire' in *Performance and Politics in Popular Drama.*
134. 'Leave aside the plan of visiting different villages, even the plan of visiting different districts with *Nabanna* could not be materialized. *Nabanna* did not go to any other place than Jessore, Behrampore, Burdwan, Midnapur and Chundernagore. It could not be performed in any village except Hatgovindpur,' writes Sudhi Pradhan, 'Loknatya Samaj Bhabna', *Lokyan Sambad, Loknatya Sankhya*, North Bengal, Mahalaya, 1391/1984.
135. Interview, Sambhu Mitra.
136. Among those who promised considerable donations were, according to Sambhu Mitra, father of Dilip Bose, father of Tarun Bose and Rangin Halder.
137. 'The Bengal Branch Report to the Central IPTA', included in Sudhi Pradhan, ed., *Marxist Cultural Movement*, vol. I, p. 251, refers to this financial crisis.
138. For example, the critic of *Amrita Bazar Patrika*, 28 October 1944.
139. See Sudhi Pradhan's 'Gananatya Andolaner Aitihya', *Samskritir Pragati*, p. 202.

140. 'Gananatya Sangathan' *Lokonatya,* first year, first issue, March 1355/1948.
141. 'Bangla Pragati Sahityer Atmasamalochana', *Marxbadi*, vol. 4, July 1949.
142. 'Gananatya Sangathan', *Loknatya*, first year, second issue, Phalgun—Chaitra, 1355/1949.
143. The article entitled 'Nabanatya Andolane Sankat'.
144. Kali Bandyopadhyay, 'Theatre Cinemay Anekdin', Baromas, Sharadiya, 1981.
145. Edgar Snow informs us that Miss Wei Kung-chih, director of the People's Anti-Japanese Red Dramatic Society of China, was sent by the Communist Party to study in France and Moscow. It seems that extensive training is not detrimental but rather helpful to the People's Theatre Movement. *Red Star Over China*, Penguin edition, 1978, p. 143.
146. Kali Bandyopadhyay, 'Theatre Cinemay Anekdin, *Baromas*, Sharadiya, 1981.
147. Though Dutta remained close to the Communist Party and continued to have a love-hate relationship with it.
148. 'Bijan Bhattacharya: Ekti Sakshatkar' (an interview taken by Kalpana Dutta and Mahendra Kumar), *Bahurupi Bijan Bhattacharya and Jyotirindra Moitra Smaran Sankhya*, May 1978. Bijan Bhattacharya's anguish about his failure to achieve what he had aspired for as an activist of the People's Theatre Movement comes out very clearly in the book *Bijan Bhattaharya, Likhan Bhashan Kathopakathan: Bishishta Bijan*, Kolkata: Manfakira, 2006.
149. During a television programme in early 1985. In this connection, I acknowledge with gratitude Sambhu Mitra's reference to my interview with him in his Introduction to *Sanmarga-Saparya*, op. cit. (1st edn, 1396/1989) Mitra did not let me record his interview, a large part of which dwelt on the economic viability of People's Theatre. But he did put this on record when he wrote in the above Introduction:

    'A few years ago a girl came with recommendation of my friend Chinmohan Sehanabis. Her question was—when you did "Nabanna", why didn't you try to make your organization economically viable? I wonder why! For self-reliance would have made your task easier....

    I told her—But I did. Some people did think of it. This was conveyed to some well-wishers. They were enthusiastic and ready to collect subscriptions with a view to building a stage. But some people did not like this idea. So it did not materialize.... Now you find out through your research who were responsible for this and for what reason, and also how reasonable that reason was.'

    I can safely claim that this girl was me.
150. We can perhaps describe the predicament of these theatre workers by borrowing the words of Steve Gooch, who tried to do 'socialist' theatre in Britain during the 1970s with the help of some left-wing theatre groups:

    'That's where the contradictions begin, because a piece of political theatre as product can make one kind of intervention in society, and the internal process which make the product are the field of another kind of intervention. It's unfortunate that our work can't all be seen as process. As it is, we are making products for audience consumption on a semi-commercial market. And one thing that is quite evident in theatre production at the moment, particularly in alternative theatre, is the conflict between those two things: getting shows out to a working-class audience, for example, on the one hand, and the problem of how you govern the internal process on the other. I remember the same kind of contradictions being in the production of socialist plays when I first started work in 'Conventional' theatre 8 years ago. The sad thing is that these contradictions often put theatre workers off, make them cynical about socialist theatre. One of our important tasks now is not to let that disillusionment recur.'

(Steeve Gooch, playwright, during a discussion with David Hare and Trevor Griffiths, 'After Fanshen: A Discussion with the Joint Stock Theatre Company', Included in *Performance and Politics in Popular Drama*, ed. David Bradby, Louis James Bernard Sherratt, op. cit.).

Gooch further said:

'I think that the question of "popular theatre" is very much a question of the social context in which it takes place, and that presumably it's theatre by and for the people—that's something you have to work on at both ends; you have to work on it at the end of the production system, you have to be working towards occupying the big theatres, the small theatres and the secondary schools and the streets—all those places where you can do theatre. . . . You have to be working, hopefully, towards a new kind of audience. And you have to be constantly examining your own work to see whether it is actually going to take your thinking about popular theatre further. But I think it would be naïve to say that there is any one place, any one answer, one kind of theatre, even one kind of audience, that can offer us a popular theatre now.'

But in Bengal, disillusionment did gradually grip the non-commercial and socialist theatre workers. The urge to acquire a popular character disappeared. Reaching out to the working class audience ceased to be even a wild dream for most of them. They catered to a restricted middle-class audience only. Then over the last fifteen to twenty years, during this era of triumphant neoliberal capitalism, the commercial theatre of the olden days disappeared and those who had once dreamt of 'non-commercial' and idealistic theatre had to operate in a ruthlessly commercial framework. The audience became further restricted. Far from trying to build up an alternative economic basis for their theatre, these theatre workers got structured in the social order surrounding them. They either suffer from a sense of disappointment or from a sense of complacency.

151. Interview, Sajal Roy Chowdhury.

152. A sister of Debabrata Biswas, the IPTA singer.

153. Kali Banerjee's article in *Baromas*, op. cit.

154. J.L. Stylan, *Drama. Stage and Audience*, Cambridge University Press 1975, p. 224.

155. 'People's Theatre in India', a discussion article, the important points of which were to be on the agénda of the coming All India IPTA Conference, *Unity*, December 1952.
156. See, for instance, the first *IPTA Bulletin*.
157. See Partha Pratim Bandyopadhyay, 'Jatra: Kayekti Ghanistha Path', *Samskriti O Samaj*, May 1984.
158. *Included in Sudhi Pradhan, ed. Marxist Cultural Movement*, vol. 2.
159. A montage of music and acting—an amusing performance which is a very popular folk-form in Maharashtra.
160. Included in Sudhi Pradhan, ed., *Marxist Cultural Movement*, vol. 2.
161. Romain Rolland, *The People's Theatre*, ed. Sudhi Pradhan, p. 99.
162. 'Rajar Kathay', *Prasanga Natya*, p. 163.
163. M.R. Anand interviewed by a reporter of the journal *Unity*, June 1951
164. 'Bangla Theatre', *Parichay*, Chaitra—Baisakh, 1357–8/1981.
165. 'I know the religion, but don't find it likeable', a famous saying, originally uttered by Arjuna in the *Gita*.
166. See Sambhu Mitra's interesting discussion on this method in his introduction to the play Bibhav, *Bahurupi*, no. 3.
167. M.R. Anand interviewed by a reporter of the journal *Unity*, June 1951.
168. Sunil Dutta, *Jibandharmi Natya Prajojanr Rup o Rekha*, p. 11.
169. Interview, Sambhu Mitra.
170. Ibid.
171. Interviewed by Kalpana Dutta and Mahendra Kumar, *Bahurupi*, *Bijan Bhattacharya and Jyotirindra Moitra Memorial Number.*
172. G.P. Deshpande, *Talking the Political and Other Essays*, Kolkata: Thema, 2009, particularly the essay titled 'Of Progress and Progressive Cultural Movement'.
173. Express letter No. 511 (13) Pr. S/100/49 dated 17 June 1949, from the Secretary to the Government of West Bengal; quoted in Sudhi Pradhan's *Marxist Cultural Movement*, vol. 2.
174. For detailed information about the Dramatic Performance Act of 1876 see *Petition to Agitation! Bengal 1857–1885* by Manju Chattopadhyay, Chapter 5 ('Repressive Measures against Bengali Public Opinion'), Section 1 ('The Dramatic Performance Act, 1876'), Kolkata: K.P. Bagchi and Company, 1985 and *Bangla Natya-niyantraner Itihas* by Dr Rabindranath Bandyopadhyay, Kolkata: Distributor De Book Stores, 1976. The latter book is also useful for the period of our study. See also *Uttar Challisher Rajnaitik Natak* by Prabhat Kumar Goswami, p. 82, Kolkata: Samskriti Parishad, 1982.
175. It is based on an interview with Sudhi Pradhan on 1 December 1984. All the relevant documents have been seen through his courtesy.
176. The Introduction of Niren Bhanja's book *Yabanika*, a copy of which was possessed by Sudhi Pradhan.
177. From the copy of the circular addressed to Sudhi Pradhan.
178. From the printed draft signed by Sachindranath Sengupta, General Secretary of the Preparatory Committee.

179. The Prospectus of Bangiya Natya Parishad, published from 25 Dixon Lane, Calcutta.
180. Sources for this last attempt: The magazine *Natya*, some issues of 1954, in Sudhi Pradhan's collection, Sudhi Pradhan's article in *Abhinay*, *Dr Sadhan Kumar Bhattacharya Memorial Number,* March–April 1974.
181. This is largely based on Talat Ahmed, *Literature and Politics in the Age of Nationalism: The Progressive Episode in South Asia, 1932–56,* London, New York and New Delhi: Routledge 2009.

4

The Political within Pictorial Art and the Pictorial Art in Politics

Towards a Realistic Art

LIKE ART ACTIVITIES in every other sphere—literary, musical or theatrical—pictorial art too entered a new era in Bengal in the 1940s. This concomitance was due to the same political, social and intellectual milieu which involved almost every practitioner of every art form some way or other.

The Neo-Indian or Renaissance School of painting, better known as the Bengal School, ushered in by E.B. Havell and A.K. Coomaraswami and headed by Abanindranath Tagore, had been dominating the art scene of Bengal for quite some time. In fact, the Bengal School movement had swept across the whole sub-continent in a flush of nationalism—avowing to rediscover the national art heritage. But just before the period of our study, doubts started creeping in. The Bengal School seemed to have become a spent force. It was generally producing two-dimensional paintings on literary or mythological themes, at best attaining some lyrical heights. Not only were the themes far removed from contemporary reality but the very attitude of softness and sentimentalism seemed anachronistic.

The critics started saying that after all the Bengal School had not naturally descended from traditional Indian art. Rather, in a modern age, it intended to fill the vacuum created by the disruption of that old art by trying to revive it, without weighing the merits of the case in its proper perspective. Doubts arose as to whether emotion and rhythm could any longer compensate for the neglect of anatomy and yet achieve the high standard that had marked ancient and medieval Indian painting. Moreover, this Bengal School style had got confused under the influence of the whirlpool of various Western art movements and was fast losing its rhythm, movement or whatever originality and excellence it could have claimed earlier. It was becoming a stale academic art smacking of mannerism.

Abanindranath himself was still continuing his experimentations. His old-age paintings—the Mangal Kavya series containing a folk flavour and the Arabian Night series where the glamour of Baghdad was interspersed with the life of Calcutta can be cited too. His greatest disciple, Nandalal Bose, too continued to be refreshing, depicting labouring people, women doing house work, dancing Santals and other aspects of civic life. But other followers of the Bengal School perhaps thought, 'What Abanindranath has done renders new experiments unnecessary.'[1]

The only other kind of art that was prevalent at that time was Western academism taught in different art schools. This meant mostly portrait and still-life, and was even less fit to provide the impetus for a new and vital art movement. Atul Bose was the only artist belonging to this school who could arouse some interest. In the West itself, perhaps as a reaction to this conservative trend of photographic representation of the theme, new methods of art were coming up every day. But these different 'ism's, impressionism, cubism, etc., had little impact on the Bengali artists. As a matter of fact, the people here had very little exposure to these arts.

A search for a way out of this impasse had already begun. Some artists had found new directions in art. The two great non-conformists came from the family of Abanindranath himself—his uncle Rabindranath and brother Gaganendranath, Rabindranath, the greatest literary figure and lyricist of his time, took to painting at the age of sixty-nine, and ceased to be literary and lyrical. Moods of melancholy, harshness, cruelty and conflict were caught in the 'volcanic eruption of paintings' during the last decade of his life. With vital colours and vigorous forms, he depicted men and animals that stand on their backbones in a world of darkness and deformity and make us shiver. These were poles apart from the Bengal School painting that had become 'effeminate and wishy-washy, bereft of any inner strength'.

Gaganendranath, another artist to break new grounds, drew sarcastic sketches on the political and social maladies of his time and thus may be called an early exponent of 'social realism' in Bengal. He was influenced in this respect by Daumier, the reputed French cartoonist of the nineteenth century. Mention may be made of the cartoons compiled in the book *Realm of Absurd* (1917) and *Reform Screams* (1921), or his drawing with the caption 'Peace declared in the Punjab', a comment on the Jallianwala Bagh Massacre, that made Lord Chelmsford, the then Viceroy, blush during his visit to an art exhibition, while the artist stood unperturbed.[2] Gaganendranath also experimented with new forms and adopted Cubism in a peculiarly Indian way.

Then there was Jamini Roy. After trying his hand with the Bengal school style and also in the Western method, he wanted to chart an independent course. He turned to the vital and persisting folk-traditions of Bengal—*Pot* art, *Alpana* and *Kantha* motifs,[3] and this 'conscious and productive home-going' (in the words of Stella Kramrisch) was indeed a 'forward solution'. Having broken loose from classicized 'Indian' art, he created his own kind of classic 'Indian' art inspired by the folk tradition. Indeed it was more classic than contemporary. His work had hardly any trace of the new socio-political reality.

Through the Kala Bhavan of Visva-Bharati, the creative centre of the Bengal School, with Nandalal Bose at the helm of the affairs, quite a few artists started exploring new ground. Satyendranath Bandyopadhyay, Benodebehari Mukherjee and Nandalal himself depicted natural scenery, village life, family life, tribal people and other subjects based on the day-to-day life experiences of ordinary people hitherto inaccessible to the fashionable painters. However, their themes were overlain with a sort of lyricism. Their language inclined towards neatness and grace.

But there emerged the sculptor Ramkinkar Beij at Kala Bhavan to make up for the deficiency of his colleagues. Absolutely true to life, his open-air sculpture signified an intimacy with the tribals in his surroundings, living in unison with nature. In their life-style he found the supreme creative principle—'stark, savage and elemental'[4]—that gives life to man and art. And to portray this, he developed a sculptural method of his own. The 'Santal Family' sculpted in 1938 was a remarkable piece. But the full blooming of his genius took place during the 1940s—the period of our study. So we will not treat him as a part of the background to the art of the 1940s, but as a direct subject of our study.

Another rebel against the Bengal School, though not a Bengali, should be mentioned here. Amrita Sher-Gil, half-Hungarian and half-Indian by birth, deplored the stagnation reached by the Bengal School. Trained in Paris, she could view art in its international context. Returning to India, she started pictorially interpreting the common Indian. She discovered a certain pathos in them and depicted that in a liberal style. But she died young at the age of twenty-nine, unknown and unsung, leaving others to fulfill her task.

The Tagores, Jamini Roy, the Kala Bhavan artists and Sher-Gil—all are widely recognized today as great artists and pioneers in the field of modern Indian art. But there are lesser known artists also who contributed their bit to modernity. Bhola Chatterjee is one of them, and what is more, he took the lead in the first collective effort at the creation of a new kind of art, forming the Rebel Art Centre which held its first exhibition on 20 April 1933. Here he was joined by Digindranath Bhattacharya, Haridhan Dutta, Barindra Nag, Annadacharan De, Haridas Ganguly, Abani Sen, Kalikinkar Ghosh Dastidar, Gobordhan Ash and a few others.[5]

The avowed aim of the Rebel Art Centre was 'to create an art that is strong, bold, virile and anti-sentimental, fearless in its desire for new adventures, a powerful advance-guard, which alone can save art in India now threatened by traditional conservation and the habitual indifference of the public.' [6] The artists wanted to connect art with science that had made long strides since the First World War, to introduce 'scientific outlooks in the techniques of art, its subject matter being Indian', 'to understand properly the underlying principles of the New Movements of Europe', 'to assimilate where possible the techniques of Western Schools to preserve the true spirit and character of Indian Art': to pay particular attention to realism in spirit'.[7] Bhola Chatterjee's drawings published in different journals of the 1930s, particularly in the *Four Arts Journal* that Chatterjee himself edited, are concrete manifestations of this spirit. The very cover of *Four Arts*, 1935—a powerful image of Viswakarma, the God of Labour, executed in modern geometric design, is a good example.

The *Anandabazar* of 4 January 1936 reviewed the third annual art exhibition of the Academy of Fine Arts held on 21 December 1935. The critic said that in the place of the conflict between conservatism and modernity in European art, here in India there was a conflict between the Eastern method (the Bengal School style) and the Western method (Western academism), a fussy fight to keep intact the purity of mannerisms, not helping in any way the development of talent. No art that could be called 'modern' had been created in India. Then the reviewer discussed the Indian and European sections of the exhibition, after which he drew the readers' attention to the works of a few young artists—Arthur Ghosh, M.L. Dutta Gupta, T. Mukherjee, Tarak Basu and others, who had given the critic an indication of the new direction that the Indian art was taking. Their subject-matter consisted of scenes, incidents and people familiar to the ordinary Bengali. Boatmen, beggars, carters, fishing folk, sweepers, coolies, rickshaw-pullers and shopkeepers figured in their art. The critic hailed the new and refreshing life that had been infused into the art of Bengal by this band of young artists. He saw in their work the promise of a great future.

The new thoughts about art stirred, however mildly, even the Indian Society of Oriental Arts (ISOA), the original breeding ground of the Bengal School. This was evident in its annual art exhibition of 1922 which had a special section representing the contemporary German paintings of the Bauhaus School. The artists represented in the exhibition included Wassily Kandinsky, Paul Klee, Lyonel Feininger, Gerhard Marcks and Georg Muche. This was arranged following a suggestion from none other than Rabindranath himself. More significantly, the ISOA arranged in 1932 an exhibition of *Patua* paintings collected from rural Bengal and in 1937 an exhibition of Jamini Roy's paintings executed in the *Pot* style.[8]

But these sporadic efforts could not crystallize into a definite trend in the art scenes of Bengal. In the late 1930s, the Bengal School style was still a predominant influence over the artists. Western academism too continued to influence them. But the rapid change in the socio-political climate was fast exposing their limitations. The Bengali upper middle-class, i.e. the landed class and the professional men, who had so far been the only connoisseurs and purchasers of the Bengal School paintings, were facing an economic crisis on account of the falling rental incomes from land and due to chronic unemployment. They were no longer complacent enough to like the unrealistic paintings of the Bengal School and nor were they rich enough to buy them. The stark reality that was staring the artists in the face was the distressed lot of the lower middle class, the urban proletariat and the rural folk. Political consciousness had been growing among these lower strata of society for some time. There was a general feeling, not essentially having any political colour, that the future lay with them. The artists too were taking up ordinary men (instead of Gods and Mughal princes) as their subject-matter. In their sufferings and struggles, in their very life-style, the artists found a genuine rhythm of life, that had been denied to the Bengal School.

Dhurjatiprasad Mukherjee, a leading leftist intellectual, contributed an article in 1938 to the *New Indian Literature*,[9] a publication of the All-India Progressive Writers' Association. There he severely castigated the Bengal School (his approach to this so-called nationalist art partly resembling the later view of the Cambridge School of historians on the question of nationalism): 'To put it bluntly, the comparative purity of Bengal painting was mainly due to the inability of its exponents to find government jobs or at best prompted by an intuitive appreciation of the crisis that had not yet ripened, mythological pictures in lyrical moods were in many ways a liberation, if not an escape.' These paintings, according to Dhurjatiprasad, fitted into a nationalism unrelated to the economic reality of the day and amounted to emotionalism. They appealed to all economic groups, particularly the buyers of the pictures—the Bengali bourgeoisie, who were very lyrical and very religious; 'painting had to be a fine art to flatter the bourgeois vanity'.

Then Mukherjee described the economic changes that had been taking place since the First World War—the classes tending towards polarization and segregation, the upper middle-class drifting into a state of decay, the non-Bengali proletariat manning the mills and the Bengali landless proletariat hovering around their paternal acres. He suggested to the artist a bus trip to Kidderpore or Barrackpore so that the latter could observe what was happening to the countryside near Calcutta, and also suggested that a new kind of sympathy was necessary to convert visual observation into motives for creating novel forms of art.

Chintamani Kar, who was to become a reputed artist later, was then pursuing 'pure art' and had no interest in politics. He went to Paris to study advanced methods of sculpture and there a French artist asked him if he was Communist, Fascist or Socialist. He replied that he was an artist and hence had nothing to do with politics. To his embarrassment, the French friend replied that an artist was not outside society and its politics; 'For example, though you are an artist, you are subservient to the British like all other people of your country.' The friend also emphasised on the role of the artist in the coming Revolution. When Kar somehow managed to reply that an artist creates and does not destroy, his French friend said convincingly, 'We engrave stones with chisel and hammer to model statues—is that destruction of creation?' Kar recounted this incident in *Agrani* (February 1940),[10] on his return to India.

Though never known to be directly political, Chintamani Kar thus became aware of social and political influences on art. In another article in *Agrani* (April 1940)[11] he talked about this in general and specially referred to the Indian national movement that had drawn the artists' attention to the life of the people and led them to a search for Indian identity in content and form. He talked about Abanindranath and Nandalal in this connection and omitted the other disciples of the former. And yet, he said, art had failed to keep pace with the changing society and its people. First, this art had been meant for the rich who had no connection with the masses and in fact exploited them. Second, the social layer that produced most artists was not the one to which the bulk of the masses belonged. Third, due to the negligence of the state, absence of museums, relative paucity of exhibitions, the masses were ignorant of art. He said, Nandalal's experiments with folk-art and Jamini Ray's with *Pot* art were not adequate to fill the gap between the masses and art. A more thorough search for national art was needed. The article thus ended; 'Will the Indian artists continue to sleep and dream? Perhaps the conflicts of the present life will strike them a blow to make them express the present, the society—the national soul.'

All these ideas were gradually gaining ground. In the early 1940s in the Communist weekly *Janayuddha*,[12] an unnamed artist wrote a short essay demanding that both in content and style art should be able to appeal to the masses of people. The writer quoted J.D. Harding: 'Art is an appeal to the mind and not addressed, as commonly believed, to the eyes,' and then added that it should appeal to the mind of all mankind and not only to a handful of people. Chittaprosad, a young Communist artist of repute, observed in *Arani*[13] that art is called 'chitra' because of its appeal to man's mind or 'chitta', and suggested that at that moment what would appeal most was a struggle against fascism on the part of the artists. Chittaprosad narrated the history of Indian art in this article in terms of social control. Some social class or other had always controlled art from ancient times. Sometimes, it was the priestly class, sometimes the rajahs and badshahs and in recent times it was the bourgeoisie inspired by nationalism. Bourgeois art found its expression in Abanindranath and the Bengal School. But this art was unable to serve the masses of people. Hence the need for a new art.

There was a feeling that if art had not a progressive role to play, it would play a reactionary one. How reactionary forces could use this powerful medium was manifest in contemporary Japanese art. The art critic for *Janayuddha*, 4 January 1945, wrote about a Japanese painting exhibited at the Paus Festival at Santiniketan. The picture called 'The Truth of Life' had been painted by Samamura and was divided in two panels. The first panel showed a wandering ascetic with everything around him being burnt by a blazing fire. In the second panel there was conflict and bloodshed, but in the tranquil sky shone a tender moon. According to the critic, Nandalal Bose had explained the picture as follows—the truth of life does not exist in seeking peace through asceticism. One should seek truth by relying on one's own power. The strong and powerful would achieve peace through his triumph over others. The weak would inevitably perish. The critic wondered whether this was not the imperialist philosophy, and whether this should have been accepted at Santiniketan of all places, since it was inconsistent with the legacy of Tagore who had been a great rebel against imperialism. Benodebehari Mukhopadhyay also says in his reminiscences how during his visit to Japan in 1938 he found an anti-Chinese sentiment dominating the artists there.[14]

History sharpened the urge for a new art as the fifth decade of the century heaped ruins upon ruins. The world was already in the grip of a war. With the Japanese attack on Chittagong, the terrible Famine and the string of events taking place in that decade, Bengal was in ferment, socially, politically and intellectually. But the most severe among the blows was the Bengal Famine in 1943. With death, destitution and decay all around, it stirred almost every Bengali artist of any consequence. The terrible human exploitation and degradation turned the romantic and peaceful landscape-painter Zainul Abedin into a rebel for the rest of his life. Prankrisna Pal, an obedient follower of the Bengal School, painted the famished figures of 'Mother and Child',[15] and henceforth his art would move in an entirely different direction. He started a new phase of his career by joining the Calcutta Group. In fact, the Famine acted as a catalyst in the blossoming of all the artists of the Calcutta Group. It provided the urge behind the formation of this collective of budding young artists pursuing a new kind of art. Then there were artists who started their career as relief-workers and artist-journalists of the Communist Party during the days of the Famine, and some of them became famous later on, e.g. Chittaprosad and Somnath Hore. Atul Bose, Indra Dugar, Tribhanga Roy, Kamal Chatterjee, Ardhendu Sekhar Gangopadhyay, Naren Mallik and others responded to the Famine in some way or other. Sudhir Khastagir's Famine

Series and Ramkinkar's painting 'Storm' and etching 'Hunger' can be cited too. Even Nandalal Bose, the doyen of the Bengal School, responded to this ghastly event, though he expressed himself in the Ajanta style and through religious symbols: a skin-and-bone Siva dancing in front of Annapurna engaged in meditation. The caption was: 'He who has Annapurna (the food-giving goddess) at his home, cries of hunger—this is indeed a great error of illusion.'

The Bengal Famine was so critical an influence on the artists that from then on the art of most of them was to be socially-humanly motivated. However, their responses naturally varied, as so many factors like the artists' personality, training and environment entered into the creative process.

The Calcutta Group of Artists

The Bengal School was not replaced by another school of art, determining the artistic style of its followers. But a group of young artists organized themselves in 1943 with some common aims—raising a voice of protest against the prevalent art situation, viewing art in its international context, exploring the modern styles developed in the West and finally showing a concern for man and society. It is a kind of like-mindedness in these respects that brought together Nirad Majumdar, Subho Tagore, Gopal Ghosh, Paritosh Sen, Rathin Moitra, Prankrishna Pal, and two sculptors—Pradosh Dasgupta and Kamala Dasgupta to form the Calcutta Group. There was no other common bond of artistic realization among them and they were all individualists in their pursuit of art. Yet, as Paritosh Sen said emphatically in an interview later in the 1980s, they had assembled under the banner of a group to meet a 'historical need'. They had a definite philosophy about art and its social role which, according to them, the Bengal School was unable to fulfil:

> I say this for the reason that today we find artists' group cropping up everyday and everywhere. The nature of group formation in our case was totally different from theirs. There is no trace of aesthetic or philosophical unity in today's groups. They form groups just because it is financially easier to organize group exhibitions than individual exhibitions. But we had a distinct viewpoint, a distinct philosophy.[16]

Later on, Ramkinkar Beij, Gobardhan Ash, Abani Sen, Sunil Madhav Sen and Hemanta Misra joined the Group.

These young and talented artists had not been feeling quite at home with the art situation of Bengal. They were groping for a fresh approach. They had started taking interest in the great changes in the Western art—not so much in Dadaism or pop arts, but in art practices like Impressionism,

German Expressionism, Cubism, etc. At first, they had learnt about these new trends from books and magazines. Then their understanding of the new art scene in Europe deepened as a result of their contact with some artists and writers from the West, who came here as members of the Allied Forces. E.M. Forster, the English novelist, the two poets—Martin Kirkman and Miller, Frederick McWilliams, Slade Professor of Sculpture in the London University, and like-minded people were in India at that time. They brought with them up-to-date books and nice prints. Rathin Moitra recalled later that these foreigners used to come to his place very often. Sometimes, the young Bengali artists would meet them at the houses of Jamini Ray and Bishnu Dey. These distinguished foreign visitors also participated in the discussions that the Calcutta Group members held every evening during the formative period about their schemes and ambitions. Their meeting places were Subho Tagore's residence at 3, S.R. Das Road and Pradosh Dasgupta's studio known as Glyptothek at Rashbehari Avenue.[17]

Thus, the artists here discovered a strange new and overpowering world that sparked off their interest in form. In the words of Pradosh Dasgupta,

> The guiding motto of our group is best expressed in the slogan: 'Art should aim to be international and interdependent' . . . During the past two hundred years the world outside of India has made vast strides in art, has evolved epoch-making discoveries in forms and techniques. It is, therefore, absolutely necessary for us to close this hiatus by taking advantage of these developments in the Western world. And this is inevitable, whether we like it or not. In our world of supersonic planes and televisions, it is not possible or desirable to preserve the lilywhite purity of our tradition, because art, like science, is also becoming an international activity.

But those Bengali artists borrowed from the West according to their individual mental make-up. Nirad Majumder inclined towards Cezanne, Gopal Ghosh took the colour of the Fauvists on the one hand and was inspired by the Japanese Hokusai artists on the other. Rathin Moitra was highly impressed by Greco, Modigliani, Matisse and the sculptor Henry Moore. Among his other favourites were Paul Klee, Mark, Munk, Picasso and Goya. Their influences made themselves felt in a very subtle way in his art. In his words, 'I took their essence keeping the Indianness intact.'

According to Rathin Moitra, on the whole, they had an open and eager mind. They looked not only into Western art, but also into their own Indian traditions. Folk arts like the toys of Bankura, the antiques kept at the Asutosh Museum, all aroused their interest. Jamini Ray was a source of inspiration. The Calcutta Group claimed inheritance of all the art movements of the East and the West from the Bengal School and Impressionism onwards, through rejection and acceptance. It took a step towards the age of world art and attempted a new synthesis between the East and the West.

But at the same time, according to Moitra, their priority was not forms of art, but grappling with the socio-economic ills. The War, the Famine, the last days of the colonial rule and the awakening among common people made the ills too glaring for the artists to ignore them. The current socio-political problems featured in their works. One can cite the numerous sketches and paintings on the Bengal Famine, for instance. The Group's regard for fellowmen was expressed in their guiding slogan—'Man is supreme. There is none above him.'

Some of the members of the Calcutta Group were driven towards the periphery of the Communist movement. Pradosh Dasgupta was involved in labour movements. Nirad Majumder was fairly close to the CPI. He covered the Netrokona Kisan Conference for the Party paper *Janayuddha* and decorated the pandal on that occasion. Rathin Moitra went so far as to become a member of the Party; perhaps the influence of his brother Jyotirindra Moitra was partly responsible for this. Gopal Ghosh too was a friend of the Communists. He even took great risks in helping them hold street-corner art exhibitions at the Wellington Square with a view to preaching communal harmony during the days of the communal riots. All the Group members contributed to leftist journals like *Arani* or *Swadhinata*. Prankrishna Pal's line-drawing 'Revolutionary Prisoner' printed in the *People's Age* (1945) is just one example. Most of them were also members of the AFWAA, the cultural front of the Communist Party.

II

It is not possible here to discuss in detail and do justice to the works of all the Group members. Though all of them featured socio-political scenes and depicted common people, there were wide variations among them. Paritosh Sen's paintings on the Bengal Famine—dying children oozing out of skeletal mothers, masquerades of death composed of strong swirling lines, expressed the anger and anguish of the painter. Gopal Ghosh's Famine sketches of short-hand brush marks and abbreviated strokes dealt with the theme more directly, as for example, that of a street dog looking up expectantly at a little naked boy, while the latter looks utterly dejected with an empty bowl in his hand, and the distressed mother and child:[18] all very touching indeed.

All the members of the Group depicted workers and peasants. To give only a few examples—Rathin Moitra's 'Majur Majurani', Nirad Majumdar's 'Peasant' (oil)[19] and his sketches of a Manipuri peasant and of Hajong tribals at the Netrokona Kisan Conference.[20] On the other hand,

Subho Tagore's 'Ploughman: The Protector of the People' was a symbolic figure in linear design—an Indian farmer standing against a palm tree with a plough in his hand and a leaf head covering on his head which is used as protection against the sun and rain. Subho Tagore's were generally symbolic patterns rather than figures suggesting human warmth. His exhibition in aid of 'Distressed Poets and Artists of China', his cover of his own verse-book *May Day & other Poems*, all suggest this.[21]

Each of the Calcutta Group members tried to develop a realistic style to cope with a wide variety of social subjects. Prankrishna Pal,[22] for example, with his love for classical beauty could not bring himself to draw the image of famished men and women reduced to skeletons. But this did not prevent him from responding to the Famine. The artist, so long used to painting miniatures in the Mughal style, simplified his art to catch the pathos of the Famine in a soothing combination of bold rhythmic lines and flat colours. As a result, his art assumed a formalistic appearance that in a way resembled that of Jamini Roy.

Many of the Group artists tried to find an Indian identity through Jamini Roy; Rathin Moitra's working men too remind us of Roy, particularly in their pillar-like legs, looking like stone-made ones, standing for self-sufficiency and vigour. The *Nuliahs* of Gopalpur or the peasant standing with his feet submerged in the paddy field (on the cover of Bishnu Dey's book of poems *Sandwiper Char*) can be cited as examples. Jamini Roy's influence was also evident in an album of eight monochrome reproductions of Nirad Majumdar's paintings, published by the Calcutta Group.[23] Majumdar admitted to a friend that the influence had once been there indeed, but when people started talking about it he angrily decided to get over it, promptly bought oil colours and painted pictures of an entirely new type.[24]

Prankrishna Pal and Nirad Majumdar had received training from the Indian Society of Oriental Arts. They joined the Calcutta Group having discarded their background. From a very different background came Pradosh Dasgupta, Gopal Ghosh and Paritosh Sen. They had all been students at the Madras School of Art with Debiprasad Roychowdhury—the legendary sculptor, painter and writer from an aristocratic background. Debiprasad's technique was not substantially different from that of the Bengal School, but his art was rather different in mood and much more down-to-earth. He had a great regard for anatomy and encouraged sketching trips to the surrounding country to develop the power of observation in his students. All this continued to shape the latter's careers, even after some of them formed the Calcutta Group.

Having always been hostile to the so-called Indian art, Paritosh Sen stood at the opposite extreme to Prankrishna Pal in his use of colours. 'The artists of our country', he said, 'are afraid to use bold colours. The artist must go on splashing colour lavishly until the very canvas seems to throb with life.'[25] And he did not use colours as complementary to the object, he used them with an eye on their harmonious juxtaposition. Hence, he would paint red trees and green men. But that such colouring is at all possible was a realization resulting from Sen's discovery of Jamini Roy.

Though much different from Paritosh Sen's, Subho Tagore's paintings too sometimes showed a riotous revelry of colour. But most of the times he used to draw linear designs and weaving patterns out of which symbolic figures took shape, and here the influence of Bhola Chatterjee was evident.

But whatever Rathin Moitra says, it remains to be examined whether reflecting upon man and society was the primary concern of the Calcutta Group members or whether they were preoccupied with the purely pictorial and formal aspects of artistic expression in an attempt to be modern. This is different from the question as to how strictly they aligned themselves with the then politics of Communism. In regard to the second point Pradosh Dasgupta later said that though they had had leftist leanings, they had never acted as cheap political propagandists and managed to steer clear of any political interference. He recounted an incident that had taken place at the annual show of their Group in 1949. Gopal Haldar, a veteran Communist leader and one of the supporters of their Group at the initial stage, felt completely out of sorts at this exhibition and asked Dasgupta whether they were straying from the cherished ideal of Socialist Realism. Dasgupta's answer was, 'We never took a pledge to follow the path of Socialist Realism. All we want is to understand life and to interpret it in terms of creative art.' Unfortunately, after this dialogue, they lost a good friend in 'Gopalda'.

Of course, understanding life or even man's situation in life and his social predicaments does not need being 'trapped by political propagandists'. Yet it seems that on the whole the Calcutta Group was perhaps motivated not so much by man and his predicaments as by a reaction against the Bengal School and by a sense of internationalism or cosmopolitanism. This sense was not only confined to study and appreciation of the Western art movements, but also involved an inclination to Communism, for Communism had become the most powerful ideology at the world level. It can perhaps be said about quite a few of them that it was not a concern for contemporary social reality that attracted them to Communism, rather it was their discovery of a bond of internationalism with the Communists that drew their attention to the contemporary reality. Moreover, they might have felt that if men like Picasso were to be recognized as masters of form, their social thoughts should be accepted as well.

In *Parichay*, Magh 1352 (1946), an art critic, Rabindra Majumder, found that the Calcutta Group members identified themselves with the change of values evident those days in all spheres of culture. Hence, they were keen on painting truthfully and not so much beautifully. But a deep and strong social consciousness was needed for fulfillment of this ideal, i.e. for the coordination between the truth of reality and the truth of art, since without such deep involvement art would just become a display of technical skill or an imitative repetition of the use of colour and line of a particular school. According to this critic, both these vices and virtues of the modern art movement were reflected in the Calcutta Group's recent exhibition. As examples of the artists' excessive attention to form, he cited Nirad Majumdar's 'Still Life' and 'Composition', where he found a sort of luxury despite the neat and nice drawing, and also in Majumdar's screen-design for the IPTA which tried too much to amaze the beholders, and that too in an obsessive imitation of Salvador Dali.

According to Pranab Ranjan Roy, a well known art critic, the social consciousness of the Calcutta Group was very superficial:

> The 'socially conscious' artists of the Calcutta Group, as Nirad Majumdar, Rathin Moitra, Prankrishna Pal and Paritosh Sen, wavered between too many mutually non-convergent preordained stylistic strands. They sought to pack in social content in formalist language, a synthesis of the urban-folk idiom of Kalighat as formalised by Jamini Roy on the one hand, and cubism on the other. The result was quite disastrous. The language-form and the meaning-content never converged. The content remained at best an illustrative element and at worst as inert motifs to formal exercises. Nirad Majumdar later became a non-abstract purist, Prankrishna Pal gave up painting and Rathin Maitra tried hard just to keep up the practice.

According to this critic, the only exception was Paritosh Sen, whose 'concern over social reality was more than skin-deep'. That this was more than a passing interest was proved by Sen's depiction of the refugees on the platform of Sealdah after Partition, his series of paintings in the late 1950s in which he sarcastically commented on the Bengali 'baboo', or by his later-day full-blooded expressionist style to objectify human figures in emotional stress, conditioned socially, though in these later works, a hiatus between the manneristic overstressing of idiom and the intellectually-conceived content is noticeable.[26]

Among the Calcutta Group artists themselves, at least Nirad Majumdar would have agreed with this critic. In a brochure published by the Calcutta Group, it was written about him: 'He thinks the fundamental point in art is Form . . . the content, expression and impression are not worth a damn: There is no formal distinction between a living animated face and the inert pot.' A friend of Majumdar wrote on the basis of a talk with him much later: 'Yet in his opinion, though big words like Famine, protest, agitation, etc., are implicated with the Calcutta Group, the matter was, in fact, formal. Influence of modern painters of other countries particularly of France (says Majumdar), was extremely vital to us—and new experimentations—urge to do something new, and so on.'[27]

Let us see what Paritosh Sen had to say about this charge against the Calcutta Group. He told me in an interview that the charge was only partially true. According to Sen, all the members of the Group had a double concern—formalist and social. They tried to bring these together in their art work, but not always with success. For some of them the formalistic urge was stronger than the social one. But at least two of them—himself and Rathin Moitra—were mainly concerned with man and society, though there was a difference between them. Moitra was closer to rural Bengal in his temperament, while the urban was stronger in Sen's work. He would usually depict city scenes or crowded places. In this interview, Sen recalled having done a series of paintings on the third class railway compartment at that time. He considered them to be pretty good both as artistic experiment and as social response.[28]

In fairness to the Calcutta Group, it may be said that its artists might not have been as socially responsive as some other artists of that time like, say, Somnath Hore whose social sensitivity preceded and perhaps gave birth to his artistic urge. But every artist worth the name is sensitive in a general sense and as such is bound to be shaken by social crises, particularly when they are as strongly manifest in specific events as during the 1940s. So, the social concern of the Calcutta Group may not be dismissed as utterly superficial, though of course, its intensity varied from artist to artist. At least in some of their works, experimentation in form and social content inextricably merged, and this is what we call successful art.

III

And above all, the Calcutta Group's was the first solid collective effort to challenge the Bengal School and to give a reorientation to Indian art in order to make it contemporary. Rabindranath, Jamini Roy and a few others had already prepared the way in this direction. But theirs were individual explorations in a spirit of adventure. They could not force a definite change in the overall art situation. Bhola Chatterjee had tried to formulate a definite art theory acknowledging the requirements of the new age and organized a group of rebel artists. It is interesting to note the strong similarity between his theory and that of the Calcutta Group. The stylistic influence of Chatterjee was very clear in the works of Subho Tagore of the Calcutta Group and at least two of the latecomers to the Group, Abani Sen and Gobordhan Ash, had once belonged to Bhola Chatterjee's Rebel Art Centre And yet, the Rebel Art Centre was very short-lived and Chatterjee almost gave up drawing during the 1940s.

So whatever the limitations of the Calcutta Group, front-ranking contemporary critics like Professor Shahid Suhrawardy, Sudhindranath Dutta and Bishnu Dey did appreciate their work. From outside Bengal, Mulk Raj Anand paid tribute to their 'brave gestures of defiance'. 'And if they achieved only a few pictures and sculptures of great worth', said Anand, 'They had shown tremendous courage in confronting the conservatives with a new direction for creative art.'[29] The Calcutta Group was able to impress some distinguished foreigners too. After returning to Britain, E.M. Forster gave a talk on Indian art on the BBC devoting a considerable portion of it to the Calcutta Group. A few years later in 1947, the art critic F.H. Baines admired the Calcutta Group in *Our Times*, London, for seeking 'to turn the uncertain lead of Jamini Roy to the expression of contemporary ideas'. Among other learned critics whom the Group attracted were Sanjay Bhattacharya, the Editor of *Purbasha*, Chanchal Chattopadhyay, Kalyan Gangooly, Kalyan Dasgupta, O.C. Gangooly, Abani C. Banerjee, Khagen De Sarkar, Abani Mukherjee, Kim Christen, Lindsay Emerson, Sheila Auden and Charles Fabri.

Another patron was Mrs Casey, the wife of the Bengal Governor, who was instrumental in bringing about their first informal exhibition at S.R. Das Road. Shortly afterwards, in 1944 the first public exhibition of the Group was held under the auspices of the Services Art Club. Praise for pioneering and criticism for denouncing the traditional that were showered on them after this exhibition clearly indicated that a new movement had been born. One of the critics groaned: 'Their national traditions appear to be submerged, full five fathoms deep, under the dirt carried by that dubious dirty wind (from Europe).' Another hailed them as 'trail-blazers, the pioneers of a new epoch in Indian Art'. Not a piece of painting or sculpture was sold at this exhibition and the artists 'comforted themselves by interpreting that as a happy sign'. But by 1948, many people took pride in possessing a painting or a sculpture from the Group members.

Having been encouraged by the local appreciation, the Group members sent two large exhibitions to Bombay in 1944 and 1945. There too they were hailed by critics like Rudolph Von Leyden, the *Times of India* art critic. And the younger artists of Bombay like K.H. Ara, who had already been feeling unsure and unsettled, were immensely inspired by a new hope. Early in 1948, the Bombay Progressive Group was formed with K.H. Ara, Francis Newton Souza, Syed Haider Raza, Hari Ambadas Gade, Maqbool Fida Husain and Sadanand K. Bakre. Leyden and the Calcutta

Group members were directly instrumental in forming them into a group. The Calcutta Group and the Bombay Progressive Group organized a joint exhibition in April 1950, at 1, Chowringhee Terrace.[30]

The Calcutta Group held quite a few exhibitions in Calcutta. The usual venue was Jatin Majumder's house at Chowringhee Terrace. One such exhibition was '5 years of Calcutta Group' in 1949, in which Rathin Mitra (not to be confused with Rathin Moitra) participated for the first time. The art of Hemanta Misra, a popular progressive artist of Assam and a late-comer to the Group, was exhibited in this same house in 1952.[31]

In 1953, the Calcutta Group had their last and most eventful show in Delhi at the All India Fine Art and Crafts Society Hall. After a decade of collective contribution to the shaping of the modern Indian art, the Group dissolved. As their common interest had already been served, the members had to break apart and go their individual ways, since, after all, their approaches to art were widely different.

Subho Tagore had left the Group long ago. Nirad Majumder and Paritosh Sen went to Paris. Pradosh Dasgupta, who had been the Secretary for a long time, tried to keep the Group alive by admitting new members and inviting guest artists at exhibitions. Thus, Gobordhan Ash, Abani Sen, Sunil Madhav Sen and Hemanta Misra became associated with the Group in its later years. Ramkinkar Beij contributed to their exhibitions as a guest artist. But then Pradosh Dasgupta himself accepted a job in Delhi, as did Prankrishna Pal. The Calcutta Group was thus dissolved.

Such artists' associations as the Calcutta Group are always destined to be short-lived, as Paritosh Sen explained to me later. Even in the West this is the general rule. As an artist proceeds toward maturity, his individuality becomes stronger and the desire to make personal statements prevails over the group interest. Moreover, Bengal tided over the great crises of the War and the Famine that had been the driving force behind the formation of the Calcutta Group. The social climate now no longer called for a collective response. Paritosh Sen himself retained a strong social concern which was the mainstay of his art for a long time to come. But he tried to express it in his own individual language. Yet, all said and done, Sen later regretted that the Group had been too short-lived to fulfill all its potential. The agitations of the 1940s gave a great push to a kind of social art. Sen wished its momentum could have continued for a longer time.

Some Committed Artists

Then there emerged some artists during the 1940s who did not belong to any art group. They, however, believed that as artists their foremost duty was to serve their fellow-men. Some of them belonged to the

Communist Party. Others were very close to the Party and its cultural front, the AFWAA.[32] In this section we will discuss four of them—Zainul Abedin, the most famous artist of the Bengal Famine, Debabrata Mukherjee, Chittaprosad Bhattacharya and Somnath Hore.

Zainul Abedin (1914–76)

Born into a poor family in Kishoregunj, Mymensingh, Abedin[33] had to struggle hard to take up an artist's career. He graduated from the Calcutta Art College, received the Governor's Gold Medal of the Academy of Fine Arts for a group of water colour landscapes in the All-India Art Exhibition. He was appointed a teacher at the Art School while still a student there.

So far he had concentrated on the study of landscapes, having drunk his fill of nature's bounty at his home in East Bengal. Then came the terrible Famine. The sight of thousands dying, humanity degraded and values collapsing like a pack of cards shook Abedin to his very roots. He expressed this traumatic experience in numerous black-and-white sketches that made him famous not only in left circles, but all over Bengal. The Communists were proud of him and highlighted his Famine sketches by holding exhibitions or writing about him in their periodicals.[34] He became a member of the AFWAA.

As a young art teacher with small earnings, he could not afford quality art materials which were scarce and dear. So he made these drawings in black ink with dry brush on the cheapest kind of paper, usually wrapping paper, slightly tinted with yellow and pink. And yet these were the most powerful sketches on the Famine. His initial preference for Western realistic art to the cool and highly-stylized Bengal School, was probably responsible for the vigorously realistic Famine sketches. The bold and harsh lines with no tonal modulation and the stark contrast between black and white revealed the starkness of human misery and had a shocking effect on the viewers. His subjects were men and animals feeding on roadside garbage, a skinny man eagerly licking a plantain leaf (that had been used as a plate in some feast and then thrown away), numerous symbolic crows—these scavenger birds moving around in abundance in a human settlement—and of course numerous mother-and-child scenes, the dying child clinging to the dead mother's breast and so on, for 'the relationship which stands at the origin of all culture, or every virtue, of every nobler aspect of existence is that between mother and child; it operates in a world of violence as the divine principle of love, of union, of peace'.[35]

Moved by a fervent passion, Abedin went on to depict the suffering have-nots of his country, particularly the villagers. Many of these drawings appeared in the pages of the *Millat*. The force and movement of the lines reflected his deep sympathy for those people and his anger at their impoverished existence. The book *In those Darkening Days* by Ela Reed was banned by the British Government for having included one of his sketches.

And this became the leit motif of his whole career as an artist. The helpless condition of the poor people continued to haunt him through the rest of his life. He opted for East Pakistan as his home after the Partition. His creation went through many changes in both thematic and stylistic terms, even verging on abstraction for some time. But the passion for the poor and the lowly never left him.

Debabrata Mukhopadhyay (1918–91)

Debabrata Mukherjee[36] got his first inspiration as an artist from traditional Indian art. Abanindranath and Nandalal had a great influence on him. Moreover, he toured famous places of pilgrimage all over India for self-training. He received formal training at the Indian Society of Oriental Arts, Art School and Academy of Commercial Art, but stuck nowhere.

Though inspired by the Bengal School movement, he did not blindly imitate its mannerisms in his own artistic pursuit. This is because belief in the Communist ideology gave his art a fresh purpose and direction. His indoctrination took place in the 1930s when socialism was generally replacing militant nationalism as the dominant political ideology among the middle-class of Midnapore, Debabrata's home district.

After some time, he came to Beleghata, Calcutta and started wandering about the streets of this city with a cloth-bag on his shoulder and a brush in his hand. In this way he discovered the subject-matter of his art in the turbulent city of the 1940s. His sketch book was like a diary. His art centred around common men, not only from Calcutta but also from remote villages—tea coolies, miners, boatmen, Lepchas, Santals, and so on.

Then there were numerous political posters and cartoons. An exhibition of his anti-communal drawings was held at the Shilpi Sabha of Beleghata in 1949, his first exhibition. Debabrata was closely associated with this local club. On the occasion of the Durga Puja of 1947 or 1948, the Nabamilan Club held an exhibition of his paintings on the distress of the refugees. His graphics on the fighting peasants of Tebhaga came into light in the 1950s.

Debabrata made covers for a number of books. *Stories about Lenin* was his first such commission (1944). The covers of *Chharpatra* and *Mithe Kara*, two books of verses by Sukanta Bhattacharya, created a sensation. The cover of the *Gananatya*, the organ of the Bengal IPTA, was also his handiwork. He also successfully carried out stage-designing and the overall decoration for many meetings organized by the Communist Party, the IPTA and other leftist organizations.

The urge to communicate with more and more people—an urge imparted by the Communist ideology—made Mukherjee experiment with different traditional methods of art, e.g. the *Shalaka Likhan* method of South India, a kind of graphic art where the artist carves palm leaves with a pointed skewer and uses ink to make the carved part prominent. He also learnt the *Pot* art of Bengal from some real Patuas as also different Japanese and Chinese methods from artists of these countries.

There was a 'den' of the Communist Party near Central Avenue (at the back of Mahajati Sadan). Here, Chittaprosad, Debkumar Roy Chowdhury, Debabrata and other Communist artists tried their hands at litho-printing, though they did not have a litho-machine. They used to place wet paper on stone, press the paper with a wooden block, then keep jumping on the block for quite some time. The impressions thus obtained made excellent posters. The Tebhaga Movement was going on at that time and a large number of posters were needed.

Debabrata Mukherjee's hard lines and their sharp tension, the close-up view of matter as well as the simplification of appearance helped him to find his conceived subjects. He broke up the ordinary human image in sharp lines, and thus twisting its frame, diffused terrific anger or vigour that rebounds from the picture directly into the heart of the viewers. They were ideal posters, not fit for drawing rooms. And still they were good art.

Debabrata was thus acclaimed by O.C. Ganguly, a leading art-critic of the time: 'He is not ultra-modern in his creative work, nor does he wholly follow the traditional path. This artist has found out a new path and method for himself, based on the old. With just ink and brush he discovers such mystery of form, brings about such deep flow of ecstasy onto the canvas, spreads such infatuating net of beauty as can hardly be found in other young artists of today.'[37]

Chittaprosad (1915–78)

Chittaprosad Bhattacharya,[38] a boy from Chittagong, was well-conversant with the traditional style of village sculptors and puppet-players and influenced by them. At the same time, he was attracted by the Bengal School trend and longed to learn art from Abanindranath at Santiniketan. But his did not materialize. Chittaprosad grew up to be a self-trained artist.

While studying at the Chittagong College, he joined the political left. During 1938–9 they held numerous poster exhibitions in rural areas in temporary sheds made of bamboo and walled-up by tatty. These drawings calling for a mass consciousness on the part of the artist forced him to strike out a new path of his own.

The grim brutality of the Japanese attack on Chittagong in 1942 resulted in a series of posters, where the Japanese looked like green-faced demons. These were intended to incite the people to resist the Japanese. P.C.Joshi, the Communist Party General Secretary, visited Chittagong at about this time and proposed that an art exhibition be held on the theme, 'Defend Chittagong'. Chittaprosad was the main artist of this exhibition. He was helped by some left-minded artist-soldiers from England, who were then camping at Chittagong on their way to Arakan. Particularly, one Mr Stevenson who had been an art teacher in London helped him a lot and taught him some important techniques of art—spraying, etc. The 'Defend Chittagong exhibition was a great success and Chittaprosad became well known.

This was followed by the Bengal Famine, 1943–4. Chittaprosad roamed the countryside and reported the horror in black-and-white sketches to the Communist Party organ *Janayuddha*. At this time, his father was transferred to Midnapore and the family accompanied him there. For some time, Chittaprosad stayed alone in Chittagong and then went to Midnapore with a commission from the Party to chronicle the Famine from there.

After some time he returned to Chittagong. But P.C. Joshi now wanted him to come to Calcutta and work for the party from a central position. At the same time, the Chittagong police ordered him out of the town for the initiative he had taken to put up a seditious play, *Abirbhav.* That brought him to Calcutta. He set up his abode at Shyama Charan De Street and devoted himself to Party work.

In 1946, he moved to Andheri, Bombay, as the costume and scenic designer of the Central Squad of the IPTA on a monthly salary of Rs. 25. That was his most creative phase. He contributed drawings to the *Unity* and the *People's War.* These included some powerful and famous ones, like the heart-rending linocut on the martyrdom of the 'Kayurs' or the sketch of two robust hands breaking shackles on the theme of the RIN Mutiny. He edited a pictorial book 'Hungry Bengal' on the Bengal Famine. Most of its copies and all the blocks were destroyed by the British police. He designed costumes, painted scenes, drew posters, political caricatures and a vast number of book illustrations for the Communist Party. Gradually linocut became his favourite way of expression, though not to the exclusion of other mediums.

In 1949, he responded to the call of the World Peace Movement. A number of linocuts were produced on this theme—smiling and playful children feeding birds or playing flutes; mother and child, both content and happy, mother reading out fairy tales to her enchanted sons or painting *Alpana* on the floor with the son on her lap. It was a happy world where flowers blossom and birds (most of the time doves, the epitome of peace) fly in abundance. And though these linocuts were just black-and-white, their joyous spirit makes them look colourful, as if by some magic. On the other hand, in 1952, the artist made a series of linocuts depicting poor Indian children with all their poverty and diseases. The collection entitled *Angels Without Fairy Tales* was dedicated to the International Conference in Defence of Children.[39] These two themes—the optimistic 'Fairy Tale' and the shocking 'Angels without Fairy Tales', together revealed the integrity of a highly sensitive artist.

Somnath Hore (1921–2006)

Born in a village of the district Chittagong, Somnath Hore[40] first gave vent to his artistic urge by copying portraits of the old masters of the European art. He was a student at the intermediate level at that time.

About 1940 he came to study B.Sc. at City College, Calcutta and came into contact with some members of the Communist Party. On account of the Japanese bombardment of Calcutta and the evacuation of the city, he returned to Chittagong. Here too he made contacts with the Communists. As a matter of fact, the local leaders whom he had always respected as militant patriots, had turned Communist. He himself did not very well understand all these political doctrines—he was too young for that. But to him these leaders were infallible.

Then came the Japanese attack on Chittagong. At Patia village, a few miles away from his home, the bombers had left marks of death and devastation which he could see with his own eyes. By this time, Purnendu Dastidar, the chief functionary of the CPI at Chittagong and Somnath's principal liaison with the Communist Party, had introduced him to the artist Chittaprosad. Somnath used to accompany Chittaprosad to the devastated villages, did relief work, helped the latter sketch the horror for the journal *People's War.* He himself made some posters and published one or two sketches in *People's War.* But what is really important, this experience aroused in him a strong desire for artistic creation, the kind of art that could play a social role.

His real initiation as an artist took place during the Famine. When I interviewed him in the 1980s, he still shivered to think of it and did not know how to describe it adequately. From Chittagong, he used to send visual reportage of the Famine for the *Janayuddha.* Particularly after Chittaprosad had left for Midnapore, the paper depended solely on Somnath to cover the Famine at Chittagong. As art works, these were nothing more than amateurish sketches, but as social documentation they were invaluable.

In 1945 he came to Calcutta as a Party artist on requests from leaders like Bhabani Sen and Somnath Lahiri. P.C. Joshi got him admitted into the Government Art College. Somnath's own interest was to have Zainul Abedin as his teacher there. By this time he was a whole-timer of the Communist Party.

About this time, Somnath was exposed to a new medium of art—wood-cut. But side by side with experimentation with wood-cut, he made posters for the Party and drew sketches. The Party sent him to Rangpur, the storm centre of the Tebhaga fighting, and this enriched him both as a Communist activist and as an artist. Some of his sketches on Tebhaga—of the determined faces of peasants and group activities showing a conviction in political endeavour—were published in the Party weeklies. During the communal riots of August 1946, Somnath was a boarder of the Communist Party commune at Dharmatala Street. He has quite a few pictures to his credit on the theme of communalism.

In the meantime, the Party faced financial difficulties. Somnath was considerate enough to withdraw himself from his whole-timer's role in the Party, though he continued to stay in its commune. He started supporting himself. Sometimes the senior Party leader Muzaffar Ahmad would get him some money by making him illustrate a few publications of the National Book Agency. At the same time, he was continuing his studies in college. He got involved in organizing political movements amongst the students.

In 1948, the Communist Party was banned. Somnath was arrested and was in jail for a few days. In 1949, he went underground fearing another arrest. In a list of police suspects prepared by the Intelligence Branch of the West Bengal police about this time Somnath Hore's appears to be the only name from the cultural front of the Communist Party. He was whole-heartedly devoted Party work at that time. His principal task was to make posters for Party meetings. Like many of his artist colleagues, he believed the words of Mao Tse-tung: 'This is not the time to do embroidery'. Socialist Realism in art was their ideal.

Ever since the time of his visual reportage on the Famine, Somnath Hore used to amplify in his art certain elements of reality, so that they assumed almost symbolic qualities. His human and animal figures were almost always skeletal with a prominent thorax appearing as a cage of ribs with each rib jutting out prominently. The children, very common in his drawings, would invariably have out-of-proportion malarious spleens, their heads would be enormous skulls with small bony faces, perched on rickety torsos. He continued with and improved this way of depiction of misery in his later career.

The Institute of Art and Culture

During the 1940s, Sitesh Dasgupta, Bani Majumdar, Tapas Dutta, Prakash Karmakar, Kamal Bose, Asoke Gupta, Chittaranjan Das and some other young and left-minded artists, more or less associated with the Socialist unity Centre of India, formed the Institute of Art and Culture.

They specialized in wood-cut and linocut, and their themes were the world-wide struggle for liberation in the post-War years, the vision of peace and so on. Later, Tapas Dutta took to sculpture.[41]

The artists of the IAC held a number of successful exhibitions. A report of *Natun Sahitya* (January 1951) spoke highly of one such exhibition. According to this report, the art works were simple and yet powerful and it was noted that such an exhibition had not taken place in Calcutta for a long time. The works especially mentioned were Tapas Dutta's 'Save the Civilization'—a woman with a stalk of corn in her hand (wood-cut), Sitesh Dasgupta's 'The Call' (wood-cut) and Chittaranjan Das's 'Mother's Family' (dry-point). In later years, reputed artists from outside used to be represented in the exhibitions of the IAC and this increased their variety and value.

An interview[42] with Sitesh Dasgupta, one of the founder-members of the Institute, threw considerable light on his personal art activities, the activities of the IAC and the atmosphere they were working in. As a child, Dasgupta used to paint Radha-Krishna, like many other children of those days. But he gave up such themes as he became more and more conscious about man, society and the subjugated state of India. The harrowing experience of the Bengal Famine further sensitized him and decided the kind of art he would prefer. In the Art College, he had as his teacher Zainul Abedin, whose Famine sketches had already appealed to him greatly. But, according to Dasgupta, Abedin did not help him much with regard to his ideological clarification. His ideological conviction came from some other source—the Culture Club near his residence in South Calcutta. It was, in fact, a local library. He used to go there to borrow books. Gradually he realized that it was an organization of the Revolutionary Socialist Party. Before this, it had been the meeting place of some revolutionary terrorists of the Anusilan Samity, who eventually formed the RSP. Political discussions amongst the elders at the club roused his interest. The books on Marxism, Leninism, labour movements, etc., broadened his horizon. During 1945–6, many comrades were released from jail—Sibdas Ghosh (who founded the SUCI), Mrinal Mukherjee and others. They started holding their study circle meetings regularly in a back room of that club house. Gradually Dasgupta was deeply involved in leftist politics under the guidance of Sibdas Ghosh. Alongside, his art activities continued. He and two of his friends, Bani Majumdar and Tapas Dutta, shared the same ideas about art and politics.[43] These three provided the nucleus for the IAC.

So far as the style of their art is concerned, Sitesh Dasgupta recalled that they had a definite preference for the Bengal School, particularly Abanindranath, Nandalal, Benodebehari and Ramkinkar. Their courage in experimentation inspired the IAC artists. Their Indianness fascinated them. Dasgupta studied Nandalal and his own work was heavily influenced by that master artist. Sometimes, people even took his strokes for that of Nandalal. One of his works done in this style was 'Ora Kaj Kare' (They Labour) which got a lot of publicity. Lady Ranu Mukherjee bought it from an exhibition, though she did not subscribe to the artist's ideological views. Dasgupta added that this did not mean that they had not been attracted by the artists of the West. Of course, the European naturalistic art never attracted them, they liked the classical artists of Europe—artists ranging from Rembrandt, Gauguin, Manet, Monet, the post-Impressionists, up to Braque and Matisse. Though Modigliani's form was to their liking, on the whole he did not appeal to them. And more recent European artists did not attract them at all. Dasgupta admitted that Dali (who inspired some of the members of the Calcutta Group) used to cause a nervous sensation and a feeling of nausea in him.

Due to attraction for the Bengal School, the IAC developed a relationship of cooperation and even organizational connection with Rupayani, another art institute working in the Indian style. Rupayani, patronized by some of the leading Bengali intellectuals like Suniti Kumar Chatterjee and Amal Hom, comprised Sunil Pal, the sculptor, Priyaprasad Gupta and a few other artists. But because they could not find any ideological rapport with Rupayani, the IAC artists were not fully satisfied while cooperating with the former. In any case, both the organizations were short-lived.

During the 1940s, the new art that was associated with political radicalism generally meant a departure from the Bengal School. The defiant attitude of the members of the Calcutta Group, proclaimed with much fanfare, was responsible for this. But this did not apply to all artists of that period. We have already seen how Debabrata Mukherjee and Chittaprosad, two artists of the Communist Party, had an initial preference for the Bengal School, and though they developed their own individual styles in the course of time, they scarcely intended to challenge the Bengal School. Even some Calcutta Group artists had come from the Bengal School background and naturally they could not wholly get over its influence. So the stand that the IAC artists took was nothing exceptional. Personally, Sitesh Dasgupta felt that those who opposed the Bengal School could not catch its essence. He considered Abanindranath to be a superb artist and the depth reached by him as unsurpassed, though, as he admitted, mere imitation of Abanindranath's art did produce bad results in many cases.

A young art historian has recently perceived the visual arts of Bengal during the 1940s as a three-trajectory development, the first emerging around the response to the man-made Famine, the second the formal modernist attempt of the Calcutta Group aspiring after an international language rather than nationalist articulations, and the third the shift within the so-called Bengal school, especially in the works of Nandalal, Benodebehari and Ramkinkar. These three often overlapping trajectories, in the opinion of this scholar, were equally vital and constituted a valid multiplicity in the visual arts of the period. I agree with him, but I think that there was a fourth trajectory—to be located in the political ambience which was largely dominated by the Communist Party.[44] However, more or less the same socialist ideology was nurtured also by some other political groups, which contributed to the visual art of the period too. The Institute of Art and Culture associated with the SUCI testifies to this.

Sculpture

India, ironically enough, lost in the modern times her proud position in the art of sculpture, and even the exponents of the Bengal School did not pay much attention to this particular aspect. Of course, the Indian Society of Oriental Art employed practitioners of stone- and wood-carving of the Orissan tradition as teachers, and Rabindranath appointed a little-known sculptor, Narayan Debal, for Kala Bhavan. But somehow or other, this art did not flourish.

Academic sculpture as taught in England, i.e. the imitation of the romantic realism of the Victorian age, enjoyed some prestige. One exponent of this style was Hiranmay Roy Chowdhury, teacher of the famous Debiprasad Roy Chowdhury. But their creativity could not go much beyond the pursuit of the Western style in image-making, mostly on commission.

Then amidst the newly awakened social consciousness emerged a few sculptors with a new content and form. The first and foremost among them was undoubtedly Ramkinkar Beij of Kala Bhavan. Another sculptor was Pradosh Dasgupta of the Calcutta Group. The latter was close to the Communist cultural and other activities, while the importance of the former was not adequately realized by the Communists.

But before we talk about the two above-mentioned sculptors, we should acknowledge the contribution of Sudhir Khastagir, Ramkinker's predecessor at Kala Bhavan. On the one hand, he had met reputed Western sculptors at Kala Bhavan, some of them students of Rodin and Bourdelle, and gone abroad to learn more about the Western style of sculpture; on the other hand, on Abanindranath's advice, he had visited the famous pilgrim spots of India—Konarak, Mahabalipuram, Elephanta, etc.—which are also seats of great sculpture. He never cared much about Gods and Goddesses. As he said, 'My love for keeping a link with our own tradition and culture in art is entirely based on intellectual foundation and not due to spiritual or religious sentimental background.' His deep thinking about art and a concern for life produced excellent results in his sculpture that was imbued with life, vigour and movement, combining Indian convention and modernity of style. *Daughters of the Soil*, executed as early as 1929, may be cited as an example. But he kept himself isolated from the art scenes of Bengal as a teacher at the far-off Doon School, and hence remained relatively less-known.[45]

Trained under no particular teacher and having imbibed no particular style, Ramkinkar cultivated sculpture by reading books, talking to the foreign guest-sculptors at Santiniketan and, above all, under the encouragement of his teacher Nandalal Bose. Through experiments he evolved an original style suited to his theme, signifying an intimacy with life and nature. His sculpture investing his figures with a solid physicality profoundly appealed to the sense-perception of the viewers, and this particular quality ushered in a new age in Indian sculpture. In the words of Bishnu Dey: 'And he seemed to have got out of the confusion of media which makes sculpture feel like painting and painting aspire after sculptural effects, and in short both appear to be more literary than plastic or chromatic.'[46] Moreover, Ramkinkar's open-air sculpture was placed in such a way as to look like an integral part of the surroundings and to be appreciated by whoever passed that spot, and not just by a few art lovers.

At the back of the students' hostel of the Kala Bhavan, on the way to the village Surul, he built the monumental 'Santal Family' in 1938; a man and his wife with their baby lying in a basket hanging from the *bank* (a long and bent pole) on the father's shoulder, and a dog following them. The rhythm of their gait, their muscular bodies, firm posture and real Santal features signify the struggle of the Santal worker's life. One cannot think of this piece of sculpture displaced from the tamarisk trees of the surroundings, frequented at that time by the local santals. These figures were natural like trees, rooted in the soil, with a tree-like stretch and build and having the tactile quality of the bark of a tree. He chose his own material to bring about this vision of physicality—cement and sand mixed with local gravels.

In 1941, Ramkinkar placed his 'Paddy-threshing', the figure of a peasant woman at work, on the right side of the huge ground lying in front of and providing a visual relief to the newly-built Havel House supposed to hold a permanent art exhibition at Santiniketan. This piece of sculpture reached a level of abstraction in search of the rhythm of life, an abstraction emanating from the experience of real life.[47]

This independent sculptor who has seldom done any requisionary work, never yearned for fame or money, had his sole loyalty to life itself—life at the grassroot level, life with its labour and love, pleasures and pains. From his bust of Rabindranath, executed towards the end of the poet's life, when the poet was smarting under a sense of 'the Crisis of Civilization', with his head bowed down and his usual majestic and dignified beauty notably absent[48] to his 'Siren of the Factory', depicting some working women, all his sculptures bear testimony to his concern for life.[49]

Pradosh Dasgupta[50] started from the base of a solid academic realism, imbibed from H. Roy Chowdhury and later from the Royal Academy of Arts in London, and then he broke away from this style as he turned his artist's vision on life as people around him actually lived. The horrors of the War and the Bengal Famine stirred him and found expression in his sculpture. Among his Famine pieces were 'The Exodus' of helpless people from the village to the city and 'Food Queue, 1944'. On the quality of these sculptures one would like to quote Bishnu Dey:

> I still think the artist himself is a little too harsh on his work of this period. He was afraid that the content of his sculptures of this phase was catchy enough to rouse easy emotions, and he was suspicious of their popular appeal and the favourable press reviews. Some of these pieces may be guilty, as he soon felt they were, of emotional excesses. But I don't think he is quite fair to call them bordering on sentimentalism. At any rate, we liked the artist's sympathy and courage to deal with real life in terms of art. And those of us who are used to the literary drama in D.P. Roy Chowdhury's sculpture were not at all upset. And, after all emotional excess is much more life-enhancing than an enforced fear of warm humanity. Prodosh moreover, never succumbs to the merely literary.

Bishnu Dey[51] also points out how Dasgupta largely succeeded in reconciling the drama of the social theme with his own formal urgency.

Prodosh Dasgupta moved forward and the next phase of his artistic progress was marked by a heightened self consciousness about basic forms. This not only showed his artistic mastery, but his mature humanness too. This is obvious from some of his pieces executed in the 1940s and the early 1950s: 'In Bondage' with its monumental quality expressing the African-American strength (1945—National Gallery of Modern Art), 'First Born (1946), 'Jai Hind' (1948), 'Mother and Child' (1949—Shri Arjun Roy), 'Condolence' (1950—Madras State Museum), 'Proud Mother' (1952), etc., and also his portraits of fellow artists—Nirad Majumder, Rathin Moitra and others. They all convey a sense of solidity, of visible and tactile physicality that is surely the essence of good sculpture.

Wood-cut, Linocut, Etching

It was the urge of the new generation of artists to make their creation available to a large number of people, and not only to a few rich ones and connoisseurs. This was the reason why Jamini Roy made numerous copies of his own works. He wanted them to find places in more homes and not to be priced high, and in this respect he proudly called himself a *Patua* with whom repetition was rather usual.

For artists connected with the Communist Movement, the multiplicity of single designs seemed all the more necessary to increase the utility of their posters quantitatively. The best, at least the most handy, way to do this was to issue prints. Sometime in 1946, an album of contemporary Chinese prints (wood-cuts) reached the cultural activists of Bengal and created quite a stir. They learnt how effectively and attractively an inexpensive and easily reproducible means of communication was being used in a country where literacy was then at about the same level as in India.

Another inspiring book was published from London during the Peace Movement of the post-War years. It contained twelve linocuts of Noel Counihan with poems by Jack Lindsay. By that time, of course, the Bengali artists had become competent printmakers. Chittaprosad excelled in linocuts on the very theme of peace.

The artists coming from middle-class families were not at all well off, and neither could the Party help them financially. As canvas and oil colours were costly, the only alternatives were drawing on paper, engraving cheap blocks or planks of wood and cutting linoleum to take prints on readily-available paper. The illegal phase of the Party particularly left the artists so down and out that they heavily resorted to print-making.

The beginners in Bengal naturally found the techniques of relief-printing mediums like wood-cut, wood-engraving, and linocut easier than intaglio methods like etching and dry-point. In the late 1940s and the early 1950s, there was a flood of wood-cuts and linocuts and the former seemed more popular. Talented artists gradually developed a medium-consciousness and tried to extract from the medium all its potency.

An article by Pranab Ranjan Ray helps us understand how Somnath Hore acquired a masterly grip over print-making through sheer hard labour. In fact, he later became known more as a print-maker than a painter. He took his first lessons in wood-cut and wood-engravings from Safiuddin Ahmed, later a well known printmaker of Bangladesh. He did his first couple of wood-engraving in 1947. One of them was 'Communal Harmony', a scene of a meeting being addressed by Gandhi (done just after the Great Calcutta killing of 1946 and the Bihar and the Noakhali riots of 1946–7). Another was 'Dukhiramer Ma', a portrait of an aged woman labourer in light and shade, done from a pen-and-ink sketch drawn earlier, from life, in a tea garden in Chittagong.

Somnath had an intimate experience of the Tebhaga struggle of Rangpur (1946–7). He returned to Calcutta with a great many sketches and images to utilize them as source materials for wood-cut and linocut. A few of them were published in the Party weeklies. By this time, he had acquired a grip over craftsmanship. He made the best use of his medium to depict group compositions of processions and congregations of resistance fighters with expressive figural gestures, though the figures themselves were fleeting impressionistic shapes in space. The light and shade used for chiaroscuristic purpose expressed the moods of the characters too, not an easy thing to do in wood-cut and wood-engraving which are basically atonal mediums. The cut-away whites and uncut blocks of the wood created rhythmic patterns in print, corresponding to the rhythm of the march of procession and of waving hands and heads in congregation. These wood-cuts were great improvement upon pieces like 'Dukhiramer Ma', which was nothing more than a mediocre academic work, though done with a lot of sympathy.

Somnath tried his hand at linocut to make posters for the Party during its illegal phase. His first pictorial linocut, as distinct from the posters, was 'A Chakma Mother and Child' (done on the basis of a 1944 drawing). He made his first multicolour wood-cut and the first black-and-white etching in 1954. And, from 1954 he was to go a long way in perfecting his print-making, particularly the intaglio methods.

Chittaprosad excelled in linocut. Apart from incarnating the hard life of toiling people, during the Peace Movement in the post-War period he envisaged happy, tender and loveable figures, especially of mothers and children representing the peace-loving humanity. In the Puja issue of *Parichay*, 1951, quite a few of these were published. In contrast with these pictures there was his album of twenty-two linocuts entitled 'Angels without Fairy Tales', depicting poor children deprived of all pleasures of life, done with equal competence.

The Communist artists did not resort to etching until much later. But an artist with no less humanitarian sympathy and perhaps greater concern for artistic experiments had started doing etching as early as the year of the Famine. This was Ramkinkar Beij. Among other themes of his etchings, picked up from the life of ordinary people, there was one captioned 'Hunger' inspired by the horror of the Famine. It shows a hungry boy, whose twisted body manifests his terrible pain. His head is big, mouth agape and eyes bulging out as if he wanted to devour the whole world to satisfy his hunger. A few other teenagers sitting in the rows of the *Langarkhana* are looking at him with eyes wide open.

Ramkinkar's experimentation with etching was, in fact, in keeping with the tradition of Kala Bhavan. Here, even before the 1940s, a spirit of all-round artistic experimentation had made the artists try their hand at print-making also. As in all other spheres of fine arts, here too Kala Bhavan had been one of the first to break new grounds. Sudhir Khastagir was another brilliant printmaker produced by Kala Bhavan. He did excellent wood-engravings and linocuts.

The Role of the Communist Party

Unlike music and theatre, the pictorial art of the 1940s did not develop under the direct auspices of the Communists. So while there were the 'People's Song Movement' and 'People's Theater Movement', there was no 'People's Art Movement' in Bengal during this decade.

There was, of course, the Anti-Fascist Writers' and Artists' Association which had a Fine Arts sub-committee headed by the artist Moni Roy.[52] It used to organize exhibitions, many of them itinerant ones, spot local talents, hold classes for the beginners and discuss contemporary art. Moni Ray provided the nucleus around whom this organization worked. Roy himself did postering, but also encouraged creative artists and tried his best to bring to the limelight the Calcutta Group of artists.[53] In 1945, the Bengal branch of the IPTA got separated from the AFWAA and the latter changed its name to the Progressive Writers' and the Artists' Association in anticipation of an imminent fascist defeat. Despite the exit of performing artists, it still retained the word 'artists' in its name, because the painters and other fine artists had become very important by that time, both quantitatively and qualitatively. According to Somnath Hore,[54] an artist's cell was formed within the Communist Party in 1948. It included Adinath Mukherjee, Bijan Chowdhury, Debkumar Roy Chowdhury, Nilratan Chatterjee, Kesab Majumdar, Moti Majumdar, Somnath himself, his wife Reba and a few others. They had close contact with Moni Roy and other Party men.

Art exhibitions were often to be a feature of the conferences and festivals organized by the Communist Party and other Communist organizations. The organizers of these exhibitions tried to make their countrymen conscious about the cruel and destructive war and Famine through pictures which were usually called posters. There were also posters on such themes as peasants resisting their exploiters, protecting the *aman* crop and so on. Soviet posters too were exhibited sometimes. Besides, they exhibited traditional handicrafts from different regions, e.g. the *Muslin* of Dhaka, the *Pot* art of Kalighat, etc. They felt it to be their duty to encourage these dying arts and their distressed craftsmen. Perhaps such dainty and refined creative works formed an illuminating contrast to the hard reality depicted in the posters and suggested peace and prosperity as the ultimate goal.[55]

In the case of music, the Communists of Bengal introduced new themes in the old folk-forms in order to enliven them all the more. They tried to do the same for handicrafts also and they knew how such restoration was being carried out in Russia and China.[56] But in the case of the Bengali Communists, such instances are very few. They made the clay-modelers of Krishnanagar model fighting peasants as well as mothers and children killed by a Japanese bomber. In an advertisement in the *Swadhinata*,[57] the manager of the Art Chamber, Krishnanagar, offered relief bust statues of P.C. Joshi and Rabindranath at a price of Rs. 10 for each five.[58] At the instance of Chinmohan Sehanabis, *Lakshmir Sara*[59] was decorated with a new motif—instead of the goddess Durga killing Mahisasur[60] it was now a militant peasant killing a jotedar looking like an *asur*. According to Sehanabis, the *Saras* were sold in Delhi for Rs. 5 each.

In 1944, The Students' Federation published a pictorial album consisting of drawings and paintings of young and old talents. This book entitled *Bengal Painters' Testimony* showed Communist appreciation of the evolution of pictorial art of Bengal in the direction of more and more social involvement, reaching a striking height during the Famine.[61]

But these direct art efforts of the Communists did not really mean much. The Party indeed played a very important role in bringing about a change in the art scenes of Bengal in the 1940s, but it did that indirectly. The heightened social consciousness that gave birth to a new art during this period owed a great deal to the Communist ideology and activities. Many artists of the new generation were associated with the Communist Party. So, though we have not called this chapter 'the Communist Art Movement' or 'the People's Art Movement', we have repeatedly referred to Communist (or leftist) artists, critics and the Party. It was not so much the 'pictorial art of politics', rather it was the 'political within pictorial art'—the political which primarily emanated from the social-human and was intensified in many cases through the hegemony of Communist ideology.

II

When we come to assess the direct role of the CPI in this phase of the art history of Bengal, its limitations become glaring. This was due to the 'politics of pictorial art' that the Party tried to conduct within its limited hold in this sphere. Most of the Party members were interested only so far as art would pay off immediately, i.e. in visual reportage and cartoons in the pages of Party periodicals and posters exhibitions to enlighten people on topical issues. The narrowness of their art interest was reflected in their demand that the artist should always concentrate on the exigency of the moment, depict specific socio-political situations, comment on aspects of social reality like the Japanese aggression or the Famine, or depict the conflict between the oppressing social classes and the oppressed. Ghulam Quddus complained in *Parichay* that Abedin's art following his Famine sketches were losing appeal and asked why the artist did not depict the contrast between jotedars and oppressed peasants in his village scenes, why he did not paint scenes of industrial strikes.[62]

Then again, a *Janayuddha* report on a poster exhibition held at 46 Dharmatala Street, proudly proclaimed: '. . . those who visited the exhibition realized that not only in politics, but in every field of art as well, the Communist Party has established its lead. At the exhibition even the most apolitical visitors found the Communist Party more prominent than the artists.'[63] So, establishing the Party's lead in the cultural field meant the Party outshining the artists in the very field of art. Certainly, this attitude would not create a condition favourable for the efflorescence of artistic latent. And it is this mentality of demanding 'ready payment' (*nagad aday* in the words of Chinmohan Sehanabis in a mood of self-criticism later) from art and artists that led the Communists to neglect great artists like Ramkinkar who was intensely sensitive to humanity and its social situation, but would not deal much with specific current problems and had nothing to do with the Communist Party.

Needless to say, social motivation does not express itself in the same way in all artists. Even the same artist can draw a specific political scene today and an ideational picture tomorrow. And yet if he is a good artist, he would successfully highlight the human significance of the political situation in the first one and retain a strong social consciousness while doing the second. Furthermore, even when the artist is in a protesting mood, the protest may not be direct and pronounced. He may protest through compelling depictions of sufferings of people (which does not conform to the then Communist aesthetic of 'socialist realism'), as in most of the Famine visuals. An artistic internalization of the external shock is a necessary condition for good art. After all, it is the sufferings of the artist himself, and not the mere representation of the actual people or event that delivers the political message to the viewers. Sometimes, even amidst a lot of social wrongs, the artist's social consciousness may seem affirmative rather than critical, such as when he is in an optimistic mood and sees himself as already representing the cherished future. Chittaprosad's linocuts responding to the peace movement and portraying happy children enjoying the plenitude and beauty of the world would exemplify the point.

Paritosh Sen was asked in an interview[64] whether after his paintings on the Famine of 1943 he did any more work on the significant subsequent occurrences of that eventful decade—the communal riots or the popular movements, for instance. Sen, who is considered as one of the leading socially conscious artists of Bengal since the 1940s, gave a negative answer and explained that social response does not always register itself so directly and sometimes even produces seemingly contradictory results. An artist may opt to shut out the stark externalities to negotiate with his disturbances within. Sen gave the example of George Braque who fought in the First World War and having been critically injured, lay in a trench for quite some time until some men came and rescued him. But strangely enough, as

Braque recovered and started painting again on his return from the war, no trace of his violent experience could be seen in his work. From then on his main theme was order and harmony.

III

The narrowness of the Communist art interest was also reflected in their intolerance of abstraction in art. In this respect, the Bengali Marxists were subject to the confusion of the contemporary world about the desirable form of visual art. A hot controversy was raging around Picasso at that time and Bengali readers were exposed to such view as that of an art critic whose article condemning some leading French artists in the *Modern Quarterly* was translated in *Arani*.[65] The critic wrote that some artists including Picasso, despite their membership of the French Communist Party and their depiction of the horrors of fascism, were obsessed with the desire to do something intelligent and in the process were alienating themselves from people. And this was the dominant view among the Communists. Those having this viewpoint were unhappy with Picasso doing the utmost violence to the human image, his tortured break-up of the human body (particularly during the ascendancy of fascism and culminating in the famous painting 'Guernica'). They saw in it an anti-human gesture of alienation rather than the artist's intense protest against the anti-human state of human order.

But as elsewhere, in Bengal also there were intellectuals who were unaffected by this anti-abstraction taboo. Bishnu Dey paid tribute to Picasso: 'He brushed aside the prevalent idea about the truth of object, and renewed the connection between the object and the subject, between the object and the seer, i.e. he who thinks on observing an object.'[66]

When some artists of the Calcutta Group were found guilty of too much abstraction, Bishnu Dey, being the friend, philosopher and guide of the Group, came immediately to their defence. He noticed a dilemma between naturalistic art and abstraction in Nirad Majumder and Rathin Moitra and was satisfied that their sense of form prevailed ultimately: '. . . that rare sense which is not scared of abstraction'. Dey asked these artists not to pay heed to the adverse criticism of some petite-bourgeois critics disguised as progressive and Marxist.[67]

An artist's visual objectification is always mixed up with his interpretation of the object. So even though he is realistic, he just cannot paint absolutely tangible things. Good art is different from photography and involves more or less abstraction. Paritosh Sen thus explained this[68]—there can be two kinds of abstraction in art. An artist can abstract a form from what he sees before his eyes or he can totally reject his observation and present something non-figurative (or non-objective). There is a big difference between these two kinds. Sen said,

> We never indulged in non-figurative abstraction. We tried to keep figures alright and to stylize them at the same time. We wanted to see how far we could remove art from reality while maintaining the reality. And this is the time-hounoured tradition in art everywhere—in Mexico, Japan, China, Egypt or Greece. Only during the Renaissance we had approximate representation of what we saw with our eyes. On the other hand, non-figurative abstraction has become obsolete even in America where it was once patronized most.

Sen further explained that the abstraction emerging out of observation is decided by what the artist sees with his mind's eyes and this in turn is influenced by the social forces of the time. When the twentieth century opened up new and glorious chapters in science, that made an impact on artists by sharpening their intellect and rationality. Artistic experiments became more scientific. According to Sen, this is what John Berger meant when he traced a connection between Cubism and the Theory of Relativity.

Perhaps, the Communists assumed that pictures designed to be seen by and to have an impact upon a wide public, i.e. peasants and workers, should be as close as possible to natural appearance. This shows an ignorance of the complexities of the process of perception; in fact, folk arts do usually involve abstraction. Even if we admit the need of a revolutionary party for a kind of propaganda art rendered as simply as possible and having an immediate and short-term effect upon the masses, we must differentiate from it the art intended to have a long-term effect, and perception and rendering of the latter would naturally involve complexities.

IV

People's art can become great art at the same time. But this would require deep thoughts about forms of art on the one hand and a certain maturity of the mass movement on the other. A good example is the mural art movement that developed in Mexico from the 1920s under the direct agency of the Communist Party.

A few words about this Mexican art would be relevant in this context. In Mexico there had been a drive to paint murals in the open exposed to the sun and rain and monumental in character, and these qualities made art more human and public and even heroic. It not only communicated with a large number of people and became public property, but the construction of such art, covering hundreds of square metres needed a considerable amount of team work, i.e. participation of the people. And all this they did by adapting the pre-Hispanic tradition of mural art in Mexico to the new theme of social revolution. The mural art movement headed by the famous trio—Orozco, Rivera and Siqueiros—found a place in the rank of the world art movement on terms of equality with Paris, the capital of the art world. For this, the Mexicans had to do their own hard thinking, even about 'tricks of technique'. The book *Art and Revolution*,[69] a collection of Siqueiros' writings, bears this out.[70] And Siqueiros admits that as they ceased to be 'Revolutionary amateurs' and became seasoned, their art attained its full bloom.

In India, instead of broadening the human and public nature of art in the process of a revolutionary struggle, the Communists tended to employ art in the immediate service of the public. Thus, they required no proper art theory to give intellectual guidance to the artists, though piecemeal attempts, sometimes thoughtful ones, were made by individuals tending to formulate such a theory. There were essays and art criticisms by enlightened intellectuals like Bishnu Dey. Then the Progressive Forum of College Street reprinted the book *On Revolutionary Art* that had been published by Messrs Wishart from London in 1935. It included essays as diverse in opinion as those of Herbert Read and A.L. Lloyd, though both justified abstraction in art.[71] Gopal Haldar, writing the introduction to this Indian edition entitled *Revolutionary Art: A Symposium*, expressed the hope that the five essays of the book would be of timely interest and lasting service in the construction of a revolutionary theory of art, 'for such theory and practice must go hand in hand and form a part of gigantic and complex process of our life and history that we call Indian Revolution'. But what Haldar saw as the 'fire' of Indian Revolution was soon extinguished. And the desirable art theory was never really constructed. If at all there was any Communist art theory in Bengal during the period of our study, it was dominated by too much of a fixation for the Soviet-type 'Socialist Realism', i.e. a kind of naturalistic art that was being officially sponsored in the Soviet Union at that time. There was little original thinking about development of art in India. The Communists were not serious about the efflorescence of art. It seems that they inherited the relative indifference about art, that had been prevalent in Bengal for a long time, and they continued with it.

In fact, if the Communists had a definite political and cultural programme, removing this lack of art-consciousness would have been one of their major tasks. They would have liked to create a new art-public, embracing not only middle-class people, but reaching down to the peasants and workers as well, to make people proud and conscious of the privilege of art, to inculcate a sense of national cultural tradition which art serves. But while they tried, however imperfectly and haphazardly, to build up a People's Theatre and a People's Song Movement, they had no plan for a People's Art Movement. The few art-exhibitions that they held were not enough.[72]

And yet if the Bengali Communists had looked at the actual art situation in Russia rather than the art theory prevalent in that country, they could have drawn some inspiration from the widespread public concern for art that was being generated there. It was a post-1917 development and was made possible by encouraging local Soviets and trade unions to commission and buy (but always through the central authority) works of art, by publishing albums, by founding and maintaining museums, by ensuring that there were references to works of art in school syllabus and so on. The public indifference to art as found in most countries including the most advanced ones of Western Europe and America would shock even the least-privileged provincial of the Soviet Union. It is another matter that the Russian art authority blocked the aesthetic development of the very public that it created for art.

V

The concept of Socialist Realism, born in post-Revolutionary Soviet Union, cast a strong influence in the world of Marxian aesthetics during the period of our study and affected all fields of arts. Here, we should form an idea about how this concept was being applied to the visual arts of Russia in the context of the history of art in that country.

In the eighteenth century, Peter the Great had autocratically imposed a kind of academism on Russian artists. This academic art had no popular roots, but was just an imitation of West European academic art—a naturalistic art that intended to present with maximum credibility the immediate scene, with the ideal aim of producing a replica. It involved no deep thoughts about forms and shirked all kinds of abstraction. By introducing this art, Peter the Great wanted to bring Russia on par with more-advanced Western Europe.

For a few years after 1917, Russian art was the very antithesis of that which had preceded it for nearly two centuries under the control of the Academy established by Peter the Great. 'We have taken by storm the Bastille of the Academy', claimed the art students. The artists served the state on their own initiative, enjoying freedom and experimented with modern methods like Cubism to enrich the Russian art.

But all this was stopped in 1932, when painting and sculpture in Russia were put under the centralized control of the Union of Artists directed by Isaac Brodsky, who had been trained in the pre-Revolutionary Academy and was already known for his very conservative attitude to art. This re-imposed a sterile academism and stifled all kinds of art except the naturalistic one. John Berger in his short but brilliant criticism of this post-1932 Russian art, later showed how the apologists for Socialist Naturalism—masquerading as Socialist Realism—tended to distract attention from the fundamental and very complex aesthetic problem of realism in visual arts.[73]

And yet the vast Russian public to whom this art was disseminated by a centralized government accepted it with apparent satisfaction. For so long they had no experience of art and now this was the only art made available to them. Moreover, it corresponded in form and style (with gilt frames even!) to the art of the old ruling class, and this flattered the ordinary people. So the new socialist art could be justified and glorified on the grounds of popularity.[74] No wonder, the Indian Communists found the naturalistic Russian art exemplary.

But the Soviet art exhibition held in Calcutta in 1952 came as an eye-opener. The large number of huge paintings created a sensation in the city. Yet, the general reaction of artists and art critics to this exhibition was one of dissatisfaction. All the critics did admit that state patronization of art was highly commendable; they also did not mind the propaganda element in Soviet art. Yet O.C. Ganguly, a leading non-leftist art-critic, found that art pictographic, an imitation of mid-nineteenth century European art and devoid of imagination. According to him, the Revolution that had taken place in Russia and in art-forms other than painting in that country had not left its mark on pictorial art. D.P. Mukherjee and Bishnu Dey were a bit more sympathetic, but hesitant in their appreciation. Mukherjee for instance, found Russian art abounding in ideal-type peasant-like Russian heroes, and because these heroes were not natural, their images involved, according to him, a certain amount of abstraction. But he found this art suffering from much inhibition and on the whole it could not captivate his mind. Only a few artists of the academic realistic school of Bengal whole-heartedly approved of the Soviet art. This included J.P. Ganguly and Atul Bose.[75]

VI

The CPI could not do much either to create an art public or to guide the artists. So it was gradually displaced from its high position in the art world of Bengal. The artists once close to the Communist Party went their own individual ways one by one. The Party could not accommodate them either materially or spiritually. The process started in the late 1940s with the break-up of the original Calcutta group.

A story narrated by Somnath Hore, a devoted and active party member even in the early 1950s, is quite revealing.[76] While Somnath was acting whole-heartedly for the Party, confusion was gradually creeping in. The first great shock came on the occasion of the Railway strike called by the Communist Party on 9 March 1949. The headstrong Party was moving in the direction of 'Revolution' without taking into cognizance the real situation, though many local activists felt that a revolutionary situation had not yet developed in their areas, and that the people were not really enthusiastic. On the day before the scheduled strike, Somnath went underground to avoid arrest. But 9 March was a total fiasco. The rashness and futility of Randive's line was proved beyond doubt.

He spent a few months in an adventurous fugitive life. Then in 1950 the Party had a *volte face*, a total reversal of the revolutionary policy. There was even more confusion. But Somnath was still working for the Party, though at the same time he was feeling the need to concentrate more on his art and improve his techniques. In 1951, he presented the Communist Party with its election symbol—sickle and corn.

In 1952, the Soviet Art Exhibition was held in Calcutta. But Somnath did not like those paintings. While he admired their handling, it seemed to him that their photographic nature prevented them from feeding the viewers' thoughts. For the first time, it occurred to him that an artist should think and rethink about the form of art. He had already seen a bit of Picasso and other so-called abstract artists of the West. But at that time he had thought in terms of Socialist Realism, and hence failed to find a rapport with such art. However, at the same time it had made him think. Discontented with the Soviet art exhibition, supposed to be the best examples of Socialist Realism, he now felt free to accept Picasso-type art. Second, Somnath felt that he would have to search for an Indian identity for his art. This was his personal feeling and probably his search for an Indian identity made him join Visva-Bharati. A new phase in his career began.

Disillusioned with the Communist Party and full of fresh thoughts about art, he gradually came away from the Communist fold in the 1950s. He did not renew his membership of the Party, but he maintained cordial relationship with individual Communists. He says that he did not miss the Party much in his pursuit of art, because, by his own admission, it was not so much the understanding of Communism as the sheer sufferings of men that moved his artist's soul. His life's work of art can be explained in terms of his experiences of the Bengal Famine. He was never able to get over it. He could not think of any other theme than wounded and dying men and animals, although he experimented with varied ways to express this theme.

Chittaprosad Bhattacharya, who remained in the Communist Party, suffered badly. He was gradually gripped by a sense of futility. The Communist fold where he had taken shelter could not give him any support, material or mental. P.C. Joshi who had acted as his mentor and given him abundant encouragement suffered humiliation at the second Party Congress in 1948 and this was a shock to Chittaprosad. He was ill-treated and cheated by some so-called Communists on different occasions. His letters to a friend written in the 1950s bear testimony to his disappointment.

> I don't remember whether I wrote to you about my plan of doing something constructive using the medium of linocut. Linocut is able to spread pictures, i.e., the story of this land all over the country, even the world, with little expenses and in no time, which we cannot do possibly by depending on exhibitions or patrons or on journals for black-and-white reproductions. But even linocut needs help of mass organizations and of a progressive press; that is, if the Party does not have art consciousness, this would be as futile as my children series, all my labour and self-sacrifice will be lost. It is here that I have come to a dead-end of heart-breaking despair.[77]

He busied himself with puppet-making to forget all disappointments. He continued to do other kinds of artistic works also. But that disappointment could not be overcome till the last day of his life.

So in the 1940s, no revolutionary art theory was born in Bengal, nor was there a great efflorescence of art as part of a broader mass movement. But this should not cause us much regret from the point of view of art. For, after all, in this decade, a new concept of art took shape—a realistic concept, or rather a humanistic concept (for, the primary and the essential subject of realistic art is human being). And that this recently-refreshed notion did not fit into definition like 'Socialist Realism' or any other 'ism' was perhaps fortunate for the art of the 1940s. It left enough freedom for individual artists to make varied experiments and thus produced a wealth of art. The relative indifference of the Communist Party to fine arts was, in a sense, good for the artists who could derive inspiration generally from the Communist ideology and yet were not subject to much control by the Party authority and the resultant bitterness that vitiated the atmosphere in other fields of creativity. They were also spared the disappointment of the break-up of an art movement, as in the cases of the 'People's Song Movement' and the 'People's Theatre Movement'.

The art of the 1940s would fit in beautifully with the definition of realistic art given by Sidney Finkelstein in the 1950s in his book *Realism in Art*, written from a Marxist point of view:[78]

> Realistic art is not simply art that portrays recognizable people and objects from nature. It reveals both the individuality of human beings and their similarity to masses of other human beings who, for all their widely different appearance and background, lead similar lives and face the same problems. It awakens people to the beauty of nature and also to the beauty of human beings. It portrays the social relationships in which people are engaged, the forces that injure them and ties that

bind them together. By its choice of subjects, it shows how the world is changing, and what is new, stirring and rising among people in society.

Finkelstein traced the relation between artistic beauty and real life in painting from its primitive origins to date. As the reality changes, so does the realistic art over the ages. At every new stage it achieves even greater and more critical reality.[79]

According to Chinmohan Sehanabis, Finkelstein's book had a deep influence on Bengali leftists in the 1950s, and whatever its limitations, the book must have helped them to overcome the inhibitions and confusions of the 1940s to some extent. This in its turn should have made it easier for them to realize at last the significance of the art of the 1940s. The Bengali artists of the 1940s overtook the Bengal School and took a step forward in the realm of reality, or rather adjusted themselves to the new reality of the day. Through them, the common people forced their life and character into art, appearing now as never before as a powerful moving force in history. And each artist chose his own form to depict the loving, suffering and fighting humanity. New thoughts started about forms of art too. Thus, on the whole, Bengali art came of age in the 1940s.

APPENDIX I

Exhibitions

A few examples of art exhibitions held on different occasions of political and peasants' meetings, as reported in the Party periodicals and other publications, are given below.

From the Janayuddha

A poster exhibition decorated the anti-fascist assembly at Dhalghat, Chittagong, on 3 August 1942. It was organized by the Students' Federation (*Janayuddha*, 19 August 1942).

An art exhibition at No. 46 Dharmatala Street was facilitated by the assembly of artists from all the districts on the occasion of the Provincial Party Conference. The reporter of *Janayuddha* says that here the posters were much more vigorous than the lifeless and anti-people national War Front posters. Chittaprosad contributed a number of posters highlighting the food-problem, calling for unity, satirizing the bureaucracy, exposing the conspiracy of the imperialists and so on. Two posters of the Students' Front were of high quality. There was also art from Soviet Russia on the Nazi oppression, rearing of babies, etc. Clay-modellers from Krishnanagar contributed models of peasants' huts destroyed by the Japanese bombers and of mothers and children killed by the Japanese (*Janayuddha*, 14 April 1943).

A huge gathering was organized by the Communist Party at the University Institute Hall. A poster exhibition was held one hour before the session. Some of the best drawings of Chittaprosad, a few pictures brought from the USSR, drawings of the District Committee workers manifesting the work and the main slogans of the Party were shown (*Janayuddha*, 7 July 1943).

The Students' Federation organized a meeting in Dinajpur on 28 and 29 April 1943. It was presided over by Sukumar Sen. Here Biren Dasgupta's posters drew attention (*Janayuddha*, 12 May 1943).

'Arrangement for protecting the *Aman*[80] crops' was the name of an art exhibition organized in Mymensingh by Moni Roy on behalf of the AFWAA. It depicted the distress of peasants on the one hand and the determination and signs of salvation on the other (*Janayuddha*, 29 December 1943).

The Communist Party held classes for art training during 19–26 January 1994 in Calcutta. The teacher was Moni Roy. Eight students attended his classes from eight different districts. Sudhin Sen of Murshidabad received the prize for the best poster (*Janayuddha*, 16 February 1944).

At the Burdwan Provincial Peasants' Conference (13 March 1945), big clay models of a peasant and a peasant woman made by Amulya Rana of Memari stood just in front of the exhibition ground. There were depictions of the miseries of the peasants on the one hand and of the glorious history of the peasants' movements on the other. Many informative posters for the peasants and handicrafts of the districts of Burdwan, Birbhum, Bankura and Darjeeling were exhibited (*Janayuddha*, 22 March 1945).

At the All-India Kisan Conference at Netrokona, Nirod Majumder and his artist friends decorated the dais with hard labour. Lakshmi Pal, a clay-modeller of Krishnanagar, made a statue of a spirited peasant modelled on Hriday Sarkar, a peasant leader of the Tank Movement,The statue was placed at the gate (*Janayuddha*, 19 April 1945).

From AFWAA Reports

The *Half-yearly and Annual Reports of the AFWAA* in its third year (1945) contained reports of the Fine Arts Subcommittee. A glance at them would reveal that the organizers used art as a powerful mass-medium.

The Bengal Squad of the IPTA visiting Punjab to convey the miseries of the Famine-stricken Bengalis and to raise funds for them, took along some drawings. The artists were Surya Roy, Lakshmi Roy, Moni Roy, Ranu Pakrashi among others.

They printed 6000 copies of three pictures of the distressed and sent them to different provinces for sale at a price of 4 *annas* each. Within three months, these were all sold out, and despite the continuing demand, no more copies could be printed due to non-availability of paper. (From an advertisement inserted by the Cultural Cell, Bengal Committee of the Communist Party in the *Janayuddha*, 17 November 1943, it is learnt that these three posters had been designed by Moni Roy of the Provincial Cultural Cell.)

Moni Roy, on behalf of the Association, toured the district of Mymensingh with 45 pictures and posters. Exhibitions were organized at Mymensingh, Netrokona, Lengura, Sherpur, Jamalpur, Kishoreganj, Katiadi, Bajitpur, Karimgunj and Muktagacha (ten places in total). On the final day, at the town of Mymensingh, the exhibition was presided over by Dr Shahidullah who took great interest in the artists' works.

Soon after the second annual conference of the AFWAA (January 1944) drawing classes were held under the leadership of Moni Roy. Ten trainees from eight districts attended these classes which were held for seven days. Here they were taught methods of drawing. The question of the artist's responsibility towards society was also discussed. Drawings of renowned artists were displayed. Emphasis was put on line-drawing. In seven days the students drew at least 60 pictures. A prize was given to the best one (Corroborated by report in *Janayuddha*).

Exhibitions were held at eight places—Naihati, Howrah, Chandannagar, Barishal, Phulbari (Dinajpur), Burdwan, Jagaddal, and Mahirampur. About 34,000 people attended. The exhibition at the Barishal Women's Conference drew almost 2,500 women, many of them living under the aristocratic 'purdah' system. The exhibition at the provincial Peasants' Conference at Phulbari had 15,000 peasant visitors. (A report of the *Janayuddha*, 8 March 1944 says that the exhibition was organized by Moni Roy and inaugurated by the Communist leader Panchugopal

Bhaduri. Inside the pavilion there was a pillar erected in the memory of the deceased peasant workers of Dinajpur.)

Two exhibition were held at the Calcutta University Institute, attended by 2,000 tram workers and 1,000 students.

In April 1944, under a project undertaken by the AFWAA, Moni Roy visited different villages of the district of Dhaka and drew 90 pictures of ailing villagers. These were sent to the exhibition called 'Bengal Gripped by Epidemic' organized at Agra. The visitors sympathized and contributed to the fund of the Bengal Medical Relief Co-ordination Committee.

In May 1944, a three-day exhibition was held in their Central office. It was named 'Bhukha Bangla', and the artists were mainly from Calcutta: Ramen Chakraborty, Satish Sinha, Zainul Abedin, Gobardhan Ash, Sunil Dasgupta, Indra Dugar, Motilal Dasgupta Makhan Dasgupta, Adinath Mukherjee, Rathindra Maitra, Bimal Majumdar, Anwarul Haq, Kamrul Hasan, Saifuddin Ahmed, Muralidhar Tali, Habibullah Khan, K. Ahmed and others. The renowned artist Atul Basu, the photographer Sambhu Saha, the critic Arun Sen and many students of the art school visited this exhibition. An American soldier bought a picture by Gobardhan Ash. Each day, there were almost 200 visitors. On the final day there was a seminar on 'Advancement of the Soviet Art', presided over by Abu Sayeed Ayub. Arun Sen (Bar at law) delivered a lecture showing slides. Radharaman Mitra talked about the responsibility of artists in the prevailing crisis. The exhibition was financed by Rathindra Moitra, a worker of the Association. Indra Dugar, Surya Roy and other artists rendered a lot of help (corroborated by a report in *Arani*, 2 June 1944).

At the Pakistan Renaissance Conference at Islamia College, the AFWAA organized an exhibition of 70 pictures. About 1,500 visitors came in three days. Each admission ticket cost 4 paise. The money collected was donated to the Relief Committee.

In 1944, the AFWAA planned to convene conferences at border regions to strengthen the organization. One such conference was held in Dhaka. On that occasion, there was an art exhibition. Pictures of the Famine and the crisis in education in East Bengal drawn by local artists and artists of the bordering districts were exhibited. The exhibition received about 5,000 visitors.

Meanwhile the People's Relief Committee sent for an artist to draw pictures of an epidemic raging in Mymensingh. Moni Roy was elected for the work. His experience of the tour of about 30 villages was depicted in 50 heart-rending pictures.

With these pictures they went to the Bengal Progressive Writers and Artists' Conference at Berhampore. Local artists were brought together and 45 of them contributed pictures to the art exhibition. (From the report of the activities of the different branches of the AFWAA, preceding the sub-committee report, it seems that this was possible because of the efficiency of the Murshidabad branch. They had already arranged a pottery exhibition on the occasion of the district conference on 16 May 1945). Besides the pictures of the Famine, there were clay models, embroidery work, silken things, letters of Maharaja Nandakumar and Rani Bhavani and a few embroidered *saris* of the Nawabi regime. Drawings by the students of the local Deaf and Dumb school were also displayed. 6,500 visitors attended. The originally planned two-day exhibition was extended for one more day on people's request. The artist Sarashi Majumdar was profusely admired. On the final day of the exhibition a meeting was convened. A permanent exhibition committee of 15, including a Hindu and a Muslim lady, was formed. This committee was to contact different artists, organize exhibitions every year and work for the advancement of handicrafts.

In November 1944, a cultural class was held at the office of the AFWAA, Students came from various districts. Rathin Moitra and Moni Roy held two classes on the art of drawing, forms, methods and drawing materials.

They held a seminar at the office of the AFWAA soon after the Puja to discuss the pictures published in various Puja magazines. It was inaugurated by Moni Roy and joined by Gopal Haldar, Swarnakamal Bhattacharya and others.

About 900 pictures and posters were handed over to the People's Relief Committee on their request for exhibitions in Bengal and other provinces. They organized 20 such exhibitions visited by 70,000 people.

In conclusion, the Annual Report delightfully acknowledged the cooperation they had received from local patriots for these mobile exhibitions, and expressed satisfaction about the way they had been able to move people. Then, it stressed the need for a permanent mobile exhibition for Bengal with more pictures, posters and magic lanterns; the need for revival of handicrafts, particularly the clay modelling of Krishnanagar, *Pot* art of Kalighat, ivory work of Murshidabad, *Pot* art of Dhaka, bell-metal art of Khagra, Palang, Arambag, Bikrampur and Islampur of Mymensingh; and finally the necessity of keeping a permanent exhibition-cum-sales room in Calcutta containing these crafts and also pictures.

From Other Sources

We have learnt about more exhibitions from contemporary periodicals. A few examples: At the AFWAA conference at Muhammad Ali Park (3–8 March 1945) an art exhibition named 'Amar Desh' (My Country) was inaugurated by Asit Kumar Haldar. Pictures by Atul Bose, Ramen Chakrabarty, Benodebehari Mukhopadhyay, Sudhir Khastagir, Zainul Abedin, Satish Sinha, Shaila Chakrabarty, Gobardhan Ash, Rathin Moitra, Makhan Dasgupta, Muralidhar Tali and Moni Roy were shown. Other exhibits were the *Muslin* of Dacca and the pottery of Krishnanagar. (*Arani*, 23 March 1945)

An art exhibition was held at Panjia showing pictures on the theme of the reconstruction of peasants' life. It was extremely informative. Samples of the fine craftsmanship of the women of Panjia were also displayed (*Swadhinata*, 21 January 1945).

The All India Peace and Culture Conference at the Park Circus Maidan (1–6 April 1952) held an art exhibition in one corner of the pavilion. The works of some young artists dealing with the theme of peace and its splendour were exhibited. There were also textiles from Kashmir and Manipur, stone-made artifacts from Agra, and the paintings of Kashmiri artists on huge flower-vases made of paper on display. In contrast, there were photographs from the *Statesman* depicting the horrors of the last World War. The exhibition was inaugurated by Mulk Raj Anand on 6 April (*Parichay*, Baisakh, 1359 and *Natun Sahitya*, April 1952).

APPENDIX II

Bengal Painters' Testimony

On the occasion of the 8th Annual Conference of the All India Students' Federation, December 1944, a picture album entitled *Bengal Painters' Testimony*, edited by Arun Dasgupta, Kamrul Hasan, Adinath Mukherjee and Saifuddin Ahmed, was published. The sale proceeds of the album, priced Rs. 5 each, were to go to the relief work of the AISF. The blue paper of its cover, decorated with the serene face of a woman by Jamini Roy, was supplied by the Mahila Atmaraksha Samity from their paper-making centre run by destitute women.

In the 'Foreword', Sarojini Naidu paid tribute to the artists of Bengal who had 'paid the homage of love and pity to the vast anonymous legion of the hunger-stricken and heroic Bengal'. In his 'Introduction' ('Visions of Bengal') to the album, Bishnu Dey traced the art history of Bengal from the days of nationalist upsurge, i.e. the Bengal School, to Jamini Roy, Rabindranath Tagore and the recent Calcutta Group. He regretted that 'Gaganendranath Tagore, the painter of slashing cartoons and poetical book illustrations who also experimented with cubist forms, could not be included in the album'.

Not all the pictures were on hunger-stricken Bengal. The Bengal School and its masters were, represented. There was even Ramendranath Chattopadhyay's wood-cut 'Peacock', in which it is difficult to find any social motive at all, though it was a good example of experimentation with a new medium that was to come in handy for the social purpose of wide circulation of pictures. On the other hand, there was Abanindranath's 'The End of the Journey', a camel collapsing flat on its face, a typical Bengal School picture in style, but the pathos and even the theme would remind the viewers of the famished villagers coming to the city and dying on the streets there. Those represented in the album were Rabindranath, Abanindranath (Tricolour), Nandalal Bose (2), Asit Kumar Haldar, Debi Prasad Ray Chowdhury (2), Ramkinkar Beij, Benodebehari Mukhopadhyay, Atul Bose, Jamini Roy, Jamini Ganguly (Tricolour), Sudhir Khastagir, Ramendranath Chattopadhyay (Wood-cut), Manindra Gupta (Tricolour), Subho Tagore, Zainul Abedin (2), Dilip Dasgupta, Gopal Ghosh, Indra Dugar, Rathin Moitra, Nirad Majumdar, Pradosh Dasgupta, Abani Sen, Kamrul Hasan, Muralidhar Tali (Wood-cut), Saifuddin Ahmed (Wood-cut), Adinath Mukherjee (Wood-cut), and Chittaprosad (Sketch).

Many of the art-works mentioned in this chapter were printed in *Bengal Painters' Testimony*.

Notes and References

1. Asit Kumar Haldar's book *Rabitirtha*, quoted by Benodbehari Mukhopadhyay in *Chitrakar*, Kolkata: Aruna Prakashani, 3rd edn., 1388/1981, p. 182.
2. It was during the annual exhibition of the Indian Society of Oriental Art, December 1919. This incident has been narrated by the famous art critic

O.C. Ganguly in his book *Bharater Shilpa O Amar Katha*, Kolkatta: A. Mukherjee and Company, 1376/1969, p. 183. Ganguly was an eye-witness to this incident.

3. *Pot* art—a sort of scroll painting used by itinerant storytellers of Bengal villages. Traditionally the themes were religious or mythological. This art also flourished near the famous Kali temple of Kalighat, Calcutta, in the nineteenth century.
   Alpana—a kind of decorative folk art, applied by the women of rural Bengal on different festive occasions in executing various designs on floors and walls.
   Kantha—cotton wrappers on which the village women used to sew exquisite designs.
4. Tapati Guha-Thakurta, 'Locating Gandhi in Indian Art History: Nandalal and Ramkinkar', *Addressing Gandhi*, New Delhi: Sahmat, 1995.
5. Asok K. Bhattacharya, 'Silpi Bhola Chatterjee', *Saraswat*, Sharadiya, 1389.
6. Introduction of the brochure published on the occasion of this exhibition; quoted by Asok K. Bhattacharya.
7. Kumar Sinha, 'Modern Movement of Indian Art', *Four Arts Annual*, 1935.
8. Asok K. Bhattacharya—'Indian Society of Oriental Art in Retrospect', *Journal of the Indian Society of Oriental Art*, 75th Anniversary Special Number, 1981–3, ed. Gopen Ray and Krishna Deva.
9. Included in Sudhi Pradhan's *Marxist Cultural Movement*, vol. II (1947–58), Kolkata: Navana, 1982.
10. In an essay entitled 'Shilpi O Samaj'.
11. This article was entitled 'Shilpe Samajik O Rajnaitik Prabhav'.
12. 'Adhunik Shilpa Alochana', *Janayuddha*.
13. Chittaprosad Bhattacharya, 'Chhabir Sankat', *Arani*, Sharadiya, 1942.
14. Benodebehari Mukhopadhyay, *Chitrakar*, op. cit., p. 38.
15. Bishnu Dey's collection.
16. Interview, Paritosh Sen, at his flat on Sarat Banerjee Road, April 1985.
17. All this is obtained from: (a) Atanu Basu, 'Rathin Moitra: Bangla Chitrakalar Palabadal', *Pratikshan*, 2 August 1983. It is, in fact, an interview with Rathin Moitra. (b) Pradosh Dasgupta, 'The Calcutta Group: Its Aims and Achievements', *Lalit Kala Contemporary*, vol. 31 (nd), sometime in the early 1980s. We will use these articles many more times in this section for reminiscences and opinions of Moitra and Dasgupta.
18. This was the most common theme for the artists depicting the Famine—Indra Dugar's 'Madona' and many more examples can be given.
19. Nihar Ranjan Ray's collection. Seen at his home in Calcutta.
20. *Janayuddha*, 19 April 1945.
21. All these art works of Subho Tagore are available in an album published sometime in the 1940s. *May Day and Other Poems* was published by the Book Emporium Ltd., Calcutta, 1945.
22. For details about Prankrishna Pal's art see: (a) Rathin Mitra, 'Prankrishna Pal: Shilpi Jibaner Ruprekha', *Ekshan*, Grishma, 1391/1984. (b) Asok Bhattacharya, 'Shilpi Prankrishna Pal', *Saraswat*, Kartik-Paus, 1376/1969.

23. *Modern Art Publication*, vol. III, way back in the 1940s.
24. Arun Sen, 'Rikhiyay Nirad Majumdar', *Parichay*, Sharadiya, 1978.
25. Quoted in the brochure published on the occasion of the last exhibition of the Calcutta Group.
26. P.R. Ray, 'To carry the Roots in the Veins', *Lalit Kala Contemporary*, New Delhi, pp. 24–5.
27. Arun Sen, 'Rikhiyay, Nirad Majumdar', *Parichay.*
28. Interview, Paritosh Sen.
29. Mulk Raj Anand, 'Prolegomena to Contemporary Indian Painting', *Marg*, 1944, quoted by Pradosh Dasgupta.
30. It must be admitted that Bombay had been progressing in a new direction of art for quite sometime and thus it was already prepared to welcome the Calcutta Group and work with it. As early as 1942, the Spartacus Group had been formed there comprising P.T. Reddy and others. They too had revolted against the Bengal School and thought in terms of internationalism. On the whole, the Spartacus Group, the Calcutta Group and the Bombay Progressive Group shared the same attitude towards art.
31. *Swadhinata*, 28 November 1952.
32. Anti-Fascist Writers' and Artists' Association.
33. For Abedin's Famine sketches and other works see *Art of Bangladesh Series, Vol. I*—Zainul Abedin, ed., Dr Muhammad Sirajul Islam, Bangladesh Silpakala Academy, The National Academy of Fine and Performing Arts of Bangladesh.
34. *People's War*, 21 June 1945. Gholam Quddus, 'Shilpi Zainul Abedin', *Parichay*, Agrahayan, 1353/1946.
35. Bachofen, *Das Mutherrecht.*
36. Sources for the art-work and the life of Debabrata Mukherjee: (a) *Mukhar* (Literary Magazine)—Debabrata Mukhopadhyay Number, ed. Dwijen Ghosh, December 1981–March 1982. (b) Brochure published on the occasion of a felicitation given to the artist at Gorky Sadan, 24 January 1984. (c) Interview, Debabrata Mukherjee, January 1985.
37. Ardhendu Kumar Gangopadhyay (O.C. Gangooly), *Bharater Shilpa O Amar Katha*, op. cit.
38. For the art-works and the life of Chittaprosad: (1) Interview, Gouri Chatterjee, the artist's younger sister. (2) Interview, Kalpataru Sengupta, a prominent Communist leader of Chittagong during the period of our study. (3) Private papers of Chinmohan Sehanabis. (4) Catalogue published on the occasion of an art exhibition of Chittaprosad at Calcutta Information Centre in November 1980, organized jointly by Chittaprosad Art Archive and the Department of Information and Cultural Affairs, Government of West Bengal. (5) 'Chittaprosader Chithi' (Letters of Chittaprosad), *Parichay*, Sharadiya 1981. (6) A recent publication, Prakash Das, ed., *Chittaprasad* (a collection of visuals a writings by Chittaprosad himself and by others on him), Gangchil, Kolkata, 2011. (7) An exhibition of Chittaprosad's works put together by Sanjoy Kumar Mallik and organized by the Delhi

Art Gallery in July 2011. Two volumes of *Chittaprosad 1915–1978: A Retrospective*, compiled and edited by Sanjoy Kumar Mallik were published on this occasion, which also saw the publication of *Hungry Bengal: A Tour Through Midnapur District, By Chittaprosad, in November 1943* (a book that had become very rare), *Yours, Chitta: Translated Excerpts from Select Letters of Chiitaprosad* and *A Sketchbook of 30 Portraits by Chittaprosad*, all of them owing to the painstaking research of Sanjoy Kumar Mallik.

39. It was published in book-form in 1969 by the Danish UNICEF Committee.
40. Sources for Somnath Hore: (a) Pranab Ranjan Ray, 'Hunger and the Painter; Somnath Hore & The Wounds' *Transactions*, vol. I, no. 2, Winter 1981, published by CRESSIDA. (b) Somnath Hore, 'Tebhagar Diary', *Ekshan*, Saradiya, 1981. (c) Interview, Somnath Hore.
41. Khudiram's statue, one of the best memorial statues in Calcutta is Tapas Dutta's handiwork.
42. November 1985.
43. Sitesh Dasgupta remembers that three of them used to meet very often at a spot near the crossing of Southern Avenue and Lansdowne Road (Extension) where there stood three palm trees, very close to each other and looking like intimate friends. They used to sit at the foot of these trees and discuss literature, art and politics. They were nicknamed BATASI (Bani, Tapas, Sitesh) by the local people.
44. I am referring to Sanjay Mallik's article 'History-Art-Art History', an earlier version of which was presented at a national seminar on 'Cultural Representations as Historical Processes' organized by the Department of History, Jadavpur University in March 2010. The article placed side by side with the present chapter will show how a scholar is guided by his/her background and the related concerns. Mallik, being an art historian and moreover a faculty member of Kala Bhavan, Santiniketan, pays special attention to the 'contextual modernism'(the phrase has been coined by R. Siva Kumar) of the Bengal school experimentation of the 1940s. I am aware of the importance of these experiments, but I have dealt with this very briefly. Rather I have paid a lot more attention to the role of Communist politics in this connection. As I have been saying from the beginning, this book is more politically than aesthetically engaged.

    I, however, quite appreciate Mallik's following example of socially-humanly motivated art independent of any political agenda—Benodebehari's mural depicting medieval Hindi saint-poets at Hindi Bhavan, Santiniketan, at a time when a communal war was ravaging the country. Mallik appropriately quotes R. Siva Kumar about this mural: 'The mural was painted against the unfolding tragedy although not in direct response to it. ... In the manner in which he depicted his protagonists and constructed his mural we see a humanity emerging that stands in counterpoint to the macabre dance of death and life he saw around him. It was his belief that art reflected the humanity of the artist, not through the obvious subject of his work but through an uncompromising exercise of freedom.'

45. Sudhir Khastagir, *Myself*, published by the author from Chandbagh, Dehradun (n.d.).
46. *Contemporary Indian Art Series*, the volume on Pradosh Dasgupta, Lalit Kala Akademi, 1961, Bishnu Dey's 'Introduction'.
47. This sculpture was uprooted in the birth centenary year of Tagore to provide space for building a girl's hostel named after a prominent industrialist.
48. Adverse criticisms were made of it since it does not fit the popular idea about Tagore's appearance.
49. Sources for Ramkinkar: (a) Sobhan Som, *Shilpi, Silpa O Samaj* (The Chapter on Ramkinkar), Kolkatta: Anustup Prakashani, 1982. (b) *Contemporary Indian Art Series—Ramkinkar*, Lalit Kala Akademi, first published 1961, repr. 1981
50. Sources for Pradosh Dasgupta: (a) *Contemporary Indian Art Series—Pradosh Dasgupta*, Lalit Kala Akademi. (b) Pradosh Dasgupta, *My Sculpture*, Calcutta: Oxford Book and Stationery, 1955.
51. *Contemporary Indian Art Series—Pradosh Dasgupta*, 'Introduction' by Bishnu Dey.
52. Though its first Secretary was Rathin Moitra, according to Sudhi Pradhan in 'Chittaprosad o Challisher Marxbadi Samskritik Andolane Chitrakalar Bhumika' in *Chittaprasad*, edited by Prakash Das, op. cit.
53. Moni Roy, who had once been a militant nationalist, joined the CPI and helped it greatly by organizing art activities. He also designed the first headpiece of *Janayuddha*. See Sudhi Pradhan, ibid.
54. Interview, Somnath Hore, October 1984.
55. See Appendix I for a list of these art exhibitions.
56. For example, in 1951 a Chinese art exhibition was held at the Indian Art School under the initiative of the India–China Friendship Organization. The reporter of the *Natun Sahitya*, June 1951, noticed that the Chinese artists were using their chisels to engrave on stone the day-to-day reality of reconstruction of China's socio-economic order instead of the traditional dragons, Gods and Goddesses.
57. 28 February 1946.
58. The statues were 5″ x 7″, to be kept on tables or walls. Special concessions were announced for the agents of *Swadhinata*, the profit being meant for the periodical's fund.
59. An earthen plate required for worshipping the goddess Lakshmi.
60. Mahisha, a demon of the Hindu mythology. He used to harass the gods. So the Goddess Durga killed him.
61. See Appendix II.
62. *Parichay*, Agrahayan, 1353/1946.
63. 'Agrani Shilpir Dal', *Janayuddha*, 14 April 1943.
64. Interview, Paritosh Sen, April 1985.
65. 31 May 1946 and 7 June 1946.
66. Bishnu Dey, 'Picasso', *Sahityer Bhabishyat*, Kolkata: Signet Press, 1952.
67. Bishnu Dey, 'Calcutta Group', ibid.
68. Interview, Paritosh Sen.

69. Siqueiros, *Art and Revolution*, London: Lawrence and Wishart, 1975.
70. His suggestion of imposition of the constructive spirit upon the purely decorative, emphasis upon geometrical structure of form and on interplay of volume and perspective which combine to create depth rather than on colour and line which are expressive elements of the decorative rank, also his working out of other and even finer details just amaze us. His warning against the naive exaltation of popular (folk) art which might just create 'Mexican Curios' to be sold to tourists and yet his urge to develop the seeds of geographical, social and racial values lying in folk art into real work of art (for folk art, however beautiful, has its limitation. After all, it is creation of the people who have been slaves for centuries) shows how mature the Mexican art movement became, and this was possible due to the maturity reached by the revolutionary movement there.
71. Lloyd, for instance, discussed how Picasso's cubism had departed from the old type of cubism in its search for reality:

    Abstract idealism building patterns out of metaphysical interpretation of bodies in space could not recover concrete and material reality. So they (great cubists like Picasso, Braque and Gris) tried to resolve by a kind of quardrature of the circle the artist's eternal problem of a reconciliation between idealism and materialism. They tried to stiffen their pictures by employing side by side with the most abstract forms, certain non-artistic materials, pieces of cut-out paper, labels, fragments of commercial lettering, etc., stuck to the canvas.
72. Sudhi Pradhan, who was an important organizer of the AFWAA and who later became closely involved in the cultural front of the CPI(M)-led government, thus commented about the art-indifference of the Communists:

    Pictorial art is still neglected in India. The W.B. government has founded so many academies. But how much money does it spend on pictorial art? How many people are involved in this sphere? This is a reflection of the general social attitude. Swarms of writers clamour their demands; hence, we have the Bangla Akademi, which caters to them. They start writing right from the moment of their birth. And if they can write poetry, then nothing more is required. Then there are middle-class theatre groups in every locality. So the Natya Akademi is very active. But who cares for the folk artists of the village? The place of pictorial art is at the bottom of the budget provision.

    The comment reveals layers of truth. First, the art-indifference of the Party. Second, the belittling attitude and harshness of the cultural leaders of the Party (Sudhi Pradhan being one of them) towards creative writers and performing artists. Third, quite paradoxically, even in its harshness the comment contains some truth. See Sudhi Pradhan in Prakash Das edited *Chittaprasad*, op. cit.
73. John Berger, *Art and Revolution: Ernst Neizvestny and the Role of the Artist in the USSR*, Penguin, 1969.
74. Though really the most popular works were the nineteenth century Russian paintings that had been painted in the same style but with great skill and

much greater sincerity and because they appealed to a sense of national tradition deriving from the past, serving ideologically the conservative nationalism which necessarily accepted the Stalinist policy of 'socialism in one country', as says John Berger.

75. For opinions on this Soviet art exhibition see: Ardhendu Kumar Gangopadhay, Atul Bose, Jamini Prakash Gangopadhyay, and Prabhat Kumar Dutta, 'Soviet Charukala Pradarshani', *Paricahy*, Baisakh 1359/1952. Dhurjati Prasad Mukhopadhay—'Russian Chitrakala Sambandhe', *Parichay*, Jaistha, 1359. (His observation was based on his recent visit to the Tetriakov Gallery in Russia. He did not have the opportunity to see the Soviet Art Exhibition held in Calcutta.) Bishnu Dey, 'Soviet Shilpa Pradarshani', *Sahityer Bhabishyat*, 1952.
76. Interview, Somnath Hore.
77. 'Chittaprosader Chithi' (Letters of Chittaprosad), *Parichay*, Sharadiya, 1981. It is collection of letters addressed to Murari Gupta of Lucknow. This particular letter was dated 23 June 1953. It was written at Andheri. All the letters show the bitterness and helplessness of the broken-hearted artist.
78. International Publishers, New York, 1954.
79. According to Finkelstein, this applies even to the portrait of Giorgione and artists of the Renaissance (not because of adequate likeness, nor because of pure form, but because they dealt with their problem socially: 'The more profound the artist's insight into a personality, the more he reveals the kinship of his subject to others, the portrait becomes at once a complete individual and a generalization of both how history makes people and people make history') and to the Romantic art of the early nineteenth century ('Great visions were conceived of human development and freedom, to the extent that they rose out of the real life and the possibilities now disclosed, this dream and visionary quality was not counterposed to realism').
80. Autumn rice.

Conclusion

One may be tempted to describe the Communist cultural movement in Bengal that is the subject of this book by borrowing the following words from the inimitable Bernard Shaw: 'Its grandioseness, neuroseness and sensationalness, its efforts, its hurry, its excitement, its aspiration without purpose, its forced and invariably disappointing climaxes, its exhaustion and decay.'[1] But the question that remains to be answered is why such a muddle in the movement? The answer lies outside the areas of arts and aesthetics. We have to turn to society and politics for our answer.

I

The Communist (or Marxist or socialist or leftist) movement in Bengal was mainly controlled by a few middle-class people, commonly called *babus* or *bhadralok*. They provided the leadership. Let us first pose the question: Why did a large section of the Bengali *bhadralok* were attracted to Communism during the 1930s?

During the decade, a number of middle-class people of England, including many intellectuals and writers (scholars like Raymond Williams, Edward Thompson and Eric Hobsbawm, poets like Auden, Spender, Day Lewis and MacNeice, and so on), turned towards Communism. George Orwell in his essay 'Inside the Whale',[2] has the following reasons behind this: (1) It was the worst of times. The debunking of Western civilization had reached its climax and disillusionment was widespread. Yet one had not necessarily got rid of the need for something to believe in. During the 1920s, a few gifted writers, e.g. T.S. Eliot, had sought refuge in the Catholic Church. And Orwell concludes, 'I do not think one need look farther than this for the reason why the young writers of the 1930s flocked into or towards the Communist Party. It was simply something to believe in. Here was a church, an army, an orthodoxy, a discipline. Here was a Fatherland and—at any rate since 1935 or thereabouts—a Fuehrer.' (2) The softness and security of the cultured middle-class life in England was another factor, according to Orwell, that contributed to 'the cult of Russia' among the English intelligentsia during these years. These writers were 'eager-mined public school boys' creating 'a Boy Scout atmosphere of bare-knees and community singing' in literature. Orwell quoted a stanza from Auden's poem 'Spain':

> *Today the deliberate increase in the chances*
> *of death,*
> *The conscious acceptance of guilt in the*
> *necessary murder...*

and says,

> All very edifying. But notice the phrase 'necessary murder'. It could only be written by a person to whom murder is at most a word. Personally I would not speak so lightly of murder. It so happens that I have seen the bodies of numbers of murdered men . . . to me, murder is something to be avoided. So it is to any ordinary person . . . Mr Auden's brand of amoralism is only possible if you are the kind of person who is always somewhere else when the trigger is pulled.

Do Orwell's views hold good for the Bengali Communists, or even for the Western Communists, for that matter? Let us first take up his theory of 'the softness and security of the cultured middle-class life'. This does seem to require some qualification. E.P. Thompson tried to refute it in his essay 'Outside the Whale' so far as the British Communists were concerned.[3] Thompson rightly points out that all the Communist intellectuals of the 1930s were not public school boys, all of them were not persons who were always somewhere else when the trigger was pulled, and that during the Spanish Civil War many of them were actually committed, as soldiers, to the activity of 'murder'. He censures Orwell for having failed to suggest that any other, more honourable, motivations might have coexisted with the trivial, and for regarding the leftist intellectual activities of that decade 'not as a political response within a definite political context (the threat of fascism and so on), but as the projection of the neuroses and petty motives of a section of the English middle-class'.

The motives that Orwell attributed to the English Communists of the 1930s are often attributed to their Bengali brethren too. There is this lay theory that these Communists came of affluent families, did not have to worry about earning their living and turned to Communism as a very good pastime within the framework of a soft and secure middle-class life. Some people argue quite differently and say that Communism was a product of the grudge of the not-so-well-off against the well-off, of the jealousy of pedestrians against those who drive cars. The two arguments, though contradictory, are grounded on the same assumption of 'neuroses and petty motives, of a section of the Bengali middle-class. The same assumption is also traceable in a police report of 1941[4] saying that half of the Indian students who became involved in Communist politics during their studies abroad 'recover balance on return, if they find employment. Those taking to subversive politics as a career, have done so because they failed in their exams or quarreled with families on other grounds (religious or matrimonial).' Some critics have gone even further, suggesting that the early leftist movement in this country meant to create a lobby to serve the interest of a group of people—in terms of prestige, if not in terms of power, economic or political.

The problems with such arguments are indeed glaring. Many of the Bengali Communists came from families struggling hard to make both ends meet. On the other hand, many affluent people joined the Communist fold. Among the Bengali Communists there were sons of zamindars and of petty clerks, though both belonged to the same *bhadralok* category. It is futile to try to explain the commitment of a group to a certain ideology solely in terms of its class-composition. If socio-economic compulsions are the chief reason behind acceptance of ideologies, then why did in the same family one brother join the Congress or militant nationalism and another become a Communist?[5]

Then, though the Bengali Communists were far away from the battle-fields of the Spanish Civil War and the Second World War and hence did not have to fight as actual soldiers, many of them risked the advantages of their middle-class background, their career, health and even life during the period of our study. Providing relief to the Famine-stricken millions was not a very 'soft' task. The young Communists who built barricades on the streets of Calcutta during the INA Release Movement did it at a great risk to their life. The way the Communist cadres tried to bring about Revolution (be it a mere illusion) during the years 1948-50 cannot but be called 'dangerous' by any middle-class standard. In the Communist movement there were people like Hemanga Biswas, a Zamindar's son, who was disowned by his father for his political activities, chose an uncertain livelihood and suffered from a nasty sort of tuberculosis. Petty middle-class interests scarcely explain so much of sufferings and sacrifices.

The historians of the Indian National Movement have already established that interpretations of an ideology in terms of self-interests or pettiness are not tenable. The old Marxist explanation of nationalism in terms of class interests of the 'bourgeoisie' and the Cambridge School analysis in terms of the narrow status aspiration of elites such as the Bengali *bhadralok* or of the Marathi Chitpavan Brahmins—both have been unfounded. Professor Sumit Sarkar, in his study of the Swadeshi Movement long back,[6] stressed the autonomous role of ideology. He applied to the English-educated elite of Bengal Gramsci's concept of 'traditional' (as distinct from 'organic') intelligentsia; men of learning, not a well-defined economic class, who 'for that very reason may be swayed by new cultural or ideological forces to the point of being won over in part by an emergent revolutionary class'. Now, we may apply this to the Communists as well, for after all, the Communists were the same class of people as the nationalists. The sons and younger brothers of the Gandhiites and the national revolutionaries turned Communists during the 1930s and the 1940s. Many people made their way to Communism from other streams of the national movement.

Not that the Bengali leftists were insincere in their ideology; however, they did not give much critical thought to it. It seems that Orwell's theory of 'the worst of times' has some truth in it. Europe as well as Bengal experienced crisis after crisis during the period of our study. The crises heightened the stark social reality in which the middle-class people were involved along with all other classes. It was a time of testing for the middle-class and quite a few members of this class reacted by turning to a certain ideology. For them, Communism was something to believe in. So Orwell's first allegation perhaps holds good for them.

Many of them sincerely believed that a better new world was in the offing. They did have a vision of such a world, howsoever vague it may have been. They were committed to this vision, but did not really have a mission, for they did not know what they could do to usher in the new world. The kind of Marxism they believed in, taught them that capitalist order would crumble soon due to its own inherent contradictions and that the cherished order would come about as a matter of rule. Indeed, the crisis of capitalism as manifest in the world-wide Depression and the War made them believe so. Thus, they approached Marxism in the believer's mode and this made any theoretical interpolation of Marxism seem unnecessary. They believed that mere faith in this ideology and some stray struggles as expressions of this faith would be enough. Again, one is reminded of Bernard Shaw's phrase 'aspirations without purpose'.

II

But before we elaborate on the above point, let us consider some other limitations of the movement. It has been pointed out that a crucial weakness of the whole leftist movement in Bengal was that the middle-class leaders failed to reach the lower rungs of society, i.e. the peasants and the workers. Dipesh Chakrabarty has put forward the theory of a dysjunction between ideology and culture to explain this failure. While writing on the middle-class leadership of the jute mill workers of Bengal,[7] Chakrabarty has explained the fact of 'so much militancy, so little organization' among these workers during the 1920s, 1930s and 1940s in terms of the 'power' of their middle-class leaders who turned out to be 'masters' instead of 'representatives' of the workers, thus rendering proper organizational discipline redundant.

Chakrabarty has applied this not only to the early non-Communist trade union leaders like Prabhabati Dasgupta, but also to the generation of socialists and Communists, who, according to him, for all their commitment and sacrifices, remained imprisoned in the *babu-coolie* relationship. Thus, Gopen Chakrabarty, a Moscow-returned Communist, who joined a jute mill at Bhatpara as a machine-man in the steam-room at Rs. 14 a month, was not accepted by the workers as one of them, and they still called him 'Union Babu'. In his conclusion, Dipesh Chakrabarty has tried to explain this by drawing a distinction between ideology and culture.

> Ideologically the Bengali left was committed to developing trade unions based on the democratic, contractual and voluntary procedures of organization that their theory of trade unionism entailed. In the culture of every day life however they, as *babus*, were related to the coolies through a hierarchy of status. Their education, their appearance, the language they spoke, the work they did, could all act as indicators of their authority and superiority over the coolies.

Did this culturally-determined relationship of power that Chakrabarty has noticed in the field of trade-unionism characterize other fields of the left movement also, including the cultural movement? We may try to argue a little with Chakrabarty in this respect, though not really against him. First, the duality that was glaring in the *babu*-worker relationship was not so obvious in the *babu*-peasant relationship. Most of the workers had come from villages of other provinces, and talked in languages which the *babus* of Calcutta hardly understood. So their relation with the *babus* was one of remoteness and uneasiness. But the *babus* of the mofussil and rural Bengal shared the same tradition of rural culture with the peasants. They had many points of affinity—folk-music, *Jatra*, *Kathakata*, language, etc. And these proved to be important, despite the educational background and the relative affluence of the *babus*. We have seen how such affinities bore rich fruits in the People's Song Movement. Hemanga Biswas is a good case in point. Though a Zamindar's son, he could mix intimately with the common people of his area and imbibe the local folk-music from his childhood. After joining the left movement, he composed songs using the dialect and the tunes of the peasants and these songs naturally became popular among them. Second, the workers coming from other provinces found themselves in a *terra incognita* here. They were bewildered and confused and hence depended on the benevolent 'Union babus' who seemed to have much more knowledge and a superior power of negotiation. But the *babus* of rural Bengal did not enjoy so much of a cultural advantage over the peasants.

But even Khaled Chowdhury, who was engaged in the People's Song Movement among the peasants, the most successful mass movement of all Communist cultural movements, brings the allegation of ideology-culture dichotomy against it.[8] And we cannot brush this aside lightly, because he was deeply involved in the movement himself and because he has the *babu*-peasant relationship as his referral framework. Chowdhury was an active member of the Sylhet IPTA Squad during the 1940s. But having spent a number of years in search of folk tradition in his later life, he now finds the people's songs of that time artificial in most cases. He says that the mere use of folk diction and tune cannot make a song reach the hearts of common people. Hemanga Biswas's song 'Oh Chasi-bhai (brother peasants), dacoits are descending on your golden paddy field' was based on folk form, but the problem is that a real peasant never addresses another real peasant as 'Chasi bhai'. This sounds artificial. Moreover, folk composers usually accept poverty quite philosophically and even make fun of it, whereas in the People's Songs of the 1940s we find crude complaints about poverty. According to Chowdhury, despite their utmost sincerity, the middle-class composers and singers of the People's Song could not bridge the gap between the peasants and themselves.

Chowdhury tells us a funny story in this connection in a mood of self-criticism. Once he and his colleagues arranged a session of People's Songs at the house of their friend Nirmalendu Chowdury, whose father was a rural zamindar of Sylhet. The peasants of the village were present there as audience. Khaled was singing a Famine song, 'Bhukha hai Bangal' (Bengal is Hungry). He had made a tableau by dabbing black smut on the body of a little girl and by making her ribs prominent by brushing them with lime. He was so carried away with emotion that tears were flowing down his cheeks. And naturally he thought that he was arousing a similar kind of emotion in the hearts of the audience. Suddenly, however, Nirmalendu came running and asked him to stop. Khaled was flabbergasted. Nirmalendu explained that he had heard the following conversation among the peasant audience. One peasant asked another: 'Do you understand the song?' The reply was: 'No. How can I? It is in Hindi!' 'Oh, the language is Hindi. But what is the content? The content is—"Muslims are *boka* (fools)".' It was a Muslim-majority locality and communal hatred was on the rise those days. The conversation had naturally scared Nirmalendu. This misinterpretation of the song is, however, easily explicable. In Sylhet, Muslims are called 'Bangal' and the word *boka* is pronounced as 'bhukha'. The IPTA artists tried to move the peasants with their Famine song, but did not pause to consider whether they would understand its meaning.

We have to admit that Chowdhury is largely right. It is true that the peasants showed enthusiasm about many a IPTA song. We also have reports that this very song 'Bhukha hai Bangal' aroused strong emotive reactions among the peasants of Punjab, for whom it was meant originally. It is also true that a number of folk poets contributed to the People's Song

Movement, and Chowdhury's criticism certainly does not apply to them. Yet it has to be admitted that the ideology-culture dichotomy and the resultant *babu*-peasant gap could not be entirely bridged. In other areas of aesthetic practices—theatre, pictorial art and literature—the gap was all the more yawning.

III

However, with due respect to Dipesh Chakrabarty and Khaled Chowdhury, I would like to raise a question here: Is the failure to bridge the above ideology-culture gap that important an obstacle for a project to change the world for the better? Should we not treat such bridging as a process subsumed under the bigger project rather than assigning it a driving and determining role? If the *bhadralok* failed to bridge the gap, was it not because something was more fundamentally wrong with their project? I say this because I cannot fail to notice that the process of bridging the gap was indeed on within the leftist movement under discussion. While it had its limitations, we have instances in which those limitations could also be overcome through an urge of the *bhadralok* 'outsiders' to be part of the life of the labouring people and to move along with the latter to a better and equitable future, and also an urge on the part of the labouring people to believe in the *bhadralok* intention and respond positively to the *bhadralok*-sponsored movement. Such instances show that this urge on either side was informed by a strong, if temporarily swelling, emotion. We can safely say that apart from ideology and culture, another factor was at work in the leftist movement of that time, and that is emotion. And an emotional moment can largely bridge the gap between ideology and culture, between the *babus* and the peasants and even the coolies. As the socio-political crises intensified, and the struggle sharpened, the emotion in the Communist cultural movement deepened too. Here are a few examples of how emotion worked wonders during the period of our study.

In 1942, the Students' Federation sent a cultural brigade on a tour of one-and-a-half months tour to East Bengal. The reminiscences of Ramakrishna Moitra, one of the members of the squad, vibrates with the emotion that helped them to break the barrier separating them from the peasant masses:

> From Sealdah to Narayangunj—by train. Music, music, music all the way. In the evening the Padma Steamer. Music again. Rice and chicken curry. Annada—organization, Arun—management and finance (which was negligible), Rama—rehearsal and agit-prop. One and a half month tour. The money that was with us at Sealdah lasted only upto Narayangunj. After that we did not have to bear our own expenses. Wherever we went, the local student-workers took charge.

Ten to twelve miles of daily walk. From one place to another. Music while walking along the shadowy paths of rural Bengal. Reach the destination in the afternoon. Function in the evening. At night food of delicious varieties at some places and coarse rice and pumpkin dish at others. Sleep sometimes on costly bedsteads and sometimes beneath the open sky . . .

One evening, function at a remote village of Noakhali. At night, we stayed in the house of a peasant comrade. Ate pumpkin curry and red and coarse rice. I still remember, before closing my eye. I whispered to Annada who was lying by my side: 'At last we have thrown away our petite-bourgeois garb and are getting merged with the proletariat'. I did not notice whether Annada smiled with a twinkle in his eyes.'[9]

Anandasankar Bhattacharya may or may not have smiled at Ramakrishna's passionate outburst. But it is a fact that some of the *babus* were largely overcoming their insularity and the peasants also responded.

Then, how easily could the peasants replace the gentlemen-leaders at critical points of time! The following story is revealing. Once the Party and the Kisan Sabha arranged a procession. Peasants from remote villages joined the procession that would finally reach the divisional town Nilfamari (North Bengal) to voice their demands. On the way they halted at Domar, where they started cooking *khhichri* for lunch. But disheartening news suddenly reached them. There was a railway town called Sayeedpur nearby and communal riots had broken out there. The procession consisted of Hindus and Muslims of different villages. Tension spread among them. The leaders were at a loss. A few young peasants approached them and said: 'Hamar hatta chhari deo. Chinta na karen (Leave it to us. Don't worry).' The leaders had no alternative but to obey them. 'Within a few minutes, a slogan was raised—'Dari-tiki (Hindus and Muslims) bhai-bhai / Laraier maidane jatibhed nai (Beard and Tuft are brothers / There is no caste-division on the battlefield). 'The whispering stopped, the climate changed instantaneously, the comrades shook off their weariness, got up, the Beards and the Tufts joined hands to finish the cooking.'[10]

The Tebhaga Movement was the high-water-mark of *babu*-peasant camaraderie. The superiority of the *babus* no longer held good. At many places, the leadership was in the hands of the peasants. We have already seen how Somnath Hore's *Tebhagar Diary*[11] brilliantly recorded the comradeship between the *babus* and the peasants in a Rangpur village during the Tebhaga Movement. The *babus* and the peasants were fighting shoulder-to-shoulder. The peasants addressed the *babus* not as 'Babu', but as 'Comrade'. Somnath Hore, an urban *babu*, used to call a local peasant leader 'Rupkantada', just as he would address any respected member of his own middle-class society. 'Dineshda', a *bhadralok* leader, lectured in the language of the peasants and the latter were thrilled. In the morning, while going to the field to harvest paddy, the peasants would sing 'Chasi, de tor lal selam lal nisanre' (Peasant, give your red salute to the Red Flag), a song composed by Benoy Roy, a *bhadralok* composer. At night, Somnath returned to the camp (the house of the Kisan Sabha) and sat down to write about his day's experience. 'But I could not write. The *Adhiyars* started coming one by one. There was no serious purpose behind their coming. They just wanted to chat with us'—a spectacle of perfect amity! Hore also writes that at such gatherings during those critical days, the peasants preferred listening to the newly-composed People's Songs of the *babus* rather than their own traditional folk songs.

But the Tebhaga Movement did not last long and so this amity was short-lived. Ultimately, the *babus* remained *babus* and the peasants remained peasants. Emotion during moments of intense struggle helped the gentlemen largely overcome the distance between themselves and the masses. But the Tebhaga movement failed due to a sort of purposelessness at the level of planning and decision-making that strangely coexisted with the aspiration of some zealous Communists at the micro-level and not so much due to any ideology-culture dichotomy. We agree that such a dichotomy was to be found more or less in all the leftist gentlemen in Bengal, but it is also true that many of them were getting over it to a large extent, aided by their emotion. Also, we must remember that emotion does not necessarily mean emotionalism, i.e. undue indulgence in emotion as absolutely opposed to reason, which, of course, is true of the left movement of that time at one extreme. But emotion ordinarily means just passion or feeling. As Lucien Febvre has put it, it is a sort of passion which is powerfully 'contagious' and 'constitutes a system of inter-individual stimuli.'[12] In any case, emotion is a very effective aspect of consciousness.

Now, should we put so much emphasis on emotion, if ultimately it did not achieve as much as the participants expected? But this rich emotion did bring about an unprecedented efflorescence in art and literature, which this study deals with. Art can transcend the socio-economic reality of its time and enter a new reality through the sheer consciousness of the artist, and what we call emotion holds a big place among the elements constituting this consciousness. So far as art is an individual artist's creation, this emotion based on the artist's humanitarian sensitivity may seem more than adequate to comprehend the cherished reality. But when art tries to become a movement, a people's movement, a movement leading to a better society, it needs strategies and tactics, organizations and activities—in a word, proper politics—with a strong sense of practicality. The writer, the directors and the actors of *Nabanna* could perhaps come close to the life and feelings of the poor peasants and establish most convincingly the need for a change in their lot. It is another matter that the peasants about whom the play had been written did not get much opportunity to watch it or get inspired by it, and that the desired change did not take place. For this, the leftist cultural leaders should have organized a strong theatrical movement and a strong political movement, which they did not. The People's Song Movement became a people's movement even without much planning and organization in the field of music, because of the peculiarity of this particular art form. Songs, if they are appealing to the people, can spread without much external promotion. But the lack of effective praxis in the field of politics made the appeal of the People's Songs ephemeral and thus the People's Song Movement ultimately failed.

Communism served to provide the Bengali leftists with emotional support, rather than with weapons useful in their practical activities. So the left here remained a mere aesthetic expression, and the whole leftist movement a leftist cultural movement, if we judge it from its positive achievements. P.C. Joshi, the General Secretary of the Communist Party seems to have realized the role of culture in mentally preparing people for a fundamental change in the social order. He thus tried to initiate a hegemonizing drive in the field of culture by creating a broad united front of writers and artists. So far the idea was good. But too much emphasis on culture at the cost of real politics defeated his purpose. Chinmohan Sehanabis says that during Joshi's tenure, critics within and outside the Party used to ask, 'Is the Communist Party just a party of music and dance?'[13] Joshi is often accused of over-enthusiasm about matters of culture. But even during the tenure of B. T. Randive, Communism did not show any practical path to action to the Bengali leftists; it remained an aesthetic exercise, just facilitating a flourish in the cultural movement. The politics remained weak, though in a different way.

Perhaps this dichotomy between emotion and practicality is something basic. Lucien Febvre says, '... as soon as the emotions occur they modify intellectual activity. And on the other hand ... the best way to suppress an emotion was to portray its motives or object in precise terms.... Making a poem or a novel of one's sorrow has probably been a means of sentimental anaesthesia for a good many artists.'[14] Perhaps emotion always contains seeds of emotionalism and seeks a cathartic outlet. I may sound sacrilegious, but in this connection I must confess to an uncomfortable feeling I have always had about the musical drama *Nabajibaner Gan* composed by Jyotirindra Moitra, which was one of the most famous creations on the Bengal Famine and a matter of great pride for the Communists. This is how Moitra has described the immediate background in which he composed it. One day he was walking down a street of the city full of destitute and dying human beings. Suddenly he saw a dead mother with her child clinging to her breast and desperately trying suck it. He was so traumatized that he ran to a friend's house nearby, pulled out the harmonium and started composing:

'Na, na, na, manbo na!' (No, no, no! We are not going to accept this!').[15] This was surely catharsis. I cannot but feel that trying to rescue the poor child who was still alive would have been a more normal and humane reaction, even if we set aside the question of the bigger politics of changing the world!

IV

So ideology without much political initiative, aesthetics without much intellection—this was what the cultural movement under discussion was. It was mostly an elitist affair with the 'people' regarded as an abstract cult. All that the Communists did to advance the cause of Revolution was attack talented writers and artists for not abiding by their aesthetic policy. This policy known as Zhdanovism demanded the most absurd things from the artists and was an imposition on their autonomy. In terms of content, it decried the despondency and despair depicted in art and literature. In terms of style, it demanded the adoption of folk forms in music and theatre, and a rejection of any kind of abstraction in pictorial art. And we have seen how after the second Party congress, the fanaticism increased, as the Communist movement entered an apparently revolutionary mode. But it was only a revolution on paper, based not on a concrete study of concrete situation, but on quotations from Lenin, Stalin and Mao Tse-tung. They came out of this revolutionary illusion very soon.

Part of the political deficiency of the Bengali Communists has perhaps to be explained in terms of the Stalinist orthodoxy that was dominating world Communism at that time. But why did the *bhadralok* Communist accept this orthodoxy without any question, without asserting their own intellectual power, without fashioning their own politics? This has perhaps to be attributed to the inherent *bhadralok* character as it had shaped since the nineteenth century under the aegis of colonialism. What we have called the 'second Renaissance of Bengal' was an 'unsatisfactory half-way house', just like the first one. In fact, for all their aspirations for the future, the Communist *bhadralok*'s self-identity remained deeply rooted in the renaissant past of the nineteenth century. This meant a legacy of the Bengal Renaissance with its over-dependence on foreign sources of ideas to the exclusion of original thinking, its dichotomy between thought and deeds, its unbridgeable gap between the elite and the masses. A leading historian of modern India observes:

> In India, full-scale colonial rule lasted the longest, and there was ample time for the growth of dependent vested interests, the elaboration of hegemonic infrastructure producing 'voluntary consent' side by side with more direct politico-military domination. The English-educated intelligentsia in its origins was very much a part

of this system, nowhere more so than in Bengal; that it later turned to nationalist and even sometimes Marxian ways did not automatically imply that the old presuppositions had been entirely and consciously overcome.[16]

Indeed, the Bengali Communists could not overcome the limitations and contradictions of their forefathers. Their over-enthusiasm in culling quotations from Lenin, Stalin, Mao and others, their writings and speeches full of platitudes and stereotypes bear this out. This prevented them from formulating any sound theory with a view to changing the world, and effective action springs only from a sound theory.

Revolution was too big an aspiration for men encumbered with such a heritage. Those Marxists were actually nothing more than reformists, even when they spoke of Revolution. They continued to inhabit the middle-class world of their forefathers, for which they expressed strong contempt, and compromised with the needs of this world every now and then in their personal lives. In every sphere of their lives, including the political, their thoughts and deeds were overlaid with middle-class proclivities. The leftist circle provided for them a middle-class enclave within middle-class society with most of the characteristics and values of that society remaining intact.

We know that the left movement did go beyond its original elite confines, but not very far. There had always been a big gulf between the *bhadralok* and the masses of people. This was quite natural, given the *bhadralok*'s English education and relative prosperity, and they cannot really be faulted on this ground. Rather, it goes to their credit that at least some individual *bhadralok* tried to temporarily close this gulf. But what was really damaging for the Communist movement was that they never took up a *purposeful and practical* programme of changing or even hegemonizing society. I hope this has become amply clear from the preceding chapters on different art forms as mediums of the Communist cultural movement. Here is one small example related to literature, which we have left out in this study. Nothing can be queerer than the way in which in a largely illiterate country like India, some educated people wanted to take literature to the masses in order to equip them for a revolutionary struggle and yet did not try to spread literacy among them. The Communist aestheticians condemned the poet fellow-traveler Bishnu Dey saying that the difficult forms used by him prevented the masses from understanding his poetry, while they admired the easy forms and hence revolutionary utility of the young poet Sukanta Bhattacharya.[17] However, while the Communists kept arguing about the relative revolutionary potential of the two poets, the illiterate masses could read neither. Of course, the idea of a literacy campaign occurred to some of the middle-class leftists, but they did not pursue the matter with the seriousness it deserved. Chinmohan Sehanabis once suggested that arranging occasional cultural programmes should not be the only task of the local branches of the Progressive Writers' Association and that they should try to spread literacy as their day-to-day work. But the suggestion went unheeded.[18]

George Orwell said that it was the softness and security of their life that made the Western middle-class literati turn to Communism during the 1930s. We have already argued that this could not be the reason behind the acceptance of an ideology. But perhaps the factor of security in middle-class life was important in preventing the leftists from fully pursuing their ideology, at least in Bengal. The middle-class life was not always soft, but it proved to be secure. During the critical forties, one could often hear in the leftist circle that the middle-class was getting declassed. But the process of being declassed did not go far enough. A few might have become poor. But the middle-class remained all right, and the leftists remained within the middle-class. Once the political context in which they had gravitated towards Communism disappeared, the prodigal sons returned home. Their family and educational background ensured for them a decent middle-class living. A large number of them got utterly disillusioned with Communist politics, if not with Communism itself. Some overtly capitulated to the forces of maintaining the status quo. Of course, many leftists stuck to Communist politics as Party members or close sympathizers. But after 1950, their slogans suddenly faded from red to pink. Their ideological compulsions progressively weakened. Another phase of revolutionary Communism came with the Naxalite Movement of the late 1960s and early 1970s. But it was short-lived and a failure. Then, with the capture of the state power in 1977, with the collapse of the Soviet Union and other Communist regimes from the late 1980s along with the retrogression of China, Communism just became a mask of self-advancement for the Bengali Communists. Thus, the left movement in Bengal became a lost cause and ceased to be a living movement. I do not know how many individual Communists today really feel guilty about being associated with the prevalent socio-economic and political system that embraces market values and nurtures inequalities, how many of them really look beyond this system and have a single vision of a just and egalitarian world, and how many of them are really eager to pursue it in a big way instead of just engaging in small protests on isolated issues. But it seems their number is not many.

When I did my research during the 1980s, there were still some Communist grandfathers sitting in their middle-class drawing rooms with Lenin's portrait hanging from the wall and chatting to their grandchildren about the heady days and the feast of art and intellect of the 1930s and 1940s. During the course of the 1990s, however, those Communist grandfathers (and certainly the next generation, i.e. the Communist fathers) became enthralled with the prospect of neo-liberal economic development the world over. They tried to participate in it to the best of their ability. If direct participation was not possible, they looked up to the next generation(s) for this—children (and grandchildren) settled in the hub of world capitalism in many cases or making good in their own country. And of course, they were greatly helped by their precious Party in power. As a result, they have been able to spend liberally on foreign trips, in buying luxurious apartments and cars, in frequenting shopping malls, and in getting admitted to five-star hotel-like hospitals if and when illness puts them down.

V

The left movement in Bengal reminds me of the following Mollah Nasiruddin story: It was night. A man was looking for something under a lighted lamp-post. A policeman came to him and asked, 'Have you lost anything?' 'Yes, my key,' answered the man. The policeman offered to help and both of them searched for the key. They searched for a long while, without any success. The exhausted policeman asked at last. 'Are you sure you've lost the key exactly on this spot?' The man said, 'Oh no. I've lost it elsewhere.' 'Then why the hell are you searching for it here?,' asked the policeman. 'But, you see, it is here where I get the light,' came the answer. The Bengali leftists searched for the key to their cherished future in the fields of art and literature, for only there could they get the light, though evidently the key had been lost elsewhere.[19]

I would only like to add a small conclusion to this story. Ultimately, the leftists found a shining key not very far from the lamp-post. It was not the key they had been looking for. But it looked even better and more attractive. They eagerly picked it up. And it enabled them to open so many doors of desires, to enter a world full of material prosperity and power. They surely thanked their luck that they had not found the original key and left satisfied with it!

Notes and References

1. Bernard Shaw, 'Revolutionary Music (1789)', in *Great Composers: Reviews and Bombardment*, ed. Louis Crompton, University of California Press, 1978, p. 21.
2. Included in *Collected Essays*, London: Mercury Books, 1961.
3. Included in *The Poverty of Theory and Other Essays*, Merlin, 1978.
4. A Report of the Intelligence Branch (Home Department), 1941.
5. Many examples come to mind—that of Ajoy Mukherjee (Congress) and Viswanath Mukherjee (CPI) in politics, that of Reba Raychowdhury (IPTA) whose elder sister had been involved in militant nationalism, and so on.
6. *The Swadeshi Movement in Bengal, 1903–1908*, New Delhi: PPH, 1973, 'Conclusion', p. 513.

7. 'Trade Union in a Hierarchical Culture: The Jute Workers of Calcutta, 1920–40', Subaltern Studies, vol. III, New Delhi: Oxford University Press, 1984.
8. Interview, Khaled Chowdhury.
9. Ramakrishna Moitra, 'Chhatra Federation: Challish Bachhar', *Chhatra Abhijan*, published by the Students' Federation on the occasion of its 40th anniversary, 1976.
10. Monikrishna Sen's reminiscences in *Tebhaga Rajat Jayanti Smarak Grantha*, published by the CPI from the office of Kalantar on the occasion of the golden jubilee of the Tebhaga Movement.
11. Published in *Ekshan*, Sharadiya, 1981.
12. Lucien Fevbre, 'Sensibility and History: How to Reconstitute the Emotional Life of the Past', repr. in *French Studies in History*, vol. 1, ed. Maurice Aymard and Harbans Mukhia, Orient Longman.
13. Interview, Chinmohan Sehanabis.
14. Lucien Fevbre, op. cit.
15. 'Amader Nabajibaner Gan', *Kalantar*, Sharadiya, 1972.
16. Sumit Sarkar, Rammohun Ray and Break with the Past', *Rammohun Ray and the Process of Modernization of India*, ed. V.C. Joshi, New Delhi: Vikas Publishing House Pvt. Ltd., 1975, p. 68.
17. I have discussed the aesthetic debates among the Bengali Marxists of the late colonial and early Independence years elaborately in my forthcoming book *Bengal Marxism: Early Discourses and Debates*, to be published by Stree-Samya, Kolkata.
18. Interview, Chinmohan Sehanabis.
19. The concept of 'culturalism' of the Bengali *bhadralok* has been very central to my explanation of the failure of the Communist cultural movement in this book. Yet I am aware that I have not been able to adequately explain this very culturalism, which is true of the Bengali middle-class life irrespective of their political affiliations. The culturalism of the post-CPI(M) regime in today's Bengal, for example, is a proof of this. Though, of course, Rabindranth has largely replaced Marx as the icon of today's culturalism. Needless to say, the acquiesces in this, because it thinks that it would thus be able to cater to the culturalism of the Bengalis in general.

    I have simply referred to Sumit Sarkar's seminal book on the Swadeshi Movement that marked the Gramscian turn in history-writing in our country by stressing the autonomous role of ideology without grounding it in any particular social interest, and again by referring to Sarkar's understanding of the dichotomy between the thoughts (or ideologies) and the deeds of the *bhadralok* as well as their alienation from the masses (in other words, what may be seen as manifestations of Bengali culturalism) in terms of their overdependence on colonial rule. But I confess that this explanation, even though based on a long and sound history of the *bhadralok* traced since the nineteenth century, does not fully satisfy me.

Can Partha Chatterjee's famous two-domain theory (vide his *The Nation and Its Fragments: Colonial and Post-colonial Histories*, originally published 1993, paperback, Delhi: Oxford University Press, 1997)—the outer domain of materialist pursuit under the colonial masters and the inner domain of assertion of national cultural sovereignty, that, according to him, had been developed by the *bhadralok* since the nineteenth century as a strategy to take on the challenge of foreign rule—be of any help to us? Didn't this inner domain, as a space of freedom from the necessity-oriented and even corrupt material world, promote culturalism? But Chatterjee's division between the outer and inner domains, though deeply insightful, appears too neatly. Indeed, his theory has been subjected to a lot of criticism. The overlapping of the so-called outer and inner domains has been pointed out by a number of scholars. The underlying equations between the outer domain and the modern on the one hand and the inner domain and the traditional (communitarian) on the other have also been questioned. And for us, the most important question is—even if the nationalist *bhadralok* had to indulge in culturalism in the face of British rule, why would their Communist descendents do that too? As Communists, they rather professed a keen awareness of material existence in all their activities, and avowed to change that materiality. Even their cultural activities were no exceptions. How could this materially-oriented consciousness go with culturalism? Evidently the *bhadralok* Communists accepted their material existence on the whole, even though they outwardly challenged it in terms of culture. But how can we explain this *bhadralok* dichotomy (if not hypocrisy)?

Recently, Andrew Sartori (*Bengal in Global Concept History: Culturalism in the Age of Capital*, University of Chicago Press, Chicago and London, 2008) has tried to explain the culturalism of the Bengalis in terms of a factor external to the *bhadralok* character. His explanation is very novel and may prove partly helpful to us. Let us try to understand it briefly. Sartori adopts a kind of Marxian approach here, via Raymond Williams. Capitalism is not just market exchanges, but a particular constellation of social practices, including subject-constituting practices. In the course of the nineteenth and twentieth centuries, capitalism thus generated a concept of culture as a truly global concept, representing a unified conceptual field that traversed the boundaries of linguistic differences and specific discourse formations. This culture as a lens for construing the world and as a whole way of life was regarded as something purifying and refining, and articulated the freedom of subjectivity from determinations of objective necessities such as biology, nature, economy and society. As a mitigating and rallying alternative, it was actually a critique of materialistic, coercive and destructive modern society. And, according to Sartori, Bengali culturalism was grounded in such social practices generated by the abstract structures of global capitalism emerging from the nineteenth century onwards. For, as he stresses repeatedly, capitalist structures meet the double criterion of meeting a historical specificity (the contingency of a colonial context, in Bengal's case) and of dynamic expansion all over the world (a colonial society is, after all, embedded in a larger imperial-cum-global context).

Sartori also gives us an internal history of Bengali culturalism. He says that the culturalist ideological paradigm emerged in Bengal from the 1880s as a reaction against the liberal ideological paradigm that had dominated in the early nineteenth century (these two are, according to him, the two historically specific forms of subjectivity that is generated by capitalism) and thus he introduces a discontinuity in the narrative of the so-called Bengal Renaissance which is usually presented as a continuous history defined around the binary of colonizer and colonized (also West/non-West, modernity/tradition). And then he traces the history of this culturalism from Bankimchandra through the Swadeshi movement to the post-Swadeshi period.

I am not comfortable with Sartori's history of Bengali culturalism, but I need not argue with him about this history in the present book. Here I would like to say only this much that his explanation of culturalism in terms of the global structures of capitalism seems to have an element of truth and what I find most interesting is his contention that the Bengalis misrecognized these structures, not because they were particularly stupid or duped, but because the very nature of modern capitalist society systematically presents itself in forms that cloak its deeper logic. This contention seems very meaningful when he touches upon the leftist project in Bengal while discussing the impact of the Swadeshi collapse. He says that the Bengalis interpreted the failure of the Swadeshi Movement as a moral failure due to too much materialistic propensity. A proliferation of the concepts of culture occurred in the post-Swadeshi years—all dissociated from and opposed to the material life of people, signifying some prestigious engagement and critiquing democracy. However, against this 'there emerged a broadly leftist project of harnessed the very popular energies that had undermined the Swadeshi Movement to a democratic project that at once sought to transcend culturalism and yet remained haunted by its shadow.' Sartori further says, 'Marxism in Bengal has long enjoyed a troubled intimacy with the culturalist tradition that renders transparent simultaneously the practical foundations of Bengali culturalism and the conceptual limitations of that form of Marxism.'

Sartori's argument that that the Bengalis had the roots of their culturalism in the global structures of capitalism unknown to themselves can perhaps explain to some extent why even the Communists of Bengal remained trapped in this culturalism. I wish he had elaborated on these structures and the social practices involved in them more clearly and empirically. But having said this, I would assert that one needs to study the Bengali middle-class character too as it has developed through history in greater depth to have a more complete understanding of Bengali culturalism. And going back to Sumit Sarkar once again, I would say that colonial subservience should be given due importance in such a study.

Bibliography

A. Contemporary Original Sources

(1) Archival

Intercepted letters, newspaper cuttings and police reports kept at the archives of the Intelligence Branch, West Bengal Police, Lord Sinha Road, Calcutta.

(In the 1980s, when I worked here, researchers were not allowed under the rules in force to see files of the post-1947 period. They were not even allowed to note down the numbers of the files they were permitted to consult. They could, however, note the dates of the letters, reports, etc. I have mentioned the dates in foot-notes in most cases.)

(2) Non-Archival

Source for Contemporary Songs

1. The richest source is note books of composers and singers of People's Songs. Priti Banerjee's note book of that period contains the Hindi songs sung by the Central Squad, with instructions written by Ravi Shankar, in some cases. An old exercise book of Hemanga Biswas contains about a hundred songs of different people—Benoy Roy, Haripada Kusari, Satyen Sen, Sadhan Dasgupta, Jyotirindra Moitra, Kanak Nukherjee, Harindranath Chatterjee, Dayal Kumar, Kshetragopal Chatterjee, Nibaran Pandit, Prabhat Bose, Nihar Dasgupta, Pradyot Guha, Surath Chowdhury (Sylhet), Tarapada Bhowmik (Nadia), Subhas Mukherjee, Gangapada Roy Chowdhury, Jiten Sen, Manik Das (Koyepara, Chittagong), Adam Ali Sheikh (Kustia) and some Hindi songs learnt from other provinces. But unfortunately, most of such copy books are lost to us. Jaya Roy, wife of Benoy Roy, writes, 'His thick song book, his treasure of songs, was known to all IPTA singers. Unfortunately this book fell into the hands of the police when they went to Surapati Nandi's house to arrest him and they took all his and Surapati's song books, which they never returned'. (Jaya Roy, 'Life Sketch of Benoy Roy', *Benoy Roy: A Tribute*). Salil Chowdhury told me in an interview that his songs of that period had mostly been occasioned by some political meeting of other, and written on the spot. Naturally most of them did not survived. Some were preserved by a comrade named Bhupen. But Chowdhury did not know anything definite about the latter's whereabouts. Of course, quite a few of his songs were of more than momentary value and won enough popularity to survive. These were later collected in books.

2. Many books of People's Songs were published during that period. Among them are—*Janayuddher Gan* published by the AFWAA, Kolkata. It ran into three quick editions. In the third edition (May 1943) there were 17 Bengali and 7 Hindi songs. The contributors were Benoy Roy, Subhas Mukherjee, Mohit Banerjee, Jolly Kaul, Bishnu Dey, Dayal Kumar, Satyen Sen, Hemanga Biswas, Harindranath Chatterjee, Rahman (a tramway worker) and also some anonymous composers.

Jatiya Sangeet, which contained a few People's Songs along with old patriotic songs, Anti-Fascist Writers' and Artists' Association, Kolkata, February 1945.

Jyotirindra Moitra, *Nabajibaner Gan*, published by Progressive Writers' and Artists' Association on behalf of the IPTA, 1945. This book was reprinted in 1978 by Indira Silpi Gosthi, Kolkata.

Hemanga Biswas, *Bishan*, a collection of 33 songs, mostly of Hemanga Biswas and also of Sudhangsu Ghosh, Surath Pal Chowdhury, Kshetra Chattopadhyay, Haripada Kusari and Benoy Roy. It was published by Deben Shyam, Assam Publishing House, Gauhati (2nd edition, May Day, 1944).

Kanak Mukherjee's *Desrakshar Dak*, Introductions by Bhavani Sen and Benoy Roy, Kolkata: National Book Agency, 1943.

Janasangeet, published by Sunil Dutta of Naya Sanskriti Prakashani, Kolkata, somewhere in the early 1950s.

Salil Chowdhury's *Ghum Bhangar Gan* (with notation), Kolkata: Naya Sanskriti Prakashani, 1358 (1951).

Hemanga Biswas and Naibaran Pandit, *Bhoter Gan*, Kolkata: National Book Agency, published before the elections of 1952.

Paresh Dhar, *Bhot Ranga*, published before the elections of 1952 (publication details not found).

Paresh Dhar, *Santi Tarja*, 1952 (publication details not found).

Songs written by folk-poets too were published. Chittagong District Kavi Samity was very active in this respect. It had two centres for publication—one at Gomdandi and the other at Lamburhat. Among its books were:

Kavir Gan, a collection of songs by Ramesh Seal, Hedayet Ali, Raigopal, Phani Barua and others (n.d.).

Ramesh Seal, *Desher Gan* (1352/1945).

Ramesh Seal, *Bhot-Rahasya* (1946).

Ramesh Seal, *Lok Kalyan* (1946, according to Sudhi Pradhan) and also other song-books by Ramesh Seal, some of them being collections of songs written before the age of People's Songs.

Nibaran Pandit's *Lok-Sangeet*, published by Mymensingh District Progressive Writers' and Artists' Association, 1st edition August 1945—5000 copies, 2nd edition September 1945—7,000 copies. Introduction by Subhas Mukherjee. I could not find Nibaran Pandit's other books.

Many other books of People's Songs are lost. We have not been able to trace Chittaprosad's song book or a single book of Sheikh Gumhani Dewan or

Ganasangeet, a very popular song book published by Pratirodh Publishers, Dacca, during the Peoples' War period.

3. Among later collections of Peoples' Songs of that period are *Ramesh Sealer Srestha Gan O Chharar Sankalan*, ed. Purnendu Dastidar, Chattagram Ramesh Seal Sambardhana Sansad, Chittagong,10 April 1964.

Salil Chowdhuryr Gan, collected by Dipa Mukhopadhyay and Suhas Chowdhury, Introduction by Hemanga Biswas, Saraswat Library, Kolkata, April 1975. *Hemanga Biswaser Gan*, Published by Mass Singers, Kolkata, September 1980. Distributor Sribhumi Publishing House, Kolkata.

Ganasangeet, A collection of Peoples' Songs of the 1940s and later period, published by Anup Kumar Das on behalf of Gananatya Utsav Committee, on the occasion of Gananatya Utsav, Kolkata,1979, with the cooperation of the West Bengal government.

Brochure published by Indian People's Cultural Association on the occasion of a function—'Presentation of Progressive Songs of the Forties'—at Mahajati Sadan, Kolkata,12 March 1979.

4. An important source is contemporary leftist periodicals like *Janayuddha*, *Swadhinata*, *Parichay* and *Natun Sahitya*.

5. Saroj Hajra, a leader of the AISF during the 1940s and later a resident of Santiniketan, sang a number of old People's Songs for me. So did Sadhan Gupta, another leader of the then AISF, a visually-challenged person who went on to become the Advocate-General of West Bengal. Sudhi Pradhan was another important source of the tunes of the old songs. Although a leading organizer of the IPTA movement, he was not known as a singer. But he used to accompany the singers on harmonium. Khaled Chowdhury too sang a couple of People's Songs when I interviewed him. But others involved in the People's Song Movement could not remember the tunes of the songs.

   Needless to say, due to the failing memories and the very nature of the People's Songs, their reconstruction was not easy for me. I found a lot of variations. Often the lyric and the tune did not go well with each other. But I tried my best to put them together with the help of my friend Jayashree Seth. For a more elaborate discussion of the tunes of the songs, see my Bengali book *Challisher Dashaker Banglay Ganasangeet Andolan*, Kolkata: Papyrus, 1992.

Sources for Contemporary Plays

Most of the plays referred to in this study are not available now. Even the playwrights have not preserved their own plays. The plays that are available are listed below:

Abhyuday, Published by Subal Chandra Bandyopadhyay on behalf of the Congress Sahitya Sangha, Kolkata (sometime in the middle of the 1940s).

Bandyopadhyay, Digindra Chandra, *Dipsikha*, Kolkata: Bengal Publishers, 1944.

———, *Antaral*, Kolkatt: Bengal Publishers, 1945.

———, *Bastubhita*, Published by Kalipada Bandyopadhyay, Desbandhu Nagar, Kolkata,1954.

———, *Taranga*, Kolkatt: Pustakalaya, 1954.

———, *Purnagras*, Kolkatt: Pustakalay. The play was written in July 1948.

Bandyopadhyay, Digindra Chandra, *Mokabila*, Kolkatt: Pustakalay, 2nd edn., September 1955 (1st edn., 1950).

———, *Masal*, Published by Kalipada Bandyopadhyay, Deshbandhu Nagar, Kolkata, 1954.

Bhattacharya, Bijan, *Agun*, the journal *Arani*, 23 April 1943.

———, *Jabanbandi*, *Arani*, 29 October 1943. Included in *Tinti Natika*, AFWAA, Kolkata, Paus, 1350/1943. Reprinted in the journal *Bahurupi Nabanna Smarak Sankhya*, vol. II.

———, *Nabanna*, there have been many editions of this play, the most useful to me had been published by Prama Prakashani, Kolkata. I saw the original script edited by Sambhu Mitra, in the private collection of Sudhi Pradhan.

———, *Jiyankanya*, Eagle Publishers, Kolkata, Baisakh, 1355/1947, written in 1351. Reprinted in *Bahurupi. Nabanna Smarak Sankshya*, vol. I.

———, *Marachand*, Kolkatt: Manisha Granthalay, 1375/1968.

Bhattacharya, Manoranjan, *Homeopathy*, *Arani*, 5 November 1943, included in *Tinti Natika*.

Bose, Manoj, *Natun Prabhat*, Kolkata: Bengal Publishers, 1943.

Chattopadhyay, Sunil, *Kerani*, printed in *Bahurupi Nabanna Smarak Sankhya*, vol. I.

Dutta, Sudhindranath, *Punarujjiban*, *Parichay*, Bhadra, 1343/1936, Reprinted in *Bahurupi Nabanna Smarak Sankhya*, vol. II.

Ghosh, Benoy, *Laboratory*, the journal *Arani*, 14 May 1943, Included in *Tinti Natika*.

Ghosh, Subodh, *Anjangarh*, printed in the journal *Bahurupi Nabanna Smarak Sankhya*, vol. I.

Jana, Sushil, *Purnagras*, Kolkata: Vidyoday Library, 1953.

Lahiri Tulsi, *Dukhir Iman*, Published by Bimal Bose, Chhotoder Asar, 16A, Duff Street, Kolkata, Jyaistha, 1354/1947.

———, *Banglar Mati*, D. M. Library, Kolkata, Baisakh, 1361/1954, Included in *Tulsi Lahirir Nirbachita Natyasangraha*, Kolkata: Jatiya Sahitya Parishad, 1388.

———, *Chhenra Tar*, included in *Tulsi Lahirir Nirbachita Natya Sangraha*.

Sen, Salil, *Natun Ihudi*, Kolkata: Indiana Ltd., May 1953.

Sources for Contemporary Pictorial Art

1. In the case of pictorial art too the researchers feel frustrated to find that a large number of the art-works have not been preserved. Artists like Somnath Hore, Debabrata Mukherjee or Paritosh Sen could not show a single art-work of theirs, done during the period of our study.

   Quite a few works of art are, however, available in the private collections of Chinmohan Sehanabis, Nihar Ranjan Ray (now his son P. R. Roy), Bishnu Dey (later his wife Pranati De) and Rathin Moitra. Lady Ranu Mukherjee was in possession of a number of lino-cuts of Chittaprosad, Sitesh Dasgupta's 'Ora Kaj Kare' (They Work) and some other works.

Debes Ray possessed a number of lino-cuts by Chittaprosad. But most of the works of Chittaprosad were dumped in a small room on a judicial order in the context of a family conflict over ownership of the works, at least at the time when I tried to find them. Recently, however, Prakash Das has recovered many art works of Chittaprosad and printed them in his book *Chittaprasad*, Gangchil, Kolkata, 2011. An exhibition of Chittaprosad's works was put together by Sanjoy Kumar Mallik and organized by the Delhi Art Gallery in July 2011. Two volumes of *Chittaprosad 1915–1978: A Retrospective* compiled and edited by Sanjoy Kumar Mallik were published on this occasion, which also saw the publication of *Hungry Bengal: A Tour Through Midnapur District, By Chittaprosad, in November 1943* (a book that had become very rare), *Yours, Chitta: Translated Excerpts from Select Letters of Chiitaprosad* and *A Sketchbook of 30 Portraits by Chittaprosad*, all of them owing to the painstaking research of Sanjoy Kumar Mallik.

2. A major source of the contemporary art-works is the leftist journals of the period, *Janayuddha, Swadhinata, Parichay, Arani, Natun Sahitya, People's War, People's Age,* etc.
3. Covers and illustrations of contemporary books are examples of the art of the period, e.g. Rathin Moitra's cover of Bishnu Dey's *Sandiper Char*, Debabrata Mukherjee's illustration of Sukanta Bhattacharya's *Mithekara*, Subho Tagore's cover of his own verse-book *May Day and other Poems,* etc.
4. Another major source is the *Bengal Painters' Testimony*, published by the AISF in 1944. For details see Chapter IV, Appendix II.

5. Other Sources:

Abedin Zainul, *Art of Bangladesh Series*, vol. I, art works of Zainul Abedin, ed. Dr Muhammad Sirajul Islam, Bangladesh Silpakala Academy, The National Academy of Fine and Performing Arts of Bangladesh (n.d., published sometime in the late 1970s or early 1980s).

Bose, Nandalal, An album published by the National Gallery of Modern Art, Jaipur House, New Delhi, on the occasion of Nandalal Bose Centenary Exhibition.

———, *Centenary Volume: A collection of Essays*, Lalit Kala Akademi, 1983.

Bhattacharya, Chittaprosad, Catalogue published on the occasion of an art exhibition of Chittaprosad at the Calcutta Information Centre in November 1980, organized jointly by Chittaprosad Art Archive and the Department of Information and Cultural Affairs, Government of West Bengal.

Dasgupta, Pradosh, *My Sculpture*, Calcutta: Oxford Book and Stationery, 1955.

Khastgir, Sudhir, *Myself*, published by the author from Chandbag, Dehradun.

Mukherjee, Debabrata, brochure published on the occasion of felicitation for Debabrata Mukherji at Gorky Sadan, Kolkata, 24 January 1984.

Mukhar, Debabrata Mukherjee Special Number, December 1981–March 1982, ed. Dwijen Ghosh.

Majumdar, Nirad, *Modern Art Publication*, vol. III, an album of eight monochrome reproductions of paintings by Nirad Majumdar, published by the Calcutta Group, Kolkata (n.d., sometime in the 1940s).

Tagore, Gaganendranath, *Realm of Absurd* (1917), a copy possessed by Chinmohan Sehanabis.

Tagore, Rabindranath, *Drawings and Paintings of Rabindranath Tagore*, Lalit Kala Akademi, 1961 (Supervised by Satyajit Ray)

Tagore, Subho, *The Art of Subho Tagore, An Album*, ed. Amal Hore, 1945.

The brochure published on the occasion of the last exhibition of the Calcutta Group.

Contemporary Indian Art Series, published by Lalit Kala Akademi, the volumes on Pradosh Dasgupta, Sher-Gil, Gopal Ghosh, Devi Prosad Roy Chowdhury, Jamini Roy, Ramkinkar Beij and others.

Sarkar, Nikhil, *A Matter of Conscience (Artists bear witness to the Great Bengal Famine)*, Kolkata: Punashcha Publication, 1998.

Contemporary and Near-contemporary Literature and Other Books
(quite a few books do not show the dates of their publication)

(This is by no means an exhaustive list. The literary works helped me considerably to get a feel of the period, but I have not included all those here, for literature is excluded from my purview. I have however, listed quite a few works related to literature that give us an idea about the aesthetic views of the period of the study.

Bandyopadhyay, Manik, *Manik Granthabali*, Kolkata: Granthalay, 1982–5.

Bandyopadhyay, Tarasankar, *Tarasankar Rachanabali*, Kolkata: Mitra and Ghosh Publishers Pvt. Ltd.,1386 (1979), 87–8 onwards.

Bhattacharya, Manoranjan, *Theatre Prasange*, Kolkata: Pragati Lekhak Organization Silpi Sangha (n.d., probably 1945).

Bhattacharya, Sukanta, ed., *Akal* (A collection of poems on the Bengal Famine), AFWAA, Kolkata, 1351/1946, Reprinted by Saraswat Library, Kolkata,1386/1979.

———, *Sukanta Samagra*, Kolkata: Saraswat Library, 3rd edn., 1376.

Bose, Buddhadev, *Fascism O Sabhyata*, AFWAA, Kolkata (n.d.).

Bose, Pratibha, *Fascism O Nari*, AFWAA, Kolkata (n.d.).

Chakrabarty, Sibram, *Moscow Banam Pundicherry*, included in *Sibram Granthabali*, Granthabali Series, Basumati Sahitya Mandir, Kolkata (n.d.).

Chowdhury, Pramatha, *Rayater Katha,* Biswa-Bidya Sangraha Series, Kolkata: Viswa-Bharati Granthalay, 1351/1944.

Dey, Bishnu, *Baishe June*, AFWAA, Kolkata, 1942.

———, *Ruchi O Pragati*, Kolkata: Eagle Publishers, 1946.

———, *Sahityer Bhabisyat*, Kolkata: Signet Press, 1952.

———, *Bachhar Panchis* (A collection of his poems from the earliest phase to *Smriti Satta Bhabisyat*, Kolkata: Biswabani Prakashani, 3rd edn., 1383/1976.

Chanda, Somen, *Somen Chanda O Tar Rachana Samgraha*, vols. I and II, ed. Dilip Majumdar, Kolkata: Nabajatak Prakashani, 1977.

(I have used this book not so much for Somen Chanda's writings as for reminiscences and other valuable documents appended to the volumes.)

Chattopadhyay, Sarat Chandra, *Sarat Sahitya Sangraha*, Kolkata: M.C. Sarkar & Sons, Pvt. Ltd., 1376/1969.

Dutta, Bhupendranath, *Sahitya Pragati*, Kolkata: Purabi Publishers, November 1945.

Ghatatak, Manish (Pen-name 'Yubanaswa'), *Pataldangar Panchali*, Kolkata: Karuna Prakashani, 1981.

Ghosh, Kalicharan, *Famines in Bengal* (1770–1943), Kolkata: Indian Associated Publishing Company, 1944.

Gupta, Jagadish, *Jagadish Gupta. Rachanabali*, vol. I, Kolkata: Granthalay, 1385/1978.

Hajra, Manoranjan, *Nongarhin Nauka*, Kolkata: Sarbahara Prakashani, 2nd revised edn.

———, *Palimatir Phasal*, 2nd edn., Kolkata: Purabi Publishers, 1945.

Haldar, Gopal, ed., *Revolutionary Art: A Symposium* (n.d., sometime in the 1940s). It was, in fact, a revised edition of *On Revolutionary Art*, published by Messrs Wishart from London, 1935.

———, *Ekada*, Kolkata: Bengal Publishers, 1959 (6th edn.).

———, *Anya Din*, Kolkata: Bengal Publishers (2nd edn.).

———, *Ar Ek Din*, Kolkata: Bengal Publishers Pvt. Ltd., 1956 (2nd edn.).

These three novels have been compiled in the book *Tridiba*, Kolkata: Saksharata Prakashan, Paschimbanga Niraksharata Durikaran Samity, 1978.

———, *Soviet Yuddher Tin Mas*, AFWAA, Kolkata (n.d.).

———, *Samskritir Rupantar*, Calcutta: Orient Book Company, 7th edn., 1965.

———, *Panchaser Pathe, Unapanchasi, Teroso Panchas*, Kolkata: Puthighar, 1945–6.

Home, Amal, *Purusottama Rabindranath*, Kolkata: M.C. Sarkar & Sons, Phalgun 1368 (2nd edn.).

Kaji Nazrul Islam, *Agnibina*, Kolkata: D.M. Library, 1377/ 1970 (21st edn.).

Mitra, Premendra, *Pank*, Kolkata: Readers' Corner, 2nd edn., 1953.

Mukhopadhyay, Dhurjatiprasad, *Chintayasi*, 1933.

Mukhopadhyay, Hirendranath and Goswami, Surendranath, eds., *Pragati*, AIPWA, Kolkata, 1937.

Mukhopadhyay, Sailanajanda, *Kaylakuthi*, Barada Agency, 1336/1929.

Mukhopadhyay, Shyamaprasad, *Panchaser Manwantar*, a collection of speeches and writings on the Bengal Famine, Bengal Publisher, 2nd edn., Kolkata, 1351.

Mukhopadhyay, Subhas and Sanyal, Hiran Kumar, eds., *Keno Likhi*, AFWAA, Kolkata, January 1944.

Pradhan, Sudhi, ed., *Kayekjan Lok-Kavi*, AFWAA, Kolkata, 1945.

Ray, Bijan (Pen-name of Sushobhan Sarkar) *Japani Sasaner Asal Rup*, Kolkata: AFWAA (n.d.).

Sen, Samar, *Samar Sener Kabita*, 5th edn., Kolkata: Signet, 1388/1981.

Sengupta, Achintya Kumar, ed., *Bede*, Kolkata: Signet,1947.

Sengupta, Jatindranath, *Kabita Sankalan*, ed. Sunilkanti Sen, Kolkata: West Bengal State Book Board, 1981.

Prachir (A Collection of anti-Fascist poems), South Calcutta Students' Federation, 1942. Dedicated to Somen Chanda's memory.

Stephens, Ian Melville, *Maladministration in Bengal, The Statesman*, Kolkata,1943.

Tagore Rabindranath, *Rabindra Rachanabali*,Viswa-Bharati.

———, *Chithipatra*, vol. XI,Viswa-Bharati, 1974.

Souvenirs, Bulletins, Speeches. Reports, etc.

Many of these have been included in Sudhi Pradhan, ed., *Marxist Cultural Movement in India*, vols. I, II and III, Kolkata. Some are included in Dilip Majumdar, ed., *Somen Chanda O Tar Rachana Sangraha*, vols. I and II. Others I saw were:

IPTA Bulletin No. I (through the courtesy of Sudhi Pradhan). In fact, this has been included in *Marxist Cultural Movement*, vol. I.

Souvenir published on the occasion of the first show of *Nabanna* (courtesy of Chinmohan Sehanabis).

Half-yearly Report of the AFWAA (January–June 1944).

Annual Report of the AFWAA (March 1945).

(Both seen through the courtesy of Sudhi Pradhan).

S.A. Dange's speech at the fourth AIPWA Conference, 1943, published by People's Publishing House, Delhi,1943. A copy possessed by Chinmohan Sehanabis.

Brochure published on the occasion of the last exhibition of the Calcutta Group. Seen through the courtesy of Asok Bhattacharya.

Annual Reports of Artists Association (1945–6, 1946–7, 1947–8), in possession of Sudhi Pradhan.

Circulars for unification of theatre groups, in possession of Sudhi Pradhan.

Diaries and Letters

Bandyopadhyay, Manik, *Manik Bandyopadhyayer Diary*, ed. Jugantar Chakravarty, *Ekshan*, 3–4 Double Special Number, 1381/1974.

———, *Manik Bandyopadhyayer Chithipatra*, ed. Jugantar Chakravarty, *Ekshan*, Sharadiya, 1382.

These diaries and letters have been compiled in *Aprakashita Manik Bandyopadhyay*, ed. Jugantar Chakravarty, Kolkata: Signet.

Bhattacharya, Chittaprosad, 'Chittaprosader Chithi', *Parichay*, Sharadiya, 1981.

Hore, Somnath, 'Tebhagar Diary', *Ekshan*, Sharadiya, 1981. Later published as a book by Subarnarekha, Kolkata, 1991.

Tagore, Rabindranath, *Chithipatra*, vol. XI (Letters to Amiya Chakravarty Viswa-Bharati, 1974).

Some letters were found in private collections.

Contemporary Journals

Agrani, Kolkata, through the courtesy of Chinmohan Sehanabis.

Ananda Bazar Patrika, Kolkata, at the library of the Ananda Bazar Group of Publications.

Arani, Kolkata, at the National Library, Calcutta.

Janayuddha, Kolkata, at the Centre for Studies in Social Sciences, also at Ajoy Bhavan, Delhi, and also Sudhi Pradhan's private collection.

Natun Sahitya, Kolkata, mostly at the house of its editor Anil Sinha and partly through the courtesy of Chinmohan Sehanabis and Gautam Chattopadhyay.

Parichay, Kolkata, at the houses of Chinmohan Sehanabis and Gautam Chattopadhyay, a few issues at the Central Library of Jadavpur University.

People's War, Micro-film copy at the Centre for Studies in Social Sciences, Kolkata. Also Sudhi Pradhan's collection.

Pratirodh, The organ of the Dacca Progressive Writers' Association, through the courtesy of Kiran Sankar Sengupta, at the house of Chinmohan Sehanabis.

Swadhinata, Kolkata, at the Muzaffar Ahmad Library, Alimuddin Street, Calcutta.

I have also seen stray copies of the following journals:

Four Arts Annual, Kolkata, 1935, through the courtesy of Asok Bhattacharya.

International Press Correspondence, 29 February 1936, through the courtesy of Sudhi Pradhan.

Lokanatya, some issues of 1355/1948, through the courtesy of Sudhi Pradhan.

Marxbadi, 2 volumes, through the courtesy of Gautam Chattopadhyay; for articles published in the remaining six volumes I have depended on Dhananjay Das' *Marxbadi Sahitya Bitarka*.

Natya, some issues of 1954, through the courtesy of Sudhi Pradhan.

New Indian Literature, one issue, through the courtesy of Sudhi Pradhan; only another issue was published.

Shilpi, Kolkata, Magh 1355, through the courtesy of Sudhi Pradhan.

Unity, 3–4 issues of 1951 and 1952, through the courtesy of Sudhi Pradhan.

Documentation

Pradhan, Sudhi, ed., *Marxist Cultural Movement in India*, 3 vols., vol. I (1936–47).

Published by Sudhi Pradhan, Kolkata, Distributor: National Book Agency, Kolkata, 1979, vol. II (1947–58), Kolkata: Navana, 1982.

Vol. III (1943–64), Published by Shanti Pradhan, Kolkata: Pustak Bipani, 1985.

Das, Dhananjay, ed., *Marxbadi Sahitya Bitarka*, 3 vols., *Bastubadi Sahitya Bichar*, Kolkata: Natun Paribesh Prakashani, 1975–8.

Majumdar, Dilip, ed., *Somen Chanda O Tar Rachana Sangraha*, 2 vols., Kolkata: Nabajatak Prakashan, 1978 (2nd edn.).

Bandyopadhyay, Dipendranath and Sanyal, Tarun, eds., *Parichay*, *Fascist Birodhi Sankhya*, May–July 1975 and its elaborated version *Pratirodh Pratidin* (dedicated to International Anti-Fascist Conference, Patna, 4–7 December 1975, Manisha Granthalay, 1975.

Sarkar, Sipra and Das, Anamitra, comp., *Bangalir Samyabad Charcha*, Kolkata: Ananda, 1998.

Banglar Fascist Birodhi Aitihya, published on the occasion of the 30th anniversary of Victory over Fascism, by Manisha Granthalay, Calcutta, in collaboration with the Indo-GDR Friendship Society, 1975.

Anti-Fascist Traditions of Bengal, An Anthology in Celebration of the Foundation of the GDR, compiled and published by Indo-GDR Friendship Society, Calcutta.

Rao, M.B., ed., *Documents of the History of the Communist Party of India*, vol. VII (1948–50), Delhi: PPH, 1976.

Sen, Mohit, *Documents of the History of the Communist Party of India*, vol.VIII, 1951–6, Delhi: PPH, 1977.

B. Other Original Sources

Interviews

When I did my research, the method of tape-recording interviews, getting them transcribed and then consented to in writing by the interviewees was not strictly followed. In any case, such a method would have limited the scope of oral history for me, as a number of persons I interviewed would not have agreed to speak into the tape-recorder. I remember the aversion of Sambhu Mitra, Hiren Mukherjee and a quite a few others when they saw me bring out the machine from my side-bag. I had to take down rapid and copious notes during such interviews. Today, however, this may make my citing of interviews appear somewhat journalistic. I apologize for this.

Bandyopadhyay, Digin, at his residence at Deshbandhunagar, Calcutta, a couple of days in December 1985.

Bandyopadhyay, Nripen, at the Centre for Studies in Social Sciences, August 1985.

Bandyopadhyay, Priti, at her residence at Jodhpur Park, January 1983.

Bhattacharya, Asok, at his residence in Salt Lake, 3 May 1985.

Biswas, Hemanga, at Mr Biswas's residence at Ganguli Bagan, Naktola.

Chattopadhyay, Gouri, at her residence on Hazra Road, September 1884.

Chattopadhyay, Gautam, at his residence at Palm Place.

Chowdhury, Khaled, at his Park Circus residence, sometime towards the end of the 1980s.

Chowdhury, Salil, at the Centre of Music Research, near Gol Park, November 1985.

Dasgupta, Sitesh, at the Trade Union Office run by the SUCI, on Dharmatala Street, November 1985.

Dasgupta, Ranesh, at the office of the journal *Santi-Swadhinata-Samajtantra*, near Park Circus, September 1982.

Ganguly, Arati, at Mrs Ganguly's, residence near Hindustan Park, 3 July 1984.

Gupta, Sadhan, at his Theatre Road residence near Kala Mandir, in March 1990.

Hazra, Saroj, at his Santiniketan residence, a number of days in 1990.

Hore, Somnath, at his house in a village near Santiniketan, October 1984.

Kaviraj, Narahari, at his house at Santoshpur, January 1986.

Mitra, Sambhu, at his flat near Park Circus, December 1984.

Mitra, Tripti, at her flat on Nasiruddin Shah Road, near Park Circus, February 1986.

Moitra, Rathin, at the Academy of Fine Arts, March 1986.

Mukhopadhyay, Debabrata, at Mr Mukhopadhyay's on Beleghata Main, January 1985, January 1986.

Mukhopadhyay, Hirendranath, at his flat in 'Saptaparni' on Ballygunje Circular Road, October 1985.

Mukhopadhyay, Hemanta, at his residence at Sarat Chatterjee Street (near Maneka Cinema), in February 1987.

Pakrashi, Amulya, at Mr Pakrashi's in Salt Lake, 12 December 1984.

Pradhan, Sudhi, at Mr Pradhan's at New Alipore.

Roy Chowdhury, Sajal and Reba, at their house in Baruipur, November 1985.

Sen, Paritosh, at his flat on Sarat Banerji Road, April 1985.

Sehanabis, Chinmohan, at his place on Sarat Banerji Road.

Sehanavis, Uma, at her house on Sarat banerji Road, January 1984.

I have interviewed many other persons associated with the leftist cultural movement of the long 1940s, e.g. the poets Golam Kuddus, Mangalacharan Chattopadhyay, Arun Mitra, Subhas Mukhopadhyay, Kiransankar Sengupta, Dhananjoy Das, Amitabha Dasgupta, Purnendu Pattrea; but I have not actually used these interviews in my dissertation, though they all helped me to form an idea of the Movement.

Digin Banerjee, Hemanga Biswas, Gautam Chattopadhyay, Sudhi Pradhan and Chinmohan Sehanabis must be especially mentioned. I have been to their places a number of times, spoken with them for several hours and gone through their private papers. Most of these visits did not mean to be formal interviews. I have not kept account of these visits. On a few occasions when I interviewed them on specific subjects and tape-recorded the interviews, I noted down the dates and these have been mentioned in footnotes in due places.

Reminiscences

Interviews and memoirs (or articles largely based on memory published in magazines or as books):

Ahmad, Muzaffar, *Kaji Nazrul Islam: Smritikatha*, 4th edn., Kolkata: National Book Agency, 1975.

Bandyopadhyay, Digindra Chandra, 'Nildarpan Punarujjibaner Nepathya Kahini', *Bangarangamancha Satavarsapurti Smarak Grantha*, ed. Azaharuddin Khan, Studies, Mahatma Gandhi Road, Calcutta, 1380/1973.

Bandyopadhyay, Kali, 'Theatre-Cinemaye Anekdin', *Baromas*, Sharadiya, 1981.

Bhattacharya, Bijan, Interview, *Kalantar*, 1374/1967.

———, *Bishishta Bijan: Likhan Bhashan Kathopakathan*, Kolkata: Manfakira, 2005.

Biswas, Debabrata, *Bratyajaner Ruddha Sangeet*, Kolkata: Karuna Prakashani, 1385/1978.

Biswas, Hemanga, 'Gananatya Andolane Amar Gan', *Prastutiparba*, 1383/1976.

———, 'Sraddhanjali: Debabrata Biswas', the journal *Baromas*, Sharadiya, 1980.

———, 'Jibaner Madhye Sur Chhariye Achhe'. (It is an interview taken by Dipa Mukhopadhyay), *Kalantar*, Sharadiya, 1982.

Chakravarty, Renu, *Communists in India Women's Movement*, Delhi: PPH, and its Bengali translation by Puspamayee Bose and Manikuntala Sen, Manisha, Kolkata, 1980.

Chowdhury, Khaled, 'Manchasajja: Prathamik Dayitva', *Parichay*, Paus, 1372/1965–6.

Chowdhury, Salil, 'Jiban Ujjiban', the journal *Pratikshan*, 1 July 1983–17 June 1984. It was later published as a book.

Dey, Bishnu, *In the Sun and the Rain*, Delhi: PPH, 1972. The book contains different types of articles. I have used some reminiscences of Dey from this book.

Dasgupta, Pradosh, 'The Calcutta Group: Its Aims and Achievements', *Lalit Kala Contemporary—31* (n.d., sometime in the early 1980s).

Dutta, Utpal, Reminiscences in *Ajker Natak O Nabanatya Andolan*, ed. Sunil Dutta, Kolkata: Jatiya Sahitya Parishad (n.d.).

Dutta, Sunil, ed., *Jibandharmi Natya Prayojanar Rup Rekha*, Jatiya Sahitya Parishad, Kolkata (n.d., sometime during the 1980s). It includes reminiscences of Dutta himself and a few others.

Gangopadhyay, Ardhendu Kumar, *Bharater Silpa O Amar Katha*, Kolkata: A. Mukherjee & Company, 1376/1969.

Ghatak, Surama, *Ritwik*, Kolkata: Asha Prakashani, 1384/1977.

Haldar, Gopal, 'Prasanga Panchaser Manwantar' (an interview conducted by Maitreya Ghatak in June 1982), published in the journal *Samskriti O Samaj*, 1st year, 1st issue.

Hore, Somnath, Interview taken by Raghab Bandyopadhyay, the journal *Desh*, 9 November 1985.

Kaul, Jolly, *In Search of a Better World: Memoirs*, Kolkata: Samya, 2010.

Khastgir, Sudhir, *Myself*, Published by the author from Chanbagh Dehradun.

Mitra, Sambhu, *Prasanga Natya*, Kolkata: Samskrita Pustak Bhandar, 1971.

———, *Sanmarga-Saparya*, M.C. Sarkar & Sons, Kolkata, 1st edn. 1980, 3rd edn., 2001.

Moitra, Jyotirindra, 'Amader Nabajibaner Gan', the journal *Kalantar*, Sharadiya 1972.

Moitra, Rathin, 'Rathin, Moitra: Bangla Chitrakalar Palabadal' (an interview conducted by Atanu Basu), the journal *Pratikshan*, 2 August 1983.

Mukhopadhyay, Binodbihari, *Chitrakar*, 3rd edn., Kolkata: 1388/1981.

Mukhopadhyay, Dhurjatiprasad, Reminiscences (1341/1934), reprinted in *Natun Sahitya*, Tagore Centenary Issue, 1961.

———, *Tori Hote Teer: Paribesh, Patyaksha O Pratyayer Brittanta*, Kolkata: Manisha, 1974.

Mukhopadhyay, Saroj, *Bharater Communist Party O Amra*, Kolkata: Ganasakti Patrika Office, May 1985.

Pradhan, Sudhi, *Samskritir Pragati*, Kolkata: Pustak Bipani, 1389/1982.

It is a collection of essays on different facets of culture, some written during the period of study and others written later. The more recent ones were largely Pradhan's recollection of what had happened during the period of our study.

———, 'Nildarpan Natak Punah-prayojaner Aitihasik Tatparja', *Natun Theatre*, vol. 2, 15 March 1973.

———, 'Artiste Association, Bengal', *Bangladesh*, Calcutta, Special Number, 3rd Year, 20th issue, 14 September 1973.

———, Reminiscences in the journal *Abhinay*, Dr Sadhan Kumar Bhattacharya Memorial Number, March–April 1974.

———, 'Loknatye Samaj Bhabna', *Lokyan Sambad*, Loknatya Sankhya, North Bengal, Mahalaya, 1391.

Pandit, Biswanath, Interview taken by Ratna Bhattacharya, the journal *Gananatya*, Sharadiya, 1985.

Ravisankar, *Rag Anurag*, Kolkata: Ananda Publishers, 1980.

Roy Chowdhury, Reba, 'Gananatya Katha', the journal *Ganantya*, Sharadiya, 1985.

———, *Jeebaner Tane Shilper Tane*, Kolkata: Thema, 1999.

Roy Chowdhury, Sajal, 'Gananatya Sangher Ek Adhyay',the journal *Gananatya*' Sharadiya, 1985.

———, *Gananatya Katha*, Kolkata: Ganaman Prakashan, 1990.

Sanyal, Hiran Kumar, *Parichayer Kuri Bachhar O Anyanya Smritichitra*, Kolkata: Papyrus, 1978.

Sehanabis, Chinmohan, *Chhechallish Nang* (No. 46), Manisha Granthalay, Kolkata (n.d.). A later edition entitled *No. 46: Ekti Samskritik Andolan Prasange* published by Research India Publications, Kolkata, 1986.

Sen, Manikuntala, 'Nabanna', *Epic Theatre*, May 1977.

———, *Sediner katha*, Kolkata: Nabapatra Prakashan, 1982.

Sen, Ranen, *Banglay Communist Party Gathaner Pratham Yug* (*1930–48*), Kolkata: Bingsha Shatabdi, 1388/1981.

Sen, Tapas, 'Theatre-e Natun Alo', *Parichay*, Paus, 1372.

Sengupta, Achintya Kumar, *Kallol Yug*, M.C. Sarkar & Sons, Kolkata, 6th edn., 1387/1981.

The following journals and books have compiled reminiscences of a number of persons. Wherever I have used any of these, the names of the essay and its writer are mentioned in foot-note. Here I am omitting these details.

The journal *Bahurupi, No. 49, Bijan Bhattacharya and Jyotirindra Moitra Smarak Sankhya*,May 1978.

The journal *Bahurupi, Nos. 33 & 34, Nabanna Smarak Sankhya*, vols. I and II, October 1969 and June 1970 respectively.

Benoy Roy: A Tribute, Delhi: PPH, 1984.

Bijan Bhattacharya SmarakGrantha, published by Nabarun Bhattacharya, Kolkata,1978.

Chhatra Abhijan, Published by the Students' Federation on the occasion of its 40th Anniversary, Kolkata,1976.

The journal *Chetanik*, Ramesh Seal Centenary Special Number, ed. Atul Chandra Bandyopadhyay, Lalbag, Murshidabad, 1976–7.

Chetanik, Gumani Dewan Memorial Special Number, 4th year, 3rd issue, Murshidabad.

Communist, Published by the CPI, on the occasion of its 50th anniversary, Kolkata,1975.

The journal *Gandharva, Bijan Bhattacharya: Banglar Theatre Andolan*, 30th issue, ed. Nripendra Saha.

Tebhaga Rajat Jayanti Smarak Grantha, Published by the CPI from the office of Kalantar, Kolkata.

The journal *Parichay*, Special Number on the occasion of Bisnu Dey's 70th birthday, May–July 1979.

Parichay, Hiran Kumar Sanyal, Bijan Bhattacharya, Jyotirindra Moitra Smaran Sankhya, February–April 1978.

Also Sudhi Pradhan, ed., *Marxist Cultural Movement in India* and Dilip Majumdar, ed., *Somen Chanda O Tar Rachana Sangraha*.

Private Papers

We have already noted how for the contemporary songs, art-works and the manuscript of *Nabanna*, we depended on private collections. Much of the published materials also were available only in private collections.

Other important unpublished materials in private collections.

Benoy Roy's statistical chart on the tour of the 'Voice of Bengal Squad' in possession of Sudhi Pradhan (this has been appended to Chapter II).

The Minute-book of the Artiste Association in possession of Sudhi Pradhan.

Letters of Benoy Roy, Sachin Dev Burman and Sheikh Gumhani Dewan, written to Sudhi Pradhan.

Letters from Nibaran Pundit to Hemanga Biswas.

'Bangla Pragati Sahityer Atmasamalochana' a handwritten report written by Chinmohan Sehanabis for discussion within the CPI, in 1954.

Articles in Later-day Journals and Books

Bandyopadhyay, Partha Pratim, 'Jatra: Kayekti Ghanistha Path', the journal *Samskriti O Samaj*, May 1984.

Basu, Amitabha (pen-name of Kunal Chattopadhyay), 'Banglay Tebhaga Andolan', the journal *Janasakti*, published serially from 16 February 1978 to 16 November 1978.

Bhattacharya, Asok, 'Silpi Prankrisna Pal', the journal *Saraswat*, Kartik-Paul 1376/ 1969–70.

———, 'Silpi Bhola Chatterjee', *Saraswat*, Sharadiya, 1389/1982.

———, 'Indian Society of Oriental Art in Retrospect', *Journal of the Indian Society of Oriental Art*, 75th Anniversary Special Number, 1981–3, ed. Gopen Roy and Krishna Deva.

Bhattacharya, Hiren, 'Sramajibi Manuser Andolan O Bangla Gan', *Sang Barta*, Published by Rajya Sangeet Academy, Department of Information and Culture, West Bengal Government, 1 March 1984.

Bhattacharya, Malini, 'The IPTA in Bengal', *Journal of Arts and Idea*, January–March 1983.

———, 'Changing Roles: Women in the People's Theatre Movement in Bengal (1942–51)' in Lata Singh, ed., *Theatre in Colonial India: Playhouse of Power*, New Delhi: OUP, 2009.

Biswas, Hemanga (under the pen-name Mohan Murmu), 'Apasamskritir Biruddhe Samskritik Jukta Fronter Swarup O Samasya', *Anik*, September–October–November 1973 and December 1973.

———, 'Lok-Kavi Nibaran Pundit', *Gananatya*, January 1976.

Chakrabarty, Sunil, 'Kavi-gan O Kaviyal Ramesh Seal', *Gananatya*, Sravan, 1374/1967.

Chattopadhyay, Baudhayan, 'Panchaser Manwantarer Karyakaran Sandhan' in the journal *Samskriti O Samaj*, 1st year, 1st, 2nd and 3rd issue, Nihar Ranjan Ray Jatiya Samhati Charcha Kendra, Kolkata.

In fact, the whole of the first issue is dedicated to the Bengal Famine of 1943–4 and includes several articles throwing light on that ghastly phenomenon. But we have particularly used Chattopadhyay's article.

Chaudhuri, Binay Bhusan, 'Organized Politics and Peasant Insurgency', *The Calcutta Historical Journal*, July 1988–9, University of Calcutta.

Chowdhury, Ramshankar, 'Asansol Gananatya Sangha o Pragati Lekhak o Shilpi Sangher Andolan', the journal *Gananatya*, October Dasgupta, Rajarshi, 'Inventing Modernity in a Colony: The Marxist Discourse on the Bengal Renaissance', *Contemporary India*, vol. 3, no. 1, 2004.

———, 'Rhyming Revolution: Marxism and Culture in Colonial Bengal', *Studies in History*, vol. 21, no. 1, February 2005.

———, 'Manik Bnadyopadhyay', *Journal of History*, University of Burdwan, vol. VI, no. I, 2005.

———, 'Marxbader Bhut Banam Marxbadir Gotra', *Ababhas*, April–September 2006.

Dasgupta, Padmanabha, 'Bajrer Swaralipi', *Parichay*, Criticism Number, 1387/1981.

De, Ramprasad, Ganantya Pratham Lekhak Jyotirmoy Sengupta', the journal *Gananatya*, Sharadiya, 1392/1985.

Ghatak, Maitreya and Mahasweta Devi, Prayata Asoke Bose Smarane', the journal *Samskrity O Samaj*, December 1983.

Ghatak, Sauri, 'Bangla Pragati Sahitya O Andolan Keno Byartha Holo?', the journal *Shiladitya*, January, February and March 1982. It is based on interviews.

Kumar, Aishwarj, 'Visions of Cultural Transformation: The IPTA in Bengal, 1940–4' in Biswamoy Pati, ed. *Turbulent Times; India 1940–44*, Popular Prakashan, Mumbai, 1998.

Majumdar, Nepal, 'Pragati Lekhak Sangha: Rabindranath O Suren Goswami', the journal *Nandan*, Sharadiya, 1390/1983.

Mallik, Sanjay, 'History-Art-Art-History', an earlier version of which was presented at a national seminar on 'Cultural Representations as Historical Processes' organized by the Department of History, Jadavpur University and submitted for publication in a volume on the same theme.

Mitra, Rathin, 'Prankrishna Pal: Silpi Jibaner Rup Rekha', *Ekshan*, Grishma, 1391.

Mitra, Sambhu, Introduction to the play 'Bibhav', *Bahurupi*, no. 3.

Mukherjee, Jaykesh, 'Howrah Jelar Gananatya Sangha: Pratham Jug', the journal *Gananatya,* January 1986.

Roy, Gopal Chandra, Essay on Bankim Chandra, and Ananda Math, in the journal *Desh* 4 December 1982.

Satyabrata Tapadar's letter to the editor, *Desh*, January 1983 and Gopal Chandra Roy's rejoinder in the same issue are important in this context.

Roy, Pranab Ranjan, 'Hunger and the Painter; Somnath Hore and the Wounds', *Transactions*, vol. I, no. 2, Winter, 1981, Published by CRESSIDA, Calcutta.

Saha, Jagat, 'Lal Sukra Oraon o Tar Katha' in *Jalpaiguri Loksamsriti Utsav Smaranika* (n.d., probably sometime in the 1970s or 1980s).

———, 'To carry the Roots in the Veins', *Lalit Kala Contemporary*—24–5.

Sarkar, Sumit, 'The Communists and 1942', in *Turbulent Times*, ed. Biswamoy Pati, Popular Prakashan, Bombay, 1998,

Sen, Arun, 'Sahityapatrer Chhabbis Bachhar', *Sahityapatra*, Baisakh 1382/1975.

———, 'Rikhiyay Nirad Majumdar', *Parichay*, Sharadiya, 1978

Sengupta, Samarendra, 'Charan Samrat Gumani Dewan', *Desh*, Kartik, 1383/1976.

A number of important articles by different persons have been included in the magazines listed in pp. 631–2, also in the journals *Bahurupi*, vol. 55 and *Mukhar, Debabrata Mukhopadhyay Number*, ed. Dwijen Ghosh, December 1981–March 1982.

Bandyopadhyay, Saroj, 'Golap Hoye Uthbe' (not an article, but a novel), published serially in *Parichay* in 1962–3.

Books

Ahmed, Talat, *Literature and Politics in the Age of Nationalism: The Progressive Episode in South Asia, 1932–56*, London, New York and New Delhi: Routledge, 2009.

Bagchi, Moni, *Sisir Kumar O Bangla Theatre*, Jijnasa, Kolkata, 1960.

Bandyopadhyay, Brajendranath, *Bangiya Natyasalar Itihas*, Bangiya Sahitya Parishat, 5th edn., Kolkata, 1386 BS (1st edn., 1340 BS).

Bandyopadhyay, Rabindranath, *Bangla Natya-niyantraner Itihas*, Kolkata: Distributor- De Book Stores, 1976.

Bandyopadhyay, Sasipada, *Prasanga Gananatya*, Published by Krisna Bandyopadhyay, 33A/1A Harekrisna Sett Lane, Calcutta-50, March 1981.

Bandyopadhyay, Satya, *Brecht O Tar Theatre*, Kolkata: Asha Prakashani, 1977.

Barucha, Rustam, *Rehearsals of Revolution*, Calcutta: Seagull books, 1984.

Berger, John, *Art and Revolution: Earnst Neizvestny and the Role of the Artist in the U.S.S.R.*, Penguin, 1969.

Bhanja, Niren, *Yabanika* (a collection of four plays) Published by Prabodh Kumar Ghosh, 2B, Shyamaprasad Mukherji Road, Kolkata, 1961.

Bhattacharya, Asutosh, *Bangiya Loksangeet Ratnakar* (4 vols.), Paschim Banga Loksanskriti Gabeshana Parishad, 32, Becharam Chatterji Street, Calcutta-34, 1966–7.

Biswas, Hemanga, *Loksangeet Samiksha: Bangla O Assam*, Kolkata: A. Mukherji & Company Pvt. Ltd., 1385(1978).

———, ed., *Folk Music and Folklore* (Anthology), vol. I, Folk Music and Folklore Research Institute, Calcutta, October 1967.

Bose, Dilip, *1942 August Struggle and the Communist Party of India*, CPI, June 1984. This is a reply to Arun Shourie's article in the *Illustrated Weekly of India.*

Bose, Sugata, *Agrarian Bengal: Economy, Social Structure and Politics 1919–1947*, Cambridge University Press, 1986.

David Bradley, Louis James and Bernard Sherratt, ed., *Performance and Politics in Popular Drama, Aspects of Popular Entertainment in Theatre, Film and Television (1800–1975).* Cambridge University Press, 1980.

Caudwell, Christopher, *Illusion and Reality: A Study of the Sources of Poetry* (originally pubished in 1937), PPH, 1981.

Chanda, Pulak, *Ganakaviyal Ramesh Seal O Tahar Gan*, Kolkata, April 1978.

Chatterjee, Partha, *The Nation and Its Fragments: Colonial and Post-colonial Histories*, Princeton University Press, 1993, Delhi: OUP paperback, 1997.

Chattopadhyay, Bankimchandra, 'Politics' in *Kamalakanta*, available in *Bankim Rachanabali*, 2nd vol., Sahitya Samsad, 1st edn., 1361/1954.

Chattopadhyay, Geeta, ed., *Bangla Swadeshi Gan*, Delhi University, 1983.

Chattopadhyay, Gautam and Manju, *Samakalin Bangla O Lenin*, Kolkata: Manisha Granthalay, 1970.

Chattopadhyay, Manju, *Partition to Agitation: Bengal 1857–1885*, Kolkata: K.P. Bagchi & Company, 1985.

Cooper, Adrienne, *Sharecropping and Share-croppers' Struggle in Bengal, 1930–1950*, Kolkata: K.P. Bagchi, 1988.

Cunningham, Valentine, ed., *The Penguin Book of Spanish Civil War Verse*, 1980.

Custers, Peter, *Women in the Tebhaga Uprising*, Kolkata: Naya Prakash, 1987.

Chowdhury, Darsan, *Gananatya Andolaner Pratham Paryay*, Kolkata: Anustup, May 1982.

Das, Susnata, *Fasci-birodhi Sangrame Abibhakta Bangla*, Kolkata: Prima Prakashan, 1989.

Dasgupta, Abinash, *Lenin, Rushbiplab O Bangla Sambad Sahitya*, Calcutta Book House, Lenin Birth Centenary, 1970.

Davidow, Mike, *The Soviet Theatre: From Box Office to Stage*, Moscow: Progress Publishers, 1977.

Deb, Chittaranjan, *Palligeeti O Purba Banga Kathakata*, Kolkata, 1360/1953.

Deshpande, G.P., *Talking the Political and other essays*, Thema, Kolkata, 2009, particularly the essay titled 'Of Progress and the Progressive Cultural Movement'.

Dutta, Utpal, *Chayer Dhonya*, Kolkata: Jatiya Sahitya Parishad, September 1979.

Elliot, Kruzik, Michaut et al., eds., *International Solidarity with the Spanish Republic* (1936–1939), Moscow: Progress Publishers, 2nd edn., 1976.

Engels, F., *Anti-Duhring*, Moscow, 1962.

Essays in Honour of Professor S. C. Sarkar, New Delhi: PPH, 1976.

Esslin, Martin, *Bertolt Brecht*, Columbia University Press, 1969.

Finkelstein, Sidney, *Realism in Art*, New York: International Publishers, 1954.

Fischer, Ernst, The *Necessity of Art*, Penguin, 1981.

Flores, Angel, The *Philosophy of Art of Karl Marx*, trans. Ralph Win, New York, 1938.

Gangopadhyay, Dwarakanath, ed., *Jatiya Sangeet*, 29 songs, Kolkata, 1876.

Gangopadhyay, Narayan, *Sahitye Chhotogalpa*, Kolkata: D.M. Library, 1374/1967 (4th edn.).

Ghosh, Chittaranjan, *Bibhutibhusan*, Kolkata: Samskrita Pustak Bhandar, 1972

Ghosh, Kalicharan, ed., *Matrimantra* Eastern Publishers, 8-Characters Raman Majumdar Street, Kolkata (n.d.).

Ghosh, Pradyot, *Gambhira Loksangeet O Utsav*, Chakra and Company, 64 Pratapaditya Road, Calcutta-26, 1376/1969.

Gopal, Priyambada, *Literary Radicalism in India: Gender, Nation and the Transition to Independence*, London: Routledge, 2005.

Greenough, Paul, *Prosperity and Misery in Modern Bengal: The Famine of 1943–1944*, Delhi: OUP, 1982.

Guha, Pradyot, *Marxiya Sahityasamalochanay Samasya*, Kolkata: Chalti Duniya Prakashani, 1975.

Guha, Ranajit, ed., *Subaltern Studies III*, Oxford University Press, 1984. (I have used the article by Dipesh Chakravarty, 'Trade Unions a Hierarchical Culture—the Jute Workers of Calcutta (1920–50)'.

Gupta, Amit, *Crises and Creativities: Middle-class Bhadralok in Bengal c.1932–52, Hyderabad:* Orient BlackSwan, 2009.

Joshi, V.C., ed., *Rammohan Ray and the Process of Modernization of India*, Delhi: Vikas Publishing House Pvt. Ltd., 1975.

Lenin, *Collected Works,* vol. X, Moscow, 1962.

———, vol. XV, Moscow, 1963.

Majumdar, Nepal, *Bharater Jatiyata O Antarjatikata Ebang Rabindranath*, vols. IV, V, VI, Distributor, Kolkata: Chatuskon Pvt. Ltd., 1971.

Mao Tse-tung, *On Literature and Art*, Peking, 1967.

Marx, Karl and Engels, Frederick *The German Ideology*, Moscow, 1964.

———, *Theses on Feuerbach, Marx and Engels, Selected Works*, 3 vols., Moscow, 1969–70, vol. I.

Marx, Karl, and Engels, Frederick, *Manifesto of the Communist Party*, Moscow: Progress Publishers, 1977.

Mitra, Saonli, *Sambhu Mitra: Bichitra Jiban Parikrama*, India, Delhi: National Book Trust, 2010.

Mukerjee, Madhusree, *Churchill's Secret War: The British Empire and the Ravaging of India during World War II*, New York: Basic Books, 2010.

Mukhopadhyay, Arup, *Utpal Dutta: Jiban o Srishti*, India, Delhi: National Book Trust, 2010.

Mukhopadhyay, Arun, *Bangla Samalochanar Itihas*, Calcutta: Classic Press, 1965.

EMS Namboodiripad, *A History of Indian Freedom Struggle*, Trivandrum, 1986.

Orwell, George, *Collected Essays*, London: Mercury Books, 1961.

Poddar, Arabinda, *Rabindranath: Rajnaitik Byaktitya. Uchcharan*, Kolkata, 1982.

Pradhan, Sudhi, *Samskritir Pragati*, Kolkata: Pustak Bipani, 1389/1982.

Rais Qamar, ed., *October Revolution: Impact on Indian Literature*, New Delhi: Sterling Publishers Pvt. Ltd. 1978.

Rasul, Abdullah, *Krishak Sabhar Itihas*, Kolkata: Nabajatak Prakashan, 3rd edn., 1982.

Ray, Nisith Ranjan and six others, eds., *Challenge*, Delhi: PPH, 1984.

Ray, Nihar Ranjan, *Krishti Culture Samskriti*, Bichitrabidya Granthama Jijnasa, Kolkata,December 1979.

Rice, Elmer, *The Living Theatre*, New York: Harper and Brothers, 1959.

Robeson, Paul, *Here I Stand*, New York: Othello Associate, 1958.

Rolland, Romain, *The People's Theatre*, ed. Sudhi Pradhan, G.A.E. Publishers, Calcutta, 1980.

Roy, Anuradha, *Sekaler Marxiya Samskriti Andolan*, Kolkata: Progressive Publishers, 2000.

———, *Challish Dashaker Banglay Ganasangeet Andolan*, Kolkata: Papyrus, 1992.

———, comp. and ed., *Shahid Sachindranath Mitra o Anya Ek Swadhinata*, Kolkata: Sutradhar, 2009.

———, comp. and ed., *Swdhinata Sangramer Gan o Kabita: Bingsha Shatabdi*, Delhi: Sahitya Akademi, 1999.

———, comp. and ed., *Swadeshprem o Swajatyabodher Gan o Kabita*, Kolkata: Pashchim Banga Bangla Academy, 2012.

Rude, George, *Ideology and Popular Protest*, London: Lawrence and Wishart, 1980.

Russell, Ralph, *Pursuit of Urdu Literature: A Select History*, London: Zed, 1992.

———, 'Leadership in the All-India Progressive Writers' Movement', in *Leadership in South Asia*, ed. B.N. Pandey, New Delhi: Vikas Publishing House, 1977.

Sarkar, Nikhil, *A Matter of Conscience (Artists bear witness to the Great Bengal Famine)*, Kolkata: Punashcha Publication, 1998.

Sarkar, Sumit, *The Swadeshi Movement in Bengal (1903–1908)*, 2nd edn., Delhi: PPH, 1977,

———, *Modern India*, Delhi: Macmillan India Ltd., 1983.

Shaw, Bernard, *The Great Composers: Reviews and Bombardments*, ed. Louis Crompton, University of California Press, 1978.

Sartre, Jean Paul, *A Philosophy of Man*, New York, 1963.

Sartori, Andrew, *Bengal in Global Concept History: Culturalism in the Age of Capital*, Chicago and London: The University of Chicago Press, 2008.

Sen, Amartya Kumar, *Poverty and Famines: An Essay on Entitlement and Deprivation*, Oxford: Clarendon Press, 1981.

Sen, Sukomal, *Working Class of India*, Kolkata: K.P. Bagchi & Company, 1979.

Sen, Sukumar, *Bangla Sahityer Itihas*, vol. IV (1891–1941), 4th edn., Kolkata: Eastern Publishers, 1976.

Sen, Sunil, *Agrarian Relations in India (1793–1947)*, Delhi: PPH, 1979.

Sinha Roy, Jibendra, *Kalloler Kal: Bangla Sahitye Palabadal*, Kolkata: Kathasilpa, 1380.

Siqueiros, David Alfaro, *Art and Revolution*, London: Lawrence and Wishart, 1975.

Slonium, M., *Russian Theatre: From the Empire to the Soviets*, Cleveland and New York: The World Publishing Company, 1961.

Smedley, Agnes, *The Great Road: The Life and Times of Chu The*, New York: Monthly Review Press, 1956.

Snow, Edgar, ed., *Red Star Over China*, Penguin, 1978.

Solomon, Maynard, ed., *Marxism and Art*, Sussex, England: Harvester Press Ltd., 1979.

Som, Sobhan, *Silpi, Silpa O Samaj,* Kolkata: Anustup Prakashani, 1982.

Srimanjari, *Through War and Famine: Bengal 1939–45*, Hyderabad: Orient BlackSwan, 2009.

———, 'War, Famine and Popular Perceptions in Bengali Literature, 1939–1945', in *Issues in Modern Indian History for Sumit Sarkar,* ed. Biswamoy Pati, Mumbai: Popular Prakashan, 2000.

Stylan, J.L., *Drama, Stage and Audience*, Cambridge: Cambridge University Press, 1975.

Thompson, E.P., *The Poverty of Theory and Other Essays*, London: Merlin, 1978.

Thompson, George Derwent, *Aeschylus and Athens*, Lawrence and Wishart, 1946.

Trotsky, Leon, *Class and Art*, Fourth International, July 1967.

White, Hayden, *Metahistory: The Historical Imagination in Nineteenth Century Europe,* Baltimore and London: The Johns Hopkins University Press, 1973.

Willett, John, tr. and notes, *Brecht On Theatre: The Development of an Aesthetic*, London: Methuen, 1964.

———, *The Theatre of Erwin Piscator: Half a Century of Politics in the Theatre*, London: Eyre Methuen, 1978.

Index